Face Perception

Human faces are unique biological structures which convey a complex variety of important social messages. Even strangers can tell things from our faces – our feelings, our locus of attention, something of what we are saying, our age, sex and ethnic group, whether they find us attractive. In recent years there has been genuine progress in understanding how our brains derive all these different messages from faces and what can happen when one or other of the structures involved is damaged.

Face Perception provides an up-to-date, integrative summary by two authors who have helped develop and shape the field over the past 30 years. It encompasses topics as diverse as the visual information our brains can exploit when we look at faces, whether prejudicial attitudes can affect how we see faces, and how people with neurodevelopmental disorders see faces. The material is digested and summarised in a way that is accessible to students, within a structure that focuses on the different things we can do with faces. It offers a compelling synthesis of behavioural, neuropsychological and cognitive neuroscience approaches to develop a distinctive point of view of the area.

The book concludes by reviewing what is known about the development of face processing, and re-examines the question of what makes faces 'special'. Written in a clear and accessible style, this is invaluable reading for all students and researchers interested in studying face perception and social cognition.

Vicki Bruce has taught and researched aspects of visual perception, particularly face perception, since completing her PhD in 1977. Vicki has held chairs in psychology at the universities of Nottingham, Stirling, Edinburgh and Newcastle.

Andy Young has more than 35 years' experience researching different aspects of face perception. He has held posts at the universities of Aberdeen, Lancaster, Durham and York, and with the Medical Research Council.

Face Perception

Vicki Bruce and Andy Young

Psychology Press
Taylor & Francis Group

LONDON AND NEW YORK

First published 2012
by Psychology Press
27 Church Road, Hove, East Sussex BN3 2FA

Simultaneously published in the USA and
Canada
by Psychology Press
711 Third Avenue, New York NY 10017

[www.psypress.com]

*Psychology Press is an imprint of the Taylor &
Francis Group, an informa business*

*British Library Cataloguing in
Publication Data*
A catalogue record for this book is available
from the British Library

*Library of Congress Cataloging in
Publication Data*
Bruce, Vicki.
　Face perception / Vicki Bruce and Andy
Young.
　　p. cm.
Includes bibliographical references and
index.
ISBN 978–1–84169–878–6 (hb)
1. Face perception.　2. Facial expression.
I. Young, Andrew W.　II. Title.
BF242.B74 2011
153.7′58—dc23
　　　　　　　　　　　　　　2011021790

ISBN: 978–1–84169–878–6 (hbk)

Typeset in Futura and Century Old
Style by RefineCatch Limited, Bungay,
Suffolk

Cover design by Lisa Dynan

Printed and bound in Great Britain by
TJ International Ltd, Padstow, Cornwall

To Pete and to Mavis

All reasonable efforts have been made to contact copyright holders, but in some cases this was not possible. Any omissions brought to the attention of Psychology Press will be remedied in future editions.

Contents

Introduction

A couple of years ago, Psychology Press asked whether we knew of any energetic young authors who might contemplate writing a new text on face recognition. In thinking about this, it struck us that the likely publication date of 2011 for anything written from scratch would coincide with the 25th anniversary of our own joint paper on face recognition (Bruce & Young, 1986), and we began to wonder about the possibility of doing something ourselves. Psychology Press were diplomatically evasive about whether this was a good idea at our age, commenting only that they had 'thought we would be too busy', but when pressed more firmly they gave us a contract.

Things have moved on to an astonishing extent across the last 25 years, during which time the scientific study of faces has moved from a fringe to a mainstream enterprise. Goldstein (1983) pointed out that in the past a remarkable array of behavioural scientists had published one or two studies on faces and then moved on to other topics, but this is no longer the case. More and more researchers have entered the area and stuck with it.

Since we are most unlikely to be in a position to take stock after another 25-year interval, we wanted to give this our best shot. It was immediately apparent to us that 'face recognition' was in itself too narrow a topic for what we wanted to do, and that we preferred to range fairly widely over the topic of how people perceive faces. Fortunately, we had done this at around the halfway point in the intervening 25 years (Bruce & Young, 1998), and our previous publishers kindly agreed we could build on that previous book. Even so, the task has been substantial. We had intended a short summary of distilled wisdom focused only on key studies, but as we struggled to bring ourselves up to date with the sheer variety and volume of work – we quickly found thousands of research studies, and well over a hundred reviews of specific topics – we realised that something longer would be needed just to achieve some kind of overview.

One reason why face perception has become such a widely adopted research area is that it impacts on so many different questions, encompassing topics as diverse as the visual information our brains can exploit when we look at faces, whether prejudicial attitudes can affect how we see faces, or how people with neurodevelopmental disorders see faces. Reflecting this diversity of topics, the whole range of behavioural and cognitive neuroscience methods can be used in different studies. This allows many different ways in which the material we want to present might be organised, and many different facets that might be emphasised. We have opted to try to keep our primary focus on the different things people can do with faces – perceiving social characteristics, recognising emotion, interpreting gaze, recognising identity, and so on.

We begin with two chapters that are intended to create firm foundations for our main sections. Chapter 1 looks at the face in its biological context – why our faces are the way they are, and how interdependent evolutionary development of the various parts (eyes, nose, mouth, etc.) has resulted in our present appearance. We also take the opportunity to introduce some of the changes that have taken place inside our heads – our brains are clearly adapted for visual perception, and perceiving faces forms an important part of this task. In Chapter 2 we review the various sources of evidence we can use to infer things about how we perceive and recognise faces, and the kinds of theory we can construct about how the process is achieved – commenting along the way on the strengths and weaknesses of the different possible approaches.

Chapters 3 to 6 then examine the core agenda of what is known about how we see different things in faces. In Chapter 3 we examine how we infer social characteristics from facial appearance – ranging from the mostly correct attribution of physical qualities (age, sex, race) to things that are often considered subjective (attractiveness, trustworthiness) but may have more of a commonality and even a 'kernel of truth' than has sometimes been thought. In Chapter 4 we look at facial movements and what they can deliver as social signals – especially facial expressions of emotion and the movements involved in speaking. Chapter 5 deals with the movements of our eyes and heads that indicate our direction of gaze – a potent social signal with a wide range of uses. In Chapter 6 we discuss the classic question of how we recognise the faces of people we know.

Chapters 7 and 8 broaden the perspective to ask how face perception relates to wider questions involving interpersonal perception in Chapter 7, and then asking how we manage to develop such sophisticated abilities in Chapter 8. The rich interplay of biology and experience found in developmental studies brings us back to where we began in Chapter 1, but the journey also allows us to comment more illuminatingly on questions about what makes faces 'special'.

As well as reviewing some of what is 'out there' in the research literature, though, we have tried to set out a point of view. To this end, there are various themes that run through more or less all the chapters of the book. Some of these themes are:

- the crucial importance of sound methods – in particular, being aware of the strong and weak points of different types of study and arriving at the best use of comparison conditions;

- converging evidence wherever possible – no method is perfect in itself, but ideas supported by several lines of evidence have a better chance of survival;
- testable theoretical positions that are capable of making predictions and being falsified;
- linking results to theory wherever possible – not just collecting random facts;
- integrating different perspectives – especially those from psychology, biology and neuroscience;
- implications of the variety of social signals we get from faces – and exploiting these to ask critical theoretical questions;
- keeping face perception within the broader perspective of person perception – asking how information from faces relates to voices, bodies and other cues we are skilled at using.

We cannot resist commenting on how extraordinary have been the changes across the last 25 years. In some ways, this has been a golden age for psychological research, in which huge technical advances have opened up previously undreamt of possibilities and considerable public interest has supported exploiting these techniques. In 1986 we had nothing to say about functional brain imaging, and even in 1998 it was sufficiently new that we cited only a handful of papers on neuroimaging of face perception – now they are everywhere. So too are the image manipulation techniques that have allowed the systematic investigation of face properties that could never be achieved with the methods available in the early 1980s – cutting up photographs or relying on drawings or artists. Even in 1998, too, conducting the research needed to write a book involved long sessions taking notes or photocopying articles in university libraries, and quite a few cups of tea while waiting for archive material to be found by helpful librarians. This time, admittedly, we had most of the old stuff already, but nearly all the more modern literature could be accessed straight from the computers on our desks.

Sadly, a consequence of the staggering volume of recent research has been that there are many, many sound and interesting studies we had to leave out because of space and because we wanted to keep some kind of overall narrative. To their authors, we sincerely apologise. Twenty-five years ago, we were able to approach the topic of face perception with a fairly thorough knowledge of the literature. Now, we cannot hope to achieve that degree of coverage, so we have opted for citing and discussing a mixture of findings that seem to us to address interesting issues and to be reasonably firmly established, or else to be sufficiently thought-provoking to merit discussion with appropriate caveats. We have also tried wherever possible to refer to solid reviews or interesting theoretical work, and to integrate as much as possible of our material within an overall point of view.

Along the way, we have received help with formulating ideas, commenting on drafts, or finding things we needed from a number of people we would like to thank, including Tim Andrews, Markus Bindemann, Mike Burton, Andy Calder, Andy Ellis, Charlie Frowd, Peter Hancock, Rick Hanley, Karen Lander, Tony Morland, Julian Oldmeadow, Debbie Riby, Peter Thompson and Frans Verstraten. Special thanks, though, must go to Stefan Schweinberger, who gave a detailed and thoughtful critique of many points and issues from a previous draft. Of course, these individuals don't agree with us about everything, and we don't hold them responsible for any of our misinterpretations. However, we have greatly missed the advice of one person who would have had plenty to offer. The untimely death of Hadyn Ellis in 2006 was a considerable personal and professional loss. We can trace modern interest in faces to his 1975 review paper, which set the scene for many of our current preoccupations (Ellis, 1975). In many other areas, too, Hadyn was there at the start with an interesting take on the evidence and a sound intuition for what would matter – always offered with the charm and wit that came so naturally. We miss his guidance, as well as his friendship and humour, very much.

Vicki Bruce and Andy Young
April 2011

Chapter 1

The face: Organ of communication

Introduction and overview

The human face provides a bewildering variety of important social signals which can be detected and interpreted, very often correctly, by another human. A face tells us if its bearer is old or young, male or female, sad or happy, whether they are attracted to us or repulsed by us, interested in what we have to say or bored and anxious to depart.

Perhaps because we must watch faces so closely for all these signs and messages, we are able to perceive the often tiny variations between individual faces which can be used to identify them. Personal identity is a further and important message conveyed by the face, and our own individual identities are bound up with our faces in a way which makes facial injury particularly traumatic to deal with.

This book is about the science of face perception. Recent years have seen huge advances in our understanding of the psychological processes involved in face perception, and we will describe many of these discoveries about how people decipher all these different messages from faces. We also now know a fair amount about the neural structures that process these myriad messages, and when appropriate we will be discussing these alongside more classically psychological evidence.

Before we can embark on a discussion of how we perceive faces, however, we must first understand what faces are for and how they may have evolved, since this places important constraints on what messages can be signalled by faces and how these can be perceived. In this chapter, we therefore begin by examining this fundamental agenda of how our faces have come to be the way they are.

The face plays important roles in many biological functions. Eyes and ears are spaced to allow us to perceive distance; nose and mouth are arranged to minimise choking; the mouth and jaws are built for chewing and swallowing, but also, in humans, for speaking and smiling. The biological functions of the face have produced a basic face 'template' which is remarkably similar across numerous different species, but with modifications that reflect the animal's behavioural needs. The particular characteristics of human faces arise, directly or indirectly, from our large brains, our position as predators and tool users, and from adaptations for vocal language. These general and species-specific factors mean that all human faces are remarkably similar in basic form. Despite this, there are subtle differences that make every face unique so that faces play an important role in the identification of individual members of our highly social species, and systematic variations of the human face pattern inform us about characteristics such as age, sex and race.

The biological functions of the face combine to create a structure of extraordinary mobility, and in this chapter we will also describe some of the ways in which our repertoire of expressive gestures may have evolved.

The different functions of the human face and its varied roles as a transmitter of social signals undoubtedly mean that faces form a unique category of visual objects, of special interest to human beings. Interpreting the various messages we get from watching people's faces is so important to us that sizeable regions of our brains get allocated to the task, raising the possibility that the evolution of the face itself might to some degree be accompanied by evolutionary changes in the brain that can facilitate the task of face perception. So in the second part of this chapter we will introduce some of the brain regions involved in perceiving faces and ideas about how these are organised, touching on the question of whether faces are so special that the human brain has evolved face-specific neural systems to help decipher their many messages (an issue to which we will return in Chapter 8).

The face as a biological structure

There is an almost universal face blueprint across different animal species. It may sound odd to suggest that human faces resemble those of other animals, but at the most general level that we can use to describe faces it is true. Virtually all animals have the same kind of face – with two horizontally positioned eyes above a single centrally placed nose and mouth. The basic similarities between human and other animals' faces have been used to suggest similarities between individual humans and the characteristics of the animals they resemble. This can be done with serious (albeit no longer credible) intent, as in Giambattista della Porta's (1586) work *De Humana Physiognomia* (see Figure 1.1), or frivolously by caricature artists to make humorous or satirical points about human personality and celebrity.

A fundamental similarity across all animals which is reflected in their faces is their symmetry, which matches the typical bilateral external symmetry of their

Figure 1.1 Similiarity between human and bovine face used by della Porta to infer psychological characteristics. Giambattista della Porta (1535–1615), page 51 from *De Humana Physiognomia*, Vico Equesne [Italy], Apud Iosephum Cacchium, 1586, engraving, Yale Center for British Art, Paul Mellon Collection.

bodies. Why should it be that the vast majority of animals have left–right symmetrical bodies and faces? Gardner (1967) argues that the near-universal bilateral symmetries of the animal world are a natural consequence of the patterns of forces which operate upon them. The force of gravity imposes a vertical differentiation (between the top and bottom of the animal), and as soon as animals evolved independent means of locomotion it was inevitable that there should be a differentiation between front (towards food) and back. However, there is nothing in the environment to force a distinction between right and left, and this is why, according to Gardner, features such as eyes and legs developed equally on each side of the animal. Intriguingly, Gardner suggests that these same considerations would mean that animals evolving on other planets would mostly share this same basic feature of bilateral external symmetry.

However, it is less clear why most animals have just two (rather than four or more) eyes and ears. For some animals it would be useful to have extra eyes in the backs of their heads, but this has never evolved in vertebrates (though spiders are amongst some invertebrate exceptions). For the reasons why, we need to explore what faces are and how their different parts depend upon each other and upon the structure of the brain.

Differences in the basic arrangement of the face generally reflect *evolutionary adaptations* to different environmental and behavioural demands. The theory of evolution developed by Charles Darwin (1859) argues that, because of natural variations within the gene pool of a species, some members will possess characteristics that make them more likely to survive and reproduce than others. This is the process Darwin called natural selection, which can result in a gradual shift in the characteristics of the species as a whole. In what follows we will discuss adaptations which have affected the shapes of faces, focusing mainly on the faces of land-living mammals, though there are similarities in overall principles of face design across birds, reptiles and many insects too.

Eyes

The eyes are an outcrop of the brain, containing the light-sensitive retina, whose specialised photoreceptor cells contain chemical compounds which respond to light. Impulses are then passed through successive layers of nerve cells (neurons) within the retina, optic nerve and cortical and other brain areas (see Figure 2.16 in Chapter 2).

The parts of eyes visible to the observer are the coloured iris and part of the white outer casing of the eye-ball. The colour of the iris is what gives a person their characteristic 'blue', 'green' or 'brown' eyes, but these variations are irrelevant to the job of seeing, though they may affect our impression of facial attractiveness. The role of the iris is to expand or contract to allow more or less light to reach the retina via the pupil, and this plays an important role in adapting vision to different kinds of lighting conditions. Pupil size also changes as a function of arousal, and dilated pupils are seen as sexually attractive.

All mammals have two eyes, but the arrangement of their eyes reflects the type of animal they are (see Figure 1.2). Animals which are preyed upon need the

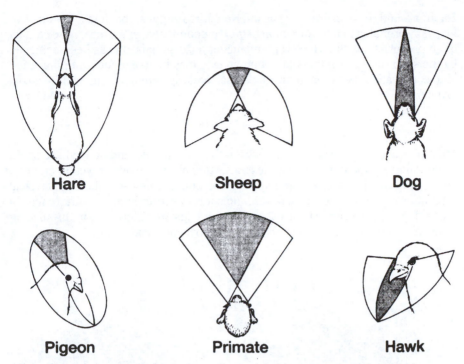

Figure 1.2 The degree of overlap of visual fields varies considerably between different species. From Kardong (2006). Reproduced by permission of The McGraw-Hill Companies.

best possible warnings that predators are approaching. Thus many herbivores, such as deer, horses and rabbits, who may be hunted by other animals, have eyes positioned on the sides of their heads in order to keep watch over the widest possible field of vision. In contrast, animals who do the hunting need good distance perception. One way that vision provides information about distance is through stereopsis, a process by which differences between each eye's image of the world are compared to indicate the relative distance of different objects. For stereopsis to work, the visual fields seen by each eye need to overlap. This is why carnivores such as dogs and cats tend to have their eyes at the front of their heads, so that their overlapping visual fields allow the stereoscopic vision useful for accurately judging the distance of prey. Primates have extremely well-developed stereo vision, which is also particularly useful for manipulating tools – try threading a needle with one eye closed!

The appearance of human eyes is rather unusual in revealing a relatively large amount of the white casing of the eye (the sclera) compared with other species. Kobayashi and Kohshima (1997) examined the eyes of 88 different primate species and showed that humans had the largest amount of exposed sclera, and the most horizontally elongated eyes, as well as being the only species of primates with white sclera – most others have sclera which match the skin colour around the eyes. Kobayashi and Kohshima suggest that it may be adaptive for many primates to have direction of gaze camouflaged, since direct eye contact often provokes attacks. However, enhancing gaze signals, as has been achieved by the shape and coloration of the human eye, may be useful for communication and cooperation between individuals, particularly when acting within social groups.

Ears

Mammals also have two ears, and where they are placed and shaped are again evolutionary adaptations to their lifestyles. Animals which are preyed upon often have large, mobile ears, which help to collect and amplify sounds. The physical separation of the ears helps localise sound sources through minute differences in the timing of signals arriving at each of the ears, just as differences in the spacing of visual images signal distance through stereoscopic vision.

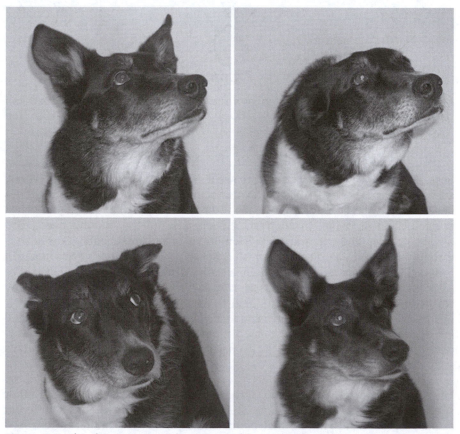

Figure 1.3 The dog's ears can be remarkably expressive as these pictures demonstrate. Photographs courtesy of Barney.

Ears tend to be an unremarkable aspect of human facial appearance unless they are noticeably unusual in shape. This is partly because our interactions are typically face-to-face, where ear shape is scarcely visible, and in any case human ears are often concealed by hair. However, ears play an important role in the expressive postures of some other animals, such as dogs, cats and horses. A dog's ears are laid back flat in anger and are lowered in appeasement or when the dog is miserable, and raised when alert (Figure 1.3).

When considering the shapes of different parts of an animal's body, there is always the temptation to assume that all variations serve some adaptive purpose. That this is not necessarily the case is illustrated rather neatly when one considers variations in the shape of ears within primates (Figure 1.4). These minor but characteristic variations from one primate species to another have not been fully explained in terms of differing function, though enhanced sensitivity to certain kinds of sounds may account for some of the differences (Coleman & Ross, 2004).

Noses

In all animals the nostrils lie above the upper jaw, thus reducing the chance of blocking airways with food. Indeed choking is almost impossible in species other than humans, because other animals breathe only through their noses, whereas the pharynx and oesophagus are arranged differently in humans – some of the many adaptations that facilitate vocal language. Other details of the shape of the

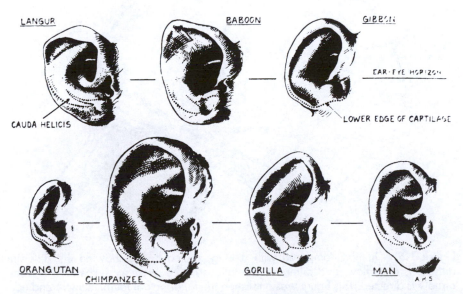

Figure 1.4 Different shaped ears in different primate species. Lenneberg (1967).

nose and the mouth/jaw region differ a great deal depending on the role of scent for each animal, whether additional sensory whiskers are present to supplement sight and scent, and on the kind of food that the animal eats.

Most mammals other than primates have pointed faces, but the elongated fleshy 'nose' of the human is rare. This adaptation ensures that the inflow of air is aimed upwards into the nasal chambers. The nerve endings which serve the sense of smell are located in the top of these chambers within the olfactory bulbs. Figure 1.5 shows the different directions in which air is inhaled in the human compared with a long-snouted mammal. In some other animals the fleshy nose serves different functions. The elongated nose of the

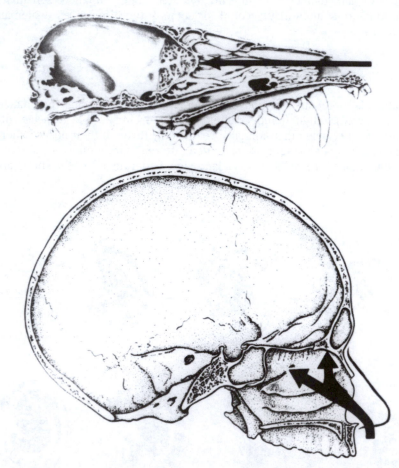

Figure 1.5 A human compared with a long-snouted head, showing the different directions of airflow, and different orientations of the olfactory bulbs to which the airflow is directed. This figure was published in *Handbook of facial growth*, 2nd ed., Enlow D. H., Figure 4–28, p. 207. Copyright Elsevier (1982).

elephant, for example, is an adaptation for foraging, but can also act as a useful hosepipe.

The horizontal positioning of the smell receptors within the olfactory bulbs of the brain is itself a consequence of the size of the brain in humans compared with other mammals. The large size of the human brain has forced the olfactory bulbs to rotate downwards, and this has had a significant impact on the shape of the human face, which is arranged vertically rather than horizontally. This interdependence of changes resulting from different selection pressures is an important feature of facial evolution.

Jaws and mouth

The mouth serves multiple functions in humans, but its primary function in all mammals is as an entry point to the digestive tract. The mouth, lips and jaws are used in the majority of mammals to catch and grasp food (some exceptions include primates who can use their upper limbs to collect food, and elephants who use their noses). The shapes of jaws and teeth reflect the kind of food an animal eats. Herbivorous mammals have jaws which move from side to side to break down vegetable matter, while carnivorous ones have powerful scissor-like jaws for catching and eating their prey. Primate jaws are relatively unspecialised and allow them to eat a wide variety of different foodstuffs. Within primates, though, there is much variation, and humans have particularly weak jaws compared with some of their closer relations among the great apes (see Figure 1.6). The modern human, *Homo sapiens*, may also be compared with other prehistoric forms of the human face seen in Figure 1.7. *Homo erectus*, an early ancestral form of human which emerged from Africa some 2 million years ago, had a weak jaw rather like modern *Homo sapiens*, but a much smaller brain. However, the jaw actually became larger in *Homo neanderthalensis*, a (presumed) descendant of *Homo erectus* (Lewin, 1993).

Once collected, food must be digested. Chewing or puncturing of food with the teeth enables the process of digestion to begin in the mouth, as enzymes can start to act on the food material. The nature and layout of teeth is a further factor which affects the appearance of an animal's face. In the human, the replacement of milk teeth with adult teeth, and associated growth of the jaw, has a significant effect on facial appearance in the developing child. In some animals teeth become elongated as ornamental features, as in elephant tusks.

Human mouths serve other functions than eating, since the tongue, teeth and lips are uniquely adapted to produce the variety of vocal signals on which human language depends. Many animals produce elaborate vocal signals, and many show emotional states with movements of their faces (e.g. by movements of the ears). Many species of primates also use their lips in expressive displays. But the human lips are particularly adapted to their role in helping to form speech sounds and these adaptations may allow them to be particularly expressive in our faces. This is a further example of the complexity of evolutionary adaptation, where a feature which emerges for one purpose (e.g. speaking) may prove useful for another (e.g. smiling).

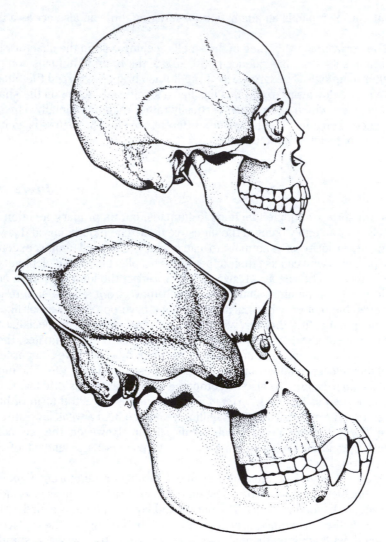

Figure 1.6 The skulls of human and gorilla illustrate the comparatively small size of the jaw in humans. From Johnson and Moore (1997).

Forehead

Human and other primate faces differ from other animal faces in a number of ways. Larger brains – particularly the frontal lobe regions – require more space, giving rise to the high brow area (compare a human face with the dog's shown in Figure 1.3). The high brow plus forward-pointing eyes for stereoscopic vision result in a relatively flat rather than a pointed face (owls and cats also have flat faces). However, this itself is made possible because there is no pointed muzzle to

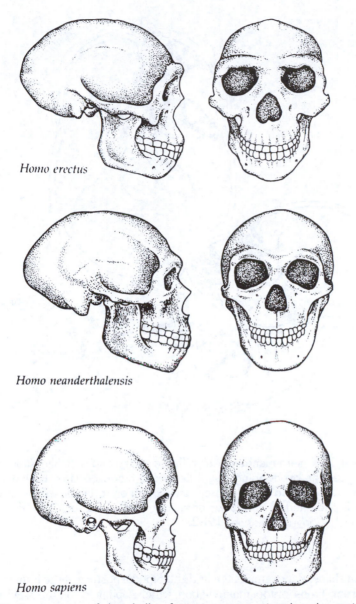

Homo erectus

Homo neanderthalensis

Homo sapiens

Figure 1.7 Comparison of the skulls of *Homo sapiens* (modern human), *Homo Neanderthalensis* and *Homo erectus*. First published in Lewin, R., 1993, *Human evolution: An illustrated introduction*, 3rd ed., John Wiley & Sons Ltd.

get in the way of the overlapping fields of vision, and as we saw earlier, the shape of the muzzle is itself an adaptation to the growth of the brain. Again, the development of different facial layouts reflects interdependent factors (see Figure 1.8). Moreover, these adaptations of the face and head also interact with other aspects

11

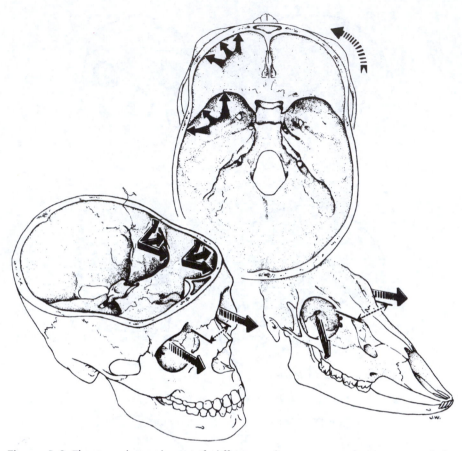

Figure 1.8 The interdependence of different adaptations to the structure of the human face. The overlapping visual fields are made possible by the change in layout of the nose and muzzle, itself an adaptation to increased brain size. This figure was published in *Handbook of facial growth*, 2nd ed., D. H. Enlow, Figure 4.3, p. 191. Copyright Elsevier 1982.

of human shape. For example, the upright, bipedal posture of the human frees the upper (front) limbs for tool manipulation, which capitalised on the 3D vision made possible by the overlapping visual fields.

Distinctive features of human faces

Many species of animal have distinctive additional features of their faces, which play roles in sexual and/or aggressive displays, such as the antlers of deer or the horns of the rhinoceros. Human and other primate faces also have some unusual features. The distribution of hair on human and some primate faces differs from most other animals. In the mandrill monkey, for example, the absence of hair has allowed the evolution of the most extraordinary facial coloration. It has a red nose and blue cheeks that mimic the red penis and blue scrotum which many species of monkey use in display to threaten males from rival groups.

Human female faces are almost hairless, with dense hair mainly only on the eye-brows and head. What is the function of these remaining areas of hair? Head hair may well serve both to prevent heat loss, and to provide protection from the sun, but the function of eye-brows is more mysterious. One suggestion is that they serve to prevent sweat dripping into the eyes. Our heads are particularly prone to sweating, which helps keep the brain area cool (Lieberman, 2011), so eyebrows might help protect our eyes from these salty secretions. An important additional function of eye-brows, however, is to enhance facial signals (Ekman, 1979; Tipples, Atkinson, & Young, 2002), and it may also be this role in interpersonal communication which has preserved hair in the eye-brow region (see Figure 1.9).

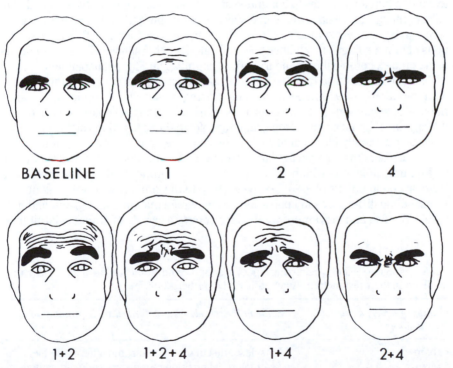

Figure 1.9 Different eye-brow movements are involved in a range of distinct human expressions such as concern, surprise and anger. The numbers signify the different groups of muscles which are active to produce each of the distinct eye-brow postures shown. First published in Ekman P., 'About brows: Emotional and conversational signals' in *Human Ethology*, Cranach et al. (Eds.). Copyright 1979 Cambridge University Press.

A number of further differences between human and other animal faces can be seen in specific adaptations for speech. The social and structural pressures which led to the evolution of vocal speech are not clear, but one interesting account (Dunbar, 1996) suggests that a crucial factor is that humans sweat, rather than pant, to regulate temperature. This happens to free the mouth and tongue for communication, and enables humans to vary their respiration in the ways necessary to use expelled air for long periods in speech. Other adaptations for language through the shape and mobility of the jaws and tongue also affect the appearance of the human face.

Many aspects of the internal and external appearance of the human face and air-passages enable us to articulate rapidly the different sounds which make up our languages (see Figure 1.10). Whether these were specific adaptations for speech or whether speech was structured by the shapes of our faces cannot be known, but there are certainly a number of unique features of our faces, not shared with other primates.

Table 1.1 lists how different features of the human face allow us to make a range of speech sounds which commonly occur in different languages. Attempts to teach non-human primates to communicate with spoken language have all ended in failure, though there has been some success in teaching them to use words using sign language or via symbols (e.g. see Bodamer & Gardner, 2002). Such explorations of primate linguistic abilities have indicated that human vocal speech depends on a complex combination of neurological, cognitive and facial adaptations.

In sum, the basic face template is similar across the majority of mammals, with variations between species usually arising as specific evolutionary adaptations. The arrangement of features in the human face reflects particular sensory, dietary and linguistic adaptations, and to perform these functions all human faces must be essentially identical in their underlying design. Artistic violations of the basic face 'schema' are particularly striking and often disturbing (Figure 1.11), and natural violations which arise from facial deformities and disfigurement can have profound effects on people's lives. Despite the similarity between all human faces, subtle differences in appearance convey information about group and individual identity, and movements of the face convey a variety of other social signals.

Table 1.1 Some widely occurring speech sounds and some of the facial structures involved in their production. Adapted from Lenneberg (1967).

Groups of widely occurring speech sounds	*Some of the structures involved in their production*
p, b, m	Muscles: muscular rim in lips; muscles of cheeks
f, v, w	Teeth: vertical position of incisors; reduced canines
t, d, n	Position of teeth
k, g	Bulging of tongue with ability to raise back
l, r	Blade of tongue with facility for changing shape of cross-section
Vowels	Muscles in corner of mouth; small size of mouth

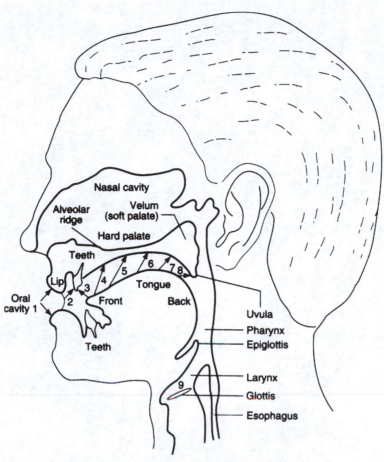

Figure 1.10 Adaptations of the vocal tract. The major features of the human vocal tract, with the different places of articulation of speech sounds numbered from 1 to 8. Reproduced from Fromkin and Rodman (1974).

Variations in the human face

The human face depends on an underlying skeleton (skull) to which the hard and soft tissues of the face are attached (see Figure 1.12). The three-dimensional shape of a particular face results from the combination of the underlying skeletal structure, the hard tissues such as the cartilage in the nose, and the soft fatty tissues, muscles and skin. Differences in these tissues, plus variations in coloration and texture of skin, eyes and hair, provide the basic information which is used to categorise the face (e.g. as a man or a woman). Because all faces must be identical in basic design, sensitivity to rather subtle differences is often needed to determine group membership and to identify individuals from their faces.

15

Figure 1.11 Violations of the face schema are disturbing for us. Rene Magritte: Le Viol (The Rape). 1934. © ADAGP, Paris and DACS, London 2011.

The orthodontist Enlow (1982) described how the growth of faces and heads is constrained by the interdependence between different aspects of their form, in ways which result in a small number of basic face types in different races. So, for example, long thin noses go with long narrow heads, and short,

16

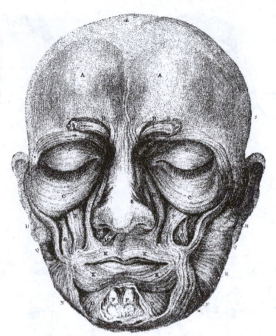

Figure 1.12 Sir Charles Bell's illustration of the muscles of the face which are attached to the underlying bony structures of the skull.

wide noses go with broad, wide heads. The two extreme forms which occur in humans are the 'dolichocephalic' head, which is long and narrow, and the 'brachycephalic head', which is wide and short. These different types of head in turn give rise to different types of face. The 'leptoprosopic' face (see Figure 1.13) is long and narrow with protrusive features, typical of faces from southern Europe, for example. The 'euryprosopic' face is broad and wide with flatter features – typical of Asian faces. So, growth of faces results in differences between basic types of faces. Next we turn to consider the nature of variation and change across the lifespan for an individual human face.

Growth of the face during childhood produces a characteristic transformation in appearance as the nose and jaws grow (Figure 1.14). In the infant, the eyes are relatively lower down the face, and relatively larger than in the adult, which gives rise to the characteristic 'cute' look of the baby and young child. The change in shape which occurs during growth was described geometrically by the naturalist D'Arcy Thompson, who argued that similar principles appear to apply to growth in a variety of biological forms.

> The form, then, of any portion of matter, whether it be living or dead, and the changes of form which are apparent in its movements and in its growth, may in all cases alike be described as due to the action of a force.
>
> (Thompson, 1917; 1961 abridged edition, p. 11)

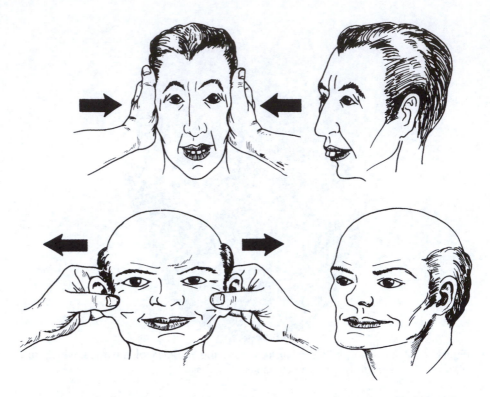

Figure 1.13 The leptoprosopic (upper) and euryprosopic faces described by Enlow (1982). This figure was published in *Handbook of facial growth*, 2nd ed., D. H. Enlow, Figure 1.2, p. 3. Copyright Elsevier 1982.

Thompson was able to demonstrate that forms that were related by growth or evolution could be shown to be related one to another by a simple deformation induced by strain operating on the original structure. In Figure 1.15, for example, Thompson illustrates the deformation needed to map the shape of a human skull onto that of other primates. Indeed some failures to produce simple mappings in this way led Thompson to draw conclusions about lines of descent:

> It appears impossible … to pass by successive and continuous gradations through such forms as Mesopithecus, Pithecanthropus, Homo neanderthalensis, and the lower or higher races (sic) of modern man. The failure … indicates that no one straight line of descent, or of consecutive transformation, exists; but on the contrary, that among human and anthropoid types, recent and extinct, we have to do with a complex problem of divergent, rather than of continuous variation.
>
> (Thompson, 1917; 1961 edition, pp. 320–321)

This conclusion is in fact consistent with contemporary views of human evolution (see also Figure 1.7 for an example of lack of continuity of evolutionary change).

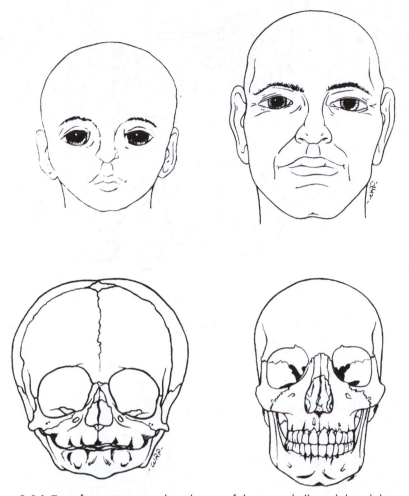

Figure 1.14 Transformations in the shape of human skull and head between infancy and adulthood. This figure was published in *Handbook of facial growth*, 2nd ed., D. H. Enlow, Figure 1.10, p. 13. Copyright Elsevier 1982.

More important here, though, is the way that psychologists have built upon Thompson's pioneering demonstrations to characterise the shape change which occurs as the face and head grows from infancy to adulthood in terms of a mathematical transformation termed 'cardioidal strain' that we describe next.

Pittenger and Shaw (1975; Shaw et al., 1974) first applied Thompson's work directly to the perception of human faces. They argued that as people seem often to be able to identify individuals despite changes produced through the ageing of their faces, human vision must be able to decipher the geometry of this non-rigid transformation and extract information that remains invariant across such

19

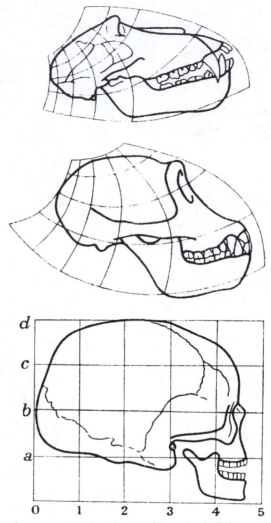

Figure 1.15 Transformations in the shape of human skull (bottom) needed to map it to the shape of a chimpanzee (centre) and baboon (top). First published in D'Arcy Thompson (1917), *On growth and form*, abridged Cambridge edition, John Tyler Bonner (Ed.). Copyright 1961 Cambridge University Press.

changes. Building upon Thompson's demonstration that strain characterises growth processes in a range of biological forms, they compared the growth of the human skull with the growth of dicotyledonous plant and vegetable structures such as kidney beans and apples, all of which expand symmetrically from a nodal point where growth is constrained (e.g. at the stem of the apple or the point of attachment of a bean to its pod). The growth of the human brain and skull appears similar, and is also constrained around the nodal point created where the brain

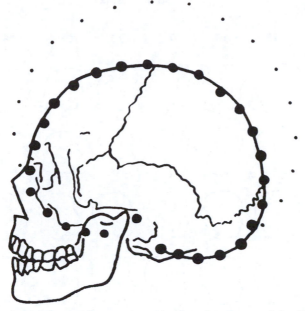

Figure 1.16 A heart shape characterises the transformation of the human cranio-facial profile as it ages. From Shaw et al. (1974).

stem meets the spinal cord. Pittenger and Shaw (1975) showed that a strain transformation called cardioidal strain (from 'cardioid' – a heart shape) characterises well the transformation of the human cranio-facial profile as it ages, as illustrated in Figure 1.16.

In addition to cardioidal strain, a 'shear' transform also models some of the changes due to human growth, in particular the change in the angle of the face between infancy and adulthood. Figure 1.17 shows a series of skull profiles which have been deformed to different levels of cardioidal strain (horizontally) and shear (vertically). Perceptual experiments have shown that observers are reasonably consistent at rank-ordering different skull profiles transformed in this way according to their apparent age, though cardioidal strain level has a much greater influence upon their judgements than does shear. The same cardioidal strain manipulation can be applied to the profiles of other animals to produce age-related transformations, as in the animal profiles illustrated in Figure 1.18.

In an interesting extension of this work, Mark and Todd (1983) obtained a 3D data-base of measurements of a girl aged 15 years, which was used to produce a computer-sculpted bust. The cardioidal strain transformation was then applied (in reverse) to yield a transformed bust which observers judged as looking several years younger. In further work using this same technique, Bruce, Burton, Doyle and Dench (1989) applied this transformation to a data-base of 3D measurements of a face obtained using a laser range-finding device. In laser scanning,

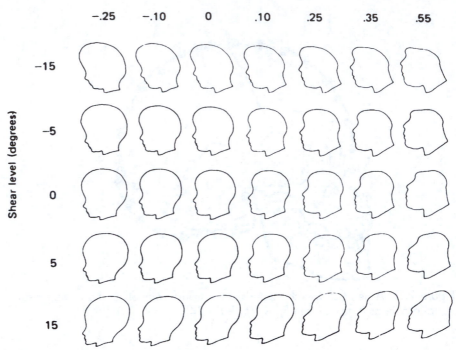

Figure 1.17 A series of skull profiles deformed to different levels of cardioidal strain (horizontally) and shear (vertically). From Pittenger and Shaw (1975). Copyright © 1975 by the American Psychological Association. Reproduced with permission.

the ins and outs of the laser beam as it is reflected from different regions of the face are recorded as the beam moves over the face, so that the face is then represented as a very large number of laser 'profiles'. The resulting measurements can then be used to display the surface shape of the face graphically (we will have more to say about this technique later in the chapter). Such data can also be transformed in a way which should make the head look younger or older. This is quite successful in transforming the apparent age of these 3D images (see Figure 1.19) although the absence of hair in these images, and the adult shape of other features such as the nose, gives rise to some strange perceptual effects.

Clearly, cardioidal strain can only provide an approximate description of one of the global changes which arises through growth. Changes in facial hair, skin texture, etc., are also important, as we will see in Chapter 3. During adolescence the facial appearance changes considerably with the emergence of secondary sexual characteristics – a prominent voice box and beard (or visible stubble) for men.

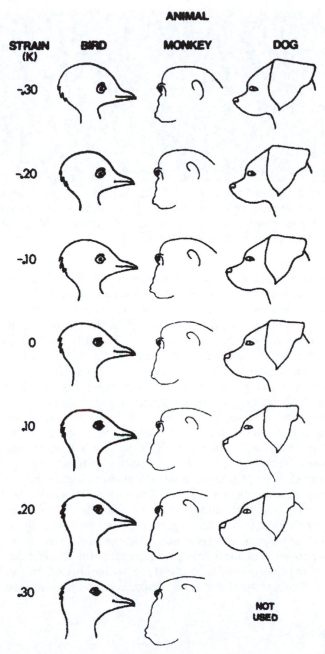

Figure 1.18 The cardioidal strain transformation applied to profiles of other animals. From Pittenger et al. (1979). Copyright © 1979 by the American Psychological Association. Reproduced with permission.

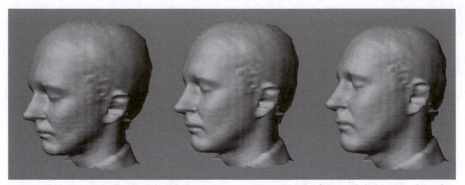

Figure 1.19 Applying cardioidal strain to a 3D model of an adult human head to yield a younger-looking model. With kind permission from Springer Science+Business Media: Further experiments on the perception of growth in three dimensions. *Perception & Psychophysics, 46,* 1989, Vicki Bruce.

As people grow still older, the appearance of their faces changes further as the skin loses its elasticity – leading to wrinkles and sagging. Thus the appearance of the face is determined in part by the shape and growth of the underlying bone structure, and in part by other factors such as the age of skin, the distribution of fat, the texture and pigmentation of the skin and so forth. Because of the interplay between bone, hard and soft tissues of the face, and the important effects of facial and head hair on appearance, it is only possible to make estimates of likely appearance from the skull alone. Nonetheless it is often important, for historical or forensic reasons, to attempt such reconstructions.

Reconstructions of possible appearance are done by adding a face surface to the underlying skeletal information. This may be added physically, using clay or other modelling materials, or, increasingly, it can be done electronically, using similar techniques to those used to simulate cranio-facial surgery as described a little later. A surface is built up based upon information about average thickness of the soft tissues in people of the same approximate age and sex as the target person. As there may occasionally be ambiguity even about the sex of a person whose skull is recovered it is clear that the process requires a good deal of guess-work. Guesses about the possible hair-style and coloration must also be made. These techniques were used by medical artists to reconstruct the face of unknown victim 115 of the London Underground tube fire in 1987 (Chambers, 2007) and to reconstruct the face of Robert the Bruce from his skull, as illustrated in Figure 1.20.

Abnormal faces

Because faces are such complicated structures, a number of different things can affect their function and/or their appearance. Clearly, sensory deficits prevent the normal functioning of the afflicted organs, but this may also affect the appearance of the face. Blind people, for example, may show patterns of eye movement which are not typical of normally sighted individuals. Although deafness has no

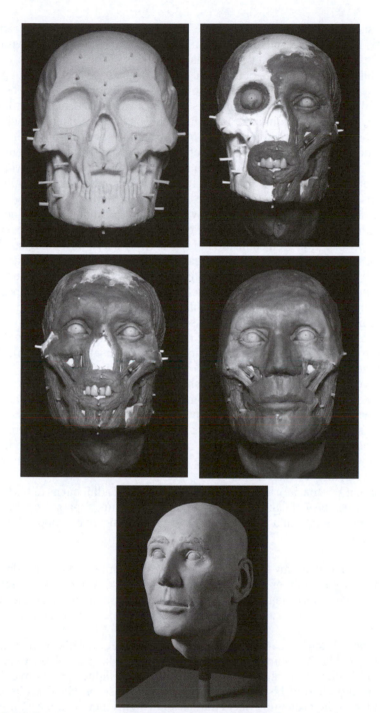

Figure 1.20 Reconstruction of Robert the Bruce's face. Stages in the sequence from skull to reconstructed head. Provided by Brian Hill, Newcastle University.

visible signs, the use of sign language rather than vocal language means that facial expressions are used differently in deaf signers, since facial expression has a linguistic function which it does not have for users of vocal language.

Malformation of parts of the head and face can arise as a result of genetic factors or accident. Cleft lip and palate affects approximately 1 baby born per 1000 births and is one of the commonest forms of facial abnormality. Its cause is not clear, though the slight increase in incidence in families where one child has already been born cleft suggests there may be some genetic component. As well as producing visible disfigurement, clefting affects speech development in the child, so early surgical correction is usually performed. However, following early correction of the cleft, later growth of the face may not be normal, and further problems for the cleft patient may arise in later life.

Other people can react badly or awkwardly in the initial stages of acquaintance with someone with a facial disfigurement. The difficulties reported by afflicted people have been confirmed in research by social psychologists. In one series of studies, Rumsey and her colleagues secretly observed the reactions of passers-by to an actress who was made up to appear with a disfiguring birthmark, and compared the reactions given to the same actress in her normal appearance. Passers-by tended to approach the disfigured person less closely, and to avoid approaching her disfigured side (Rumsey, Bull, & Gahagan, 1982). In another study where the actress was collecting money for charity, fewer people donated when the actress appeared with the disfigurement (Rumsey & Bull, 1986), though those that did donate gave larger sums of money in this condition.

Given such reactions, it is probably easier, and more satisfactory to the disfigured individuals themselves, to intervene surgically to try to make faces more normal in appearance than it is to try to change the behaviour of bystanders. Certain surgical procedures, such as that for cleft palate, are remarkably successful and conducted routinely in most countries. Correcting the kinds of damage which can occur to the face as a result of road traffic accident or fire, however, remains a major challenge.

Simon Weston, a British soldier who suffered dreadful burns to his face and hands during the Falklands war, underwent numerous separate operations in order to restore to him a face which is still far from normal in appearance (see Figure 1.21.):

> I can joke about my looks now, but there was a time when every glimpse of myself in the mirror was enough to send shivers down me. I was frightened I looked so terrible that no one would ever look at me or touch me again.
>
> (Weston, 1992, p. 16)

Simon Weston became very well-known in the UK for his bravery, and his story was told in TV documentaries and in his own books. His celebrity continues through his charity work, and the whole country delighted in his marriage in 1990 and the birth of his first child in 1991. His case provided a high-profile illustration of the profound effects that facial disfigurement can have on an individual's life, and the importance of developing improved techniques for facial surgery and skin grafting.

Figure 1.21 Falklands War veteran Simon Weston. Courtesy of Press Association Images.

> Face and hands – these are the bits that really define you as an individual in the eyes of other people, the bits that everyone notices, that can't be covered up...
>
> (Weston, 1992, p. 4)

Many of the standards which have been used to plan and assess surgical interventions to the face were based on two-dimensional assessments and measurements of the cranio-facial profile. However, the human face is a complex three-dimensional surface, and operations must be conducted on complicated 3D bone structures. Improvements in surgical technique are arising through better ways of understanding and describing three-dimensional shape.

Over the past 20 years there has been remarkable progress at producing representations of bone and skin surfaces in 3D interactive computer graphics. Three-dimensional images of the facial bones can be obtained using a number of modern imaging techniques, and surface images of the skin surface can be obtained by stereophotometry or by measuring the undulations of the face with a laser beam. Figure 1.22 shows the 3D profile as measured by the laser down the midline of the human face. The points on different profiles can then be joined together to form a wire mesh model of the face. This model can be displayed as a smooth surface by showing how a model with all these facets would look if illuminated by light from a particular direction.

A data-base of surface measurements obtained by laser can be positioned over a skull to show how the surface of the face would be affected by some underlying restructuring of the bones. One of the many advantages of these techniques is that it means that surgeons can 'try out' different operations electronically, and

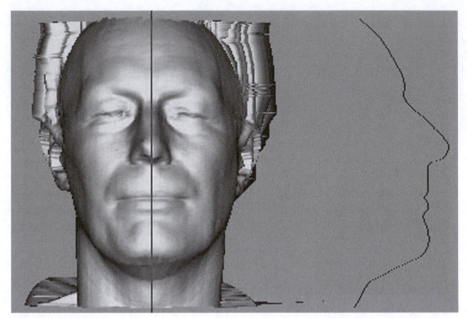

Figure 1.22 How a laser scanner measures the shape of one profile – displayed on the right. Image provided by Alf Linney for Bruce and Young (1998).

then redisplay the surface of the face to view the effects of a hypothetical operation. Moreover, the face can be viewed from any angle to see the effect on appearance (Linney et al., 1989). In this way, surgeons can plan operations systematically to produce the most effective (in terms of minimising patient trauma and medical costs) means of producing a particular outcome. The same technique of pulling facial surface measurements onto a skull can be used to try to reconstruct the actual appearance of a face from recovered bones (Vanezis et al., 1989). Figure 1.23 shows an image of a skull, and a surface image to be fitted over it. The triangulation patterns drawn on the face and skull are used to bring appropriate points on the two images into correspondence. The reconstructed face can then be viewed from any angle (Figure 1.24). These images were produced for us by Alf Linney at University College London, whose team developed many of the first interactive graphical techniques for 3D measurement and display of face images (e.g. Coombes et al., 1991; Fright & Linney, 1993).

One problem with these ways of displaying faces is that until fairly recently these facial surfaces lacked pigmented 'features'. Research has shown that such featureless surfaces can be very difficult to identify (see Chapter 6). Newer techniques involve 3D stereo-photogrammetry to allow the texture as well as 3D shape to be measured and displayed, opening up new possibilities for future surgical prediction (see Kau, Richmond, Incrapera, English, & Xia, 2007, for a review). However, any attempt to add pigmented features onto the reconstructed faces from skulls of missing persons will still involve a lot of guesswork, and could be misleading if the wrong choices are made.

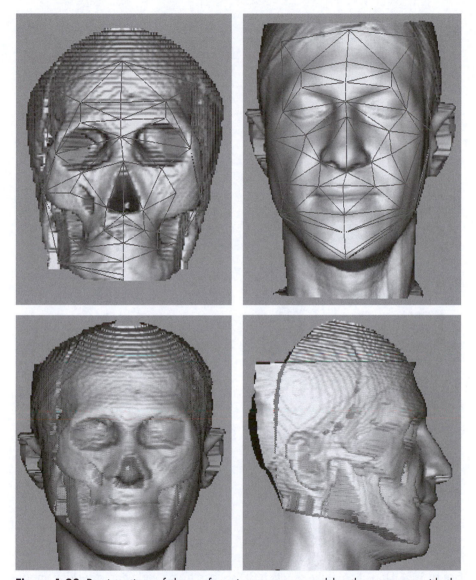

Figure 1.23 Registration of the surface image measured by the scanner with the skull. Image provided by Alf Linney for Bruce and Young (1998).

Successful facial surgery involves more than 3D remodelling. For example, for burns victims much of the repair requires grafting skin from other areas of the body on to damaged areas of the face. Differences in the texture and appearance of grafted skin can make a repaired face look strange even when its underlying shape has been restored. 'Natural' variations in the skin surface such as

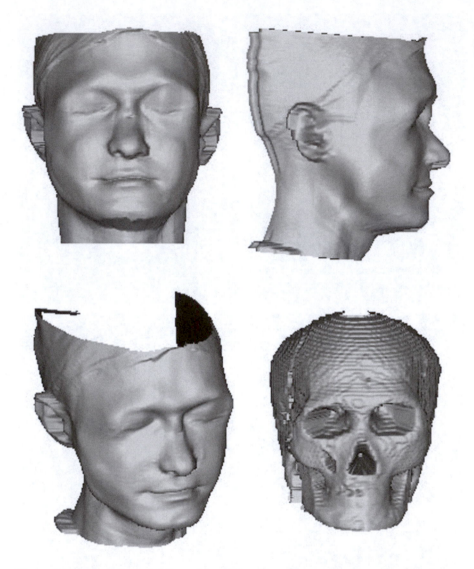

Figure 1.24 Depiction of the resulting 3D surface from overlaying a surface image on an image of the skull. Image provided by Alf Linney for Bruce and Young (1998).

port-wine stains ('birthmarks') can also have considerable impact on people's social interactions, as we described earlier.

In the past few years a small number of pioneering attempts have been made to correct serious facial disfigurement by using facial transplants – the grafting of (usually part of) a face from a deceased 'donor' to a recipient. The first such operation was reported by a French surgical team in 2007 (Dubernard et al., 2007). The recipient was Isabelle Denoire, a French woman whose face had been destroyed by her dog while she was unconscious following a drugs overdose. The transplant of new tissue was to restore nose, cheeks, lips and chin. The procedure raises a number of complex ethical issues (see Morris et al., 2007). Transplantation is usually used to address a life-threatening condition, and so the risks of complications due to rejection, or the toxicity of the drugs to prevent rejection, need to be set in this context. A damaged face is not always life threatening, and so the costs and benefits must be carefully weighed. For these reasons the procedure is still an experimental one and its long-term efficacy unknown. The results of several of the ten cases reported to date are encouraging in terms of viability and aesthetic impact. However, two of these ten patients have died.

As well as the face appearing more normal it is critical that it can function correctly. Isabelle Denoire was able to drink without dribbling after 12 months and recovered sensitivity to heat and cold within the first few months. Recovery of motor function was slower, but she was able to smile normally 18 months after the operation. The complexity of the muscles and nerves that support facial movements renders these results truly remarkable. It is to these aspects of the face that support expressive movements that we turn next.

The muscles and expressive movements of the face

While the hard and soft tissues of the face produce the individual variations in appearance which are important for categorisation and identification, it is movements of the face which are responsible for its ability to transmit a range of other social signals. Expressive movements provide information about emotional states, eye and head movements provide information about the direction of attention, and movements of lips, tongue and jaws provide information which aids speech perception. All these different kinds of movements are controlled by a bewildering variety of muscles (see Figure 1.25).

The different functions of the human face – looking, eating, breathing and sending social signals – all require muscular movements. For example, muscles are needed to control the lips, tongue and jaws during speech, to chew or expel food, and to adjust the posture of external sensory organs. Darwin argued that emotional expressions of the face build upon these other kinds of activity rather than involving specific muscles which have developed solely for expression.

> there are no grounds, as far as I can discover, for believing that any muscle has been developed or even modified exclusively for the sake of expression.
> (Darwin, 1872; 1904 edition, p. 377)

Interestingly, although there are clear similarities in the anatomy of the facial muscles between humans and chimpanzees (Parr, Waller, & Vick, 2007), a recent study by Waller, Cray and Burrows (2008) may slightly qualify Darwin's conclusion. Waller et al. (2008) note that although textbooks of human anatomy describe a precise anatomical arrangement of facial muscles, there are actually individual differences between people in the muscles themselves. Some muscles

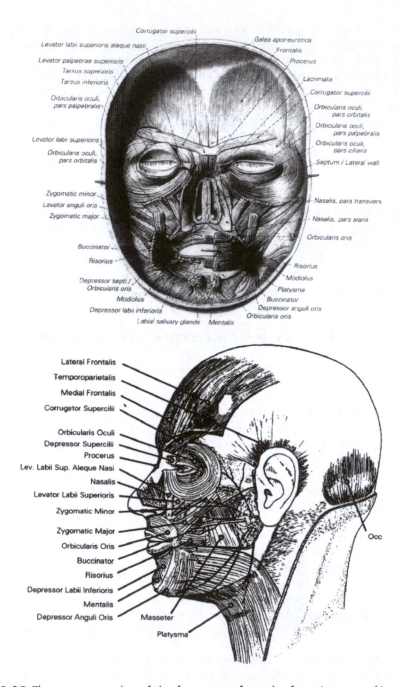

Figure 1.25 The major muscles of the face, seen from the front (as a mask) and from the side, as adapted by Fridlund (1994). This figure was published in *Human facial expression: An evolutionary view*, A. J. Fridlund. Copyright Elsevier (1994).

are not present in some individuals, and some muscles can be asymmetric – larger or absent on one side of the face. Through a careful anatomical study of the arrangement of facial muscles in 18 cadavers, Waller et al. (2008) showed that those muscles involved in producing the facial expressions of what Darwin, Ekman and others have considered 'basic' emotions that are recognised in all cultures of the world (see Chapter 4) were present in all 18 cadavers and only showed minimal asymmetries. This raises the possibility that, although these muscles may well have originally developed for other purposes, they are now subject to a selection pressure that facilitates communication.

According to Darwin and others since, our specific human expressive movements are explicable as remnants of behavioural responses to emotionally arousing events. In Chapter 4 we describe the painstaking research by Ekman and his colleagues to understand the effects of movement in different muscle groups in the expression of different emotions. This is, of course, the knowledge that underpins studies such as Waller et al. (2008), but it has wide applications. Applying such knowledge, for example, computer graphics artists are able to animate facial expressions by applying a model of human muscle action to distort the skin surface of the human face as represented by a mesh of 3D data points (see Figure 1.26). With techniques like these, computer-animated films can now achieve astonishing levels of natural-looking expression, even when the characters are not human (e.g. Shrek). The surface representations used in such animations are similar to those used to reconstruct faces electronically.

Darwin's thinking on the origin of emotional expressions through evolution was influenced by Sir Charles Bell's careful anatomical study of expressions which we have illustrated here (e.g. Figure 1.12). However, while Darwin was a great admirer of Bell's work, he was also critical that Bell did not attempt to explain *why* certain muscle movements characterised the different expressions: 'why, for instance, the inner ends of the eyebrows are raised, and the corners of

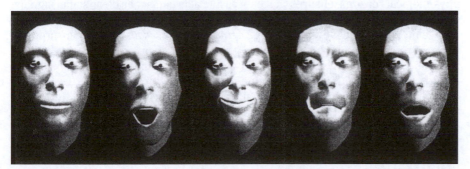

Figure 1.26 Computer animation of facial expressions. Surface texture is 'mapped' from a photograph of a person's face onto a 3D model and deformed by simulating the effects of muscle movements on this surface. First published in Waters, K., Terzopoulos, D. The computer synthesis of expressive faces. *Philosophical Transactions of the Royal Society of London, B335*, 87–93 Figure 3, p. 90. Copyright (1992) The Royal Society.

the mouth depressed, by a person suffering from grief or anxiety' (1872 edition, p. 9).

It was this question which formed the basis of Darwin's own examination of the nature and origins of facial expressions. In *The expression of the emotions in man and animals*, Darwin produced an early and thorough analysis of the origins and nature of facial expressions. Darwin disagreed with the prevailing view that each individual species was uniquely created with a specific repertoire of behaviours, emphasising the continuity of expressive behaviours across species, and the origin of human facial expression in more primitive evolutionary stages:

> some expressions, such as the bristling of the hair under the expression of extreme terror, or the uncovering of the teeth under that of furious rage, can hardly be understood, except on the belief that man once existed in a much lower and animal-like condition.
>
> (1872; 1904 edition, pp. 13–14)

In his treatise, Darwin claimed three important fundamental principles of expressive acts, which he deduced from observations of expressions in a number of species. The first principle is that of *service*. An action which accompanies some biological act (such as grimacing with pain, or spitting out foul-tasting food) becomes habitually associated with the accompanying emotion. This does not mean that how to make each expression must be learned by each individual during their lifetime. Darwin was clear that such expressive 'habits' are inherited in humans just as other complex behaviours are instinctive in other species.

Darwin's second principle was that of *antithesis*. When habitual and physiological tendencies give rise to one set of expressive acts to accompany one emotion, there is a tendency for opposite expressive acts to accompany an emotion of opposite kind. Emotional expressions are contrastive, so that the expressions which accompany friendliness, for example, are distinctively different from those accompanying hostility. This principle, while arising for physiological reasons, ensures that expressive acts can act as clear social signals, since there will be maximum visible contrasts between opposite emotions.

The final principle is that *direct action of the nervous system* can produce expressive actions which do not arise through habit or antithesis, but simply from as yet unexplained physiological responses. Examples given by Darwin include trembling with intense emotion or blushing with shame.

There have been many valiant attempts to describe the origins of human facial expressions in the expressive actions of primate relatives. Not all such comparisons are convincing, and this is perhaps not surprising given that there is considerable diversity within non-human primates. Chimpanzees are thought to be most similar in their facial musculature and expressions to humans (Parr et al., 2007).

The commonest expressions among primates are threat faces, grimaces, the play-face and lip-smacking. The threat face, grimace and the play-face are all rather similar one to another, yet they have very different functions. The primate play-face is similar in structure and function to the human laugh. What is more controversial is whether the human smile is also linked to the play-face in some diminutive way or, as some would argue, more closely related to monkey threat and grimace gestures.

It may be oversimple to seek a single origin for the human smile, since there are many different varieties of smile. Ekman and Friesen (1978) go so far as to claim that there are over 180 different smiles which are distinguishable anatomically and visually. In particular, Duchenne (1862) and later Ekman draw important distinctions between genuine smiles and false smiles used to hide other feelings, and there is no doubt that smiling can be used in a nervous or threatening way by humans. Interestingly, Darwin devotes some discussion to 'grinning' in dogs: 'A pleasurable and excited state of mind, associated with affection, is exhibited by some dogs in a very peculiar manner; namely, by grinning' (1872/1904, p. 121).

This was not mere fancy on Darwin's part, since the same was noted by Bell: 'Dogs, in their expression of fondness, have a slight aversion of the lips, and grin and sniff amidst their gambols, in a way that resembles laughter' (1844, pp. 140).

Such observations may suggest that there are more fundamental linkages between pleasurable arousal and movements of the lips across a range of species – or else that we read more into dogs' expressions than we should!

Human facial displays of anger also differ. Where teeth are visible the anger face may reflect a relic of pre-human ancestral fighting with teeth. Other comparisons may be made between the closed mouth human angry face and the tense mouth display in primates.

The human fear face resembles the primate grimace. Similar muscles are involved in each, and these are quite different from the smile musculature. However, neither sadness nor disgust are so easy to compare with other primate gestures. The disgust face may have evolved from the movements which physically accompany the ejection of foul-tasting substances from the mouth, and a wrinkled-up nose to prevent the inhalation of foul-smelling air. Sadness as well as disgust involve a turned-down mouth which is not evident in other primate signals. The expression of adult sadness seems to originate from the more dramatic facial movements which accompany crying, but why these particular movements occur is not so clear.

Other recognisable facial expressions include surprise and interest, but these do not have the same emotional content as others. Some have argued that the particular facial actions which signal these states may reflect the orientation of the sense organs – eyebrows raised and eyes wide in surprise as though to take in as much external information as possible, and eyes narrowed in interest in order to focus on the object of attention.

Whatever the specific reasons for the repertoire of facial expressions exhibited by humans, there is some remarkable consistency in both the display and 'universal' understanding of these different signals across different cultures. Later (Chapter 4) we will discuss the extent and possible significance of the 'universality' of facial expressions, and consider the relationship between the perception of expression and the experience of emotion.

Brain regions involved in visual perception

So far, we have described how the human face has evolved both to serve basic survival functions and to send social messages. But these messages must be interpreted by the perceiver and there is evidence that the brain inside our heads has evolved to enable it to decipher facial signals just as much as the facial surface has evolved to facilitate sending them. We therefore need to delve beneath the skull to introduce some of the neural structures involved, before elaborating on their various contributions in later chapters.

We begin with the simplest, indisputable fact – parts of the brain are adapted for vision. We already mentioned that the retina of each eye is, in effect, a bit of brain tissue moved to a convenient location for photoreception. It has a complex intrinsic organisation of light-sensitive rods and cones linked to ganglion cells and the optic nerve, meaning that analysis of the pattern of light in a visual image begins as soon as it falls on the retina.

What is more surprising to a lay person is the sheer amount of the brain's cerebral cortex that is involved in vision – an amount that makes clear visual perception is one of the brain's crowning achievements, reflecting a long history of evolution. The optic nerves project to primary visual cortex in the occipital lobes at the back of the brain. Primary visual cortex, however, turns out to be only the start of a large network of interconnected regions of cortex involved in the task of seeing. This network encompasses pretty well all of the occipital lobes and large parts of the temporal and parietal lobes. In the earlier stages, there is a clear succession of retinotopic maps (e.g. see Bruce, Green, & Georgeson, 2003). For the human brain, these retinotopic regions have been largely established from functional Magnetic Resonance Imaging (fMRI) – a technique that can measure regional cerebral blood flow (McKeefry, Gouws, Burton, & Morland, 2009). We will say more about the basics of fMRI in Chapter 2. Calling a brain region 'retinotopic' means there is an orderly spatial mapping between light falling on a specific part of the retina and activation of neurons in a corresponding part of that region.

As one moves further from the primary visual cortex, brain regions whose neurons are still clearly activated by visual stimuli become less obviously retinotopic. Often this happens because the region of visual field that can engage them seems to get larger, but the response becomes more selective – whereas part of the occipital lobe may respond to any pattern of light falling at a specific retinal location, a region in the temporal lobe may respond to an appropriate pattern at any retinal location but become more selective as to which kinds of pattern are of interest to it.

The pattern of cortical regions involved in vision turns out to be astonishingly intricate. Much of the evidence is derived from studies of the neurophysiology of monkey brains (Felleman & Van Essen, 1991), but there is no reason to think that the human visual system will be less complex. A search for general simplifying principles that might help us to understand the overall organisation has therefore become an important task. One such widely used principle is that the cortical visual areas seem to lie along two discernibly distinct processing streams (Milner & Goodale, 1995; Ungerleider & Mishkin, 1982), as shown in Figure 1.27.

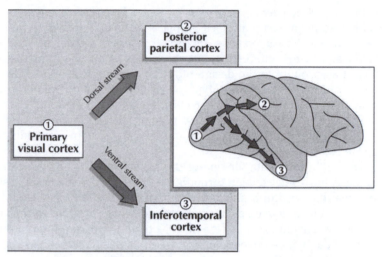

Figure 1.27 Dorsal and ventral cortical pathways – adapted from Goodale et al. (1994). *Current Biology*, Vol. 4, Melvyn A. Goodale, John Paul Meenan, Heinrich H. Bülthoff, David A. Nicolle, Kelly J. Murphy, Carolynn I. Racicot, Separate neural pathways for the visual analysis of object shape in perception and prehension, pp. 604–610. Copyright (1994), with permission from Elsevier.

Each of these visual processing streams originates in the primary visual cortex. The ventral stream then runs through the occipital and temporal lobes – it subserves pattern and object recognition and conscious awareness of the visual scene. Much ventral stream processing relies on input from 'parvocellular' retinal ganglion cells that code particularly for fine detail and colour. The other, dorsal, stream runs through occipital and posterior parietal lobes. It takes input from 'magnocellular' retinal ganglion cells responsive to larger scale shape and rapid movement, and subserves acting in the visual world and manipulating objects (Milner & Goodale, 1995).

Brain regions selectively responsive to faces

What we have described so far is a general organisation of brain regions involved in visual perception, rather than adaptations that might be more specifically tailored to perceiving faces per se. However, many scientists now take seriously the idea that some parts of the brain have become adapted specifically for the task of perceiving faces. Much of the force of this point of view comes from studies that have followed pioneering work by Kanwisher.

The landmark study was by Kanwisher, McDermott and Chun (1997) who used fMRI to study brain regions responsive to faces. What fMRI does (see Chapter 2) is to measure haemodynamic changes across a grid of small, brick-shaped regions of brain called voxels, and to use these changes in blood flow as a proxy for neural activity. If, however, you simply measure haemodynamic changes when someone looks at a face compared to when they look at nothing in particular, you will find a response across the broad swathe of voxels that form the visual system – interesting, but not especially exciting. The main twist Kanwisher et al. brought to the design of the experiment was to look for brain regions that respond more to one type of visual pattern (in this case faces) than to another (which might be objects, houses, or something else – see Figure 1.28). In this way, they got rid of regions that are active to any visual stimulus, and highlighted any voxels within the visual system responding more selectively to faces.

Figure 1.28 shows data for one of the participants in Kanwisher et al.'s (1997) study. A horizontal section through the lower part of the brain is shown, with the areas that produced significantly greater activation for faces than the comparison stimuli marked on a blue-yellow scale, where brighter (more yellow) regions indicate an increased difference. Note that we have mirror-imaged Kanwisher's radiological-convention images, so that in Figure 1.28 the right hemisphere of the brain is shown on the right side of the display.

Two key points clearly stand out in Figure 1.28. First, there are regions that are more responsive to faces than the comparison stimuli. Second, their distribution does not seem accidental. For each of the three contrasts shown, there is a medial region in the fusiform gyrus of the right hemisphere (the upper right bright spot in each image – highlighted with a green surround) and a more lateral region in the occipital cortex of the right hemisphere that respond strongly to faces, and there seem to be equivalently located but less differentially responsive regions in the left hemisphere. The case for these being face-responsive regions is appealing, because some alternative possible explanations are ruled out by the data – the intact versus scrambled faces contrast shows the regions respond more to the whole face than its constituent parts, and the faces versus houses contrast shows this is not a response based on symmetry or to making any within-category discrimination between similarly-shaped stimuli.

These face-responsive areas are located along the ventral visual processing stream shown in Figure 1.27, which as we noted is thought to be involved in visual recognition. Kanwisher et al. (1997) placed particular emphasis on the region in the fusiform gyrus, which they dubbed the Fusiform Face Area – a term which has stuck and is now widely abbreviated to FFA. They had good reason for doing this, because the occipito-temporal cortex, and the fusiform gyrus in particular, was already considered to be the critical locus of damage in the neuropsychological condition of prosopagnosia, in which brain-injured patients lose the ability to recognise familiar faces (Damasio, Damasio, & Van Hoesen, 1982). This created a promising convergence between evidence from neuro-psychology and functional brain imaging.

The parallel runs deeper, too. In prosopagnosia, the damage to the occipito-temporal cortex is usually bilateral, affecting both sides of the brain, and in Figure 1.28 we can see that there is evidence of a left as well as a right FFA. If the FFA is involved in face recognition, it therefore makes sense that it has to be damaged in both cerebral hemispheres to create a recognition deficit as severe as prosopagnosia, in which overt recognition of virtually all faces is lost (but see

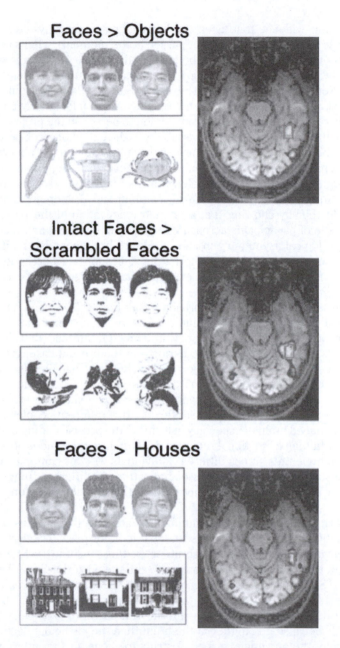

Figure 1.28 See colour plate. Face-responsive brain regions in Kanwisher et al.'s (1997) study. Note that the right hemisphere of the brain is shown on the right of this figure.

Chapter 7 for evidence that faces can be recognised covertly – an interesting point whose implications we will not pursue at the moment). That said, the right FFA shows up more clearly than the left FFA in Figure 1.28 and it seems that, occasionally, prosopagnosia can follow a purely right hemisphere lesion (Barton, 2008; De Renzi, Perani, Carlesimo, Silveri, & Fazio, 1994). The point of interest here is that Figure 1.28 only shows the results for one (albeit fairly typical) participant. There is a bit of variability from person to person in the precise location of the FFA in the fusiform gyrus, and variability in the extent of cerebral asymmetry favouring the right hemisphere. This seems comparable to the observation that most prosopagnosic patients have bilateral fusiform damage, but in a minority of cases a right hemisphere lesion alone may create a severe face recognition problem. An intriguing study by Yovel, Tambini and Brandman (2008) pushed this idea further by showing that asymmetric activation of the FFA is a stable characteristic of participants across fMRI scanning sessions, and that this functional neurological asymmetry in an individual's brain correlates with a behavioural measure of cerebral hemisphere differences for face perception based on a chimaeric face procedure (we will explain behavioural studies of cerebral asymmetry in Chapter 2).

Kanwisher et al.'s (1997) approach forms the basis of what has become a widely-used technique in fMRI studies, known as a 'functional localiser'. A functional localiser defines a neurological Region Of Interest (ROI) in which the brain voxels meet some specified criterion – in the present case, greater activation to faces than to everyday objects. This ROI will usually also meet some *anatomical* constraint – we wouldn't call it the FFA if it wasn't in the fusiform gyrus – but the principal determinant is its *functional* characteristics. What the functional localiser does is to allow for the fact that different people have slightly differently shaped brains – especially in terms of the precise folding of the cortical surface. By finding a functional region, we can then ask questions about how this same region operates across different individuals without running the risk that we are mistakenly comparing bits of brain that do different things (as could happen if we only estimated the location of the functional region from gross anatomy).

It turns out that a smallish number of face-selective regions of brain are easily identified by fMRI localiser scans that look for greater activation to faces than other visual stimuli. In the cerebral cortex, these include the FFA (as already discussed), the Occipital Face Area (OFA), and the posterior Superior Temporal Sulcus (STS). The OFA is the second of the face-responsive regions shown in Figure 1.28 (the more laterally positioned region, nearer the back of the brain and hence lower in the picture), but the posterior STS can't be seen in Figure 1.28 because it is higher in the brain than the particular section chosen. Subcortically the amygdala, a medial structure beneath the anterior temporal lobes, also shows clearly on many face localiser scans. We will look in more detail at the amygdala in Chapter 4, but concentrate on the cortical regions for the moment. Note that the OFA, FFA and STS may not be the only face-selective regions – this is a rapidly advancing field of research (Tsao, Moeller, & Freiwald, 2008). They are, though, the cortical regions that show up in almost all studies.

Organisation of face-responsive regions

What contributions do the functionally localisable brain regions OFA, FFA and STS make to perceiving faces? The honest answer is that it is too early to be confident, but a clever suggestion was offered by Haxby, Hoffman and Gobbini (2000). Although much remains to be established we will use Haxby et al.'s neurological model at several points in this book, showing how it can help interpret an impressive range of findings, linking them to a broadly-based perspective.

Haxby et al. (2000) suggested that OFA, FFA and STS form a core system involved in face perception, as depicted schematically in Figure 1.29. Unfortunately, the terminology used by Haxby et al. (2000) can be a bit confusing, as most researchers now use slightly different labels. For present purposes, the inferior occipital gyri in Figure 1.29 largely correspond to what we have called the OFA, the lateral fusiform gyrus to FFA, and by the superior temporal sulcus they mainly mean posterior STS.

In Haxby et al.'s model, the OFA is involved in perceptual analysis to provide input to the other two regions. From OFA there is a bifurcation of neurological pathways. One pathway goes to FFA and is involved in decoding information that can be gained from relatively invariant aspects of facial form (those that only change slowly over time) – recognising identity would be a prime example, but so would perceiving sex or age. The other pathway goes to posterior STS and is involved in abilities that rely more on changeable characteristics of our faces that can vary from moment to moment – these include perceiving gaze and expressive movements. We will have more to say about these pathways in later

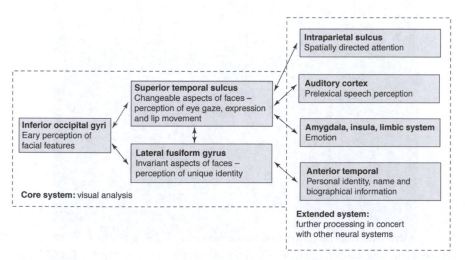

Figure 1.29 Haxby et al.'s (2000) model of the core and extended neural systems for face perception. Reprinted from *Trends in Cognitive Sciences*, Vol. 4, Haxby, J. V., Hoffman, E. A., & Gobbini, M. I., The distributed human neural system for face perception, p. 230. Copyright (2000) with permission from Elsevier.

chapters of this book – in Chapter 3 and Chapter 6 for invariant characteristics, and in Chapter 4 and Chapter 5 for the changeable characteristics.

Haxby et al. (2000) also describe a more extended network of other structures that may be involved in perceiving faces and people – for example the amygdala, insula and limbic system which are involved in emotion, and the anterior temporal lobes which are critical to knowledge about the identities of familiar people. We will also have more to say about these in later chapters, but it is the core system we will concentrate on at the moment.

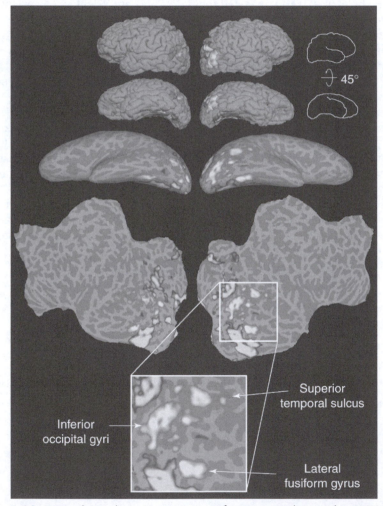

Figure 1.30 See colour plate. Brain regions forming Haxby et al.'s (2000) core system for face perception. See text for further explanation. Reprinted from *Trends in Cognitive Sciences*, Vol. 4, Haxby, J. V., Hoffman, E. A., & Gobbini, M. I., The distributed human neural system for face perception, p. 230. Copyright (2000) with permission from Elsevier.

Figure 1.30 shows the anatomical arrangement of the components of Haxby et al.'s (2000) core system, using an illustration based on one of the participants in a study reported by Haxby et al. (1999). This figure shows well how the three-dimensional folded structure of the cerebral cortex can make it difficult to make sense of functional imaging findings, and some of the techniques that are used in modern research to show the underlying pattern more clearly. The top row of Figure 1.30 is a conventional view of the left cerebral hemisphere (on the left of Figure 1.30) and the right cerebral hemisphere (on the right), seen from a side view. The regions of stronger activity to pictures of faces (in this case, compared to pictures of houses) are coloured on a red to yellow scale. You can see that these regions are mostly located low down and towards the back of the brain, forming part of the occipital and temporal lobes. You can also see that the face-selective regions are a little more clearly evident in the right hemisphere than the left, but they are clearly present in both hemispheres. However, this sideways view doesn't include the FFA, so in the second row of images the view of the brain is rotated through 45 degrees, so that we are looking at it from slightly under-neath, making the FFA (in the lateral fusiform gyrus, on the brain's underside) more visible. Even this does not reveal the true picture of regional activation, however, because some of what is going on is hidden from view within the brain's sulci. The next row of images therefore moves to an artificial representation in which the view of each cerebral hemisphere is 'inflated' by computer image manipulation, as if it had been blown up like a balloon and the wrinkly folded bits are now all on a smooth exterior surface. In this inflated brain representation, the sulci and gyri are coloured in different shades of grey, so you can see where they are relative to the more conventional anatomical representations. Only now can you clearly see the structure of Haxby et al.'s (2000) core system. The final row of images takes this a step further by flattening the entire cortical surface of each hemisphere, as if it had been rolled out like a sheet of pastry. This makes the relative positioning of the face-selective OFA (in the inferior occipital gyri), FFA (in the lateral fusiform gyrus) and posterior STS regions very clear, but it becomes harder to interpret their location in the brain (for which the third row is most useful).

By cross-referring between Figure 1.30 and Figure 1.27, you can see Haxby et al.'s (2000) OFA to FFA core pathway lies on the ventral visual stream, whereas their FFA to posterior STS pathway is more closely aligned with the dorsal stream. Does the difference between neural pathways for perceiving faces simply reflect this more basic division? Intuitively, this seems to make overall sense, but the precise relationship between FFA/STS and ventral/dorsal is not straight-forward. As we will see later, while the processing of changeable aspects of faces such as gaze and expression does involve processing of dynamic information (dorsal stream), these also involve fine-grained static pattern analysis too, which would be seen as more 'ventral stream' activities. It seems that face perception may be organised within the brain in a way that keeps it broadly in line with aspects of other visual perception, but that it could have some specific require-ments of its own that need to be accommodated as well.

In the above discussion we have, for now, avoided confronting the tricky question of whether these really are face-*specific* regions or whether they may play a role in other kinds of processing. We will have more to say about specialisation of these areas in the final chapter of this book.

Concluding remarks

To conclude, faces are intricate structures, the product of complex evolution, which deliver many messages. Our brains have evolved to decipher these messages with some elaborate, perhaps purpose-built, machinery. In the remaining chapters of this book we will explore these mechanisms in detail before returning at the end of the book to reconsider the question 'Are faces special?' Before we move on to the substantive topics of face research, however, we need to do further groundwork by considering the various research techniques that can be used to understand face perception. This forms the topic of Chapter 2.

Further reading

Calder, A., Rhodes, G., Haxby, J. V., & Johnson, M. (Eds., 2010). *Handbook of face perception*. Oxford: Oxford University Press.
This is a comprehensive and up-to-date compendium of review chapters which touch upon virtually all the topics we cover in this book. Recommended to provide supplementary reading for any chapter in this textbook – but we mention it just the once here.

Ekman, P. (1998). *Charles Darwin: The expression of the emotions in man and animals.* Third Edition with an introduction, afterword and commentaries by Paul Ekman. London: Harper-Collins.
A definitive edition of Darwin's classic study of facial expressions. Ekman provides a valuable Introduction (pp. xxi–xxxvi) explaining the originality and importance of Darwin's approach, and an interesting Afterword (pp. 363–393) on his own involvement in some of the consequent disputes.

Haxby, J. V., Hoffman, E. A., & Gobbini, M. I. (2000). The distributed human neural system for face perception. *Trends in Cognitive Sciences, 4*, 223–233.
An elegant neurological model specifying brain regions that seem to be critically involved in perceiving faces, and what they might contribute. Particularly useful because it has the potential to integrate important behavioural observations with findings from cognitive neuroscience and neuropsychology. We will be using this model a lot.

Kanwisher, N., McDermott, J., & Chun, M. M. (1997). The fusiform face area: a module in human extrastriate cortex specialized for face perception. *Journal of Neuroscience, 17*, 4302–4311.
A seminal paper that showed the power of fMRI to reveal the organisation of face perception.

Leiberman, D. E. (2011). *The evolution of the human head*. Cambridge, MA: Harvard University Press.
Describes in detail the complex factors that have affected the evolution of heads (but says more about underlying bony structures than about the soft tissues that form faces),

particularly as these have developed in hominids, and elaborates on a number of the topics we touch upon in this chapter.

Leopold, D. A., & Rhodes, G. (2010). A comparative view of face perception. *Journal of Comparative Psychology, 124*, 233–251.
Describes how different animals perceive faces and the special status of faces for primate, and particularly human, brains. Reviews some fascinating studies of non-primate face perception, in, for example, sheep, birds and even insects, and poses questions about the evolution of these abilities.

Chapter 2

The science and methods of face perception research

Knowledge is always hard won, and gaining knowledge in psychology can be particularly tricky because we naturally make all kinds of assumptions that seem like common sense and are validated by our own experience. For faces, most of us think that we can recognise people we know without much difficulty and usually almost instantaneously. We don't expect face recognition to be susceptible to error, and we think that photographs or videos are accurate records of an individual's appearance that present no problems of interpretation. These experiences are encapsulated in sayings like 'I never forget a face' or 'the camera doesn't lie'. When carefully investigated, though, some of these assumptions turn out to be misleading or only partly correct, making everyday experience something that remains obviously relevant but has to be treated cautiously.

If experience can mislead, what might we put in its place? Broadly, the answer is 'scientific evidence'. However, there are many potential sources of scientific evidence and, like experience, each has its own strong and weak points. So, to evaluate an idea in psychology we need carefully to consider what evidence supports it and, critically, how that evidence was obtained.

In this chapter, then, we look at the basics of the science and methods of face perception research. We begin by considering what kinds of information we might use – these include normal errors and mistakes, persistent errors due to brain injury, reaction times for carrying out different tasks, habituation and adaptation. Techniques for manipulating visual images in systematic ways will also be described – these have had a revolutionary impact on what can be investigated and in this context we discuss some of the basic processing in the visual system which contributes to face perception. To provide background to theories of face perception we introduce some basic principles of functional and computational modelling. Finally we discuss another area in which there has been immense progress – brain imaging. Structural brain imaging with MRI and measures of brain function based on haemodynamics or electrophysiology will be introduced, and we look at where they fit in the broader picture of face research.

Technical matters such as these are not everyone's favourite topics, but they are central to any reasoned evaluation of what we do and don't know. They underpin nearly everything we discuss in other chapters of this book – if you don't get to grips with the ins and outs and the pros and cons of different techniques, your understanding will remain superficial. Students therefore ignore Chapter 2 at their peril, but we can understand you may choose to approach it in bits, or keep returning to it as you learn more.

To err is human: And it can be highly informative

Eyewitnessing is a good place to begin. It represents one of the obvious applications of face research, and it shows clearly why scientific evidence is so important. Intuitively, recognising someone you previously saw committing a misdemeanour from a police line-up or in a court room seems very persuasive that they were indeed the guilty party, and unless otherwise directed juries tend to put a lot of weight on identification evidence. Yet there are many well-documented examples of miscarriages of justice based on witness identification.

In one such case, which is well known because it formed part of the basis of a public enquiry in the 1970s, Laszlo Virag was sentenced to 10 years' imprisonment for a series of offences involving theft, using a firearm to resist arrest, and wounding a police officer. The conviction was made in 1969, on the basis of identification evidence. The case had some loose ends. There was no physical evidence linking Mr. Virag to the crime, and he produced witnesses who said he was elsewhere on at least one critical occasion. He also claimed to be unable to drive, yet a police chase had been involved.

The evidence that led to Laszlo Virag's conviction hinged on two identification parades to which the police had invited 14 witnesses. These identification parades seemed to be fair; Mr. Virag had a legal representative present, and everyone in the line-up wore a trilby hat because the suspect had worn a trilby. Three of the witnesses were unable to identify anyone in these line-ups, and three chose one of the innocent participants, but eight separate witnesses picked out Laszlo Virag. Some of these identifications were made with considerable confidence; one police witness testified that 'his face is imprinted in my brain' (Davies, 1996).

In 1971, whilst Laszlo Virag was serving his sentence, a man named Georges Payen was arrested for another matter, and found to have in his possession the firearm and other items from the incidents for which Virag had been convicted. At first, police thought Virag must have had an accomplice, but investigations showed that they had never met and that Payen had been solely responsible for the crimes for which Virag had been convicted. Laszlo Virag was pardoned in 1974.

Such miscarriages of justice show that eye witnesses can be wrong. Worse still, witnesses can be wrong even when they are confident that they are right. This shakes our faith in the 'evidence of our eyes', and shows that we need to understand how witnesses can make such serious mistakes. Importantly, Georges Payen and Laszlo Virag were not 'lookalikes'; there was a passing but not striking resemblance between them.

So what might have led so many witnesses to be mistaken? Many possibilities would need to be looked at to know the answer. Did they get a really good view of the criminal at the time of the incidents? Were they distracted or threatened at the time? For how many weeks did they have to remember his face before the line-ups were conducted? Had they seen photos of suspects that might have included Virag? Did they feel under pressure to pick out someone? And so on.

With a real-life case, it is impossible to weigh the relative contributions of such a wide range of potential factors, so an obvious step is to try to set up carefully conducted studies that would allow the influence of a particular factor to be evaluated whilst other factors are held constant. Formal experiments have thus become a key source of information about our ability to recognise faces and its fallibility. For some questions, the experimental set-up has to be contrived to be as close to 'real life' as possible, whereas other questions can be tackled using procedures that may not need to mimic real-world conditions.

An outstanding example of the value of a cleverly designed, realistic experiment was conducted by Kemp and his colleagues. This evaluated another widely made common-sense assumption, that it is easy to match the appearance of a person to their photograph. This assumption has often led to the suggestion that, to reduce fraud, credit cards should show a photo of the holder's face.

To test the usefulness of photos on credit cards, Kemp, Towell and Pike (1997) conducted a study in a supermarket, using its own cashiers at a time when the shop was closed to real customers. The cashiers were told that the aim of the study was to investigate how quickly and accurately they could process credit cards that included photographs of the bearer. They were paid for their work, and they knew that a bonus payment would be made to the person with the best performance. The 'shoppers' were students issued with specially created credit cards showing a correct photo (a picture of them taken within the last 6 weeks) or an incorrect photo (a picture of someone else). The correct photos showed the person with an unchanged appearance from how they presented themselves in the study, or with a change in 'paraphernalia' (for example, adding or removing glasses, or changing hairstyle), and incorrect photos were of individuals who were judged to be either similar (matched foils) or dissimilar in appearance to the bearer (unmatched foils). 'Shoppers' presented 10 to 12 items at the till, and the cashier totalled these in the usual way and then checked the shopper's credit card, calling a supervisor if the photo was incorrect.

This was therefore a highly realistic study, but the cashiers knew they were taking part in an experiment and were therefore presumably particularly alert to the possibility that some people would have incorrect cards. The main results are shown in Table 2.1, in terms of the average error rates across six cashiers. Note that errors when the card shows someone else's face involve failing to detect a potential fraud.

Two points stand out. First, shoppers were challenged by the cashiers on around 10% of occasions even when they presented a card with a genuine photo of themselves. Second, many of the cards that showed someone else's face were accepted as valid, and most were accepted if there was some similarity in appearance (the matched foil condition). The implication is very clearly that comparing a photo of a face to the face of the person standing in front of you is not as easy as we usually take it to be.

Kemp et al.'s findings again underscore the importance of testing what might seem obvious, instead of relying on intuition or 'common sense'. For the purpose of evaluating the usefulness of showing photos on credit cards, the experiment's realism is a definite asset, but for understanding why so many

Table 2.1 Percentages of incorrect cashier decisions to different types of card in Kemp et al.'s (1997) study.

Cards showing the bearer's face:	
Unchanged appearance	7%
Paraphernalia change	14%
Cards showing someone else's face:	
Matched foil	64%
Unmatched foil	34%

errors were made by the cashiers, it isn't actually necessary. A relatively simple demonstration is enough to see that there might be a problem.

Look at Figure 2.1a. The picture on the left is that of a person who may or may not be among the 10 photos on the right. Is he there? The pictures all show faces taken from the same angle, with much the same expression, and photographed on the same day, so it doesn't seem like it should be that difficult. Yet the error rate reported by Bruce, Henderson, Greenwood, Hancock, Burton and Miller (1999) was around 30%. Answer: he is there, at number 3.

What seems to make the task so tricky is that the target photo and the pictures from the choice array were taken under different lighting conditions by

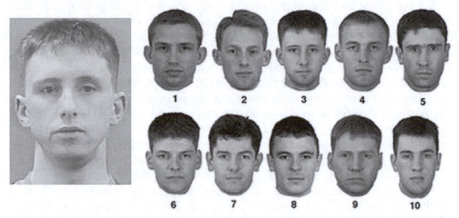

Figure 2.1a Unfamiliar face matching. Is the person on the left shown among the 10 photos on the right? Reprinted from *Trends in Cognitive Sciences*, Vol. 4, Peter J. B. Hancock, Vicki Bruce, A. Mike Burton, Recognition of unfamiliar faces, pp. 330–337. Copyright (2000) with permission from Elsevier.

Figure 2.1b Familiar face matching. Is the person on the left shown among the 10 photos on the right? David Cameron, courtesy of Press Association Images.

different cameras. We find it surprisingly hard to work out which differences in the pictures reflect changes in lighting, and which are due to genuine differences between the faces (Hancock, Bruce, & Burton, 2001).

Now try again with Figure 2.1b. If you know the target person, the task becomes almost trivially easy.

The bottom line is that we are not as good at recognising faces as we like to think. Or, more precisely, we are not very good with the unfamiliar faces of people we haven't seen before. For familiar faces, recognition is much more robust and able to cope with such variations. Even familiar face recognition is not perfect, though. Errors collected from diary studies where people record instances where they failed to recognise people (Young, Hay, & Ellis, 1985) or from formal studies recording identification of photos of famous people (Hay, Young, & Ellis, 1991) show that there are times when we may slip up even with very familiar faces, though usually such mistakes are quickly corrected.

Why, then, are most of us so over-confident in our ability to recognise faces? One contributory factor is probably that our relatively good recognition of familiar faces misleads us into thinking that we will be as good with all of the faces we encounter. But psychology researchers are just as guilty of falling into the trap. One of the paradoxes from the spate of face recognition research in the 1970s triggered by examples such as Laszlo Virag's wrongful conviction was that laboratory studies did seem to bear out that we are remarkably good at recognising faces we have only seen once before, which for a while made it even more puzzling how wrongful convictions based on witness identification might arise.

These studies mainly used variants of a recognition memory paradigm in which participants looked at a series of photographs of unfamiliar faces and were then asked to pick out the faces they had seen before when they were mixed in with previously unseen distractor faces. In tasks like this, high recognition accuracies can be obtained even when large numbers of faces are looked at for only a few seconds each. However, researchers often had access to only one photograph of each of the test faces, and so the same photograph was studied in the first part of the experiment as was used to test recognition in the second part. If, in contrast, the study and test photos are different pictures of the same person, performance drops dramatically (Bruce, 1982; Longmore, Liu, & Young, 2008). What these experiments show is therefore that we are very good at remembering unfamiliar *photographs* (excellent performance at picking out the pictures we saw before), but we are actually not very good at remembering unfamiliar *faces* (poor performance at recognising a different picture of one of the faces we saw before). This simple but important distinction between photograph/picture recognition and face recognition substantially qualifies the widely used idea that, because of our everyday interest in faces, we are all face experts. Instead, although we certainly do acquire considerable expertise for many of the things we do with faces, this acquired expertise has its limits. Understanding the limits of perceptual expertise may offer useful insights.

Errors therefore form an important source of information. We have seen how they can be used in more or less realistic studies of eyewitness testimony, in diary studies, and in purely laboratory-based studies. These include recognition memory paradigms, and various types of perceptual matching task.

Errors can also offer insight into other things we can do with faces apart from recognising them. We can study errors in recognising people's facial expressions, in perceiving where they are looking, in telling their age or sex, and so on. Investigating errors is a powerful general technique for gaining insight into abilities we often take for granted.

Unavoidable errors: The effects of brain injury

The errors we have considered so far are those everyone makes occasionally, but against a pattern in which we can often get things right and avoid mistakes. A limitation of this is that, because errors may be infrequent, it can be difficult to study them systematically. Techniques such as limiting the presentation time of experimental stimuli can sometimes be used to increase error rates, but at the risk of distorting what is being investigated. A particularly compelling version of the approach of studying errors therefore involves investigating the effects of brain injuries, which can sometimes dramatically increase the frequency of a particular type of error.

For example, there has been a lot of interest in prosopagnosia, a neuropsychological condition caused by damage to the occipito-temporal cortex in which patients become unable to recognise familiar faces (Ellis & Florence, 1990). Even the most familiar faces may go unrecognised, including family, friends and the patient's own face when seen in a mirror. Yet people who suffer prosopagnosia have not forgotten the identities of familiar people; they can often recognise them from other cues such as voice or name, and they don't have problems using such cues to recall what they know about a person.

One way to think about prosopagnosia is that it may be like a very exaggerated form of the problem all of us have from time to time when we fail to recognise someone we know (Young, Hay, & Ellis, 1985) – you don't realise it happened until your friend says something like 'Hey, you walked right past me in town yesterday!' In prosopagnosia, however, this becomes a severe and relatively permanent problem, making it possible to document thoroughly just what exactly it is that the person with prosopagnosia can and cannot do when s/he looks at a face. The key concept is that prosopagnosia is a dissociable deficit, in the sense that some abilities are defective yet others are relatively intact. For example, we have seen that memory for people is relatively intact in prosopagnosia, and still accessible from voices or names; it is recognising faces that presents the problem. But this raises all kinds of interesting questions that we will address elsewhere in the book. Is the face perceived normally (for example, in terms of ability to see age and sex)? Is the recognition problem specific to faces, or does it affect other types of visual object? What about recognising facial expressions of emotion? And so on.

By studying cases of prosopagnosia, we can therefore arrive at an understanding of which deficits are commonly found together with the problem in recognising faces (*associated* deficits) and which deficits need not co-occur (*dissociable* deficits). Interestingly, it turns out that perception of unfamiliar faces may be relatively intact in prosopagnosia – patients sometimes perform as well as non-prosopagnosic control participants on matching unfamiliar faces using tasks like that shown in Figure 2.1a (Barton, 2008).

This single dissociation (preserved unfamiliar face matching with impaired familiar face recognition) could suggest that to recognise a face we must first create an adequate percept of what the face is like, as is shown schematically in Figure 2.2a. The idea would be that an adequate facial percept would permit successful matching of photographs of unfamiliar faces, so that only the second (recognition) stage is compromised in cases of prosopagnosia with preserved ability to match unfamiliar faces. If this were true, patients who cannot create an adequate percept (i.e. those who are poor at unfamiliar face matching) should always be prosopagnosic as well. Interestingly, this straightforward prediction turns out to be false – people who have suffered brain injuries that compromise their ability to match photographs of unfamiliar faces are not usually prosopagnosic (Benton, 1980). This pattern of a *double dissociation* of deficits across different patients offers evidence that familiar face recognition and unfamiliar face matching are in some respect functionally independent from each other, as shown in Figure 2.2b.

The method of carefully studying brain-injured individuals to look for theoretically interesting dissociations therefore offers important insights. In later chapters, we will look at other important dissociations, including facial identity recognition versus facial expression recognition, overt and covert recognition of identity, and name retrieval compared with accessing other forms of semantic information. All of these dissociations arise in the context of brain injury acquired in adulthood, and the method of studying dissociable deficits due to adult brain injury is usually called 'cognitive neuropsychology'. Characteristic of this approach is the attempt to relate the consequences of brain injury to some form of model of the normal pattern of organisation of the ability investigated, as in Figure 2.2 – the type of diagrammatic representations used in Figure 2.2 are often called 'functional models'. Moreover, we have seen from Figure 2.2 that cognitive neuropsychology can be interpreted as consistent with one functional model (Figure 2.2b) and falsifying another (Figure 2.2a).

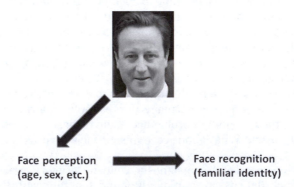

Face perception
(age, sex, etc.)

Face recognition
(familiar identity)

Figure 2.2a Schematic representation of sequential model for face perception (needed for matching images of unfamiliar people) and face recognition. Courtesy of Press Association Images.

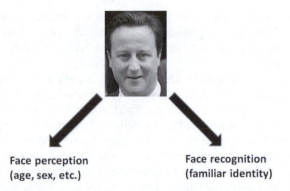

Face perception
(age, sex, etc.)

Face recognition
(familiar identity)

Figure 2.2b Schematic representation of parallel model for face perception (needed for matching images of unfamiliar people) and face recognition. Courtesy of Press Association Images.

Cognitive neuropsychology, then, views brain injury as a kind of heartless natural experiment that can potentially offer striking insights into the organisation of our normal cognitive abilities. It is not, however, without difficulties. Whilst nature may be heartless, psychologists should not be, so there are a number of ethical issues concerning the welfare and dignity of participants with what are often disabling and distressing conditions. There are also technical and interpretive problems that need to be faced. Ideally, one would only want to claim a dissociable deficit when a person with a brain injury is completely unable to do one thing and perfectly able to do another. This, though, will in turn depend on the brain injury's having abolished one of the functional components involved, whilst leaving the other totally spared. For a variety of reasons, this seldom happens in practice; a more common pattern is that one ability seems to be more affected than another, creating a relative rather than a perfect dissociation (Shallice, 1988).

You can see why quite easily if you think about the effects of strokes, one of the more common causes of brain injury. In a stroke, blood supply to a region of brain is interrupted, leaving the brain cells in that region starved of oxygen. Unfortunately, without oxygen, brain cells quickly die, creating a region of damage called a lesion. But, of course, the location and extent of this lesion will depend on the location and duration of the interruption of blood supply, which is in turn affected by the arrangement of blood vessels in that part of the brain. The lesions created by strokes can therefore show considerable variability, and the possibility of affecting one critical component of mental abilities without also having at least some impact on other components seems unlikely. Kanwisher (2000), who has been a strong proponent of the idea that a region of brain may be specialised for face perception, used the analogy that the chance that a stroke might destroy this specialised face region without affecting nearby cortical areas 'is similar to the chance that an asteroid hitting New England would obliterate all of the state of Rhode Island without affecting Massachusetts or Connecticut' (Kanwisher, 2000, p. 760).

For this kind of reason, a lot of the emphasis in cognitive neuropsychology is placed on relatively rare patients whose deficits come close to the pattern predicted by a theory, rather than on the more typical patients who may have multiple problems.

Brain injuries acquired in adulthood reflect damage to what was presumably a well-organised system. However, a recent development has been to turn the cognitive neuropsychological spotlight toward neurodevelopmental disorders. For example, it turns out that a small proportion of people grow up unable to recognise faces very well; they suffer from a developmental (as opposed to adult-acquired) prosopagnosia. In the research literature, the labels 'congenital prosopagnosia' and sometimes 'developmental prosopagnosia' are used interchangeably to refer to this condition. Interestingly, congenital prosopagnosia can run in families, implying the possibility of a genetic link (de Haan, 1999; Duchaine, Germine, & Nakayama, 2007; Schmalzl, Palermo, & Coltheart, 2008).

A lot of the questions that can be asked about acquired disorders can also be asked of neurodevelopmental differences. In congenital prosopagnosia, for example, we can again investigate ability to tell age and sex from faces, whether the recognition problem is face-specific, and whether facial expressions of emotion can be recognised. There are important differences, though, in what the findings can be taken to mean (Bishop, 1997), because they arise in the context of a system that has itself developed along an atypical or abnormal trajectory. For this reason, the implications of studies of congenital disorders are not simply the same as those of studies of acquired impairments; they need to be carefully thought through.

The time it takes to do things: Reaction times and what they can tell us

We have seen that errors, either in the form of everyday or laboratory-induced slips or of more intractable problems created by acquired brain injury or neurodevelopmental abnormalities, offer valuable sources of information, though they also have their limitations.

A useful adjunct to studying errors can be to investigate reaction times. In cognitive neuropsychological studies the ideal is to demonstrate well-preserved, normal performance of one task and contrast it with highly deficient performance of another task. But what counts as normal? Often, accuracy scores that fall within the range of a comparison group of neurologically normal individuals (usually called a 'control group') or that meet some statistical criterion (such as a z-score with a probability greater than a specified cut-off value) are taken as evidence of normality, but these can themselves be influenced by technical properties of the measures (especially ceiling performance by normal controls, which can suggest the test is too easy to be able to discriminate at the higher-scoring end). It is also sometimes necessary to question the assumption that a normal score reflects normal cognitive mechanisms. Newcombe (1979) noted that although her prosopagnosic patient RB could match pictures of unfamiliar faces, he took a long time to do this and seemed to rely on careful feature by feature comparison. This led Newcombe to suggest that RB's apparent dissociation between impaired familiar face recognition and preserved unfamiliar face matching might reflect the availability of alternative strategies in face-matching paradigms. From this point of view, reaction time measures might form a useful additional source of information, since unusual strategies will often be time-consuming. The danger, of course, is that people with brain injuries may often be slow and careful for reasons other than that they are deploying unusual strategies. In fact, as noted from Figure 2.1a, studies of neurologically normal people tend to show that matching photos of unfamiliar faces is sufficiently tricky that all of us try various techniques to see which will help solve what can be a surprisingly problematic perceptual puzzle (Hancock et al., 2001). If, however, an individual with prosopagnosia can achieve *both* normal accuracy *and* speed of unfamiliar face matching, as did Sergent and Poncet's (1990) patient, this is impressive evidence that the dissociation is unlikely to be strategic in origin. More generally, looking at the relation between speed and accuracy can offer insight into strategic factors across a range of paradigms.

Importantly, though, the time it takes to do things can be a useful source of information in its own right. This applies especially to experiments with neurologically normal participants, where reaction time measures can be used in a variety of ways.

First, we can look at the time it takes to reach different types of decision. Consider again the possible sequence represented in Figure 2.2a. How might we assess when each stage has been completed? The second stage (recognising the face) doesn't seem too problematic; we can simply use a task that can only be successfully performed if the face is recognised, such as deciding whether or not the face is that of a familiar person. Assessing the first (perceptual representation) stage is a bit more tricky. One possibility that we already looked at would be to use a face-matching task, but we saw this is unsatisfactory because people tend to make lots of errors and use a ragbag of strategies when asked to match pictures of unfamiliar faces. A better way might be to ask participants to carry out a task they can perform well even with unfamiliar faces, but one that is sufficiently tricky that it requires an accurate perceptual representation. An example would be judging the sex of a face; we can do this very accurately, even though the differences between men's and women's faces can be fairly subtle (see Chapter 3).

So, let's try to measure the time it takes to complete each of the stages shown in Figure 2.2a. To do this, we can set up an experiment in which people see a series of photographs of unfamiliar and familiar faces, one at a time. We will need two different experimental conditions. In the first condition, each time a face is presented the participant presses one button if it is a man's face and another button if it is a woman's face. We record the reaction time (from onset of the face photograph) and accuracy of these button presses, in order to calculate the average reaction time needed to determine a face's sex across a number of trials. In the second condition, the participant's task is to press one button if the face is a familiar person and another button if it is an unfamiliar person; again, we record accuracy and reaction time across a number of trials.

Having completed such an experiment, it is usual to find that reaction times to determine a face's sex are faster than those for determining its familiarity (Bruce, Ellis, Gibling, & Young, 1987). Importantly, the experiment can be designed in a way that will eliminate potentially uninteresting possible explanations of this result. For example, we can record the critical reaction times from the same finger, so that any difference between conditions isn't something to do with the required button-pressing movement. We can use the same photographs in each condition, to ensure that it isn't something to do with the pictures themselves. We can even make the comparison photograph by photograph (instead of using overall mean reaction times across photographs) to determine for what proportion of the faces themselves the decision about sex is faster than the decision about identity. In all, we can be confident that it is a 'genuine' finding.

However, being a genuine finding and arriving at the correct interpretation are not the same thing. One obvious limitation of the reaction times recorded in our hypothetical experiment is that they contain some indeterminate mix of the time needed to decide what was asked (i.e. whether the face is male or female, or whether it is familiar or unfamiliar) plus the time needed to make the button-press response. However, as we already noted, the button-press response is common to both experimental tasks (recognising sex, and recognising identity), so any *difference* between reaction times for each task should not be created by the button-press time itself. In fact, if we are confident that Figure 2.2a is correct, we can deduce that the reaction time to determine a face's sex consists of the time needed to perceive the face plus the time to press the button, whereas the reaction time to determine a face's familiarity consists of the time to perceive the face plus the time to recognise it plus the time to press the button. On this basis, we could simply subtract the reaction time for recognising sex from the reaction time for recognising facial identity, to arrive at the time needed for the face recognition stage.

This important technique of *cognitive subtraction* was devised by the Dutch physiologist Franciscus Cornelis Donders in the nineteenth century. Its correct application depends, though, on the components investigated mapping neatly onto the tasks used, and on their taking place in sequence, as in Figure 2.2a, rather than taking place in parallel, as in Figure 2.2b. If the processes take place in parallel, the result of subtracting the time taken for one from the time taken for the other has little meaning.

What grounds does our experiment offer for favouring the sequentially organised Figure 2.2a over the parallel organisation shown in Figure 2.2b? The fact that we can tell a face's sex more quickly than we can tell its identity is certainly *consistent* with Figure 2.2a, but a bit of thought shows it does not prove that Figure 2.2a is correct. An alternative possibility is that sex and identity recognition take place in parallel (as in Figure 2.2b), but at different speeds.

So how can we use reaction times to distinguish these possibilities? One trick is to do something that will affect what should be the first component in the sequence; in our example, the process of recognising the face's sex. If sex and identity recognition take place in sequence (Figure 2.2a), then anything that affects seeing a face's sex will also have an impact on seeing its identity. If sex and identity

Table 2.2 Average reaction times in milliseconds for correctly classifying unfamiliar and familiar male faces of highly masculine or less masculine appearance as male or female ('Judge sex') or as familiar or unfamiliar ('Judge familiarity') from one of Bruce et al.'s (1987) experiments. See text for explanation.

'Masculine' appearance:	Unfamiliar faces			Familiar faces		
	High	*Low*	*'M benefit'*	*High*	*Low*	*'M benefit'*
Judge sex	532	694	+162	558	682	+124
Judge familiarity	1056	1113	+57	911	883	–28

recognition take place in parallel (Figure 2.2b), we may find that it is possible to alter reaction times for seeing sex without any effect on seeing identity.

Exactly this logic was used by Bruce, Ellis, Gibling and Young (1987), who took advantage of the fact that some faces are naturally harder to classify as male or female (i.e. more androgynous in appearance) than others. If (say) it is harder (and therefore takes longer) to see that Leonardo di Caprio's face is a man's face than it takes to see that Clint Eastwood's face is a man's face, then if Figure 2.2a is correct we would expect that it will also take longer to recognise Leonardo di Caprio as familiar.

Table 2.2 shows average reaction times for correctly classifying unfamiliar and familiar male faces as male or female ('Judge sex') or as familiar or unfamiliar ('Judge familiarity') from one of Bruce et al.'s (1987) experiments. These correct reaction times (RTs) are tabulated separately for faces that are of highly masculine or less masculine appearance, with the differences between RTs to high and low masculinity faces used to estimate any advantage of stereotypically masculine appearance for the relevant decision (the 'M benefit'). The critical data are those for familiar faces, where it is clear that looking masculine makes it easier to judge a face's sex yet has no substantial effect on determining its familiarity. This lends support to the arrangement shown in Figure 2.2b.

Priming and interference: Important and widely used paradigms

Widely used variants of cognitive subtraction involve phenomena known collectively as 'priming' and interference. Priming refers to manipulations that will facilitate whatever you are asked to do with an item. A commonly used form of priming involves repetition of a stimulus. Repetition priming studies look at the benefit of having encountered an item before, usually (but not necessarily) the benefit of having seen it fairly recently. In a face recognition study, we might show a set of *training* faces and ask participants to look at them or maybe rate them for some characteristic, then follow this with a task of deciding whether or not each of a *test* series of faces is familiar. The familiar test faces can include 'primed' faces that were presented in the training set, and 'unprimed' faces that were not in the training set, with any increase in speed of response (i.e. faster reaction time) for primed compared with unprimed items indicating the benefit of having recently seen the faces.

This can be a useful way of probing the representations involved in recognition. For example, studies of repetition priming show that seeing Clint Eastwood's face will facilitate later recognition of Clint Eastwood's face, whereas reading Clint Eastwood's name confers no benefit on later recognition of Clint Eastwood's face (Bruce & Valentine, 1985). Conversely, seeing Clint Eastwood's name does facilitate later recognition of Clint Eastwood's name, whereas seeing Clint Eastwood's face confers no benefit on later recognition of Clint Eastwood's name. The simplest interpretation of this pattern is that distinct perceptual representations are needed for name and face recognition. Importantly it also shows that our ability to recall what we have seen before is not the primary determinant of our ability to recognise things. Participants can often remember perfectly well whether Clint Eastwood was in the training set and even whether it was his face or name that they saw, yet it is only having seen Eastwood's face that affects later recognition of his face.

Another form of priming effect looks at the benefit conferred by something that is closely associated with the target – for example, the benefit of seeing Cherie Blair on recognising Tony Blair. This phenomenon, known in the literature as associative priming or as semantic priming, turns out to have instructively different properties from repetition priming, as we will see in Chapter 7.

Priming effects involve facilitation compared to a baseline (unprimed) condition, whereas in interference paradigms performance is often impaired (slower reaction times and/or more errors). The difference between what will lead to priming or to interference is not always obvious, but a common feature is a difference in relative timing – in priming paradigms the prime is usually presented before the test stimulus, whereas in interference paradigms the interfering and test stimuli are usually presented together.

A well-known example of interference is the Stroop task, in which people are asked to name the colours of written words. Naming the colour 'green' (for example) is slower if the word happens to be 'red' than if the word is 'green' – we aren't able to suppress the tendency to read the word, which then competes with the (requested) response of naming the colour of the ink. Closely related paradigms can be used to investigate properties of face recognition through testing interference between faces and names (Young, Ellis, Flude, McWeeny, & Hay, 1986). For example, by comparing the time taken to name David Beckham's face when it is presented alongside the written name 'David Beckham' to the time taken to name David Beckham's face when it is accompanied by the written name 'Madonna', we can investigate whether the presence of an irrelevant name will slow naming a familiar face (it does). We can then examine what exactly causes the interference by using names that are more or less closely related to the face in different ways (e.g. other men, other footballers, members of the same team, his wife).

In the above examples, interference is measured between competing classes of stimuli that may need to access the same semantic representations (coloured inks and colour words, or faces and names), but it is also possible to create competition between different forms of perceptual representation. A widely used variant of this for studies of face perception is Young, Hellawell and Hay's (1987) composite paradigm, which exploits the idea that faces can be analysed as wholes ('holistic processing') or in terms of their constituent parts (features).

Look at the images in Figure 2.3. The first (left) column shows the faces of British politicians David Cameron and Ed Miliband. Images in the second and third columns are made by recombining the top and bottom halves of their faces. When these face parts are slightly misaligned, as in the third column, it is easy to see which half comes from which face. But if the two parts are aligned with each other to create a composite face, as in the central column, the perception of a new whole face makes it harder to recognise whether the top half or the bottom half belongs to Cameron or Miliband. It isn't impossible to see this (perception of the parts isn't abolished), but it is more difficult (because seeing the whole gets in the way of analysing the parts). This face composite effect (as measured by the difference in performance between aligned and misaligned stimuli) offers an estimate of the influence of holistic perception (via its ability to interfere with

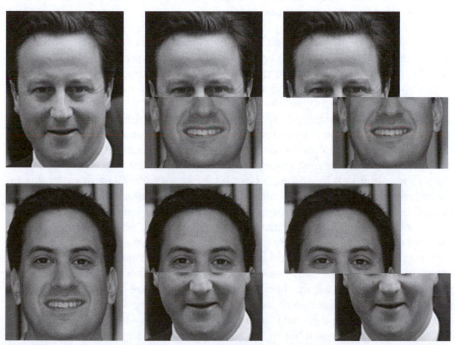

Figure 2.3 Face composite technique used by Young, Hellawell and Hay (1987). The left column shows the faces of David Cameron and Ed Miliband. In the centre column, the top and bottom halves of their faces are exchanged to create new 'composite' faces. In the final column, the parts of the composites are 'misaligned' so they don't form an overall face configuration. It is more difficult to identify the constituent parts (i.e. the top half or the bottom half) of composite than misaligned images. Courtesy of Press Association Images.

feature-based processing) that can be applied to a range of things we perceive in faces (sex, race, identity, expression, etc.).

Another widely adopted interference paradigm in face perception research derives from Garner's influential approach – Garner was not himself studying faces, but his technique is adaptable to many questions (Garner, 1974). In Garner interference, participants judge stimuli on one of two dimensions (in face research, this will be some specific characteristic of a face). Trials are grouped into blocks that map the two dimensions to each other in different ways. In the 'correlated' condition, a particular value on the dimension to be judged is always paired with a particular value on the irrelevant (non-judged) dimension, whereas in the 'orthogonal' (non-correlated) condition, the values on each dimension vary independently. Often a control condition (called the 'constant' condition) will be included, in which the irrelevant dimension does not vary at all. The logic of the Garner interference paradigm is that a difference in performance between the correlated and orthogonal conditions indicates that the participant cannot analyse the dimensions as completely independent channels – compared to the baseline constant condition there may be facilitation (faster and more accurate responses) for the correlated condition, and interference (slower, less accurate responses) for the orthogonal condition.

The Garner interference method was first applied to face research by Etcoff (1984), to demonstrate that right-sided brain injury reduced the degree of independence of perception of a face's identity and its expression. Her technique was slightly unusual in that she measured the overall time needed to sort sets of faces across different conditions, rather than the more typical measure of reaction times for responses to each trial recorded in most other studies (Schweinberger & Soukup, 1998). However, outlining Etcoff's procedure will probably help make the Garner technique a bit easier to understand. In separate sets of trials, participants were asked to classify (sort) faces either by identity or by expression. The stimuli consisted of photos of two women posing two expressions (happy and sad). In the correlated condition of Etcoff's study one value on the expression dimension was consistently paired with one value on the identity dimension – for example, pictures of woman A with a happy expression inter- mixed with an equal number of pictures of woman B with a sad expression. In the constant condition only one dimension varied, with the other remaining constant – for example, the pictures would be of one woman showing the two expressions when the task was to classify the expression, or of the two women showing one expression when the task was to classify the identity. In the orthogonal condition, equal numbers of pictures were used in which both expressions and both identi- ties were combined in the four possible ways.

As we noted, the aim of the Garner approach is to investigate how well we can separate the two dimensions concerned. If they function as completely inde- pendent channels, there will be no differences in performance between the correlated, constant and orthogonal conditions. What is less clear is what exactly the presence of interference signifies. Garner called this evidence that the dimen- sions have *integral* properties, which might be taken to imply that they are perceptually integrated. Etcoff, in contrast, used interference as a measure of selective attention to each dimension – of course, failures of selective attention would be expected if there is perceptual integration of the dimensions, but it is important to recognise that they can also have other causes. A more neutral way to put things is therefore that demonstrations of Garner interference show some form of crosstalk between the dimensions. As we will see in later chapters, the inability of Garner interference techniques to pin down the precise nature of this crosstalk can create contention.

Other sources of information: Preferences and adaptation

Errors and reaction times are not the only measures we can use. Some interesting technical demands arise in studies where participants can't be given verbal instructions as to what they are required to do, such as in studies of infants. Considerable ingenuity has gone into finding ways round such difficulties. An important insight is that one way to solve the problem is to find an informative naturally occurring behaviour.

For instance, most of us prefer to look at things we find pleasant than things that are less pleasing. So if we show two pictures to an infant and it spends longer looking at one than the other, we can infer that it has a preference for that stimulus, provided that we use appropriate counterbalancing and other techniques to eliminate obvious confounds such as the possibility that the baby just likes to look in one direction more than another.

The existence of a looking preference demonstrates something important, because a baby cannot prefer one thing over another unless it can see a difference between them. Moreover, preferences very often go in the direction of favouring things that are familiar over the unfamiliar or novel. So, if we want to know whether babies know something about human faces, we might try investigating whether they prefer looking at human faces to monkey faces; if we want to know whether they can recognise their mother's face, we might investigate whether they look longer at her face than at a stranger's, and so on. Such studies require painstaking, meticulous attention to tricky procedural factors that range from ensuring the babies are suitably alert to eliminating extraneous cues such as odours if the baby's own mother is present. These are cues that can seem trivial or undetectable to adults, but that doesn't mean they are as unimportant in the baby's perceptual world!

Although careful studies of infant looking preferences have offered valuable insights,there is a limitation on the inferences that can be drawn. A positive finding of a preference implies that an infant has registered some difference between a pair of stimuli, but unfortunately the negative finding of absence of a preference doesn't imply that it can't tell the difference. It is conceivable that an infant might see differences yet have no preference, leaving negative results tricky to interpret. Here, habituation studies are useful, because they can offer a more sensitive measure.

Habituation studies take advantage of our decreasing interest in something that we come across repeatedly. For example, if you show someone a series of ten pictures and the first nine happen to be all the same, the chances are that they will spend less time looking at the ninth picture in the series than they spent inspecting the first picture, because it has lost its novelty. If, however, the tenth picture in the series differs from the previous nine, there will be a recovery of interest and increased inspection time. But, of course, this recovery of interest will only arise if the person can see the difference between the novel (tenth) picture and the repeated (first to ninth) pictures. So, we can use recovery of interest following habituation as an index of whether or not a particular change is detected. Habituation has been used to study recognition of faces in the developing infant, as we describe in Chapter 8.

A related technique that has become popular in studies of adults is known as 'adaptation'. This depends on the observation that if you look at a fixed type of visual stimulus for a while, you seem to adapt to its presence in a way that can affect looking at something else. Adaptation has been used to explore lower and higher levels of the representation of faces by the adult visual system.

The visual system is built in a way which responds to change, and hence to informative aspects of visual input. Information about boundaries between objects in the world, and the shapes of objects, is carried by spatial pattern information in the image (e.g. a difference in intensity across the image) and information about events in the world is conveyed by changes over time – the temporal pattern. Cells early in the visual system respond in ways that emphasise discontinuities in space via *lateral inhibition* (Hartline, Wagner, & Ratliff, 1956) in a way which helps reveal important boundaries between regions of the image. And cells early in the visual system will adapt over time to continuous unvarying stimulation in a way which makes them less responsive after a few minutes' exposure. For example, cells in the visual system respond with a burst of activity when a light comes on, but then their rate of firing diminishes if the pattern remains unchanged.

If you stare at a bright light or patch for a minute or so, and then look at a uniform field, you will see a dark patch or 'after-image' which corresponds to the area of the retina which was stimulated by the original bright part. A rather striking example of this is illustrated in Figure 2.4. Stare at the left panel for at least a minute. Try not to move your eyes at all by fixating the central dot. After a minute, look at the blank area to the right. You will see a famous face! This dramatic effect is quite easy to explain. You should be able to understand why the famous face is seen once you are told that the upper panel contains a negative image of the face, with light and dark areas reversed from the original image. Adaptation of cells stimulated by the bright region means that when gaze is transferred to the uniform field, a positive version of the original face will be seen in the pattern of the after-image. The 'illusion' relies on the fact that faces are difficult to recognise in photographic negative images (and hence the initial identity of the image is concealed in Figure 2.4), but readily identified from black on white images, provided these contain appropriate regions of light and dark (see Chapter 6).

With adaptation effects, careful controls are needed to determine the precise nature of the observed adaptation. You can verify that this particular effect arises early on in the visual system by repeating the demonstration, but this time closing one eye when you stare at the adapting figure. After one minute, transfer your gaze and now compare the after-effects seen by the adapted and unadapted eye. Only the adapted eye sees the after-effect, confirming that the

Figure 2.4 A face illusion seen in a visual after-image. See text for viewing instructions. The after-image is easier to see if you blink your eyes when looking at the blank region. From Bruce and Young (1998)

effect arises because of activity in cells prior to the combination of information from the two eyes.

Low-level after-effects like this rarely arise in everyday life, as our eyes do not normally remain still enough for selective adaptation to occur. The eyes are in constant motion, darting from one part of the visual scene to another through large-scale movements called 'saccades', through smoothly following moving objects, and also through making continuous tiny flicks and tremors. All these movements mean that retinal receptors are rarely exposed to constant stimulation.

However, adaptation effects can also be found for what seem to be complex, multidimensional aspects of the visual environment, and studies of face perception have provided important demonstrations of effects that seem to demand a higher-level explanation. Figure 2.5a shows stimuli used in a seminal study by Webster and MacLin (1999). The image from the centre of the display is distorted in the horizontal (x distortion) or vertical (y distortion) dimensions by expanding or contracting it around the centre of the image (more or less, the middle of the nose) in a way that makes the degree of change greatest for the regions closest to this central point in the image. By doing this, changes in the shapes of internal features are maximised whilst leaving the overall face shape, hair and background relatively unaffected.

Webster and MacLin taught participants to recognise the original, undistorted image and then asked them to use keyboard buttons to scroll through the x and y coordinates of the image array in order to move from a distorted image back to this undistorted original. Their choices ('nulling matches') are shown as the

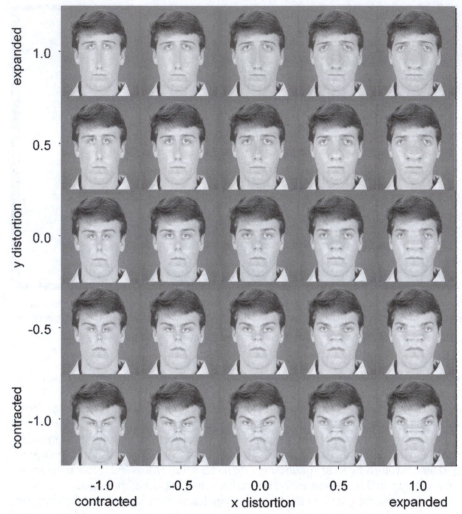

Figure 2.5a Stimuli used by Webster and MacLin (1999). See text for explanation. With kind permission from Springer Science+Business Media: Figural after effects in the perception of faces, *Psychonomic Bulletin & Review*, 6, 1999, Michael A. Webster.

'before' curve in Figure 2.5b for stimuli distorted along the x dimension. As might be expected, this is a flat line, showing that participants know what the undistorted image looks like. More interesting is the 'after' curve, which shows choices of what is perceived as undistorted following adaptation from prolonged viewing of an image that was distorted in the x dimension. Now the choice of undistorted image is shifted in the direction of the adapting image – showing a change in perception of other images in the array resulting from adaptation. Similar findings were made with arrays based on other faces, and for changes along the x and y dimensions.

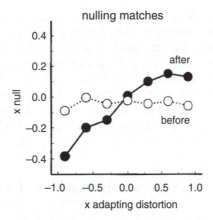

Figure 2.5b Data from Webster and MacLin (1999). See text for explanation. With kind permission from Springer Science+Business Media: Figural aftereffects in the perception of faces, *Psychonomic Bulletin & Review*, 6, 1999, Michael A. Webster.

As we will see in later chapters, the adaptation technique has become a widely used method for exploring our perception of faces. A range of interesting and sometimes remarkably selective effects can be revealed, offering potentially important insights. Where the technique can run into difficulties, though, is in pinpointing exactly what underlies a particular adaptation phenomenon. Both low-level and high-level neural mechanisms may be involved, and it is also possible that some effects might reflect a change in a participant's criterion for what counts as a good example of the category in question. Teasing apart these various alternatives requires painstaking and sometimes ingenious use of appropriate comparison conditions.

Eye movements: Where you look, and why it matters

Studies of preferential looking take advantage of the fact that our eyes are constantly darting from one part of the visual scene to another through movements called saccades. A useful tactic can be to investigate more closely where these saccades are targeted in a visual display.

The reason why we need saccadic eye movements is that only a small central region of the retina of each eye (the fovea) has a sufficiently dense concentration of cones for the high acuity vision that can allow us to see fine detail. This means that we are constantly moving our eyes to regions of interest in a visual scene, and in consequence the brain uses highly sophisticated systems to control eye movements (Carpenter, 1988).

A useful side effect of this arrangement is that by studying where we look (i.e. by monitoring the patterns of eye movements) we can make inferences about how we integrate critical details into a scene and where our eyes/brains think they will find them. As everyday observers of other people's faces we do this naturally, taking advantage of gaze direction to infer (among other things) what interests someone (see Chapter 5). Many recent research studies have pursued this approach more formally, encouraged in part by technical developments that have made accurate and automated eye-movement recording both simple and affordable. None the less, it is important not to underestimate how much we can do without foveal information – for faces, a surprising amount can often be taken in with a single glance, largely because (as we will soon explain) the brain makes use of information from different spatial scales.

Understanding and manipulating images: Contributions of computer graphics

We have seen that faces are a rich visual stimulus, containing a multiplicity of cues. Many of these cues are very difficult to quantify, and this has been a serious obstacle to identifying what is or is not important. For more than a century, accurate images of the patterns of light and shade falling across a face have been available via photography. The existence of photographs has been invaluable in face research, but it has also led to some blind alleys. The clearest (though still underappreciated) of these blind alleys is created by the assumption that because they are relatively veridical records of patterns of light and shade, the interpretation of photographs by human perceivers will be unproblematic. Instead, findings such as those of Kemp et al. (1997) and Hancock et al. (2001) show we can find it very difficult indeed to work out which parts of the light pattern shown in a photo accurately reflect the characteristics of a depicted face and which are face-irrelevant effects of lighting conditions and camera properties.

To do good science it is essential to be able to control and manipulate the inputs to the visual system to examine the changes in perception or recognition that result. One reason for the dramatic advances in our understanding of face perception over the past 30 years is that it has become possible to use computer graphics to vary face patterns systematically in a way that was just not possible with photographs. We have already seen one example of this in the materials used in Webster and MacLin's (1999) adaptation studies (see Figure 2.5a). In this section we review the different kinds of contributions that have resulted. We will focus on three important areas – the analysis of the spatial structures in two-dimensional (2D) face images; the development of techniques for morphing and caricaturing facial images; and finally we consider how cues within images and image sequences can specify three-dimensional shape and movement.

2D spatial analysis

A visual pattern can be described at different levels of detail or scale. If you look close up in the mirror, you will notice every wrinkle and blemish on your own face, but if you blur your eyes or look at a more distant mirror image only larger scale features are visible. Our visual system appears to operate in a way that separately analyses or 'filters' different spatial scales. Here we give only the sketchiest of introductions to this complex technical area (see Bruce, Green, & Georgeson, 2003 for more detail).

At each stage of visual processing in the retina, lateral geniculate nucleus and visual cortex of mammals, cells are activated by light falling within localised areas known as their 'receptive fields'. Receptive fields are organised so that cells respond to discontinuities rather than to uniform input, so that a cell is excited by light in one part of its receptive field and inhibited by light falling elsewhere. For example, 'on'-centre retinal ganglion cells have concentric receptive fields where light falling towards the centre excites the cell and light falling in the periphery of the field inhibits it ('off'-centre ganglion cells have the opposite organisation). 'On'-centre cells will not respond at all to a uniform field – since inhibition from the surround will cancel excitation from the centre – but will respond strongly to local spatial changes in the image. This is an essential first stage in the process by which the visual system locates important image features such as 'edges' that might signify important structures in the world (e.g. object boundaries).

Importantly, while retinal ganglion cells pool information across their receptive fields, these receptive fields can themselves be of different sizes. When receptive field sizes are relatively large, fine spatial detail is lost and a set of ganglion cells with large receptive fields effectively 'blurs' the image, removing all fine detail but preserving the coarse-scale features of the image. When receptive field sizes are small, then finer spatial detail is preserved but coarser scale information – such as how the intensity changes across a region of the image – is lost. The ganglion cells with larger receptive fields are often near the edge of the retina (the periphery), whereas ganglion cells in the centre of the retina have much smaller receptive fields, and there is much less pooling, making this central area – the fovea – especially responsive to fine detail.

Such pooling of activity across receptive fields occurs at many stages in the visual system. In cortical area V1, for example, pooling of responses to ganglion cells yields receptive field structures that will respond maximally to more complex image features while also filtering the image at different spatial scales.

The French mathematician Fourier showed that any complex waveform can be described as though it were constructed from the sum of a set of simpler patterns known as sine waves. A visual sine-wave pattern is one whose brightness varies in the way shown in the top two rows of Figure 2.6. The graphs on the left describe the sine-wave undulations in the pattern of intensity which are drawn out in the images on the right. The image on the top right has a frequency of one-third that of the pattern below it, but an amplitude (the 'contrast' between the darkest and lightest parts) three times as great as the one below. Because these are patterns whose frequency varies across space, we described them as sine waves with different 'spatial frequencies'. These two sine-wave patterns can be added together to form more complex patterns, as shown in the bottom two rows. These differ in terms of their phases. At the bottom, the sine waves have been added so that their peaks and troughs coincide to provide an apparently higher overall contrast between the darkest and brightest parts. In the row above, however, the two patterns have been added so that their peaks do not coincide.

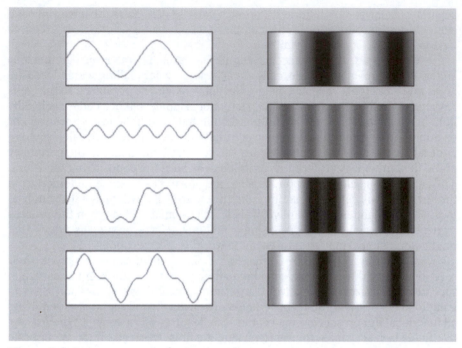

Figure 2.6 Decomposition of complex patterns into sine-wave components. See text for explanation. From Bruce and Young (1998).

Since any complex pattern can be decomposed into sine-wave patterns in this way, one way of transmitting a complex signal would be to decompose it into its constituent frequencies. Evidence that the human visual system filters the images it receives through distinct spatial frequency channels was obtained in classic experiments in which the contrast in patterns of stripes is varied to measure how much contrast is needed for human observers just to be able to detect that stripes are present. For example, Campbell and Robson (1968) found that the amount of contrast needed to see a complex pattern of stripes (like those in the bottom two rows of Figure 2.6) was almost the same as that required for the detection of each of the individual sine-wave components presented individually, suggesting that the complex pattern was detected by combining the outputs of channels which selectively responded to distinct component frequencies.

Another series of experiments by Blakemore and Campbell (1969) showed that observers can selectively adapt to different frequencies of patterns. For example, if an observer stares for a minute or so at a high-contrast pattern of stripes at a frequency of six stripes per inch, they will then find it much harder to detect a faint pattern of stripes at this same frequency, but not at other frequencies. Such effects of spatial frequency adaptation, unlike those of after-effects of brightness that we described earlier, do not depend on the eye being kept fixated on the adapting image.

It therefore appears that the human visual system filters its input in a way that keeps different spatial scales separate. This filtering operation could be achieved if the outputs of cells with similar receptive field sizes are pooled together. Figure 2.7 (from Bruce, Green, & Georgeson, 2003) shows how the image of Albert Einstein's face might be seen by four distinct spatial frequency filters. The receptive field sizes and properties (excitatory inner portion, inhibitory outer portion) of the cells whose outputs would be pooled to produce these filters are shown at the bottom right of each image. The separate outputs of these four frequency channels can transmit virtually all the information from the original image, as seen by the reconstruction of the original from the average of the four filter outputs shown in the top right of Figure 2.7.

If face images are filtered, as in Figure 2.7, to produce outputs that preserve information at different spatial scales, it can be shown that much information which is important for face perception is captured by the very coarse-scaled (blurred) representation (e.g. the centre left panel from Figure 2.7). A striking early demonstration of this was provided by Harmon and Julesz (1973) using a portrait of Abraham Lincoln (see Figure 2.8).

A picture is displayed on a computer as a grid of 'picture elements' or pixels, each showing a specific intensity or 'grey level' (for monochrome pictures). The more pixels are used to display a picture, the better will be the reproduction of the fine-scale information from the original. As the number of pixels used to display a picture is reduced, so the finer-scale details of the original are lost. Harmon produced an extremely coarse-scale version of a portrait of Abraham Lincoln by radically reducing the number of pixels used to display the image, replacing the specific intensity within each of the original pixels with the average intensity over a larger block. With block sizes set large then the image is severely degraded compared with the original, and this 'coarse pixellation' technique effectively blurs out the fine-scale information from the original image. However, unlike the smooth filtering that can be obtained with centre-surround filters, or simulations of these as in Figure 2.7, the resulting 'pixellated' images have sharp edges between each of the blocks, which seem to conceal the identity of the face. These sharp edges are due to irrelevant fine-scale detail, introduced by the divisions between the large blocks, superimposed on the coarse-scale information. If you look at Figure 2.8 you may find that you are able to recognise the original face behind the pixellated disguise by blurring your eyes. Blurring your eyes filters out the fine-scale block edges, and leaves the coarser-scale information unaffected. This demonstration shows how this coarse-scale information alone can contain information sufficient to identify a face, and relatively coarse-scale information can often allow faces to be categorised in other important ways – for example, according to their age and sex (see Chapter 3).

Figure 2.9 shows an intriguing illustration of the different information contained in different spatial scales – it superimposes the high spatial frequency information from one face onto the low spatial frequency information from another face. Look at Figure 2.9 close up. What/who do you see? Now place the book against a wall and look at it from a distance of a couple of metres. What/who do you see now? At close distance, your visual system is able to see the high spatial frequencies in which Tony Blair's face is depicted. At a distance, this fine

Original   Average

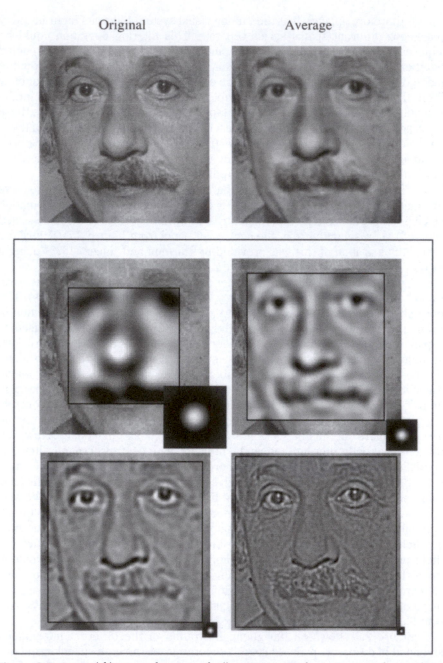

Figure 2.7 Spatial filtering of image of Albert Einstein's face. See text for explanation. Republished from Bruce, V., Green, P. R., & Georgeson, M. A. (2003). *Visual perception: physiology, psychology and ecology.* Figure 5.9, p. 96, Psychology Press.

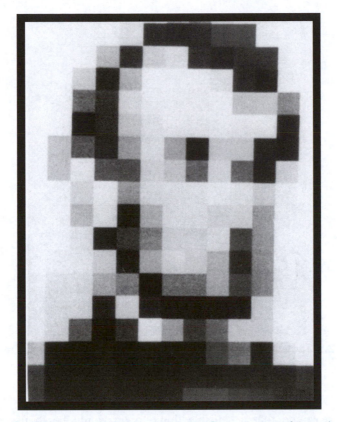

Figure 2.8 Pixellated version of Abraham Lincoln's face. See text for explanation. From Figure 1, p. 1194 in Harmon, L. D., & Julesz, B. (1973). Masking in visual recognition: Effects of two-dimensional filtered noise. *Science, 180*, pp. 1194–1197. Reprinted with permission from AAAS.

detail cannot be seen and the low spatial frequencies of Margaret Thatcher's face dominate.

Computer manipulation of face images to remove or display different spatial scales has provided important information about the nature of visual information used to identify faces, as we will see in Chapter 6.

Morphing and caricaturing

Another way of manipulating 2D images of faces is to blend them together into a composite image – for example, to try to find what is common or average across several faces. Of course, if you simply slap one random image of a face on top of another, you will probably get an unintelligible mess, so you need to find a meaningful way to put the images together. In the nineteenth century, Galton

Figure 2.9 Thatcher/Blair composite produced by Philippe Schyns and Aude Oliva. See text for explanation. Courtesy of Philippe Schyns.

(1879) reasoned that a sensible thing to do would be to use only full-face photographs and align the positions of the eyes in each image. He then exposed several different images onto the same photographic plate, to create a face-like composite showing the average of all these images. Examples are shown in Figure 2.10.

Techniques in essence like Galton's can still be used, but with the image blending done by computers instead of photography. A problem, though, is that the image loses sharpness as more and more pictures are blended together, because even when you align the eyes the other parts of the different full-face images won't align very well with each other.

An important way of dealing with this problem was developed by Perrett, Benson and their collaborators (Benson & Perrett, 1991; Tiddeman, Burt, & Perrett, 2001). This involves identifying a large number of what are called fiducial points on each image to delineate locations of facial features (see Figure 2.11). This is usually done manually. Some of the fiducial points are specified fairly exactly (the pupil of the eye, the tip of the nose, the corners of the mouth, etc.), whilst others are simply spread evenly around particular features (eyes, eyebrows, mouth, nose, face outline, etc.). The delineated face image can then be considered to consist of these fiducial locations and an overlaid mesh of small triangle-shaped regions (tesselations) of colour and brightness between the fiducials, as shown in Figure 2.11.

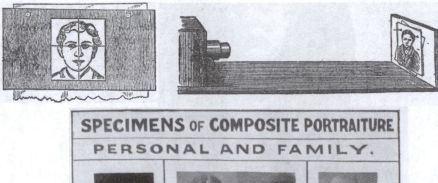

Figure 2.10 Galton's photographic technique for averaging images by aligning their eyes and superimposing them onto the same negative, with some examples of the composite portraits he produced.

To average several images of different faces using this technique, we can first measure the average position of each fiducial point across the images, and then deform the shape of each of the tesselations present in the images to the average shape of that tesselation before blending them together. The result is a photo-realistic face-like image with the average shape and texture of the constituent faces.

Please note carefully that the images that this kind of averaging delivers are different from those created by Galtonian averaging. The term 'average' needs to be interpreted strictly in terms of the technique that lies behind the construction of the averages – it is essential to understand that an 'average' image created using averaging technique A need not be the same as the 'average' created with averaging technique B. A similar but more obvious point is that what is meant by a 'composite' image derived from Galton's method (Figure 2.10) is a very different kind of face composite from the top plus bottom composites we described earlier for Young, Hellawell and Hay's (1987) composite paradigm (Figure 2.3) or, indeed, the composite images generated by eyewitnesses to crimes we discuss in Chapter 6. Terms like 'composite', 'average' and (as we will see) 'prototype' or 'caricature' are widely used in image manipulation studies, but need always to be interpreted in direct relation to the underlying techniques.

The new image-averaging methods allow us to manipulate facial images in many different ways. We can create averaged images that show average male or average female faces, average old or young faces, average attractive or

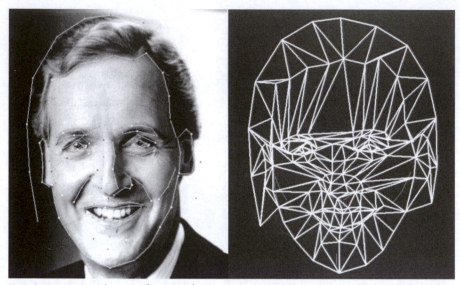

Figure 2.11 Tesselation of image for accurate image manipulation. Fiducial points are placed on the image (left panel) and used to divide it into a large number of deformable regions (right panel). Different images can then be brought to a common shape (in terms of the locations of fiducial points) before being combined – allowing averaging without substantially blurring features and contours. The averaged images can then be reshaped to the average shape of constituent images, the individual shape of one of the constituent images, or any other desired shape. Images courtesy of David Perrett and University of St. Andrews – www.perceptionlab.com.

unattractive faces, and so on. These averages are often called 'prototype' images for the characteristic that has been averaged. Prototype images can be very useful because any consistent characteristic in the set of images that are averaged to create the prototype will still be present in the prototype, whereas characteristics that are idiosyncratic to particular faces will tend to be averaged away.

We can then take two different prototype images (face averages) and create evenly-graded transitions between them (*morphing*) to evaluate the perceptual effects of gradually making each prototype more like the other – for example, to see whether changing an average male face to an average female face results in a smooth transition or gives a sudden switch from overall male to overall female appearance ('categorical perception'). Morphing can be used in the same way with individual face images.

Alternatively, we can use one prototype image (or an individual face image) as a reference norm and increase any differences between this norm and another face image (which might itself be another prototype, or just an individual face) to produce realistic *caricatures*. In this way, we can make an average male face look even more masculine (by increasing differences from the female average) or we can make a female face look more feminine (by increasing differences from the male average). Or we might caricature an individual face's identity by making it less like the average face.

These changes do not need to be global. We can restrict the changes to particular visual cues to investigate their roles – for example, by taking the 2D shape of one face image (i.e. the locations of the fiducial points) and transposing onto it the colour and brightness information from another face to create a new face that has the shape of one image and the texture of another. And so on. The existence of such techniques has completely transformed our ability to generate systematic approaches to important questions about face perception.

A particularly widely used application of image manipulation techniques is in studies of categorical perception of different face properties. The phenomenon of categorical perception arises when items which come from the same category seem more perceptually similar to each other than they actually are, while items from different categories seem more dissimilar. For example, in colour perception, two different wavelengths which are both considered shades of 'red' will be judged as visually more similar to one another than two wavelengths which are physically no further apart (in terms of the difference in wavelength) but which span the boundary between a red and an orange.

Figure 2.12 shows images of faces morphed in 25% steps between an average young male and young female face, between two famous identities, and between two facial expressions (Sprengelmeyer et al., 1996). Mathematically, each of the morphed images marks a 25% change in the positioning of feature points and blending of textures from the images at the ends of the continuum. But the combination of this myriad of linear changes in shape and texture can be perceptually non-linear. To find out whether this is the case, two main criteria can be applied. First, we can test whether *identification* of the images is non-linear – that is whether images from the left of each row are identified as the leftmost prototype and images from the right of each row as the rightmost prototype, with a fairly abrupt shift near the centre of the continuum. Second, we can test whether *discrimination* of the images is also non-linear – whether is easier to see that pairs of images that straddle the category boundary are different from each other than it is to see that equally-spaced pairs from within a category are different. So, in Figure 2.12, do the 25% and 75% morphs from each row look more different than do the 0% and 50% or 50% and 100% morphs, even though there is a constant 50% difference in each case? Such discontinuities in identification and enhanced discrimination at the category boundary are phenomena that are hallmarks of categorical perception.

Beyond 2D images

The above analysis of spatial structures treats the image in two dimensions. But we can think of the faces we see as a surface pattern of colour and brightness values from the pigmentation and reflectance of skin, eyes, hair, etc., superimposed onto an underlying three-dimensional shape. As we saw in Chapter 1, the human face is a complex 3D surface deriving from the combinations of muscles,

Figure 2.12 Examples of morphed continua created by computer image manipulation, showing transitions across perceived sex (young male to young female), identity (Cary Grant to Humphrey Bogart), and expression (sad to happy). Reproduced from Sprengelmeyer et al. Loss of disgust: Perception of faces and emotions in Huntington's disease, *Brain*, 1996, *119*, 5, pp. 1647–1665 by permission of Oxford University Press.

fat deposits, skin and hair placed on the underlying bony surface of the skull. Variation in the specific shapes and relationships of protruberances and concavities helps specify the age, race and sex of the face (see Chapter 3). These undulations of the facial surface combine with the effects of lighting direction to moderate the amount of light reflected from different regions and hence affect the 2D images of faces we see. Our opening examples from this chapter show that we are not good at discounting image variations due to lighting changes when it comes to matching face images for identity. Moreover it is difficult to recognise even very familiar faces when these are lit from below, a fact well-known to children playing with underlighting from torches to make their faces look grotesque. Nonetheless we are able to interpret a 2D image of a face as showing an underlying 3D structure and for this some analysis of the 3D effects of variations in lighting and shade must be implemented.

When lighting comes from above, e.g. from the sun or from an overhead room light, parts of the surface higher up will reflect more light than parts lower down. Where one part of a surface blocks light, it will cast a shadow. The patterns of shading and shadow across a surface are therefore informative about the three-dimensional shape of a surface, and the visual system can use this information to retrieve a description of surface shape provided that some information about the direction of the light source is known. The direction of the light source needs to be known because any particular pattern of shading is ambiguous.

For example, consider the simple shapes shown in Figure 2.13. This pattern of shading could arise if a domed shape were lit from above, *or* if a hollow shape were lit from below. Unless light direction is either known or assumed, the pattern cannot be interpreted. Moreover, it is often possible for the interpretation of such an image to shift, either spontaneously, or as a result of some other change of conditions, such as a change in the apparent direction from which the surface is lit.

Ramachandran (1995) has demonstrated three simple principles that are usually sufficient to explain our interpretation of patterns of shading. These are that light usually comes from above, that there is a single light source in a scene, and that shapes are usually convex rather than concave. However, exceptions are made when other assumptions about likely events in the world are stronger. If we are presented with a hollow facial mask, then provided that we view this at a distance too great for stereo vision to work, we will see this as a real face, with its nose sticking out towards us, rather than as the mask it actually is – see Figure 2.14. This hollow face illusion, popularised by Gregory (e.g. see Gregory, 1973), appears first to have been described by Brewster (1826; see Wade, 1983).

Three-dimensional shape can be measured accurately by laser scanning, allowing the shape of a person's head to be recorded and stored as a series of xyz spatial coordinates (see Chapter 1). These coordinates can then be used to look at the effects of changes in face shape on a person's appearance (Bruce, Burton, Doyle, & Dench, 1989). This is both scientifically interesting and of practical

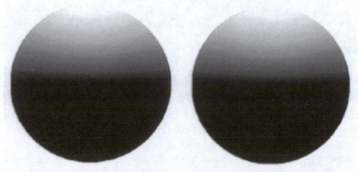

Figure 2.13 Humps or dents? See text. From Bruce and Young (1998).

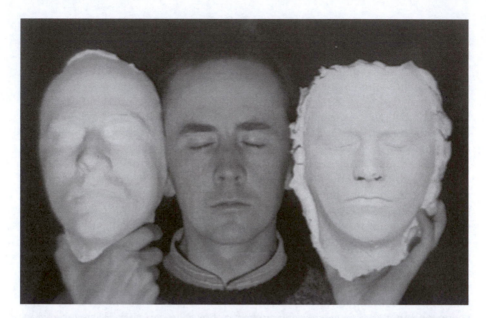

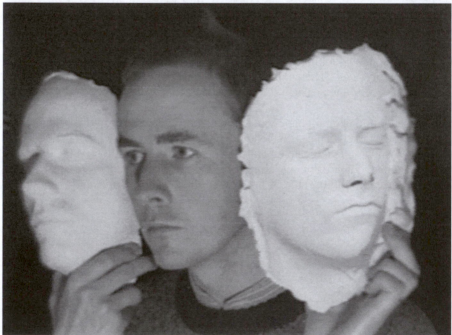

Figure 2.14 The hollow face illusion. Ben (centre) holds a plaster cast of his face (left of picture) and a hollow mould (right of picture). When facing the camera (top row) both the cast and the mould look like faces, though apparently lit from different directions. As the camera turns (lower row) the hollow mould seems like a solid face that has turned in the opposite direction. Pictures courtesy of Ben Craven and Harold Hill.

benefit in predicting the effects of cranio-facial surgery. Using 3D images of this kind allowed Hill and Bruce (1996) to investigate systematically the effects of changing the direction of lighting on the matching of 3D face surfaces.

Laser scanning, however, only records 3D shape, leading to a volumetric representation that lacks surface pigmentation, like the bust of a Roman Emperor. Measuring colour and brightness values themselves is relatively straightforward, but synchronising these with the three-dimensional coordinates of the head is more tricky, and recording the colour and brightness values independently of lighting direction is harder still. Solving these technical problems is essential to creating and manipulating realistic and accurate three-dimensional face images. Although scientists seem to be closing in on this goal (Smith & Hancock, 2008), it has yet to be fully realised. Nevertheless some experiments have been able to separate out and recombine 3D shape and pigmentation as we describe in Chapter 3, and to apply caricaturing in three dimensions by averaging together and then exaggerating 3D, rather than 2D, shape descriptions (O'Toole, Vetter, Volz, & Salter, 1997; O'Toole, Price, Vetter, Bartlett, & Blanz, 1999).

The observation that photographs convey likeness so well might suggest that *movement* is unimportant for face perception. However, this conclusion would be premature. One remarkable way to illustrate the important information conveyed by motion is to present displays where motion is about the *only* information present. A technique to do this was introduced by the Swedish psychologist Johannson (1975), using 'point-light' displays of human motion. In these displays, points at the major joints in the body are illuminated; for example, lights are placed on the shoulders, elbows, wrists, hips, knees and ankle joints. It is possible to film this display as the actor moves in the dark, so that all the viewer can see is a moving set of these 12 points. A still frame from such a film looks completely unrecognisable as a human figure – more like a Christmas tree, perhaps. Yet, once the film is animated, observers immediately see that it is a human and can describe how it is moving.

A similar technique was applied to faces by Bassili (1978), who scattered a large number of small bright spots over the surface of a human face, and then filmed the face as it moved in the dark, with the camera set to pick up just these brightest spots. Bassili was able to show that, when seen moving, people were highly accurate at recognising what facial expression was displayed from this moving point-light display. In follow-up experiments, Bruce and Valentine (1988) made point-light displays of a small number of their colleagues and asked other department members to try to identify these individuals. When the tapes were seen moving, there was some modest ability to recognise individuals from these point-light displays, though performance was highly inaccurate overall. People also showed some ability to tell if the displays were male or female. These results can be explained if motion allows the human brain to build a better representation of the facial surface than can be obtained from static individual frames.

On theoretical grounds, we might expect a role for motion in face processing. This is because many of the characteristics of face perception – the importance of coarse-scale information containing patterns of overall lightness, and the relative unimportance of hue (colour) – are characteristics of a major visual pathway (termed the 'magnocellular' pathway) in the brain which also codes information about movement. Moreover, research has already revealed that there may be important information in the fine timing of expressions which helps us to decipher such things as whether an expression is genuine or posed (see Chapter 4). You may be able to convince yourself of this by remembering how a 'forced' or 'insincere' smile may be over-quick or too slow in comparison with a genuine smile of pleasure. Pollick, Hill, Calder and Paterson (2003) demonstrated the importance of these temporal characteristics by caricaturing these dynamic patterns of expressive movements in a temporal extension of the techniques we described earlier (see also Hill, Troje, & Johnston, 2005 for related work on facial speech movements). Recent evidence also suggests that there may be information in the dynamics of face action which can help to identify known individuals too (see Chapter 6).

Functional and computational models: Key types of theory

As well as developing ways of investigating what happens when we look at faces, we need to be able to put the findings into systematic order and communicate them to other people. This can be done verbally, of course, but that can be a clumsy and long-winded way of doing things. A more effective technique is often to condense what is claimed into a simple diagram, as we did in Figures 2.2a and 2.2b. In psychologists' jargon, this approach is often called 'functional modelling'.

Functional modelling offers some substantial advantages. If done well, it can bring together a range of observations into an easily understood, concise pattern. It can also be testable and falsifiable, as we saw from Figure 2.2, where the pattern of evidence favours the model shown in Figure 2.2b over that shown in Figure 2.2a.

The most well-known functional model of face perception is that suggested by Bruce and Young (1986), shown in Figure 2.15. We will briefly introduce key features of this model here, to provide an overview that gives the context for more detailed discussion of specific aspects elsewhere.

In common with many models of this type, Bruce and Young (1986) suggest that face perception is achieved by separable functional components (shown as 'boxes' in the diagram) linked by processing pathways ('arrows'). The overall aim is simply to spell out what (some of) these components might be, and how they relate to each other. Following perceptual analysis ('structural encoding') of the face, it is proposed that recognition of facial expression ('expression analysis' – see Chapter 4), facial speech movements (which play a role in speech perception – see Chapter 4), directed visual processing (to determine characteristics such as age and sex from facial appearance – see Chapter 3) and face recognition (Chapter 6) are to a substantial degree independent of each other and proceed in parallel. For face recognition, however, a more elaborate specification of the pathway is offered, spanning a sequence proceeding from recognition of the appearance of a familiar face ('face recognition units' – Chapter 6) through access to identity-specific semantic information ('person

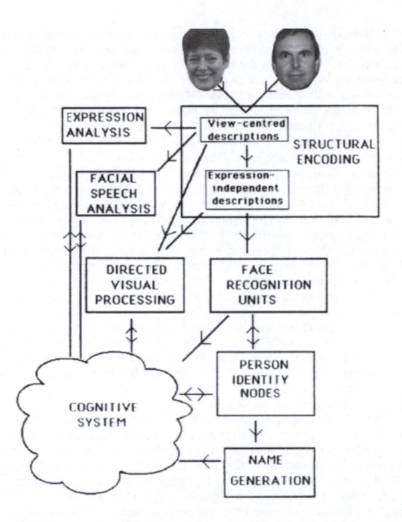

Figure 2.15 Functional model of face perception proposed by Bruce and Young (1986). Understanding face recognition. *British Journal of Psychology*, 1986, Volume 77, Issue 3, pp. 305–327, Figure 1, p. 312, John Wiley & Sons.

identity nodes' – Chapter 7) to retrieval of the person's name ('name generation' – Chapter 7).

Note that some of the functional components of this model seem to involve faces per se (e.g. face recognition units) whilst others (e.g. person identity nodes) are likely the same as those involved in perception of other socially relevant information – such as recognition from the voice (Chapter 7). Note too that all of the information gets brought together in the (conventionally cloudy, because little understood) 'cognitive system' – there is no claim that the different pathways are unable to interact with each other.

In 1986, we offered this model to summarise what we thought was known and to make a guess at some of the things about which we knew very little. Rather to our surprise, it has stood the test of time relatively well, and is still used to frame research questions. However, the functional modelling approach also has limitations. Its main weakness is that diagrammatic representations can leave important details unspecified. For example, what exactly is intended by the sequential organisation shown in the face recognition pathway? Does the facial percept have to be fully formed for familiar face recognition to take place, or might some faces be of sufficiently unusual appearance that they can be recognised from a relatively incomplete percept? Is it really exactly the same percept that is needed to determine age and sex, and to match photos of unfamiliar faces?

We could go on to spell out other questions, but the point is in essence a simple one. A functional model is a convenient way of representing what is happening overall, but it will often fall short when detailed predictions are needed. The diagrammatic convention simply cannot capture everything that is going on.

An effective solution can be to create a version of the functional model that can be implemented as a computer simulation. For example, as we will see in Chapter 7, Burton, Bruce and Johnston (1990) devised a computer program that simulated some of the key properties of the familiar face recognition pathway in Bruce and Young's (1986) functional model. They did this because the Bruce and Young model proved unable to offer satisfactorily precise predictions concerning patterns of priming and related effects that were being reported. It was clear that priming effects could be fitted to the model (and therefore loosely 'explained') post hoc, but there were few constraints in the model itself that could predict patterns of priming in advance of data collection.

The advantage of a computer simulation is that it avoids this kind of imprecision. A computer program won't run if key parameters are not specified, and it makes predictions or fits data based on its inputs and outputs, not on what might be a selective human interpretation. In designing their simulation, Burton et al. (1990) therefore had to choose how to implement a number of properties that Bruce and Young (1986) had left vague or simply not discussed, and this highlighted new research questions that the original functional model had not foreseen. Even more impressively, it proved possible to extend Burton et al.'s general approach to encompass other previously puzzling phenomena such as findings of non-conscious 'covert' recognition in cases of prosopagnosia (Burton, Young, Bruce, Johnston, & Ellis, 1991; Young & Burton, 1999).

We will look at Burton et al.'s simulation in more detail in later chapters. For now, the key message is that implementing a theory as a computer simulation can offer powerful advantages of increased precision and ability to predict and interpret complex phenomena.

That said, computer simulation is not free from technical problems of its own. We will mention two here. First, what is achieved is what is intended – a *simulation* of key features of a theory. Computer simulation programs like Burton et al.'s (1990) do not actually recognise faces – they just try to mimic certain properties of how human face recognition is organised. So the fact that a simulation seems to work is a good start, but it doesn't prove the simulation correct. Like any theory, it must be tested against as wide a range of evidence as possible.

The second problem is that how a computer simulation works (i.e. how it generates mappings between specified inputs and calculated outputs) is not always transparent; in other words, the simulation may depend on some property of the program whose significance we don't notice. This is obviously the case with more complex simulations, but it is found even with fairly simple simulations that rely on 'distributed representations'.

Consider, for example, how we might represent familiar faces in a simulation. Most people can probably recognise hundreds, if not thousands of familiar faces. One way to represent this would simply be to have one representation for each of the familiar faces the person knows (i.e. one representation for Madonna's face, one for Barack Obama, one for Wayne Rooney, and so on). This type of model uses what are called 'local' representations. Alternatively, and at the opposite extreme, we could instead have a pool consisting of a large number of 'face units', and represent each familiar face as a different pattern of activation across these face units. This type of arrangement is called a distributed representation, because there is no particular unit that corresponds exactly or specifically to Obama or to Madonna.

At first sight, modelling with distributed representations may seem preferable, because it seems closer to how we think the brain is likely to approach the task; indeed, such models are often (and usually misleadingly) referred to as 'neural networks'. In practice, though, any gain in neural plausibility is more than offset by the fact that it can be very difficult to be certain how a network with distributed representations achieves its results (Page, 2000; see also Bowers, 2009).

Recording what happens in the brain

The techniques we have described so far are very useful for answering questions about the psychological mechanisms involved in perceiving and recognising faces, but they don't directly tell us what is happening in the brain. For example, the Bruce and Young model shown in Figure 2.15 tells us about the possible relation between facial expression perception and face recognition, but says nothing about where or how this is achieved in the brain.

One reason for this was purely historical. In the 1980s, good information on localisation of function was hard to obtain (Young, 2011). The locations of brain injuries that caused particular neuropsychological problems could only be determined with high accuracy from (rare) autopsies because CT (computed tomography) scans didn't show enough detail, and the techniques for studying localisation of function in the normal brain were very indirect. The most widely used method for studying normal organisation of brain function involved exploiting the anatomy of the visual pathways by briefly presenting stimuli in the left visual hemifield (the part of your field of vision falling to the left of a vertical line through the point of fixation) or the right visual hemifield.

This 'divided visual field' technique works because, as long as a person is fixating centrally, the retina of each eye projects its responses to stimuli from the left visual field to the primary visual cortex of the right cerebral hemisphere and

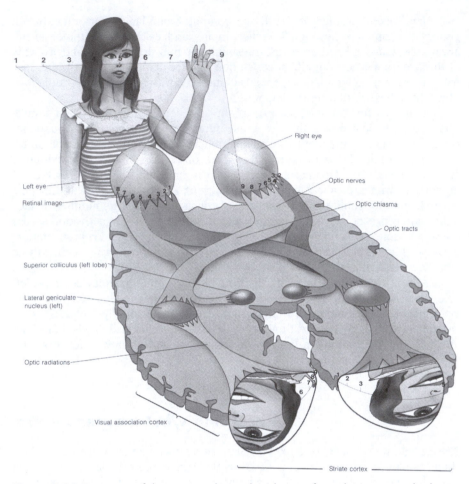

Figure 2.16 Diagram of the principal visual pathways from the retina to the brain. Note how the retinal image is split at the point of fixation (the woman's nose). The pictures superimposed on the brain's primary visual cortex (striate cortex) show how the retinal image is projected in topographic form, but divided at the midline and crossed, so that the left side of the image goes initially to right visual cortex, and vice versa. From Frisby (1979).

responses to stimuli from the right visual field to the primary visual cortex of the left cerebral hemisphere, as shown in Figure 2.16. So, in theory, we can compare the abilities of the left and right cerebral hemispheres to process stimuli such as faces (Rizzolatti, Umilta, & Berlucchi, 1971) or words (Young & Ellis, 1985). In practice, this comparison is limited by the need for a presentation time that is short enough to prevent any eye movement that would bring the stimulus into central vision (Bourne, 2006; Young, 1982) and complicated by the fact that we know little about how and when 'information' is transferred from one hemisphere to the other once it has reached the cerebral cortex. The technique still has its uses, though (Bourne, Vladeneau, & Hole, 2009). Typically, words are better recognised from the right visual field (projected to the left cerebral hemisphere) and faces from the left visual field (projected initially to the right cerebral hemisphere), reflecting the phenomenon of cerebral asymmetry of function.

Consequences of cerebral asymmetry can be found without needing to resort to lateralised presentation under certain conditions. The most extensively studied of these involves creating 'chimaeric' faces by combining the left side of a photo with its mirror image, or the right side with its mirror image, as in Figure 2.17. Surprisingly, for right-handed viewers the left side plus mirror image ('left' here means the side falling to the viewer's left) usually looks more like the original photo than does the right side plus mirror image (Bourne, 2008a; Gilbert & Bakan, 1973; Kolb, Milner, & Taylor, 1983). The phenomenon is not due to the asymmetric properties of the face itself because the preference for which looks more like the original is reversed if the original photo is mirror-reversed – it is what falls to the viewer's left or right that matters. Left-handed perceivers don't show such a consistent perceptual bias, pointing to cerebral asymmetry as the likely cause (their brains are often less asymmetrically organised), but exactly how this operates is unclear. It seems that right-handed people have learnt to prioritise facial information from the left sides of faces. This bias is linked to the parts of the face that are fixated, but the relationship is not strong and it is uncertain whether scanning biases are the cause or consequence of the representational asymmetry (Butler et al., 2005; Walker, Findlay, Young, & Lincoln, 1996).

A second reason why functional models like Bruce and Young (1986) often don't refer directly to brain regions or functions is to do with the underlying logic. This has been expressed with characteristic incisiveness by Coltheart (2006), who draws a sharp distinction between facts and theories about psychology, and facts and theories about the brain. His point is that, even if we know which of the models shown in Figure 2.2 is broadly correct, this tells us little about the underlying neural mechanisms. Conversely, and perhaps less easy to see, many facts about the brain are equally unable to constrain theories expressed at the psychological level. For example, and purely for the sake of argument, even if we discovered that only a tiny part of our brains is critical to the perception and recognition of faces, it could still be organised in either of the ways shown in Figure 2.2.

This logical distinction between psychological and neurological levels of explanation is important because advances in brain imaging techniques now allow us to ask many different types of question about the brain. For example, we can use structural brain imaging methods to get a detailed anatomical view of the inside of someone's head. The key technique is magnetic resonance imaging (MRI), which involves using a powerful magnetic field to measure the density of hydrogen atoms at different locations in your body. Because hydrogen is one of the constituents of water, and water density varies in different types of body tissue, these differences in density can be used to create remarkably detailed anatomical images.

Structural brain imaging has many uses. In research, a key technique is to use MRI to visualise which regions of the brain have been affected when someone

Figure 2.17 The top row is a drawing of the photographer James Craig Annan. The middle row shows composite portraits made from the left side of the original and its mirror image (on the left of the display), or the right side and its mirror image. To most right-handed perceivers, the left side plus mirror image composite looks slightly more like the original. The bottom row shows the original (top row) image in mirror-reversed form. Now, the right image in the middle row looks slightly more like the bottom row image to right-handed perceivers. This reversal of which image looks more like the original shows that the cause lies in a differential emphasis on information from the side of the face to the viewer's left. Original portrait courtesy of the Scottish National Portrait Gallery, Edinburgh. William Strang, James Craig Annan, Scottish National Portrait Gallery.

suffers a brain injury, allowing us to relate the region of damage to observed deficits in behaviour and cognition – we no longer need autopsies to be able to do this. This principle of comparing deficits to the region of damage is usually called the 'lesion' method – lesion being the medical term for a region of cell death. It is potentially very informative about what functions different brain areas may serve, though it is sometimes possible to make incorrect inferences because the damaged region will seldom overlap exactly with the neural representation of a particular ability, and because different brain areas interact with each other in ways that may mask the underlying pattern of function when a part is damaged.

These complications of the lesion method make it important to have techniques for studying organisation of function in the normal, intact brain. Remarkably, the MRI scanner used to create a structural image of a person's brain can also be used to measure brain function by functional magnetic resonance imaging, or fMRI. In essence, it uses haemodynamic changes linked to blood flow as a proxy for neural activity. The brain's neurons require a constant supply of oxygen and, when a region of brain is working hard, oxygen uptake from blood haemoglobin in that region increases. However, oxygenated and deoxygenated haemoglobin have different magnetic properties, allowing the MRI scanner to measure a blood oxygen level dependent (BOLD) response from different brain regions.

Because neurons need oxygen all the time, and different regions of brain have different blood vessels and resting oxygen needs, the BOLD response has to be measured in terms of a relative change in oxygen uptake in a particular region. In essence, fMRI looks for regions where performance of a particular task is correlated with a change in the BOLD response. That is, it doesn't measure brain function directly, but instead uses haemodynamic changes as a proxy for neural activity. This sets limits to the spatial and temporal resolution of fMRI. Spatial resolution refers to the size of a region of activity that can be detected. In fMRI, brain activity is measured across a grid of three-dimensional 'voxels'. Each dimension of one of these voxels is not usually less than 2 mm, and the data are often smoothed across adjacent voxels to improve the signal to noise ratio. What this means in practice is that fMRI is recording the activity of regions of brain that, whilst small compared to the whole brain, may none the less contain millions of neurons.

Temporal resolution involves the duration of the time period across which brain activity can be recorded. Because fMRI measures changes in blood oxygen content, there is always going to be a time lag between changes in neural activity and changes in the BOLD response. In fact, the BOLD response turns out to itself involve different components, including initial depletion of oxygenated haemoglobin as the neurons begin working hard followed by an increased flow of blood to the active region. In practice, these changes mean that the temporal resolution of fMRI is of the order of a few seconds. This is still impressive, but much slower than the speed of neural events. One way to deal with the limited temporal resolution is to use a block design, in which the BOLD response is measured across a sequence of trials of the same type. However, event-related designs investigating neural responses to individual stimuli ('events') are also increasingly used. Compared to block designs, event-related paradigms are technically demanding (but not impossible) with fMRI. Other functional brain imaging methods based on haemodynamic techniques, such as positron emission tomography (PET), have even more limited temporal resolution and are restricted to block designs.

The absolute level of BOLD response in fMRI is not in itself very meaningful, since neurons are always active and different brain regions vary considerably in their blood supply. What matters is changes in the BOLD response in a given region. In particular, studies look for BOLD changes that correlate with some important feature of the experimental task or presented stimuli. This is where psychological theories and knowledge are vital to designing sound functional brain imaging experiments.

Two of the techniques we have looked at already are especially important; *subtraction* and *adaptation*. In the same way that cognitive subtraction can be used to separate out a particular mental component from patterns of reaction times, the subtraction method can be used to compare the BOLD response between two different experimental conditions that are intended to differ in only one respect. For example, as we discussed in Chapter 1, if we want to find brain regions involved in face perception we might start by identifying regions that show increased BOLD signal to faces compared to other visual stimuli. That way, we eliminate regions involved in any aspect of seeing (they are common to both tasks, so subtract to zero) and are left with the face-responsive bits. But which other visual stimuli do we choose for this comparison? They might be everyday objects, or maybe objects that come from categories that (like faces) have a degree of visual homogeneity (flowers, cars, houses), or maybe we should just use pictures of scrambled faces? These choices are not theoretically neutral – each presupposes a slightly different background conception as to why we might find face-responsive regions in the brain, and what they might be doing.

Adaptation paradigms offer a different way to approach the question – the technique is now widely used (Krekelberg, Boynton, & van Wezel, 2006), and often referred to as fMR-adaptation. The basis of fMR-adaptation is that if we present the same visual stimulus repeatedly across a block of trials, the BOLD response is reduced across some brain regions in comparison to a condition where the stimulus changes for every trial in the block (Ewbank, Schluppeck, & Andrews, 2005). In other words, the BOLD response shows a form of adaptation to stimulus repetition, and a release from adaptation when stimuli vary. The comparison of conditions that create adaptation or release from adaptation of the BOLD response in a particular brain region can thus be used to infer something about what that region is doing. The logic is that release from adaptation can only occur when stimuli are treated by the region as in some way different from one another.

Through these kinds of clever techniques, paradigms such as fMRI have become very sophisticated and led to important findings. But in essence the inferences made are correlational in nature, because it is haemodynamic changes that are recorded, not brain activity itself. Techniques that can directly record brain activity are therefore also needed. Mainly, these involve electrophysiology.

Electroencephalography (EEG) is the most well known. It uses sensors placed on a person's scalp to record electric currents created by post-synaptic neuronal activity. For a measurable overall current to be generated, many thousands of neurons must fire at the same time. By averaging together large numbers of EEG records to a specific event (such as the presentation of a picture of a face), an averaged event-related potential (ERP) can be plotted to show the evolution of these synchronised neural responses across time. Typically, ERP studies will look at the size of peaks or troughs in recorded current that occur at specific times. For example, a particularly clear response that is often found for faces involves a negative current flow at around 170 ms after stimulus presentation (Bentin, Allison, Puce, Perez, & McCarthy, 1996) – electrophysiological studies call this the N170 (N for negative, 170 for the timing of the response peak).

The advantages of EEG and ERPs are that they record neural events with excellent temporal resolution, so they can be particularly useful for investigating hypotheses about the time course of neural events. A disadvantage is that it is impossible to achieve an unambiguous way of identifying brain sources from the recorded activity of external sensors without making simplifying assumptions – a difficulty known as the 'inverse problem'. Moreover, the electrical currents do not follow straight-line pathways from their sources to the recording sensors, making it even more difficult to infer exactly where they came from in the brain, with consequent limited spatial resolution. The more recently introduced technique of magnetoencephalography (MEG) tries to circumvent this problem by recording the magnetic fields created by the electric currents resulting from neural activity, using superconducting sensors (known as SQUIDs) positioned around the head. Unlike electric currents, magnetic fields pass transparently through brain, bone and body tissue, making the spatial resolution of MEG potentially better than that of EEG/ERP whilst retaining the excellent temporal resolution.

Both EEG and MEG can only record the activity of many thousands of neurons firing in synchrony. It is possible to record the activity of individual neurons, but only by placing electrodes into the brain, an invasive procedure reserved for studies of non-human species or of human patients needing brain surgery.

In essence, functional brain imaging techniques are correlational – they record brain events and correlate these with some behaviour or mental function of interest. This point is obvious when the recorded signal is a proxy for neural activity (such as haemodynamics in fMRI), but in fact it applies equally to techniques (like ERP and MEG) that measure neural events themselves. Famously, psychologists have long recognised that correlation does not necessarily imply causation, so it is useful to confirm functional brain imaging findings with normal participants against the effects of brain lesions affecting the identified regions. A relevant recent development is Transcranial Magnetic Stimulation (TMS), which uses a coil positioned above the head to create a local magnetic field that is sufficiently strong to temporarily disrupt regional brain activity (Hallett, 2000). The TMS can be in the form of a single pulse or more sustained, repetitive stimulation. Not all brain areas are suitable for studying with TMS, and determining the extent of the TMS disruption is seldom straightforward, but the possibility of creating a kind of temporary, reversible 'lesion' in the affected area holds sufficient promise that TMS is becoming widely used. The combination of studies involving fMRI to identify potentially important regions with TMS to demonstrate that disrupting these regions affects the ability of interest is potentially very useful scientifically (McKeefry, Gouws, Burton, & Morland, 2009).

The broader picture

We have seen that a range of different techniques can be used to investigate how we perceive and recognise faces. All of these methods have their strengths and weaknesses – there is no perfect, incontestable method. What is impressive, instead, is the sheer diversity of methods that can be used.

This diversity is useful in cases where different lines of evidence point to the same conclusion. When this happens, the ways in which each line of evidence might be at fault are themselves quite different. Hence, as more lines of evidence are adduced in support of a particular conclusion, the alternative that all of the various sources of error apply simultaneously (and in the same direction) starts to look unlikely.

This technique of putting the weight on what is consistently indicated across findings made using different methods is often called 'converging operations'. It doesn't give a privileged status to any one line of argument – instead it tries to weigh the evidence by how consistently it points in the same direction. Of course, this doesn't guarantee we will reach the right conclusion, but it does enhance confidence that a phenomenon is interesting and important.

So there is a strong case for bringing together data from different methods. However, not all methods address the same issues. In this respect, brain imaging has proved particularly contentious. As we noted, Coltheart (2006) draws a sharp distinction between testing theories expressed at the psychological level and localising functions to specific brain regions. He recognises that neuroimaging studies have provided plenty of data relevant to the localisationist enterprise but argues that, to date, they have not successfully been used to distinguish psychological theories. In contrast, Henson (2005) sees neuroimaging as a useful adjunct to other ways of gaining evidence that can be used to test psychological theories. Henson's (2005) view is that, as long as there is some systematic mapping between psychological functions and underlying brain structure, functional neuroimaging findings can be used in the same way as other data to test psychological theories.

The debate is important because the neurological model of face perception by Haxby and his colleagues (Haxby, Hoffman, & Gobbini, 2000), which we introduced in Chapter 1, was created largely around data from brain imaging. Yet Haxby et al.'s (2000) model actually relates well to explicitly 'functional' models such as Bruce and Young (1986), as Calder and Young (2005) point out. Figure 2.18 shows a simple spatial realignment of the Bruce and Young (1986) model that makes clear its underlying similarity to Haxby et al. (2000). In effect, 'structural encoding' corresponds to 'early perception of facial features', 'expression analysis' and 'facial speech analysis' share properties with Haxby's pathway for perceiving changeable aspects of faces, whereas 'directed visual processing' and 'face recognition units' reflect relatively invariant aspects.

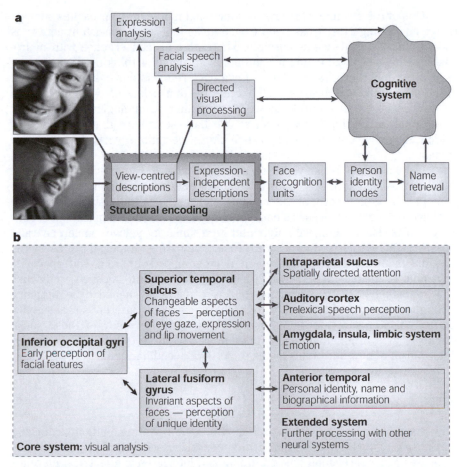

Figure 2.18 Realignment of the Bruce and Young (1986) model as depicted by Calder and Young (2005) to make clear its underlying similarity to Haxby, Hoffman and Gobbini (2000). See text for explanation. Reprinted by permission from Macmillan Publishers Ltd: *Nature Reviews Neuroscience*, 6, pp. 645–651, Understanding the recognition of facial identity and facial expression, Andrew J. Calder and Andrew W. Young, copyright (2005).

Something that is particularly appealing about Haxby et al.'s (2000) position, though, is that by emphasising the differences between those aspects of face perception that depend on the interpretation of cues that are changeable from moment to moment (e.g. emotional expression, gaze direction, facial speech) or relatively invariant (age, sex, identity) it explains a potential organising principle underlying part of the 'division of labour' in face perception noted by Bruce and Young (1986). Moreover, this can be linked to the more general system of visual pathways for perceiving motion and static form in the cerebral cortex we introduced in Chapter 1, making the neuroanatomy and psychology fit neatly alongside each other.

One of the strongest features of functional modelling approaches such as Bruce and Young (1986) has been to use ideas that were consistent across as wide a range of evidence as possible. The emerging convergence with neuro-anatomy thus seems to us to give additional grounds for thinking the approach of bringing together different lines of evidence remains our best way forward. More specifically, Coltheart's (2006) criterion that a line of evidence should be able decisively to arbitrate between competing psychological theories if it is to be taken on board is very strict. We have seen here that most lines of evidence in practice fail to live up to such high expectations, yet can remain very valuable.

Our view, then, is that the diversity of questions and approaches that can be used to investigate face perception is a considerable strength. In many ways, face perception is a microcosm of wider issues in psychology. Understanding how we perceive and interpret faces has both theoretical and practical applications. Faces are complex visual stimuli with high inter-item similarity, yet we can perceive and classify many of their properties with ease. They are so important to us that is possible (many think likely) that evolution has equipped our brains with specialist apparatus for the task of perceiving them. Notwithstanding any such predisposi-tion, our ability to perceive many aspects of faces is shaped by experience throughout our lives. Importantly, the face carries many different social signals, leading to interesting questions about whether the diversity of these social signals or their origination in a common physical source (the face) is the major determinant of how our brains tackle the task of decoding them.

Summary

This chapter introduced key research methods, commenting on their strong and less strong features. The research methods discussed included performance measures (errors, reaction times, priming and interference effects), preference and adaptation paradigms, effects of brain injury, and functional brain imaging. Some aspects of visual perception were introduced including receptive field organisation, spatial filtering, and the perception of 3D shape and biological motion. The differences between functional, computational and neurological models and theories were discussed, together with the implications of these differences.

We also introduced important computer graphics techniques that can be used for manipulating visual images to create stimuli with systematically varying stimulus properties – these have had a profound impact on face research.

There have been two overarching themes to the chapter. The first has been that students (and researchers) ignore issues of method at their peril! All of the evidence from studies of face perception (we could equally say all evidence in psychology) needs to be carefully evaluated against the methods used to ensure it is reasonably interpreted. The second theme has been that there is no single road to understanding. All methods have their own strengths and weaknesses – it is very important to put the greatest weight on the conclusions that can be supported from independent lines of converging evidence.

Further reading

Bruce, V., Green, P. R., & Georgeson, M. A. (2003). *Visual perception: Physiology, psychology and ecology* (4th ed.). Hove: Psychology Press.
Here, we can only touch on our understanding of the mechanisms of visual perception. Textbooks like Bruce et al. (2003) cover visual perception more generally.

Hancock, P. J. B., Bruce, V., & Burton, A. M. (2001). Recognition of unfamiliar faces. *Trends in Cognitive Sciences, 4*, 330–337.
A review paper discussing in more detail the problems inherent in unfamiliar face matching highlighted by studies such as Kemp et al. (1997).

Hole, G. J., & Bourne, V. J. (2010). *Face processing: Psychological, neuropsychological, and applied perspectives*. Oxford: Oxford University Press.
The appearance of a rival textbook while we were finishing writing this one was a real blow for us! It's good, too. The methods used in face perception studies are mainly discussed in Hole and Bourne's (2010) Appendix (pp. 335–345), but the entire book is worth reading because it never does any harm to get more than one perspective.

Kemp, R., Towell, N., & Pike, G. (1997). When seeing should not be believing: photographs, credit cards and fraud. *Applied Cognitive Psychology, 11*, 211–222.
The study of the value of identity cards we discussed. An outstanding example of how wrong 'common sense' can be. If this doesn't convince you to question anything that *isn't* supported by evidence – however sensible it may seem – then nothing will.

Krekelberg, B., Boynton, G. M., & van Wezel, R. J. A. (2006). Adaptation: From single cells to BOLD signals. *Trends in Neurosciences, 29*, 250–256.
A review of the importance of adaptation techniques and what can be inferred from them, with an emphasis on fMR-adaptation.

Webster, M.A. and MacLeod, D.I.A. (2011). Visual adaptation and face perception. *Philosophical Transactions of the Royel Society, 366*, 1702–1725.
An excellent up-to-date review of the adaptation method with a sophisticated discussion of its psychological implications.

Social categories

Our faces convey a lot of information about our social identities. From looking at someone's face we can infer some details of their racial background and decide whether they seem old or young, male or female, attractive or unattractive, friendly or unapproachable, intelligent or unintelligent, and so on. Some of these inferences (such as age or sex) are remarkably accurate, others (such as approachability or intelligence) can turn out to be really wide of the mark, yet we all carry on making them.

The pervasiveness of social categories

Consider an instructive study carried out by Cook (1939). He took photographs under standard lighting conditions and gave an intelligence test to 150 male students who had just started at university. When he asked people to estimate the intelligence of these students from their photographs, their estimates were found to be unrelated to the intelligence test scores or the students' performance on their courses. However, Cook also demonstrated that even though they therefore did not seem to be valid, people's estimates tended to agree with each other. In other words, there was something about the faces that Cook's participants were fairly reliably picking out, but this did not seem to be valid for the task of esti-mating intelligence. As far as Cook could tell, the factors which seemed to lead to judgements of high intelligence were symmetry of facial features, seriousness of expression, and tidiness of appearance (remember, this was in 1939, though we would not be overly surprised if some of the same factors still operate).

The literature on psychological judgements to faces is full of similar exam-ples. It seems that while we may not be accurate in our judgements, there is nonetheless a good deal of agreement about those that we make. Strikingly, too, they are often snap judgements – Willis and Todorov (2006) found that trait infer-ences of attractiveness, likeability, trustworthiness, competence and aggressive-ness based on an exposure duration of only 100 ms correlated well with judgements made without time constraints.

Stereotyping is an obvious place to look for the causes of such effects. For example, the rather dubious history of studies of the 'criminal face' has shown that there is little validity in our ability to predict criminal behaviour from facial appearance, but remarkable agreement between different observers about which faces look more 'shifty'. We will say more about this later – for now it is enough to note that some of this agreement is undoubtedly perpetuated by stereotypes derived from several sources, including the portrayal of different types of character in mass media. Actors with villains' faces will tend to play villains' roles, thus reinforcing the impressions that all of us hold of the face of villainy.

However, more subtle judgements about faces can also be made with a high degree of agreement. Bull and his colleagues (Bull & Hawkes, 1982; Bull, Jenkins, & Stevens, 1983) demonstrated that people tended to agree on their judgements of the political views of faces shown. In each study, photographs of clean-shaven male British Conservative and Labour politicians were collected, with careful matching of the groups in terms of their approximate age, the presence or absence of spectacles, facial expression, and so forth. Volunteers, who were unaware that the faces were those of politicians, were asked to rate each face for its intelligence, sincerity, social class, political inclination and attractiveness. There was a fair degree of agreement between observers in the judgements made of the political inclination of the faces. The rub was again that not all these judgements were accurate. In Bull and Hawkes' (1982) study, for example, of six faces which were judged to be most extremely 'Conservative', two were of Labour politicians, and of five judged clearly 'Labour', two were actually Conservative. However, while actual political allegiance did not discriminate between the two extremes, other associated factors did. The 'Conservative' faces were judged as more intelligent, of higher social class, and as more attractive than the 'Labour' faces, and these judgements did not differ according to the political inclination of those making the judgements. Bull et al. (1983) found a similar pattern of effects.

These studies predate the rebranding of political parties from projects such as 'New Labour', but the important point is that judgements about which political party a person supported were closely associated with their rated attractiveness and apparent intelligence and social class, yet these factors were not themselves affected by the political persuasions of the people doing the judging. Somehow, we seem all to be skilled at using social stereotypes, but this also makes us susceptible to misattributions we can derive from them.

The standard view in psychology, derived from classic theorising of Lippmann (1922) and Allport (1954), is that stereotyping is useful to the person doing the stereotyping. An obvious benefit is that it creates cognitive shortcuts based on past experience, but it also has more social functions in establishing social identities or justifying the status quo (Hilton & von Hippel, 1996). Noticing that someone is a man or woman, or young or old, establishes a set of expectations that can save some of the mental effort of dealing with everyone you meet as a truly unique individual. The downside, of course, is prejudice, where you don't look beyond the stereotype.

For many stereotypes, it is tempting to think that there might be some 'kernel of truth' that underlies them, and the 'cognitive shortcuts' hypothesis tends to imply that this should be the case. In the case of political affiliation, recent studies have shown that judgements based on facial appearance can be above-chance – American participants could tell whether U.S. Senate candidates and even college students were Democrats or Republicans (Rule & Ambady, 2010), and students from the University of Basel could tell whether unknown German and Swiss politicians had left-wing or right-wing views (Samochowiec, Wänke, & Fiedler, 2010). These studies do not, of course, unearth high success rates for such estimates – the point is only that they are not completely at chance level. In part, these political judgements seem to derive from weighing up factors like the individual's personality, for which evidence pointing to above-chance validity is also emerging (Kramer & Ward, 2010; Little & Perrett, 2007). Even so, the importance of social as well as cognitive factors and the history of human prejudice should make us doubt that a kernel of truth is always there to be found, or that when found it will amount to much. This is also evident from studies that show how easily stereotypes can be acquired.

Lewicki (1986) carried out experiments where people were exposed to remarkably simple co-occurrences of certain types of social information with

Figure 3.1 Stimuli used by Lewicki (1986). See text for explanation. Courtesy of Pawel Lewicki.

certain physical features, to see how readily these would be picked up. Figure 3.1 shows the faces Lewicki used. The top row faces were carefully matched to the bottom row faces for perceived attractiveness, and to have comparable ranges of pose, expression, gaze direction, clothing, etc. What differed was hair length – the hairstyles of the people in the top row having longer hair than those of the people in the bottom row.

In one of Lewicki's experiments, participants were shown three of the faces from the top row, one at a time, while a brief vignette of each person was read out. These vignettes were actually invented, but the experiment was carried out in a manner which would make people suppose that the vignettes were genuine, and that the photographs were of people who were remarkably *kind*. For example:

> No one could ever call her self-centred. She does a lot for other people; she is sensitive and helpful. She knows how to treat each individual so as to make him or her feel really good.
>
> (Lewicki, 1986, p. 146)

A further three faces from the bottom row were also presented, together with vignettes which emphasised how *capable* each person was. For example:

> She is very intelligent and effective. She knows very well how to make the best use of her particular talents, so she usually wins. She likes to be on a tight time schedule and she hates to waste her time.
>
> (Lewicki, 1986, p. 146)

So, during this procedure, three faces with long hair were shown accompanied by descriptions emphasising their kindness, and three faces with short hair accompanied by descriptions emphasising their capability.

Later on, participants were shown the other two faces from the top row, and the remaining two faces from the bottom row, and they were asked to evaluate whether each person was 'kind', and whether each was 'capable'. The times they took to make such decisions to these entirely novel faces were measured, and are shown as Condition I in Figure 3.2, where they are plotted with solid lines.

The result of the experiment is clear. When people were judging the kindness of new faces, they spent longer evaluating those with long hair, and when judging capability they spent longer evaluating those with short hair, regardless of the eventual decision they reached. It therefore seems that from as few as three training trials with kind long-haired faces and three trials with capable short-haired faces the participants had become sensitive to the potential link between hair-length and these traits. Yet, when quizzed about this, no-one explicitly stated that they used such a rule. It was acquired in a non-conscious manner – influencing people's judgements without their being aware of the source of the influence.

As a check that the results did not reflect pre-existing stereotypes participants brought to the experiment, Lewicki also included Condition II, in which a different group of participants were exposed to the opposite set of contingencies – with long-haired faces being characterised as 'capable', and short-haired as 'kind'. This exactly reversed the pattern of response times to the new faces (see

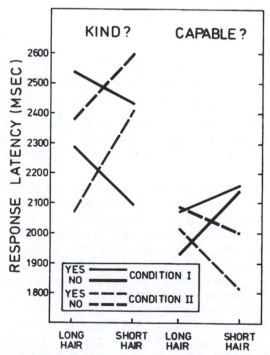

Figure 3.2 Response latencies from Lewicki (1986). See text for explanation. Courtesy of Pawel Lewicki.

Figure 3.2), showing that it was indeed what participants had learnt during the experiment (albeit non-consciously) which influenced their behaviour.

All the time, then, we pick up social cues from the faces of others and use them to support a variety of inferences. To look in more depth at how we assign faces to social categories, we will consider the cues used in perceiving physical characteristics such as age, sex and race, then move on to consider attractiveness and various kinds of social inference.

We begin with age, sex and race – characteristics that are usually easily and accurately determined from facial appearance. The underlying physical differences between people that might be exploited to achieve this involve the shape of the bone structure of the skull, the presence and positioning of subcutaneous muscles and fat, and the surface texture and pigmentation of the skin itself. All seem to come into play in different ways.

Physical differences between faces: Cues to age

In Chapter 1 we described how the shape of our skulls changes across our lifetimes, and how this change can be modelled with a mathematical cardioidal strain transform, allowing the creation of realistic changes in apparent age of 2D drawings or 3D laser-scanned heads. Drawings and laser-scanned heads, though, lack realistic surface texture or pigmentation (see Figure 1.19, in Chapter 1). From one perspective, this lack of texture and pigmentation is valuable, since it shows that shape differences created by cardioidal strain are sufficient in themselves to influence our perception of age. What it leaves open is whether these other cues can also be effective.

A nice study by Burt and Perrett (1995) shows that they can. Burt and Perrett (1995) set out to investigate the relative contribution of gross shape compared with surface texture/coloration in the perception of the age of adult faces. They made use of clever computer graphics techniques to do this. First they collected together a number of different male faces spanning a range of 25 years within seven distinct age groups; 20–24, 25–29, 30–34, 35–39, 40–44 and 50–54 years. Participants were reasonably good at judging the age of these original images.

The different faces within an age-band were then combined into an 'average' face for that age-group, using the morphing techniques described in Chapter 2. Briefly, by careful alignment of feature landmarks identified on each face, faces can be averaged together without blurring. This is achieved by deforming each of the images into a common average shape, in which the locations of the feature points are those of the average for the set, before blending them together. The age averages are shown in Figure 3.3. Burt and Perrett found that the apparent ages of these age-group averages were related to the ages of their constituent faces in an orderly way, though each age-group average face was judged as younger in appearance overall than the average age of the faces it contained. This may be because the averaging technique softens the impact of the different wrinkles and skin texture changes from each of the individual contributing faces.

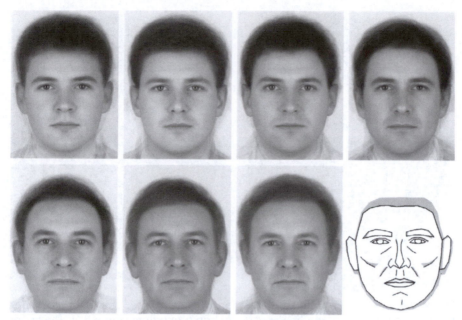

Figure 3.3 See colour plate. Face blends of seven different age groups from 20 to 24 years (top left) to 50 to 54 years (third from left in bottom row). Differences between the 25–29 and 50–54 age groups are shown by the shaded areas in the line-drawn figure at bottom right. The positions for the younger age group are shown with dark lines, and the edge of each shaded area shows the movements of these locations with age. The older group has a higher forehead (receding hair), fatter face, thinner lips, etc. First published in Burt, D. M, Perrett, D. I., Perception of age in adult Caucasian male faces: Computer graphic manipulation of shape and colour information. *Proceedings of the Royal Society, London, B: Biological Sciences, 259,* pp. 137–143. Copyright (1995) The Royal Society.

By examining how each age-group average face differed from neighbouring averages, we can form an idea of how the faces of one age group differ from others. However, Burt and Perrett's techniques made it possible to approach this more systematically. For instance, they were able to exaggerate the differences between age group averages to produce a computer 'caricature' of age-related changes (see Chapter 2 for a fuller description of computer caricature techniques). In Figure 3.4, the differences between the average 50–54-year-old face (left panel) and the average male face across all age groups have been exaggerated to give the more aged-looking face shown on the right. This ageing transform involves changes both to the face image's shape, and in terms of its texture/colour. Using the same techniques, however, Burt and Perrett were also able to take an individual face and apply a transformation to move a face image's shape, or its colour characteristics, or both, towards that of a different age-group (see Figure 3.5). Their work shows clearly that colour and texture differences

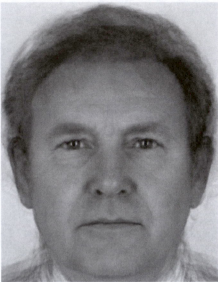

Figure 3.4 See colour plate. Exaggeration of cues to age. The left hand image shows the face blend of the 50–54-year-old age group from Figure 3.3. The image to the right exaggerates the differences between this and the average of all age groups. First published in Burt, D. M, Perrett, D. I. Perception of age in adult Caucasian male faces: Computer graphic manipulation of shape and colour information. *Proceedings of the Royal Society, London, B: Biological Sciences, 259*, pp. 137–143. Copyright (1995) The Royal Society.

resulting from changes in hair, skin pigmentation and elasticity are, like 2D and 3D shape, important cues to age.

The presence of such a variety of cues to age in our faces helps to make age estimation both accurate (M. Rhodes, 2009) and remarkably insensitive to changes (inversion, photographic negation, image blurring) that we will see in Chapter 6 can have a considerable impact on face recognition (George & Hole, 2000).

Sex differences between faces

We are also remarkably accurate at deciding whether faces are male or female. Even if hairstyle is concealed, men are shown clean-shaven, and cosmetic cues are avoided, people are still around 95% correct at deciding whether faces are male or female. Moreover, we are so good at classifying faces by sex that doing this makes few attentional demands and is little affected by having to undertake an attentionally demanding task at the same time (Reddy, Wilken, & Koch, 2004). Research studies have investigated the possible basis of this performance, both by carefully measuring and comparing male and female faces, and by examining how our perceptual judgements are affected when some sources of information are missing.

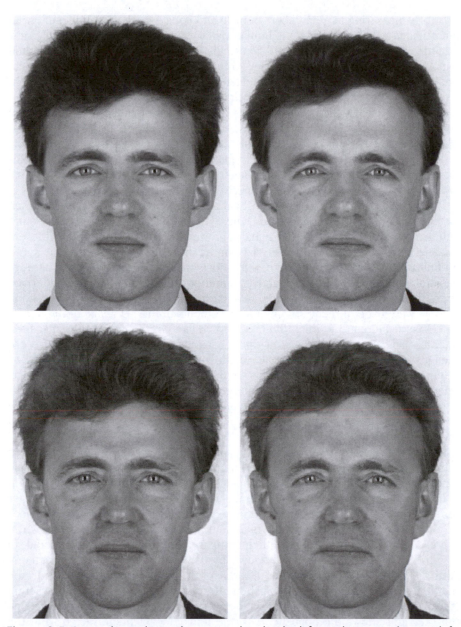

Figure 3.5 See colour plate. The original individual face shown in the top left panel has been aged by transforming its shape (top right), its colour/texture (bottom left), or both (bottom right) in the direction characterising older faces. First published in Burt, D. M, Perrett, D. I. Perception of age in adult Caucasian male faces: Computer graphic manipulation of shape and colour information. *Proceedings of the Royal Society, London, B: Biological Sciences, 259*, pp. 137–143. Copyright (1995) The Royal Society.

By measuring large numbers of male and female faces we can identify what information *might* be used by the human visual system to classify the sex of faces. Identifying what information might be used is, however, only a first step in finding out what is actually useful or necessary for the task. For example, one measurement that differs quite a lot between male and female faces is overall head size, since men are generally taller and broader than women. However, the size of the face is not necessarily a useful cue to determine its sex, and in experiments where faces are all standardised to the same overall size, people are no slower or less accurate at deciding their sex, suggesting that whilst head size is a cue we might conceivably use, in practice it is actually relatively unimportant for human vision. This makes sense in everyday life, where if absolute size were to be used as a cue the visual system would have to compensate for perceived distance in order to use it.

To discover what other physical variables might form the basis of human sex judgements Burton, Bruce and Dench (1993) collected pictures of 91 young adult males and 88 young adult females and made a large number of different measurements of these faces. The sizes of the different features were measured in full-face images (e.g. the length of the nose or the width of the eyes), as were separations between different features. A number of different ratios were derived from these full-face measurements. In addition, profile photographs of the same people were used to recover some measurements of the 3D shape of the heads, such as the amount by which the nose protruded. On the basis of the measurements made, Burton et al. found that it was possible to classify 94% of these images correctly as male or female (a similar success rate to that achieved by human observers) using a total of just 16 different measurements. The measurements included some simple, local features such as the thickness of the eyebrows (thicker in men) and the distance between the eyes and brows (greater in women – particularly if eye-brows have been plucked), as well as more complex, 3D measures such as the protruberance of the nose.

A picture of the overall differences in 3D shape which are found between male and female faces can be obtained by comparing 3D surface images of male and female heads obtained using the laser-scanning technique described in Chapter 1. Linney, Fright and colleagues at UCL were able to average together different surfaces obtained from a number of different male and female faces in order to produce the 'average' male and 'average' female surface shown in Figure 3.6. These surfaces were then compared and their differences noted. In Figure 3.6 these differences are shown by using the colours of the spectrum, with red showing extreme positive differences through to violet showing extreme negative ones. The image on the left shows the differences obtained by subtracting the average male surface image from the average female surface image. The one on the right shows the opposite, with the female surface subtracted from the male one. Thus the left hand image has violet, blue or green areas (negative differences) where the right hand one has red, orange or yellow ones (positive differences). Examining these images we can see that the male face has a more protruberant nose and brow and broader chin and jaw-line than the female face (red on the right, violet on the left). The female, in contrast, has somewhat more protruberant cheeks and a fleshier pad on the chin (yellow on the left, green on the right).

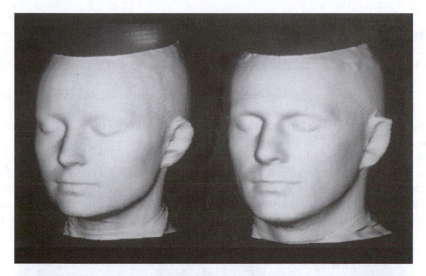

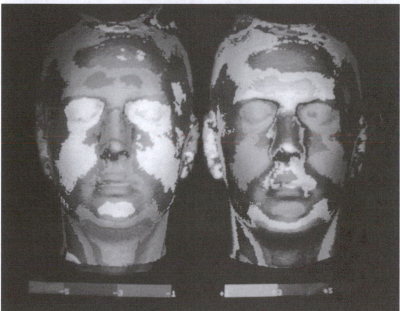

Figure 3.6 See colour plate. The upper panel shows average female (left) and male (right) surface images obtained from laser scanning. The lower panel compares the average male and female 3D shapes – lower left is female minus male, and lower right is male minus female, with positive and negative differences plotted using the colour scale shown beneath (increasingly negative differences in violet to increasingly positive in red). Bruce, V., Burton. A. M., Hanna. E., Healey. P., Mason. O., Coombes, A., Fright, R., Linney. A., 1993, 'Sex discrimination: How do we tell the difference between male and female faces?' first published in *Perception*, 22(2), pp. 131–152. Courtesy of Pion Limited, London.

These differences between men's and women's faces have a variety of causes. For example, Enlow (1982) relates the differences in shape between men and women in the nasal area to their differing oxygen requirements. Because men are larger than women they require a greater air-flow, and hence a differently shaped nasal passage.

The discussion so far suggests that, as for age, there may be different kinds of features that are useful in the perception of the sex of faces – superficial or 'local' features such as the thickness of eye-brows or the texture of the skin in the beard region (where even clean-shaven men often have visible hair follicles or beard 'shadow'), and overall shape features such as the 3D shape of the nose and brow region. Perceptual experiments support the idea that both these sources of information are important. For example, Bruce et al. (1993) compared how accurately people were able to make sex judgements when shown just the 3D surface information derived from laser scanning (see Figure 3.7) with the accuracy obtained to the

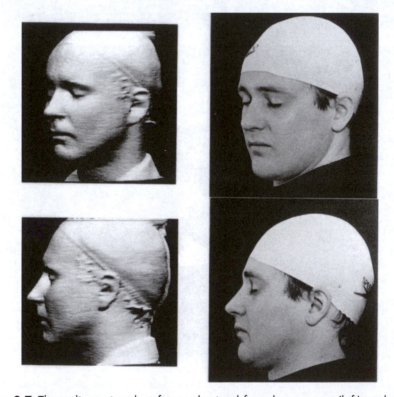

Figure 3.7 Three-dimensional surfaces obtained from laser scans (left) and photographs of the same person as scanned (right). The images to the right contain information about surface texture and pigmentation not available in the laser scans. From Bruce, V., Burton. A. M., Hanna. E., Healey. P., Mason. O., Coombes, A., Fright, R., Linney. A., 1993, 'Sex discrimination: How do we tell the difference between male and female faces?' first published in *Perception*, 22(2), pp. 131–152. Courtesy of Pion Limited, London.

same set of faces shown in the manner in which they were scanned – with hair concealed with a bathing cap and with eyes closed. The surface images contain all the same 3D structural information as the photographs of the people being scanned, but lack the local surface information – for example about brows and skin texture. Accuracy with the surface images was very much better than chance (84%, for example, when ¾ pictures were shown), but it fell considerably below that found with the photographs (94% in ¾ view pictures). This shows that the additional texture information (eye-brows, visible hair, stubble and skin texture) in the photographs adds significant information to that contained within the 3D surface alone. Although the surface images were judged quite accurately in ¾ view, where their 3D shape could be seen, the accuracy of judging these images dropped a great deal when they were shown in full face (75% correct), while accuracy with photographs remained at 95% correct in full-face images. The local texture cues of eyebrows and stubble etc. are equally visible in full-face and ¾ photographic images, while cues to 3D shape such as nose and chin protruberance are much less visible in full-face images and must be derived entirely by an analysis of shape-from-shading.

The subtle differences in shape and surface texture between male and female faces are often exaggerated by the use of cosmetics to enhance femininity. Fashions in cosmetic application change across time, but women have often plucked their eye-brows, thus maximising differences in the hairiness of the brow between men and women. Eye-shadow is used to alter appearance of the eye region. Shading may also be used on the cheeks to enhance the apparent prominence of the cheek bones, again in line with natural differences in the male and female norm. In fact, women's faces typically exhibit a greater contrast in brightness between the eyes and lips and their surrounding skin than do men's faces (Russell, 2003). This effect is often enhanced by cosmetics, and the interesting illustration devised by Russell (2009) reproduced in Figure 3.8 shows how an androgynous face can be made to look more like a man or more like a woman simply by decreasing (more masculine looking) or increasing (more feminine looking) contrast in these regions.

Of course, there are significant variations in the actual shapes of the individual faces of men and women, and considerable tolerance on the part of the human observer. Some very feminine women have bone structures quite unlike the prototypes we have been discussing, yet misclassifications are rare when all relevant information is present. The human visual system rapidly weighs up all the evidence from the particular constellation of surface and shape features and comes up with a decision about the person's sex which is remarkably accurate. Usually, of course, there will be additional information from hairstyle, body shape, clothing and posture which will support the impression gained from the face, and these can help even the most masculine-looking of men to get away with passable female impersonations (e.g. Jack Lemmon in *Some Like It Hot*; Robin Williams in *Mrs. Doubtfire*) by a combination of cosmetics, clothing and mannerism. However, a striking example of how different facial cues are themselves immediately integrated comes from evidence that combinations of cues that specify a face's sex are used holistically.

Baudouin and Humphreys (2006) used Young, Hellawell and Hay's (1987) composite face technique (see Chapter 2) to show holistic processing of a face's

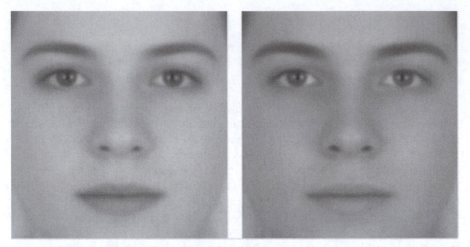

Figure 3.8 Illusion of sex. The facial features are unaltered in each image – only the skin tone is changed by being made lighter to feminise the face (left) or darker to masculinise it (right). From Russell, R., 2009, 'A sex difference in facial contrast and its exaggeration by cosmetics' first published in *Perception, 38*(8), pp. 1211–1219. Courtesy of Pion Limited, London.

sex. They combined top and bottom halves of images of male and female faces into face composites where both halves were of the same sex or both halves came from faces of different sexes, as in Figure 3.9. When participants had to identify the sex of the top or bottom half of a composite face, this was more difficult in the mixed-sex images. Importantly, a control condition with images in which the parts were misaligned (and therefore did not look like faces) did not show this effect, demonstrating that the interference with part processing for the composite faces comes from seeing them as whole faces – it is not simply due to the presence of competing elements in the display.

Racial differences between faces

Race is a different type of categorisation from age or sex because, despite its pervasiveness in modern culture, it is a relatively new concept historically. The genetic differences between people from different racial groups are actually small and surprisingly difficult to pin down consistently – race is a social rather than a biological construct, and modern approaches to biogenetic diversity focus more on geographically defined subpopulations. Even so, people belonging to what are generally considered different racial categories have faces with different characteristic appearances. Skin and hair pigmentation provide the most obvious differences. On the whole, Caucasian Europeans have light skin and light hair in the north, darker hair in the south; Japanese have somewhat darker skin and straight black hair; Africans dark skin and black curly hair, and so on.

Male face   Linked faces   Composite   Noncomposite

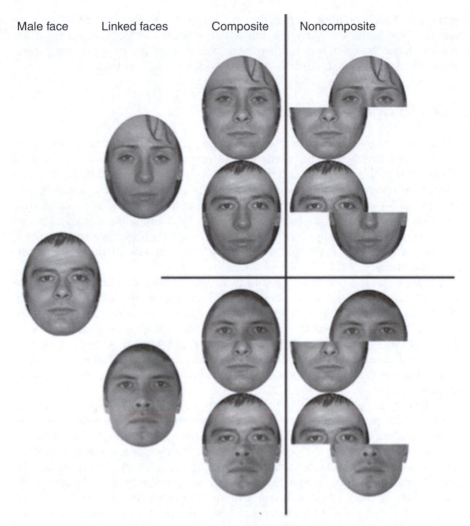

Figure 3.9 Method used by Baudouin and Humphreys (2006) to create mixed-sex composite and misaligned (non-composite) images. The example shows how the top or bottom part of a male face is linked to the top or bottom of another face, which can itself be male or female. Baudouin J.-Y., Humphreys, G. W., 2006, 'Configural information in gender categorisation' first published in *Perception*, *35*,(4), pp. 531–540. Courtesy of Pion Limited, London.

The faces of different races differ in average shape as well as hair and skin colour (Farkas, Katic, & Forrest, 2005). For example, Asian faces are flatter than European ones, and African faces have broader noses than European ones (see Chapter 1 for Enlow's description of some of the different basic types of face). However, the physical differences associated with race have been less extensively studied than have cues to age or sex – Farkas et al.'s (2005) work is a notable exception. This is no doubt in part due to the fact that these physical differences seem so obvious in everyday life, but it also reflects the fact that much of the interest in perception of race has revolved around social issues concerning stereotyping and prejudicial attitudes – issues to which we will return later.

Using cues to age, sex and race

While we have discussed separate cues to age, sex and race of faces, there are actually many interactions between these different dimensions because of shared characteristics that arise through the ways that different faces are structured and grow. Look again at the differences between the average male and female shape in Figure 3.6 – you should also be able to see that the average female shape has a slightly more youthful appearance than does the average male shape. Female faces are a bit more 'baby-faced' than are male faces – they have smaller chins and noses and their eyes appear larger (a consequence of the lesser brow protruberance).

As well as the overlap between the visual features of youthful appearance and femininity, there is some overlap in the characteristics of different racial groups and those of different sexes. Japanese faces are to Western eyes more feminine in appearance, as their nasal areas are less protrusive. Consistent with this, observers are faster and more accurate at judging the sex of 3D surface images of Japanese females and Caucasian males, whereas Japanese males and Caucasian females are slightly more difficult for observers to judge as male or female (Hill, Bruce, & Akamatsu, 1995).

Hill et al. (1995) examined the separate effects of 3D shape and surface colour on the perception of sex and race. They made use of a more advanced form of the laser-scanning equipment used for the measurement of 3D surfaces of faces that recovered the colour from each point on the surface as well as recording its 3D position. Each face scanned in this way can therefore be described as an array of 3D surface co-ordinates, plus an array of colours, as in Figure 3.10. To reconstruct a 3D image of the face, the colour information can be superimposed on the 3D coordinates to give a 3D model on which texture and coloration has been reinstated. This allows us to see what happens if the sources of 3D and colour information are mismatched – for example a 3D shape from a male face combined with a colour map from a female one, or a 3D shape from a Japanese face combined with a colour map from a European one. By comparing the effects of mismatched versus matched 3D shape and texture information we have a way of finding out which source of information is the more important in determining the sex and race of faces.

Hill et al. (1995) obtained scans of four clean-shaven male and four female Japanese and four clean-shaven male and four female European faces. Using the 3D information alone they found that observers were on average 72% correct at judging the sex of the surfaces. This performance is a little less accurate overall than performance described by Bruce et al. (1993), but as half the faces were of another race, and judging faces of another race is more difficult (O'Toole, Peterson, & Deffenbacher, 1996) this may explain this discrepancy. However,

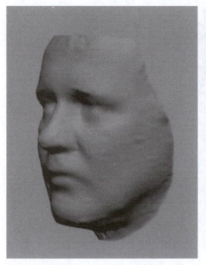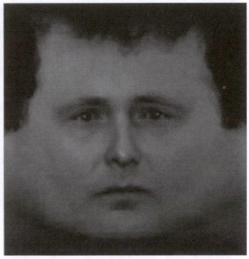

Figure 3.10 See colour plate. Three-dimensional surface coordinates of head from laser scan (left), and colour texture overlay map needed for a photo-realistic 3D representation. From Hill, Bruce and Akamatsu (1995) as illustrated by Bruce and Young (1998).

observers were 88% correct at classifying the 3D surfaces as Japanese or European. When just the colour information was presented in a second experiment, flattened out to minimise the cues to shape embedded within the colour, observers were highly accurate at judging the sex (97% correct) but less accurate on the race (90% correct). The very high performance on the sex judgement task probably arises because of a number of residual superficial cues in these colour images (for example some visible stubble on several of the male faces, plucked eye-brows on the women, etc.).

Hill et al. (1995) then examined the effects of combining 3D shape and colour information so that the sources of information about sex or race matched or mismatched. Figure 3.11 shows examples of the matched and mismatched face images used in these experiments. In each block of four, the top left and bottom right images have matched colour and shape, and the top right and bottom left are mismatched. When sex judgements were made, the effect of mismatching information from the 3D shape was relatively small, confirming that, with these images, the task was dominated by the superficial cues from the colour cues. However, when race judgements were made, judgements were influenced substantially by the 3D shape.

The experimental results are shown in Figure 3.12. Participants had to decide the race (top panel) or sex (bottom panel) of faces shown in full-face (FF), three-quarter (TQ) or profile (PR) views. The graphs plot the percentage of trials where the decision was consistent with the shape information. For matched trials (white bars), where shape and colour are consistent on the dimension judged, then performance is nearly 100% consistent with the shape. When shape and colour mismatch (shaded bars), the lower performance indicates the contribution

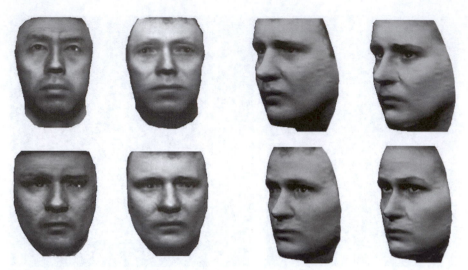

Figure 3.11 See colour plate. Stimuli from Hill et al. (1995) as illustrated by Bruce and Young (1998).

The full-face images show four faces in which race is matched or mismatched:
    Top left: shape and colour from male Japanese.
    Top right: shape Japanese, colour Caucasian.
    Bottom left: shape Caucasian, colour Japanese.
    Bottom right: shape and colour from male Caucasian.
The ¾ view images show faces in which gender is matched or mismatched:
    Top left: shape and colour from Caucasian male.
    Top right: shape Caucasian male; colour female.
    Bottom left: shape Caucasian female; colour male.
    Bottom right: shape and colour Caucasian female.

of the mismatching colour information. The *higher* the shaded bars, the *greater* the contribution of the shape to the decision. It can be seen that the shape has a greater effect for race (upper) than sex (lower) decisions, and that its effect is least when faces are shown in full-face (where 3D shape is hardest to see).

Categorical perception and adaptation effects for physical characteristics

It is clear that we are very skilled at combining multiple sources of information to evaluate age, race and sex from facial appearance. Often, though, we will only need to make fairly broad categorisations such as man, woman, Asian, African, European, child, young adult, middle-aged adult, elderly adult. The importance of such categories can be seen in studies of categorical perception of faces (see Chapter 2 for a brief description of such paradigms).

Categorical perception of race has proved particularly easy to demonstrate, and has now been reported from a number of studies. Figure 3.13 shows images

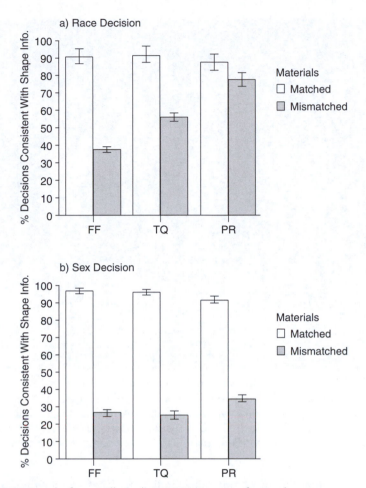

Figure 3.12 Results from Hill et al. (1995). See text for explanation.

depicting an average young male African face and an average young male East Asian face, and morphed images in 10% steps between these averages. The techniques involved in creating such images are described in Chapter 2 – they involve using reference points to control the shapes of images and blend their textures in the required proportions.

The key phenomena of categorical perception are evident in Figure 3.13. Identification of the images as African or Asian is non-linear, with a fairly abrupt shift from African-looking to Asian-looking near the centre of the continuum. Discrimination of the images is also non-linear – it is easier to see that pairs of images that straddle the category boundary are different from each other than it is to see that equally-spaced pairs from within a category are different.

One of the first studies of categorical perception of race was reported by Levin and Angelone (2002). Their procedure was different from that shown in

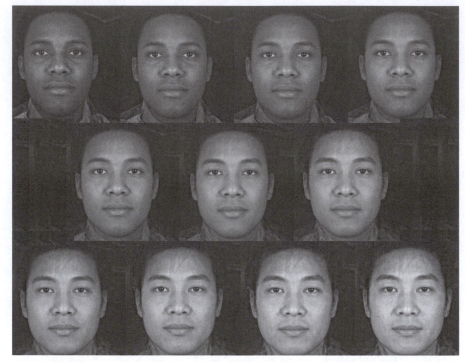

Figure 3.13 See colour plate. Morphed continuum of images in 10% steps from average young male African to average young male East Asian facial appearance. Top row 0% (African prototype) to 30% East Asian images, middle row 40% to 60%, bottom row 70% to 100% East Asian. Images courtesy of David Perrett and University of St. Andrews Perception Lab – www.perceptionlab.com.

Figure 3.13 in that they used unfamiliar individual faces (rather than the averaged faces of Figure 3.13) and found enhanced discrimination of cross-boundary pairs from morphed continua that ran between a black and a white face compared with discrimination from continua running between two black or two white faces. This shows that categorical perception of race has an effect over and above categorical perception phenomena that might reflect the temporary learning of any pair of face images.

Results for categorical perception of sex are a bit more mixed. The critical effects can be obtained (Campanella, Chrysochoos, & Bruyer, 2001), but they are modulated by factors such as familiarity with the images (Bülthoff & Newell, 2004; Viviani, Binda, & Borsato, 2007). This makes sense because changing the apparent sex of an image will also inevitably change its identity, and categorical perception of familiar identities is to be expected (see Chapter 6). To show an effect of categorical perception of sex over and above any effect of identity requires a degree of cunning – for example contrasting categorical perception effects between continua of same sex (identity change only) and opposite sex (change of sex and identity) images (Viviani et al., 2007).

Adaptation effects to salient physical characteristics are also readily found. Webster and his colleagues created morphed continua of images that ran from male to female or from Japanese to Caucasian appearance – exactly the same stimuli as would be used in a categorical perception study (Webster, Kaping, Mizokami, & Duhamel, 2004). They identified where the perceived category boundary fell in each continuum (i.e. the point at which the images become ambiguous between perceived male and female, or between Japanese and Caucasian), and then studied whether this boundary still fell in the same place after adaptation to an image from one end of a continuum. Their results showed a shift in perception that enhanced perception of non-adapted characteristics – in effect, shifting the category boundary towards the adapted image. For example, adaptation to a male face made what had previously been judged to be an ambiguous face look female, or adaptation to a Japanese face made what had previously been judged to be an ambiguous face look Caucasian.

A key question in adaptation studies concerns what exactly is adapted? If we take Webster et al.'s (2004) findings for adaptation to a male face as a starting point, there are at least three different possible reasons why the pattern of results might arise. First, participants may shift their criterion for what counts as male, noting that the ambiguous face is nothing like as masculine as the face they saw before. This explanation is particularly difficult to rule out, but it doesn't seem to fit well with the subjective feeling when you participate in such an experiment that you really do 'see' the ambiguous face differently following adaptation. A second possible reason is that low-level visual features are being adapted, since some of these will be those that are common to the male adapting face and the ambiguous test face. This has appeal because we already know that low-level adaptation can occur with other visual features. The third possible reason is that adaptation is actually to the constellation of features that specifies a perceptual category. This would make the phenomenon relatively novel and of considerable theoretical interest.

In Webster et al.'s design, the second and third explanations can't be disentangled, because morphing the images from male to female changes category-defining and other low-level features at the same time. Attempts have therefore been made to tease these explanations apart by manipulating images within rather than between male and female categories (for example, by increasing the masculinity of an already male face) to see whether adaptation effects might be 'category-contingent' (our possible reason 3) as well as 'structure-contingent' (our possible reason 2). Results have been mixed, but offer support to the idea that both mechanisms may operate (Bestelmeyer et al., 2008; Jaquet & Rhodes, 2008; Little, DeBruine, & Jones, 2005; Little, DeBruine, Jones, & Watt, 2008). Similar findings have been reported for adaptation to race, in which the perceived racial category has an influence that is larger than for equivalently different stimuli that seem to lie within a common racial category (Jaquet, Rhodes, & Hayward, 2007).

Understanding adaptation mechanisms has become very important because adaptation has proved so useful in functional brain imaging studies – in fMRI adaptation, we can infer whether or not a particular brain region might be sensitive to something by seeing whether it adapts to repetition of that characteristic (see Chapter 2). In Haxby, Hoffman and Gobbini's (2000) neuro-logical model, the inferior occipital gyri and the lateral fusiform gyrus are parts of the core system that are involved in analysing invariant aspects of faces (see Chapter 1, Figure. 1.29). These regions are often equated with brain regions that are highly responsive to faces in fMRI studies – the occipital face area, OFA (part of the inferior occipital gyri) and the fusiform face area, or FFA (part of the lateral fusiform gyrus). Since characteristics like sex or race are clearly of the 'invariant' type, we might therefore expect substantial fMRI adaptation to sex or race from OFA and FFA. However, when Ng, Ciaramitaro, Anstis, Boynton and Fine (2006) identified regions of cortex that showed adaptation to a face's sex or race, they found these were relatively widely distributed across occipital and fusiform cortex – extending well beyond more localised regions such as OFA and FFA. To understand why this might happen, it is important to grasp that OFA and FFA are *functionally* rather than purely anatomically defined regions – they are identified in individual brains by fMRI localiser scans (see Chapter 1) that find regions of cortex within a fairly general anatomical area (such as the fusiform gyrus) that respond maximally to faces compared to some other type of visual stimulus (such as objects or houses). Ng et al. (2006) pointed out that this procedure for identi-fying face-selective brain regions may actually maximise the likelihood of finding regions containing neurons that are generally responsive to faces (and therefore respond to all faces in the localiser scan), rather than neurons tuned to a partic-ular face type (as these would only respond strongly to some of the faces used in a localiser). The point is similar to Haxby et al.'s (2001) demonstration that infor-mation about faces may be more widely distributed across occipital and fusiform cortex than is often thought (see Chapter 8).

Freeman, Rule, Adams and Ambady (2010) used a categorical perception paradigm to study how the sex of a face is neurally represented. Participants viewed images of faces that were at different levels of morphing between male to female appearance whilst regional cerebral blood flow was recorded with fMRI. A localiser scan was used to define the FFA as a region of interest, within which Freeman et al. (2010) could then determine whether neural activation (as indexed by the BOLD response) was more accurately modelled by physical changes in the stimuli (i.e. graded levels of morphing) or by perceived sex (with a discontinuity near the centre of each morphed continuum). Consistent with Ng et al.'s (2006) findings, the FFA proved more sensitive to physical than category changes. A whole-brain analysis showed responses to sex category in orbito-frontal cortex – a brain region which is also involved in perception of attractiveness.

Perception of attractiveness

Characteristics like age, sex and race are in large part objective – it is not a matter of opinion whether you are 20 or 30 years old, even though you may look a bit younger or older than you really are – or try to! As well as perceiving these rela-tively objective traits, we also see some faces as looking more attractive than others. In fact, attractiveness is remarkably salient in our (conscious and non-conscious) reactions to faces, as shown by Olson and Marshuetz (2005). They presented pictures of faces for a very brief 13 ms each, and used forward and backward masking to prevent their conscious perception. Yet when participants were invited to 'guess' the attractiveness of each face on a 10-point scale, with no feedback as to how well they were doing, higher mean ratings were given to attractive (5.79) than to unattractive (4.71) faces. These ratings of subliminal faces showed less discrimination than for supraliminal faces – with 1000 ms presentation, the mean rating was 7.44 for the attractive faces and 2.45 for the unattractive faces. None the less, something about facial attractiveness was being picked up even when the faces were not consciously perceived.

As for other facial characteristics, adaptation paradigms have been used to study attractiveness. Rhodes and her colleagues investigated the effect of adapting to slightly distorted faces on what looks normal (i.e. what looks average) and what looks attractive (G. Rhodes, Jeffery, Watson, Clifford, & Nakayama, 2003). Adaptation to a distorted image shifted what seemed normal and what seemed attractive towards the adapted image – showing a correlation between perception of attractiveness and averageness (see later). These adaptation effects were found even when the adapting and test images differed in orientation by 90 degrees (with one oriented 45 degrees left of vertical and the other 45 degrees right of vertical), showing that any low-level mechanisms involved are not orientation-specific (i.e. not very 'low-level'!).

A variant of the composite paradigm has also been used to study attractiveness. Abbas and Duchaine (2008) found that the top half of a composite face image was judged more attractive when combined with an attractive bottom half face than when the same top half face was combined with an unattractive bottom half.

In terms of critical brain regions for evaluating attractiveness, the orbitofrontal cortex shows up consistently in fMRI studies (Ishai, 2007; O'Doherty et al., 2003; Winston, O'Doherty, Kilner, Perrett, & Dolan, 2007). This is a brain region that is widely interpreted as being involved in the neural circuitry for stimulus reward value, but it falls outside Haxby et al.'s (2000) core system. Consistent with this, facial attractiveness can be perceived by individuals with congenital prosopagnosia (Carbon, Grüter, Grüter, Weber, & Lueschow, 2010), despite their problems with face recognition.

However, a potentially complicating factor in studying attractiveness is that what is considered attractive can vary according to individual tastes, and that these tastes themselves are subject to strong cultural influences. For example, within the last few hundred years pale skin and a degree of plumpness were considered highly attractive in Europe, whereas now many Europeans want to be tanned and relatively thin. The shift may reflect changes in how socioeconomic factors link to status. In the pre-industrial era food was more scarce and people worked outdoors, creating the perception that plumpness and light skin indicated higher social status. Now, some of these correlations of status and appearance operate in the other direction.

So, there is clearly a subjective element to the perception of attractiveness. The philosopher David Hume famously argued that beauty 'is no quality in things themselves: it exists merely in the mind which contemplates them; and each mind perceives a different beauty' (Hume, 1757, pp. 208–209).

What this shouldn't be taken to mean, though, is that the perception of what is beautiful or attractive is *entirely* learnt or culturally created. Fascinatingly, modern studies have instead uncovered a core of factors involved in perception of attractiveness that seem to be relatively universal. Despite the easily demonstrated individual differences in taste which we have discussed, there is actually a degree of agreement between people from different cultures as to which faces are attractive if one uses averaged responses (Langlois & Roggman, 1990). Hence, although there can certainly be wide variation between the views of any two individuals as to what is attractive, they vary around an underlying norm which is surprisingly consistent across cultures. Although it is important not to overstate this degree of commonality of responses (Hönekopp, 2006), what initially proved surprising was that it existed at all. In this respect, a particularly striking phenomenon is that when babies who are less than a year old are shown faces adults consider attractive or unattractive, they spend longer looking at the attractive faces (Langlois et al., 1987). We will discuss this infant preference for attractive faces in more detail in Chapter 8. For now, all we need to note is that babies show this preference at an age where they could not have tapped into cultural aesthetic standards.

We therefore need to consider what factors create consistency in judgements of attractiveness, and how we might account for their influence. It is still too early to give a definite answer, but some interesting ideas have been put forward.

In a study which generated a great deal of interest, Langlois and Roggman (1990) took photographs of faces with standard pose, expression and lighting. These were then scanned into a computer and adjusted to all have the same distance between the eyes and lips. Each image was then divided into a very large number of tiny squares (pixels), and the brightnesses of corresponding pixels in different faces of the same sex were averaged to create computer-composite images. In its essentials, this is very like the technique Galton (1879, 1883) had used with superimposed photographs in the nineteenth century (see Chapter 2). Examples of male or female composite faces made from 4, 8, 16 or 32 faces are shown in Figure 3.14.

When people were asked to rate the attractiveness of these composite faces, they rated them as increasingly attractive as more faces went into each image – in other words, perceived attractiveness increases as one moves downwards in Figure 3.14. This applies both to the male and to the female faces. In fact, Galton had noticed the same thing – commenting that 'all composites are better looking than their components' (Galton, 1883, p. 224).

The mathematical consequence of increasing the number of faces used to create a composite image (as in Figure 3.14) is to move the brightness values in that image closer to the average brightness values of the entire set. This happens because the more images are used, the more the idiosyncrasies of particular faces which may be unusual become ironed out. This is clearly evident in Figure 3.14, where the same-sex faces in the lower rows are much more similar to each other than are the same-sex faces in the upper rows.

It seems, then, that moving a facial image closer to the average (in effect, moving it in a downward direction in Figure 3.14) increases its perceived attractiveness. We must now ask, why?

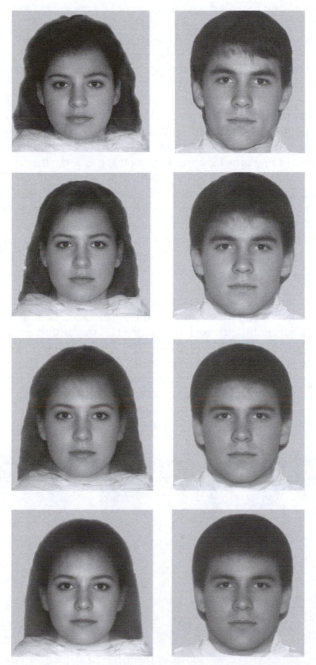

Figure 3.14 See colour plate. Computer composite faces created by combining female (left column) or male (right column) faces. From top to bottom, the rows show composites created by averaging 4 faces of each sex (top row), 8 faces, 16 faces and 32 faces (bottom row). Courtesy Judith Langlois.

One rather uninteresting possibility is that it may derive from this specific method of averaging brightness values. A technique often used in photography and cinema has been to defocus the image a little in close-up shots of the face, to hide surface blemishes and create a slight aura of mystery. Perhaps something similar happens when more faces are put into a computer-composite based on pixel brightness values?

This was what Galton had thought – he pointed out that 'the averaged portrait of many persons is free from the irregularities that variously blemish the looks of each of them' (Galton, 1883, p. 224). It is likely to be a contributory factor, but it is not the full explanation because the same effect is found when the locations of features in line drawings are moved closer to or further away from their average locations in a set of faces (Rhodes & Tremewan, 1996), using the computer caricaturing and anti-caricaturing techniques described in Chapter 2. These line drawings are free from surface blemishes, yet they still become more attractive as their shapes get closer to the average. Moreover, using the more modern technique that uses fiducial points to align feature positions before averaging (see Chapter 2) also replicates Langlois and Roggman's finding that the more faces are averaged, the more attractive the result. A particularly neat study was that of Little and Hancock (2002). First, they showed that the averages of 3, 6 or 12 young adult male faces were seen as increasingly attractive – see Figure 3.15. In these images, both the shape (i.e. the positions of the fiducial points used to define the facial landmarks) and the texture (i.e. the brightness values in each region defined by the fiducials) are averaged at the same time, but of course each of these can be varied independently of the other. Figure 3.16 shows the effect of transforming a face in terms of its shape only (using the 12-face average shape but retaining the original texture), its texture only (using the 12-face average texture but retaining the original shape), or both at the same time (which is, of course, the same as the 12-face average from Figure 3.15). As can be seen, shape

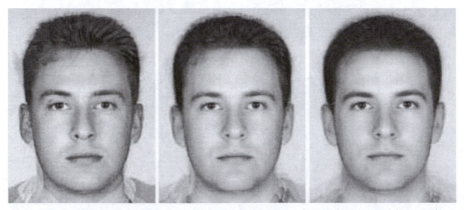

Figure 3.15 Composite images showing averages of 3 (left), 6 (middle) and 12 (right) male faces. See text for explanation of averaging technique. First published in Little, A. C., & Hancock, P. J. B. The role of masculinity and distinctiveness in judgments of human male facial attractiveness. *British Journal of Psychology*, 2002, *93*, pp. 451–464. John Wiley & Sons.

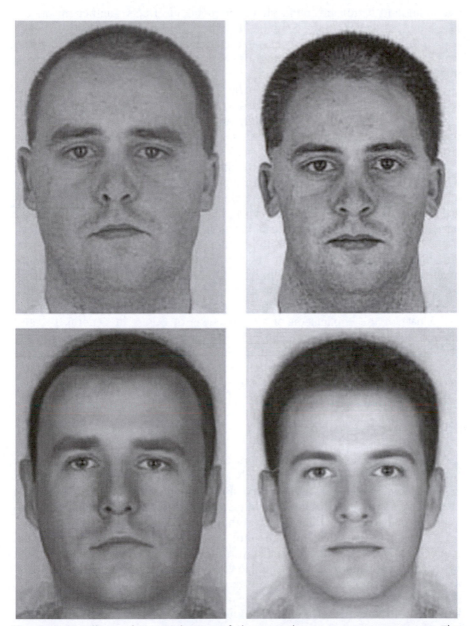

Figure 3.16 Effects of manipulations of shape and texture on attractiveness. The individual male face shown in the top left panel has been changed by transforming its shape to the 12-face average shape from Figure 3.16 (top right), its texture to the 12-face average texture from Figure 3.16 (bottom left), or both (bottom right). Adapted from Little, A. C., & Hancock, P. J. B. The role of masculinity and distinctiveness in judgments of human male facial attractiveness. *British Journal of Psychology*, 2002, *93*, pp. 451–464, John Wiley & Sons.

averaging and texture averaging have independent effects – either makes the face more attractive, but the combination of both is particularly effective.

The relation of attractiveness and averageness therefore seems to represent a genuine phenomenon, though it needs to be treated cautiously. So what might be its basis?

One possible contribution is from our preference for things that are familiar to us. The importance of familiarity has been extensively investigated by Zajonc (1980), who considered it as intimately linked to affective reactions which are often the very first reactions of the organism, and which are the dominant reactions for many species.

Surprisingly, several studies have shown that we will prefer visual stimuli we have seen before even when we have no recollection of having seen them at all (Bornstein, 1989)! The mechanisms which lead us to prefer a familiar stimulus are therefore separate from those involved in consciously remembering that we have seen it before – these two kinds of familiarity are quite different.

This form of preference without inference may contribute to perceived attractiveness. Although you may never have seen before the actual composite images from the bottom row of Figure 3.14, their closeness to the average of the faces you *have* seen may suffice to create a preference based on a comforting sense of ease. Some form of preference based on familiarity of averages does seem to be part of the explanation of attractiveness of things in general, because Halberstadt and Rhodes (2000) showed a correlation between rated averageness and rated attractiveness for drawings of items from a variety of perceptual categories (birds, dogs and wrist watches). These correlations of averageness and attractiveness were comparable to those obtained in studies using images of faces.

Attractiveness and evolution

Other potential explanations of factors underlying facial attractiveness come from evolutionary psychology. Mostly, these link attractiveness to factors associated with selection based on sexual reproduction. From this point of view, attractiveness can have a signalling value to other members of the species, who in turn evolve to be able to make use of this signal.

Most of us don't give much thought to why most animals come in male and female versions, reproducing sexually rather than by some form of cloning (asexual reproduction) – it's a fact of life we tend to take for granted. The reason seems to lie in the fact that whereas asexual reproduction aims to transmit 100% of the parent's genes to the offspring, sexual reproduction transmits 50% from the father and 50% from the mother. The mechanism used to copy genes during reproduction is very slightly susceptible to error, and these gene copying errors (mutations) are important in introducing new characteristics into the gene pool, but only a minority of the mutant genes turn out to be useful. Because sexual reproduction combines the genes of males and females in the offspring, it allows beneficial mutations to spread quickly through the gene pool of the species – conferring better adaptability to challenges such as changes in environment or the capabilities of parasites and predators.

The complexity and intricacy of the genetic control of the development of the hard and soft tissues of the skull and face is evident in the many congenital syndromes which affect the appearance of the face, such as Down's syndrome. Most of the relevant genes have not yet been identified, but clinicians can become remarkably skilled at recognising their different characteristic effects on a person's appearance (Baraitser & Winter, 1983). So it is at least plausible that your face signals something about your genetic make-up.

Langlois and Roggman (1990) had recognised this possibility – they suggested that individuals with characteristics that are close to the average of the population might be preferred because they are less likely to carry harmful genetic mutations. However, subsequent findings such as Halberstadt and Rhodes' (2000) demonstration that averageness confers gains in attractiveness on other types of stimuli (not just faces) weakens the case for an evolved mechanism for detecting good genes being behind the finding that averages are attractive. It may be, though, that more than one mechanism is involved. 'Attractiveness' is a concept that could include preferences based on familiarity, aesthetics and sexuality (Franklin & Adams, 2009). From this point of view, averageness may be more closely related to preferences derived from non-sexual origins whereas sexual attractiveness is a different phenomenon.

At first sight it seems surprising that a lot of research has looked at facial attractiveness in the context of sexual selection when the bodily differences between men and women are so much more obvious than the relatively subtle differences in their faces. In evolutionary terms, however, there is evidence for a 'redundant-signals' approach in which multiple features signal different aspects of mate quality that will be used together in arriving at an overall evaluation (Fink & Penton-Voak, 2002). Of course, the complexities of choosing a mate are such that many factors other than attractiveness will also enter into such evaluations (Miller & Todd, 1998).

Returning to the issue of averageness and attractiveness, common observation suggests that people who become film stars or sex symbols are not noticeably average in appearance, and recent psychological research has also shown the 'attractiveness is only averageness' position to be too simple.

Direct evidence that there is something other than averageness involved in facial attractiveness comes from elegant work reported by Perrett and his colleagues (Perrett, May, & Yoshikawa, 1994). They found that whilst averageness is indeed attractive, it is not optimally attractive. Instead, images created from the average shape of a set of attractive faces were rated as more attractive than images created from the average shape of the set of faces from which the attractive faces had been selected.

Figure 3.17 shows Perrett et al.'s technique. First, the average shape of the faces of 60 Caucasian females aged 20–30 was calculated by marking the locations of 224 feature points (such as the end of the nose), and calculating their average positions. This is shape a in Figure 3.17. The same process was then carried out with the 15 faces rated as having the highest attractiveness – the average shape of these 15 attractive faces is shape b in Figure 3.17. The differences between the locations of feature points in shapes a and b were then calculated, and then each was increased by 50% to create shape c – these changes are

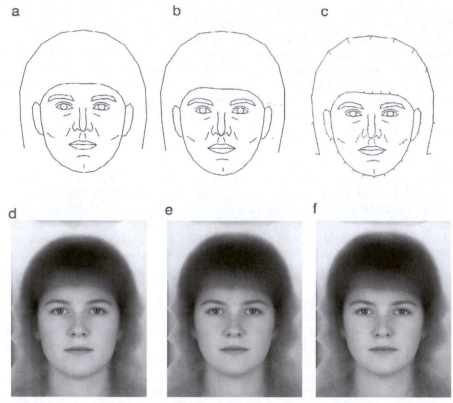

Figure 3.17 See colour plate. Averageness and attractiveness in Caucasian female faces. See text for explanation. Reprinted by permission from Macmillan Publishers Ltd: *Nature*, Perrett, D. I., May, K. A., & Yoshikawa, S. Facial shape and judgements of female attractiveness, *368*, pp. 239–242, copyright (1994).

indicated by the short lines. Finally, an average pigmentation was mapped onto each face shape, to create face images *d–f.*

When British people were asked whether image *d* or image *e* was the more attractive, they consistently preferred *e* to *d*, and when the choice was between image *e* and image *f* they preferred *f.*

These findings show there is something more to attractiveness than just averageness. If attractiveness was entirely due to averageness, there would be no difference between face shapes *a* and *b*, and hence face images *d* and *e*. This is because the highly attractive faces used to create shape *b* and image *e* would themselves be close to the average of the whole set (shape *a* and image *d*). Instead, the average derived from highly attractive faces is more attractive than the average of the entire set from which they were taken.

The same point was apparent when the difference between the average shape of attractive faces and the average shape of the entire set was increased.

The effect of such a change would be to make the resulting faces more different from the average – yet it increased perceived attractiveness.

Perrett et al. also found exactly the same pattern of results for Japanese faces (Figure 3.18), regardless of whether their attractiveness was judged by Japanese or by British people. There is clearly something pan-cultural about attractiveness.

A further study by DeBruine, Jones, Unger, Little and Feinberg (2007) has shown that attractiveness and averageness are not the same thing by comparing ratings of how 'normal' a face looks (its averageness) to its rated attractiveness (they are different), by showing that attractive faces that differed in equal but opposite ways from the average could be discriminated (this would not be possible if attractiveness is just averageness), by confirming that caricaturing (making a face non-average) can enhance attractiveness, and by showing different patterns of adaptation effects for judgements of face normality and facial attractiveness.

Such findings mean that the evolutionary psychology viewpoint has to be taken seriously. But why might a response to see some faces as more attractive than

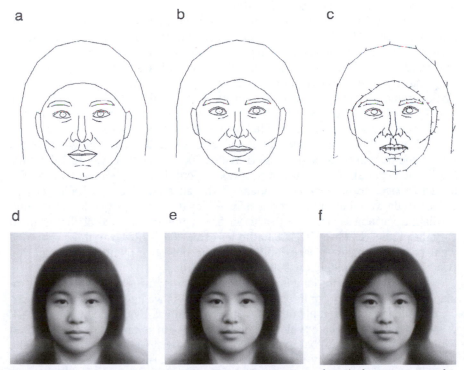

Figure 3.18 Averageness and attractiveness in Japanese female faces. See text for explanation. Reprinted by permission from Macmillan Publishers Ltd: *Nature*, Perrett, D. I., May, K. A., & Yoshikawa, S. Facial shape and judgements of female attractiveness, *368*, pp. 239–242, copyright (1994).

others have evolved? This is always a tricky kind of question to answer. Indeed, it may be in principle unanswerable – evolution does not have a purpose beyond the replication of genes or species, so it doesn't need to proceed along the fixed trajectory assumed by any reason based on a specific factor. The pitfalls are neatly illustrated in a paper by Ramachandran (1997) on why gentlemen might prefer blondes, which argues that the lighter skin tone of blonde women helps reveal health, age and hormonal status – a constellation of factors pertinent to reproductive status. This was intended as a spoof – a parody of facile evolutionary arguments – but it was close enough to the mark to deceive at least some of its readers.

A variety of evolutionary hypotheses have been proposed – some apply to faces of men and women, whilst others are more obviously applicable to one sex. An obvious starting point is that attractive female facial features may signal youthful sexual maturity, and hence fertility (D. Jones, 1995). This fits the facts, and may well be correct, but it is not specific enough to offer strong predictions.

A related alternative is that facial features which are attractive signal health and the likelihood of offspring with improved parasite resistance (Thornhill & Gangestad, 1993). Certainly, faces that look healthier are judged to be more attractive, even if the manipulations only involve superficial characteristics such as skin tone (Perrett, 2010). What is more difficult to establish is whether attractiveness is a valid marker of health.

Kalick, Zebrowitz, Langlois and Johnson (1998) sought to test this using photos of over 300 adolescents for whom health records were available from adolescence, middle and late adulthood. They found that facial attractiveness was unrelated to actual health. A problem with such studies is that modern medicine may mask any evolved relationship between health and attractiveness. The matter remains open because Zebrowitz and Rhodes (2004) found that a reanalysis of the same data showed a moderate association of attractiveness at age 17 and later health for faces of below median attractiveness.

Other studies also have not found strong relationships between actual health and perceived attractiveness (Rhodes, 2006; Rhodes, Chan, & Zebrowitz, 2003; Rhodes et al., 2001). However, it does seem that people *expect* those with attractive faces to be healthier – many of the attractive faces in Kalick et al.'s (1998) study were incorrectly rated as healthier than unattractive faces. Beyond mediating variables such as attractiveness, symmetry or sexual dimorphism (Rhodes, Chan, & Zebrowitz, 2003; Rhodes et al., 2001), however, the question of what precisely makes a face look healthy is only beginning to be explored (Coetzee, Perrett, & Stephen, 2009; Perrett, 2010).

A more surprising idea is that female facial features which are attractive may increase paternity confidence (Salter, 1996). As we have seen, facial appearance is under a considerable degree of genetic control. Everyone knows this – it is still common to debate which of the baby's features are like its father, and which like its mother. What gives this an added twist is the fact that since the baby has been carried by its mother, it will necessarily have 50% of its genes derived from her genetic make-up. The other 50% come from its natural father. But bringing up a human child is a protracted process, representing a considerable parental investment – this makes it a potentially important issue whether the father who helps nurture the infant is its biological father.

To see why this might be important, we need to understand a little about a discipline which has come to be known as sociobiology. In everyday life, we usually think of reproduction as a way of ensuring the survival of the species. From this (species) perspective, it does not matter whether the baby is looked after by its biological father or not. But several recent findings have suggested that it may be equally near (or nearer) the truth to think of the species as a way of ensuring the continuation and development of particular sets of genes, and from this perspective it is very important whether a person is the baby's natural father (with 50% shared genes) or not (much smaller proportion of shared genes).

This perspective – the 'selfish gene' theory (Dawkins, 1976) – has been useful in providing accounts of otherwise puzzling phenomena such as altruism. Acts of altruism are often puzzling because individuals act against their (narrowly defined) self interests, and in ways that do not always seem directly to enhance the prospects of survival of the species. But many instances of altruism fit the selfish gene hypothesis, because it turns out that acts of altruism between one individual and another are on average related to the extent to which they have genes in common.

Such ideas are not always popular, because they seem to many people to take away something of the humanity from human beings. In our view, that is a misconception. The claim of selfish gene theory and related sociobiological accounts is not that altruism is nothing but gene survival, or that foster or step-parents will always be the enemies of their children. On the contrary, it is accepted that through our great capacity for learning, symbolisation and cultural development there will be many counter-examples to these rather basic rules of our animal nature – but these counter-examples should not blind us to the fact that the influences of fundamental genetic mechanisms can still be revealed when one looks at what happens across the average of many instances.

Paternity confidence, then, is a potential issue for males in a monogamous species where parental investment is high. The mother knows it is her baby, carrying her genes, but the father wants reassurance that it is his. It is therefore conceivable that men try to mate with more average-looking women because this allows their own genetic contribution to be more readily discerned in the baby's appearance. Being 'average-looking' is therefore a compliment in this sense.

We are not endorsing this hypothesis as correct – it would be very difficult to achieve satisfactory standards of proof. But it does fit with evidence that, for similar sociobiological reasons, many animal species have developed mechanisms of kin recognition (Fletcher & Michener, 1987). If, for example, you are going to help those who share your genes more than those who don't, you need a way to estimate genetic similarity (Lieberman, Tooby, & Cosmides, 2007). How humans might do this remains controversial, and is complicated by the fact we use deductive as well as perceptual information. For example, Bressan and Dal Martello (2002) found that the pattern of estimated resemblance between photos of adults and children was affected by whether people were given information to indicate that the adult and child were or were not related, regardless of whether this information was true or false. In other words, participants' *beliefs* influenced the way they judged resemblance.

Perceptual factors do also seem to be involved, but their influence is subtle and best shown in paradigms where participants are unaware of what is manipulated (DeBruine, 2004). A particularly interesting study is that by Bressan and Zucchi (2009), who investigated participants who were twins to establish whether self-resemblance or family resemblance is the key variable. They used computer morphing to blend an image of each of the members of pairs of twins with that of a same-sex stranger in the proportions 35% participant's face and 65% stranger's face. These proportions were craftily chosen so that the morphed faces would still look like the stranger's face, even though each was blended with (and hence resembled) one of the twins. The morphed images involving a twin's own face or their co-twin's face were then presented together, and the participant was asked which person they would prefer in contexts indicating altruism or long-term likeability. Both dizygotic and monozygotic twins showed a slight but statistically significant preference for self-morphed over twin-morphed faces in both contexts – knowing the appearance of one's own face therefore trumps the influence of family members in any putative kin-recognition template.

The findings for the monozygotic twins (of which there were 17 pairs in Bressan and Zucchi's study) are particularly persuasive because monozygotic twins are genetically identical – hence they show an own-face influence over and above genetic relatedness per se. This offers only limited support for a sociobiological account, and actually presents some problems too. A keen sociobiologist might argue that your own face is a good template from which to estimate relatedness in everyday circumstances (monozygotic twins being rare). But how could a mechanism that incorporates your own face have evolved? Mirrors are a recent cultural invention, we doubt that our ancestors spent large amounts of time studying their reflection in pools of water, and anyway pools are only occasionally sufficiently still to take a really good look! One possibility is that our modern narcissistic interest in our own faces superimposes these onto a mechanism that was originally triggered mainly by relatives, but you can see that once again this is getting difficult to falsify.

The difficulty of testing the hypotheses of evolutionary psychology has led many researchers to worry that it will prove unscientific, but that seems to us an over-reaction. A number of the hypotheses are grounded in well-established biological theories and principles applicable across many species, which adds considerably to their plausibility. A different form of objection comes from those who maintain that, because of language and culture, our biological background is mostly irrelevant to human behaviour. This view usually leads to overstated claims in the opposite direction from those of evolutionary psychology, but it still has a grip on a lot of journalism and everyday thinking. Here are the views of the popular anthropology writer and photographer Ted Polhemus:

> A male baboon has a fixed idea of what a desirable female baboon should look like. A certain shape and colour of backside is essential, and male baboons battle with each other to get access to those females which fit this ideal most perfectly. The same general principle is true of any animal which

reproduces by sexual selection. But there is an important difference between baboons and ourselves. For other animals the physical ideal is 100% instinctively determined. Thus all baboons of a particular species pursue the same ideal (which is biologically produced at a particular point in the female menstrual cycle). For humans, on the other hand, ideals of beauty are learned.

(Polhemus, 1988, p. 8)

Developing this theme a bit more, Polhemus asserts that 'there is no such thing as natural human beauty'. Of course, this is intended as popular writing and his book was published before a lot of the work we are discussing here. None the less, it expresses particularly clearly a point of view that remains widely voiced even though the facts do not really fit such claims. In trying to draw a firm line between humans and other animals it overestimates the role of learning in human perception of attractiveness, and underestimates its importance to other species. On the one hand, the studies we have reviewed make clear that there is indeed some kind of 'natural human beauty'. Later, too, we will discuss evidence that perception of attractiveness does relate to the menstrual cycle in humans – though in an unexpected way. On the other hand, many studies show that learning often plays a large role in the acquisition of standards of attractiveness among non-human animals – in particular, early experience influences later mate choice via mechanisms such as imprinting (Immelman, 1975).

An interesting hypothesis put forward by Bateson (1978) suggested that sexual imprinting and kin recognition are closely related, serving to create a balance between the genetic costs and benefits of inbreeding and outbreeding (inbreeding maximises genetic similarity, but can perpetuate harmful mutations) by allowing an animal to select a mate that is optimally different from its imprinted individuals. This led to demonstrations that mate preferences can be influenced by infant experience of parental characteristics in a variety of species, and Perrett et al. (2002) found an effect of this type in humans in the form of an influence of their parents' age on participants' attractiveness ratings for averaged faces of different ages.

It is clear that the exploration of sociobiological hypotheses is at an early stage. In addition, it should be noted that any evolutionary selection pressures which operate to influence attractiveness may actually work in the opposite direction to selection pressures relating to other facial functions (such as respiration or ingestion, see Chapter 1) – this could limit the extent to which attractive faces might deviate from the population average (Perrett et al., 1994). But the sociobiological approach clearly holds promise, and it has already generated some interesting predictions and findings.

A good example concerns facial symmetry and attractiveness. Biologically, animal bodies have two kinds of asymmetry – directional asymmetries are consistent in more or less all members of a species (for example, your heart is on the left side of your body), whereas fluctuating asymmetries vary from person to person. Nearly all faces show some degree of fluctuating asymmetry – they are slightly or not so slightly asymmetric around the vertical midline. An interesting controversy in the nineteenth century involved asymmetries in the face and body of the Venus de Milo statue, stimulating the first systematic studies of facial asymmetries (Güntürkün, 1991). The controversy centred on whether asymmetries noted in the face of the Venus showed it was modelled from life, and whether they rendered it more or less attractive.

From a biological perspective, directional asymmetries are unproblematic, whereas fluctuating asymmetries can be a marker of anomalous genetic make-up or developmental problems, so we might expect a degree of symmetry to be attractive (Perrett et al., 1999). In fact, symmetry is such a powerful cue that even photographs of faces with only slight asymmetry can be made more attractive if they are altered to be perfectly symmetric (see Figure 3.19).

Impressively, this preference for symmetric faces was predicted and discovered from the theory that the basis of attractiveness is to be found in the need to produce offspring with optimal parasite resistance (Thornhill & Gangestad, 1993). The ability to generate clear, testable predictions is one of the hallmarks of a good scientific theory. However, the finding is consistent with other variants of sociobiological accounts, and it is also difficult to separate effects of averageness and symmetry – if fluctuating asymmetries characterise our faces, symmetrical faces are going to tend to be more average.

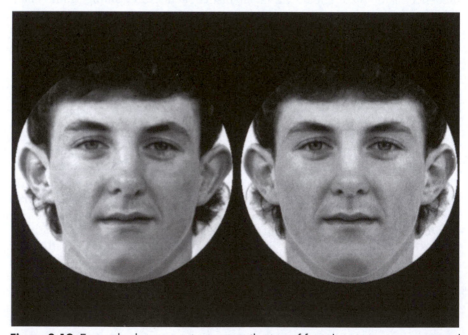

Figure 3.19 Example demonstrating a contribution of facial symmetry to perceived attractiveness. The face on the left is a normal photograph, whereas that on the right has been altered to make it perfectly symmetric. Courtesy of Gillian Rhodes.

Hormonal influences on attractiveness

Another intriguing line of evolutionarily inspired research concerns hormonal influences on perceived attractiveness. From a straightforward evolutionary perspective, more stereotypically masculine features signal high levels of the sex hormone testosterone and should therefore make male faces more attractive to women because testosterone in men is related to strength and resistance to disease. Conversely, more feminine features signal high levels of oestrogen and should make female faces more attractive to men because oestrogen in women is related to youth and fertility. Perrett et al. (1998) tested this theory by using computer graphic techniques to make faces more masculine or feminine in shape. Figure 3.20

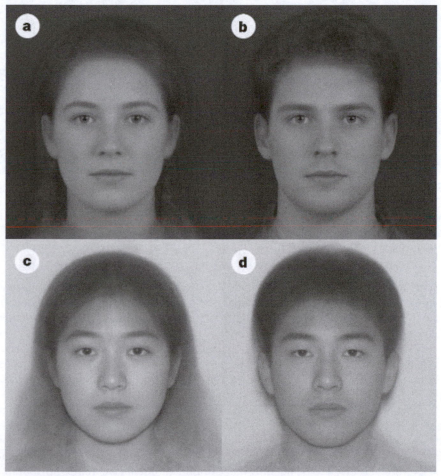

Figure 3.20 See colour plate. Average faces of male and female Caucasian and Japanese young adults. Reprinted by permission from Macmillan Publishers Ltd: *Nature*, Perrett, D. I. et al. Effects of sexual dimorphism on facial attractiveness, *394*, pp. 884–887, copyright (1998).

FEMALE FACES: MALE FACES:

feminised   masculinised   feminised   masculinised

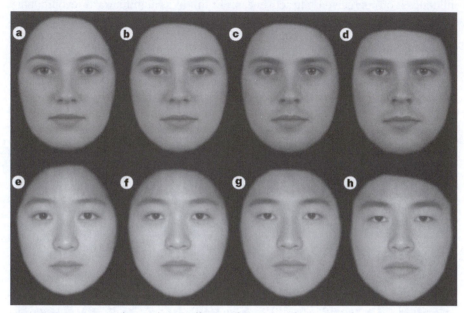

Figure 3.21 See colour plate. Effects of making features of male and female Caucasian and Japanese young adults more 'masculine' or more 'feminine' in shape. Reprinted by permission from Macmillan Publishers Ltd: *Nature*, Perrett, D.I. et al. Effects of sexual dimorphism on facial attractiveness, *394*, pp. 884–887, copyright (1998).

shows average faces of male and female Caucasian and Japanese young adults, and Figure 3.21 shows the effects of making their facial features more 'masculine' or more 'feminine' in shape. Consistent with Perrett et al.'s (1998) prediction, Caucasian and Japanese men (and women, but this is not so important to the theory) preferred female faces with an enhanced feminine shape. This general pattern was consistent across cultures, but slightly enhanced for own-race faces. Surprisingly, though, and counter to the prediction, women (and men) also preferred male faces with a slightly feminine face shape.

So, men find a more feminine face shape attractive in women, but women also seemed to find a more feminine face shape attractive in men. One finding fits the evolutionary perspective, whereas at first sight the other does not. However, Perrett et al. noted that when masculine facial characteristics were enhanced, the faces were perceived to be not only more dominant but also acquired attributions of characteristics such as coldness or dishonesty which might impact on assessments of parenting skills and likely parental investment.

This paradox has potentially been resolved by further work by Penton-Voak et al. (1999), who looked at female preferences for male faces across the phases of the menstrual cycle associated with a higher or lower risk of conception. Remarkably, they found that women in the phase of the menstrual cycle carrying a high risk of conception preferred more masculine-looking male faces, whereas women at low risk of conception preferred 'feminised' male faces. In a separate experiment, Penton-Voak et al. asked women to choose the most attractive male faces for a 'short-term sexual relationship' or a 'long-term relationship' from a continuum ranging from 50% feminised to 50% masculinised. More feminine-looking faces were preferred for a long-term partner, and more masculine-looking for a short-term relationship.

Penton-Voak et al. suggested that a preference for masculine faces when there is a high risk of conception may confer benefits in terms of offspring resistant to disease, but has costs in terms of the likelihood of decreased paternal investment. This offers a characterisation of female sexuality that many people may find unflattering – it is saying that women will take a long-term partner who seems likely to help look after their children, yet be tempted to cheat on them from time to time to get some better genes for the next child. Of course, no-one is claiming that women have to give in to such urges, but if the hypothesis is correct men have grounds for worrying. In fact, genetic studies have thrown up estimates of population rates for non-paternity that are by no means negligible (Neale, Neale, & Sullivan, 2002) – though these may have a range of possible causes.

Importantly, the finding of changes in preference linked to the menstrual cycle has been replicated in other studies (B. Jones et al., 2008), and even access to stereotypical information about men seems to be enhanced when there is a high risk of conception (Macrae, Alnwick, Milne, & Schloerscheidt, 2002). Moreover, other hormonally-mediated effects on the perception of attractiveness have also been found in contexts relevant to parenting and reproduction. For instance, women of child-bearing age are able to make very consistent discriminations of small changes in the 'cuteness' of babies' faces that elude men and can no longer be made by post-menopausal women (Sprengelmeyer et al., 2009). There is clearly a variety of things pertaining to hormonal influences on face perception to be explored and explained.

Other social characteristics

We have seen that there is a surprising degree of inter-individual agreement about attributions such as personality, intelligence or even political persuasion that we make based on facial appearance, and that some of these attributions may have a degree of validity (Kramer & Ward, 2010; Little & Perrett, 2007; Rule & Ambady, 2010; Samochowiec et al., 2010). Historically, there have been many attempts to tell people's psychological make-up from their faces – a discipline that used to be known as 'physiognomy' and is now largely dismissed as a pseudo-science. The first physiognomic writings are usually attributed to Aristotle. He noted several previous attempts by others, but was cautious about their validity. Aristotle thought that the key to character lay in comparing the features of people with those of animals – a nose might be fat like a pig's and therefore indicate stupidity, or flat like a lion's to indicate generosity, and so on.

Aristotle's views were resurrected in the Renaissance by Giambattista della Porta, whose *De humana physiognomonia* (1586) synthesised Hippocrates' typology of four temperaments (sanguine, phlegmatic, melancholy, choleric) with the idea that these could be revealed in the facial features, and again suggested that the correct interpretative technique involved comparison to animal species (see Figure 1.1 in Chapter 1).

The most famous physiognomist was Johann Kaspar Lavater, who worked in Zurich in the eighteenth century and attained great fame, being consulted and befriended by the poet Goethe, and having an influence which extended into the depiction of character in nineteenth-century fiction (Tytler, 1982). Lavater (1793) argued that character could be read from facial features – he considered the nose to be the indicator of taste, sensibility and feeling, the lips of mildness and anger, love and hatred, the chin the degree and species of sensuality, the neck the flexibility or sincerity of the personality, and so on.

Lavater claimed that his views were based on observation, but he also insisted that physiognomy required a special talent to interpret these observations. This insistence that special qualities were needed in a good physiognomist no doubt contributed to Lavater's influence at the time, but ultimately proved the undoing of his system after his death. Without its inventor, and with no basis in science or systematic record, who was to decide which were the skilled and which the unskilled practitioners?

Fortunately, progress has been made. We saw earlier from Lewicki's (1986) work that it is remarkably easy to get people to learn to associate facial attributes with social characteristics – even when the associations are created in a purely arbitrary way – and that in such circumstances people will often have little or no insight into what precisely they have learned. Given this, it seems likely that many of the more complex social attributions we make might be based on stereotyping from other attributes like those we already discussed – age, sex, race and attractiveness.

There is a lot of evidence that this kind of stereotyping happens. For instance, studies of what is often called 'baby-facedness'. As was discussed in Chapter 1, the facial features of the young child are relatively lower down the face than those of the adult. Compared with adults, 'baby-faces' have high foreheads, relatively large eyes and small chins. There is evidence that subtle variations in the apparent immaturity of people's faces within a particular age-group can affect the way that other people judge and interact with them.

For example, in a rather alarming study, McCabe (1984) compared the facial appearances of a sample of children who had suffered physical abuse with the appearance of a control group of children drawn from a similar geographical region who had not suffered harm. The abused children had faces with more adult-like proportions than the non-abused ones – as reflected in relatively shorter foreheads and longer lower faces than the control group children. This finding was replicated with further samples of children and found to apply within each of a number of different age-groups spanning toddlers through to teenagers. Thus, for 12–15-year-old children as well as for 2–7 year olds, children with faces which are relatively more adult in proportion were more likely to have suffered from abuse.

There are a number of potential explanations for such a finding, and we should be cautious before drawing simplistic conclusions about the causes of abuse from such a study. Nonetheless, some of the potential explanations merit discussion since it is possible that any or all of these factors may play some role in some circumstances. One possibility is that children who appear older than their chronological age may tend to be attributed inappropriately grown-up characteristics, and hence may be more likely to be punished for what appear to be immature (though actually age-appropriate) behaviours. Another possibility, offered by those who favour biologically-based explanations, is that 'baby-faced' attributes act as a trigger that produces caregiving in adults. If key attributes of 'babyness' are lacking, then the infants or children may be more likely to suffer aggression. For example, McCabe (1988) draws the analogy between the facial characteristics of the human baby face and the white tail tufts in juvenile chimpanzees. As long as young chimps retain the white tail tufts which signal their youthful status they rarely suffer aggression from adults, but as soon as the tufts turn black – like the adult – then adults will be aggressive towards them. Another possible explanation for McCabe's results is that the facial characteristics that she measured in her studies co-vary with some other factor or factors which are linked with abuse. For example, children with more adult-like faces may be less attractive than those with more baby-like ('cute') faces, and as we will see, perceived attractiveness can also have profound effects.

The degree to which a face shows apparently mature or immature proportions has impacts on the impressions of adult as well as children's faces. If adult faces are altered in ways which mimic these 'baby-faced' features, then their apparent age is changed as a result (see Figure 3.22, for an illustration). Moreover, baby-faced adults are attributed properties which tend to be associated with immaturity. For example, McArthur and Apatow (1983/4) manipulated realistic line-drawings of adult faces to have more or less babyish characteristics, by varying three separate aspects of appearance – vertical feature placement (baby-faced features are lower down the face), eye size (baby-faces have larger eyes) and feature length (baby-faces have shorter noses). All three separate

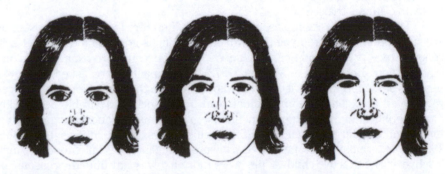

Figure 3.22 Schematic adult faces in which the central female face has been altered to have more baby-faced (left) or more mature (right) characteristics. From McArthur and Apatow (1983/4).

manipulations affected the impressions made to faces, but their combination had the greatest effect of all. The manipulations affected judgements of physical strength (baby-faces were judged as weaker), social submissiveness (baby-faces were judged as submissive) and intellectual naivety (baby-faces were more naive). In a related study using real faces, Berry and McArthur (1985) found that variations in baby-facedness (as measured by variations in chin width and eye size, which were strongly related to rated facial maturity) were positively correlated with the perceived warmth, honesty, kindness and naivety of the faces.

In a further study (Berry & Zebrowitz-McArthur, 1988), mock jurors were asked to judge the guilt or innocence of a defendant accused of a crime of negligence (forgetting to issue a product warning) or intentional deception (deliberately omitting the warning in order to secure the sale of a product). The other variable in the study was the appearance of the defendant, whose photograph was attached to the description of the incident. Photographs of young men were selected in such a way that they were matched on perceived age and attractiveness, but differed in the extent to which the face shape shown had 'baby-faced' or 'mature' proportions. Berry and Zebrowitz-McArthur predicted that the baby-faced young men would be more likely to be considered guilty of the crime of negligence and the mature-faced young men to the crime of deliberate intent. The results fitted this prediction.

These studies illustrate the impact of a particular variation in facial appearance which usually characterises changes occurring during the growth of a child. For reasons unrelated to their chronological age, some children, and some adults, have faces which are more baby-like or less baby-like, and these differences can influence other impressions which are made to these faces.

Similar points pertain to facial attractiveness. For those of less fortunate appearance, the literature on the social psychology of attractiveness makes depressing reading. A remarkable number of our evaluations of people can be shown, on average, to be directly influenced by their physical attractiveness (Bull & Rumsey, 1988). These influences range from professed satisfaction with a blind date, through evidence that simply being with an attractive person enhances one's social status, to findings that beautiful people are thought to possess other desirable psychological attributes, and that they are even less likely to be found guilty in criminal trials!

There are many examples in the research literature to show that most of us are susceptible to a stereotype that 'what is beautiful is good'. Some of the classic reports were by Dion and her colleagues – we will use just two examples. In one study (Dion, Berscheid, & Walster, 1972), participants were asked to assess people's personal characteristics from photographs of their faces – attractive faces were rated as belonging to individuals with more socially desirable personality characteristics, higher occupational status, greater marital and parental competence, and greater social and professional happiness. In the other study (Dion, 1992), a description of an aggressive act was accompanied by a picture of an unattractive or an attractive child. Adults were more likely to attribute the reasons for the aggressive act to character dispositions in the unattractive child and to circumstances for the attractive one – in other words, they tended to assume the unattractive child was nasty but the attractive one was having an off day.

Stereotype activation

Although stereotypical thinking based on assigning other people to categories is clearly widely used, we need to know a lot more about the conditions under which stereotypes will be activated and the extent to which their influence can be controlled (Macrae & Bodenhausen, 2000). One such question concerns whether all potential social categories are automatically activated whenever we encounter a face. Given the multiplicity of categories we might use, this seems unlikely, but how might we map what *is* activated? Asking people won't do, because the questions themselves may activate the categories whose spontaneous use is what we are interested in investigating.

Santos and Young (2005) used the isolation effect to get at this question. The isolation effect (also known as the von Restorff effect, after its originator) is a memory phenomenon in which items that stand out as somehow different from other items that are being studied will be better remembered – memory for them is enhanced by their isolation from the other items. For example, a man's face might be easy to remember if it is one of the only male faces among a list that is mainly females. Conversely, the same man's face would be less well remembered if the other faces in the list were mainly males too, whereas a woman's face would be well remembered under such circumstances.

So, in an isolation paradigm, one kind of item occurs frequently in the studied set, whereas another (isolated) kind of item is rare. To the extent that participants notice whatever characteristic it may be that distinguishes the isolated items, they will remember them better – the memory improvement is due to the item's standing out from others, not its intrinsic properties. The isolation paradigm thus provides a way to find out which characteristics of faces get noticed by participants. From the participant's point of view, a set of faces simply have to be learnt – nothing need be mentioned about isolated items, social categories, and so on.

With no instruction other than to remember the faces, Santos and Young (2005) found strong isolation effects for age and sex, weaker effects for distinctiveness and attractiveness, and no clear isolation effects for intelligence and trustworthiness. This suggests that not all categories are automatically activated whenever we encounter a face – as might be expected, those that are automatically activated seem to correspond to categories that are both frequently used in everyday life and have highly reliable physical correlates. Even for these categories, though, evidence from other studies is mixed. Wiese, Schweinberger and Neumann (2008) used ERPs to demonstrate that information about age is encoded regardless of task demands, whereas with ERPs (Wiese et al., 2008) and with behavioural reaction times (Quinn & Macrae, 2005) it has been reported that the encoding of a face's sex can sometimes be more flexible.

What seems to emerge is therefore that social categorisation is a complex process that can show a degree of flexibility to adjust to prevailing circumstances and needs. The same point is clearly seen in a further experiment using the isolation paradigm. Although Santos and Young (2005) did not find any isolation effect of apparent intelligence when participants were instructed simply to remember the faces they had seen, a clear isolation effect for intelligence was obtained when participants were asked to judge intelligence as they studied the faces to be learnt, with isolated faces of high-intelligence appearance or isolated faces of low-intelligence appearance then being better remembered – showing that the categorisation is readily activated when circumstances demand.

The activation of racial categories and their associated stereotypes has been particularly extensively investigated. We noted earlier that race is not a genuine biological concept, but it is socially highly pervasive and operates even at a perceptual level. For example, faces with African-American features are perceived as having a darker overall skin tone than faces matched for skin tone but with more stereotypically Caucasian features (Levin & Banaji, 2006) – seemingly because our visual systems have become so attuned to conjunctions of properties that exemplify racial differences that they exert some form of top-down influence which alters perceived skin tone in the expected direction. In fact, a difference as small as changing the hairstyle of a racially ambiguous face can be enough to make it appear slightly more African or Hispanic – see Figure 3.23. MacLin and Malpass (2003) noted that in some parts of the world this will lead to profound differences in other attributed characteristics – their U.S. participants thought the faces with stereotypical 'Afro' hairstyles had darker complexions, deeper eyes and wider mouths, they associated negative or positive characteristics to what they perceived as 'other-race' or 'own-race' faces, and they showed better memory for 'own-race' faces. The own-race memory bias is particularly

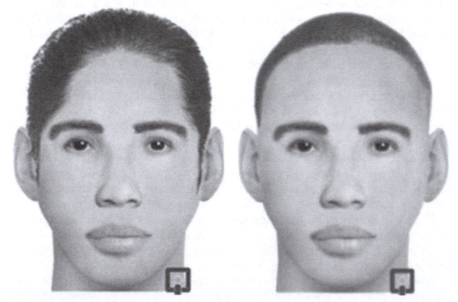

Figure 3.23 Changing the hairstyle of a racially ambiguous face to make it appear more African or Hispanic. From MacLin, O. H., Malpass, R. S., 2003, 'The ambiguous race face illusion' first published in *Perception, 32*(2), pp. 249–252. Courtesy of Pion Limited, London.

interesting because it is happening for faces whose features are mainly identical (only the hairstyle changes) – showing that part of the 'other-race' effect discussed in Chapter 6 may derive from assigning the face to a racial category.

Other studies have used faces to address the question of prejudicial stereotyping directly. Blair, Judd, Sadler and Jenkins (2002) showed that simply possessing some 'Afrocentric' facial features led to attributions of stereotypically 'African American' attributes by US observers, and this happened even when the faces were discernibly 'White' in overall appearance.

As well as having an impact on the relatively fixed characteristics investigated in the studies just described, effects of racial prejudice extend to perception of changeable characteristics like expression. Hugenberg and Bodenhausen (2003) created movies using computer animation software to show a Black or a White face changing from a hostile to a friendly (happy) expression. The faces were matched for facial structure and expression, with only skin tone, skin colour and hairstyle differences being used to create the perception of a racial difference – see Figure 3.24 for sample frames. Each movie lasted 16 seconds – making the change in expression quite slow. Participants were asked to view the movies and signal via a key press when the target face no longer expressed its initial emotion.

Hugenberg and Bodenhausen (2003) used an indirect measure of racial prejudice involving an IAT (Implicit Association Test) procedure. The IAT is a widely used measure of automatic activation of attitudes. In this case, participants have to press two different response keys to stereotypically Black or stereotypically White names, and to pleasant words or unpleasant words. The mappings are set up so that pleasant words and White names are assigned to one response key and unpleasant words and Black names are assigned to the other response key (for participants who are prejudiced against Black people, this will be a highly *compatible* mapping), or so that pleasant words and Black names are assigned to

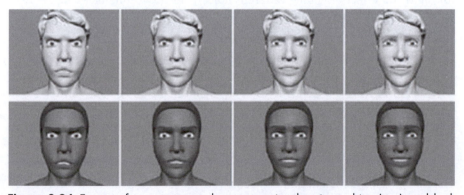

Figure 3.24 Frames from angry to happy movie showing white (top) or black (bottom) faces. See text for explanation. Kurt Hugenberg, Galen V. Bodenhausen, *Psychological Science*, 14, 6, pp. 640–643, copyright © 2003 by Sage Publications, Reprinted by Permission of SAGE Publications.

one response key and unpleasant words and White names are assigned to the other response key (for participants who are prejudiced against Black people, this will be a highly *incompatible* mapping). Any difference (in either direction) between these two critical conditions will show implicit prejudice by revealing whether White or Black names are more easily associated with responses that also take in pleasant or unpleasant words. Hugenberg and Bodenhausen (2003) found that European Americans who were high on implicit prejudice against Black people were slower to see the change from hostility in Black than White faces, and quicker to detect hostility in Black than White faces in a second experiment in which the movies went from a neutral to a hostile expression. Such findings are important because they point to the likelihood that racial prejudices can become self-fulfilling prophecies in which perceived hostility will attract attention and promote reciprocation.

Another interesting approach was used by Dotsch, Wigboldus, Langner and van Knippenberg (2008). This adopted an ingenious technique for finding critical regions of the face that may underpin different perceptual decisions that was devised by Mangini and Biederman (2004). In Mangini and Biederman's method, random visual noise is added to an ambiguous base image and participants are asked to classify the picture representing the base image plus noise in various ways – for example, as male or female. Since the noise is added to the same base image to create every one of the pictures judged in the experiment, the information that is critical to a particular decision (in our example, critical to deciding whether the face is male or female) can be inferred from the difference between the average noise patterns that lead to one decision (male) or the other (female). As Mangini and Biederman (2004) put it: 'our method allows an estimate, however subtle, of what is in the subject's (rather than the experimenter's) head'.

Dotsch et al.'s (2008) use of this technique is illustrated in Figure 3.25. They investigated the perception of Moroccans – a stigmatised immigrant group in the Netherlands. Image (a) is their base image, and the images in row (b) show the effect of adding different noise patterns to this base image. Row (c) shows the effect of asking participants in the Netherlands to select images that looked either Moroccan or Chinese. The row (c) images are based on averaged 'Moroccan' or averaged 'Chinese' choices – they serve to show that the method works to find recognisable perceptual cues to racial appearance.

Dotsch et al.'s (2008) critical step was to then use an IAT measure of implicit attitudes to Moroccans to divide the participants into those who showed high, moderate or low levels of implicit prejudice against Moroccans. They then recalculated the average 'Moroccan' face classification image for each group, as shown in row (d). These images were rated by an independent group of observers for criminality (stereotypically high in Moroccans for prejudiced individuals) and trustworthiness (stereotypically low in Moroccans for prejudiced individuals). The ratings showed that prejudiced observers had selected faces that were more stereotypically 'criminal' and 'untrustworthy' as corresponding to 'Moroccan' appearance.

This fascinating study begs as many questions as it answers. In particular, what does it mean to evaluate a face as looking 'criminal' or 'untrustworthy'?

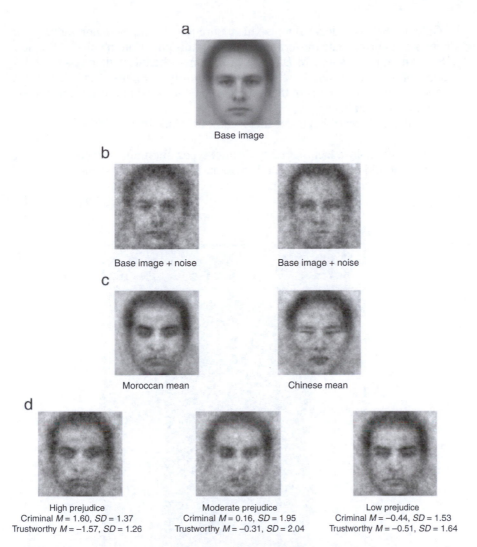

a

Base image

b

Base image + noise   Base image + noise

c

Moroccan mean   Chinese mean

d

High prejudice
Criminal $M = 1.60$, $SD = 1.37$
Trustworthy $M = -1.57$, $SD = 1.26$

Moderate prejudice
Criminal $M = 0.16$, $SD = 1.95$
Trustworthy $M = -0.31$, $SD = 2.04$

Low prejudice
Criminal $M = -0.44$, $SD = 1.53$
Trustworthy $M = -0.51$, $SD = 1.64$

Figure 3.25 Appearance stereotyping by prejudiced individuals. See text for explanation. Reproduced from Ron Dotsch, Daniël H.J. Wigboldus, Oliver Langner, Ad van Knippenberg, *Psychological Science, 19,* 10, pp. 978–980, copyright © 2008 by Sage Publications, Reprinted by Permission of SAGE Publications.

Faces that look untrustworthy or threatening: The role of the amygdala

Like some other aspects of face research, the question of judging trustworthiness or untrustworthiness from appearance was first approached systematically by Galton (1883). He decided to use his technique of composite portraiture (see Chapter 2) to investigate the 'criminal face'. To this end, Galton enlisted the help of Sir Edmund du Cane, HM Director of Prisons, who allowed access to photographs of inmates taken by the prison authorities. Figure 3.26 shows two composite portraits. One is of the faces of men convicted of murder and violent crime, the other of thieves.

Galton held great hopes for this technique, since he considered that

It is unhappily a fact that fairly distinct types of criminals breeding true to their kind have become established, and are one of the saddest disfigurements of modern civilisation.

(Galton, 1883, pp. 10–11)

Figure 3.26 Examples of Galton's (1883) composite photographs of criminals' faces.

This type of approach reached its zenith in the work of Lombroso (1911), who claimed that the 'born criminal' was characterised by facial asymmetry, a low sloping forehead, prominent brows and anomalous teeth. However, systematic results have not favoured such theories. Instead, it seems more likely that to the extent to which such characteristics were present in institutionalised criminals, they were also shared by many underprivileged but law-abiding people of the time. In line with this, Galton's own results were probably a great disappointment to him – the composite portraits (Figure 3.26) look mainly like somewhat undernourished men, as might be expected if there was no particular validity to his premise.

Galton's and Lombroso's lack of success should make us appropriately sceptical of modern studies that in some ways hark back to their agenda. None the less, some of the recent findings are intriguing and impressive. Again, a key observation is that different observers agree about which faces look more or less trustworthy, irrespective of whether such opinions are valid. Even more remarkably, our brains seem to rely on the same neural region to evaluate trustworthiness, and they do this automatically, whenever we look at a face. The critical structure is the amygdala, located in the medial anterior temporal lobes, which is part of Haxby et al.'s (2000) 'extended system' (see Chapter 1) and thought to form a key component of the 'social brain' (Bickart, Wright, Dautoff, Dickerson, & Barrett, 2011).

A seminal study by Adolphs and his colleagues showed that three brain-injured patients with bilateral amygdala damage were impaired at evaluating the trustworthiness and the approachability of faces (Adolphs, Tranel, & Damasio, 1998). What is meant by being impaired in this context is that their evaluations of faces differed from those of participants who did not have amygdala damage. But patients with bilateral amygdala damage can usually recognise familiar faces (Calder, Young, Rowland et al., 1996; Young et al., 1995), so Adolphs et al.'s (1998) finding makes an interesting double dissociation when set alongside the observation that people with congenital prosopagnosia can perceive face trustworthiness relatively normally (Todorov & Duchaine, 2008).

The importance of the amygdala to our evaluations of trustworthiness has been confirmed using fMRI with neurologically normal participants. Winston, Strange, O'Doherty and Dolan (2002) found that untrustworthy-looking faces led to greater amygdala activation than trustworthy-looking faces, regardless of whether participants were evaluating the faces for trustworthiness or for age. The finding of increased amygdala activation to untrustworthy faces even when age (rather than trustworthiness) is being evaluated suggests that the engagement of the amygdala by untrustworthy faces is automatic, and this has been confirmed with other indirect tasks that do not require judging trustworthiness per se (Engell, Haxby, & Todorov, 2007). The amygdala's responsiveness even extends to faces that have acquired their untrustworthy status during the experiment, through playing a 'Prisoner's Dilemma' game (Singer, Kiebel, Winston, Dolan, & Frith, 2004).

In Chapter 4 we will look more closely at some of the functions of the amygdala, but to interpret the findings we are discussing at the moment it is sufficient to know that it is a brain structure with a long evolutionary history and that it seems to be involved in the appraisal of danger and physical threat. This makes it easy to see why the amygdala might be involved in evaluating the potential trustworthiness of seen individuals. Engell et al. (2007) even report that average estimates of trustworthiness across a group of participants are a better predictor of amygdala responses than are the more idiosyncratic responses of individual participants – paradoxically, group averages will predict your own amygdala's activation better than your personal trustworthiness assessments! This is probably happening because the group averages offer an excellent way to home in on those things that are relatively invariant across trustworthy or untrustworthy-looking faces.

A provocative series of studies initiated by Phelps and her colleagues used fMRI to measure amygdala activation (blood flow) to faces of different races. In Phelps, O'Connor, Cunningham and Funayama's (2000) first experiment, they presented Black and White male faces with neutral expressions to White American participants. An IAT procedure similar to that already described for Hugenberg and Bodenhausen's (2003) study was used to measure implicit racial prejudice. White participants who showed more prejudicial attitudes to Black people on the IAT also showed relatively large amygdala activation for Black compared to White faces – as if their brains are set to evaluate Black faces as potentially untrustworthy or threatening.

On a more positive note, it is worth pointing out that in a second experiment Phelps et al. (2000) found that faces of famous Black people who were positively regarded by their participants did not elicit a differential amygdala response – suggesting that the amygdala's response is modifiable in the light of experience. Subsequent studies (Eberhardt, 2005) also demonstrate that there is considerable interplay between initial automatic and slightly later, more controlled responses. For example, in Cunningham et al.'s (2004) study a presentation time of 30 ms created greater amygdala activation to Black than White faces, but increasing the presentation time to 525 ms substantially reduced this difference and led to greater activations in regions of frontal cortex involved in cognitive control.

Much of this literature on race effects may reflect a more general tendency to exaggerate differences between members of a social in-group and an out-group, with stereotyping and superficial processing of the out-group members. A thought-provoking example comes from recent work by Hugenberg and Corneille (2009) who told participants that White faces were those of students at the same university (in-group) or at another university (out-group). The cue to in-group or out-group membership was simply the colour of the background behind the face (red or green). Using a variant of Young, Hellawell and Hay's (1987) composite face paradigm (see Chapter 2), Hugenberg and Corneille (2009) found more holistic processing of the faces seen as in-group than out-group members.

A systematic approach to social perception

Some of the findings we have discussed are remarkable, but something that is lacking from many of the studies is an overarching theory. Mostly, they tend to show that social categories involving things like age, sex, race or attractiveness can get used to underpin more complex social inferences and attributions – which is interesting and important – but often they don't systematise these in any way that can lead to a strong prediction of what exactly might be expected to happen in a particular study.

In this respect, the recent work of Todorov holds promise (Oosterhof & Todorov, 2008; Todorov, Said, Engell, & Oosterhof, 2008). Todorov and his colleagues looked at the underlying structure of attributions we make to faces. They began by asking people to rate images of emotionally neutral faces on a number of traits – most of these traits were taken from other participants' spontaneous descriptions of what they saw in the faces. They then used a Principal Components Analysis (PCA) of these ratings to simplify the dimensional structure of the ratings and find any underlying order. Two orthogonal Principal Components (PCs) emerged, as shown in Figure 3.27, which summarises the 2D PC solutions for 66 photos of faces (top panel). In this figure, the smaller the angle between a trait dimension and one of the (vertical or horizontal) PCs, the more closely it relates to that component, so Todorov and his colleagues consider the first (the horizontal axis of Figure 3.27) to correspond well to 'trustworthiness' and the second PC (the vertical axis of Figure 3.27) to be approximated by 'dominance'. The PCs themselves, of course, are only descriptions of the regularities in the data set – labelling them as approximates of trustworthiness and dominance is just a way of trying to give them some kind of psychological meaning.

The lower panel of Figure 3.27 shows an equivalent PCA for trait ratings made to 300 computer-generated faces created using a morphable model of 3D facial structure that was itself developed by Blanz and Vetter (1999) from a PCA of laser scans of heads of young adults with an overlaid RGB texture map. Impressively, the solutions for the trait ratings of these computer-generated faces and the natural face photos are closely comparable.

Figure 3.28 takes this a step further, by using the 2D space defined by the Principal Components to modify an individual synthetic face in ways that affect its perceived trustworthiness or dominance. By implication, this should transform the synthetic face on all of the other dimensions incorporated into the PCA that created the 2D model – showing that it is a powerful conception.

When Todorov and Engell (2008) used fMRI to investigate amygdala responses to the 66 photos of neutral expression faces that had been used for the PCA shown in the top panel of Figure 3.27, they found that amygdala responses were correlated with the first PC (approximated by trustworthiness) but not with the second PC (dominance). Although the amygdala does not therefore seem to be interested in the second PC, the psychological reality of Todorov's second PC is evident from the remarkable finding that around two-thirds of the 2004 elections to the US Senate and House of Representatives were won by the candidate whose face was judged to have a more 'competent' appearance by raters with no prior knowledge of the candidates (Todorov, Mandisodza, Goren, & Hall, 2005)! In Todorov's model, competence is a trait that (like dominance) is a fair approximation of the second PC.

A further strength of Todorov's approach is its close links to the theories of Fiske, who has hypothesised that perceived warmth (closely related to approachability and trustworthiness) and competence (closely related to dominance) are

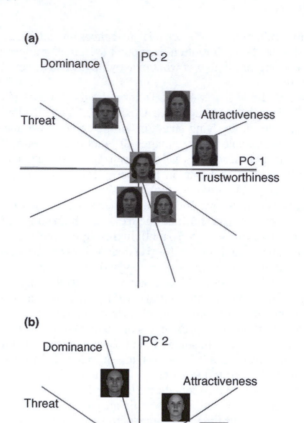

Figure 3.27 See colour plate. Dimensional structure for ratings of characteristics from face photographs (top) and computer-generated faces (bottom). Reprinted from *Trends in Cognitive Sciences, 12*, Alexander Todorov, Chris P. Said, Andrew D. Engell, Nikolaas N. Oosterhof, Understanding evaluation of faces on social dimensions, pp. 455–460, Copyright 2008, with permission from Elsevier.

universal dimensions of social cognition derived from our primate ancestry (Fiske, Cuddy, & Glick, 2007). Social animals need to be able to determine quickly whether they are encountering a friend or foe (warmth) and how effectively any such intentions might be enacted (competence). This places the social

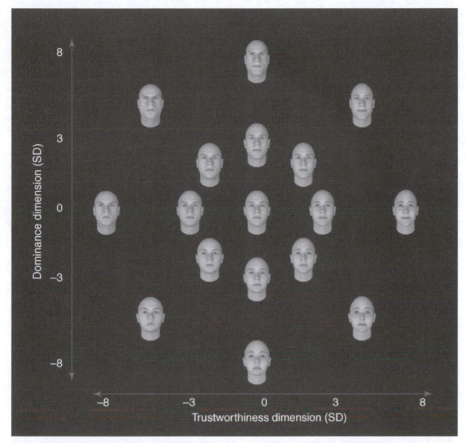

Figure 3.28 See colour plate. Modifying a synthetic face to change its perceived trustworthiness or dominance. Reprinted from *Trends in Cognitive Sciences, 12*, Alexander Todorov, Chris P. Said, Andrew D. Engell, Nikolaas N. Oosterhof, Understanding evaluation of faces on social dimensions, pp. 455–460, Copyright 2008, with permission from Elsevier.

evaluation of faces into a clear context of potentially evolved mechanisms with functional significance for types of social interaction that are widespread in primate species, which Fiske then uses to account for common forms of human interpersonal and inter-group relations and associated social emotions such as admiration, envy, pity and contempt.

A limitation of Todorov's approach at present is that it doesn't explicitly incorporate interactions between its PC-based structure and obvious social categories and signals we use all the time – age, sex, race and of course facial expression. Will we need a more complex arrangement to accommodate these, or might they fit somehow under the existing PCs? Note, too, that attractiveness results from a combination of PC1 and PC2 in Figure 3.27 – this generates easily testable predictions concerning this much-studied trait.

In principle, these kinds of details can be worked through if the basic approach is valid, and the parallel with Fiske's work (much of which is concerned with evaluations of social characteristics more broadly than just from faces) suggests it may well stand the test of time. To sound a cautionary note, though, we will see in Chapter 4 that two-dimensional models are not always successful in capturing what can turn out to be important facets of complex phenomena. To date, the kinds of experiment that undermined the credibility of two-dimensional accounts of facial expression recognition (described in Chapter 4) have not been applied to Todorov's model – it will be interesting to see how it fares. Whatever the outcome of such tests, Todorov's approach is valuable because it systematises the field of study and makes clear, falsifiable predictions – this is a key way in which science makes progress.

We also know that social learning can play a role in the perception of characteristics like trustworthiness – a study by DeBruine (2002) found that trustworthiness judgements were affected by similarity to the perceiver's own face (a potential marker of genetic relatedness). As was evident for attractiveness, though, these influences of learning may be superimposed on a biological substrate that becomes evident from averaged responses.

To get a clearer idea of how different cues are used to infer social characteristics from faces, Santos and Young (2008) studied how inversion (i.e. turning the photo upside down) and negation (i.e. making the image into a photographic negative) affected judgements of age, sex, distinctiveness, attractiveness, approachability, trustworthiness and intelligence. Examples of Santos and Young's (2008) stimuli are shown in the upper row of Figure 3.29. Their aim was to include characteristics that ranged from those with a well-established physical basis (e.g. age, sex) to those whose basis is at present indeterminate (e.g. intelligence). In an attempt to ensure that as many as possible of the potential cues that might be used in everyday interactions were present in the stimuli, the face photographs were of men and women of a wide range of adult ages and with no constraints on pose or facial expression.

Santos and Young's results showed that effects of inversion and negation were independent, but a further experiment (using stimuli as in the lower row of Figure 3.29) showed that the effects of negation were mainly due to reversing brightness (changing light regions to dark, and vice versa) rather than to reversing colour values (changing reddish hues to green and blue to yellow). On this basis, Santos and Young (2008) suggested that information about both surface properties (affected by brightness negation) and holistic or configurational properties (affected by inversion) is important, and that the similar effects of these changes on most of the judgements implies that the different characteristics are mostly inferred from a common perceptual representation.

The importance of holistic processing is underlined by studies reported by Todorov, Loehr and Oosterhof (2010) who applied the top plus bottom face composite procedure (Young, Hellawell, & Hay, 1987) to the perception of trustworthiness by creating aligned and misaligned versions of images in which one half came from a trustworthy-looking face and one half from an untrustworthy-looking face. Evidence of holistic perception of trustworthiness was found for upright images, in the form of better performance in identifying the

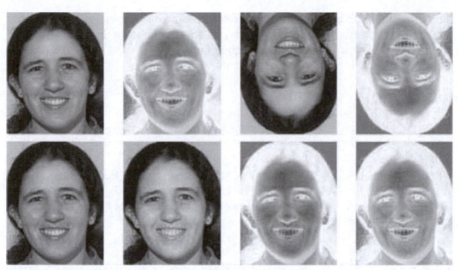

Figure 3.29 See colour plate. Manipulations of photographic images. Upper row: inversion and negation (left image original, second image negated, third image inverted, right image inverted and negated). Lower row: reversing colour and brightness (left image original, second image colour-reversed, third image brightness-reversed, right image colour-reversed and brightness-reversed). Reproduced from Santos, I. M., Young, A. W., 2008, 'Effects of inversion and negation on social inferences from faces' first published in *Perception, 37*(7), pp. 1061–1078. Courtesy of Pion Limited, London.

trustworthiness of parts of misaligned than aligned stimuli – in misaligned stimuli, there is no face whole to interfere with analysing the constituent parts. As expected, this effect was reduced for inverted stimuli (holistic processing is hard to apply to inverted faces).

Summary

This chapter is intended to convey some idea of the wide variety of social inferences we make based on facial appearance. These range from inferring physical characteristics (age, sex, race, etc.) based on a wealth of cues we have become very skilled at interpreting, to attributing social attributes whose validity has often been questioned (trustworthiness, intelligence, and so on), though several researchers now take seriously the 'kernel of truth' point of view.

The evolutionary background to some of these evaluations was discussed – especially for perception of attractiveness, where it has been intensively researched. Provocative findings have also come from brain imaging studies, which (given sufficient ingenuity – and this remains a considerable caveat) offer the possibility of measuring reactions we might prefer to conceal in many circumstances.

Overall, these topics are among the 'hottest' in contemporary cognitive science, but a lot of the action involves piecemeal accumulation of findings rather than fitting them to an overall perspective – in some cases generating more heat than light. We discussed Todorov's work as a good example of the value of a more integrative, theoretically-driven research agenda.

Further reading

Eberhardt, J. L. (2005). Imaging race. *American Psychologist, 60*, 181–190.
Reviews brain imaging studies of responses to faces of different races, and discusses their implications.

Macrae, C. N., & Bodenhausen, G. V. (2000). Social cognition: thinking categorically about others. *Annual Review of Psychology, 51*, 93–120.
Links the questions addressed in this chapter to wider issues in the fields of social cognition and person perception.

Rhodes, G. (2006). The evolutionary psychology of facial beauty. *Annual Review of Psychology, 57*, 199–226.
A wide-ranging and authoritative review offering a broad perspective on studies of facial attractiveness.

Todorov, A., Said, C. P., Engell, A. D., & Oosterhof, N. N. (2008). Understanding evaluation of faces on social dimensions. *Trends in Cognitive Sciences, 12*, 455–460.
An ambitious attempt to develop a general model to account for our social evaluations of faces that can stimulate future studies and offer a testable framework for their interpretation.

Webster, M. A., Kaping, D., Mizokami, Y., & Duhamel, P. (2004). Adaptation to natural facial categories. *Nature, 428*, 557–561.
A pioneering study showing how adaptation paradigms can be used to investigate a range of social characteristics we perceive in faces.

Messages from facial movements

Our faces are moving most of the time – we don't keep them still for long. These movements fall into two different broad types – rigid movements that don't alter the shape of facial features (for example, movements of the head), and non-rigid movements of the facial features themselves (moving the lips, widening the eyes, raising an eyebrow, and so on). Rigid movements of the head (and, independently, the eyes) often signal the direction of social attention, a topic that has become so important in its own right that we will consider it in a separate chapter. Here, we will primarily be concerned with social signals conveyed through non-rigid facial movements, the most obvious of which are speaking and using our faces to signal moods and feelings.

This separation of the roles of rigid and non-rigid movements is clearly relative rather than absolute. Rigid movements can be involved in some social signals, such as lowering the head to indicate deference or submission, or simply nodding in agreement. Likewise, gaze direction (signalled through a combination of rigid movements of the eyes and head, see Chapter 5) can interact with the interpretation of other signals – when someone looks angry and is staring at you it will be more threatening than if they are staring at the television.

The roles played by the movements themselves can also vary. In talking, the mouth and lips move rapidly and, as we will see, the patterns and timing of the movements can convey critical information. In contrast, although facial expressions of emotion also result from movements of the facial muscles, they can often be interpreted relatively well from the apex of the movement itself. Paradoxically, this means that many studies of facial expression recognition can be conducted using static, photographic stimuli.

We will begin by considering the production and perception of facial expressions of emotion from a variety of perspectives, before turning to speech movements and then considering the question these raise of how the integration of signals from different sources and sensory modalities is achieved.

The facial muscles

While the hard and soft tissues of the face produce the individual variations in appearance which are important for categorisation and identification, it is movements of the face which are primarily responsible for its ability to transmit a range of other social signals. These movements are controlled by a bewildering variety of muscles. In Chapter 1 we noted how the different functions of the human face – looking, eating, breathing and sending social signals – all require muscular movements and introduced Darwin's view that emotional expressions of the face build upon these other kinds of activity.

The anatomy of the muscles was discussed by Sir Charles Bell – the first edition of his book was published in 1806, but he later prepared an expanded version (Bell, 1844). Bell arrived at several plausible hypotheses about how the facial muscles function to signal emotion, but the only source of evidence he had was careful observation and deduction. Observation should never be belittled, but it has limitations with such a complex system.

The earliest systematic experimentation on muscle movements was by the French physician Duchenne (1862), who studied a man who had lost feeling in his face through damage to the nerves. By applying small electric currents to the sites of the different facial muscles, Duchenne could make them move independently and study the effect of moving each muscle without his unfortunate participant feeling any unpleasant sensation.

This line of research has been considerably enhanced through the work of Ekman, who developed the Facial Action Coding System (FACS) for recording which muscles in the face are moved when a person displays a facial expression (Ekman & Friesen, 1978). The FACS system can be used to code the facial muscles involved from videos or from purely static photographs of expressions. Systems such as FACS form important research tools, since they allow us to develop highly controlled stimuli instead of simply relying on actors to portray particular emotions. There is always the worry, too, that how an actor chooses to communicate an emotion may only partially reflect how it is displayed in everyday life, and FACS allows us to check whether such suspicions are warranted or groundless. In addition, FACS has potentially important applications – for example, it can be used to tell genuine from posed expressions. However, most readily recognisable facial expressions of emotion involve the simultaneous activation of more than one muscle group (Eibl-Eibesfeldt, 1989; Ekman, 1972). None the less, FACS has good psychometric properties (Sayette, Cohn, Wertz, Perrott, & Parrott, 2001) and a recent study following Duchenne's approach by using intramuscular electrical stimulation has confirmed the validity of FACS (Waller et al., 2006).

The universality thesis

In his landmark book on facial expressions, Darwin (1872) proposed that certain facial expressions have clear biological origins, and that these will therefore be universally recognisable. Certainly, perusal of Darwin's illustrations (see examples in Figure 4.1) shows that the meanings of these facial expressions have not changed in the last 125 years. Darwin was not the first to propose the universality thesis, but

Figure 4.1 Pictures of facial expressions from Darwin (1872): joy (left), grief (centre), contempt (right).

he gave it an entirely new twist by linking it to evolution. For previous authorities, such as Bell (1844), universal aspects of facial expressions were taken to reflect the 'fingerprints of the creator', rather than the product of evolutionary history.

Whilst it would nowadays be unusual to invoke the creator in a scientific hypothesis, a sceptic might want to argue that one of the reasons we can still recognise the emotions from the pictures in Darwin's book is not our biological endowment but the fact that printing, photography, cinema and television are so dominant in western culture that they have forced us all to learn a fixed set of conventions. To make a proper test of the idea that the expressions of emotion are universal, Ekman therefore visited a preliterate culture in New Guinea, where people had not seen photographs, magazines, cinema or television, and had been visited by few outsiders. They would therefore have had little opportunity to learn about the facial expressions of people from other cultures. Figure 4.2 shows

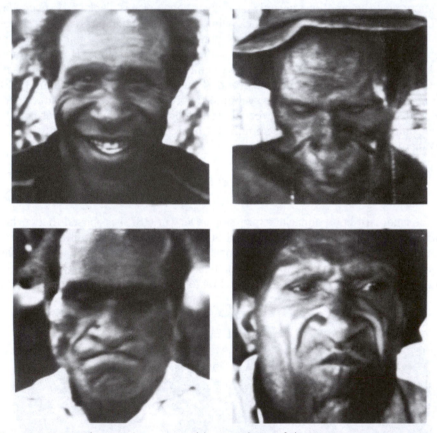

Figure 4.2 Facial expressions posed by members of the Fore community in New Guinea in response to the stories 'your friend has come and you are happy' (top left), 'your child has died' (top right), 'you are angry and about to fight' (bottom left), or 'you see a dead pig that has been lying there a long time' (bottom right). From Ekman (1972). Courtesy of Paul Ekman, Ph.D./ Paul Ekman Group, LLC.

people from this culture demonstrating what their faces would look like in response to different story vignettes. Even without the benefit of television, their expressions are essentially the same as would be seen anywhere else in the world (Ekman, 1972).

Ekman and his colleagues also tested recognition of facial expressions (Ekman, 1972). This is a tricky thing to do because there are huge cultural differences in the words and concepts people use to describe emotions. This undisputed anthropological fact was probably part of the reason that the universality thesis had not been greeted with unanimous enthusiasm – if people from different cultures can *think* about emotion in very different ways, why should we expect any commonality in how they *recognise* them? Moreover, even when members of the same culture are simply asked to describe or label facial expressions, they can give very variable responses which can themselves require considerable interpretation – how do we decide whether or not two people mean the same thing if one calls an expression 'shock' and the other calls it 'fear'?

To get round these difficulties, Ekman adopted a forced-choice procedure in which people were asked to assign photographs to one of a fixed number of categories, and he used little stories (as in the example given earlier) to make clear what each category entailed. He also took great care to ensure that the facial expression stimuli were photographs of people moving exactly the right muscles for each emotion.

With such precautions, the work of Ekman and many others has shown reasonably good recognition of a small number of basic emotional categories in nearly all cultures. These basic emotions include happiness, sadness, anger, fear and disgust. Surprise was also included in Ekman's original set of basic emotions, but it has turned out to be confusable with fear, possibly because surprise does not have the full status of a basic emotion – you can be pleasantly or unpleasantly surprised, indicating that surprise may not be a simple emotional state. More recent studies have sometimes included contempt as another basic emotion.

As already noted, from a purely intuitive reasoning it is perhaps a little surprising that *photographs* of facial expressions should be so well recognised, since it is natural to think that the pattern of movement of the facial muscles will itself convey important information. We need to keep in mind that the fact that expression photographs are recognisable does not mean that movement is unimportant – on the contrary, there is evidence that the timing of facial movements is carefully balanced between the needs of the sender and the intended recipient, even for a facial signal as apparently simple as raising the corners of the mouth in a smile (Leonard, Voeller, & Kuldau, 1991). For expressions that are too subtle to be easily seen in static displays, too, a clear role for patterns of movement has been found – movement can draw attention to small but critical changes (Ambadar, Schooler, & Cohn, 2005). However, the good recognition of photographs of normal intensity basic emotions shows that, for these emotions at least, either the apex of the set of muscle contractions forms a recognisable configuration of the facial features or that we are very skilled at estimating the implied motion (Martinez, 2003).

A set of photographs of facial expressions of basic emotions (happiness, sadness, fear, anger, disgust, surprise and also neutral expressions) posed by a number of different models (the 'Pictures of Facial Affect') was published by Ekman and Friesen (1976) and has been used in many subsequent studies. Advantages of the Ekman and Friesen photograph set include their care in establishing that appropriate muscles were moved in posing each expression (by using instructions like 'narrow your eyes' rather than 'look sad') and validation of good recognition rates for each image as the intended emotion.

Findings of universal recognition of facial expressions of emotion have not gone unchallenged – largely on the grounds that they seem to be observed most often with the particular combination of methods Ekman used (forced-choice responses, stories to back up the response categories, careful selection of target photos). These challenges seem to us, though, to miss the main point, which is that with appropriately careful testing there is evidence of an impressive degree of commonality across cultures in the interpretation of certain emotions. In making this point, Ekman has never sought to deny the richly diverse contributions from culture and upbringing.

An example of diversity involves what Ekman (1972) calls display rules. These concern the circumstances in which it is appropriate or inappropriate to display emotion – and they vary widely across the world. The important point is that although display rules concerning when it is appropriate to express certain emotions are culturally determined, the forms of the facial expressions of basic emotions themselves do not vary substantially.

An additional important point is that many of the facial expressions we encounter in our daily lives do not belong to basic emotional categories, yet we are often able to interpret them. Moreover, we can use facial expressions intentionally to elicit a particular kind of response from someone, or even to deceive them. Expressions have become part of a complex non-verbal communication system, and as such are susceptible to a range of cultural influences. These influences include social factors related to whether the expressions belong to individuals construed as in-group or out-group members (S. Young & Hugenberg, 2010). None of this, though, contradicts the evolutionary origin of some emotional expressions.

Perceiving and producing facial expressions of emotion

Although we can reconstruct a plausible evolutionary history for at least some basic emotions and their facial expressions, this doesn't tell us much about how we perceive and produce them. What it does, though, is to point towards the possibility that at least some aspects of facial expression might be 'wired in' to our brains.

Some observations fit this idea. A long line of neuropsychological studies points to the involvement of the right cerebral hemisphere in facial expression recognition. This is evident from studies of the effects of right-sided brain injury (Borod et al., 1998), from visual hemifield studies finding a left visual field superiority with neurologically normal participants (Ley & Bryden, 1979) (see Chapter 2 for a description of the technique and its rationale), and even from a left-sided bias in free viewing of chimaeric faces (Levy, Heller, Banich, & Burton, 1983). A widely used variant of the free-viewing task is shown in Figure 4.3. The stimuli are made from one side of a smiling and one side of a neutral face. The participant's task is

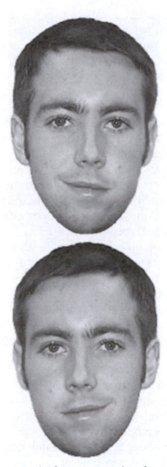

Figure 4.3 Chimaeric faces made from one side of a smiling and one side of a neutral face. Which looks happier? Copyright © 2008 by the American Psychological Association. Reproduced with permission. Victoria J. Bourne, Examining the relationship between degree of handedness and degree of cerebral lateralization for processing facial emotion. *Neuropsychology, 22*(3), pp. 350–356.

simply to decide which looks happier. Right-handed participants show a small but consistent overall bias toward choosing the face whose smiling part falls to their left. Why this might implicate the right hemisphere was explained in Chapter 2 – a particularly important pointer to the bias being due to cerebral asymmetry is that it is influenced by handedness (Bourne, 2008a; Levy et al., 1983).

Effects of brain injury on producing facial expressions also show a system that is organised by biological rather than solely experiential factors. Again, effects of cerebral asymmetry are evident (Borod, Santschi Haywood, & Koff, 1997), but even more striking are differences between voluntary and involuntary expressions. Sometimes adults with neurological diseases affecting subcortical regions suffer attacks of pathological laughing or crying (Rinn, 1984). These behaviours look emotional yet they can be triggered by nothing in particular, they can last a long time, the patients are unable to stop them, and they often experience them as irritating and unpleasant rather than emotional per se. It seems as if the motor patterns underlying such emotional behaviours are somehow elicited without appropriate circumstances, and that they are not under voluntary control.

The effects of damage to the cerebral cortex are markedly different. Diseases such as strokes often affect the cortex on one side of the brain only, and if the motor cortex is affected this creates a degree of paralysis on the opposite side of the body. So, damage to the left motor cortex affects movements of the right side of the face, whereas damage to the right motor cortex affects the left side of the face. This unilateral paralysis, though, is often more pronounced for voluntary expressions (Rinn, 1984) – a patient with damage to the left motor cortex may only smile on the right side of his or her face when asked to do so, but can show a happy expression on both sides of the face when genuinely laughing.

It seems that voluntary and involuntary expressions are, to some degree, separately represented in our brains. Yet when we perceive facial expressions we often don't seem to notice the consequences of this – it is tricky to tell a real from a false smile, or to detect that someone is lying. However, the observations of neurological differences in how voluntary and involuntary expressions are produced lend credibility to the idea that through using FACS or similar systems to analyse carefully the patterns of muscle movement a trained observer might be able to detect real from simulated emotion. Ekman (1996) describes an interesting approach based on looking for cues to different ways in which we try to hide our feelings – for example by trying to mask one expression with another (smiling through gritted teeth), trying to suppress a spontaneous expression, or just faking a non-genuine emotion. What isn't immediately obvious, though, is why we can't also become better at detecting such deceptions in our daily lives if reliable cues are available, especially if we are in an occupation where evaluating a person's sincerity is important. A plausible but somewhat unflattering speculation is that much of our social lives requires some degree of insincerity – you are polite to your obnoxious boss, you try not to hurt your friend's feelings, and so on. So we all become reasonably good deceivers, and since failures to detect these deceptions are common in everyday life, we perhaps don't get a good enough evidence base from which to learn the cues.

One of the most striking observations suggesting an evolved neural substrate for the production of facial expressions is that babies who have been blind from birth produce some recognisable facial expressions even though they have never seen other people's expressions to imitate (Tröster & Brambring, 1992). This repertoire of expressions is limited, and their use is not supported by mechanisms that would arise commonly in sighted social interactions, so the frequency with which blind infants produce facial expressions is often low. None the less, for at least some expressions, it is clear that production of the expression can be independent of ability to perceive and interpret it.

We can also ask about the relation between perception and production of expressions the other way round – would we be able to recognise expressions that we cannot produce? There are reasons to favour either possibility – that is, reasons can be adduced to suggest that perceiving facial expressions is independent of our ability to produce them, or reasons for thinking that perception and production are linked in some way.

A body of opinion among several modern philosophers and psychologists is that some kind of 'mental simulation' forms an important component of how we interpret other people's moods and feelings. That is, it may help us to interpret facial expressions that we know how we would feel if we looked that way (Goldman & Sekhar Sripada, 2005; Keysers & Perrett, 2004). The existence of 'mirror neurons' in primate brains, which respond when a monkey sees another monkey performing a certain action as well as when the monkey itself performs the action, shows a link between percepts and actions that is consistent with the simulationist perspective (Gallese, Keysers, & Rizzolatti, 2004) (see also Chapter 5). Moreover, when Adolphs, Damasio, Tranel, Cooper and Damasio (2000) mapped the regions where brain injury consistently led to problems in recognising facial expressions for a large group of brain-injured patients, they found that these included the right somatosensory cortex and adjacent areas. We already noted that the finding of right cerebral hemisphere involvement in emotion recognition is fairly common, but demonstrating the involvement of somatosensory areas was relatively novel. A study using rTMS (repetitive transcranial magnetic stimulation – see Chapter 2) has confirmed that rTMS of the face region of the right somatosensory cortex disrupts facial expression perception (Pitcher, Garrido, Walsh, & Duchaine, 2008). Research on patients with 'locked-in' syndrome, who are unable to make voluntary movements of their facial muscles, has confirmed that, as a 'simulationist' account would predict, recognition of facial expressions is impaired (Pistoia et al., 2010).

These studies certainly make a good case for some degree of commonality between mechanisms involved in facial expression production and comprehension. However, an importantly different perspective comes from Mobius syndrome, a rare congenital disorder that leads to underdevelopment of some of the cranial nerves, and especially cranial nerves VI and VII. Since these innervate the facial muscles, the affected person has a paralysed, unexpressive and mask-like face. They can't smile, frown, or even close their eyes, and they have problems controlling eye movements as well. Inability to move the lips also creates problems with activities like talking (though understandable speech is possible), sucking and eating.

People with Mobius syndrome, then, have never been able to move the muscles of their faces, and never produced a recognisable facial expression of their own. How will they fare in recognising the facial expressions of other people? Two studies (Bogart & Matsumoto, 2009; Calder, Keane, Cole, Campbell, & Young, 2000) show that there are no serious abnormalities of facial expression recognition. With a neurodevelopmental disorder, this finding needs to be interpreted in the light of the possibility that people with Mobius syndrome may have developed ways of interpreting facial expressions that are not the same as those used by people who can use their facial muscles, but as a minimum it shows that being able to produce facial expressions is not *essential* to being able to interpret them – there are other ways to recognise emotional expressions than facial mimicry.

Dimensional models of facial expression recognition

So how do we recognise facial expressions? Although a small number of basic emotions seem to be recognised throughout the world, we noted that there are many facial expressions which do not correspond precisely to one or other of these categories. Even with basic emotions the expressions can actually be fairly variable – there are different kinds of smile or, as we will see later, different varieties of disgust (Rozin, Lowery, & Ebert, 1994). So, in everyday life, we make considerable use of the contexts in which expressions occur to assist interpretation. To demonstrate this, look at Figure 4.4. What is the young woman feeling? Absolute terror?

The answer can be found opposite, in Figure 4.5. She was photographed in the audience at a pop concert. Once this context is clear, it is easy to interpret her expression as one of great excitement.

We have cheated a bit with this example, because there is a curious relationship between fear and excitement – the queues for the white-knuckle rides are always the longest at theme parks. However, less dramatic effects of context on the interpretation of expressions are common – quite possibly the norm. Indeed, if the contextual information is strongly discrepant, people will reinterpret other basic emotions as well as fear (Russell & Fehr, 1987). Facial expression perception does not deal in absolute certainties. We modify how we read people's feelings on the basis of any other pertinent information available at the time, and the context in which the expression occurs is a natural part of this (Aviezer et al., 2008; Barrett & Kensinger, 2010).

Since even basic emotions can sometimes be misinterpreted, and because many facial expressions do not in any case correspond exactly to specific basic emotions, many people have thought that what we may be doing when we perceive facial expressions is to locate their positions along general dimensions of emotion.

This idea was made popular among psychologists through the textbook of Woodworth and Schlosberg (1954), which was for many years a key textbook of experimental psychology. Woodworth and Schlosberg (1954) tried to make sense

Figure 4.4 What is the young woman feeling? First published in J. Liggett. *The human face.* Copyright London: Constable (1974).

Figure 4.5 Facial expressions at a pop concert. First published in J. Liggett. *The human face*. Copyright London: Constable (1974).

of the bewildering array of findings from the pre-Ekman studies of expression recognition which had looked at the spontaneous labels given to highly diverse sets of faces. They noticed that whilst people's responses in such tasks were clearly varied, they were not random. The key to putting them into a more systematic order was to realise that only a certain range of responses would tend to be used for each face. For example, people might say that a particular face showed fear, suffering, grief, even surprise, but no-one would describe it as joy, happiness, disgust or contempt. By grouping together some labels which seemed to them to be used almost interchangeably, and studying the patterns of responses, Woodworth and Schlosberg were able to arrange the emotions into a circle which had the property that those expressions most likely to be confused with each other were placed in adjacent parts of its perimeter. The resulting scheme is shown in Figure 4.6.

A simple way to describe locations in a two-dimensional diagram like Figure 4.6 is in terms of their positions along two fully independent (orthogonal)

Figure 4.6 Emotion circle proposed by Woodworth and Schlosberg (1954), adapted by Izard (1977) with examples of facial expressions which would fall at different points around the circumference. Springer and Plenum, *Human emotions*, 1977, C. Izard with kind permission from Springer Science+Business Media B.V.

axes, just as we do when plotting a graph. When they studied their facial expression circle it seemed to Woodworth and Schlosberg that two axes could be identified. These involved the difference between expressions which are associated with *pleasant* or *unpleasant* feelings, and between expressions which involve increased *attention* to the external world or *rejection* and shutting it out. They therefore suggested that our perception of facial expressions is achieved by the visual system coding them on pleasant–unpleasant and attention–rejection dimensions. Schlosberg (1952) collected data to support this idea by showing that ratings of pictures of facial expressions on pleasantness–unpleasantness and attention–rejection could be used to reconstruct the original approximately circular arrangement.

Since Woodworth and Schlosberg, other variants of the two-factor approach have been suggested – the most well-known is Russell's (1980) circumplex model. Interestingly, this was derived from multidimensional scaling of emotion words, but Russell clearly saw straight away that it could also be used for facial expressions (Russell, 1980). The exact details do not matter here, though; what is important is that all such models share the perspective that facial expressions are considered to vary continuously along the dimensions proposed, each shading smoothly into the next.

These two-dimensional accounts of facial expression recognition are not without merit. As we have seen, they offer a neat description of errors in facial expression recognition, making it clear which emotions are more or less likely to be confused with each other. They also offer an easy interpretation of how expressions can be expressed more or less intensely, since less intense expressions will fall towards the centre of the circle shown in Figure 4.6, and more extreme ones at the circumference. At the origin, where the two axes intersect, the expression will be completely neutral.

That the scheme can work in the way described is easily demonstrated with computer graphics techniques (Calder, Young, Rowland, & Perrett, 1997). If we take a neutral expression from Ekman and Friesen's (1976) Pictures of Facial Affect, it should approximate the origin of Woodworth and Schlosberg's two-dimensional space, whilst the expressions of different basic emotions should fall at appropriate points around the circumference. So, if we use computer image manipulation to morph between a neutral and an emotional image, we should get a fairly smooth change in intensity going from neutral to the depicted emotion. The technique (see Chapter 2) involves placing a number of fiducial points on each image (in this case, a neutral face and an emotional face) and then using these to warp the image from one shape (defined by the positions of the fiducials in the neutral image) to the other (the positions of the fiducials in the emotional image) whilst blending the textures of local regions in the tesselated mesh resulting from connecting the fiducial points to each other.

Figure 4.7 shows that this works well. In effect, we can use computer image manipulation to create a series of images that seem to travel along a radius from the centre of the circular representation (a neutral face) to a point on the circumference (an emotional face). Interestingly, if we then use computer caricaturing to increase (i.e. exaggerate) the differences between a depicted emotion and its neutral equivalent, the apparent intensity of the emotion can be smoothly increased to levels beyond that shown in Ekman and Friesen's photographs, as shown in Figure 4.7 (Young, Perrett, Calder, Sprengelmeyer, & Ekman, 2002). In this case, we seem to have travelled along a radial line that continues beyond the circumference drawn in Figure 4.6.

So far, so good for two-dimensional models. But they turn out to have other properties that do not fit the facts so well. To see this, let's think about travelling across a diameter of the circular representation. For example, moving from disgust to surprise, which are opposite each other in Woodworth and Schlosberg's Figure 4.6. We know we can do this by putting together two

000 025 050 075 100 125 150

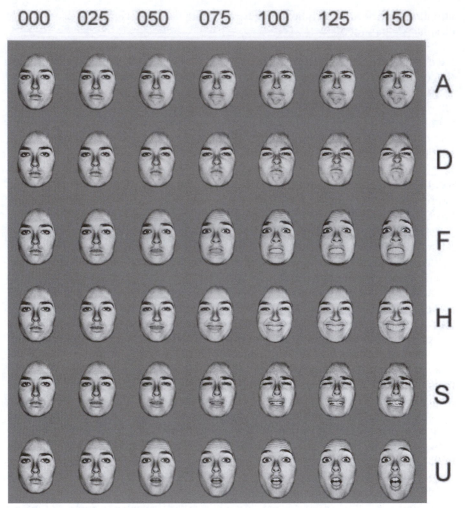

Figure 4.7 Continua of facial expression images from neutral to a basic emotion – showing how morphing and caricaturing can be used to create graded intensities of perceived emotion. Images created from a face from the Ekman and Friesen (1976) series showing neutral – anger (row A), neutral – disgust (row D), neutral – fear (row F), neutral – happiness (row H), neutral – sadness (row S) and neutral – surprise (row U). The neutral pose (0% intensity of emotion) is shown on the left of each row, with the prototype (100% intensity) Ekman emotional expression in the fifth column. The second, third and fourth columns show interpolated 25%, 50% and 75% morphed images. The sixth and seventh columns use computer caricature procedures to enhance the intensity of the expression by +25% (125% intensity column) and +50% (150% intensity column). From Young et al. (2002).

computer-manipulated radii (i.e. by joining a continuum of disgust to neutral morphs to a neutral to surprise series). But what happens if we simply morph the images directly from disgust to surprise? If the Figure 4.6 diagram is correct, there is no reason why this would be any different from joining the two radial series. To move in a straight line from disgust to surprise in Figure 4.6, you have to pass through the centre of the circle, so when you morph a continuum of images between these two emotions (i.e. if you simply take an image of a disgust expression and morph it into a surprised expression) the resulting sequence of images should pass through a neutral region near the middle.

Figure 4.8 shows what actually happens if you morph images of disgust to surprise. There is no neutral region. The images just look less and less disgusted and then more and more surprised. The central region of the continuum becomes a bit ambiguous (it might be disgust or surprise), but it doesn't look like a neutral face (Young et al., 1997).

Part of the reason for this could be that we are mistaken in thinking that neutral faces should lie at the centre of the circle, and that instead they should be placed at the periphery as a distinct expression in their own right (Shah & Lewis, 2003). However, this seems unlikely to be all that is going on because much the same findings arise if we move in a direction that does not form a radius or diameter of the circular space – for instance by morphing an expression of disgust to one of fear. In Figure 4.6, a straight line from disgust to fear will cross a region where the expression should become one of low-intensity anger, but as Figure 4.8 also shows this isn't the case. Instead, the images switch smoothly from disgust to fear, with the central region of the continuum again ambiguous between disgust and fear, but not looking like anger.

A potential reason for our lack of success in predicting these effects of morphing disgust to surprise or disgust to fear might be that the positioning of the emotions around the circumference of the circle in Figure 4.6 isn't entirely correct. To check this, Young et al. (1997) created every possible morphed

90:10   80:20   70:30   60:40   50:50   40:60   30:70   20:80   10:90

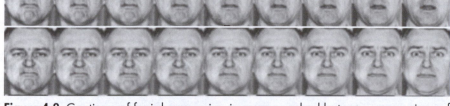

Figure 4.8 Continua of facial expression images morphed between expressions of disgust and surprise (upper row), and between disgust and fear (lower row). In each row prototype expressions (not shown in the figure) from the Ekman and Friesen series are blended in proportions 90:10, 80:20, 70:30, 60:40, 50:50, 40:60, 30:70, 20:80 and 10:90. From Young et al. (1997).

continuum between pairs of the six emotions (happiness, surprise, fear, sadness, disgust and anger) from the Ekman and Friesen (1976) Pictures of Facial Affect. Doing this leads to a total of 15 continua (happiness–surprise, happiness–fear, happiness–sadness, and so on; there are 15 rather than 30 such continua because happiness–surprise involves the same images as surprise–happiness). Images from these 15 continua were then mixed together, and participants were asked to identify which of the six emotions was depicted in each image. For every one of the 15 continua, Young et al. (1997) found that images were identified as one or other of the prototypes used to create the continuum. That is, images from the happiness–surprise continuum would be identified as happiness or surprise, with few responses from any other emotion category. Importantly, images from the central region of each continuum were not seen as looking like any other emotion than the prototypes from which the continuum in question was created.

Exactly the same pattern of results was found when Young et al. (1997) added the six continua from each emotion to neutral in their set of stimuli, and allowed 'neutral' as a possible response. They found that images were seen as neutral only when they came from a continuum created with one neutral prototype (e.g. disgust–neutral) and not when they came from emotion to emotion continua (such as disgust–fear).

These findings show that there is something more fundamentally wrong with Figure 4.6 than just the relative positioning of the emotions around the circle's circumference. You can't position seven points (corresponding to six emotions plus neutral) on a two-dimensional surface in such a manner that none of the straight lines that can be drawn between any possible pair of points will never pass near one of the other points. Yet that is what the data show – all of the morphed continua seem to travel directly from one prototype expression to another.

So, we can see that a satisfactory two-dimensional model of facial expression recognition is impossible. At a minimum, we would need to add extra dimensions to achieve something realistic. To be fair to Schlosberg, he also recognised problems with the two-dimensional account, and in a paper that is now less well-known he suggested the possible existence of a third dimension which might alleviate some of the problems we have discussed (Schlosberg, 1954). The more radical alternative, though, is that dimensional accounts will never work properly because they ignore the point that we perceive emotions as belonging to distinct categories.

Category models of facial expression recognition

Central to Ekman's work on facial expressions has been the idea that these can correspond to different emotional *categories*. From this perspective, the way we recognise facial expressions is through *combinations* of features which have become communicative signals – eyes opened wide or narrowed, brows raised or lowered, mouth open or closed, corners raised or lowered, teeth showing or behind the lips, and so on. Each of these features might itself be encoded as a continuous dimension, but the effect of using several different dimensions simultaneously is to create distinct categories based on specific feature constellations.

An implication is that recognising expressions is not dependent only on the presence or absence of a single feature – even something as apparently simple as upturned corners of the mouth need only be seen as a smile if the other features are appropriate.

When stimuli can be encoded with a single feature, they are highly noticeable when placed in a background of stimuli which differ on that feature. Look at Figure 4.9. The misoriented stimulus is quickly detected – it seems to 'pop out' of

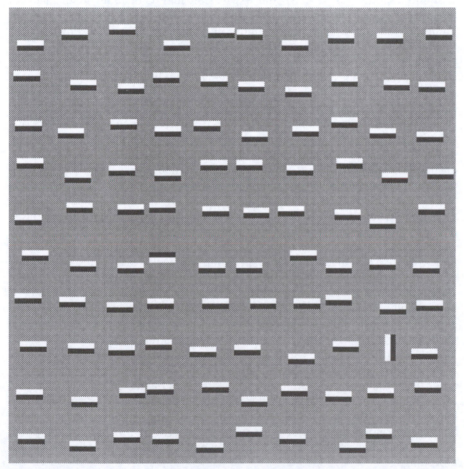

Figure 4.9 Demonstration of the phenomenon of 'pop-out' in visual search. The differently oriented bar is almost immediately obvious. Note that there is a second target which differs from the other bars, but this (upside-down) bar has to be carefully sought. From Nothdurft, H.-C., 1993, 'Faces and facial expressions do not pop out' first published in *Perception*, 22(11), pp. 1287–1298. Courtesy of Pion Limited, London.

the display. (We have more to say about such 'pop-out' effects with faces in Chapter 5.)

In contrast, pop-out is not found for facial expressions (Nothdurft, 1993). Try finding the sad face among the happy faces in Figure 4.10a, or the happy face among the sad faces in Figure 4.10b. It is not easy!

Now go back to Figure 4.9. As well as the misoriented bar, there is another one which is discrepant, but finding it usually takes some time. This is because it shares a common feature (horizontal orientation) with the other bars, and only differs in a secondary characteristic which requires putting the elements together (white over black, instead of black over white). Similarly, the need to put the elements together to perceive the expression may contribute to the lack of pop-out for facial expressions. This conclusion does not follow directly from Figures 4.10a and 4.10b, because finding a single up-turned and down-turned mouth shape amongst opposite-shaped distractors would have caused a little difficulty even without the rest of the face. But the point is clear in Figure 4.10c, where one still needs to search a bit for the face with the discrepant mouth, even though the circular shape would be fairly immediately obvious among the other curves if no other facial features were present.

These observations point to the idea that we encode facial expressions holistically, rather than in terms of specific features. This can be tested directly using Young, Hellawell and Hay's (1987) facial composite effect. We already encountered this effect in Chapter 2, where we noted that if the top half of a picture of one person's face is combined with the bottom half of someone else's face, we seem to perceive a new face and it actually becomes difficult to recognise the constituent halves. Young, Hellawell and Hay (1987) originally used this phenomenon to demonstrate holistic perception of identity, but it can equally show holistic processing of expression by combining facial features from the upper part of a face displaying one expression with features from the bottom half of another face displaying a different expression (Calder, Young, Keane, & Dean, 2000; White, 2000). This makes it difficult to see the expression in the top half or bottom half of the face, because perception of the strange composite expression shown in the whole face interferes with recognising the expressions from its parts (see Figure 4.11). If the parts of the face are misaligned, so there is no impression of a coherent whole face, the expression displayed by the top or bottom half is easier to see (for examples of misaligned composite images, see other figures showing the composite effect, such as Figure 2.3).

Holistic perception of facial expressions can provide a perceptual basis that helps in seeing the expressions we recognise as belonging to distinct categories. Strong support for the categorical perception hypothesis comes from additional findings of studies using computer image manipulation through caricaturing and morphing.

We saw that caricaturing an emotional expression by exaggerating differences from a neutral expression worked well to increase the perceived intensity of the caricatured emotion (Figure 4.7), and we noted that this fits a two-dimensional account such as Figure 4.6. In a two-dimensional model, however, caricaturing should only work relative to a small number of starting points that come either from the centre (i.e. neutral) or from an opposite region of the

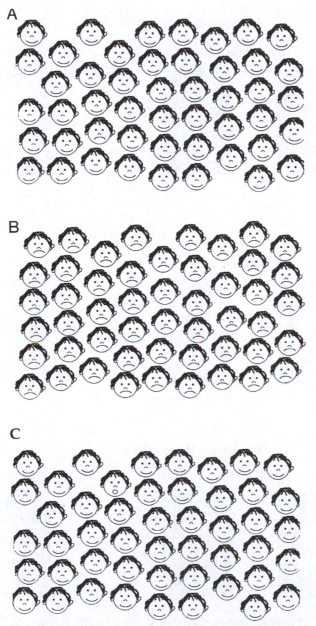

Figure 4.10 Lack of pop-out for facial expressions. It is not easy to find a sad face among happy faces (A), or a happy face among sad faces (B). An open-mouthed expression among closed-mouth expressions (C) is a bit easier, but still does not pop out. From Nothdurft, H.-C., 1993, 'Faces and facial expressions do not pop out' first published in *Perception, 22*(11), pp. 1287–1298. Courtesy of Pion Limited, London.

Different expression/Same identity

Prototypes   Composite

Same expression/Different identity

Prototypes   Composite

Different expression/Different identity

Prototypes   Composite

   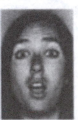   

Figure 4.11 Composite expressions from Calder, Young, Keane and Dean (2000). See text for explanation. Copyright © 2000 by the American Psychological Association. Reproduced with permission. Calder, Andrew J., Young, Andrew W., Keane, Jill, Dean, Michael, Configural information in facial expression perception. *Journal of Experimental Psychology: Human Perception and Performance, 26*(2), pp. 527–551.

two-dimensional space. This turns out to be incorrect – Calder and his colleagues showed that any emotion can be caricatured by exaggerating how it differs from any other emotion (Calder, Rowland et al., 2000). Figure 4.12 shows examples, in which expressions of anger or sadness are caricatured relative to norms involving expressions of fear or disgust. Notice that the fear and disgust norm faces look very different from each other, yet the caricatured faces that emphasise differences between anger and either norm look increasingly angry, and the caricatured faces that emphasise differences between sadness and either norm look increasingly sad. The way in which anger or sadness is expressed in the caricatured faces looks a little different, depending on the norm used, but these are still highly recognisable expressions of anger and sadness. Perceived emotions behave like categories – increasing the difference between one category and any other category simply makes it stand out more clearly.

An engaging illusion due to category assignment was created by Seyama and Nagayama (2002). Look at Figure 4.13. Which of the faces in each row has the larger eyes? In general, the happy faces in the right column seem to have slightly bigger eyes than the surprised faces in the left column – but in fact the eyes are identical for each row! Only the bottom half of each image is changed to make it look happy or surprised overall – in the top row the top half (eyes) comes from a surprise expression, in the middle row from a happy expression, and in the bottom row from a neutral expression. The mouth (bottom half) cue is sufficiently strong to create an overall judgement of happiness or surprise, but the perceived category affects interpretation of the eyes – possibly because the eye size gets judged against what one would expect to see for the assigned category.

Image morphing also supports Ekman's idea that facial expressions of basic emotions belong to discrete categories. We saw already (Figure 4.8) that the perceptual transitions between emotional expressions created by morphing do not fit the pattern that dimensional accounts would predict. Instead, there are abrupt discontinuities in identification along any morphed continuum, rather than smooth transitions, with the morphed images always looking like one or other of the expressions from which they were created. Even more persuasive evidence against the dimensional view comes from a direct test of categorical perception applied to these faces. As we noted in Chapter 3, the phenomenon of categorical perception arises when items which come from the same category seem more perceptually similar to each other than they actually are, while items from different categories seem more dissimilar. If emotions are perceived categorically, then pairs of faces which fall within the range of faces identified as the same emotion should be judged as being more visually similar to each other than equally similar pairs of faces which straddle the boundary between being perceived as one emotion and another. Studies using a range of techniques for measuring visual similarity and discriminability have found that this is the case (Bimler & Kirkland, 2001; Calder, Young, Perrett, Etcoff, & Rowland, 1996; Etcoff & Magee, 1992; Young et al., 1997), and phenomena of categorical perception of expressions are evident even in infants (Kotsoni, de Haan, & Johnson, 2001; Leppänen & Nelson, 2009).

Categorical perception effects are known to exist in other domains, such as colour perception (where perceived colour changes more abruptly across some

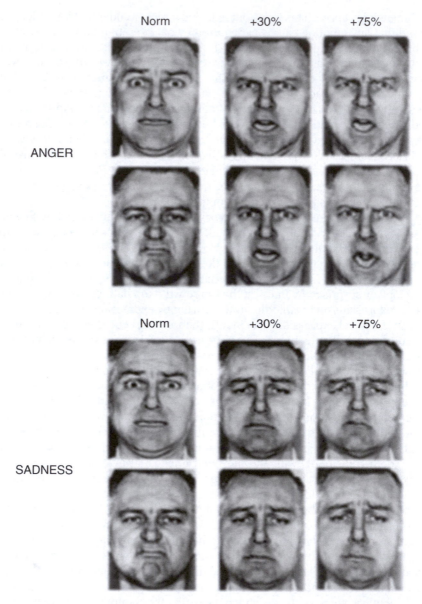

Norm   +30%   +75%

ANGER

Norm   +30%   +75%

SADNESS

Figure 4.12 Caricaturing facial expressions by increasing their difference from other expressions; the images show +30% and +75% caricatures of anger or sadness relative to a fearful or disgusted norm face. Note that the caricaturing works to intensify perceived anger or sadness whichever norm is used. Reprinted from *Cognition*, 76, 2, Calder, A. J., Rowland, D., Young, A. W., Nimmo-Smith, I., Keane, J., & Perrett, D. I., Caricaturing facial expressions, pp. 105–146, Copyright 2000, with permission from Elsevier.

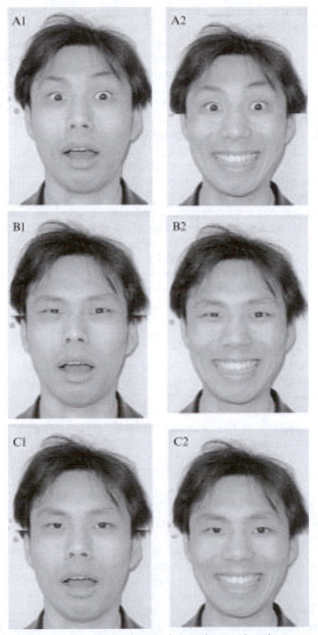

Figure 4.13 The faces in each row have identical eyes, but the eyes in the happy faces (right column) can seem larger than the eyes in the surprised faces (left column). From Seyama, J., Nagayama, R. S., 2002, 'Perceived eye size is larger in happy faces than in surprised faces' first published in *Perception, 31*(9), pp. 1153–1155. Courtesy of Pion Limited, London.

wavelengths than others) and speech perception (where the perceived consonant can also shift suddenly as voice onset time is altered). It is likely that they also apply to certain other aspects of face perception, such as the perception of race (see Chapter 3) and identity (Chapter 6). Categorisation confers a range of benefits (Brosch, Pourtois, & Sander, 2010) and a potentially important theory is that one of these is to assist perception under suboptimal conditions (Feldman, Griffiths, & Morgan, 2009). However, it is important not to over-interpret categorical perception results. Although observed discrimination performance for images of facial expressions peaks at category boundaries, we can still see within-category differences even though we are more sensitive to differences between categories. Seeing some facial expressions as belonging to distinct categories is useful to us, but it is not the only thing that needs to be explained.

Approaches based on computer simulation have helped in understanding properties of facial expression recognition (Dailey, Cottrell, Padgett, & Adolphs, 2002; Susskind, Littlewort, Bartlett, Movellan, & Anderson, 2007). We will focus on Dailey et al. (2002), who developed a neural network implementation that simulates a number of the effects relevant to perceiving and classifying facial expressions. Their neural network involved three feed-forward layers. The first ('perceptual') layer filtered images of facial expressions from the Ekman and Friesen (1976) series in a way thought to approximate characteristics of early stages of the visual system (Gabor filtering at five spatial scales and eight orientations, using a grid of overlapping filters), the second layer reduced the dimensionality of the Gabor-filtered data into 50 principal components through PCA (Principal Components Analysis), and the third level learnt to classify the weightings from these 50 principal components into basic emotion categories. This model was able accurately to simulate patterns of data found in studies using categorical perception or multidimensional scaling paradigms, and recognition and discrimination data for the morphed images of all combinations of basic emotions reported by Young et al. (1997). It therefore represents a very promising approach.

Emotion-specific mechanisms

Perhaps the most striking examples of category-based influences on facial expression perception involve what seem to be emotion-specific mechanisms.

Adaptation effects offer an example. Hsu and Young (2004) asked participants to view an image showing a facial expression of happiness, sadness or fear and then asked them to decide whether a low-intensity version of one of these three expressions (created by morphing the expression prototype towards a neutral image) showed happiness, sadness or fear. They found emotion-specific adaptation effects, where seeing a face showing a particular emotion reduced the tendency to report seeing that emotion in the following morphed image – as if the initial viewing of the emotional expression had somehow fatigued receptors dedicated to finding that emotion. Similar effects were reported at the same time by Webster, Kaping, Mizokami and Duhamel (2004), together with the adaptation effects for perception of sex and ethnicity described in Chapter 3.

A thorough investigation of the relationships between different emotion categories revealed by adaptation was conducted by Rutherford, Chattha and Krysko (2008), using basic emotions as adapting images and briefly presented neutral expressions as test images. Their findings confirmed that adaptation effects can be category-based, with different emotions showing asymmetric adaptation effects on the perception of neutral images – for example, adapting to a fear face makes a neutral image look slightly happy, whereas adapting to a happy face makes a neutral image look slightly sad.

A later study by Skinner and Benton (2010) has pushed the point further. They used an image representing the average of six basic emotions to create a set of 'anti-expressions' by linearly morphing each of the six original expressions through this average along a trajectory that took each image away from the original prototype expression (an anti-caricaturing procedure). Adaptation to these anti-expressions led to the average image being perceived as the source expression from which the anti-expression was derived – for example, adapting to anti-fear led to the average expression being seen as fear.

Furl, van Rijsbergen, Treves, Friston and Dolan (2007) used MEG to identify whereabouts in the brain facial expression adaptation effects arise. The advantage of MEG for this purpose is that it has both reasonable spatial resolution and excellent temporal resolution (see Chapter 2) – allowing analysis of brain responses to specific morphed expressions following adaptation. Responses from the right posterior STS were found to be sensitive to differences between adapted and test (morphed) expressions, and to correlate with behavioural after-effects. This region is, of course, part of Haxby, Hoffman and Gobbini's (2000) neural pathway for analysing changeable aspects of faces (see Chapter 1).

However, STS is clearly not the only brain region involved in perceiving facial expressions, and a recent meta-analysis of fMRI studies has shown that basic emotions of happiness, sadness, fear, anger and disgust all have distinct neural correlates to some extent (Vytal & Hamann, 2010). We will concentrate here on fear and on disgust, which have attracted particular interest.

Striking findings of some kind of emotion-specificity come from work on the contribution of the amygdala to recognition of emotion. As introduced in Chapter 3, the amygdala is a small structure lying beneath the temporal lobe. It contains a number of anatomically distinct nuclei, and may therefore have a variety of functions, potentially including differing social and emotional functions, but in recent decades its strong involvement in the emotion of fear has become clear (LeDoux, 1995).

Adolphs and his colleagues studied patient SM, a woman with Urbach-Wiethe disease, a rare neurodegenerative disorder that leads to bilateral amygdala damage from a build-up of calcium deposits (Adolphs, Tranel, Damasio, & Damasio, 1994). They showed facial expressions from Ekman and Friesen's (1976) Pictures of Facial Affect series and asked SM to rate the intensity of each of the basic emotions in each picture. This method offers a sophisticated insight into facial expression perception, because it taps not only which emotion SM saw in each face (i.e. which emotion she rated as strongest for each image) but also which emotions she saw as most similar to each other. For example, normal observers will rate a disgusted face as perhaps showing some anger, but not happiness or surprise. From a number of different analyses, it was clear that SM was markedly poor at seeing fear.

Further studies of recognition of facial expressions of emotion after amygdala damage support the view that recognition of fear is particularly severely impaired (Adolphs et al., 1999; Broks et al., 1998; Calder, Young, Rowland et al., 1996), though recognition of other negative emotions (especially anger) can also be affected to some degree (Graham, Devinsky, & LaBar, 2007; Sato et al., 2002).

For example, Calder, Young, Rowland et al. (1996) studied the ability of two people with amygdala damage to recognise facial expressions of emotion. The stimuli for one of their tests are shown in Figure 4.14. Facial expressions from the Ekman and Friesen (1976) series were computer-manipulated through morphing to create a hexagon of faces whose expressions were evenly graded between happiness and surprise (top row), surprise and fear (second row), fear and sadness (third row), sadness and disgust (fourth row), disgust and anger (fifth row), and anger and happiness (bottom row).

Images from this emotion hexagon were presented one at a time – each had to be recognised as most like happiness, surprise, fear, sadness, disgust or anger. In total, each of the 30 images from Figure 4.14 was presented five times, in random order.

Figure 4.15 shows the rate at which each image was recognised as each emotion. The top graph shows recognition by neurologically normal people – there is a clear sequence of abrupt transitions between regions which are consistently perceived as each of the six emotions.

The lower graph in Figure 4.15 shows the average recognition rates for the two people with amygdala damage. The recognition of happiness, surprise and sadness is not too different from normal performance, but there are signs of some difficulty with disgust and clear problems in recognising anger and fear.

Such findings demonstrate that the amygdala may be more involved in the evaluation of some emotions than others – especially fear and anger. We will briefly defer discussing why this may be whilst we point out that similar implications come from studies of blood flow when normal people look at facial expressions. Morris et al. (1996) created computer-manipulated images of facial expressions with increasing intensities of happiness or fear. Participants were asked to look at a series of such faces and classify them as men or women whilst regional cerebral blood flow was recorded with positron emission tomography (PET). When the cerebral blood flow was analysed to find the brain structure which required more blood as the face became more afraid, it was the left amygdala.

Numerous other functional imaging studies have shown that the amygdala responds to fearful facial expressions (Calder, Lawrence, & Young, 2001). Note that in Morris et al.'s (1996) experiment regional cerebral blood flow for different intensities of one facial expression (fear) was contrasted with another (happiness). In this way, any amygdala responsiveness to faces per se was eliminated, making clear the differential response to a particular emotion. This is important

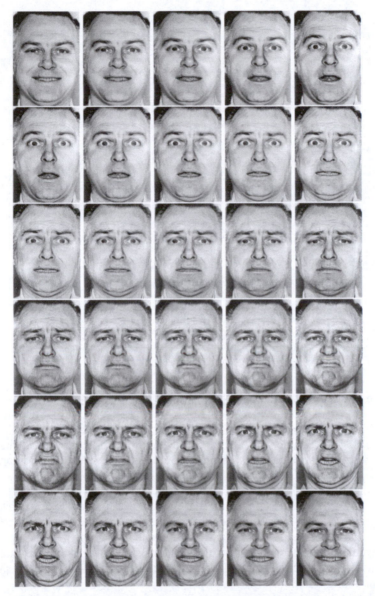

Figure 4.14 Images used to test facial expression recognition by Calder, Young, Rowland et al. (1996). From left to right, the columns show 80%, 70%, 50%, 30% and 10% morphed images along each continuum. From top to bottom, the continua shown in each row are happiness to surprise (top row), surprise to fear (second row), fear to sadness (third row), sadness to disgust (fourth row), disgust to anger (fifth row), and anger to happiness (bottom row). First published in Facial emotion recognition after bilateral amygdala damage: Differentially severe impairment of fear, Andrew J. Calder, *Cognitive Neuropsychology*, 1996, reprinted by permission of the publisher (Taylor & Francis Group, http://www.informaworld.com).

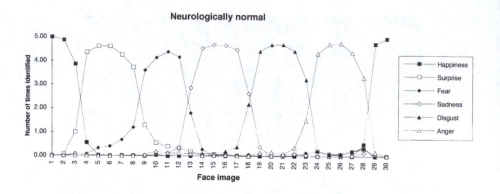

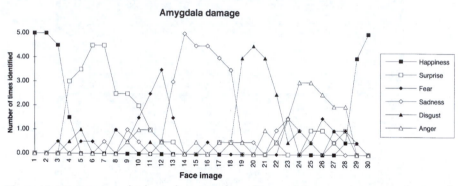

Figure 4.15 Rate at which each image from Figure 4.14 was recognised as each emotion in Calder, Young, Rowland et al.'s (1996) study. The images are numbered 1 to 30 going from left to right and from top to bottom of Figure 4.14. The upper graph shows recognition by neurologically normal participants and the lower graph the average recognition rates for two people with amygdala damage.

because the amygdala is a structure that responds to all images of faces to some extent, regardless of their expression, and it also shows some degree of response to emotions other than fear (Sergerie, Chochol, & Armony, 2008). Contrasting the amygdala's response to fear with its response to another emotion thus shows that it has a particularly strong response to fear, over and above any response to the contrasting emotion.

Note, too, that nothing was actually asked about emotion in Morris et al.'s study – the participants' task was just to decide if the face was male or female. This suggests that the amygdala is automatically responsive to displays of fear by others – it is not something we can switch on or off at will. A striking demonstration of this was by Vuilleumier et al. (2002), who studied case GK, a patient with a right inferior parietal lesion. Like many patients with this type of brain injury, GK showed 'extinction' of the left side of a perceptual display containing items positioned to the left and right. So, if GK was shown a display with a picture of a face on the left and a picture of a house on the right, he only reported seeing the house. However, his cerebral blood flow (recorded with fMRI) increased in his left amygdala if the 'extinguished' face showed a fearful rather than a happy expression. The amygdala response does not seem to relate exclusively to the conscious recognition of emotion.

Similarly, Whalen and colleagues recorded blood flow with fMRI for neurologically normal participants who were shown very brief (17 milliseconds) masked presentations of eye whites or 'eye blacks' from fearful or happy faces (Whalen et al., 2004). What is meant by eye whites is shown in the second row of Figure 4.16. The point of interest is that the whiteness of the sclera of the human eye seems to be an evolutionary adaptation involved in social communication (see Chapter 5), and the eye-widening that is characteristic of fearful faces shows the white sclera very clearly. The 'eye blacks' (third row of Figure 4.16) are simply photo negatives of the eye whites, and hence a useful point of comparison with the same underlying shape but lacking the regions of dark and light that make the stimuli compellingly eye-like. Amygdala blood flow was enhanced for fearful compared to happy eye whites, with no difference for the 'eye black' stimuli.

Whalen et al.'s (2004) study was intended to do two things. First, it showed that a single cue (enhanced salience of the whites of the eyes) can be sufficient to trigger the amygdala's response, and it used a clever control (the eye blacks) to demonstrate that this is to do with eyes per se. Intriguingly, this links an aspect of facial expression perception to gaze perception, an area in which the amygdala is also thought to play an important role, as we will see in Chapter 5. Second, by using 17 ms presentation and an immediately following pattern mask it tried to rule out the possibility that participants consciously saw the eye stimuli. Whether this second aim was successfully achieved has been brought into question (Straube, Dietrich, Mothes-Lasch, Mentzel, & Miltner, 2010), but the importance of the eye region has received striking confirmation from a further study of case SM by Adolphs et al. (2005).

By recording SM's eye movements, Adolphs et al. (2005) found that as well as showing impaired recognition of fear from facial expressions, SM didn't fixate the eye region spontaneously when she looked at faces. Remarkably, her recognition of fear temporarily improved when SM was instructed to look at the eyes, suggesting she has some ability to use cues from this region if she fixates it. However, when left to her own devices, SM reverted to not looking directly at the eyes.

These are intriguing findings, but they need to be carefully interpreted. They show that they eye region is important to the amygdala's response to fear, but they don't show that the amygdala only uses information from this region. By masking different parts of the face, Asghar et al. (2008) were able to show with fMRI that the amygdala responds more to fearful than to neutral expressions even in pictures of faces where the eye region was totally obscured. It seems that it is interested in a range of cues that signal fear, not simply eye-widening.

This may happen because the amygdala plays a more general role in the appraisal of danger (LeDoux, 1995; Zaretsky, Mendelsohn, Mintz, & Hendler, 2010). We noted already that it responds to other negative emotions, including anger, as well as fear – facial expressions of fear and anger are important

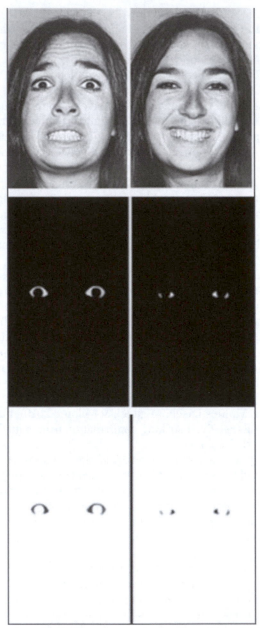

Figure 4.16 Examples of fearful and happy stimuli used by Whalen et al. (2004). Top row facial expressions, middle row eye region from top row images ('eye whites'), bottom row brightness reversed eye whites ('eye blacks'). Adapted from Whalen, P. J., Kagan, J., Cook, R. G., Davis, F. C., Kim, H., Polis, S., et al. (2004). Human amygdala responsivity to masked fearful eye whites. *Science, 306*, p. 2061. Reprinted with permission from AAAS.

indications of the presence of danger in the immediate environment. As Darwin (1872) pointed out, basic emotions represent important evolutionary adaptations – Ekman (1992) characterised them as facilitating rapid responses to funda-mental life-tasks in ways which have enhanced our fitness to survive. For example, if an animal comes into contact with something dangerous it may become frightened and flee, or it may aggressively stand its ground – danger induces a basic emotion, fear, and a set of preparatory responses that aid in the preservation of life. One can suppose, then, that any animal that can experience fear (or, at least, mobilise a fear response) under the appropriate circumstances will be better equipped to survive than one that cannot. Similarly, an animal that is sensitive to perceiving fear or anger in other animals is in a better position to decide when a rapid exit or a display of aggression could pay off. This may help explain why facial expressions are often treated as belonging to distinct categories by our perceptual systems – different categories require the mobili-sation of different types of response. It is not to deny that emotions like fear will also involve learning and cultural influences, but these are likely built upon an evolved substrate.

Fear is a response to danger in the form of immediate physical threat, but we also face other kinds of danger, one of which is the risk of disease. The rele-vant emotion here is disgust, which is experienced in relation to things we should not eat. There are several lines of evidence that point to the possibility that disgust helps us to avoid disease (Curtis, Aunger, & Rabie, 2004; Oaten, Stevenson, & Case, 2009), and Darwin (1872) pointed out that the disgusted facial expression incorporates elements of our response to offensive foods.

Social transmission of information about foods that might make you ill is potentially of survival value to an omnivorous species, and like fear, disgust seems to involve specific brain mechanisms. A critical region is the anterior insula and underlying basal ganglia, which shows up consistently in studies using fMRI to measure cerebral blood flow to facial expressions of disgust (Calder, Lawrence et al., 2001; Phillips et al., 1997). This is interesting because the insula is both evolutionarily old and forms part of gustatory cortex – so it makes sense that a response from this area should be elicited by a particularly relevant facial expression.

In neuropsychological studies, patients with insula and basal ganglia damage show deficits in recognising facial expressions of disgust. This applies both to single case studies of circumscribed regional brain damage (Calder, Keane, Manes, Antoun, & Young, 2000) or less focal lesions (Adolphs, Tranel, & Damasio, 2003), and in cases of neurodegenerative Huntington's disease (Gray, Young, Barker, Curtis, & Gibson, 1997; Sprengelmeyer et al., 1996) where fMRI has also shown reduced insular response to facial expressions of disgust (Hennenlotter et al., 2004) and the magnitude of the disgust recognition impair-ment is correlated with the extent of insular damage revealed by structural brain imaging (Kipps, Duggins, McCusker, & Calder, 2007).

Although disgust is considered to be a basic emotion, it has some complex properties (Rozin, Haidt, & McCauley, 1993). Many of the foods we find disgusting would not actually harm us – they have become cultural prohibitions, and this seems to apply particularly to which animals can be eaten. Likewise, although

Darwin was probably correct in thinking that the emotion has its origins in bad tastes, the feeling of revulsion you get when you find a half-eaten worm in your apple isn't really triggered by the taste of the worm itself. Moreover, disgust seems also to apply beyond offensive foods to things that create a sense of purely moral offence. We say that we are disgusted by the expenses claims of politicians, or the lack of effort from some well-paid footballers. In this sense, disgust can involve a moral outrage that is also a kind of anger (Nabi, 2002), but the link to offensive foods remains when we say things like 'it left a bad taste in my mouth' – a metaphor that has proved accurate, since recent research has shown evidence of a degree of continuity between facial expressions created by moral disgust and gustatory distaste that would be expected from Darwin's hypothesis (Chapman, Kim, Susskind, & Anderson, 2009).

Evolutionary continuity notwithstanding, disgust can take distinguishable forms that are evident in individual differences in what is considered disgusting (Haidt, McCauley, & Rozin, 1994; Tybur, Lieberman, & Griskevicius, 2009). Neat studies by Rozin and his colleagues used faces whose expressions were coded in terms of Action Units from Ekman's FACS system to identify facial cues that are related to different varieties of disgust (Rozin et al., 1994). Their observations imply that the wrinkled nose is linked to bad smells (and, to a lesser extent, bad tastes), lip pursing and tongue protrusion signal food contamination (real or imagined), and a raised or retracted upper lip (which is also found in expressions of contempt and anger) is more closely linked to moral offence. Recent findings by Calder et al. (2010) suggest that it is the significance of upper lip retraction as a sign of social disapproval that is particularly misinterpreted in cases of Huntington's disease.

Identity and expression

Who someone is (identity) and what they are feeling (expression) are two of the most important things we can tell from people's faces. To what extent do these rely on the same perceptual mechanisms, and to what extent are they independent from each other? As a starting point, some degree of inde-pendence seems likely given that we can readily interpret the facial expressions of strangers – we don't need to recognise the face to read its expression.

An extraordinary demonstration of this relative independence between identity and expression arises in Thompson's (1980) 'Margaret Thatcher' illusion – shown in Figure 4.17. Here, the eyes and mouth in a smiling face are cut out and turned upside-down. When the result is viewed with the face in its usual orientation, it appears to have a grotesque expression. If it is viewed upside-down, however, it is difficult to see that there is anything at all abnormal about the face!

Of course it does not *need* to be Margaret Thatcher's face for the illusion to work, but Thompson's (1980) choice of such a famous face makes clear that the effect is about expression, not identity – you can still easily see it is Margaret Thatcher despite the expression, and despite its being an expression you probably never saw before – she never quite achieved it even in her frostiest moments.

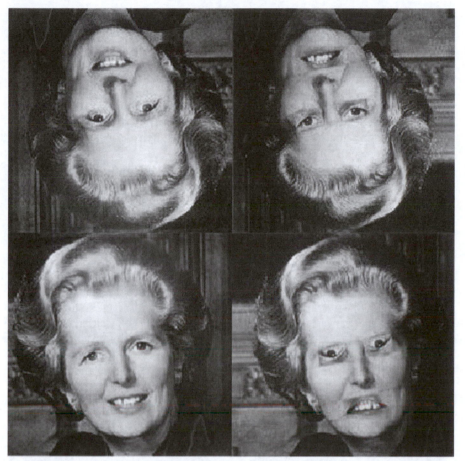

Figure 4.17 Thompson's (1980) Margaret Thatcher illusion, created by inverting the eye and mouth regions of the face. Notice how the grotesque expression evident when the face is upright is almost invisible in the inverted face. Thompson, P., 1980, 'Margaret Thatcher: a new illusion' first published in *Perception*, 9(4), pp. 483–484. Courtesy of Pion Limited, London.

Explaining why the upside-down Thatcher images look so alike is tricky (Thompson, Anstis, Rhodes, Jeffery, & Valentine, 2009). Clearly, the relationship between the different face features which is so apparent in the upright head is almost invisible in the inverted one. But why? The standard explanation is that we can't see configural information in upside-down faces (see Chapter 6 for an extended discussion of this). It seems to be on the right lines, but it is incomplete. For example, other upside-down expressions can be recognised with a bit of difficulty (McKelvie, 1995), but the Thatcherised expression just disappears. The standard counter to this point is that we still have some ability to process upside-down features, and this explains why well-known expressions can be identified in an inverted face. Yet the difference between the features in the upside-down Thatchers (the mouths especially) is substantial. So why can't we see it more easily? We really don't properly understand this.

Bartlett and Searcy (1993; Searcy & Bartlett, 1996) explored the Thatcher effect systematically by asking volunteers to rate how grotesque different faces appear to be when presented upright and upside-down. Grotesqueness due to spatial alterations such as those in the Thatcher illusion is virtually abolished by inversion. However, if local changes are made to faces, by blacking out or otherwise manipulating teeth to produce grotesque 'vampire' faces, these remain grotesque when seen upside-down.

A possibly important clue to the mechanism involved is that the effect is created by the eyes and mouth – the face frame created by the external features (hair, chin, face outline) can itself be upside-down, as in Figure 4.18 (Valentine & Bruce, 1985). This makes sense in that the internal features of a face primarily carry its expression, but it is none the less interesting that it is mainly the eyes and mouth that seem to act as the frame of reference for seeing the illusion.

Studies of holistic perception also show a perceptual segregation of identity and expression. Look again at Figure 4.11 from Calder, Young, Keane and Dean's (2000) study. The composite and misaligned images show top and bottom halves that vary in expression, identity, or both. When Calder, et al. (2000) conducted their research, the composite effect for identity was already well-known (Young, Hellawell, & Hay, 1987) – it is harder to recognise the

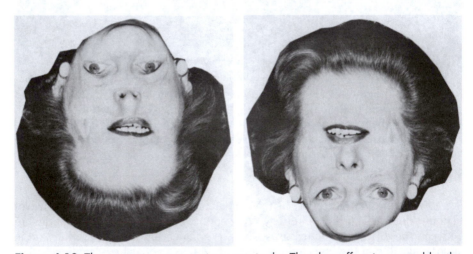

Figure 4.18 The grotesque expression seen in the Thatcher effect is created by the orientation of the internal features only, since it is still seen when the face frame of the external features is itself upside down, as in the image on the left. Conversely, the presence of an upright frame does not create the grotesque expression if the internal features are inverted (right image). From Valentine, T., Bruce. V., 1985, 'What's up? The Margaret Thatcher illusion revisited' first published in *Perception*, 14(4), pp. 515–516. Courtesy of Pion Limited, London.

identities of the top or bottom part-faces from composite images in the same expression with different identity condition than from equivalent misaligned stimuli, because the presence of parts from two different faces seems to create a new identity. Calder et al. (2000) established that there is an equivalent composite effect for expression – it is harder to recognise the emotional expressions of the part-faces from composite images in the different expression with same identity condition than from equivalent misaligned stimuli, because combining parts from two different expressions seems to create a new expression.

What Calder et al. (2000) also noted, though, was that these composite identity and composite expression effects were independent from each other. The composite effect for identity recognition is no greater when the expressions are different than when they are the same (i.e. the effect of identity doesn't differ between the same expression with different identity condition and the different expression with different identity condition), and the composite effect for expression recognition is no greater when the identities are different than when they are the same (i.e. the effect of expression doesn't differ between the different expression with same identity condition and the different expression with different identity condition). It is as if facial identities are perceived holistically and facial expressions are perceived holistically, but these holistic effects are independent from each other.

A classic way to investigate the relation between perception of facial identity and facial expression is by examining the effects of brain injury. In some cases of prosopagnosia there is a very severe impairment of facial identity recognition yet recognition of facial expressions can be well-preserved (e.g. Bruyer et al., 1983). Conversely, brain-injured patients who have problems with recognising facial expressions may be better at recognising facial identity (Parry, Young, Saul, & Moss, 1991).

These observations of double dissociations (one patient recognises expression but not identity, the other recognises identity but not expression) support the idea of separable brain mechanisms for the perception of identity and expression, but they are often limited by the fact that different tests will be used to investigate different patients, creating the possibility that the different patterns of deficit may not be directly comparable. In addition, the dissociations are often of a form in which one ability is more severely impaired than the other, but *both* are actually below normal – these can present substantial problems of interpretation (Shallice, 1988).

To achieve a more systematic study Young, Newcombe and their colleagues studied the face perception abilities of 34 ex-servicemen who had suffered injuries affecting the left or the right cerebral hemisphere during the last years of the Second World War (32 cases) or in the Korean War (two cases). These ex-servicemen formed a uniquely important group for several reasons; they were injured when young and fit, they had plenty of time to recover (most of the people tested were again leading normal lives), and the shrapnel wounds produced injuries which affected discrete regions of brain tissue.

The face perception tests were carried out in the 1980s, which would generally be around 40 years after these men were injured. Six different tests were used (Young, Newcombe, de Haan, Small, & Hay, 1993). Two tests examined ability to recognise familiar faces – these involved deciding whether or not faces were of famous people or giving the occupations of several famous faces. A further two tests involved ability to match views of unfamiliar faces – in one test a target face had to be matched to six simultaneously presented choices (Benton, Hamsher, Varney, & Spreen, 1983), and in the other test slides of unfamiliar faces were presented one after the other, to be judged as those of same or different people. The final pair of tests examined ability to recognise facial expressions of emotion – in one test by matching a target expression to one of four simultaneously presented expressions, and in the other by recognising facial expressions of six basic emotions.

The logic of using two tests of familiar face recognition, two tests of unfamiliar face matching, and two tests of facial expression recognition was to look for cases of selective impairment – defined as poor performance on both tests of a particular ability and normal performance on the other four tests. Several cases of selective impairment were found among the ex-servicemen, and these included cases of selective impairment of each ability – familiar face recognition, unfamiliar face matching, and facial expression recognition.

Such findings support the idea that these abilities each involve at least partially separable neurological pathways in the brain – a consequence of this would be that brain injury can compromise one type of ability whist sparing the others. Because of the considerable importance attached to the various forms of social information we derive from the faces we see, the most efficient method for analysing the different types of social signal may be to farm out parts of the task to specialist sub-components, each of which can then be optimally tuned to analyse a particular kind of information.

An important difference between identity and expression is that they have different dependence on patterns of movement. Facial expressions are constantly changing, whereas the cues that signal identity from facial appearance only alter slowly throughout our lives and can be more or less unchanging for fairly long periods of time. This distinction is central to Haxby et al.'s (2000) neurological model, which postulates a core system for face perception in which changeable aspects of faces (such as gaze and expression) involve a pathway from the inferior occipital gyri (OFA) to posterior superior temporal sulcus (STS), whereas non-changeable aspects of faces (such as identity) involve a pathway from the inferior occipital gyri to the lateral fusiform gyrus (FFA). According to Haxby et al. (2000) this core system feeds extended systems dedicated to more specific purposes, such as the amygdala and insula (see Chapter 1).

The emphasis on changeable aspects of faces in Haxby's neurological model highlights the paradox we referred to that so much of the evidence we have about facial expression perception comes from studies using static images. Although these studies are often underpinned by FACS analysis of patterns of muscle activity, and the clear results obtained make it likely that at least part of how the brain must analyse facial expressions is in terms of feature configurations that result from characteristic patterns of muscle movements, studies with static stimuli leave uncertain to what extent movement itself can make a separate contribution. The question is only beginning to be addressed in functional brain imaging work, but it is clear that dynamic properties such as the tempo at which facial expressions unfold are important (Kamachi et al., 2001). A pioneering study by Said, Moore, Engell, Todorov and Haxby (2010) used fMRI to record blood flow in STS to dynamic facial expressions of basic emotions. Impressively, they were able to demonstrate that the pattern of activation across STS voxels could be used to predict which expression was seen at above-chance levels, and that the similarity structure of activation of each voxel in posterior STS by each emotional expression was correlated with rated perceptual similarity of the expressions themselves. Both findings support the idea that STS plays an important role in the perceptual analysis of facial expressions.

Not all lines of evidence support a total separation of identity and expression, however. Indeed there are loose ends in some of the lines of work we have already described that leave scope for further investigation. In Newcombe's cases of ex-servicemen with shrapnel injuries, for instance, impairments were demonstrably selective, but they were not total (Young, Newcombe et al., 1993). For example, none of these ex-servicemen had face recognition deficits that approached the severity of those found in cases of acquired prosopagnosia, in which virtually all familiar faces can go unrecognised (see Chapter 6). Studies of acquired prosopagnosia show that perception of facial expressions is often better than perception of face identity, but it is seldom demonstrably normal (Calder & Young, 2005; Humphreys, Avidan, & Behrmann, 2007). In cases of congenital prosopagnosia, however, facial expression recognition can be clearly at normal levels of performance (Humphreys et al., 2007), but these individuals may have developed compensatory strategies and (possibly for this reason) their face recognition deficits are not as severe as those found in acquired cases.

Perceptual adaptation effects offer an important insight. Fox and Barton (2007), Ellamil, Susskind and Anderson (2008) and Campbell and Burke (2009) followed up Hsu and Young's (2004) finding of reduced sensitivity to a facial expression following adaptation to that expression by asking whether it mattered if the adapting and test expressions were displayed by the same individual. All three studies found emotion-specific adaptation whether the identities of the adapting and test faces were same or different, but this effect was enhanced for the same identity condition.

These findings are reminiscent of results obtained using the Garner interference paradigm by Schweinberger and Soukup (1998). In Garner interference (see Chapter 2), participants judge stimuli on a particular dimension (in this case identity or expression) whilst a second dimension is always correlated with the judged dimension (for example, the participant judges identity but Tom's face is always smiling and Harry is always unsmiling), constant (the participant judges identity but Tom and Harry always smile) or orthogonal to the judged dimension (the participant judges identity but Tom's face or Harry's face can be smiling or unsmiling). What Schweinberger and Soukup found was an asymmetric relation between perception of identity and expression, in which irrelevant variations in expression did not affect judgements of identity, but irrelevant variations in identity could affect judgements of expression. A later study by

Schweinberger, Burton and Kelly (1999) used morphed images to control the relative speed of classifying identity and expression, demonstrating that the asymmetric relationship between identity and expression perception was not simply due to relative processing speed.

These adaptation and interference effects show that identity can exert an influence on analysing facial expressions. The same point may be demonstrable with brain mechanisms themselves. Martens, Leuthold and Schweinberger (2010) used ERPs to reveal a broadly parallel architecture for facial identity and expression analysis in which the analysis of facial expression none the less relies on information about identity. Studies using fMR-adaptation (see Chapter 2 for a description of this method) to investigate the roles of STS and lateral fusiform gyrus (FG) in the perception of facial identity and expression report that regions of STS are sensitive to the interaction of identity and changeable cues such as expression. With an event-related design (see Chapter 2), Winston, Henson, Fine-Goulden and Dolan (2004) found that FG and a relatively posterior part of STS were sensitive to repetition of facial identity, whilst a more anterior region in STS was sensitive to repetition of expression. Studying adaptation with a block design, Andrews and Ewbank (2004) found that right posterior STS showed a larger response to images of the same face showing different head directions and expressions than to images of different faces with different head directions and expressions. Andrews and Ewbank (2004) interpreted this as consistent with Haxby et al.'s (2000) view that STS is involved in coding changeable aspects of faces, but showing that it is particularly interested in changes occurring within an individual's face – the types of change (expression, gaze direction) that can function as social signals.

This makes sense in that when we analyse changeable aspects of faces (such as expression) it is important to relate these directly to identity – i.e. to keep track of who looks unhappy now who didn't a few seconds ago. What is less clear is how these interactions between identity and expression arise. On the one hand, some limited aspects of expression perception seem to impact on the system that recognises identity – Kaufmann and Schweinberger (2004) found that familiar faces were slightly easier to recognise when they had relatively typical (as opposed to unusual) emotional expressions. On the other hand, we have seen that both logically and in terms of abundant evidence facial identity can interact strongly with facial expression perception.

Does this mean that the separation of identity and expression in functional and neurological models has been overstated? Perhaps. A PCA (Principal Components Analysis) of the Ekman and Friesen series of facial expression pictures showed some PCs corresponding to identity and expression but others reflecting both characteristics to greater or lesser extents (Calder, Burton, Miller, Young, & Akamatsu, 2001). This offers a basis in image statistics for there being less than perfect separation between representations needed in identity and expression perception, but doesn't prove this is the case. Equally possible (and difficult to rule out) is that at least some of the effects we have discussed here reflect cross-talk between components of Haxby et al.'s (2000) core system – especially the lateral fusiform gyrus and superior temporal sulcus.

Talking and lipreading

We have looked in detail at facial expressions, but for most people their most frequent facial movements are probably those involved in talking. Our faces show a number of evolutionary adaptations which are important for speech (see Chapter 1). The internal and external structure of the face, mouth and air-passages enable us to articulate rapidly the different sounds which make up our languages. Whether these were specific adaptations for speech, or whether speech has been structured by the shapes of our faces cannot be known, but there are certainly a number of features of our faces that are not shared with other primates.

When someone is talking to us, we can see the movements of their lips and, at moments when their mouth is open, we can also see their teeth and tongue. With skill, these cues can allow a deaf person to follow a conversation through lipreading with some degree of success. But people with normal hearing can understand someone talking on the telephone, or behind their backs, and we know that blind people do not seem to have problems in following a conversation. Such facts indicate that visual input is not essential for speech perception. But does it follow that a visual input is irrelevant to speech perception?

One of the most surprising findings of modern experimental psychology has been that the common-sense view is wrong, and that even people with entirely normal hearing make use of lipreading to support speech perception. We will discuss some of the findings, and their implications.

First, lipreading is something of a misnomer, because cues are available from seen movements of the lips, teeth and tongue (Summerfield, MacLeod, McGrath, & Brooke, 1989) – a more correct term would be 'speechreading'. However, lip movements are certainly a major cue to interpreting seen speech, so we will stick with the widely used sense of 'lipreading' here to cover interpreting any cues to what a person is saying emanating from the mouth region.

One reason for thinking that lipreading might be of some use in speech perception is that we find it disconcerting to watch a foreign film with a dubbed soundtrack. However, this does not provide strong evidence, because it may simply be relatively gross mismatches between the soundtrack and the seen face movements that are picked up (e.g. if the lips move fast when only a few different words are heard). A more impressive result is that seeing the speaker's face helps in understanding speech heard against background noise (Miller & Niceley, 1955; Sumby & Pollack, 1954). Sumby and Pollack's (1954) data showed that the effect of seeing the speaker approximated to an increase of 15 decibels in the auditory signal to noise ratio – a substantial benefit. Hence seeing the speaker does have some role in speech perception.

However, the most dramatic evidence for involvement of visual information in speech perception has come from an effect discovered by McGurk and MacDonald (1976), now known as the McGurk effect. This involves a compelling illusion in which you see the face of a person mouthing one phoneme but a different phoneme is spoken on a synchronised soundtrack. Remarkably, the phoneme you hear is neither the auditory component (i.e. the phoneme on the soundtrack) nor the visual component (the visually mouthed phoneme), but a fusion of the two. For example, if the seen face makes the articulatory movements involved in saying 'ga', and the soundtrack is 'ba', most people perceive the fusion as 'da' (see Figure 4.19). Contrary to our intuition, both auditory and visual information are used for speech perception, if available.

There are limits to when the McGurk effect will occur, but it is robust to some temporal misalignment of the auditory and visual channels (van Wassenhove, Grant, & Poeppel, 2007), and the illusion can still be experienced even when the channels are perceptibly out of synchrony (Soto-Faraco & Alsius, 2009). It can also survive a degree of degradation of the visual input (MacDonald, Andersen, & Bachmann, 2000; Munhall, Kroos, Jozan, & Vatikiotis-Bateson, 2004), and looking away from the face has little effect until your gaze is deviated by more than 10 degrees (Paré, Richler, ten Hove, & Munhall, 2003) – both observations suggest low spatial frequencies are critical.

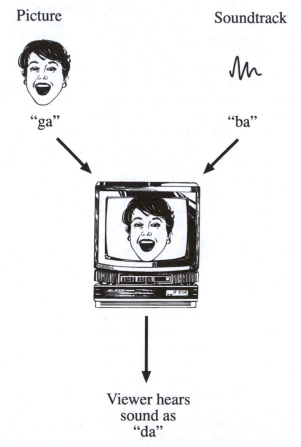

Picture   Soundtrack

"ga"   "ba"

Viewer hears
sound as
"da"

Figure 4.19 The McGurk effect. Video frames showing a person articulating a phoneme ('ga' in this example) are combined with the sound of a different phoneme ('ba'). When viewing the resulting video, you may *hear* a sound ('da') that is a blend of the auditory and visual stimuli. From Bruce and Young (1998).

Like many illusions, the mechanisms responsible for the McGurk effect are largely outside our conscious control – knowing how the stimuli are made doesn't stop you experiencing the illusion. However, it does seem that it requires some attentional resources – an unrelated but demanding visual or auditory task can affect the McGurk illusion (Alsius, Navarra, Campbell, & Soto-Faraco, 2005).

The McGurk effect is a powerful demonstration that speech perception is an inter-modal rather than a purely auditory phenomenon. The auditory input does not take precedence over the visual input, as one might expect. Instead, heard and seen inputs combine to form a percept that is a fusion of both, but no longer corresponds to either input.

Although widely described by the shorthand term 'lipreading', these effects involve more than just perceiving movements of the lips (Summerfield et al., 1989). Experiments have demonstrated that whilst seeing the lips alone certainly provides a lot of useful information, there are also contributions from seeing the way in which the teeth (i.e. jaws) and tongue are moving as well. An interesting study by Rosenblum, Yakel and Greene (2000) showed that 'Thatcherising' the mouth region by inverting it (comparable to what is done to the mouth in Figure 4.17) had a particularly deleterious effect on audiovisual integration when presented within an upright face context (see Figure 4.20 – top row). To rule out the possibility that their results were simply due to an interaction between mouth orientation and screen position (for example, if participants expect that a mouth should be upright when it is low in the picture frame), Rosenblum et al. (2000) compared the face stimuli to the 'mouth region only', as shown in the lower row of Figure 4.20.

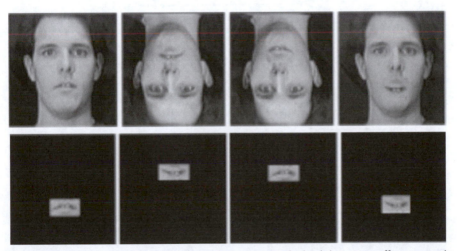

Figure 4.20 Inverting the mouth region has a particularly deleterious effect on audiovisual integration when presented within an upright face context. See text for explanation. Copyright © 2000 by the American Psychological Association. Reproduced with permission. Rosenblum, Lawrence D., Yakel, Deborah A., Green, Kerry P, Face and mouth inversion effects on visual and audiovisual speech perception. *Journal of Experimental Psychology: Human Perception and Performance*, 26(2), pp. 806–819.

However, it would be interesting to know whether the critical context in this respect is the upright face frame or the upright internal features, as for the Thatcher illusion itself (cf. Valentine & Bruce, 1985 – see Figure 4.18).

Most demonstrations of the McGurk effect use consonants, but we can also ask which parts of speech are perceived intermodally. Are fusion effects only found in the perception of consonants, or do they also apply to vowels? The answer is that what seem to be analogous effects can occur in the perception of vowels.

Summerfield and McGrath (1984) synthesised sounds to represent 10 equal steps between 'booed' and 'bard', 10 equal steps between 'bard' and 'bead', and 10 equal steps between 'bead' and 'booed', by changing the parts of the sounds (fundamental frequencies of the first, second and third formants) which determine the vowel, as shown in Figure 4.21. These synthesised sounds were

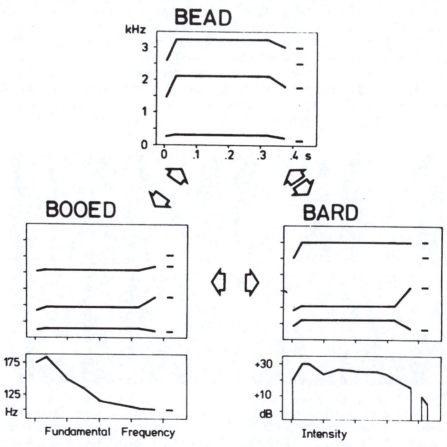

Figure 4.21 Changes to fundamental frequencies of the first, second and third formants used to modify the perceived vowel in synthesised sounds by Summerfield and McGrath (1984). See text for further explanation.

synchronised to videotapes of people saying either of the two syllables at the end of each continuum. For example, a sound lying along the booed-bard continuum would be paired with a videotape of a person saying 'booed', or with a videotape of a person saying 'bard'. Perception of the sound as 'booed' or 'bard' was then found to be influenced in the direction of the accompanying visual cues, even when observers detected the discrepancy and were instructed to report only what they heard.

This effect is clearly an analogue of that found for consonants by McGurk and MacDonald (1976), in that the observer's percept is determined by a combination of the visual and auditory inputs, but in this case the fusion simply biases perception towards one of the original inputs, rather than creating a novel percept.

Why do we lipread?

A key finding in understanding lipreading concerns the order of difficulty for lipread or heard phonemes. To understand its implications, we need to think about how speech sounds are produced (see Chapter 1). They depend mainly on the place of articulation (at the lips, or within the mouth), the manner of articulation (the way in which the airflow from the mouth is obstructed across time), and voicing (the involvement or non-involvement of the vocal chords).

A demonstration may help. To understand the importance of place of articulation, try saying 'b' or 'p', which are articulated at the lips (bilabial consonants); contrast these with 'd' or 't', formed by placing the tongue against the alveolar ridge near the front of the roof of the mouth (alveolar consonants). To understand manner of articulation, try 'b' and 'p' again, noting that these are stop consonants in which the airflow from the mouth is completely obstructed for a period of time and then released; contrast these with 'f' or 's', which are fricatives, in which the airflow is obstructed but not completely stopped. For voicing, try saying 'b' or 'z', in which the vocal chords are kept together so that the air passing through vibrates them, making a voiced sound; contrast these with unvoiced sounds in which the vocal chords are kept apart, as in 'p' or 'f'.

When you have completed this little self-tutorial, you are ready to grasp why lipreading is useful. Sounds that are easy to lipread are those whose distinctiveness rests heavily on place of articulation (since articulation at the lips is easily visible), whereas manner of articulation (how the airflow is obstructed across time) is harder to see. It turns out that the sounds that are easiest to lipread tend to be those where the differences are the most difficult to hear, because they generally involve rapid acoustic changes of relatively low intensity. This point had been grasped by Miller and Niceley (1955, p. 352) from their work on perception of speech in noise: 'The place of articulation, which was hardest to hear in our tests, is the easiest of features to see on a talker's lips. The other features are hard to see, but easy to hear.'

This suggests a simple hypothesis as to why these lipreading skills have been developed by people with normal hearing – they are probably of great value in infancy, when the baby is learning the sounds of its native language. Much communication is then face to face, and the use of lipread information will assist in disambiguating the sounds that are auditorily the more difficult. To check the plausibility of this hypothesis, we need to know whether or not infants can lipread.

A technique for investigating this was developed by Kuhl and Meltzoff (1982). Babies were shown simultaneous videos of two faces, and heard one of two possible sounds ('a' or 'i'). One face articulated the sound the baby was hearing, and the other face articulated the unheard sound in synchrony with it. Kuhl and Meltzoff (1982) measured whether babies showed any preference for looking at one face rather than the other. They found that 4–5-month-old infants looked longer at the face articulating the vowel they heard ('i' or 'a') than at the same face articulating the other vowel ('a' or 'i'). Hence infants are sensitive to the mismatch between the seen and heard information, even though at this age they cannot produce speech themselves.

Further studies of infants have found comparable effects down to as young as 2 months old with Kuhl and Meltzoff's technique (Patterson & Werker, 2003). Using purely visual talking faces as stimuli, Weikum et al. (2007) showed that 4 month olds could visually discriminate speech in their native (English) language from a foreign language (French) – showing that they are learning about the visual patterns they see on talkers' faces. With ERPs Kushnerenko et al. (2008) were able to demonstrate differential brain responses to audiovisual McGurk stimuli that do or do not fuse perceptually (for adults) in 5 month olds.

The importance of infancy to our lipreading abilities is also shown clearly in work on recovery from early visual deprivation (see also Chapter 8). People born with dense bilateral cataracts will not receive patterned visual input in infancy, but the problem can later be surgically corrected (to some extent). Putzar, Goerendt, Heed, Richard, Büchel and Röder (2010) found that participants who had experienced visual deprivation in infancy due to bilateral cataracts were poor lipreaders. Because cataract surgery improves but does not entirely restore visual function, Putzar et al. (2010) also tested participants with equally poor vision whose deficits arose later in life, confirming they were better at lipreading than the participants with early visual deprivation.

When and where does audiovisual fusion occur?

The McGurk effect seems to be stronger for meaningless sounds or single syllables, rather than coherent, fluent speech (Easton & Basala, 1982). Hence, when there is a great deal of contextual information as to what is likely to come next, the discrepant visual cue may somehow be over-ruled (Rosenblum, 2008), but even so the McGurk effect still operates to some extent for meaningful speech. However, a thought-provoking study by Tuomainen, Andersen, Tiippana and Sams (2005) found that integration only occurs when the stimuli are perceived as speech. To do this, Tuomainen et al. (2005) used distorted sounds (sine wave replicas) that could be perceived as speech or as non-speech. Participants who were trained to classify these sounds as if they were speech showed audio-visual fusions, whereas participants who were trained to classify them as non-speech did not. Consistent with this, other studies also report that the degree of audio-visual fusion can be influenced by participants' expectations (Windmann, 2004).

The McGurk effect operates even when the face and the voice are of different sexes (e.g. a male face with a female voice, or vice versa). It is interesting that auditory and visual information should be integrated despite such obvious incongruities, showing again the relatively automatic nature of the effect (Green, Kuhl, Meltzoff, & Stevens, 1991). However, there are limits to how far this will happen – if the face of a highly familiar person is combined with a different voice, the degree of fusion between the face and voice inputs is reduced in comparison to when the face is unfamiliar (Walker, Bruce, & O'Malley, 1995). More generally, switching to a different talker affects speechreading from silently mouthing faces (Yakel, Rosenblum, & Fortier, 2000), and this task is easier with familiar faces (Lander & Davies, 2008). Schweinberger and Soukup (1998) used the Garner interference paradigm to show that irrelevant variations in facial identity affected facial speech perception, demonstrating a degree of interdependence of facial speech and facial identity perception reminiscent of their finding (using the same paradigm) of some interdependence for facial expression and identity. The same pattern held for moving faces with the Garner paradigm (Kaufmann & Schweinberger, 2005).

Adaptation studies offer a particularly intriguing insight into audiovisual fusions in speech perception. Classic studies of adaptation effects to purely auditory stimuli support the idea of auditory feature detectors. Consider, for instance, the consonant sounds in 'da' and 'ta'. The difference between them is that 'd' is voiced, 't' is unvoiced, so voicing begins earlier when you say 'da' than when you say 'ta'. Put more formally, the voice onset time is shorter for 'da' than 'ta'. This difference in voice onset time was exploited by Eimas and Corbit (1973), who adapted people to 'da', by presenting it continuously across a 2-minute period. They demonstrated that following this adaptation participants were more likely to perceive some of the stimuli which they would otherwise have classified as 'da' as 'ta' – as shown in Figure 4.22. You can see that adaptation shifts the boundary for the phoneme change, consistent with adaptation of a feature detector.

Roberts and Summerfield (1981) used adaptation to study what happens in the McGurk illusion. In essence, their research question was if the soundtrack is 'ba', the face mouthes 'ga', and the participant perceives 'da', which of these will she or he adapt to? Their findings showed that the phonemic boundary shifts according to the presented auditory stimulus, even though this is not what is perceived. This suggests that the integration of auditory and visual information takes place at a relatively late stage in speech perception, beyond the stage at which adaptation to the auditory stimulus takes place, but prior to conscious perception.

Whereabouts in the brain might multimodal speech perception be taking place? A pioneering study by Campbell and her colleagues suggested that the left cerebral hemisphere may be particularly involved (Campbell, Landis, & Regard, 1986). The question of cerebral asymmetry for lipreading is particularly intriguing because although the left hemisphere is heavily involved in speech perception (to which lipreading contributes), the right hemisphere is often found to be

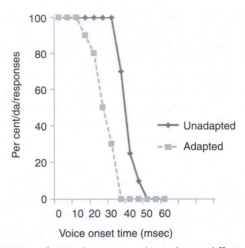

Figure 4.22 Percentages of sounds perceived as 'da' at different voice onset times (solid line), with percentages perceived as 'da' following adaptation to the sound 'da' (dotted line). Adaptation to 'da' shifts the category boundary towards perceiving 'ta' instead. Reprinted from *Cognitive Psychology*, 4, 1, Peter D. Eimas, John D. Corbit, Selective adaptation of linguistic feature detectors, pp. 99–109. Copyright 1973, with permission from Elsevier.

better at perceiving faces (from which the lips get read) – so it is interesting to know which factor will prove the primary determinant of cerebral lateralisation for lipreading in hearing participants.

Campbell et al. (1986) studied two participants with brain injuries. One of them had suffered a posterior lesion affecting the occipito-temporal cortex in the right cerebral hemisphere. She was unable to recognise familiar faces (she was prosopagnosic – see Chapter 6) and could not categorise facial expressions correctly. Yet she could judge correctly what phonemes were being mouthed in photographs of faces, and she was susceptible to the McGurk illusion. The second person had suffered a posterior lesion affecting the occipito-temporal cortex in the left hemisphere – a type of brain injury that often leads to inability to read (alexia). As well as being alexic, she was impaired at making phoneme judgements to face stimuli and was not susceptible to the McGurk illusion, yet had no difficulties in recognising faces or facial expressions.

The double dissociation of lipreading and expression processing in these two cases was one of the main reasons that led Bruce and Young (1986) to identify these as separable components in their functional model (see Chapter 2, Figure 2.15). The finding is particularly striking since both types of information are derived from a similar area of the face – the main difference is that for expression, eyes and eyebrows are involved as well as mouth and lips. Hence, in this case it seems to be the use to which the information is put, rather than the region of the face being analysed, which is crucial in determining whether or not a separable functional subsystem is dedicated to the task.

Studies using visual hemifield presentation (Campbell, de Gelder, & de Haan, 1996) and chimaeric faces (Burt & Perrett, 1997) have confirmed the left hemisphere's involvement in lipreading with neurologically normal participants. The Burt and Perrett (1997) findings are particularly striking since they created chimaeric faces (see Chapter 2 and Figure 4.3 above) whose left and right sides varied on age, sex, attractiveness, expression or speech. Only for interpreting speech was there evidence of a bias to attend to information from the side of the chimaeric face falling to the participant's right (evidence of left hemisphere involvement in lipreading) – for everything else, the left side was preferred (right hemisphere involvement).

Further evidence suggestive of left hemisphere involvement in audiovisual integration comes from MacKain, Studdert-Kennedy, Spieker and Stern (1983) – and points to its being present from an early age. They replicated Kuhl and Meltzoff's (1982) findings of sensitivity to congruence between auditory and visual stimuli with 5–6-month-old infants, but they also found that the preference for the 'matched' face plus vowel combination was stronger when the matching face fell on the right of the display, implicating left hemisphere involvement by analogy with other effects of cerebral asymmetry found in free viewing (see Chapter 2).

Functional brain imaging studies offer better precision in identifying which regions of the left hemisphere are involved in lipreading. Calvert and her colleagues initiated an important series of studies of brain regions involved in the integration of lipreading into speech perception (Calvert et al., 1997). Their first study used fMRI to measure blood flow in different regions of the brain when people looked at a speaking face (without sound) or listened to a voice (without seeing the face). The part of the brain which was activated both by seen speech and by heard speech was in the auditory cortex – in other words, merely seeing a person speaking activates brain regions which are involved in hearing.

In this initial study, Calvert et al. (1997) used as their criterion for a region of interest any part of the brain that was activated both by seeing a speaking face and by hearing a voice – Calvert (2001) later called these co-responsive regions. This criterion will find brain regions that respond to the face and to the voice, which makes them candidate regions but doesn't actually establish that their function is that of audiovisual integration. Calvert, Campbell and Brammer (2000) and Calvert, Hansen, Iversen and Brammer (2001) therefore introduced the criterion that an unequivocally multimodal region will show a supra-additive interaction effect for audiovisual stimuli. In the case we are discussing, audio-visual integration, a supra-additive activation will show more activation to an audiovisual stimulus (AV condition) than the sum of its responses to purely auditory stimuli (A) or to purely visual stimuli (V). More formally, the region's response will have the property $AV > A + V$, though it is possible that regions of sub-additive response suppression ($AV < A + V$) could also have an important role (Wright, Pelphrey, Allison, McKeown, & McCarthy, 2003).

A region that has repeatedly been found to meet Calvert's supra-additive criterion in audiovisual integration studies using talking faces is in the left posterior superior temporal sulcus, close to or likely part of Haxby et al.'s (2000) core system that they identify as heavily involved in perceiving changeable aspects of faces (see Chapter 1) and itself an area heavily involved in the perception of biological motion (Hein & Knight, 2008; Pelphrey, Morris, Michelich, Allison, & McCarthy, 2005). Supra-additivity is a strict criterion for claiming that a region's function involves audiovisual integration – some researchers think it may be too strict (Laurienti, Perrault, Stanford, Wallace, & Stein, 2005). In Calvert et al.'s (2000) study, they added the stipulation that the region identified must respond supra-additively to temporal congruence of the face and voice and sub-additively when they were incongruent (i.e. when they are mistimed with respect to each other – the effect you get with a badly dubbed film).

A recent study has confirmed the importance of left posterior STS to audio-visual integration by showing that TMS to this region disrupted the McGurk effect (Beauchamp, Nath, & Pasalar, 2010). Even so, the posterior left STS should not be overinterpreted as the only region involved in audiovisual integration of speech – it clearly forms part of a larger network that is apparent in studies that have used different criteria (Hall, Fussell, & Summerfield, 2005; Macaluso, George, Dolan, Spence, & Driver, 2004; Wright, Pelphrey, Allison, McKeown, & McCarthy, 2003). This network includes other regions along the superior temporal sulcus and superior temporal gyrus that include classical auditory areas. However, the advantage of the supra-additivity criterion is that it makes a cogent case for brain regions that do meet it – we will return to the implications of the overlap with Haxby et al.'s core system later in this chapter.

Multimodal recognition of emotion

The evidence of audiovisual integration in speech perception naturally makes one wonder whether analogous phenomena might be found for recognition of emotion. De Gelder has been one of the researchers who has most energetically pursued this possibility. In an early study, de Gelder and Vroomen (2000) investigated the possibility of an emotion equivalent of the McGurk effect. They asked participants to classify morphed images of faces from a happy–sad continuum as happy or sad, as might be done in a standard identification paradigm from a categorical perception study. However, the face was either presented on its own or accompanied by a semantically neutral sentence read with a happy or sad tone of voice. Participants were instructed to ignore the voice but, as Figure 4.23 shows, they were unable to do this (de Gelder & Bertelson, 2003). The figure shows the proportion of 'sad' responses to each morphed image in each condition – it is clear that compared to the 'no voice' baseline the proportion of sad classifications is increased by the sad voice and decreased by the happy voice.

A further experiment by de Gelder and Vroomen (2000) showed that the interaction between faces and voices is bidirectional. They took sentences with neutral content spoken with a happy or a fearful intonation and then created transitions in voice tone by simultaneously changing their duration, pitch range and pitch register. When participants were asked to classify these vocal continua as happy or afraid, the proportion of fear responses was influenced by an accompanying happy or fear face that participants were again instructed to ignore.

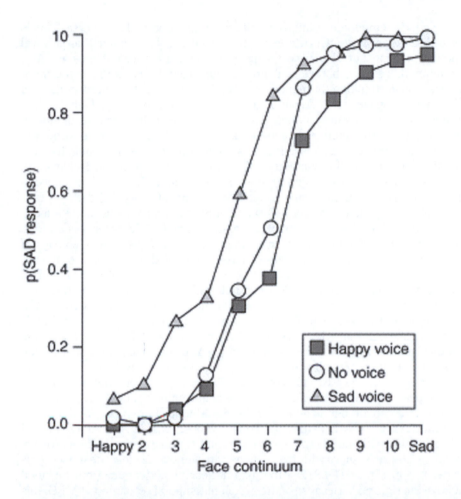

Figure 4.23 De Gelder and Vroomen's (2000) demonstration that emotional voices influence the categorisation of facial expressions. Morphed images of faces had to be classified as happy or sad, but each face was either presented on its own or accompanied by a sentence read with a happy or sad tone of voice. The figure shows the proportion of 'sad' responses to each morphed image in each condition. Compared to the 'no voice' baseline the proportion of sad classifications is increased by the sad voice and decreased by the happy voice. Reprinted from *Trends in Cognitive Science, 7*, 10, Beatrice De Gelder, Paul Bertelson, Multisensory integration, perception and ecological validity, pp. 460–467. Copyright 2003, with permission from Elsevier.

So facial emotion can interfere with vocal emotion and vice versa. This is not the same as the McGurk effect – the result is a bias rather than a novel emotion percept, but of course the face stimuli are static, not moving. At a minimum, this shows that we can't ignore cues from either channel, and there are grounds for thinking there might be some integration at the perceptual level (Hietanen, Leppänen, Illi, & Surakka, 2004). A study by de Gelder, Bocker, Tuomainen, Hensen and Vroomen (1999) used the excellent time resolution of ERP to demonstrate interaction between an emotional face and voice within the first few hundred milliseconds following stimulus onset. Like lipreading, the abilities that underpin audiovisual integration of emotion seem to be developed in infancy – Grossman, Striano and Friederici (2006) found ERP evidence of cross-modal responses to audiovisual emotion in the brains of 7 month olds.

What ERP studies do less well is to identify the spatial locus of the effects. Using fMRI, which has good spatial resolution, Kreifelts, Ethofer, Grodd, Erb and Wildgruber (2007) therefore investigated brain responses to video clips of actors speaking neutral words with different emotional intonations to identify regions showing a stronger response to bimodal (auditory + visual, or AV) than to either version of unimodal (A or V) stimuli. This showed bilateral activation of the superior temporal gyrus (STG), and activation of this region was correlated with the degree of behavioural enhancement of emotion recognition in the AV condition. The criterion is less strict than Calvert's supra-additivity, but the region identified is close to the region Calvert found to be involved in audiovisual speech integration in the left hemisphere and also included an equivalent region in the right hemisphere. Since Kreifelts et al. (2007) used speech stimuli, it is possible that the bilateral activation reflects separate contributions of the left hemisphere to speech perception per se and from the right hemisphere to something more 'emotional'. A recent MEG study by Hagan, Woods, Johnson, Calder, Green and Young (2009) with purely non-verbal stimuli (Ekman faces and non-verbal sounds) showed a supra-additive response to audiovisual fear (fear face plus scream) from right STG/STS – this had a clear posterior focus but included much of the right STS. Because of the excellent temporal resolution of MEG, this activation could be seen to have peaked within 200 ms of stimulus onset, as shown in Figure 4.24.

These findings show that, like speech perception, emotion recognition is to some extent a multimodal phenomenon, and they suggest that whereas the left posterior STS/STG region is implicated in audiovisual integration of speech (Calvert, 2001) an equivalent region on the right side of the brain is implicated in audiovisual integration of emotion. This right posterior STG/STS region is again close to or overlapping with Haxby et al.'s (2000) posterior STS region hypothesised to be involved in analysing changeable aspects of faces. As for lipreading, though, we should note that this is likely to be only a (critical) part of a more extensive network for multimodal analysis.

It may be important, too, that some of the audiovisual emotion integration studies combine static faces with temporally changing vocal expressions, whereas in the speech integration studies such combinations would themselves often be considered to form 'incongruent' stimuli because of the lack of temporal synchrony. It would be worth exploring whether temporal synchrony is more

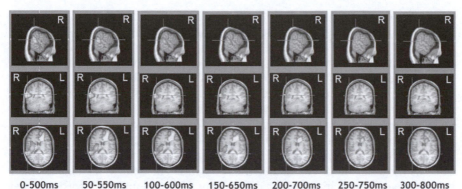

0-500ms   50-550ms   100-600ms   150-650ms   200-700ms   250-750ms   300-800ms

Figure 4.24 See colour plate. Supra-additive MEG response to audiovisual fear (fear face plus scream) from right STG/STS. The response is shown across a series of 500 ms time windows, in steps of 50 ms from stimulus onset. Images are shown in radiological convention, with the left side of the brain on the right side of each image. Reproduced from Hagan, C. C., Woods, W., Johnson, S., Calder, A. J., Green, G. G. R., & Young, A. W. (2009). MEG demonstrates a supra-additive response to facial and vocal emotion in the right superior temporal sulcus. *Proceedings of the National Academy of Sciences, USA, 106*, pp. 20010–20015.

important in speech perception, where critical changes often take place across tens of milliseconds.

A close relationship between facial and vocal expression processing is also evident in neuropsychological studies. For example, in studies of cerebral asymmetry, patients with lesions of the right cerebral hemisphere perform less well than patients with left hemisphere lesions at recognising emotion from facial expressions and from vocal prosody (Borod et al., 1998). The prosody finding is particularly interesting, of course, because prosody is an integral part of communication through language, which is usually considered to be a strongly lateralised function of the left hemisphere. Problems in interpreting emotional prosody following right cerebral injury therefore point strongly to an important role for the right hemisphere in interpreting emotion. Studies of cerebral asymmetries in neurologically normal participants confirm right hemisphere involvement in recognising emotion in prosodic and in non-verbal emotional auditory stimuli (Carmon & Nachshon, 1973; Ley & Bryden, 1982).

Studies such as Borod et al. (1998) contrast the performance of groups of patients with different brain lesions. Another important approach is to look at the performances of individual cases, to see whether deficits in facial expression recognition dissociate from other aspects of emotion recognition. Keane, Calder, Hodges and Young (2002) studied patients with frontal variant fronto-temporal dementia (fvFTD), a degenerative disease known to affect recognition of facial expressions (Lavenu, Pasquier, Lebert, Petit, & Van der Linden, 1999). As expected, they found that fvFTD led to problems in recognising facial expressions of all six of the basic emotions from the Ekman and Friesen (1976) series, whereas recognition of facial identity (as tested by familiar face recognition and ability to match photos of unfamiliar faces) could be well preserved. This dissociation is of a type that might be described as indicating preserved recognition of facial identity with impaired recognition of facial expressions. This is in one sense a correct description of the data, but Keane et al. (2002) found that it is also a bit misleading because the fvFTD patients performed just as badly when tested for recognition of non-verbal auditory expressions of the same emotions (laughter for happiness, screams for fear, and so on). Their problem was therefore one of *emotion* recognition – not a specific problem with *facial* expressions.

Something similar seems to happen neurodevelopmentally. Hefter, Manoach and Barton (2005) studied the recognition of identity and expression in a group of adult participants with a range of social developmental disorders. They found that ability to recognise facial identity was unrelated to ability to recognise emotion from facial or from non-facial cues, whereas ability to recognise emotion from the face was related to ability to recognise emotion from a range of non-facial cues. Hefter et al. (2005, p. 1620) concluded that 'Deficits in perceiving facial expression may be related to emotional processing more than face processing'.

A comparable point arises with respect to the amygdala's involvement in emotion, where again problems are not restricted to facial expressions. Further testing of DR (Calder, Young, Rowland, et al., 1996; Young et al., 1995), a person with bilateral brain lesions in the region of the amygdala who was poor at recognising fear and anger (see Figure 4.15), showed that she was also poor at recognising vocal expressions of fear and anger (Scott et al., 1997), implying that the amygdala is involved in a general way in the recognition of these emotions regardless of the type of input (face or voice). Consistent with this, strong amygdala responses to auditory signals of fear and anger have been found in an fMRI study of participants who were blind from birth (Klinge, Röder, & Büchel, 2010).

And of course it is not just face and voice – the neurologically normal amygdala responds to fearful body postures (Hadjikhani & de Gelder, 2003) and fear can be misperceived in body posture as well as from face and voice following amygdala damage (Sprengelmeyer et al., 1999). For a few years, it seemed like Adolphs et al.'s (1994) case SM would be an exception – her deficits were initially reported to be face-specific (Adolphs & Tranel, 1999). However, a later study has established that SM is poor at recognising fear conveyed in scary music (Gosselin, Peretz, Johnsen, & Adolphs, 2007) confirming that her problem also extends beyond faces.

Such findings fit well with the idea we mentioned earlier that the amygdala plays a role in the appraisal of danger (LeDoux, 1995; Zaretsky et al., 2010). Reports of the behaviour of a person with amygdala damage, YW, are consistent with this view (Broks et al., 1998). YW showed impaired recognition of facial expressions of fear in a laboratory test, but we will focus here on her real-life behaviour. While on holiday, YW and her husband were returning to their hotel after an evening out when they were mugged by some youths. In the ensuing struggle (during which, at one stage, YW was physically accosted) her husband's wallet was seized. He resisted and managed to retrieve it, and the youths eventually made off empty-handed. As well as the physical struggle, there was a loud and aggressive verbal exchange. Although closely involved, YW, according to her husband, showed no sign of concern – 'She seemed to think they were just larking around'. In contrast to this, a couple of months later YW became terrified when watching a mildly aggressive exchange between two female characters in a fictional television programme, and in the days that followed she displayed episodes of inappropriate fear. Once when her husband innocently entered the room YW cowered, hands over face, pleading 'Don't hit me', and she responded in a similar fashion on other occasions involving her son and her care assistant.

These incidents reinforce the view that appraisal of danger is a key function of the amygdala, and recent work with case SM also shows a lack of fear in everyday life (Feinstein, Adolphs, Damasio, & Tranel, 2011). However, YW's episodes of inappropriate fear also show that fear responses can be initiated and sustained under certain circumstances without the involvement of the amygdala, whilst what characterises all of the observations is that the fear response (absent to a mugging, excessive to a TV programme and some everyday behaviours) was out of line with an appropriate evaluation of the dangers inherent in each incident. The idea that the amygdala plays an important role in the appraisal of danger thus provides a perspective which can integrate observations of real-life behaviour after amygdala damage with findings of impaired recognition of the emotions expressed by others.

A comparable pattern is evident for disgust recognition. Calder, Keane, Manes, Antoun and Young (2000) studied case NK, a person with a brain injury affecting the left insula and underlying basal ganglia – regions that functional brain imaging studies had shown were responsive to facial expressions of disgust (Calder, Lawrence, & Young, 2001; Phillips et al., 1997). They found that NK was poor at recognising disgust from facial expressions, non-verbal sounds and from emotional prosody (neutral words said in a 'disgusted' way). Moreover, questionnaires suggested that NK had reduced experience of disgust in everyday life, whereas his everyday experience of fear and anger seemed normal. In Huntington's disease, perception of disgust has been found to be impaired for a wide range of elicitors as well as for facial expressions – these include olfaction, taste, vocal expressions and pictures of emotion scenes (Hayes, Stevenson, & Coltheart, 2007; Mitchell, Heims, Neville, & Rickards, 2005).

Bringing the neurology and the psychology together

This is a good moment to stand back and take in the bigger picture. We have seen that emotions often belong to distinct categories, some at least of which serve functions with a strong evolutionary background. Although the research literature has kept a strong focus on facial expressions as key determinants of emotion perception, in everyday life these are often accompanied by contiguous signals from voice and body posture. There is evidence that when brain injury affects recognition of emotion, it can compromise some emotional categories more than others and that in such cases there are usually parallel impairments of vocal and body expression recognition, together with abnormal experience of emotion in everyday life.

This pattern has taken a long time to become clear – in part because we have been looking for the wrong thing. In Chapters 6 and 7 we will discuss impairments of facial identity recognition, including the paradigmatic neuropsychological deficit of prosopagnosia (inability to recognise familiar faces after brain injury). We will describe how prosopagnosia affects the recognition of more or less all familiar faces, whilst recognition of familiar voices is largely unaffected. Because prosopagnosia has been such a well-known deficit of facial identity recognition in the research literature, there has been a strong tendency to look for an equivalent deficit of facial expression recognition – that is for patients who recognise hardly any facial expressions but are able to recognise vocal expressions without difficulty. It is striking that no convincing cases showing this pattern have emerged after more than 25 years in which researchers have sought them.

So in prosopagnosia all faces are affected but voices aren't, whereas in emotion recognition deficits some emotions may be more affected than others but the problems will extend to voices too. Why might this be?

Lipreading offers a clear clue. We saw that a major driver of audiovisual integration in speech perception is that the signals evolve rapidly across time and that information that is hard to hear can be easy to see, and vice versa (Miller & Niceley, 1955). Signals of emotion can also change in an instant during a social encounter, and there is a high premium on detecting and responding quickly to such changes. Pooling information from as many sources as possible is likely to offer an optimal solution to these requirements. In contrast, recognition of identity is relatively unconstrained – often we see someone we know before they speak (e.g. at a distance), and once they have been recognised their identity is an unchanging feature of a social encounter – they don't have to be recognised again while you are with them.

Consistent with this line of reasoning, we saw that the part of Haxby et al.'s (2000) 'core system' that deals with changeable aspects of faces is either very close to or itself a multimodal region capable of integrating information from vision and hearing (Calder & Young, 2005). Looked at in this way, the neurology and psychology dovetail neatly – as we believe they should.

The other pathway in Haxby et al.'s (2000) core system is for relatively invariant aspects of faces. It is clearly a more exclusively visual pathway and, as we will see, it is the pathway that seems mainly to be damaged in cases of prosopagnosia. This raises interesting questions, though, about what happens when we recognise facial identity from patterns of movement. Normally, recognition of any image of a familiar face is so good that we can't see whether there is any benefit for face recognition from patterns of movement. However, in Chapter 6 we describe elegant studies by Lander and her colleagues showing that recognition from patterns of movement can sometimes be achieved if recognition is made difficult.

So what is happening in Haxby's model when we recognise someone's identity from the movements of their face? Are the characteristic movement patterns that can identify individuals stored in the core system's STS pathway because they relate to changeable facial movements, or are they stored in the

FFA because they relate to invariant facial identity (O'Toole, Roark, & Abdi, 2002)? A fascinating study by von Kriegstein et al. (2008) suggests that information about patterns of movement may get stored in the functional pathway that needs it. Von Kriegstein et al. (2008) investigated the benefit of watching and listening to a person's talking face for 2 minutes on later auditory recognition of the person's speech (i.e. what they are saying) and identity (whose voice it is). For neurologically normal participants, both tasks benefited from having previously seen the person's talking face, and fMRI showed that the benefit on speech recognition was correlated with activation in the left STS, whereas the benefit on speaker's voice recognition was correlated with activation of the FFA. The latter finding shows an interesting interaction between voice perception and what is usually thought of as a purely visual region (the FFA). For participants with congenital prosopagnosia, however, von Kriegstein et al. (2008) reported that the benefit on speech recognition was correlated with activation in the left STS but that there was no improvement in recognising the speaker's voice. Studies like this push theorising beyond what is known, and keep things moving on by making us think hard about how such patterns of findings might arise.

Summary

Facial movements are important in interpreting people's moods and feelings, and (somewhat counterintuitively) they make an important contribution to understanding what they are saying. There is evidence that basic emotion categories play a role in our interpretation of many facial expressions, with categorical perception effects evident in identification and discrimination tasks. However, we remain sensitive to within-category differences between expressions, and computer simulation is beginning to show how to reconcile the paradox that when perceiving expressions we can both heighten differences between emotion categories and maintain sensitivity to within-category changes.

In the case of lipreading, the visual input is combined with auditory information in a way that facilitates analysis of what is in effect a multimodal signal, and there are clear ecological reasons why this is an effective strategy for interpreting speech. We suggest that similar contingencies operate in the case of emotion recognition, and point out lines of evidence that indicate facial expressions are not analysed in isolation from other signals of emotion conveyed by a person's voice or body posture.

Further reading

Brosch, T., Pourtois, G., & Sander, S. (2010). The perception and categorisation of emotional stimuli: A review. *Cognition and Emotion, 24,* 377–400.
Reviews evidence that we assign emotional stimuli to categories – both in terms of what the claim means and how and why we do it.

Calder, A. J., & Young, A. W. (2005). Understanding the recognition of facial identity and facial expression. *Nature Reviews Neuroscience, 6,* 645–651.

Discusses the relation between perception of facial expression and facial identity in more detail than we have space for here.

Calvert, G. A. (2001). Crossmodal processing in the human brain: Insights from functional neuroimaging studies. *Cerebral Cortex, 11*, 1110–1123.
Discusses brain regions involved in lipreading, setting them in the context of other forms of crossmodal perception and explaining why supra-additive responses offer an important criterion for assessing whether a region has a genuinely multimodal function.

Campbell, R. (2008). The processing of audio-visual speech: Empirical and neural bases. *Philosophical Transactions of the Royal Society, London, B: Biological Sciences, 363*, 1001–1010.
A review of behavioural and neuroimaging studies of lipreading that tries to identify more precisely than usual what contribution seeing a talker's mouth can make to speech perception.

Phelps, E. A. (2006). Emotion and cognition: Insights from studies of the human amygdala. *Annual Review of Psychology, 57*, 27–53.
Detailed review of the amygdala's role in emotion and cognition, explaining the implications for understanding the relation between cognition and emotion.

Gaze and attention

This chapter is about the perception of gaze – how we perceive and understand where another face is looking, and the implications of these perceptions for our social and cognitive activities. Human eyes, like those of many other animals, are remarkably mobile. We have to move our eyes in order to bring different objects or areas of interest onto the fovea – the area of the retina with highest acuity. Faces themselves attract our gaze more than most other items in the world, as we discuss later on in this chapter. But most of the chapter is about how we decipher patterns of gaze in the faces we encounter, and the impacts observed gaze patterns have on us. In humans and some other animals eye movements are used for directly communicative or affiliative acts. Being stared at may be attractive, irritating or intimidating depending on the context, and the effects of being looked at can have powerful consequences that have been appreciated and used throughout history. Looking away from someone is also a social signal with multiple potential meanings that may be interpreted as an act of rudeness, untruthfulness, shyness or distraction.

The multiple uses of gaze, and the importance of the environmental and social contexts in which eye movements occur, make the study of gaze perception potentially rich but at the same time particularly complicated. For some questions about gaze perception, standard experimental techniques of presenting stimuli out of context and asking people to decide things about them or recording neural responses will work satisfactorily. We begin by considering studies of this type, which are often directed at the issue of how we determine where someone is looking. For many other questions about gaze, though, the same approaches can give muddled, confusing results because of our flexibility and skill at interpreting the meaning of gaze direction, gaze shifts and gaze duration according to the contexts in which these take place. Under these circumstances, careful and ingenious experimental designs are needed, often including more naturalistic features (Kingstone, 2009), and we will see how the best researchers have risen to the challenge. At present, the study of gaze perception and the cognitive neuroscience of these social-cognitive processes is expanding rapidly, so we provide an introduction to one of the hottest topics in our field.

How do we know where someone else is looking?

Being looked at directly can have powerful effects. Many animals react defensively to direct gaze from other animals that might eat them (Leopold & Rhodes, 2010). In many cultures, including some quite modern ones, people believe that a look from 'the evil eye' can literally kill … or at least make you feel rather poorly. Such beliefs fit with an idea used by the ancient Greeks, where one theory of vision held that seeing occurred when rays sent out from the eyes landed upon objects, and in this context it seems less bizarre to assume that these rays might convey malign intent. More recently, direct gaze provided an iconic example of political persuasion in the First World War recruitment poster in which Kitchener's face and arm both pointed to the viewer above the message 'Your country needs YOU'.

Research studies have shown just how clever the Kitchener poster was. Direct gaze, even from a picture, can provide a persuasive context. Bateson,

Nettle and Roberts (2006) monitored how much payment for tea and coffee was made to an honesty box in the common room of a University Psychology Department. The tea and coffee prices were displayed on a notice board behind the honesty box, and on alternate weeks Bateson et al. (2006) placed either a picture of some flowers or a pair of eyes with gaze directed toward the viewer on this notice board. The pictures they used each week are shown in Figure 5.1,

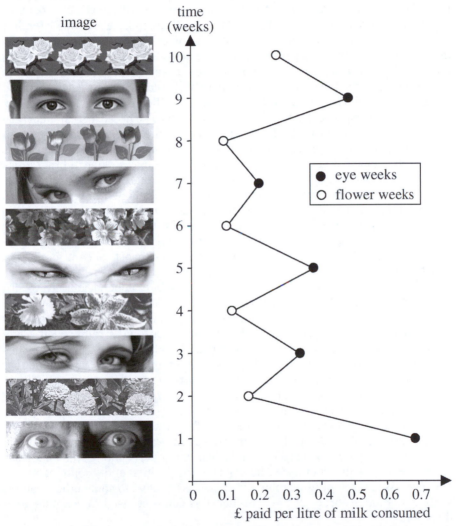

Figure 5.1 To the left is shown the picture displayed above the honesty box in each week of Bateson et al.'s (2006) study. To the right is shown the amount of money taken in the box each week with milk usage used as an index of weekly consumption. First published in Bateson et al., *Biology Letters*, 2(3), pp. 412–414. Copyright (2006) The Royal Society.

together with the amount of money paid per litre of milk consumed as a measure of the tea and coffee drinkers' 'honesty'. The figure clearly shows that honesty was higher in weeks where a pair of eyes was shown above the box than in weeks where pictures of flowers were shown.

Direct gaze is sufficiently important to us that it may well be a priority signal for our brains. In the brain, a key structure for perceiving someone's gaze *direction* seems to be the Superior Temporal Sulcus (STS). Recall that Haxby, Hoffman and Gobbini's (2000) neurological model proposes that perceiving gaze, like other changeable aspects of faces, involves a pathway from OFA to posterior STS in their core system (see Chapter 1). We will say more about this later. For now, we simply note that whether or not STS is critical to gaze perception in general, it is clear that other parts of neural systems engaged in face processing are sensitive to *direct* gaze. George, Driver and Dolan (2001) showed that faces with direct gaze elicited stronger activation in the fusiform gyrus than did averted gaze, even though Haxby et al.'s (2000) model links the fusiform gyrus to perception of invariant aspects of faces. George et al. (2001) also noted a greater correlation between activation in the fusiform gyrus and the amygdala for faces with direct gaze, and the amygdala is implicated in social and emotional processing as we saw in Chapter 3 and Chapter 4. So, *direct* gaze may influence brain areas involved in perceiving a range of facial characteristics. This might, of course, reflect interaction between posterior STS and other components of Haxby et al.'s (2000) model. Alternatively, some researchers have suggested that eye contact is such an important cue that we have evolved a 'fast track' subcortical route for detecting it (Senju & Johnson, 2009b). The latter hypothesis is interesting in that it brings in infant work (see Chapter 8) on potential subcortical contributions to face perception, but direct evidence is scant.

Whatever the neural pathways there is no doubt that, behaviourally, we are remarkably accurate at deciding correctly whether or not another person's face is looking directly at us or not. Look at the images in Figure 5.2. You should be able to tell whether they seem to be staring at you, or to your right or left. Cline (1967) showed that observers could detect gaze deviations as small as 1.4 degrees at a distance of about a metre, and Anstis, Mayhew and Morley (1969) found that at the same distance displacements of the iris of about 1.8 mm could be spotted.

How can we do this? Compared with the eyes of many other species, including other primates, human eyes have a very large area of white sclera visible, creating a high degree of contrast with the darker iris and pupil (Kobayashi & Kohshima, 1997). You really can clearly see the whites of our eyes, and this may be an evolutionary adaptation that facilitates our perception of the important social cue of gaze direction (see Chapter 1). If the position of the contrast border between iris and sclera (the limbus) is measured relative to some other feature, such as the inner corner of the eye, then this could be used to compute gaze direction.

However, such an approach does not readily explain the considerable distances over which gaze direction appears to be visible. Watt, Craven and Quinn (2007), for example, showed that gaze direction discrimination remained constant over viewing distances up to about 15 metres. Nor would a system based only on the position of a contrast boundary very easily explain why reversal of contrast

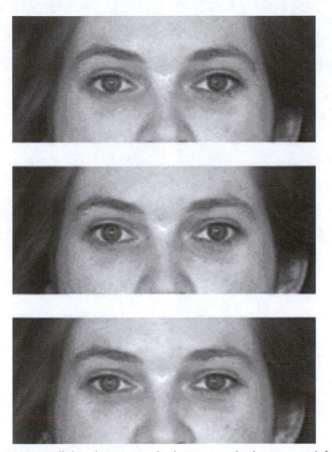

Figure 5.2 We can tell that the eyes at the bottom are looking to our left and those at the top straight ahead. Slight variations of gaze direction shown in items used by Watt et al. (2007). First published in A role for eyebrows in regulating the visibility of eye gaze direction, Roger Watt, Ben Craven, Sandra Quinn, *The Quarterly Journal of Experimental Psychology*, 2007, reprinted by permission of the publisher (Taylor & Francis Group, http://www.informaworld.com).

around this boundary (for example, in a photographic negative image) can affect gaze perception. Ricciardelli, Baylis and Driver (2000) investigated how gaze perception is affected by reversing the usual contrast polarity of the eyes within a face. Participants were shown pictures of a person gazing straight ahead, or 30 degrees to their left or to their right, with their head pointing in one of these three directions as well (so that a person with head pointing right would have their eyes oriented towards the viewer in the 'straight ahead' condition). Participants had to decide if each image showed the person looking left, straight ahead, or right, and they were shown images in which the eyes were shown in positive or negative versions (see Figure 5.3).

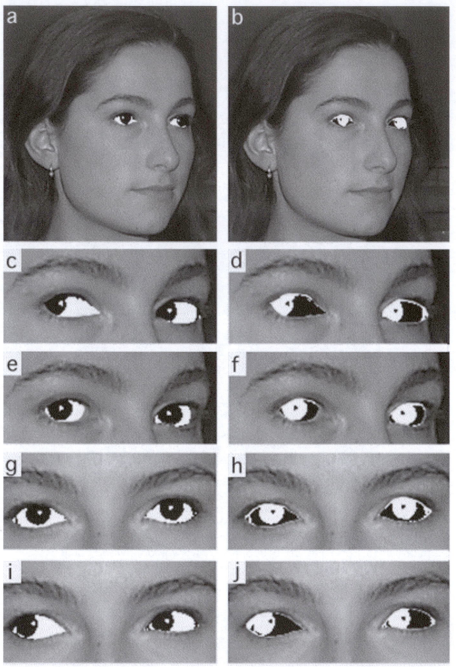

Figure 5.3 Examples of materials used in Ricciardelli et al.'s (2000) first experiment. (a) Positive eyes, with head and gaze both directed 30 degrees to the observer's right; (b) same as in (a), but with eyes now in negative polarity. Illustrations in lower rows show just the eye region to illustrate other looking angles used in the experiment. Reprinted from *Cognition*, *77*, 1, Paola Ricciardelli, Gordon Baylis, Jon Driver, The positive and negative of human expertise in gaze perception, B1–B14. Copyright 2000 with permission from Elsevier.

Overall, Ricciardelli et al. (2000) found that participants were much less accurate at these decisions for negative (52.3%) than positive (93.5%) images. Subsequent experiments showed that this was true if the whole face was in negative and not just the eyes (as in Figure 5.3), and that it was not simply because negative eyes look 'unusual'. Eyes shown with a dark red iris on a light green sclera are also in a form most of us have not encountered, yet these still led to accurate responding unless their contrast polarity was reversed. Indeed, there was only one condition in Ricciardelli et al.'s (2000) experiment in which responses to negative eyes could be made accurately. This was when both eyes and head were facing ahead, so that the 'direct' eye condition showed completely symmetrical iris/sclera areas.

Perhaps gaze direction is computed not from the geometric arrangement of a feature such as the limbus that should be unaffected by contrast polarity, but by something simpler that responds to the balance of white on dark pattern? When looked at face-on, the arrangement of these bright and dark areas could provide a very simple signal about whether or not gaze is direct. Langton, Watt and Bruce (2000) showed how the outputs of cortical simple cells – the earliest cortical stage in face perception – would show sensitivity to changes in gaze direction. Certainly such a system would be sensitive to contrast polarity. The 'Bogart illusion', reported by Sinha (2000), provides a demonstration of the importance of contrast polarity. A picture of the actor Humphrey Bogart in which his eyes look to the observer's right may appear to look in the opposite direction when the picture is negated (Figure 5.4).

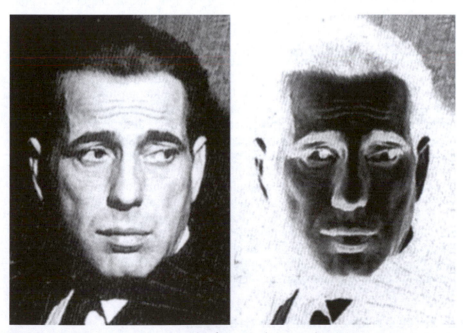

Figure 5.4 The 'Bogart illusion'. The face in photographic negative may seem to look in the opposite direction. First published in *Perception*, 29, pp. 1005–1008, Sinha 2000, The perception of gaze direction courtesy of Pion Limited, London.

215

Additional support for a mechanism based upon the balance of light and dark comes from Ando's 'bloodshot' illusion, in which a slight darkening of the visible sclera on one side of the iris – as might be seen at a distance if this part of the eye was very bloodshot – biased participants' judgements about the direction that the eye was looking (Ando, 2002). However, Ricciardelli et al. (2000) point out that the effects of contrast reversal overall suggest that gaze perception must rely on some higher level processes or assumptions as well as on low-level image features – for example an assumption that it is the darkest region that does the 'looking'.

Studies of perceptual adaptation to gaze direction have provided evidence of how we represent gaze signals. R. Jenkins, Beaver and Calder (2006) explored the effect of prolonged adaptation to eye gaze directed to one side of an observer on subsequent ability to discriminate small deviations of gaze from the straight ahead direction. In a pre-adaptation phase, participants saw faces whose gaze varied from 10 degrees leftward to 10 degrees rightward in steps of 5 degrees. They were asked to decide if each face was looking left, right or straight ahead. Accuracy was almost 100% for the 10-degree shifts, though only 71% for 5-degree shifts, which were often judged as straight ahead. Straight-ahead faces were judged correctly on 87% of trials. Following about 5 minutes of adaptation to a series of different faces seen gazing consistently 25 degrees to the left or 25 degrees to the right, there was a clear direction-specific after-effect on the judged direction of gaze in a post-adaptation test. Now the majority of faces looking 10 degrees or 5 degrees in the adapted direction were judged as looking straight ahead. Figure 5.5 plots the results of this experiment.

In fact, Figure 5.5 shows both an expected and an unexpected pattern. The expected pattern is that adaptation to leftward or rightward eye gaze affected subsequent perception of gaze in the adapted direction (as we have described), but the unexpected pattern is that judgements in the direction opposite to adaptation remained largely unaffected. In other words, adapting to a face with eyes looking to the right affected later perception of faces with rightward gaze, but did not affect perception of faces with leftward gaze. This is unexpected because it is different from the results of other face adaptation studies, where the typical pattern is one of an after-effect in a direction that is simply the opposite of whatever was adapted. The typical adaptation result therefore suggests some form of opponent-coding of facial properties, whereas the results for gaze adaptation are a better fit with a multi-channel system in which separate pools of cells code leftward, direct or rightward gaze (Calder, Jenkins, Cassel, & Clifford, 2008), allowing one of these cell populations to be fatigued independently from the others. As Calder et al. (2008) point out, there may be more than just three channels, but the case for some kind of multichannel system offers a potentially valuable way of gaining insight into the mechanism involved.

Gaze involves more than just the eyes

So far we have discussed the perception of gaze as though the eyes were seen in isolation, but actually the entire context within which eyes are perceived is

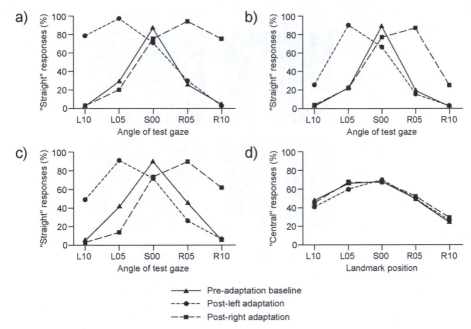

Figure 5.5 Results of the pre- and post-adaptation tests in experiments reported by R. Jenkins et al. (2006). In graph (a) is shown the proportion of times the gaze was judged as 'straight ahead' at each of the five different gaze angles (X axis) as a function of adapation to leftward or rightward gaze. Adaptation is unaffected by a change in size (b) or head orientation (c) between adapting and test faces. In contrast (d) shows that adapting to gaze does not influence the judged spatial position of non-social stimuli (lines). Rob Jenkins, John D. Beaver, Andrew J. Calder, *Psychological Science*, 17.6, pp. 506–513, copyright © 2006 by Sage Publications, Reprinted by Permission of SAGE Publications.

important. As this chapter develops, we will describe some rather complex contextual influences. For now we start with the local physical context of the rest of the face and head.

J. Jenkins and Langton (2003) examined how sensitivity to gaze shifts was affected by the orientation of the eye region and head, with these manipulated independently (see Figure 5.6) so that the eye region and the head could each be presented upright or inverted. Participants were presented with pictures of the eye region (a horizontal strip with both eyes and the eyebrows) showing a gaze direction that was any one of 48 directions varying from 13.8 degrees leftwards to 13.8 degrees rightwards, including straight ahead. The eye region was either presented in isolation or accompanied by a 'full-face' view head, which could be upright or upside down. Participants were asked to decide whether the eyes in each image were looking to their left or to their right. If they were unable to tell, then they would respond on average only 50% correctly to a given gaze displacement. As the displacements away from direct gaze became more visible, so

Eyes Upright   Eyes Inverted

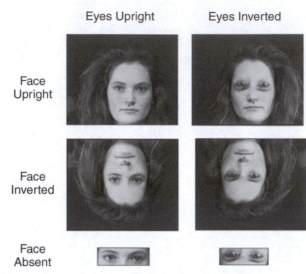

Face Upright

Face Inverted

Face Absent

Figure 5.6 Materials used by Jenkins and Langton (2003). First published in *Perception*, 32(10), pp. 1181–1188, Jenkins, J., Langton, S. R. H., 2003, Configural processing in the perception of eye-gaze direction, courtesy of Pion Limited, London.

performance would increase until at large displacements participants would be 100% correct. This psychophysical approach thus allowed the calculation of threshold displacements for the detection of leftwards or rightwards direction. Thresholds could be calculated from individual participants for the average gaze displacement that yielded 75% correct 'rightward' decisions to right-gazing eyes and 25% 'rightward' decisions to left-gazing faces.

Jenkins and Langton's (2003) results are summarised in Figure 5.7. The performance thresholds were affected by the orientation of both the eye region and the head. When the eyes were presented alone, thresholds were marginally higher (i.e. performance was less accurate) when the eye region was inverted than when it was upright. When there was a face context for the eyes, though, the effect of inverting the eye region was much greater – remarkably, this happened whether the face context was upright or inverted. So the impairment of gaze perception that results from inverting the eye region is amplified by providing a facial context – pointing to the involvement of some kind of analysis that tries to combine information from the eye region with the rest of the face in detecting where someone else is looking. Put simply, we can use information from the eye region if it is presented in isolation, but if a face context is added, this does not get ignored. What is remarkable, though, is that the face context can itself be upright or inverted – either seems to make the inversion of the eye region more noticeable (see Figure 5.6). There are aspects of Figure 5.6 that are reminiscent of the Thatcher illusion (Figure 4.17) – and at present just as inexplicable!

A pointer to why the eyes do not get analysed completely in isolation from the rest of the head may lie in the fact that everyday shifts in gaze direction often involve turning both the eyes and the head. In Jenkins and Langton's study, all

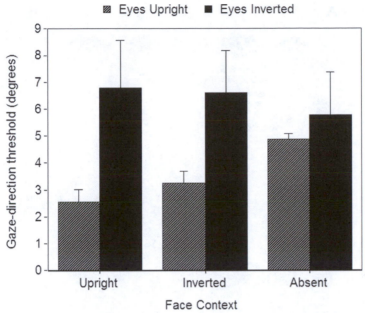

Figure 5.7 Results obtained by Jenkins and Langton (2003). See text for description.

the head views were full-face and the overall orientation of the framework of the head within the picture plane affected the perception of eye gaze rather little, but the presence or absence of this framework made a difference. Real heads, however, rotate from left to right in three dimensions, and movements within the picture plane are more limited. What is the effect of *head turning* on the perceived direction of gaze?

A fascinating demonstration was constructed by William Wollaston (1824; see Wade, 1998). Figure 5.8 shows illustrations taken from Wollaston's paper. In the upper two pictures, the face on the left seems to look directly at the viewer, whereas the face on the right seems to look slightly to one side. In fact, however, the eye regions of both pictures are identical – only the lower part of each drawing has been changed. The same effect is apparent in the lower two pictures in Figure 5.8, which show that even with realistic photographic stimuli one gets the same impression. Wollaston (1824) pointed out that this phenomenon demonstrates that we do not base our judgement of gaze direction *solely* on the position of the iris and pupil relative to the whites of the eyes – instead, this is combined with information about head direction.

> ...the apparent direction of the eyes to or from the spectator depends on the balance of two circumstances combined in the same representation, namely first – the general position of the face presented to the spectator; and secondly – the turn of the eyes from that position.
> (Wollaston, 1824, as reproduced by Wade, 1998, punctuation updated by us)

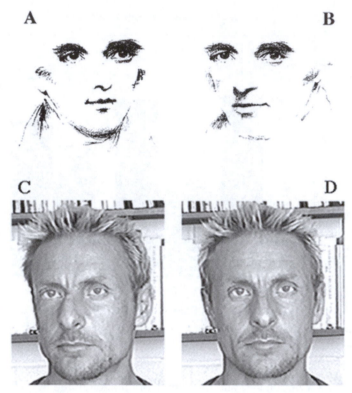

Figure 5.8 The two faces drawn at the top, and photographed below, appear to look in different directions. In each pair, the eyes are identical, but are shown in different face contexts. From Langton et al. (2004). With kind permission from Springer Science+Business Media: The influence of head contour and nose angle on the perception of eye-gaze direction. *Attention, Perception & Psychophysics*, 66, 2004, Stephen R. H. Langton.

Langton, Honeyman and Tessler (2004) showed that Wollaston was substantially correct. They investigated systematically the influence of the rest of the head on the apparent direction of the eyes within it. In a series of experiments, participants were shown brief, masked pictures and asked to decide whether or not the eyes were looking straight ahead. The displays showed eyes alone, or eyes accompanied by a context of the external head outline, the internal feature of the nose, or both. This context provided by the head outline, nose outline, or head plus nose could indicate a gaze direction that was *congruent* with the eye direction, or *incongruent* (see Figure 5.9 for an illustration of some of these conditions).

Langton et al. (2004) found that decisions about whether the eyes were looking straight ahead were made more accurately when the context shown was congruent than when it was absent, showing that the context can enhance gaze direction even when it gives the same information as the eyes alone. Conversely, incongruent contexts made gaze direction detection worse than when the eyes

Absent   Congruent   Incongruent

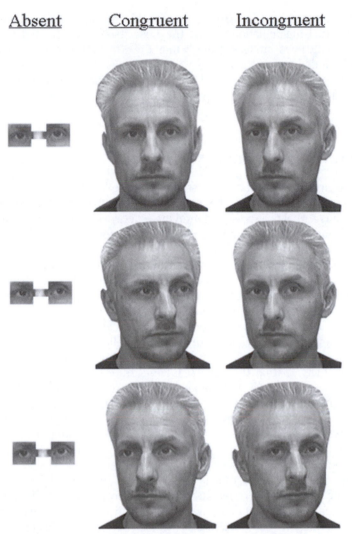

Figure 5.9 Materials used by Langton et al. (2004) in their first experiment to examine the effect of context (head plus internal features) on gaze direction decisions. With kind permission from Springer Science+Business Media: The influence of head contour and nose angle on the perception of eye-gaze direction. *Attention, Perception & Psychophysics, 66*, 2004, Stephen R. H. Langton.

were seen alone – indicating that the contextual influence cannot be ignored. Langton et al.'s (2004) first experiment showed this effect strongly when the context was the head and internal facial features. Their second experiment showed similar results when the context was provided only by the head profile with internal features apart from the eyes rendered invisible. In a third experiment the head profile remained oriented in a constant – face-on – direction, but the direction pointed by the nose within the head was altered by image-processing (giving the impression of a broken nose within the face in some conditions). This contextual manipulation of just the nose itself also affected accuracy of responses to the eyes, but less strongly than the effects shown when head outline was also included within the context. So it looks as though the computation of where someone is looking does not rely only on information about eye position, but automatically combines this with other relevant information about head direction.

Neural mechanisms of gaze perception

The recent upsurge in behavioural studies of gaze has been accompanied by a great deal of interesting research into the neural mechanisms of gaze perception. These studies reveal progress in identifying a network of different areas that are implicated and some of their functional contributions, but with various unanswered questions at the time of writing.

Much of the more recent research builds upon pioneering work on face-responsive cells in macaque monkey cortex. These cells were first noted by Gross, Rocha-Miranda and Bender (1972), and later studied in detail by Gross and colleagues (C. Bruce, Desimone, & Gross, 1981), and by Perrett, Rolls and Caan (1982). The studies involve electrophysiological recording from single cells in the monkey's brain – usually in the temporal lobes, and often along the STS. Early studies were (necessarily) devoted to establishing the existence of a degree of face-selectivity, in that the cells responded more strongly to faces than to images of other symmetrical, arousing (e.g. snakes), or important (e.g. food) objects. Some of the face-responsive cells initially investigated by Perrett and colleagues seemed to be viewpoint-specific – e.g. responding to full-face but not profile views of faces, and vice versa. Others seemed to be identity-specific – e.g. responding to any view of, say, Perrett's face more than to faces of other humans or monkeys.

Single-cell recording studies are important in that they measure brain activity directly, but they are also difficult to interpret correctly. The most widely studied region, STS, is a structure that runs the entire length of the temporal lobe and contains many millions of neurons. Making sense of the firing patterns of a small selection of these neurons is fraught with potential pitfalls. One of the earliest pitfalls proved to be inferring from the observations presented above that these studies were tapping into a neural network that represented the identities of individual faces in an increasingly viewpoint-independent fashion. This seemed appealing in terms of then fashionable hierarchic models of the representations needed for visual recognition based on Marr's (1982) ideas, but it immediately faced two substantial problems. First, STS is not a critical region of damage in human cases of acquired inability to recognise faces (prosopagnosia). Precisely how problematic this was depended on how much one expected homology between the functional organisation of monkey and human brains – an issue that remains incompletely resolved (Tsao, Moeller, & Freiwald, 2008). More serious, though, was the second problem, which was that surgically removing parts of STS where face-responsive cells are located did not make monkeys prosopagnosic (Heywood & Cowey, 1992) – this made a persuasive case that monkey STS is performing some other task than recognising face identity.

Perrett's studies of face-responsive cells had always been strongly grounded in astute ethological observation, and Perrett et al. (1992) pointed out that many of the cells that responded to specific face viewpoints might be better understood as cells that coded for a particular direction of attention. In support, they pointed out that cells that 'liked' full-face images often stopped responding if the eyes in the face were averted. Conversely, some of those that responded best to an angled view stopped responding if the eyes gazed towards the camera from that angled view.

This work helped pave the way for frameworks such as Haxby et al. (2000) which see the STS as implicated in the processing of dynamic changes in faces, particularly as these are relevant for social cognition. Consistent with this, although surgical ablation of the STS region in monkeys did not lead to deficits in face recognition, it did create deficits in gaze perception (Campbell, Heywood, Cowey, Regard, & Landis, 1990; Heywood & Cowey, 1992). Note, though, that it is mainly the posterior part of STS that is included in Haxby et al.'s (2000) core system (see Figure 1.30). There is no doubt that posterior STS is an important region, but as we will see there is also evidence from human as well as primate research that the entire STS is involved in gaze perception. Separating the contributions of different parts of STS has proved tricky, but we will look at some of the factors that may be involved.

Key studies for the development of Haxby et al.'s (2000) model were conducted by Hoffman and Haxby (2000). In their first experiment, participants were asked to detect whether or not successive face images matched one another on gaze direction or on identity. Examples of Hoffman and Haxby's (2000) stimuli are shown in Figure 5.10. Trials were presented in blocks, with a cue at the start of each block instructing the participant to attend to gaze or to identity. When the task was to attend to face identity, fMRI activation was stronger in regions corresponding to the OFA and FFA (see Chapter 1 for an explanation of OFA and FFA, and their roles in the Haxby et al. model). When the task was to match gaze direction, activation was strongest in the left posterior STS. A particularly interesting aspect of this first experiment is that regional brain activity seems to be modulated by what the participant is doing – not simply by the stimuli themselves. However, a second experiment with passive viewing of the stimuli showed that posterior STS but not OFA and FFA showed sensitivity to whether gaze was direct or averted.

Human neuropsychological evidence is consistent with the suggestion that whilst the fusiform gyrus is involved in perceiving identity it does not contribute substantially to perception of gaze, whereas STS is very important to gaze perception. However, the studies are not as extensive as might be expected, given the importance of the issue.

What happens if there is damage to the STS region in humans? Akiyama, Kato, Muramatsu, Saito, Nakachi, and Kashima (2006) report an interesting case study of a Japanese woman, MJ, who suffered a stroke which resulted in damage confined almost entirely to the superior temporal gyrus (the upper bank of STS) in her right hemisphere. The most striking aspect of MJ's behaviour was her

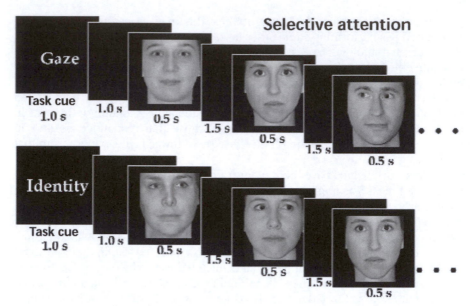

Figure 5.10 An illustration of the trial structure used in Hoffman and Haxby's (2000) study. Reprinted by permission from Macmillan Publishers Ltd: *Nature Neuroscience*, Elizabeth A. Hoffman and James V. Haxby, Distinct representations of eye gaze and identity in the distributed human neural system for face perception, *3*, 1. Copyright 2000.

difficulty in maintaining eye contact with another person. She was also hemianopic, so her ability to make judgements of gaze direction was compared with three hemianopic patients as well as normal control participants. She was significantly more impaired at gaze judgements than any of the comparison participants. This rare neuropsychological case thus adds support to the proposal that the STS region may play a key role in gaze perception in humans, though this single case alone may be open to other interpretations (Nummenmaa & Calder, 2009).

An obvious contrast to make is with case studies of acquired prosopagnosia, where the critical region of occipito-temporal damage that creates a severe deficit of face recognition is near the bottom of the brain and does not usually extend to STS. We might therefore expect that perception of gaze direction could be spared in prosopagnosia.

The evidence to date is limited. The first study was reported by Campbell et al. (1990) who investigated gaze perception in two cases of prosopagnosia. Their first case, KD, had suffered a right posterior cerebral artery stroke, leading to an acquired prosopagnosia. In a test of deciding which of two faces was looking directly at the viewer, KD was able to make correct decisions when the difference in gaze was as large as 20 degrees, was more than 80% correct with a 10-degree difference, but was at chance level (50% correct) once the difference reached 5 degrees. She therefore showed relatively (though not entirely) preserved perception of gaze direction compared to identity.

In contrast, Campbell et al.'s second case, AB, was very poor both at recognising identity and at judging gaze direction. However, AB was a congenital case, so to what extent her neurodevelopmental problems might have extended to STS was unknown. She did, though, show a very interesting behavioural dissociation – Campbell et al. (1990) showed that AB could judge the direction in which a line was pointing and make discriminations between eye-like stimuli. Examples of Campbell et al.'s (1990) stimuli are shown in Figure 5.11 – the tasks are to choose which dot the arrow points to, or identify which of the configurations of circles is the odd one out. Remarkably, AB scored 20/20 correct on both of these tasks. She was therefore able to judge the direction of a line – showing that her problem with gaze direction was not part of a generalised spatial deficit. She could even make discriminations between the eye-like circles stimuli – which contain cues comparable to some of those needed to judge gaze direction. Yet AB's perception of direction of gaze was at chance in the forced-choice task of deciding which of two faces was looking at her.

Fascinating though these behavioural findings for case AB may be, a recent report by Duchaine et al. (2009) shows they are atypical. Duchaine et al. (2009)

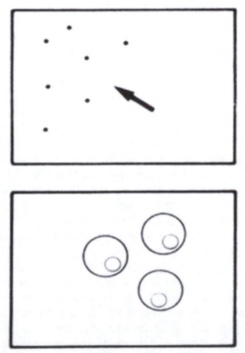

Figure 5.11 Examples of test materials used by Campbell et al. (1990) in the tasks described in the text. Reprinted from *Neuropsychologia*, *28*, 11, R. Campbell, C. A. Heywood, A. Cowey, M. Regard, T. Landis, Sensitivity to eye gaze in prosopagnosic patients and monkeys with superior temporal sulcus ablation, pp. 1123–1142. Copyright 1990 with permission from Elsevier.

225

studied seven prosopagnosic individuals, of whom six were congenital cases and one had an acquired brain injury from a ruptured aneurysm in the posterior right hemisphere and consequent subarachnoid haemorrhage. This type of case series approach is a useful way of demonstrating what patterns of spared and impaired abilities are typical or relatively unusual for a given neuropsychological condition. All seven of the individuals studied by Duchaine et al. (2009) showed normal discrimination of eye gaze direction despite face identity recognition impairments of varying severity. Moreover, all seven showed a normal pattern of adaptation to eye gaze direction with the behavioural paradigm used by Jenkins et al. (2006). This is important because we saw in Chapter 2 that neuropsychological patients can sometimes achieve a normal overall level of performance on a specific task by deploying an unusual strategy. The normal pattern of adaptation noted by Duchaine et al. (2009) showed that the mechanism for perceiving gaze as well as the level of performance was normal.

Such findings make an interesting contrast with recent claims that it is perception of the eye region that is particularly impaired when people with prosopagnosia try to recognise identity (Barton, 2008; Caldara et al., 2005). This could be of real theoretical significance if we knew whether the prosopagnosic individuals who have particular problems in perceiving the eye region do or do not have equivalent problems interpreting gaze direction. There is a lot of scope for further studies.

In the meantime, it is clear that recognition of gaze perception can be relatively spared in prosopagnosia. However, in discussing why even Campbell et al.'s (1990) relatively intact case KD might not have shown such well-preserved gaze perception as the individuals they studied, Duchaine et al. (2009) drew attention to a potentially important procedural point. In their tests of gaze direction perception, Duchaine et al. (2009) asked their participants to judge gaze from full-face photographs, whereas Campbell et al.'s (1990) test stimuli included differences in both eye and head orientations. The gaze findings may therefore fit an overall pattern that comes up persistently in other studies of prosopagnosia – namely that whilst familiar face recognition is severely impaired and other face perception abilities are relatively spared, the spared abilities are seldom completely normal when thoroughly investigated. The point is worth keeping in mind because of the evidence that, behaviourally, eye and head orientation cues are integrated in normal gaze perception (Jenkins & Langton, 2003; Wollaston, 1824). Again, there is a lot of scope for future work.

Given the evidence from behavioural findings that information about eye and head position is combined in perceiving gaze direction, it is interesting to know that this also seems to hold for face-responsive cells in monkey STS. For example, a cell described by Perrett et al. (1992) responded to a head looking downwards, or to eyes pointing downwards, but not to the same face looking at the camera or upwards. It therefore seemed to be interested in a downward gaze direction, rather than head or eye position per se. Moreover, body postures could also affect some of the same cells (see Figure 5.12). The cell that responded to a head looking downwards also responded when a human figure was shown in quadrupedal position with its head pointing down, even if the head itself was occluded, but did not respond if the figure was standing upright (for a monkey

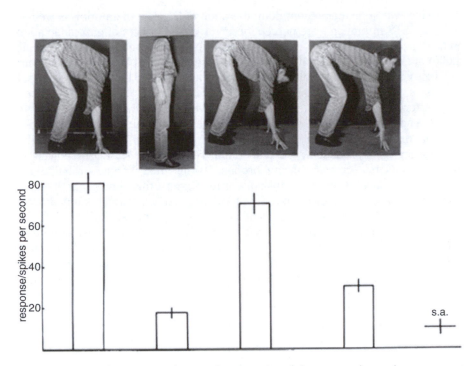

Figure 5.12 At the top are shown photographs of the materials used to test sensitivity of cells in Perrett et al.'s (1992) studies. Below is shown the response for one particular cell which was most responsive to quadrepedal posture but not when the head was pointing upwards. First published in Perrett, D. I., Hietenan, J. K., Oram, M. W. and Benson, P. J. Organization and functions of cells responsive to faces in the temporal cortex. *Philosophical Transactions of the Royal Society of London Ser. B, 335*, pp. 23–30. Copyright (1992) The Royal Society.

this would mean it was attending to the horizon, not the ground) or if the body was on all fours but the head pointed upwards.

Consistent with these primate findings, Lee et al. (2010) used complementary fMRI and MEG neuroimaging methods to demonstrate human brain responses to shifts of gaze signalled from a combination of eye and head movement along the entire length of the STS. The MEG data showed a response that extended along the entire STS but peaked in the right anterior region within the first 500 ms of stimulus presentation, pointing to a definite role for anterior as well as posterior parts of the STS in the analysis of shifts in social attention. A similar combined fMRI and MEG study by Sato et al. (2008) showed an even earlier posterior STS response (within 200 ms) to gaze direction signalled by the eyes only, without any change of head orientation. More broadly, fMRI studies find that posterior superior temporal cortex includes a mosaic of regions responsive to biological motion, in which neural activity can be elicited by eyes, mouths, bodies, hands and even pointing fingers (Allison, Puce, & McCarthy, 2000; Materna, Dicke, & Thier, 2009; Pelphrey, Morris, Michelich, Allison, & McCarthy, 2005).

However, a further recent demonstration of the role of anterior as well as posterior STS in human gaze perception involves the effects of gaze adaptation on fMRI activity. The behavioural adaptation effects described by R. Jenkins et al. (2006) are mirrored in responses measured using fMR-adaptation in the anterior STS (see Chapter 2 for an explanation of fMR-adaptation and the BOLD response) and also in the inferior parietal cortex (an important area in attention more generally). After adaptation to faces with leftward eye gaze, BOLD responses to leftward but not rightward-gazing faces were reduced in the anterior STS and inferior parietal cortex (Calder et al., 2007). Conversely, adaptation to faces with rightward-gazing eyes produced a corresponding reduction in BOLD responses in these regions to rightward-gazing probes. As for their behavioural findings (Calder et al., 2008), Calder and his colleagues suggest this shows that the anterior STS in humans is involved in coding gaze direction via distinct populations of neurons tuned to different directions of face gaze (Calder et al., 2007).

An interesting idea proposed by Hein and Knight (2008) is that some (but not all) of the apparent differences between regions of STS may not be entirely due to a fixed set of functional subdivisions, but instead reflect more flexible task-related interactions with other parts of the frontal and temporal lobes. This may help to make sense of the diversity of findings that are resulting from functional imaging studies of this sophisticated region, and brings us to important issues concerned with the different uses we make of perceived gaze.

What uses do we make of gaze?

So far, we have mainly discussed how brains interpret where images of faces and eyes are looking. It is obviously fundamental to understand this. But now we must move on to the remarkable, almost bewildering, variety of uses we can make of information from other people's gaze.

One way to approach the issue is to ask how gaze interacts with other cues. In this respect, a particularly important potential interaction is between gaze and expression. In Haxby et al.'s (2000) neurological model, of course, both gaze and expression are changeable aspects of our faces. Gaze, however, is signalled from rigid movements of the eyes and head (rigid in the sense that they do not change shape as they rotate), whereas expressions are communicated through non-rigid movements of internal facial features, as discussed in Chapter 4. In the light of this it is interesting that Engell and Haxby (2007) found that STS responses to gaze and expression were only partially overlapping.

Unfortunately, the standard Garner interference technique has produced mixed results for gaze and expression – Graham and LaBar (2007) found that expression interfered with gaze judgements but expression judgements were not affected by gaze, whereas Ganel, Goshen-Gottstein and Goodale (2005) reported symmetrical interference between gaze and expression. Adams and Kleck (2003) found that direct gaze facilitated the perception of anger and happiness, while averted gaze facilitated fear and sadness. Other behavioural techniques also show complex interactions between gaze and expression (Bindemann, Burton, &

Langton, 2008) and gaze and other aspects of person perception (Macrae, Hood, Milne, Rowe, & Mason, 2002; Mason, Tatkow, & Macrae, 2005).

Some of these interactions of gaze and expression are easy to understand – if someone looks angry and they are looking at you, it is more intimidating than if they are staring at someone else! Similarly, amygdala responses to fearful facial expressions can be modulated by a gaze direction that suggests danger in the environment (Hadjikhani, Hoge, Snyder, & de Gelder, 2008). Other findings are less immediately obvious, but make sense. When we see someone look at something, we tend not only to look at it too, but even to like it more (Bayliss, Paul, Cannon, & Tipper, 2006). Conversely, if a face gives us unreliable cues to the location of a target, we deem it untrustworthy – especially if it was smiling when it misled us (Bayliss, Griffiths, & Tipper, 2009).

However, in listing such findings we are only scratching the surface of a complex topic. We just hope we have scratched it hard enough for you to see that the question of what uses we make of other people's gaze sounds simple, but the answer is actually complicated. We need a way to tease apart some of the things we can do with gaze. A shift from eye contact to an averted gaze may direct our attention so that we look at what another person looks at, and this is an important ingredient of sharing attention (you and I are now looking at the same thing). The basic skill of using gaze direction to infer what a person is looking at is developed in infancy, and used to establish shared foci of attention between babies and their carers – most 9-month-old babies can do it (Scaife & Bruner, 1975). This use of eye gaze as a 'pointer' is likely to facilitate the acquisition of vocabulary items, and facilitates other kinds of activities that require that one person alerts another person to some item or area of space.

But averted gaze may also occur when someone we are talking to is thinking or lying or feeling ashamed, and we are unlikely to follow their gaze heavenwards or down to the floor under such circumstances. Direct gaze which results in mutual eye contact is an important ingredient in interactions between babies and their caretakers, but may be used by adults (and parents!) to exercise social control or to threaten, as well as being used between lovers to express their intimacy. So, the same physical cue of direct gaze from someone can lead you to look away, or to look back – depending on the context and the person doing the looking. Gaze is also used in complex ways in conversation. It is part of how we regulate turn-taking, where establishing slightly longer than usual eye contact at the end of an utterance is one of the signals that it is the listener's turn to speak, or we can glance at another person to check their understanding or approval, or look at them to seek information or clarification (Kleinke, 1986).

People therefore become very adept at using gaze and eye contact to make inferences about liking and attraction, attentiveness, competence, credibility and even the mental health of others. In recent years, cognitive scientists have suggested that gaze perception is at the heart of more profound abilities still – our understanding of how other people's minds have beliefs, desires and intentions different from our own.

In many circumstances, different uses of gaze will be inextricably intertwined. To organise and make sense of the range of findings, though, we will separate them according to different kinds of use highlighted above – attentional mechanisms, social functions, and mental state inferences. We begin with mental state inferences.

Gaze and mental state

It is easy for us to use patterns of gaze to infer which person is *thinking* in Figure 5.13 (top), or which object the cartoon character *wants* in Figure 5.13 (bottom),

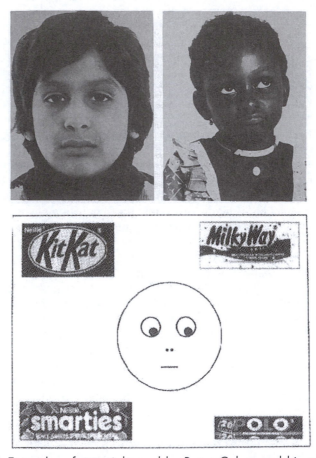

Figure 5.13 Examples of materials used by Baron-Cohen and his colleagues. At the top, which of these faces is 'thinking'? At the bottom, which sweets does the person in the middle 'want'? Top panel from Simon Baron-Cohen, Pippa Cross, Reading the eyes: Evidence for the role of perception in the development of a theory of mind, *Mind & Language, 7*, pp. 172–186. Copyright 1992 John Wiley & Sons Ltd. Bottom panel from Baron-Cohen, S., Campbell, R., Karmiloff-Smith, A., Grant, J. & Walker, J (1995) Are children with autism blind to the mentalistic significance of the eyes?. *British Journal of Developmental Psychology, 13,* pp. 379–398, John Wiley & Sons.

despite the schematic face depicted there. Baron-Cohen and his colleagues (e.g. Baron-Cohen, Campbell, Karmiloff-Smith, Grant, & Walker, 1995; Baron-Cohen & Cross, 1992) have shown that typically developing children can answer questions like these very accurately at about 4 years old.

Baron-Cohen and his colleagues have suggested that the perception of gaze is a fundamental building block of our capacity to understand other people's mental states, just as the perception of emotion is a key building block in our capacity to empathise – to understand other people's emotional states. These capacities develop over the first few years of life, but the normal developed system proposed by Baron-Cohen (2005) is shown in Figure 5.14.

According to Baron-Cohen (e.g. 2005), three initial core abilities are required to understand other mental and emotional states fully. These are The Emotion Detector (TED), the Eye Direction Detector (EDD) and the Intentionality Detector (ID). Via the Shared Attention Mechanism (SAM), which develops by the age of about one year, the typically developing infant and later adult can understand other mental states via the Theory of Mind Mechanism (TOMM), and also empathise using TESS – The Empathising SyStem (*sic*). The details of this theory are speculative and hence controversial – evidence for some of the suggested mechanisms is largely a matter of interpretation. The important point for our purposes here is only that, according to this theory, face perception and shared attention form foundational skills upon which more complex social competence depends. It therefore predicts a strong link between gaze perception and the understanding of mental states – an ability now widely known as 'theory of mind'. This predicted relationship has generated a lot of interest.

Investigations into theory of mind have been important and wide-ranging and we cannot in this book do justice to the range of developmental,

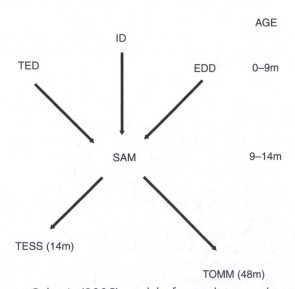

Figure 5.14 Baron-Cohen's (2005) model of mentalising and empathising. See text for the key to these acronyms.

neuropsychological and comparative questions studied on this topic (Apperly, 2010; Emery & Clayton, 2009). However, we do need to look at work on autism, which has been of central importance. Autism is a disabling neurodevelopmental disorder characterised by a triad of symptoms involving impaired social interaction, poor communication, and restricted interests and repetitive behaviours. Autism was originally associated with low intelligence, but modern diagnosis has become less categorical and brought this range of deficits under the umbrella title 'Autistic Spectrum Disorder' (ASD) which includes Asperger's syndrome, a related but less disabling condition. People with ASD can therefore vary in overall intellectual ability from severe impairments to average or above average intelligence. This wide spectrum of characteristics and abilities has to be borne in mind when interpreting studies of their social cognitive abilities.

Theories attempting to account for autism were palpably unsatisfactory until the seminal work of Baron-Cohen, Leslie and Frith (1985), who suggested that a core deficit in autism is in theory of mind – that is, in understanding that other people can have different beliefs, desires and intentions from your own. To demonstrate this, Baron-Cohen et al. (1985) used a task involving two dolls, Sally and Anne, who act out a short scenario in which Sally puts a marble in a basket and then leaves, but Anne takes the marble while Sally is gone, and puts it in a box. The experimental task is for the participant who has watched this scenario to decide where Sally will look for her marble when she comes back. As you can see, to answer correctly you have to understand that Sally doesn't know the marble has been moved, and use the implications of her belief that the marble should be where she left it to discount your own knowledge of where it really is now. Control questions are also used to establish that what happened was understood and remembered, but the key question concerns where Sally will look for her marble. Children with autism will often fail this task, whereas normally developing 4 year olds and children with other conditions that result in intellectual impairments (such as Down's syndrome) can usually pass it. The problem for people with autism seems to be with understanding other people's mental states, not a lack of intelligence per se.

Of course the Sally-Anne task used by Baron-Cohen et al. (1985) is not directly to do with gaze perception at all – it (deliberately) forms a relatively pure test of theory of mind. The reason we are discussing it is because Baron-Cohen's overall theoretical position postulates a strong link between gaze perception and theory of mind. So if theory of mind ability builds upon understanding gaze and shared attention, how do people with autism fare on such tasks? To approach this issue, we need to separate ability to perceive gaze direction (i.e. to know where someone is looking) from ability to interpret the meaning of gaze (that is, to make inferences about why they are looking in that direction). With this in mind, we turn to the evidence.

Participants with autism are usually able to perceive gaze direction in simple displays. For example, Baron-Cohen et al. (1995) showed that children with autism of about 13 years of age could answer correctly which item the person was looking at in displays like Figure 5.13. Leekam et al. (1997) conducted a more systematic study of eye gaze perception by school-aged children with autism. The two groups were equally good at deciding which of three rods, which varied in separation by different amounts, was being looked at by a photographed person, where head and eye gaze cues were varied so that head direction alone could not be used to solve the task. So it seems that people with autism are capable of perceiving the geometric properties of gaze. However, Baron-Cohen et al. (1995) and Riby, Doherty-Sneddon and Bruce (2008) found participants with autism to be less good at answering questions about gaze direction in naturalistic photographs in which head as well as eye directions varied, suggesting their abilities in this sphere are not entirely normal.

There are clear impairments in participants with autism when the questions to be answered are about which item in a display like Figure 5.13b the schematic person *wants* – a question that requires a mental state inference. Baron-Cohen et al. (1995) found that their ASD group averaged only 60% correct on average at choosing the sweets that Charlie was looking at as being those he wanted, compared with scores of over 90% correct in a typically developing group of 4 year olds and learning disabled control groups (aged around 6) of similar mental age to the much older people with autism.

One problem with interpreting these initial findings was that correctly answering a question like 'which sweets does Charlie want?' requires that the child's own preference and desire for, say, Smarties, must be overcome in order to say that Charlie wants the Polo mints he is looking at. Ames and Jarrold (2007) replicated and extended Baron-Cohen et al.'s (1995) initial findings by examining systematically how much salience and preference for particular items might be responsible for choices which departed from the 'correct' one. While salience and task-relevant learning clearly played a role in performance of these tasks, Ames and Jarrold nevertheless replicated the earlier results. Their teenaged participants with ASD (aged around 14 years) performed substantially worse both than much younger (aged about 5–6 years) typically developing children with similar intellectual level to the ASD group, and than a group with moderate learning disabilities (aged around 14 years).

So individuals with autism seem to lack understanding of what gaze signifies in mentalistic terms. Moreover, children with autism often avoid eye contact and other kinds of shared attention. In Leekam et al.'s (1997) study such children were less likely to follow an adult's change in head and eye direction than control children were. Such problems appear to be evident early in development. While diagnoses of ASD are not given until a child is two years old or older, Nation and Penny (2008) review retrospective observations of home videos of babies later diagnosed with autism, and prospective studies of babies known to be at risk of autism, that reveal abnormalities in their social orientations. Babies who will later be diagnosed with ASD spend less time looking at people or making eye contact than typically developing babies. Chawarska, Klin and Volkmar (2003) demonstrated this very clearly in naturalistic but structured interactions with 2-year-old children with autism. Fifteen such children were tested. All of them attended to a toy when it was placed in front of them or made to move, but not one of them looked at the toy when the experimenter looked at it. They all failed the kind of test of shared attention that typically developing children of the same age pass.

Older children with autism engage in eye contact less than their typically developing peers. Senju and Johnson (2009a) review theories of why this may be.

'Hyperarousal' models (e.g. Dalton et al., 2005) propose that eye contact is actually aversive for people with ASD, though this is not fully supported by evidence. But there is certainly lots of evidence that ASD participants are, at best, indifferent to faces and do not look at them in contexts where control participants do. Riby and Hancock (2008) recorded eye movements to investigate where children looked when shown natural pictures of scenes including people under no specific constraints or instructions. Typically developing children tended to look at faces but also looked at other objects in the visual scenes. In marked contrast to typically developing children of the same age, or of the same non-verbal ability, ASD participants looked anywhere except at the human faces in the scene. Either they were actively avoiding faces, or faces simply don't have the significant properties that draw the attention of typically developing people.

Senju, Yaguchi, Tojo and Hasegawa (2003) compared 12-year-old children with autism with typically developing children of the same age in a detection task where the children were asked to detect rarely occurring 'odd' faces in a series of faces where most looked downwards. Odd ones showed gaze averted to left or right or direct gaze to the camera. The typically developing children spotted the direct gaze targets better than the averted gaze targets but the children with autism showed no difference between direct and averted gaze targets. They detected the averted targets as well as the control children, but failed to show the facilitation from the direct gaze. A follow-up ERP study by Senju, Tojo, Yaguchi and Hasegawa (2005) revealed electrophysiological differences between the two groups. An occipito-temporal negative component that was lateralised to the right hemisphere in the control group and greater in amplitude for direct gaze faces was not lateralised, and not sensitive to direct gaze, in participants with autism. However, children and adults with autism can show strong effects of direct gaze with schematic faces and are less affected by inversion of faces, suggesting that they process gazing faces in a more piecemeal way and are less affected by the whole face context (Senju, Hasegawa, & Tojo, 2005; Senju, Kikuchi, Hasegawa, Tojo & Osanai, 2008).

Other functional neuroimaging studies also show neural correlates of problems with gaze interpretation in autism. A particularly impressive study by Pelphrey, Morris and McCarthy (2005) used fMRI to demonstrate abnormalities in the right STS response to the meaning of a gaze shift for participants with autism. In Pelphrey, Morris and McCarthy's (2005) paradigm, participants watched a computer-animated face whilst a small flickering chequerboard pattern appeared in the character's field of view. The character's eye gaze then shifted towards or away from the flickering pattern, in a way that was congruent (shift gaze to see what is going on) or incongruent (shift gaze away from the new focus of interest) with normal gaze behaviour. In neurologically normal participants, the incongruent trials generate larger neural response in right STS – presumably as participants try to make sense of the aberrant gaze shift. In participants with autism, right STS responded to changes in gaze but did not differentiate between congruent or incongruent shifts.

So people with autism have some proficiencies with basic gaze perception, but striking problems in terms of the significance that gaze has for them. Once again, data implicate STS as a critical region, and fMRI studies of neurologically normal participants also point to this region's importance in evaluating as well as perceiving gaze (Pelphrey, Morris, & McCarthy, 2005; Pelphrey, Singerman, Allison, & McCarthy, 2003). However, STS is not the whole story. An important hypothesis proposed by Brothers (1990) is that STS forms part of an evolved 'social brain' network for social cognition that includes other regions of temporal and orbito-frontal cortex, as well as the amygdala. Functional imaging studies of gaze perception often find activation in this more broadly defined network (Calder et al., 2002), and neuroimaging studies also point to the temporo-parietal junction's involvement in theory of mind (Saxe & Kanwisher, 2003). In reviewing the social brain literature Frith (2007) noted that it still fits Brothers' perspective surprisingly well, though research attention has predictably shifted to what sepa-rable contributions the components of this social brain network might be making. Apperly, Samson, Chiavarino and Humphreys (2004) identified theory of mind deficits in false-belief tasks for neuropsychological patients with temporo-parietal or frontal lobe lesions, but showed that different contributory factors underlay these impairments – consistent with the idea that theory of mind is itself a constel-lation of abilities, not a specific 'mental module' (Apperly, Samson, & Humphreys, 2005).

Brain damage affecting the amygdala – a key component of Brothers' social brain system – also impacts on gaze perception and theory of mind. Remember, too, evidence presented in Chapter 4 that people with amygdala damage often do not fixate the eye region of faces, and that they have problems interpreting facial expressions. The amygdala is a structure with multiple nuclei and a long evolu-tionary history, richly interconnected with anterior temporal and frontal cortex. Evidence from fMRI studies of the monkey amygdala shows differential patterns of responding of amygdaloid nuclei to gaze and to expression (Hoffman, Gothard, Schmid, & Logothetis, 2007).

Human patients with amygdala damage have been found to be impaired at determining direction of gaze from eye and head position (Young et al., 1995), and at interpreting mental states and feelings from gaze direction (Adolphs, Baron-Cohen, & Tranel, 2002; Stone, Baron-Cohen, Calder, Keane, & Young, 2003). However, their problems extend beyond gaze perception to theory of mind itself. Stone et al. (2003) found impairments on a theory of mind task that involved no gaze component, in which participants listened to a short story and had to explain which of the characters made a faux pas and why they shouldn't have said what they did.

Taken together, then, a wide range of evidence supports Baron-Cohen's contention that perception of gaze is intimately connected with our ability to make sense of other people's minds. However, this evidence is mainly correla-tional – people who have problems with theory of mind also have problems with gaze – which leaves open a range of possibilities as to the underlying causal rela-tionships. Gaze perception does not appear to be *essential* to theory of mind, though it may help its initial development. Consistent with Baron-Cohen's theory, blind children show some developmental delay in passing theory of mind tests (e.g. Brown, Hobson, Lee, & Stevenson, 1997; Peterson, Peterson, & Webb, 2000) but eventually appear to compensate for this initial disadvantage. Bedny, Pascual-Leone and Saxe (2009) have recently demonstrated that congenitally blind adults were able to reason as well as seeing adults about mental states and also that the same brain regions were activated in blind and sighted adults engaged in such reasoning. Despite this evident compensation in the brains of blind people, the strength of the links between gaze perception and inferences about mental states for normal, sighted individuals is impressive.

In the next section we turn to review another area of gaze perception, gaze cueing – where the direction of someone's gaze can be shown to facilitate reactions to something appearing in that direction. Gaze can act as a pointer to an object, with or without mentalistic significance. As we will see, people with ASD can perform quite normally at such non-mentalistic use of gaze.

Gaze cueing and attention

The environment we perceive is generally complex and cluttered, and our capacity to deal with different demands is quite limited. We must therefore attend selectively to different things at different times, and we need ways to prioritise the things that require our attention right now. In this section we review research that shows that where another person is looking can be a powerful cue to direct our selective attention. Before we describe the experiments on social attention cueing, we must first introduce some of the experimental methods used to look at cued attention.

Since seminal work by Posner and colleagues (reviewed in Posner, 1980), researchers have drawn distinctions between reflexive or exogenous shifts of attention and voluntary or endogenous shifts. A simple example of a reflexive shift is when your attention is grabbed by a sudden movement or flash of light in the periphery. An example of a voluntary shift occurs when you are asked to 'look over there'. Although eye movements are a common consequence of an attention shift, the effects of an exogenous shift in our internal attentional window can be detected over time intervals too short to have allowed an eye movement to occur.

Posner and Cohen (1984) examined in detail the properties of reflexive attentional orienting in a simple task where participants were encouraged to maintain fixation on a central location and asked to press a button as soon as they noticed a target appear in the centre of a box placed at one of two peripheral locations. Just before the target appeared, one or other of these possible target locations was cued by a brief illumination of the box. This could happen in the location where the target later appeared (the 'cued' location) or in the opposite location, in which case the target then appeared in the 'uncued' location. Reaction times to the onset of the target were faster when the target appeared in a cued than an uncued location. These effects of peripheral cues were found only at very brief intervals between the onset of the cue and the onset of the target (known as the Stimulus Onset Asynchrony, or SOA). So with an SOA of 50 ms, the response to the target is faster in a cued location. This effect declines as SOA increases from 50 ms and is not seen by 300 ms (Muller & Findlay, 1988). Moreover, at longer SOAs, responses to cued locations actually become slower, an effect known as 'inhibition of return' (e.g. Maylor, 1985).

One of the most important criteria of reflexive attentional cueing is that the effects at short SOAs are not sensitive to whether the cue is actually helpful or not. If there is only a 50% chance that the target will appear in the cued location then clearly it should make no difference to target detection if attention is shifted there or not, and yet strong cueing effects are obtained by peripheral cues at short SOAs even when these are not predictive.

These reflexive characteristics of peripheral cues are not found with central cues which create voluntary shifts of attention. A central cue – such as the word 'LEFT' presented in advance of a target that then appears to the left or right of fixation – takes effect more slowly, and it can be ignored by participants when the cues are not predictive of the target location on a majority of trials. Jonides (1981) contrasted the effects of peripheral cues with those of arrows located centrally, at fixation, which could also point towards the target (valid cue) or one of the other letter (invalid cue) locations. With centrally placed arrow cues, which were valid on only one trial in eight, participants were able to ignore these when instructed and this abolished any advantage for valid trials compared with invalid ones. This study by Jonides clearly suggested that centrally placed arrow cues shifted attention in a way that was under voluntary control.

Given this well-established background, and particularly the pattern of cueing effects obtained with arrows placed centrally, it was very interesting when in the late 1990s several studies suggested that a centrally located face cued attention *reflexively*. Three independent groups demonstrated this in variants of the Posner cueing task, with the cue provided by a centrally located face seen gazing in one direction or another. Friesen and Kingstone (1998) had participants respond in different blocks of trials to the presence, location or identity of letter targets. Prior to each target's appearance, a schematic face was shown, with its eyes gazing in the direction the target would appear (cued location), in the opposite direction (uncued target location) or straight ahead (neutral condition). SOAs were varied from 105 through to 1000 ms. In all three tasks there was a clear cueing effect, with responses to cued target locations made more quickly than in the uncued or neutral conditions, which did not differ. Although there was no interaction with SOA, post-hoc analyses revealed that there was not a significant cueing effect for the longest (1000 ms) SOA, consistent with reflexive rather than voluntary cueing.

Similar results were found with realistic face images presented centrally by Driver et al. (1999), whose task required on each trial that participants discriminate whether the letter T or the letter L was presented peripherally. A centrally located face whose eyes could look towards or away from the target letter equally often appeared 100, 300 or 700 ms before the onset of the target letter. The face gaze direction was not predictive of the location of the letter and was irrelevant to its identity. In their first two experiments, Driver and colleagues found significant gaze-cueing at 300 ms and 1000 ms SOA, but not reliably at 100 ms SOA. When, in a third experiment, participants were told that the target was four times more likely to appear on the side the face was *not* looking towards, significant cueing effects were still observed at 300 ms SOA (consistent with a reflexive cueing effect) but the effect of the cue reversed at 1000 ms – participants were then better at responding to the letter that appeared away from the direction of gaze.

This showed that by 1000 ms participants could use the gaze cue informatively and look away from the direction of the eyes to gain a benefit in their response time to the target, but at 300 ms they were unable to do this.

Langton and Bruce (1999) showed a cue in the form of an angled head oriented to right or left (see Figure 5.15) and found strong cueing effects even from non-predictive cues at short (100 ms) SOAs, but no such effects at 1000 ms SOA (nor at 500 ms SOA in their first experiment, which included all three SOAs). Consistent with Driver et al.'s (1999) findings, cueing effects at 1000 ms SOA could be influenced by the predictive validity of the cues – as the cues became more likely to predict the location of the target, so the 1000 ms cueing effect was strengthened. The 100 ms SOA effect was uninfluenced by this manipulation of predictive validity. These effects were abolished when the head cues were

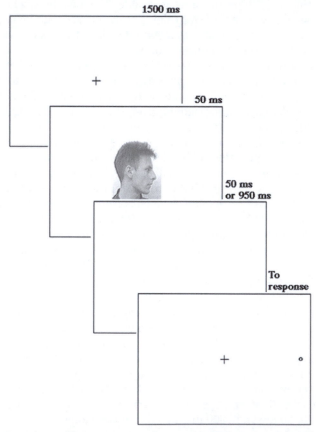

Figure 5.15 Stimuli used by Langton and Bruce (1999) to examine effects of head/gaze cues on speed of detection of a peripheral target. First published in Reflexive visual orienting in response to the social attention of others, Stephen R. H. Langton, Vicki Bruce, *Visual Cognition*, 1999, reprinted by permission of the publisher (Taylor & Francis Group, http://www.informaworld.com).

inverted, suggesting that the rapid cueing effect arose as a result of the face being processed as a face, rather than as a result of the asymmetrical 'arrow' shape of the profile in the inverted face.

When these 'social' gaze cueing effects were first discovered, a great deal of emphasis was placed on the contrast between the 'reflexive' cueing effects found with centrally placed faces and the 'voluntary' cueing effects obtained with centrally placed arrows. Akiyama et al.'s (2006) patient with gaze processing deficits showed normal attentional cueing effects to arrows, but not to gaze cues, consistent with the idea that her STS damage had created a deficit specific to gaze, and that face-cueing and arrow-cueing are different in nature (Akiyama, Kato, Muramatsu, Saito, Umeda, & Kashima, 2006). However, subsequent studies have shown that centrally placed arrows (though not other kinds of symbolic central cues) can give effects in some respects similar to those of faces. Perhaps this should not surprise us. An arrow is surely a symbolic cue invented to provoke an attention shift like that created by natural pointing with arms or faces (Tipper, Handy, Giesbrecht, & Kingstone, 2008). Nevertheless, such observations dilute what appeared initially to be simple distinctions between reflexive and central cueing, and complicate the question of whether or not cueing effects from gaze shifts in faces really arise because of some special form of socially relevant processing.

It turns out, too, that gaze cueing effects are more labile than a hypothesis in terms of a special form of processing for gaze might suppose. For example, they are affected by cues that enhance the salience of the eyes (Tipples, 2005). A particularly compelling study by Ristic and Kingstone (2005) showed a top-down influence in which the same physical stimulus could create different cueing effects according to whether it was interpreted as a pair of *eyes* or as the *wheels* of a car. This sets a clear limit on the extent to which these effects are truly 'automatic' or reflexive in nature. Indeed, some other aspects of gaze cueing are unlike other reflexive (peripheral) cueing effects. Gaze cueing does not result in inhibition of return, for example. Frischen, Bayliss and Tipper (2007) review this rather complex set of findings and conclude that the distinction between the nature and mechanisms of 'reflexive' and 'voluntary' attentional shifts is too simple. Many different neural networks are involved in detecting, perceiving and responding to attention cues and the objects of attention and the resulting patterns are likely to vary depending on the ways in which cues and targets engage these different regions.

A further complication that has come to light more recently is that there are individual differences in susceptibility to gaze cueing effects. Bayliss, de Pelligrino and Tipper (2005) found that gaze cueing effects were stronger for female than for male participants, perhaps explaining why it has not always proved easy to replicate some of the basic gaze cueing findings. There were no sex differences in peripheral cueing effects, but sex differences *were* also observed in responses to centrally placed arrows, where male participants showed no cueing effects. Such individual differences make it even harder to interpret patterns of deficit observed in a single case such as that of Akiyama et al. (2006), as we do not know whether this person showed the typical effects of gaze cueing before her brain injury.

What of gaze cueing effects in autism? Nation and Penny (2008) review 12 experiments in which gaze cueing effects found for participants with autism have been compared with those found in typical control participants and report that the majority find no difference in gaze cueing effects between the two groups. However, most of these studies used relatively high functioning and mature participants who may have learned how to use such information from eyes, rather than doing it naturally. More convincingly, the same 2 year olds with autism who failed to show shared attention when studied in naturalistic interaction by Chawarska et al. (2003) showed a cue validity effect in terms of speed of looking at a target when cued by a face looking in that same direction. That is, they looked more quickly to a picture of a toy or a cartoon character when a central face on a screen looked in its direction than when it looked in a different direction. These data strongly support the idea that children as well as adults with autism can use facial cues to attend selectively, but do not use them to 'share attention' with others in more natural situations. This is further evidence that typical 'face cueing' experiments using pictures or films of faces are not necessarily the best way to test the more socially meaningful aspects of gaze perception in real life.

Even for what seem to be studies of simple cueing effects, then, we underestimate the sophistication of human perceivers at our peril. In a recent development that he terms 'cognitive ethology', Kingstone (2009) has argued forcefully that typical gaze cueing experiments in which laboratory participants look at disembodied faces pointing at discrete and mostly meaningless peripheral targets are the wrong way to tap into what is interesting about social attention to faces. One of his arguments is that what differentiates faces from arrows is that in a cluttered and natural environment, faces grab our attention and arrows do not (Birmingham, Bischof, & Kingstone, 2009). So, he argues, we should be looking at this face-*grabbing* effect to elucidate special attentional effects involving faces rather than at gaze-cueing.

In the discussion above we have described how – to a greater or lesser extent – a face gazing in a particular direction grabs an observer's attention and redirects it to its own focus of attention. Indeed, at a more general level, faces capture our attention whether or not they are gazing in a particular direction. In the next section we briefly digress to review what is known about how readily, and why, faces engage attention compared with other complex or important objects.

How faces grab our attention

For all the reasons we have reviewed in this book faces are important to us and we detect them very readily. We may see faces in clouds, vegetation or moonscapes, and real faces seem to 'pop out' from the background in which they appear. Other things (such as size and contrast) being equal, we are faster and more accurate at detecting human faces than other kinds of objects (Hershler & Hochstein, 2005). Our ability to detect faces accurately is impaired, though, if their colour is unnatural (Bindemann & Burton, 2009) or if they are shown in profile rather than frontal or near-frontal views (Burton & Bindemann, 2009).

Some researchers have gone further than asserting that faces are detected relatively easily, to argue that faces are detected in a qualitatively different way from other objects – that faces 'pop out' of a display. In Chapter 4 we already looked at whether particular facial expressions will show 'pop-out' characteristics compared to other expressions, but in the present context the question is rather whether faces pop out in a display of non-face items. 'Pop-out' can be defined formally in terms of the pattern of results obtained when the task is to find specified targets in a larger array of items (Treisman & Gelade, 1980). Search that requires that each potential target is examined in succession will take longer the more items there are in the display. Serial search is typically found when the target is specified in terms of a conjunction of features also found in distractor items – e.g. the target is a red letter H and the background items are green Hs and red Ts. However, if some particular attribute makes the target stand out from the rest without requiring attention to be paid serially to each item, then search time and accuracy is unaffected by the number of items in the display. Such parallel search or 'pop-out' effects are found, for example, if the task is to find a red target among yellow and green distractors.

Using this kind of reasoning a number of claims have been made that a face target 'pops out' from background distractors. There are actually few persuasive demonstrations that *faces* pop out in this very strict sense because there are often simple visual features (e.g. bright white teeth in a smiling face) that could be responsible for the observed effects. Hershler and Hochstein (2005) overcame many of the limitations of the earlier studies by using a wide variety of natural and manufactured objects as distractor items in displays in which target faces could appear. They found that detection of a human face target was unaffected by display size varying from 16 to 64 items, while detection of animal faces or of other target objects was slowed by an increase in display size. Even in this case, though, Van Rullen (2006) was able to demonstrate that the ease of detecting faces could be accounted for by relatively low-level visual image properties of faces compared with other kinds of object.

Whether or not faces can be claimed to 'pop out' (and see Lewis and Edmunds, 2005, who outline the more complex theories of visual search that have arisen since Treisman and Gelade) they are certainly very salient. Moreover, their presence in a display impacts on other items.

For example, Langton, Law, Burton and Schweinberger (2008) asked participants to decide whether or not a picture of a butterfly was present within a circular array of six different pictured objects. If a face was present as one of the distractor objects, the latency of responding that the butterfly was present was slowed compared with the latency obtained to an array which did not contain a face. This can be explained if a face captures attention in a way which slows down the processing of the other items to establish if each of them is a butterfly or not. However, this slowing was not observed when arrays were inverted, suggesting that it was not some low-level image features of the faces that were attention-grabbing.

In this context, it is interesting to note that in experiments on gaze cueing where people with autism show normal cueing effects, they often have faster latencies than control participants. For the control participants it seems that faces grab attention as well as direct it elsewhere. For people with ASD, faces act more like arrows.

However, there appear to be capacity limitations in the processing of gaze, which may not be processed *unless* it forms the focus of attention. Burton, Bindemann, Langton, Schweinberger and R. Jenkins (2009) explored whether unattended gaze could influence decisions made to centrally located directional cues. In their experiments participants made speeded decisions according to whether a centrally located target was directed to the left or right. The targets were either gazing faces or pointing hands. Distractor items were presented beside the targets and these also showed faces or hands, which could be oriented in the same (congruent) or a different (incongruent) direction from the target. A series of experiments showed congruency effects when the distractors showed pointing hands, but not when distractors were gazing faces. This suggests that processing eye gaze direction itself requires attention (see also Bindemann et al., 2005, for other work on capacity limitations in face processing that demonstrate that we can only process categorical information from a single face at a time).

To sum up: faces grab attention, in a way which leaves other faces in the vicinity unable to be processed to any depth. But when an individual face has our attention, it may then redirect it to the object that is the focus of its own attention. For such a gaze cue to work, though, it must be the focus of our attention at the time. The implications are that when we look at a crowd of faces we have only a limited ability to extract information, including gaze (or expression, as discussed in Chapter 4), from one of them at a time – thus ensuring perhaps that we are not constantly distracted by what other faces are doing when interacting with one of them. The attention-demanding aspects of engaging with a particular face will become very relevant later in this chapter when we turn to consider reasons why we may sometimes need to look away from faces.

We have already mentioned how, for people with autism, faces and eyes in particular appear not to hold the significance or attraction that they do for typical children and adults. An interesting contrast can be made with the rarer genetic disorder of development, Williams syndrome (WS), which presents a very different profile of social interaction (see, for example, Jones et al., 2000; Tager-Flusberg, Plesa Skwerer, & Joseph, 2006). Williams syndrome individuals have overall learning disabilities (their IQs typically range between 40 and 90) but are particularly poor at non-verbal processing with relatively good language skills accompanied with an interpersonal interaction style that is extremely, indeed 'hyper'-sociable.

Riby, Doherty-Sneddon and Bruce (2008) compared a group of people with WS, a group of young people with ASD and appropriately matched control children on a range of face-perception tasks including identity-matching, expression, lipreading and gaze tasks. The WS group were better than mental age matched controls at tasks involving expressions and gaze, consistent with their hyper-sociable profiles. When Riby and Hancock (2008) examined eye movements in free scanning of natural scenes containing faces, WS participants looked at faces virtually to the exclusion of all other objects, and more than typically developing children (who tended to look at some other things as well as the faces in a scene). Riby et al. (2011) have used a number of search and detection tasks to investigate this fixation with faces in WS. Participants with WS are no different from controls in finding face targets in search arrays, or in the amount a task-irrelevant face distractor slows search for a butterfly in a task like that of Langton et al. (2008). However, when targets had to be detected in one of two locations that had previously been cued with a picture of a face or an object, the WS group showed a very great difference between the cost of a face compared with an object on invalid trials. It appears, then, that WS participants find it particularly difficult to *disengage* from a face once it has been fixated. WS people find faces as readily as controls, but once they have spotted them, they seem less able to move on.

The social context of gaze

A persistent theme we have used in this chapter is that humans are very skilled and flexible at interpreting gaze, and that a key determinant of how it will be interpreted is the social context of the interaction within which gaze is used. We will not dwell further on this, except to note that the point is as important in neuroimaging studies as in studies of behaviour. Although there is clear evidence that the STS is somehow involved in the perception of social attention, there are various inconsistencies in the research findings. This may again be in part because many of the studies assessing STS activation in humans have used static faces and rather artificial tasks.

Sophisticated studies by Pelphrey and his colleagues have demonstrated how the STS is highly attuned to different social contexts in which biologically meaningful movements occur – it is involved with coding intention rather than just gaze direction. Pelphrey, Viola and McCarthy (2004) created virtual reality displays in which synthetic characters apparently walked towards the participant in the scanner and then either engaged in eye contact or averted their gaze. This sequence produced BOLD activation in both the right STS and the right FFA, but only the STS activity was modulated by whether the person looked at or away from the participant. The FFA appeared to be unaffected by gaze direction in this set up – in contrast to George et al. (2001), who used static faces and found prolonged direct gaze increased activation in FFA. Pelphrey et al. (Pelphrey, Singerman et al., 2003; Pelphrey, Morris, & McCarthy, 2004) showed that STS responses were also modulated by whether a synthetic character's gaze or hand reached towards or away from a target. STS activation was greater when the character's activity violated expectations, by looking or pointing away from the location of a target. This STS sensitivity to incongruity was shown to be still more complex in a study reported by Wyk et al. (2009) where participants were scanned as they viewed film of an actress demonstrating positive or negative affect towards one or two objects and then reaching for one or the other. Where the actress reached for an object that she had indicated she did not like, or avoided an object that she had seemed to like, the action was deemed 'incongruent' and it was again these incongruent actions that gave rise to greatest activity in right posterior STS.

Looking away: Why we sometimes need to avert our gaze

We do not look at each other all the time. We are now beginning to understand that, perhaps *because* faces, and their gaze patterns, are so attention-demanding, there are moments when it is cognitively advantageous to look away. Glenberg, Schroeder and Robertson (1998) reported a series of experiments in which student volunteers were asked to provide answers to autobiographical, general knowledge or arithmetic problems. Their gaze was monitored, and they were found to look away more often when attempting to answer moderately difficult questions than easy ones. Moreover, when gaze was manipulated, so that participants were requested either to gaze at the face of the experimenter or to close their eyes when trying to answer questions, performance on items of moderate difficulty was better when eyes were closed than when gaze was directed to the questioner's face. Glenberg et al. dismissed accounts based purely on the distraction created by embarrassment by showing in a final experiment that free recall of the middle items in word lists was better when participants stared at simple pictures than if they looked at a silent movie clip at the same time as attempting their recall. It should not be embarrassing to look at a movie clip, but it showed dynamic faces which seem to have interfered with cognitive processing more than looking at simple non-face pictures.

Glenberg et al.'s findings are interesting because they suggest that a behaviour (gaze aversion) that can be interpreted in some contexts as indicating that someone is lying may instead simply reflect the cognitive demand of the question being posed. Of course, this might come down to the same thing if you assume that lying will often require a degree of mental effort. However, there are some problems in the interpretation of these experiments as they stand. For example, a silent movie clip may be more demanding of central executive resources not because it contains faces, but because it implies a plot which simple pictures do not.

Nevertheless, Doherty-Sneddon and her colleagues have replicated and extended Glenberg's findings. Doherty-Sneddon, Bruce, Bonner, Longbotham and Doyle (2002) showed that children aged 5 years did not regulate their gaze with question difficulty, but that this behaviour was exhibited by 8 year olds. To follow up Glenberg's suggestion that the effects were primarily cognitive rather than social in origin, Doherty-Sneddon and Phelps (2005) investigated gaze aversion in face-to-face compared with video-mediated communication. Since video communication should increase social distance (and see below), it should prove less necessary for people to avert gaze if the driving reason is embarrassment. Consistent with this, 8-year-old participants were more likely to avert their gaze when answering questions face to face than via a video-link. However, in both face-to-face and video-mediated communication, gaze aversion was strongly related to question difficulty, showing that it serves a cognitive as well as a social purpose. In the next section we explore in more detail the similarities and differences between face-to-face and video-mediated conversations. For now we note that these experiments suggest that gaze aversion is an important way that older children and adults modulate the cognitive demands of the

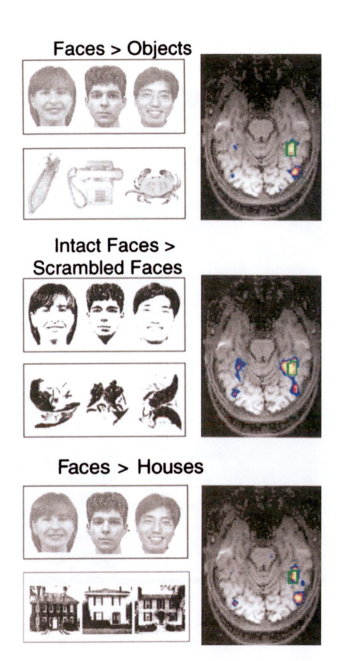

Figure 1.28 Face-responsive brain regions in Kanwisher et al.'s (1997) study. Note that the right hemisphere of the brain is shown on the right of this figure.

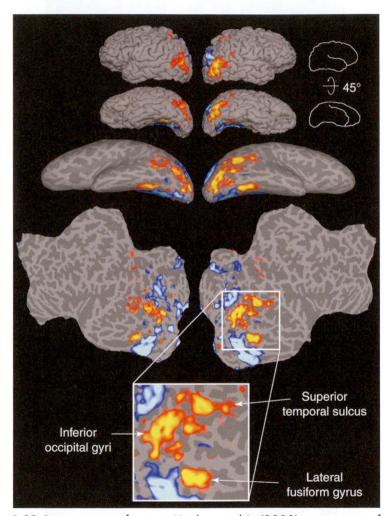

Figure 1.30 Brain regions forming Haxby et al.'s (2000) core system for face perception. See text for further explanation. Reprinted from *Trends in Cognitive Sciences*, Vol. 4, Haxby, J. V., Hoffman, E. A., & Gobbini, M. I., The distributed human neural system for face perception, p. 230. Copyright (2000) with permission from Elsevier.

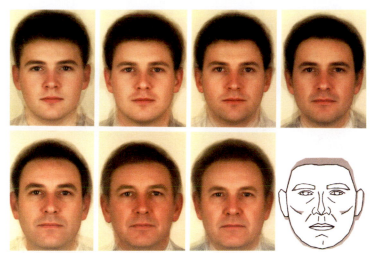

Figure 3.3 Face blends of seven different age groups from 20 to 24 years (top left) to 50 to 54 years (third from left in bottom row). Differences between the 25–29 and 50–54 age groups are shown by the shaded areas in the line-drawn figure at bottom right. The positions for the younger age group are shown with dark lines, and the edge of each shaded area shows the movements of these locations with age. The older group has a higher forehead (receding hair), fatter face, thinner lips, etc. First published in Burt, D. M., Perrett, D. I. Perception of age in adult Caucasian male faces: Computer graphic manipulation of shape and colour information. *Proceedings of the Royal Society, London, B: Biological Sciences, 259*, pp. 137–143. Copyright (1995) The Royal Society.

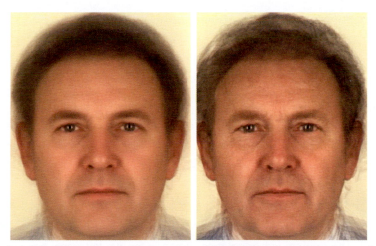

Figure 3.4 Exaggeration of cues to age. The left hand image shows the face blend of the 50–54-year-old age group from Figure 3.3. The image to the right exaggerates the differences between this and the average of all age groups. First published in Burt, D. M., Perrett, D. I. Perception of age in adult Caucasian male faces: Computer graphic manipulation of shape and colour information. *Proceedings of the Royal Society, London, B: Biological Sciences, 259*, pp. 137–143. Copyright (1995) The Royal Society.

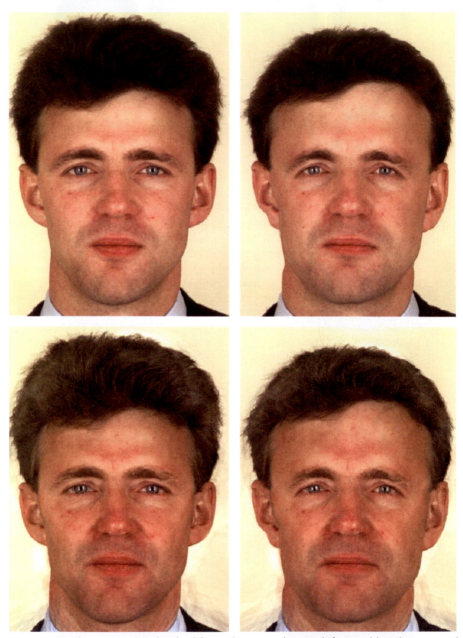

Figure 3.5 The original individual face shown in the top left panel has been aged by transforming its shape (top right), its colour/texture (bottom left), or both (bottom right) in the direction characterising older faces. First published in Burt, D. M., Perrett, D. I. Perception of age in adult Caucasian male faces: Computer graphic manipulation of shape and colour information. *Proceedings of the Royal Society, London, B: Biological Sciences, 259*, pp. 137–143. Copyright (1995) The Royal Society.

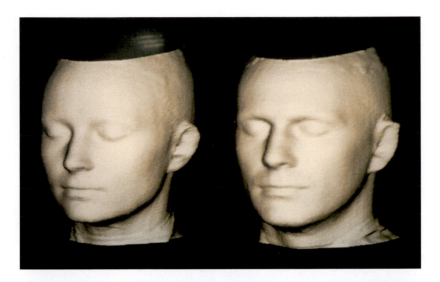

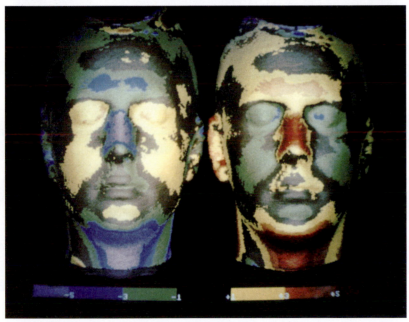

Figure 3.6 The upper panel shows average female (left) and male (right) surface images obtained from laser scanning. The lower panel compares the average male and female 3D shapes – lower left is female minus male, and lower right is male minus female, with positive and negative differences plotted using the colour scale shown beneath (increasingly negative differences in violet to increasingly positive in red). Bruce, V., Burton, A. M., Hanna, E., Healey, P., Mason, O., Coombes, A., Fright, R., Linney, A., 1993, 'Sex discrimination: How do we tell the difference between male and female faces?' first published in *Perception*, 22(2), pp. 131–152. Courtesy of Pion Limited, London.

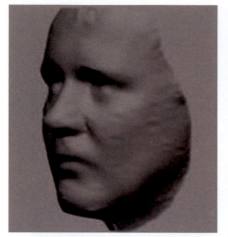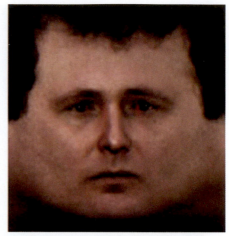

Figure 3.10 Three-dimensional surface co-ordinates of head from laser scan (left), and colour texture overlay map needed for a photo-realistic 3D representation. From Hill, Bruce and Akamatsu (1995).

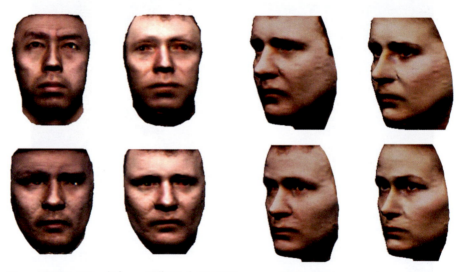

Figure 3.11 Stimuli from Hill et al. (1995).

The full-face images show four faces in which race is matched or mismatched:
    Top left, shape and colour from male Japanese.
    Top right: shape Japanese, colour Caucasian.
    Bottom left: shape Caucasian, colour Japanese.
    Bottom right: shape and colour from male Caucasian.
The ¾ view images show faces in which gender is matched or mismatched:
    Top left: shape and colour from Caucasian male.
    Top right: shape Caucasian male; colour female.
    Bottom left: shape Caucasian female; colour male.
    Bottom right: shape and colour Caucasian female.

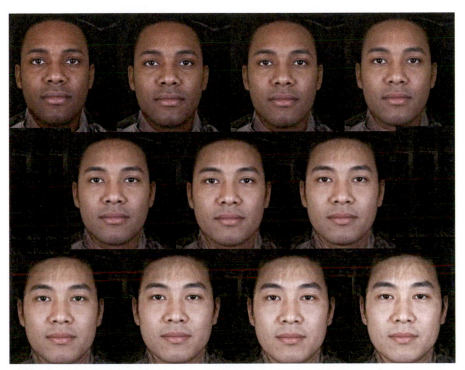

Figure 3.13 Morphed continuum of images in 10% steps from average young male African to average young male East Asian facial appearance. Top row 0% (African prototype) to 30% East Asian images, middle row 40% to 60%, bottom row 70% to 100% East Asian. Images courtesy of David Perrett and University of St. Andrews Perception Lab – www.perceptionlab.com.

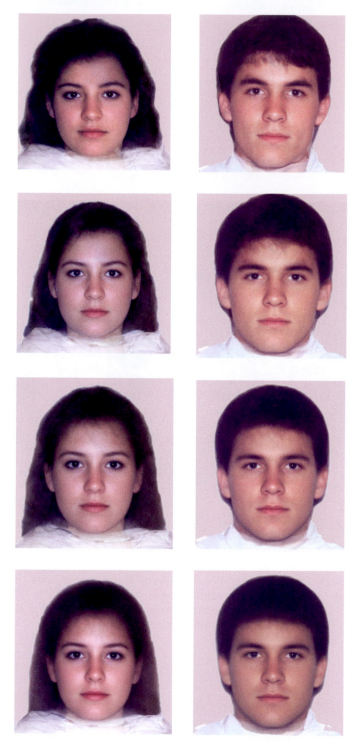

Figure 3.14 Computer composite faces created by combining female (left column) or male (right column) faces. From top to bottom, the rows show composites created by averaging four faces of each sex (top row), eight faces, sixteen faces, and thirty-two faces (bottom row). Courtesy Judith Langlois.

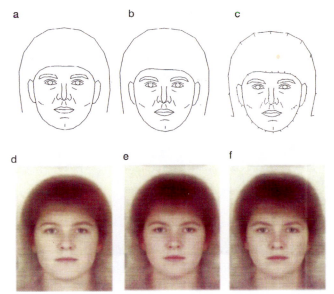

Figure 3.17 Averageness and attractiveness in Caucasian female faces. See text for explanation. Reprinted by permission from Macmillan Publishers Ltd: *Nature*, Perrett, D. I., May, K. A., & Yoshikawa, S. Facial shape and judgements of female attractiveness, *368*, pp. 239–242, copyright (1994).

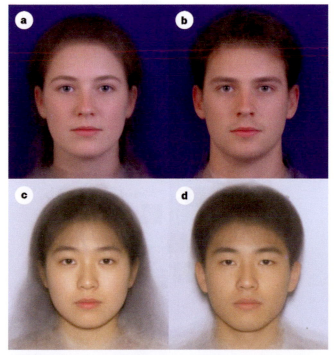

Figure 3.20 Average faces of male and female Caucasian and Japanese young adults. Reprinted by permission from Macmillan Publishers Ltd: *Nature*, Perrett, D. I. et al. Effects of sexual dimorphism on facial attractiveness, *394*, pp. 884–887, copyright (1998).

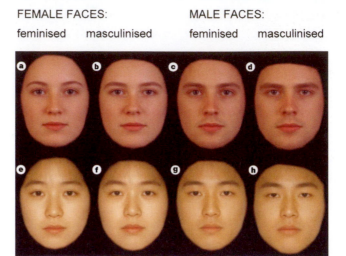

Figure 3.21 Effects of making features of male and female Caucasian and Japanese young adults more 'masculine' or more 'feminine' in shape. Reprinted by permission from Macmillan Publishers Ltd: *Nature*, Perrett, D. I. et al. Effects of sexual dimorphism on facial attractiveness, *394*, pp. 884–887, copyright (1998).

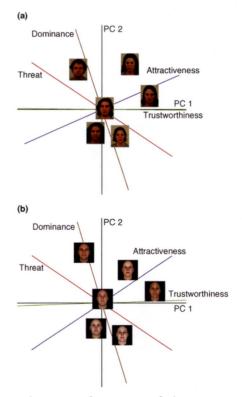

Figure 3.27 Dimensional structure for ratings of characteristics from face photographs (top) and computer-generated faces (bottom). Reprinted from *Trends in Cognitive Sciences, 12*, Alexander Todorov, Chris P. Said, Andrew D. Engell, Nikolaas N. Oosterhof, Understanding evaluation of faces on social dimensions, pp. 455–460, Copyright 2008, with permission from Elsevier.

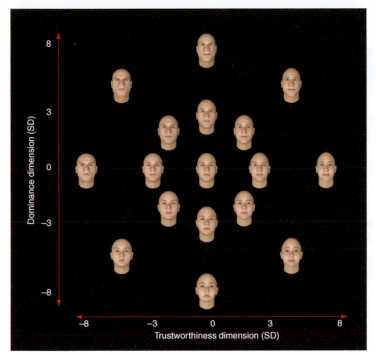

Figure 3.28 Modifying a synthetic face to change its perceived trustworthiness or dominance. Reprinted from *Trends in Cognitive Sciences, 12*, Alexander Todorov, Chris P. Said, Andrew D. Engell, Nikolaas N. Oosterhof, Understanding evaluation of faces on social dimensions, pp. 455–460, Copyright 2008, with permission from Elsevier.

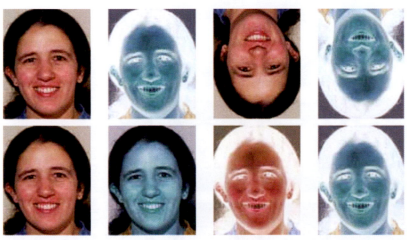

Figure 3.29 Manipulations of photographic images. Upper row: inversion and negation (left image original, second image negated, third image inverted, right image inverted and negated). Lower row: reversing colour and brightness (left image original, second image colour-reversed, third image brightness-reversed, right image colour-reversed and brightness-reversed). Reproduced from Santos, I. M., Young, A. W., 2008, 'Effects of inversion and negation on social inferences from faces' first published in *Perception, 37*(7), pp. 1061–1078. Courtesy of Pion Limited, London.

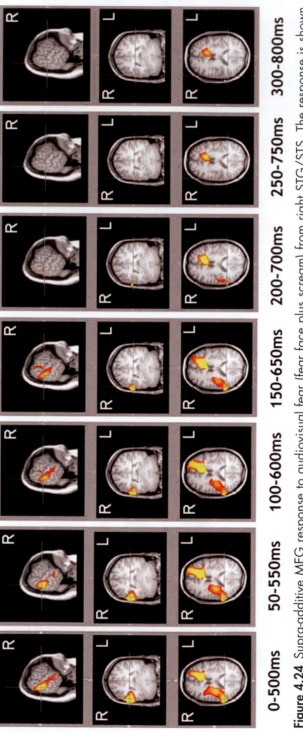

Figure 4.24 Supra-additive MEG response to audiovisual fear (fear face plus scream) from right STG/STS. The response is shown across a series of 500 ms time windows, in steps of 50 ms from stimulus onset. Images are shown in radiological convention, with the left side of the brain on the right side of each image. Reproduced from Hagan, C. C., Woods, W., Johnson, S., Calder, A. J., Green, G. G. R., & Young, A. W. (2009). MEG demonstrates a supra-additive response to facial and vocal emotion in the right superior temporal sulcus. *Proceedings of the National Academy of Sciences, USA, 106*, pp. 20010–20015.

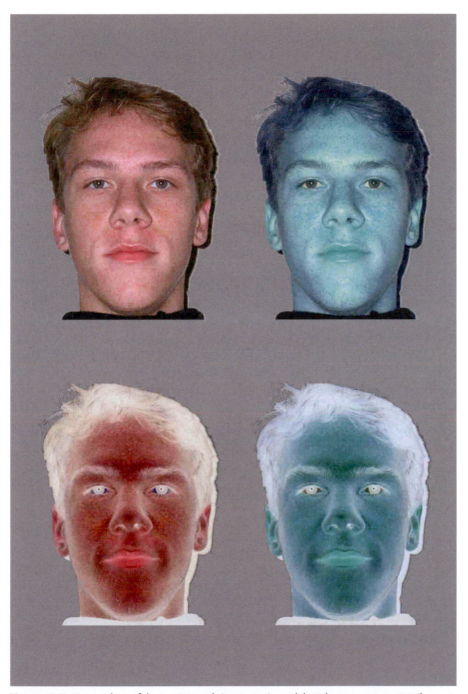

Figure 6.7 Examples of hue reversal (top row) and brightness negation (bottom row) used in experiments by Kemp et al. (1996). Courtesy of Richard Kemp.

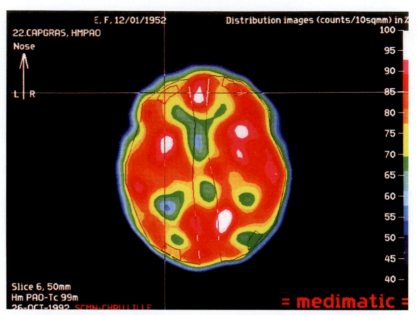

Figure 7.6 Image showing blood flow in the brain of a person with Capgras delusion, showing abnormal blood flow in parts of posterior cortex. First published in Lebert, F., Pasquier, F., Steinling, M., Cabaret, M., Caparros-Lefebvre, D., & Petit, H. (1994). SPECT data in a case of secondary Capgras delusion. *Psychopathology*, *27*, pp. 211–214. Courtesy S. Karger AG, Basel.

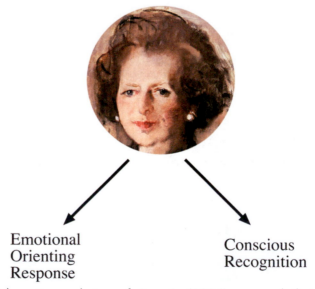

Figure 7.7 Schematic rendering of Bauer's (1984) proposal that emotional orienting responses and conscious recognition of identity are mediated by different neurological pathways. In Bauer's (1984) model, it is mainly the pathway to conscious recognition which is compromised in prosopagnosia.

Figure 8.13 Frames producing the highest activation in the face-responsive region of the fusiform gyrus (ROI shown red on underside of inflated brain). From figure 3, p. 1637 in Hasson, U., Nir, Y., Levy, I., Fuhrmann, G., & Malach, R. (2004). Intersubject synchronization of cortical activity during natural vision. *Science, 303,* pp. 1634–1640. Reprinted with permission from AAAS.

Figure 8.14 Frames producing the highest activation in the place-responsive region of the collateral sulcus (ROI shown green on underside of inflated brain). From figure 3, p. 1637 in Hasson, U., Nir, Y., Levy, I., Fuhrmann, G., & Malach, R. (2004). Intersubject synchronization of cortical activity during natural vision. *Science, 303,* pp. 1634–1640. Reprinted with permission from AAAS.

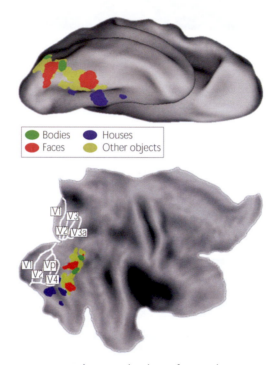

Figure 8.15 Regions responding to bodies, faces, houses and other objects. Reprinted by permission from Macmillan Publishers Ltd: *Nature Reviews Neuroscience*, Interpreting fMRI data: Maps, modules and dimensions, Hans P. Op de Beeck, Johannes Haushofer and Nancy G. Kanwisher, 9, 2, pp. 123–135, copyright 2008.

environment – the attention-demanding aspects of faces – when trying to answer difficult questions.

These observations about gaze aversion in turn raise an interesting question about the cues we think are an indication of whether or not people are telling the truth. As we noted, looking away is often seen to be a sign that someone is lying. Einav and Hood (2008) presented participants with short clips in which young adult females answered simple questions about daily activities. They either looked straight at the camera (and hence observers) when answering or averted their gaze sideways and downwards while replying. These clips were shown to younger (6 years) and older (9 years) children and adults who were asked to judge whether the person in each clip was lying or telling the truth. Adults thought that 90% of the gaze-averted clips showed lies compared with only 18% of the direct gaze clips. This was a significantly greater effect of gaze direction than was shown by 9 year olds, for whom 84% of gaze-averted clips were seen as lying compared with 41% of direct gaze. These children in turn were affected by gaze more than were the 6 year olds, who judged 68% of the gaze-averted clips as lies compared with 54% of the direct gaze clips. The 6 year olds showed a strong sex difference, with girls but not boys at this age showing sensitivity to the direction of gaze in the audiovisual clips. However, a follow-up experiment showed that 6-year-old boys did show sensitivity to gaze direction when the sound track of the clips was muted, so that they had only the face to go on. These results suggest either that girls develop sensitivity to the visual aspects of audiovisual signals sooner than boys, or that they may be better at integrating information across these different modalities.

So this and other studies show that the stereotypical attribution of 'shifty looks' with dishonesty is held by adults and develops during childhood. And yet in real communicative behaviour, gaze direction is not a reliable cue to honesty. This may be because people who want to tell convincing lies are aware of the stereotype and will work hard to maintain eye contact with their interlocutor (Vrij, 2004). But it may also be because gaze aversion signals other things too. We have already described studies showing that to answer difficult questions accurately as well as honestly may *require* that gaze is averted. Typically developing children aged 4 and above understand that someone whose eyes are oriented away from the viewer and upwards may be 'thinking' (Baron-Cohen & Cross, 1992), and in the Einav and Hood study they were careful that gaze was shifted in a downwards direction in the potential 'lying' condition. What we do not know from the reported studies by Glenberg, Doherty-Sneddon and others reviewed here is whether the gaze shifts induced by cognitive load are indeed shifts in the upwards direction.

Doherty-Sneddon, Phelps and Clark (2007) looked at where as well as when children looked when they averted their gaze when answering difficult questions. Studies of lateralisation by Kinsbourne (1972) found that right-handed adults tend to look to the right when thinking about verbal and numerical problems – predominantly left hemisphere activities. Consistent with this, Doherty-Sneddon et al. (2007) found that the 8 year olds in their experiment tended to look towards the right when answering verbal and arithmetic questions, but their eyes moved rightwards and downwards as often as upwards. If further research confirms the use of downwards as well as upwards gaze movements this will confirm that inferences about the truthfulness of witnesses, particularly important when these are children, should not be based on these non-verbal behaviours.

Beyond gaze: Face-to-face communication and video-mediated communication

Face-to-face communication involves the integrated use of all the flexible cues we have described so far – gaze, facial expressions, lipreading (see Chapter 4) – and then some more. These other facial gestures include nodding or shaking the head to indicate agreement or disagreement, frowning for puzzlement, raised eyebrows for questioning, and so on. Some of these gestures, like certain facial expressions, seem to be universally understood, others vary across cultures. Eibl-Eibesfeldt (1989) has given an especially thorough analysis of the functions of the apparently simple gesture of raising the eye-brows (see Figure 5.16).

Such gestures are often called 'paralanguage', because they supplement and complement the information conveyed by speech. McNeill (1985) has argued forcefully, by analysing the speech and gestures of people describing cartoon movies, that gestures are not just redundant rhythmic accompaniments to speech, but modify our interpretation of its content. These gestures include a range of arm, head and facial movements. Intriguingly, Holle, Obleser, Rueschemeyer and Gunter (2010) have recently presented evidence that the posterior STS and adjacent superior temporal gyrus provide the locus for the integration of information from speech with that from 'iconic' hand gestures which convey information about meaning, such as a circular hand movement accompanying the word 'around'.

To study the way in which non-verbal signals can complement speech in everyday face-to-face communication, researchers need to examine both verbal and non-verbal behaviour in a task which produces naturalistic dialogue, but which also allows performance and behaviour to be measured. One task that has been used to explore how visual and verbal signals are used together is the Map Task (Brown, Anderson, Yule, & Shillcock, 1984).

In this task, one participant is given a map with a series of landmarks and a route drawn on it, and their task is to describe the route to another participant so that they can reproduce it on their own version of the map, which shows the landmarks but not the route (see Figure 5.17). However, there are some crucial differences between the landmarks shown on the two maps. Some are absent, others in different locations, and the two partners must negotiate the correct route by trying to work out the differences between the maps. The task gives a measure of performance (how close the drawn route was to the target route) as well a producing natural, though task-directed, dialogue.

Doherty-Sneddon and her colleagues (Doherty-Sneddon et al., 1997) compared the structure of the dialogues produced when participants in the Map Task could see each other with the dialogues obtained when they communicated

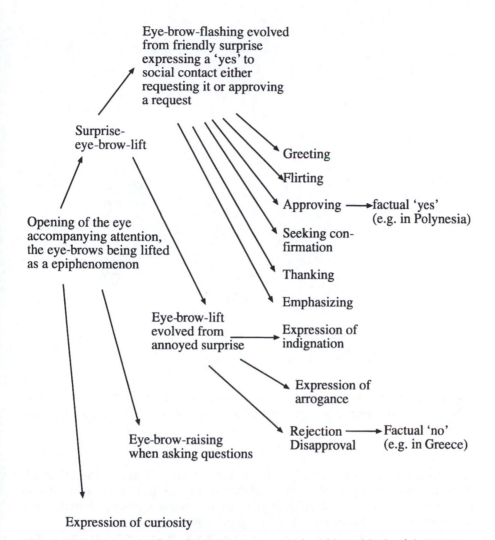

Figure 5.16 Functions of eye-brow raising, as analysed by Eibl-Eibesfelt (1989).

only with words. When participants were hidden from each other, more words were needed to complete the task successfully, and these words were used particularly to provide or elicit certain forms of feedback. For example, if the instruction giver says 'You know that wee curve?' they are seeking confirmatory feedback from their partner. If their partner says 'yes', they are providing the requested feedback. Both these kinds of speech activities were more common in the audio-only group. When participants interact face to face, they can substitute glances, nods or other non-verbal behaviours for these speech acts. Interestingly, however, when dialogues were conducted via high quality video-links, only some of these features of face-to-face interaction were preserved. Video-links, particularly where eye contact is made possible through careful arrangements of cameras and mirrors,

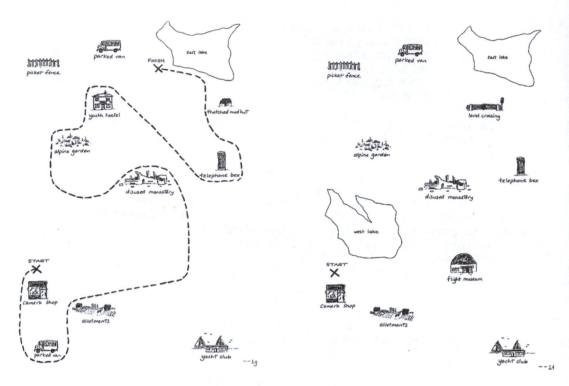

Figure 5.17 Examples of materials used in the 'map task' by Doherty-Sneddon et al. (1997). The sender (left map) describes the route to the person with the map on the right.

seem to provoke, at least initially, some behaviour which is not characteristic of normal face-to-face interaction. One possible reason for this is that participants linked by video can see each other, but they cannot see each other's environments and therefore cannot see to which objects participants are paying attention.

Video-mediated communication technologies are increasingly important, allowing teaching and counselling services, for example, to be delivered to geographically remote locations. It is important that we understand the rather subtle interactions that there may be between people's natural interpersonal behaviours and particular technological configurations, so that we can exploit the advantages of these technologies and minimise their disadvantages.

There are some clear advantages of using video-mediated rather than face-to-face communication in certain circumstances. It has become accepted practice in criminal trials in different parts of the UK and elsewhere to allow child witnesses to give their evidence via a video-link so that they are less likely to be intimidated by the formal setting of the courtroom and/or the presence of a defendant who has allegedly abused the child in some way. Some children can be examined via video-link who simply would not be able to be questioned in open court (Flin, Kearney, & Murray, 1996).

Soon after this kind of video evidence became permitted, several studies examined the usage and acceptability of these 'live links' on the testimony elicited from child witnesses, with somewhat mixed results. Davies and Noon (1991) reported that, although video interviews took considerably longer than similar interviews in court, children interviewed via video were less stressed and rated as more fluent compared with those interviewed in the usual courtroom setting. Judges, however, appeared to have less empathy with the child interviewed by live link. In a study in the Scottish courts, Flin et al. (1996) found there were some communication difficulties when video links were in use – the children's evidence was not as detailed or accurate, and the children were less resistant to leading questions over the video links. Davies and Noon (1991), however, found children were rated as more resistant to such questions. The problem with these studies, of course, is that any differences observed between the conditions are inevitably confounded with the particular cases using video versus open courtroom testimony. Where children are given a choice between forms of interview, there may be differences between those children who choose courtroom compared with video. In the Scottish studies, some children who requested live links were denied them and asked to testify in open court, making it unlikely that the sample of cases and/or witnesses in open courtroom testimony were very well matched to those in the live links comparison. Moreover, in the study based on courtrooms in England and Wales, comparisons between the live link testimony and open court relied on trials in Scotland to provide the open court room comparison.

Such problems are inevitable in real-life studies, and do not diminish their importance. What they do, though, is to underscore the value of complementing field studies of the use of such links in situ with more formally controlled, experimental studies. These can involve interviews about an incident where the events and details are known and can be compared across different formats, with children allocated at random to one or other condition. Doherty-Sneddon and McAuley (2000) made such a comparison between video-mediated and face-to-face interviews of 6- and 10-year-old children about a series of incidents that had occurred earlier that day on the way to the interview. The child's journey to the interview room was carefully choreographed so that all children experienced the same series of events. As a further control, children came in pairs and one child from each pair was randomly allocated to the video interview condition, the other to face-to-face, so any differences between particular journeys and events occurring would be balanced out across conditions. The adult experimenter questioned the child in an open-ended way, and also via a series of specific closed questions, three of which were misleading (e.g. 'It's really fun coming up in the lift in this building, isn't it?' – the correct answer being that the children didn't come up in the lift). Doherty-Sneddon and McAuley found importantly that 6 year olds were more accurate in their answers to the misleading questions via video-link (an average of 2.27 or 76% correct) than face-to-face (1.4 or 47% correct), while the 10 year olds in the study were equally accurate in both conditions (83% via video and 81% face-to-face). On other measures there were few differences between the two kinds of questioning, though older children produced more information in free narrative face-to-face than via video, but more incorrect information was produced by both age-groups in specific questioning face-to-face as well.

The younger children appeared to be more relaxed when interviewed via the links, and required more 'management' as a result, reflected in a significant increase in non-task-relevant speech from the adult in the video condition with younger children. A follow-up study by Doherty-Sneddon and McAuley (2000) seemed to back this up. Adult participants who viewed clips of the interviews rated children in the video-mediated condition somewhat more confident and less nervous than in the face-to-face condition. Children in the video-mediated condition smiled significantly longer than those in the face-to-face condition. Doherty-Sneddon and McAuley's study therefore seems to add weight to the idea that small children may be less intimidated when questioned via links than face-to-face. While the rationale for video-links in the courtroom is about reducing intimidation from the setting and the presence of an alleged abuser, Doherty-Sneddon and McAuley's research suggests that the mere physical presence of an adult authority figure can appear to influence a young child into behaving in an acquiescent manner – even if that means agreeing with something that is incorrect.

Similar effects may be evident for adults in a study reported by Tachakra and Rajani (2002) on conversations between health professionals and patients. In each discourse a nurse and a patient spoke with a doctor, and what varied was whether the doctor was in the same room as the other two participants or was linked via video from a remote location. No differences were reported between the patient and nurse interactions in the two conditions, but there were significant differences in the interactions with the doctor. For both the patients and the nurses the interactions with the doctor were longer and more interactive, with more interruptions from the patient, when the doctor was located remotely and the interaction was via video. This could arise if the patient was less intimidated by the doctor when he or she was not physically present.

It is not only humans that engage in face-to-face communication. Some intriguing recent research on domestic dogs suggests that we have selectively bred, from wolves, traits that make dogs engage with us visually in a remarkably human-like way. Miklósi, Kubinyi, Topal, Gácsi, Viranyi and Csanyi (2003) showed that domestic dogs used gaze patterns to engage their owners' attention to get help when they encountered an obstacle. Dogs and hand-reared wolves were taught a novel task that led to food reward. Their progress towards their goal was then blocked, and it was observed that the majority of the dogs (but few of the wolves) looked directly at the humans, and then back at the goal. Any reader of this who has a dog might try this at home when the dog's toy gets out of reach under the sofa – your dog may well look directly at you as though 'asking' you to sort it out. Border collies are notorious for 'staring' – anecdotally at animals such as sheep they are herding – and seem particularly good at using such face-to-face engagement to communicate with humans too.

Other studies go further to suggest that dogs have some kind of implicit understanding of what people use their faces for. Gácsi, Miklósi, Varga, Topal and Csanyi (2004) studied dogs who were variously required to fetch balls or toys, or who begged for food. The owners of the dogs faced towards or away from the dogs in different conditions, and had their eyes concealed with a blindfold in some trials. Dogs did not retrieve balls to owners who turned their backs on them, and brought other objects round to the front of owners who were seated with their backs to the dogs. Dogs were much less likely to beg for food to blind-folded than non-blindfolded people, and showed hesitant behaviour in other tasks when the owner was blindfolded. Schwab and Huber (2006) found that dogs were more obedient at remaining lying down after instruction when their owner continued to watch them, than when the owner did something else such as watch the television, or turned their back on them. Again, this suggests that dogs are sensitive to their owner's attentional state from some combination of their facial or postural cues.

So, it is not just humans who can use our facial and other postural cues as information about attentional state. Domesticated dogs were initially bred to help in hunting and herding tasks that require collaboration. The result, enhanced by further selective breeding, is an animal that is sensitive to non-verbal signs of human attention in a way that serves us (and them) very well in the companion roles that most now play.

Summary

In this chapter we have reviewed how we derive information from patterns of eye and head movements to tell us where someone else is attending. The face both attracts our attention and redirects it to items of potential mutual interest. Investigations by cognitive neuroscientists have begun to identify the neural circuits involved in social cognition and how neurodevelopmental disorders, particularly ASD, may affect gaze processing and mindreading. We have only been able to scratch the surface of what is now an enormous, complex and rapidly growing field.

Further reading

Birmingham, E., & Kingstone, A. (2009). Human social attention: A new look at past, present and future investigations. *Annals of the New York Academy of Science, 1156,* 118–140.

An up-to-date and readable review of recent findings in this area.

Frischen, A., Bayliss, A. P., & Tipper, S. P. (2007). Gaze cueing and attention: Visual attention, social cognition and individual differences. *Psychological Bulletin, 133,* 694–724.

This is a thorough and scholarly survey of the gaze-cueing literature, which reviews the comparisons between face and arrow cueing, and observed individual differences in gaze cueing.

Frith, C. D. (2007). The social brain? *Philosophical Transactions of the Royal Society, London, B: Biological Sciences, 362,* 671–678.

Sets the issues discussed here in the broader theoretical context created by Brothers' (1990) idea of the 'social brain'.

Nation, K., & Penny, S. (2008). Sensitivity to eye gaze in autism: Is it normal? Is it auto-matic? Is it social? *Development and Psychopathology, 20,* 79–97.

The autism field is huge. This careful review looks systematically at the specific question of whether or not people with autism show normal patterns of gaze cueing.

Nummenmaa, L., & Calder, A. J. (2009). Neural mechanisms of social attention. *Trends in Cognitive Sciences, 13*, 135–143.

A recent summary of some of the cognitive neuroscience we have reviewed in this chapter.

Senju, S., & Johnson, M. H. (2009). The eye contact effect: Mechanisms and development. *Trends in Cognitive Sciences, 13*, 127–134.

Reviews the neural consequences of eye contact and how these neural circuits may develop.

Chapter 6

Recognising faces

Recognising the identities of people we know is fundamental to being able to interact with them in terms of our past experience of them as individuals, so recognition from the face is an ability at which we become very skilled as we grow up. Nonetheless it is puzzling how we achieve this, given the constraints on the underlying biological structure of a human face (see Chapter 1). If all faces must essentially fit a common overall template, how do they also convey so accurately our individual identities? As long ago as 1883, Sir Francis Galton expressed the problem as follows:

> The difference in human features must be reckoned great, inasmuch as they enable us to distinguish a single known face among those of thousands of strangers, though they are mostly too minute for measurement. At the same time, they are exceedingly numerous. The general expression of a face is the sum of a multitude of small details, which are viewed in such rapid succession that we seem to perceive them all at a single glance. If any one of them disagrees with the recollected traits of a known face, the eye is quick at observing it, and it dwells upon the difference. One small discordance overweighs a multitude of similarities and suggests a general unlikeness.
>
> (Galton, 1883, p. 3)

Since Galton's speculations about the process, the sources of information used in face recognition have been carefully explored, offering useful insights into how we achieve this feat. Because faces are the most important key to identity, scientific understanding of face recognition has applications in several forensic contexts – for example, reconstructions and drawings of the face play an important role in detective work.

In this chapter we will review what is known about the visual representations which allow us to recognise faces, and how these may change as faces become familiar. We will describe how images of faces can be used to help identify criminals and some of the difficulties that arise in such contexts. Finally we will consider individual differences in face recognition and matching and the implications of these differences for eyewitness testimony.

Face features and configuration

When we are asked to describe a face, or to speculate on how individual faces may be represented in memory, there is a temptation to do this in terms of a list of separate features such as 'large green eyes' or 'hooked nose'. This tendency is undoubtedly created in part because our language has vocabulary items for the different functional parts of the face.

However, these linguistic terms may have arisen because these different features serve different functions – the eyes see, the jaws chew – as we discussed in Chapter 1. It doesn't necessarily follow that they are also the best way to represent differences in identity.

Clearly the different face features can be important ingredients in our representations of faces – especially if someone has a very distinctive part of their face, such as Mick Jagger's famous lips – though not all face features are remembered equally well. When unfamiliar faces must be recognised, the external features of hairstyle and head shape dominate our memory, perhaps because these occupy a large and relatively high contrast part of the visual image. When faces are familiar, there is a shift in memory so that the internal face features become relatively more salient (H. Ellis, Shepherd & Davies, 1979; Young, Hay, McWeeny, Flude, & A. Ellis, 1985). This shift to relying more on the internal features of familiar faces may take place because hairstyles can vary across encounters with familiar faces while internal features do not, and because internal features must be attended to in face-to-face communication, allowing us to create a more robust representation. We will return to this distinction between familiar and unfamiliar face recognition later in this chapter.

It is most unlikely, though, that the visual system describes faces in the way that we do in language – as sets of discrete features. If you cut the parts out of pictures of faces and present them in isolation, then for most individuals they become difficult to recognise – you can see that Paul McCartney's nose is *a nose*, but will often have real problems identifying it as Paul McCartney's nose (Farah, 1991). On this basis, there is nothing to suggest that recognising Paul McCartney's face is achieved solely by recognising its component parts.

Many behavioural studies show that face patterns are treated more as wholes or as inter-relationships between different features than simply as a list of their features. Our sensitivity to spatial inter-relationships between face features is evident in Figure 6.1. In these images, the face features are kept much the same, but distances between features have been altered to produce striking differences in appearance. As we will see later, these kinds of effects can have real-life consequences. It has proved remarkably difficult to produce good likenesses of faces using 'kits' of face features such as the Photofit system, in which a witness to a crime tries to recreate an image of the perpetrator's face by choosing their eyes, nose, mouth and so on from a collection of different face parts. The limited success of such approaches may be because they do not naturally tap the processes that human brains use to describe and retrieve faces.

Strong experimental evidence that we do not process features independently from each other comes from the face composite technique introduced by Young and his colleagues (Young, Hellawell, & Hay, 1987: see also Chapter 2). They divided faces horizontally into upper and lower halves. Although people may be quite accurate at identifying the isolated top half of a face when it is seen on its own, when it is combined with a wrong lower half it becomes harder to recognise to whom the upper features belong (see Figure 6.2). It seems that the impression created by, say, the eyes and forehead is modified by the features seen elsewhere in the face. This 'composite' effect is found only when the two half faces are aligned into an overall face shape. If the two halves are both present, but misaligned with each other so they do not form a whole face, then identification of each half is unaffected by the presence of the other one (see Figure 6.2). This comparison of 'face composite' and 'misaligned' conditions is important in demonstrating that the problem in identifying the parts of the composite faces is due to their being placed in an overall facial configuration – apart from this difference, the composite and misaligned stimuli are the same.

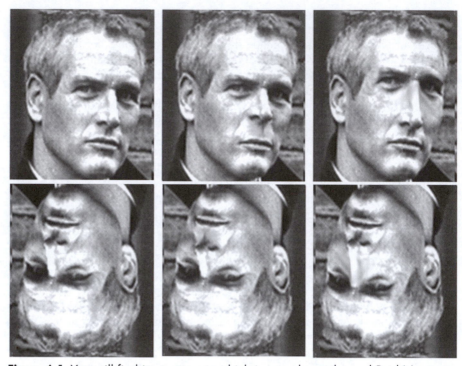

Figure 6.1 You will find it easy to see which image shows the real Paul Newman, though the distortions are much easier to see in the upright than inverted versions. Figure created by Helmut Leder for Bruce and Young (1998).

Such findings – and others we will describe – fit a distinction introduced by Carey and Diamond (1977) between *piecemeal* representation of face parts and *configurational* representation of properties of the whole face. The idea of configurational (often nowadays called configural) representation of faces has been enthusiastically adopted by many subsequent researchers, but unfortunately it can carry different meanings (Maurer, Le Grand, & Mondloch, 2002). Three logically distinct senses are the first-order relational configuration that the eyes are above the nose and this is above the mouth, the 'holistic' or 'gestalt' configuration resulting from the combination of different parts, and the second-order relational configuration resulting from the spacing of the parts themselves (i.e. their positions within an overall first-order configuration). As we will see, these different forms of configural representation cannot be distinguished in all studies – making it easy for them to be conflated or simply confused, especially for the second and third meanings – but Maurer et al. (2002) emphasise the value of keeping them separate where possible.

There is a good deal of other evidence that the whole face is more than the sum of its parts (Tanaka and Gordon, 2011, provide a more detailed recent review). Tanaka and Farah (1993) asked volunteers to learn the names of a set of faces constructed from a 'kit' of face features so that each face had different features

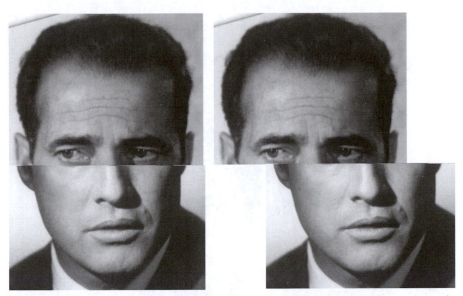

Figure 6.2 Humphrey Brando or Marlon Bogart? It is easier to see the two people whose faces are combined when the two halves are misaligned.

(see Figure 6.3). Later, the volunteers had to try to identify which face feature belonged to a particular target character. For example, they would be asked to answer the question 'Which is Larry?' and shown two alternatives to choose from, where the only difference lay in the specific nose which was depicted. People were much better at doing this when the nose was shown in the context of the whole face than when the nose was shown in isolation (so the question became 'Which is Larry's nose?'; see Table 6.1). This is persuasive evidence of holistic configural processing, because the second-order relational configuration was not substantially changed – parts of the face were swapped, but kept in much the same positions. Consistent with this, when the faces had been learned with scrambled features (a violation of the first-order configuration) so that they could not be learned holistically as faces, the effects reversed, and participants were then better when tested with isolated features than a whole (scrambled) face context.

Given the demonstrable importance of configural representations in behavioural studies of face recognition, it is natural to consider how they relate to the components of the core system of Haxby, Hoffman and Gobbini's (2000) neurological model of face perception – the OFA, FFA and STS (see Chapter 1 for a description of Haxby et al.'s model and an explanation of terms we use to refer to the different brain regions involved). In particular, the FFA is of interest because it is identified by Haxby et al. (2000) as central to the perception of invariant characteristics of faces, which of course includes face identity.

The importance of first-order configural representations for FFA was clearly established in Kanwisher et al.'s (1997) classic study that identified FFA as a functional brain region (see Chapter 1). Recall that the FFA is defined as the part of the fusiform gyrus that shows a stronger BOLD response to faces than

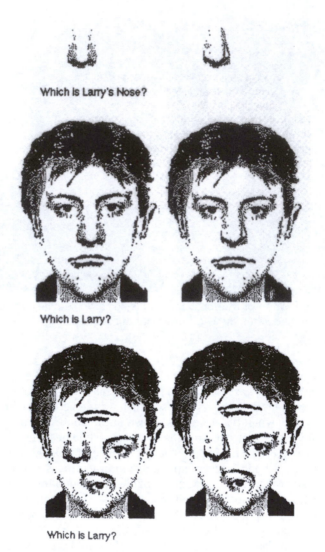

Figure 6.3 Examples of the parts, whole and scrambled face items used by Tanaka and Farah (1993).

Table 6.1 Percent correct responses to questions of the type 'Which is Larry?' or 'Which is Larry's nose?' in conditions tested in Experiment 1 from Tanaka and Farah (1993).

Learned items:	*Regular faces*	*Scrambled faces*
Probe:		
Isolated feature	62	71
Whole face	73	64

other visual stimuli (typically, objects or buildings) in an fMRI localiser scan. However, it can also be identified as the part of fusiform gyrus that shows a stronger response to faces than to scrambled faces – as Figure 1.28 shows, this fMRI contrast reveals essentially the same region. So we have known for some time that FFA is highly sensitive to first-order configuration, and many later studies bear this out. Interestingly, however, Liu, Harris and Kanwisher (2009) found that the other components of Haxby et al.'s core system – OFA and posterior STS – were as sensitive to the presence of face parts as they were to the parts being in the correct first-order configuration.

Identifying that FFA is responsive to changes in holistic configural and to second-order configural information has been a more recent development, mainly achieved through the fMR-adaptation technique (see Chapter 2). First, we will look at holistic processing. Andrews et al. (2010) used composite faces that combined the inner features of one face with the outer features of another (see Figure 6.4 for example materials). Behaviourally, Young, Hellawell and Hay (1987) had already shown that inner plus outer feature composites behave in much the same way as the top plus bottom half face composites shown in Figure 6.2. That is, combining one face's inner features with another face's outer features creates what looks to an observer like a new face – masking the identities of the component parts. The value of this for an fMRI study is that two images can look like different faces even when a substantial part of each of the images is actually the same (if they share internal features but not external features, or vice versa).

What Andrews et al. (2010) did was to use fMR-adaptation to ask which components of Haxby et al.'s core system show this behavioural effect of sensitivity to specific pairings of internal and external features (holistic processing) at the expense of loss of sensitivity to the parts themselves? The logic of the technique is that if the same face image is presented repeatedly, fMRI activation in a region interested in faces decreases over successive trials, as the neuronal responses giving rise to the fMRI activation adapt to the repetition of the same stimulus. On the other hand, if a series of different faces is presented, activation will stay strong in any brain region that can code the differences between the faces (release from adaptation). So, if a series of face images appears to be the same to a particular brain region, its activity will reduce across successive presentations (adaptation), but if the difference is picked up by that brain region, activation will stay strong (release from adaptation). In this way, we can investigate what characteristics of face images will lead a face-responsive region to treat them as same or different, offering an insight into what the region is capable of encoding.

When the internal features of a face were held constant across the stimuli presented in a block of trials but shown with different external features, or when constant external features were shown with changed internal ones, Andrews et al. (2010) found a release from adaptation of BOLD fMRI responses in the FFA and OFA, but not in STS. This shows that OFA and FFA – the components Haxby et al. see as critical to perception of identity – respond to the novel holistic pattern created by pairing part of one face with part of another face. Interestingly, Andrews et al. (2010) found that this pattern did not hold for combinations of faces and upper body clothing – the OFA and FFA represent faces holistically, but (sensibly) don't care whether the person changes their shirt! Less flippantly, this

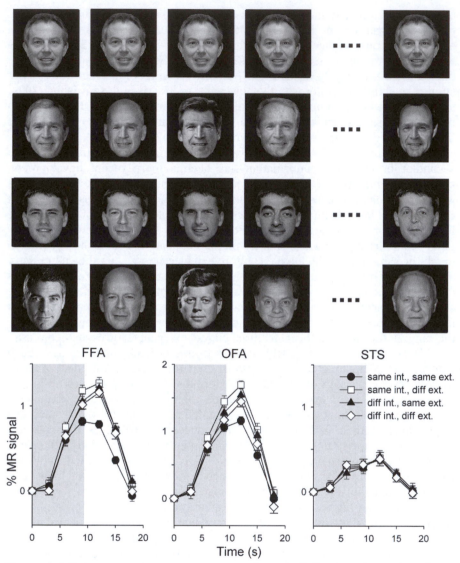

Figure 6.4 Relative activation over time in the FFA (left), OFA (centre) and STS (right panel) found by Andrews et al. (2010) when face patterns were varied. FFA and OFA both show sensitivity to changes in holistic face patterns whether created by changing external features (second row), internal features (third row) or both (bottom row). With kind permission from the Society for Neuroscience.

demonstrates that these brain regions seem to be interested in changes in faces, not to any change in an image per se.

There is also evidence that the FFA is responsive to changes in second-order configuration. Rhodes, Michie, Hughes and Byatt (2009) made use of the fMR-adaptation procedure to investigate how different face processing areas responded to changes in feature spacing. Participants viewed a series of faces and the activity in OFA, FFA and posterior STS was measured over separate blocks of trials. In one type of block of trials, the identity of the face changed on every presentation within the block, and this produced high activation in the FFA in both hemispheres, and relatively high activation in the OFA in the right hemisphere. In another block, the same face image was repeated within a block, and all areas showed little average activation. The critical blocks were where the successive faces showed spacing variations of the features within the same underlying identity (cf. Figure 6.1). When such spacing variants were presented upright, the FFA in both hemispheres remained as active as when different identity faces were presented on each trial. This shows that left and right FFA are sensitive to feature spacing. The same was found for the OFA in the right hemisphere, whereas STS activation was low across all kinds of blocks, consistent with its hypothesised role in dynamic social processing rather than static form-based identity.

These are interesting findings, but we need to keep in mind that whilst they show that FFA and right OFA are sensitive to image changes resulting from feature spacing, this might simply reflect sensitivity to any changes between face images. An important control used by Rhodes et al. (2009) was therefore to turn the images upside down. Turning pictures of faces upside down leaves them physically the same, yet makes them hard for our visual systems to recognise. When images showing the same spacing changes were presented upside down, Rhodes et al. (2009) found a reduced response to spacing changes across all face regions. This shows that FFA and right OFA are mainly sensitive to spacing differences in upright faces, possibly because inversion impacts differentially on configural processing.

Comparisons of performance between upright and inverted faces have become widely used in studies of face perception and face recognition. We therefore need to look in more detail at what is known about face inversion effects.

Why are upside-down faces hard to recognise?

The previous section has introduced some of the evidence that our skill at recognising faces seems to depend at least in part upon sensitivity to the facial configuration – which may include the spacing and relationship between different features. However, this ability to perceive subtle aspects of face configuration depends upon faces being seen in their normal, upright orientation. For example, in Figure 6.1 you will find it relatively difficult to notice the changes in the placement of the face features when the images are upside down. Despite carrying the same physical information as upright faces, upside-down faces look strange to us, and we find them harder to recognise. Bruce and Langton (1994) presented famous faces along with a list of names of the people they might belong to (the names were shown to prevent problems in name retrieval complicating the interpretation of the results). Using this procedure, faces shown upright were identified correctly on 95% of trials, while the same images upside-down were identified on only 70% of occasions.

There is something about how we perceive faces that makes them particularly sensitive to inversion – Yin's (1969) classic demonstrations of the inversion effect in face recognition showed that recognition memory for unfamiliar faces was more severely affected by inversion than the recognition of various other kinds of pictured item. None the less, faces are not the only things we have trouble recognising upside down – words are another obvious example, and body postures turn out to be problematic too (Reed, Stone, Bozova, & Tanaka, 2003) – but we still need to know how inversion affects face perception. The consensus is that our difficulties in recognising upside-down faces arise at least in part because we are relatively insensitive to the configural properties of upside-down faces, and it is these which carry much of the information about personal identity.

Consistent with this suggestion, the composite effect (Figure 6.2) disappears when the face is inverted. Young, Hellawell and Hay (1987) showed that people are actually better at identifying one of the half-faces in an inverted composite than in an upright one! While this may seem paradoxical, given that upside-down faces are harder to identify, the paradox can be resolved as follows. The reason that half a face within an upright composite is difficult to identify is because a new face identity arises from the combination of the upper and lower face features. If the perception of configural information is particularly impaired by inversion, an inverted composite does not get seen as a novel configuration, making it relatively easier to access the identity belonging to the top or bottom features alone.

The disproportionate effect of inversion on face recognition is often considered a hallmark of our expertise in face recognition, since inversion appears to disrupt the configural processing of faces that many researchers think distinguishes face recognition from the recognition of other kinds of object. Studies of prosopagnosia fit this position well. Prosopagnosia is the term used to describe severe deficits in face recognition which may result from acquired brain injury (Bodamer, 1947; Bornstein, 1963) or may be present throughout life, perhaps as a result of genetic factors (see Duchaine, Germine, & Nakayama, 2007). As we discuss further in Chapter 7, prosopagnosic individuals may be unable to recognise familiar people via their faces but able to recognise the same people from their voices or names. Despite severely impaired ability to recognise faces, people with prosopagnosia may have relatively spared abilities to read other messages from faces, such as emotions or facial speech (see Chapter 4). This suggests that their problem is not a generalised deficit in perceiving faces, but rather linked to some more specific aspect of face perception needed to recognise individual identity.

Of most relevance here is that people with prosopagnosia often have particular difficulties processing configural information and, perhaps as a result, are relatively unaffected by the inversion of faces. Busigny and Rossion (2010) report an extensive study of face inversion effects for PS, a woman who acquired prosopagnosia following a head injury in 1992. She was severely impaired at recognising familiar faces and at remembering and matching unfamiliar ones, while remaining able to recognise objects normally. Across a range of tasks, her performance did not differ substantially between upright and inverted faces. Busigny and Rossion

(2010) reviewed the literature on face inversion effects in acquired prosopagnosia to show that this lack of a face inversion effect is the typical pattern. They argue that relatively rare instances in which prosopagnosic patients actually perform better with inverted than with upright faces (Farah, Wilson, Drain, & Tanaka, 1995) may be linked to problems created by upper visual field defects.

Other studies of prosopagnosic individuals have shown that they are less sensitive to the configural properties of upright faces than are controls. Ramon, Busigny and Rossion (2010) report further work with PS, looking at her holistic configural processing abilities. In their first experiment Ramon et al. (2010) carried out a whole-part face task similar to that of Tanaka and Farah (1993), described earlier. Participants saw an intact whole target face for 1500 ms and after a short delay were shown the target alongside a distractor that varied only in a single feature. The test pair could be whole faces or isolated features. Control participants showed, on average, higher accuracy and faster responses to whole than part test pairs. PS, however, was more accurate on part than whole trials. In other experiments Ramon et al. (2010) made use of the composite effect (cf. Figure 6.2) and showed that while control participants were generally less accurate and slower when the two halves of composite faces were aligned, or when the irrelevant bottom half of the face showed a different identity to that of the relevant top half, this was not observed for PS.

But – identifying the nature of configural processing is not quite so easy!

The demonstrations noted above make a strong case for there to be something beyond a list of isolated features in our internal representation of an upright face. But we noted that there is sometimes confusion or ambiguity in the literature about what is meant by configural processing – especially as to whether this is taken to mean the spatial relationships between different face features (e.g. the distance between the eyes, or between the eyes and the mouth), or that the face is processed in a holistic way (in which features and their arrangements may not be made explicit at all).

In part, some of this confusion comes down to the fact that these different logical meanings are tricky to separate in practice. If we take Young, Hellawell and Hay's (1987) composite effect, for example, it might be hard to identify the top half of a composite when the two halves are aligned because (as we have tended to emphasise here) the aligned composite presents a new holistic pattern which fails to activate the representation stored for either of the component identities, but it might also be because the composite changes some of the spatial arrangements between distant features (e.g. the spatial relationships between the eyes and the mouth). On either account, misalignment of the two halves of the composite prevents the emergence of critical configural information and hence removes the interference from the other half of the face.

We noted that in Tanaka and Farah's (1993) method the artificial stimuli make it possible to replace one pair of (artificial) eyes with another pair in an equivalent spatial position, and this seems mostly to be how the technique is operationalised. To the extent that this is achieved (on which, more later), it is mainly tapping the holistic configuration. In contrast, the kind of manipulation shown in Figure 6.1 is mainly targeted at the second-order configuration.

Leder and Bruce (2000) took this further and attempted to distinguish the processing of the spatial relationships between different features from the perception of the holistic pattern created by the face. They did this by constructing sets of faces within which individual faces were distinguished only by unique relational features or by combinations of the pigmentation of local features. So in a 'relational' set of six faces, one face had eyes spaced widely, one had eyes close together, one had a large distance between nose and mouth, and so on. In the 'local' feature versions, one face had red lips with dark hair, another red lips with light hair, a third pale lips with light hair, etc. Importantly, to recognise one of the 'local' versions the *whole* face pattern would have to be inspected, since the unique characteristics of the face were distributed across it. Despite this, there was little or no inversion effect when faces were identifiable on the basis of these local feature combinations. As expected, there were substantial inversion effects when faces could be identified only by differences in the feature placement, suggesting that the key ingredient in 'configuration' in this study was the spatial relationships between features. However, part of the reason for the lack of a holistic inversion effect may have been that the distributed local feature differences used by Leder and Bruce (2000) were (intentionally) not particularly subtle.

However neat the apparent distinctions between processing local features, wholes and second-order configuration, though, we must offer some caveats. First, most changes in configuration have effects on component features as well. For instance, an increase in the distance between the nose and the mouth can turn an average-sized chin into a small one, or moving the eyes and mouth further apart vertically will change (elongate) the nose. So there can be no hard and fast distinction between featural changes and different types of configural change except through the use of contrived materials such as those of Tanaka and Farah (1993) and Leder and Bruce (2000). From this rather narrow perspective, the use of stimuli with limited ecological validity might have some advantages, but it brings problems too, in knowing how much the findings become determined by the constraints of the experiment. These problems of stimulus control may explain why several studies have shown that the face inversion effect can involve more than just the processing of configuration. Moreover, it is possible that there could be relatively local configural effects affecting some parts of the face – as seems also to happen in studies of gaze (see Figure 5.6) or expression (Figure 4.17). For example Rhodes, Brake and Atkinson (1993) found that manipulations of the local features of eyes and mouth gave rise to large inversion effects, while changes to features such as facial hair or glasses did not.

McKone and Yovel (2009) provide a detailed meta-analysis and review of how inversion affects the processing of facial features compared with spacing changes. They demonstrate very clearly that inversion affects the processing of face features just as much as it affects their spacing, except under certain conditions. These are when the feature changes are pronounced (as in Leder & Bruce,

2000), or where experimental conditions favour a 'piecemeal' processing strategy – for example if the features are presented without a face context, or if a very small number of items is used which might lead participants to home in on localised characteristics to do their task. McKone and Yovel's conclusion is that the specialised style of face processing which is harmed by face inversion, and upon which face processing expertise appears to be built, actually involves holistic rather than second-order configural processing.

In line with this, we think that it is not easy to work out how our brains might use second-order configural information for face recognition. Feature-spacing information is fixed from the perspective of a full-face view, but when someone simply moves their head upwards or downwards, or from side to side, this will affect the perceived spacing unless your brain actively corrects for this. What demonstrations such as Figure 6.1 show is that we are very sensitive to spacing changes in upright compared to inverted faces – which is interesting and potentially important. What they don't show directly is that this information is critical for face recognition – actually, you can recognise all the upright images in Figure 6.1, even though some look distorted.

Data strongly support this contention. Hole, George, Eaves and Razek (2002) showed that faces remain recognisable despite severe distortions of their second-order spatial configuration produced by laterally or vertically stretching or squashing the face (see Figure 6.5). Such stretched faces can yield behavioural responses not significantly different from the unstretched originals. Moreover, Bindemann, Burton, Leuthold and Schweinberger (2008) showed that such distorted faces can yield electrophysiological as well as behavioural responses indistinguishable from the original photographs of these people. One potential explanation might be that these responses are based on local features unaffected by such gross distortions. This explanation can be dismissed, however. In a follow-up study Hole et al. (2002) showed that a face to which a stretching distortion was applied to just the top or bottom half of the face, leaving the other half undistorted, was much *harder* to recognise than the original. If local features were being used then these 'half-distorted' faces should be easier, since more features are left intact. Furthermore, stretched faces which are blurred are only slightly harder to recognise even though blurring leaves spatial configural information intact and seriously degrades the detail of local features. So, these stretching effects cannot be explained in terms of local feature recognition. However, they also put further constraints on 'configural' processing. Simple 2D relationships are not preserved in stretched faces, but nor are 'holistic' patterns obviously preserved either. Should a 'half-distorted' face not match a simple holistic template better than a fully stretched one?

Hole and his colleagues' impressive findings show clearly that recognition is not based on any absolute coding for feature spacing, but more complex relational codes might be entertained. Sinha, Balas, Ostrovsky and Russell (2006) suggest that the resilience of recognition to stretching and compression implies that the human visual system codes faces in terms of 'isodimension ratios' (ratios of distances within the same dimension, i.e. horizontal or vertical), and that this might be one way that the brain can ignore some of the distortions that arise in the visual image of the face as the head turns or nods. Up to a point,

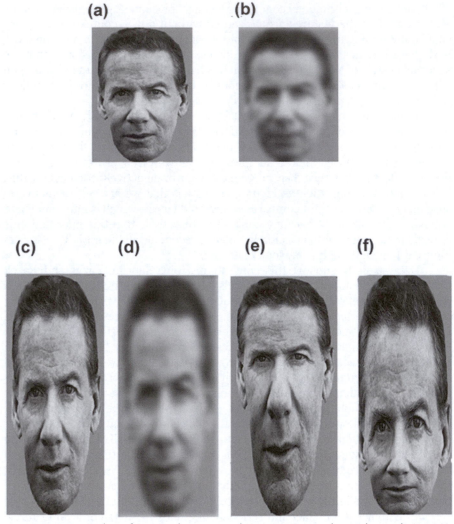

Figure 6.5 Examples of manipulations used in experiments by Hole et al. (2002). Compared with the normal face shown at (a), recognition remains high with global distortions such as the vertical stretch at (c) and is affected little by blurring as in (b) and (d), but is poor when distortions are applied to only parts of the faces as in (e) and (f). Courtesy Graham Hole.

such facial movements in depth approximate two-dimensional compressions. Any theory of representation processing of faces must accommodate these observations too.

McKone and Yovel (2009) go further. They maintain that there is no evidence that the brain processes the distances between face features separately from the shapes of these features themselves, nor any evidence that the features for which we happen to have names have some privileged status in face representation. Potential implications for our understanding of face processing are that either the spatial relationships coded from faces must be based on a very sophisticated set of coordinates, which encompass the coding of the shape of individual features as well as more distant spacing, or that faces are not decomposed via these kinds of explicit measurements at all – for example, they might be analysed as something like arrays of pixel intensities, though some kind of pre-processing would still be needed to accommodate the stretching effects we have just discussed. We will return to consider these kinds of representational hypotheses when we describe norm-based coding and image-based representations later in this chapter. At that point, the attractions of this view will become more clear.

There are other demonstrations too that our stored memories of faces are remarkably resilient. In Figure 6.6, Salvador Dali conveys a clear likeness of the

Figure 6.6 Mae West, by Salvador Dali. Art Institute of Chicago, Gift of Mrs Gilbert W. Chapman in memory of Charles B. Godspeed. (c) ADAGP. Paris and DACS, London 1998.

actress Mae West despite depicting each of her features as an item of interior decor. This image shows how powerfully the face schema overcomes other distorting influences, and shows that even individual identity can be preserved in such arrangements. Such demonstrations may suggest that face representations must have multiple redundancies too. We need to consider some of the other cues to identity that are available, and which of these can be used.

More potential cues to identity: Shape and surface pigmentation

In Chapter 1 we described how the appearance of an individual face results from a combination of its underlying bone structure, the thickness of the layers of muscle and fat between bone and skin, and the texture and pigmentation of skin and hair. The consequence is that different sources of information, from the 3D shape of the face to the superficial features of its skin coloration, might all contribute to the process of identification.

We have seen in earlier chapters the importance of 3D and surface pigmentation for the perception of such things as the sex or attractiveness of faces. But does the human visual system use this information for *recognising* faces? The 3D shape of the face is revealed from a combination of the surface features which are visible and the pattern of light and shade which can be used to derive surface information (see Chapter 2). Some evidence that 3D shape might be important in face recognition comes from the advantage sometimes found for ¾ views rather than full-face images in face recognition. An angled view reveals more about the way that a face is structured in depth. The shape of the nose in particular is very difficult to see in a full-face image and much clearer from an angle. Perhaps this forms part of the reason why full-face portraits are rare in art – artists seem naturally to prefer a viewpoint which reveals more about the shape of the face. However, where experiments have shown advantages for the ¾ view in face recognition, it tends to be in memory for previously unfamiliar faces where only a single view of the face has been learnt. In contrast, familiar face recognition seems to be equally easy from full face and ¾ views (e.g. Bruce, Valentine, & Baddeley, 1987). This suggests that the ¾ view may be useful in unfamiliar face tasks because it allows generalisation to a broader range of views than does a full-face image (see Liu & Chaudhuri, 2002). When a face is already familiar, our exposure to a wider range of views when we interact with someone, or see them on TV, may help offset any slight advantage given by the angled view.

Although the effects of viewpoint suggest some role for 3D shape in human face recognition, it is actually remarkably difficult to identify faces when *only* the 3D shape is available. Bruce, Healey, Burton, Doyle, Coombes and Linney (1991) asked a number of their university colleagues to have their faces measured using a laser scanner. Surface images of these faces were then depicted using the techniques described in Chapter 1, and the resulting images shown to friends and students. Identification rates were remarkably low, compared with the rates of identification of the same people shown in photographs with their eyes closed and wearing bathing caps – the same state they were in for the laser measurement – and lower for female faces than for male ones. This demonstrates the importance of superficial features and skin pigmentation for our normal recognition processes.

One of the most disruptive transformations we can make to a face image is to put it into photographic negative. Upside-down faces are difficult to recognise, but photographic negatives are even harder. In the experiment mentioned earlier, Bruce and Langton (1994) compared the effects of inverting and negating famous faces and found negation had an even more detrimental effect than inverting the image. Upright faces were named correctly 95% of the time, and inverted 70%. But negated images were named only 55% on average and inverted negatives only 25%. Indeed the effects of inversion and negation were additive, suggesting they affect distinct aspects of the face or distinct processing stages. If inversion prevents configural processing, negation must hurt something quite different.

Normal photographic negatives reverse two separable aspects of the image – the brightness and the colour values. However, it is possible to manipulate these separately, reversing only brightness (making the light regions dark, and dark regions light) or colour (making red hues green, blue hues yellow, and so on). Figure 6.7 illustrates the manipulations of hue negation, luminance negation and full negation (reversed colour *and* brightness) on an image of a human face (Kemp, Pike, White, & Musselman, 1996). You can see that colour negation has less effect than you might have expected (mainly, the person looks very ill indeed), whereas brightness negation is very disruptive of information about the face's identity. As we have seen throughout this book, different cues seem important for different purposes. Colour information can be useful in judging health, and even age (see Chapter 3), but it contributes little to recognising identity. For identity, the brightness values seem critical.

There are different things that brightness negation may affect. At least part of the difficulty may arise because negatives make it difficult to derive a representation of 3D shape from shading. Another factor may be that negative images reverse the brightness of important pigmented areas, so that light skin becomes dark, and dark hair becomes light, potentially 'disguising' the face. This account was favoured by Bruce and Langton (1994) who found that negation did not reduce the (already poor) recognition rates of non-pigmented 3D surface representations of faces, suggesting the effects on the normally pigmented images of faces are more to do with the patterns of surface pigmentation than shape from shading.

But other factors may also be important. The reversal of brightness in the eyes may make it difficult to encode the face, in the same way that classical sculptures seem to suffer so much from their 'white' eyes (see Figure 6.8). A dramatic recent demonstration by Gilad, Meng and Sinha (2009) has shown that the detrimental effects of negating photographs are largely eliminated if the eye regions *alone* are rendered positive within otherwise negated images to produce what they label 'contrast chimeras' (see Figure 6.9). This means that face representations must significantly favour, or be built around, 2D ordinal contrast relationships around the eyes. We saw in Chapter 5 how critical contrast

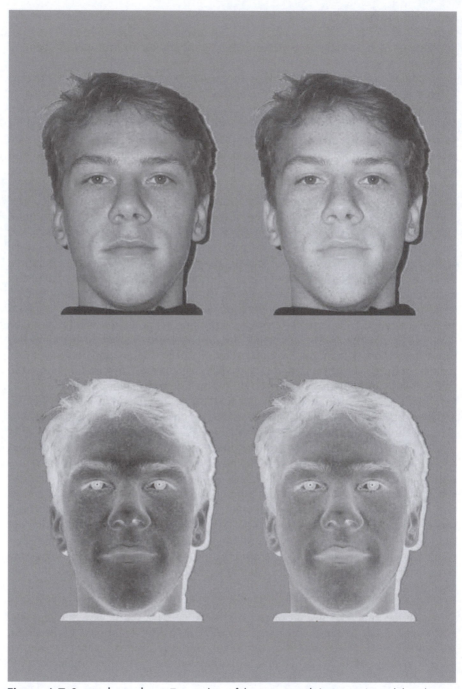

Figure 6.7 See colour plate. Examples of hue reversal (top row) and brightness negation (bottom row) used in experiments by Kemp et al. (1996). Courtesy of Richard Kemp.

Figure 6.8 Original (top) and computer-manipulated versions of the bust of George Combe by Lawrence MacDonald, courtesy of the Scottish National Portrait Gallery. Bottom – original bust of Combe (left) with pupils darkened (centre) or added by etching (right), produced by Helmut Leder for Bruce and Young (1998).

relationships are to perception of the eye region. However, it is not sufficient just to show positive eyes in an otherwise blank head silhouette, demonstrating that the positive eye regions allow useful additional information to be coded from the remainder of a negated face. In fMRI, Gilad et al. (2009) found the right FFA also responded equally to full images and to the contrast chimeras, and much less strongly to full negatives or images showing just the eyes in an otherwise blank silhouette. Later in this chapter we will return to examining evidence demonstrating the importance of internal features, particularly the eyes, as faces become familiar.

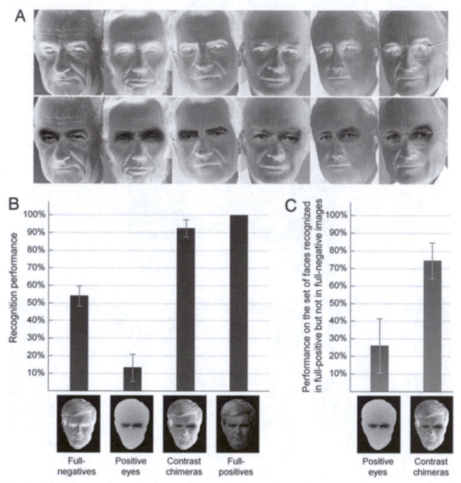

Figure 6.9 Example images and recognition results from Gilad et al. (2009). A. Negative images of some famous faces above 'contrast chimeras'; B. Recognition performance on full negatives, positive eyes in blank surround, contrast chimeras and full positives. C. Recognition of positive eyes compared with contrast chimeras for a set of faces never recognised in full negatives but always recognised in full positives. First published Gilad, S., Meng, M., & Sinha, P. (2009). Role of ordinal contrast relationships in face encoding. *Proceedings of the National Academy of Sciences of the United States of America, 106*(13), pp. 5353–5358. Copyright 2009 National Academy of Sciences, U.S.A. Part A images: Images from the White House website, www.whitehouse.gov.

Movement and face recognition

Much of the research on face recognition has focused on the process of recognising a static photograph. This is partly because experiments recording accuracy and speed of recognition are easy to conduct with static images, but become more complicated when moving images are to be used. But partly it reflects the theoretical perspective that recognition is based upon the enduring or invariant characteristics of a person's face – a perspective that tends to imply that the changes which occur when a face speaks or expresses are something that must largely be ignored in recognising who the person is.

It was therefore interesting when Knight and Johnston (1997) first demonstrated positive effects of movement on recognition success. In their experiment, participants were shown famous faces that were made difficult to recognise by presenting them in photographic negative or upside down. When these formats were shown as movie clips, successful recognition was much more frequent than when the faces were shown statically. The effects were stronger for the faces presented upright than inverted, which led Knight and Johnston to conclude that the effect was not simply due to the addition of extra 'static' information in the moving clips.

Lander and colleagues have since extended this research in a series of investigations (e.g. Lander, Christie, & Bruce, 1999; Lander & Bruce, 2000; Lander & Chuang, 2005). The studies first demonstrated that beneficial effects of motion can be seen on recognising famous faces in a range of different degraded formats – negative images, upside-down images, or simply images converted to two-tone, black-on-white through 'thresholding'. This degradation is necessary to reveal effects of motion which would otherwise be concealed by ceiling effects – because a familiar face is so easily recognisable from a normal static photograph, it is not possible to measure any beneficial effect of movement on accuracy without degrading the images, and the tactic of measuring speed of recognition would be tricky to use when comparing static with dynamic presentation.

Lander and her colleagues went on to demonstrate convincingly that there were beneficial effects of movement over and above those obtained with the addition of extra static form. For example, Lander, Christie and Bruce (1999) showed that an animated sequence of nine frames was recognised more accurately than the same nine frames seen together in a static array and studied for the same total time as the sequence was presented. Lander and Bruce (2000) showed that recognition was best if the moving sequence preserved the dynamic pattern of the original – the same frames rearranged temporally did not yield the same benefits.

What information, then, is movement adding? One potential benefit might be that it reveals more about the face's 3D structure – even though we have already seen that evidence for an important role of 3D structure in recognition is limited, this is a possibility that must be considered. However, sequences presented speeded up or reversed were not recognised as well as sequences that mirrored the original tempo (Lander & Bruce, 2000). If the beneficial effects of movement were due to additional information about 3D shape it is not clear why precise tempo information would be so critical. Instead, Lander and Chuang (2005) demonstrated clearly that the important dynamic information for the recognition of familiar faces comes from distinctive patterns of non-rigid expressive or speech movements rather than rigid head movements. Non-rigid movements should, if anything, be less informative about 3D shape than is rigid motion. These findings suggest that the dynamic movements characteristic of particular individuals are somehow represented in memory, which as we saw in Chapter 4 may have interesting implications for the organisation of Haxby et al.'s (2000) core system for face perception.

Distinctiveness and caricature

Although all faces are built to the same basic template, some faces deviate more from the average or prototype face, while other faces have a more average or 'typical' appearance. Experiments on human face recognition have shown that faces which are more deviant or 'distinctive' in appearance are recognised better than those which are more typical (e.g. Light, Kayra-Stuart, & Hollander, 1979; Bartlett, Hurry, & Thorley, 1984; Vokey & Read, 1992).

Effects of facial distinctiveness can be revealed in a number of different tasks. For famous faces, it has been found that those which are rated as distinctive in appearance can be recognised as familiar more quickly than those which are rated as more typical in appearance, even though performance is very accurate for all the faces. So, a relatively distinctive face like that of Prince Charles will be recognised as familiar faster than that of the more typical-looking David Cameron, for example (Valentine & Bruce, 1986). Using unfamiliar faces, distinctiveness gives advantages on tests of memory – distinctive faces are more likely than typical faces to be recognised correctly when the task is to decide which of a set of faces were studied earlier. If distinctive faces are placed among the non-studied items in the test series, they are less likely to be remembered falsely than more typical faces (e.g. Bartlett et al. 1984).

However, when the task is changed from one of recognition to that of classifying the face as a face – if, for example, normally arranged faces are interspersed with jumbled faces or other non-face objects, and you press a button as quickly as possible whenever you see a face – then for both famous and unfamiliar faces, typical faces have the advantage. So, the pattern of results found in face identification tasks is reversed, and people will now be slower to decide that Prince Charles' face is a face than to decide that David Cameron's face is a face (Valentine & Bruce, 1986).

One way to understand the effects of distinctiveness is the 'face-space' framework introduced by Valentine (1991). This theory proposes that any face can be described by its value along each of a number of dimensions of facial variation. Usually, as here in Figure 6.10, proponents of the face space model simplify this by showing just two dimensions, but the expectation is that a large number of dimensions will be needed to fully characterise facial appearance. Dimensions could be simple characteristics such as nose length, or global characteristics such as age or face elongation. Faces which are rated as more typical will tend to have values on the dimensions which are true of many faces (e.g. a nose of average length), while those which are rated more distinctive will have more extreme values (e.g. very long or very short noses). In the diagram in Figure 6.10, then, typical faces will tend to cluster more closely together within the space, while distinctive ones are scattered around the periphery.

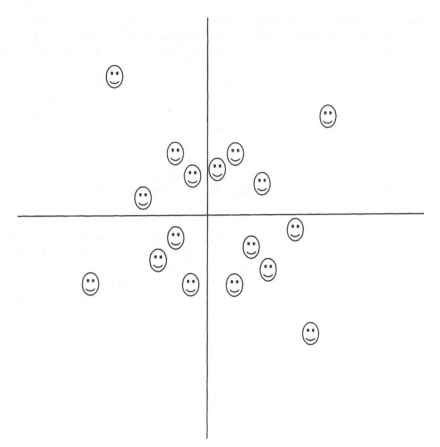

Figure 6.10 A schematic diagram of a two-dimensional face space in which the values on two dimensions locate each individual item in the 'space' of variation. See also Figure 3.28 for an illustration of two possible dimensions in such a space.

In the face-space model, the task of identifying a face requires a comparison of the dimensions of a to-be-recognised face with dimensional descriptions of faces which have already been stored, to see whether a stored face can be found which shares this same set of physical dimensions. Where there are many stored faces with similar physical characteristics it will be more difficult to distinguish true from false matches – more precision will be needed on each of the physical dimensions and so the process may take longer, or be more prone to error. Because there will be few competing descriptions in the area of space occupied by distinctive faces, matching the description can be achieved more readily than for typical faces. So the classic finding of easier recognition of distinctive than typical faces seems to fit this model fairly easily. However, if the task is to classify the pattern as a face (rather than a non-face), then the question is whether a test pattern conforms to the characteristic of the basic face template. A test pattern which is a typical face will resemble a large number of similar faces within the face space, allowing a relatively fast positive response to be made. A distinctive face, in contrast, will resemble few other patterns in the space, and therefore will get less immediate support for the positive decision, which will therefore take longer to reach.

The face-space metaphor offers an ingenious way to think about typicality and distinctiveness. Many people find it useful, but in a multi-dimensional rather than two-dimensional space the predicted distribution of faces becomes more complicated than might be supposed – your (non-mathematical) intuitions can be misleading. In particular, it can be shown that *extremely* typical faces (i.e. those which are average on all their dimensions) will actually be rather rare (Burton & Vokey, 1998). This seems to mesh with Galton's (1883) anecdotal observation about the rarity of what he describes as a typical 'John Bull' (Englishman):

> One fine Sunday afternoon I sat with a friend by the walk in Kensington Gardens that leads to the bridge, and which on such occasion is thronged with promenaders. It was agreed between us that whichever first caught sight of a typical John Bull should call the attention of the other. We sat and watched keenly for many minutes, but neither of us found occasion to utter a word.
>
> (Galton, 1883, p. 4)

Distinctiveness may help us to understand how caricatures work – by exaggerating an individual's idiosyncratic features, caricatures exploit distinctiveness by making that face less like others. Caricatures of ex-President Richard Nixon (Figure 6.11), for example, exaggerated the extended bulb of his nose, and the

Figure 6.11 Line drawing (left) and caricature (right) of ex-President Richard Nixon. From Perkins (1975). Courtesy of David Perkins.

bags under his eyes. Goldman and Hagen (1978) studied caricatures produced of Richard Nixon by 17 different artists during 1972–1973, and found that there was a great deal of consistency across different artists in terms of what features of the face were distorted in their drawings, though considerable variation in the extent of the distortions. Importantly, in making caricatures, artists were deliberately creating non-veridical representations. Nixon's nose was not *that* big, nor his eyes *so* baggy – yet these changes rendered the representations better able to characterise Nixon than other faces!

In terms of the face-space framework, the caricature produces a description which is more extreme (further out in space) than the actual Nixon, but in consequence this representation becomes less likely to be confused with any face other than Nixon's. This insight underlies the generation of line drawn and photograph-quality caricatures by computer. We briefly introduced the basics of computer caricature in Chapter 2 – now we need to discuss the results of computer caricaturing face identity.

Brennan (1985) first reported a technique for generating caricatures automatically by computer, and her technique rests on the suggestion that a caricature 'is a symbol that exaggerates measurements relative to individuating norms' (Perkins, 1975). Brennan digitised photographs of faces and located a set of 186 key points which described the major face features. For example, points within the set of 186 included the inner and outer corner of each eye and a small set of additional points along the upper and lower eye-lids. These points could be linked together to form a line-drawing of the original face, as shown in Figure 6.12. If the same set of points is measured for a large number of faces, and the coordinates of all these faces scaled to coincide at the pupils, then the average locations of

Figure 6.12 A line drawing and computer-generated caricature (right) of former President Ronald Reagan, courtesy of Susan Brennan.

each point can be computed, to produce a line-drawing of the 'average' or 'norm' face. To caricature a specific face, the locations of the individual points for that face are compared with the average and exaggerated by multiplication. The effect of this multiplication is that large deviations from the norm are increased more than small deviations, producing distortions which will be greatest for the most deviant aspects of the face. Figure 6.12 shows a resulting caricature of ex-President Ronald Reagan's face, which is much more recognisable than the line drawing to the left which is based on Reagan's uncaricatured point locations.

Rhodes, Brennan and Carey (1987) produced line-drawn caricatures like this, using smooth curves rather than straight lines to join up the points. The stimulus faces were personally familiar to the participants in their experiments, and Rhodes et al. (1987) were able to confirm that positive caricaturing of this kind made line drawings of faces more recognisable. It is also possible to make faces less recognisable by making 'anticaricatures' that shift the features towards the average face – in effect making a face more typical in appearance. Faces can be caricatured and anticaricatured to greater or lesser extent by exaggerating or reducing the difference between the face and the norm by smaller or larger percentage changes.

Figure 6.13 shows a sequence of caricatures and anticaricatures of the British comedian, Rowan Atkinson, which clearly demonstrates the enhanced likeness achieved with modest degrees of positive caricaturing. These images have been additionally enhanced, and become better representations as a result, by filling in the dark areas of the hair. Rhodes and Tremewan (1994) showed such enhanced line drawings of high school students' classmates in caricatured and anticaricatured versions and found that 30% and 50% positive caricatures were recognised significantly better (75% correct on average) than the original drawings (62%).

This technique of describing a face by a fixed set of key coordinates (known as fiducial points) and smoothly moving the face towards or away from some other set of coordinates (in this case, the coordinates corresponding to the average face) is the principle which underlies the now common technique of computer 'morphing' which allows smooth transformation from one image through to another, as we described in Chapter 2. This technique was anticipated by early caricature artists, however, as illustrated by the famous political cartoon 'Les Poires' (Figure 6.14).

This cartoon was produced by Charles Philipon in 1834, in protest at his prosecution for adopting 'La Poire' as an emblem for the French King Louis-Philippe – an emblem which played upon the pear-like shape of the monarch, using the slang word for 'fathead'. In Les Poires, the gradual 'morph' between the image of the King and of a pear was created by Philipon to protest that all pear-like images would have to be banned in order to avoid offence. The censors were apparently persuaded by this argument and proceeded to ban pears (Rhodes, 1996)!

As we described in Chapter 2, the same techniques can be applied to full photographic-quality images as well as with line-drawings, to produce morphs and caricatures of face images that have been used in many of the

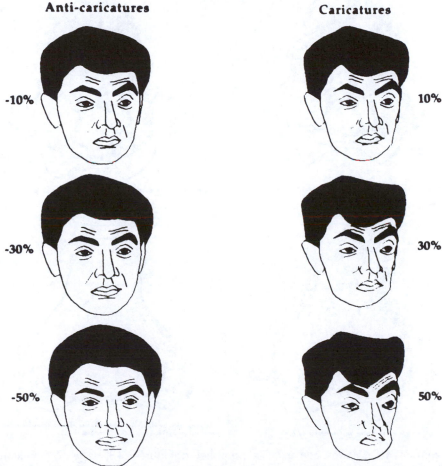

Undistorted Drawing

0%

Anti-caricatures   **Caricatures**

-10%   10%

-30%   30%

-50%   50%

Figure 6.13 Computer-generated caricatures of a line drawing of the British comedian, Rowan Atkinson. First published as Figure 3.4, page 43 in Gillian Rhodes, *Superportraits* (Psychology Press, 1996), reprinted by permission of Taylor & Francis Group, http://www.informaworld.com.

LES POIRES,

Faites à la cour d'assises de Paris par le directeur de la CARICATURE.

Vendues pour payer les 6,000 fr. d'amende du journal le *Charivari*.

(CHEZ ALBERT, GALERIE VERO-DODAT)

Si, pour reconnaître le monarque dans une caricature, vous n'attendez pas qu'il soit désigné autrement que par la ressemblance, vous tomberez dans l'absurde. Voyez ces croquis informes, auxquels j'aurais peut être du borner ma défense :

Ce croquis ressemble à Louis-Philippe, vous condamnerez donc ?

Alors il faudra condamner celui-ci, qui ressemble au premier.

Puis condamner cet autre, qui ressemble au second

Et enfin, si vous êtes conséquents, vous ne sauriez absoudre cette poire, qui ressemble aux croquis précédents

Figure 6.14 Les Poires. See text. First published as Figure 2.18, page 36 in Gillian Rhodes, *Superportraits* (Psychology Press, 1996), reprinted by permission of Taylor & Francis Group, http://www.informaworld.com.

experiments we have discussed in this book (e.g. morphs and caricatures of facial expressions of emotion in Chapter 4). All that is needed for photo-realistic image manipulation is a way to combine the surface textures of the images with the set of tesselated regions that results from the positions of the fiducial points.

Intriguingly, a computer-caricature of a photograph of a person's face produces an image which in some circumstances is judged as more like the person than their actual photograph (Benson & Perrett, 1991). When first discovered, this seemed like an impressive confirmation of the implications of face-space type models. However, further studies show that the recognition advantages of full photographic caricatures are found only infrequently and under circumstances where recognition is made more difficult (e.g. brief presentation – see Rhodes, 1996 for a review).

The beneficial effects for recognition of caricaturing line drawings of faces are much more clear, but it now seems this is because a line drawing hugely reduces the information available to the perceiver, leaving more scope for recognition to be aided by the exaggeration of distinctive features. In this respect, the benefits of caricaturing on recognition of familiar faces are not unlike those of movement. If faces are made difficult to recognise then adding something can help, whether it is through exaggerating their distinctive shapes, or adding characteristic movement. Under most everyday conditions, though, it seems that the face provides such a multiplicity of cues to its identity that a quick glance is all we need.

Other-race and other-age effects

The preceding discussion of 'distinctiveness' effects may have created the impression that distinctiveness is an objective property of a face – based only on the extent to which its characteristics resemble those present in the rest of the population of faces. However, there are related variables that affect face recognition which illustrate clearly that distinctiveness is itself more malleable – to a certain extent, it exists 'in the eye of the beholder'. We are better at distinguishing between faces that are common in our immediate social environments than between faces of a kind that are rarely encountered, but this can also be influenced by social psychological factors alongside differential experience.

The 'other-race' effect has been known for some time (e.g. Malpass & Kravitz, 1969; Brigham, 1986; Meissner & Brigham, 2001). Participants are usually more accurate in recognition memory studies when trying to recognise members of their own race than when recognising other-race faces. Explanations in terms of relative discriminability of the faces of one face or another can be discounted since these effects are symmetrical – it really isn't the case that there are races in which 'they all look the same'. Instead, where studies have used participants of two different races, each will tend to find the faces of their own race easier than other-race faces. Explanations for the other-race effect range from more social accounts, in terms of prejudice and stereotyping, through to more perceptual-cognitive accounts. We touched on these issues in Chapter 3.

Stereotyping accounts suggest it may be 'convenient' for us to fail to learn things about other-race faces, whereas perceptual-cognitive accounts point out that the optimal cues for identifying individual faces may differ between races, leading to suboptimal recognition if these cues are sought in other-race faces. These explanations need not be mutually exclusive. A number of studies have demonstrated that meaningful exposure to faces of another race – as might be gained by living in an integrated culture for several years – can reduce or eliminate the other-race effect (e.g. Chiroro & Valentine, 1995).

More recently, an 'other-age' effect has also been noted, in which participants are sometimes found to be better at recognising faces of their own than other age groups. For example, Wiese, Schweinberger and Hansen (2008) found that young adults were poorer at recognising faces of older adults than those of their own age group, while the older adults in the study were equally good at the younger and older faces. Arguably an older adult has considerable experience (through their own youth) and enduring interest (through their children and grandchildren) of faces of younger as well as older adults, while those who are younger have more restricted experience of older faces (their parents and teachers but not, yet, their peers). Similar effects have been found with children. Anastasi and Rhodes (2005) for example found that children and older adults recognised faces of their own age more accurately than those of other ages. Harrison and Hole (2009) showed that while undergraduate students were worse at recognising faces of 8–11 year olds than faces of their own age-group, this difference was not found for trainee teachers who were just as good at the children's faces as the adult ones. This lends support to the idea that contact with the 'out-group', whether of another age or another race, helps develop the attention to and/or knowledge of facial characteristics needed to discriminate between them successfully.

Something that is especially interesting about other-age effects is the way that they can change across the lifespan. We tend to think of our expertise with faces as if it is something that just gets better and better as we become more and more expert. Other age effects give the lie to this simple idea. Expertise is not just a box of tricks to which you keep adding. Sometimes, you might actually discard or modify tricks that no longer suit your purposes. When you are 18, you probably have a pretty shrewd idea who else is 18 and who isn't when you go to a pub. When you are older, you find that you can't do that any more, but you can now differentiate faces of older adults who just look 'past it' to the 18 year olds. We will return to these issues of development and expertise in Chapter 8. The other-age effect shows neatly that change continues throughout our lives.

Other-race and other-age effects can be accommodated broadly by assuming that faces are represented within a multi-dimensional space where the coding dimensions reflect the faces to which the observer has been exposed and are refined by experience of more faces. The face-space model is clearly of this type, and one of its early successes was its integration of effects of race and distinctiveness within a common framework (Valentine, 1991), but it is under-specified with respect to what the dimensions might be. Later in this chapter we will consider how a more precisely defined space built around the Principal Components of face variation might be able to model such effects.

However the dimensions of a face space are construed, there are two different ways that such a space might operate in coding seen faces. In one variant, known as an 'exemplar-based' system, each face is coded independently of the rest. In the other variant, known as 'norm-based' coding, the central tendency of the face space – the 'prototype' – assumes a key role in representation in which individual faces are stored as deviations from this prototype. In the next section we consider how experiments on the formation of prototypes, and on identity adaptation effects, have influenced our thinking about these different potential implementations of face space.

Prototypes and adaptation effects

Solso and McCarthy (1981) provided one of the first demonstrations of prototype effects in face memory. Their participants were shown faces made up from different combinations of eyes, noses, mouths, etc. from the Photofit kit. Each of the studied faces was a variation of an underlying 'prototype' face, but (importantly) this prototype was itself never studied. At test, however, participants found the previously unseen prototype faces more familiar than any of the items that had actually been studied. A similar effect was found by Bruce, Doyle, Dench and Burton (1991), whose participants studied a set of faces whose configuration varied by moving the internal features upwards and downwards. At test, participants remembered seeing faces with features placed in a location which was the average for the studied series, even though this prototype face had again never been studied. Cabeza, Bruce, Kato and Oda (1999) replicated and extended these findings using photographic quality images. In their studies participants remembered seeing the prototype of a set of within-view face feature variations, but did not remember seeing a viewpoint that fell midway between studied angles. This suggests that the mechanism responsible for false memory for a prototype operates more strongly within than between viewpoints. Later in this chapter we describe a theory of the development of representations of familiar faces based upon averaging different exemplars of a face together, which could work only within broadly similar viewpoints.

The prototype effects outlined above involve both variations of an individual face identity (e.g. remembering the central tendency of several variants formed from the same face features moved around the face) and variations across identities (different combinations of Photofit features giving rise to familiarity of an unseen but prototypical combination of these features in Solso's studies). Prototype effects are one piece of evidence for a 'norm-based' representational theory, in which faces are represented as their deviations from an underlying norm or average. Some versions of the face-space framework see an explicit norm or prototype forming the heart of the space, with individual faces represented as departures from this norm (see Rhodes, 1996, for a discussion of caricature effects in these terms). But many effects that can be explained by the emergence or use of a prototype can also be explained by the storage of individual exemplars, because a prototype pattern at test can resemble more exemplars more closely than any individual exemplar does (e.g. Hintzman, 1986;

Nosofsky, 1991). This tension between 'abstractive' and 'instance-based' accounts is something to which we return later in this chapter.

However, the idea that prototypes are at the heart of representations of faces has some appealing features. First, faces are not usually encountered as discrete exemplars, but as moving, expressing visual patterns. Given this, it is difficult to see where one exemplar would stop and another would start outside of the bounds of an experiment using pictures of faces. Second, connectionist models of representation which appeal to neuron-like properties do not store anything at all beyond a changed set of connection weights – and it is easier to think of these as capturing prototypes than 'exemplars'. Lastly, the idea that there are one or more 'norms' at the heart of face representations makes it *intuitively* easier to understand a range of adaptation effects that have recently come to the fore.

In previous chapters we have introduced studies in which adaptation from prolonged viewing of a face affects the perception of items which follow immediately afterwards. So, after prolonged viewing of a female face, an androgynous face looks male (Webster et al., 2004, see Chapter 3) and after prolonged viewing of a happy face, a neutral face looks slightly sad (Rutherford et al., 2008, see Chapter 4). Similar adaptation effects have been found for facial identity, and the precise characteristics of these effects seem consistent with the 'norm-based' coding idea.

We have described how caricatures and anticaricatures can be made by shifting an image of a face away from or towards the representation of an 'average' face. This average can be constructed from a set of faces of similar overall age and sex to the face to be caricatured. Using the same principles, it is possible to construct faces that are placed on opposite sides of the 'average' so that for each face – e.g. Jim – it is possible to produce an 'anti-face' that is its reflection in face space (e.g. anti-Jim). If Jim, for example, has a long nose then anti-Jim will have a small one. If Jim's face is fat, then anti-Jim's will be thin, and so on. Leopold, O'Toole, Vetter and Blanz (2001) demonstrated that if participants are adapted to 'anti-Jim' they then became readier (post-adaptation) to recognise 'Jim' in an ambiguous face. So adapting to anti-Jim makes the average face seem more like Jim afterwards.

In this kind of experiment the comparison/control conditions are critical if explanations in terms of simple physical after-effects are to be dismissed. While Leopold et al. (2001) compared adapting to 'anti-Jim' with adapting to an unrelated face, it is possible there might have been physical differences that accounted for the results. Rhodes and Jeffery (2006) therefore followed up this demonstration and showed that such effects were down to deviations within face space rather than simply to overall similarity. They achieved this by constructing face triplets where the control item 'Fred' was rated as being as dissimilar in appearance to 'Jim' as was the 'anti-Jim' item. Using such materials Rhodes et al. still demonstrated clear adaptation effects that were identity-specific (between Jim and anti-Jim), lending strong support to the idea that face identities are coded with reference to an overall prototype or 'norm' face. But on what kinds of measurements or dimensions are these norm-based representations based? This is the question we turn to next.

Visual representation of faces in memory

What are the dimensions of face space? It is possible to think of the space of facial variation as describing dimensions of individual facial features, but such a description would not mesh well with the clear evidence already discussed that faces are represented configurally.

There are in fact a number of ways to capture the visual information in whole face images in a way that delivers 'dimensions' of variation. Here we will focus on one technique, Principal Components Analysis (PCA). Mathematically, PCA provides a way of reducing the storage requirements for a set of images – this would be useful, for example, if we wanted to store faces efficiently in a computer. Some psychologists have argued that the brain may do something similar to PCA when it encodes faces. To explain this requires that we describe the PCA technique in more detail.

A computer stores a monochrome image of a face as the intensity or 'grey' level in each of the array of pixels used to display the image (for colour images the intensity of three different colours is separately coded). With a typical face image spanning many thousands of pixels, raw face images will therefore take up a great deal of memory. However, by analysing the statistical variation across different pixels in a large number of different face images, a more economical way of coding individual faces can be derived.

Across a series of faces, there will be variation in the intensity shown within each pixel. For example, some men have receding hairlines, and so the pixels at the upper forehead will be light (skin), while others have a full head of dark hair and the corresponding pixels may be dark. By analysing the patterns of correlation between the grey-levels in these different pixels across a series of faces, the Principal Components of this variation can be extracted.

This may be made clearer with an example from a different domain. Suppose we test a large number of children aged 10 to 16 years on the time it takes them to swim one length of a pool using different swimming strokes, and the time it takes them to walk or run different distances. If we correlate all these different measures of walking, running and swimming along with the height and weight of each child, we will be able to extract some underlying dimensions that account for the variation more economically. The first component in our hypothetical example would probably correspond to the age of the child – as age rises so children will tend to be taller, heavier, and able to move faster, however tested. However, there would be other components too. Once age is accounted for, a second component might reflect overall athletic ability – children may tend to be relatively good or relatively poor at all the field and pool tests. Further 'higher-order' components might reflect specific swimming or running abilities, and so forth.

Returning to faces, individual faces are like the different children in our example above, and the greyscale value of each pixel is like the score on each different test. From this large amount of data, a more economical set of components can be extracted which accounts for the majority of the variance in the image pixels. The extent to which each pixel within the set of faces contributes to a particular component can be represented graphically by depicting extreme contributions in white and black. Such graphic ways of depicting the different components of variation are called 'eigenfaces'. The top row of Figure 6.15

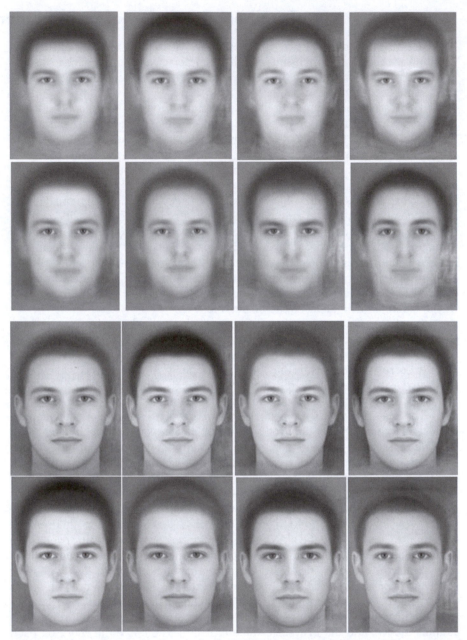

Figure 6.15 Illustrating the first four Principal Components extracted from a set of 150 male faces. Each vertical pair shows the extreme values for one dimension of variation. At the top are illustrated PCs obtained by aligning images only via the eyes. Notice these PCs capture variations of hairstyle and face shape. At the bottom are the PCs obtained from fully aligned 'shape-free' faces. Note that variation of the shape of the face is eliminated for the shape-free sets. Courtesy of Peter Hancock.

illustrates the first four Principal Components (PCs) extracted from a set of 150 male faces brought into alignment with each other by making the eye positions correspond in each image.

These first PCs, which capture the most variance between the set of faces, seem to extract interesting overall variations between sub-groups of faces. For example, in Figure 6.15 these early components capture gross variations in hair-style, face size and shape. If the set of images analysed contains female as well as male faces, the early components seem to code overall variation in male–female properties (O'Toole et al., 1993), and so forth. Higher-order eigenfaces seem to capture idiosyncratic details of individual, or small numbers of, faces within the set.

If a set of eigenfaces is derived from a set of face images, then any face can be mathematically described as an appropriately weighted sum of this set of eigenfaces. If eigenfaces represent pictorially the different dimensions of varia-tion, the weights represent the location of an individual face within this dimen-sional space. The eigenface representation can thus provide an economical method of coding large numbers of faces in 'face space'.

Of more interest to psychologists is evidence that the human brain may itself do something rather like an eigenface analysis when storing faces. O'Toole, Abdi, Deffenbacher and Valentin (1993) showed that there is a strong correlation between human memory for individual faces and how well they can be reconstructed using PCA. Moreover, O'Toole and her colleagues (O'Toole, Deffenbacher, Valentin, & Abdi, 1994) showed that a PCA-based model produced a good simulation of the other-race effect that we described earlier in this chapter. A PCA-based model exposed mainly to faces of one race will code faces of another race less successfully, reflecting the fact that some of the variation between faces is race-specific.

Mathematically, PCA just takes the pixel values in each image as input. So if you do a PCA of 200 face photographs which are each 1000 pixels high and 500 pixels wide, it treats these as 200 lists (photographs) of 500,000 numbers (the pixels in each array). It knows nothing about where the mouth is, the nose, and so on. All the PCA does is to analyse the intercorrelations between pixels in the same positions in each image – that is, it treats each pixel (1, 2, 3, 4, etc. up to 500,000) in the list as if each one has some arbitrary fixed location. So you can see that for PCA to work well, the face images must be brought into some kind of alignment. Otherwise, for example, the grey-level in the pixel for the tip of the nose in one face will be compared with that for the upper lip of another. Clearly, if there is to be a sensible interpretation, like must be compared with like.

In practice, simply positioning the eyes a fixed distance apart is enough to create eigenfaces of the quality shown in the upper rows of Figure 6.15. To improve the alignment of face images, however, faces can be morphed to a common shape before PCA is carried out – allowing analysis both of the grey-levels in the 'shape-free' (morphed) images, and of the shape vectors (the trans-formations needed to restore the original shape to the face). The lower rows in Figure 6.15 show the first four PCs extracted after all the 150 male faces were morphed to a common shape. Note the absence in the lower rows of any varia-tions around the bottom of the face. Hancock and his colleagues (Hancock,

Burton, & Bruce, 1996; Hancock, Bruce, & Burton, 1997) have shown that separating shape information in this way leads to a better PCA model which improves the correlation between the PCA-based analysis of individual faces and human performance in terms of memorability and perceived similarity of the face images.

While point-by-point alignment of faces does not seem very likely to find a close analogue in the human brain, the eyes do play a key role in the perception of faces, and in representing familiar ones, perhaps by providing something akin to an alignment function. In this respect Gilad, Meng and Sinha's observations with photo-negation are particularly intriguing (see Figure 6.9). If the eyes are used to calibrate our face representations this might explain why having this region in the correct polarity enables other areas of the face to be coded even if these are contrast reversed. It is possible, too, that it is some kind of alignment function that allows the human brain to compensate for certain kinds of 'stretching' distortion (Hole et al., 2002) only when it is applied across the whole face, and not to part of it (see Figure 6.5).

PCA is one of a number of techniques for coding faces in terms of their image-properties rather than more abstract descriptions of face features such as nose length or 3D shape. It has led to some interesting findings and, as we saw in Chapter 4, it offers promising ways to think about how the brain might code facial expressions as well as identities (Calder, Burton, Miller, Young, & Akamatsu, 2001; Dailey et al., 2002), and even how identity and expression might be represented within a common coding system (Calder, Burton et al., 2001).

What PCA offers is a useful method for finding the kinds of regularity and variability in a set of images that the brain might exploit. That said, it is unlikely that the brain uses PCA as such – it isn't suggested that it performs a formal analysis of image statistics – the idea is more that it is doing something similar through neural computation (in the rather loose sense of 'computation' used by many neuroscientists). Importantly, other techniques that can complement PCA have also been developed, based more closely on the known image-filtering properties of the human visual system that we introduced in Chapter 2 (e.g. Lades et al., 1993). As we noted there, the early stages of the human visual system describe patterns simultaneously at different spatial scales. We can think of this as analysing the image through lots of different filters set to capture information at different levels of detail – for example, if filters were like pixels, coarse scales would look at average intensity in a small number of large pixels and fine scale would look at intensity variations in much smaller sized pixels.

It is clear, from quite a large body of work investigating how face perception and recognition may rely on different scales or ranges of spatial frequencies, that there is some flexibility in the deployment of information at different scales depending upon their diagnosticity for the task in hand (Schyns & Oliva, 1997; Ruiz-Soler & Beltran, 2006). However, there is rather poor generalisation *across* different spatial scales. Liu, Collin, Rainville and Chaudhuri (2000) showed that matching of faces was more dependent on the extent to which study and test facial images matched in their spatial frequency bands than on the range of frequencies within a band.

In a striking observation, Biederman and Kolocsai (1997) showed that our representational system for face recognition, but not object recognition, is sensitive to the precise spatial frequency *components* seen in images. Biederman and Kolocsai decomposed faces and images of other kinds of objects into a set of spatial frequency components of different frequency and orientation. By adding back different subsets of these components it was possible to produce complementary image pairs, where each member of an image pair was built from distinct, alternating, but non-overlapping spatial frequency components (see Figure 6.16). Such complementary image pairs *look* very similar to a human

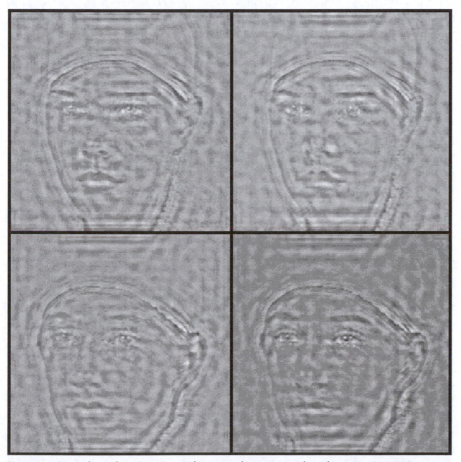

Figure 6.16 Filtered images used in Biederman and Kalocsai's (1997) experiments. The rows show two different people. To the left and right in each row are two 'complementary' versions of the same picture of each person's face – see text. First published in Biederman and Kalocsai, *Philosophical Transactions of the Royal Society B: Biological Sciences, 352* (1358), p. 1203. Copyright (1997) The Royal Society.

observer, yet Biederman and Kolocsai found that where the image complements were made from faces they behaved in matching and repetition priming experiments (see Chapter 7) as though they were different pictures! Moreover, Yue, Tjan and Biederman (2006) found that changing from one to a complementary image of a face pair yielded modest but significant release from fMRI adaptation in the right FFA, suggesting that this face-responsive area is sensitive to precise visual image characteristics (see also Xu, Yue, Lescroart, Biederman, & Kim, 2009). However, complementary image pairs made from common objects (Biederman & Kolocsai, 1997) or complex 'blobs' on which participants had been trained to become expert (Yue, Tjan, & Biederman, 2006) did not behave like different pictures on behavioural measures. Nor was the FFA differentially activated by blobs when participants were expert rather than novice blob perceivers, though blobs yielded more activation in an area critical for object recognition – the lateral occipital complex (LOC) – for experts than novices. In blob experts there was a slight, but not significant, difference in release from fMRI adaptation in the right LOC when successive images showed complementary rather than identical spatial frequency components.

The above observations suggest that visual descriptions of faces may be surprisingly 'raw' compared to what was supposed in cherished theories of the 1980s (Bruce & Young, 1986; Marr, 1982). If faces were redescribed internally in terms of, say, measurements of features or distances between features then it is not obvious why such sensitivity to matching between spatial frequency bands and components would be observed. If the visual system analyses faces in terms of dimensions of variation derived from underlying image properties, as in PCA, it is clear that this analysis must preserve something about different scales of variation too.

How do faces become familiar?

The work evaluating PCA has mostly used the equivalent of unfamiliar faces. Behaviourally, however, there are striking differences between what we can do with familiar and unfamiliar faces. Recall from Chapter 2 how difficult it is even to match photographs of unfamiliar faces (Figure 2.1a) – a task that presents no difficulty with a familiar face as the target (Figure 2.1b). When faces are unfamiliar, we find it hard to see which differences in the pictures reflect changes in lighting, and which are due to actual differences between the faces (Hancock, Bruce, & Burton, 2001).

The same point is clear from studies of face learning that have used photographs as stimuli. Representations of once-viewed photographs of unfamiliar faces, or even of previously unfamiliar faces presented several times in a restricted range of photographs, retain characteristics of the particular viewpoint or picture and generalise only weakly to novel views (Bruce, 1982). This led Bruce and Young (1986) to emphasise the difference between picture recognition (i.e. remembering a photograph you studied previously) and face recognition (remembering the face itself) and they suggested that 'pictorial' codes mediated picture recognition while 'structural' codes were needed for true face recognition. The defining achievement of genuine face recognition is to be able to recognise the face from different views, whereas performance based on picture recognition (i.e. on remembering the photo of a face) may be very good for the picture studied but will quickly fall off if the test image differs from the studied image. In experiments investigating how people learn to recognise faces they have only encountered in photographs Longmore, Liu and Young (2008) repeatedly demonstrated limited generalisation from one picture of a face to another – for example, a fall in performance in trying to recognise a test view of a face that was simply a 15-degree rotation of the learnt view. This limited generalisation to novel views was found regardless of how well the face photograph was learnt in the first place – even after many exposures to a photograph, with recognition of that picture effectively at ceiling, performance fell off in line with the degree of rotation of the test image despite there being no changes between the images in lighting or other factors.

Somehow our exposure to faces in our everyday worlds allows us to build more robust representations that are not so picture-specific. If familiar faces are represented in a multidimensional space capable of describing their essential characteristics then we need to consider the nature of the representations derived from multiple images of the same face.

Representations of unfamiliar faces are dominated by external features, particularly hairstyle (Ellis et al., 1979) while the internal features of familiar faces assume relatively greater importance (Young, Hay, McWeeny et al., 1985). Bonner, Burton and Bruce (2003) showed that relatively modest periods of familiarisation of faces from videos or multiple viewpoints selectively enhanced the accuracy of matching based on internal features, while matching of external features remained at the same (high) level as faces became familiar. O'Donnell and Bruce (2001) demonstrated that the eye regions particularly benefited in the early stages of familiarisation when participants were shown videos of faces and asked to learn a name for each. In their task, participants were asked to decide if two faces were identical or slightly different. Differences made to the eye region – whether to the detail of the irises of the eyes or to their spacing – were detected very poorly when the faces were unfamiliar, but became detected with high accuracy for a set of familiarised faces. Detection of changes made to hair, chin and mouths were unaffected by familiarisation and remained respectively high (for hair) and low (chin and mouths). Brooks and Kemp (2007) reported results consistent with these. They found enhanced sensitivity to changes to the vertical placement of eyes and noses, but not mouths, for familiar compared with unfamiliar faces.

Burton, Jenkins, Hancock and White (2005) offered a particularly appealing approach to the issue of face familiarity that could explain some of these observations as arising from incremental exposure to more instances of faces as they become familiar. They showed how a robust representation of a familiar face can be created simply by averaging different full-face photographs of that face (see Figure 6.17), if the various face images are first aligned with each other using the techniques we described above (see Figure 6.18). Participants were (on average) faster at recognising and verifying the identities of 'average' images of famous faces than they were at responding to individual exemplars.

Figure 6.17 Original images of Tony Blair (A), transformed to common shape (B) and then averaged (C) Reprinted from *Cognitive Psychology*, Vol. 51, A. Mike Burton, Rob Jenkins, Peter J. B. Hancock, David White, Robust representations for face recognition: The power of averages, pp. 256–284. Copyright 2005, with permission from Elsevier.

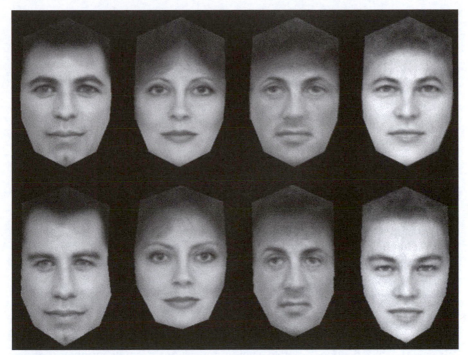

Figure 6.18 Average images of celebrities in shape free (top row) and with their individual shapes added back (bottom row). Left to right John Travolta, Susan Sarandon, Sylvester Stallone and Leonardo di Caprio. Reprinted from *Cognitive Psychology*, Vol. 51, A. Mike Burton, Rob Jenkins, Peter J. B. Hancock, David White, Robust representations for face recognition: The power of averages, pp. 256–284. Copyright 2005, with permission from Elsevier.

Furthermore, the more individual instances were included in the average, the better their performance. Intriguingly, the same advantage for average images was found in computer recognition of faces using a PCA recognition system. Moreover, in an extension of this idea Jenkins and Burton (2008) showed that probing data-bases of stored images using an average of several target photographs yields much better recognition performance than individual image probes. What seems to happen is that averaging across images preserves the information that is diagnostic of identity and gets rid of irrelevant variation created by differences in lighting, camera characteristics, expression, and so on.

Notice that Burton et al. (2005) were simply averaging 2D representations of each face, and that the instances that make up an average were first made 'shape-free', so that the features were in alignment across the images, before being averaged together and then returned to the shape of that person's face. The averaged representations (see Figure 6.18) therefore emphasise the texture and pigmentation of each image rather than properties like feature spacing. In the top row of Figure 6.18, the images are actually all morphed to a common shape, yet the different identities can still be seen to some extent. This shows that texture and pigmentation patterns can convey identity even when any potentially diagnostic second-order relational information due to spacing variations has been removed.

On Burton et al.'s averaging account, the relative advantage of internal over external features of familiar faces could arise because the internal features of the face remain constant as external ones – particularly hairstyle – change, and so the average will represent these invariant features most clearly. Also, selective attention to the internal features of faces when we interact with people, and their key role in constructing a representation, means we may encode a higher resolution of internal compared with external features.

Burton et al.'s averaging model works well for the full-face viewpoints they have explored, but in everyday life we can recognise familiar faces from a wide range of viewpoints. How might this be achieved? A simple way would be to create distinct averaged representations for a range of different viewpoints, and there is some evidence of view-specificity from experimental studies. Jeffery, Rhodes and Bucey found that adaptation to shape transformations made on an unfamiliar face in one viewpoint did not transfer to a different viewpoint even when this was a mirror image (left ¾ to right ¾ view). Cabeza et al. (1999) found prototypes formed for transformations within but not between different viewpoints of unfamiliar faces. If such effects are indicative of how representations for familiar identities are built up, then it may turn out that familiar identities are represented based upon separate averaging around a small number of viewpoints. From this perspective, findings such as Longmore et al.'s (2008) demonstration of highly picture-specific learning from photographs of faces with limited generalisation to novel views may reflect the natural learning mechanism – it is just that in everyday life it gets offered enough views for the limited generalisation to be less of a liability.

Somewhat surprisingly, the striking behavioural differences between familiar and unfamiliar faces have not proved so easy to trace in the brain. In Haxby et al.'s (2000) neurological model, the OFA-FFA pathway in the core system is involved in processing relatively invariant aspects of faces, so it is here that we might expect to find effects of face familiarity emerging, and especially in the FFA. There is evidence from functional brain imaging studies that is consistent with the FFA's playing an important role in facial identity perception. In fMRI studies, FFA activation correlates with the size of the face inversion effect and with face identification (Grill-Spector, Knouf, & Kanwisher, 2004; Yovel & Kanwisher, 2005), and with fMR-adaptation the FFA has been found to adapt to potential dimensions of 'face space' (Loffler, Yourganov, Wilkinson, & Wilson, 2005). Moreover, as we discussed earlier, FFA responses are sensitive to configural properties of faces. In line with this evidence from functional brain imaging, we saw in Chapter 1 that the brain lesions that cause *acquired* prosopagnosia point to the fusiform gyrus (which includes the FFA) as a critical region for recognising faces, and we will have more to say about this in Chapter 8.

However, whilst these lines of evidence show an important role for FFA in coding aspects of faces highly relevant to recognising them, they do not conclusively point to its being the locus of familiar face recognition itself. Instead, functional imaging studies of FFA in normal participants have produced equivocal findings concerning face familiarity. Recall that the FFA is identified with a functional localiser that finds the region in the fusiform gyrus that responds more to faces than other stimuli (usually buildings or everyday objects – see Chapter 1). But the face images used in localiser scans are nearly always unfamiliar faces. So are the FFA's responses any different for familiar faces? Gobbini and Haxby (2007) reviewed the evidence and noted it was inconsistent at the time, with no clear overall pattern.

Andrews and his colleagues have since begun to look at this question systematically, mainly using fMR-adaptation (Andrews, Davies-Thompson, Kingstone, & Young, 2010; Davies-Thompson, Gouws, & Andrews, 2009; Ewbank & Andrews, 2008; Ewbank, Smith, Hancock, & Andrews, 2008). We already noted that in fMR-adaptation studies FFA responses show considerable image-dependence (Yue et al., 2006; Xu et al., 2009), but does this differ between unfamiliar and familiar faces? Andrews and his colleagues found pronounced image-dependence for FFA responses to unfamiliar *and* to familiar faces with fMR-adaptation (Davies-Thompson et al., 2009) and with the M170 MEG response that probably originates from a similar cortical location (Ewbank et al., 2008). The fMR-adaptation paradigm used by Andrews' group involves a block design, in which adaptation is measured across a sequence (block) of images lasting a number of seconds. A block design has the advantages that it will be sensitive to any build-up of adaptation across multiple trials and that it allows for the slowish time course of the BOLD response (see Chapter 2).

In Davies-Thompson et al.'s (2009) study, release from fMR-adaptation in the FFA was as large for different images of the same familiar face as it was for images of different faces, showing that the FFA's response was dominated by differences between images rather than by the identities of the faces. Figure 6.19 shows examples of Davies-Thompson et al.'s (2009) stimuli. In the top row, a block of trials consists of the same face repeatedly shown in the same image, the middle row has the same face in different images, and the lower row is different faces and different images. Blood flow change across these different types of blocks of trials is shown in Figure 6.19 for FFA, OFA, and posterior STS, but here we will ignore STS because it is not part of Haxby et al.'s (2000) pathway for invariant properties. The same-face same-image blocks form a point of comparison for what would be expected to be maximal fMR-adaptation. In the FFA and OFA there is a clear release from adaptation in the other two conditions, which do not differ from each other even though one of these conditions consists entirely of (different) images of the same familiar face. The same pattern for FFA and OFA was found with unfamiliar faces. Note that in this study, the different images of the same face had substantial differences in lighting, hairstyle, and so on. None the less, the familiar face images would be recognised as the same person in a behavioural study, yet there was no evidence of adaptation based on familiarity in the condition that used different images of the same face.

There are hints from other studies, though, that FFA cares about face familiarity and has some of the capabilities that characterise face recognition. With a

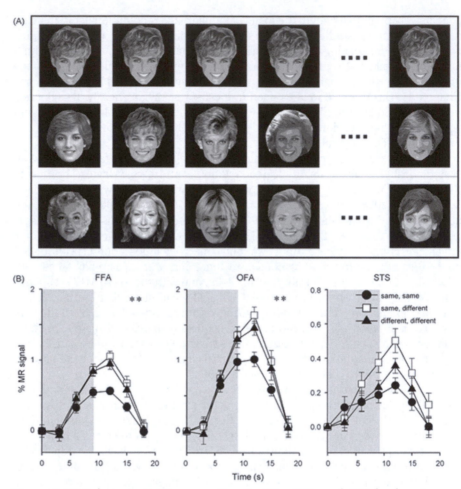

Figure 6.19 Relative activation over time in FFA, OFA and STS for face images which show the same celebrity in the same picture (top row), the same celebrity in different pictures (middle row), or a series of different celebrities (bottom row). Reprinted from *Neuropsychologia*, Vol. 47, Jodie Davies-Thompson, André Gouws, Timothy J. Andrews, An image-dependent representation of familiar and unfamiliar faces in the human ventral stream, pp. 1627–1635. Copyright 2009 with permission from Elsevier.

restricted range of viewpoint changes, evidence of some invariance in the FFA's response to rotated familiar faces was established by Ewbank and Andrews (2008). Figure 6.20 shows examples of their stimuli, which were created by using computer image manipulation techniques to rotate a face in the picture plane by up to a maximum of 8 degrees. You can see they are only rotated by relatively small amounts, and that changes in lighting and so on are effectively avoided – the only differences between images in the same identity (top row) condition are

Figure 6.20 Images used by Ewbank and Andrews (2008) – different images of the same celebrity (top row) or different celebrities (bottom row). Reprinted from *NeuroImage*, Vol. 40, Michael P. Ewbank, Timothy J. Andrews, Differential sensitivity for viewpoint between familiar and unfamiliar faces in human visual cortex, pp. 1857–1870. Copyright 2008 with permission from Elsevier.

those due to changing the viewpoint slightly. With equivalent unfamiliar face stimuli, Ewbank and Andrews (2008) did not find any view invariance in the FFA's response to these small rotations – it treated each rotated unfamiliar face image as if it was novel.

Taking together the findings of these studies, it is clear that the responses of FFA are often image-dependent, even for familiar faces. When there were substantial differences between images of the same face – as in Davies-Thompson et al.'s (2009) study (Figure 6.19) – the size of these image-dependent responses seems to have masked differences between the FFA's responses to familiar and unfamiliar faces that became evident when the variability of the different images was reduced (Ewbank & Andrews, 2008).

The image-dependent responses from FFA are problematic for models that propose recognition is based on some form of 'abstractive' representation that captures *only* the essence of a familiar face and discards any evidence of individual or recent exemplars. Bruce and Young's (1986) idea of 'Face Recognition Units' (FRUs) as analogous to Morton's (1969, 1979) 'logogens' was probably dangerously close to this category – a logogen is activated by *any* evidence consistent with the item it represents. The problem is that the face essence of Diana Spencer is present throughout the second row of Figure 6.19, but the FFA doesn't seem to take any notice of it. It is possible, of course, that FFA is *not* the locus of face recognition, and some researchers are looking elsewhere in the temporal lobes (Kriegeskorte, Formisano, Sorger, & Goebel, 2007; Tsao, Moeller, & Freiwald, 2008). We may not yet need this radical alternative, however. Studies since Bruce and Young (1986) have consistently shown that a more 'instance-based' concept of how an FRU might operate offers a better account of observed data (Ellis, Young, Flude, & Hay, 1987). For example, repetition priming of familiar face recognition turns out to be image-dependent (see Chapter 7), and we saw earlier how view-specific face adaptation can be. Ellis et al. (1987, p. 207) concluded that the benefits of repetition of behavioural studies 'arise from some form of advantage that accrues to the encoding of stimuli similar to those that have already been encoded' – a view that sits easily alongside the FFA findings. Likewise, Burton et al. (2005) noted that some images of familiar faces proved to be easier to recognise, 'better likenesses' than others. Put simply, evidence of image-dependent recognition is actually abundant, even for familiar face recognition – it just attracts less attention from researchers because the overall performance levels with familiar faces are so impressive.

If this perspective is correct, then effects of face familiarity in the FFA should be more clear when image variability is minimised. We will offer two further examples that fit this idea. First, in Andrews et al.'s (2010) study, described earlier, holistic responses were evident to images with recombined internal and external features of familiar and unfamiliar faces in the FFA, but the level of fMR-adaptation was greater to repeated images of internal features of familiar than unfamiliar faces, which parallels the behavioural finding of increased importance of internal features for familiar face recognition (Ellis et al., 1979; Young, Hay, McWeeny et al., 1985).

Our second example comes from an ingenious study by Rotshtein et al. (2005). They measured blood flow in fMRI while participants saw successively presented pairs of same or different face images which were drawn from morphed continua between famous faces – for example, images that were morphed between Marilyn Monroe and Margaret Thatcher. In essence, Rotshtein et al.'s (2005) procedure mimics some of the features of a categorical perception study. Within a morphed continuum it is possible to have different pairs of images that are an equivalent number of physical steps apart on the continuum but which appear to belong to the same or to different identities. For example, 20% and 40% morphs might both look like Marilyn Monroe, but 40% and 60% morphs might look like Monroe (40%) and Thatcher (60%). Note that Rotshtein et al. (2005) used an event-related design that measured change in neural response from the first to the second image of a sequential pair. This is more difficult to implement than a block design, and requires accurate assumptions about the time-course of the BOLD signal. What they found was that activity in the right fusiform gyrus did not differ between same and different images when the different pairs would be categorised as being the same person, but activity was greater when the second face in a pair straddled the boundary where one identity switched into another. In contrast the OFA responded when there was any change to the image, irrespective of whether it crossed the category boundary. Replication of these findings will be important to being confident that this pattern really does fit Haxby et al.'s model as neatly as it seems at present.

Although fMRI studies have not decisively resolved these issues, a persuasive case has built up in the ERP literature that a component now known as the N250r is sensitive to face repetitions and stronger for familiar than unfamiliar face repetitions. Source localisation with ERP is tricky (see Chapter 2), but results are consistent with the N250r being generated in ventral temporal cortex, most likely in the fusiform gyrus region (Schweinberger, Pfütze, & Sommer, 1995; Schweinberger, Pickering, Jentzsch, Burton, & Kaufmann, 2002; Herzmann,

Schweinberger, Sommer, & Jentzsch, 2004; Schweinberger, Huddy, & Burton, 2004).

The way things are moving, then, is towards the idea that the key to what makes a face familiar is the simple one that we have seen enough instances of that face across a sufficiently wide range of conditions. Interesting developments are being made in how these more 'instance-based' kinds of account might operate – paradoxically, these show how being able to respond to the 'invariant' properties of faces may not require any explicit search for these invariants. Overall, the FFA is showing properties that could fit this trend well, though there are enough caveats to make it unwise yet to assume that FFA will be the sole locus of recognition – it may act in concert with other cortical regions to create a more distributed face recognition system, or it may be 'preprocessing' the input into a form that will make it more easily recognised.

At a functional level, Burton et al.'s (2005) interesting theory and impressive data suggest that successive images may be averaged together to yield more robust representations. But other behavioural evidence suggests sensitivity to individual instances too. Importantly, both the averaging-based and the instance-based conceptions show that qualitative differences between familiar and unfamiliar face representations can arise incrementally, from the quantity and nature of the images we are shown. Whether averaging or separate storage of instances proves theoretically more fruitful remains to be seen. Indeed it may be that a combination will prove the best way forward: averaging similar images within views, while also retaining separately discrete memories of these encounters, as in Bruce and Young's (1986) explicit distinction between structural codes and pictorial codes for familiar faces. An intriguing early computer model by Baron (1981) offered an algorithm for recognition that contained both these key ingredients.

For the rest of this chapter, we will turn our attention mainly to applied questions about face recognition. There are a range of applications of face research, and new ones keep turning up. For instance, a few years ago we were surprised to be asked to what extent someone who received a face transplant would look like the donor? At the time, face transplants had not been carried out, and the question had been raised by members of a hospital Ethics Committee who were mindful of the possible implications of a proposed transplant for the donor's relatives. It was a question that brought together many of the issues we have been discussing – especially the relative roles of underlying 3D structure and more superficial pigmentation patterns in determining what you look like. Since then, of course, transplants have taken place (see Chapter 1).

The applied issues we will concentrate on here are those that arise in legal and forensic contexts. These have been extensively investigated, since they can have crucial implications for justice and for criminal investigations. We value these applied questions not because they allow us to show off what can be done with pure research, but because they create a virtuous circle in which the findings and theories of pure research are put to a severe test that can feed back to improving them. Practical questions can quickly show the flaws or gaps in work that might have seemed neat in a laboratory context.

When faces are not remembered: Everyday memory for faces and eyewitness testimony

Laboratory experiments have shown that people can be remarkably accurate at remembering briefly viewed, previously unfamiliar faces, typically scoring over 90% correct when asked to decide which of a large set of faces were previously studied. But this high accuracy at recognising pictures of unfamiliar faces seems to be at odds with our sometimes surprising failures to recognise or identify faces in everyday life. In Chapter 2 we recounted the false conviction of Laszlo Virag because of the testimony of several mistaken witnesses – and this was not an isolated case. Much of the recent research interest in the processes of human face recognition was stimulated by some of these high-profile cases of mistaken identity in criminal investigations in the UK which prompted a public enquiry chaired by Lord Devlin (1976).

Why is there this apparent inconsistency between accurate memory for faces in laboratory experiments and inaccurate memory in everyday life? One important factor we have already encountered is that laboratory experiments tend to test memory for identical pictures of faces, and thus confound picture memory with true face memory. If recognition memory for faces is tested with different pictures of the same people shown in the study and test phases, recognition accuracy drops dramatically. For example, in an early study by Bruce (1982), recognition was 90% correct when faces were shown in identical views at study and test, but dropped to only 60% correct when the viewpoint and expression were changed from study to test, even though the particular faces used in that study had distinctive hairstyles and clothing was not obscured. Other factors which have been shown to influence face recognition, and which are likely to affect an eyewitness, are a change in the context between the place where the face was originally encountered and where memory for the face is subsequently probed, with context broadly defined to include such things as the clothing of the person to be identified (e.g. see Smith & Vela, 1992, 2001). Moreover, most criminals attempt to disguise their faces somewhat when committing a crime, even if only by wearing a hat or hood over their hair. Hairstyle is such an important determinant of the representation of an unfamiliar face that even crude disguises of this sort will make the later memory task much more difficult. One striking aspect of the comparison between Mr Virag and Mr Payen was that any resemblance between them was closer for the lower halves of their faces, and in the original incident the gunman wore a hat, thus perhaps concealing those aspects of appearance which might most readily have distinguished Mr Virag.

While all the above factors are likely to contribute to poorer memory for faces in everyday life than in the laboratory, another important set of factors which affects the reliability of investigatory and forensic evidence involving faces arises through the methods that are typically used to probe witness memories. These methods fall broadly into two groups – reconstruction and identification – and there are problems within each group.

Witness reconstructions of faces

Reconstruction is used when criminal investigators attempt to produce, from a witness description, some image of the suspect for circulation to other police forces or to the general public. The traditional method for producing such likenesses used a police artist, who somehow converted the description given by a witness into a sketched portrait, which could then be refined in further discussion with the witness. However, a disadvantage of this method is that trained police artists are relatively few and far between. It is therefore not surprising that there has been such enthusiasm for alternative methods.

A number of methods have been devised in which a witness, alone or with a trained operator, tries to construct the target face using a 'kit' of isolated facial features. This method is reminiscent of Leonardo da Vinci's attempt to construct an inventory of all possible face features in order to instruct people how to draw portraits from a single glance at a face (the letters refer to illustrations which accompanied the text):

> To start with the nose: there are three shapes – (A) straight, (B) concave and (C) convex. Among the straight there are only four varieties, that is (A1) long, or (A2) short, and (A3) at a sharp angle or (A4) at a wide angle. The (B) concave noses are of three kinds of which some (B1) have a dip in the upper part, some (B2) in the middle, and others (B3) below. The (C) convex noses again show three varieties: some (C1) have a hump high up, others (C2) in the middle and others (C3) at the lower end.
>
> (Leonardo's *Trattato*, quoted by Gombrich, 1976)

However, as noted by Gombrich (1976), even da Vinci risked becoming exhausted with the complexity of this undertaking:

> The middle parts of the nose, which form the bridge, can differ in eight ways: they can be (1) equally straight, equally concave or equally convex, or (2) unequally straight, concave or convex, (3) straight on the upper and concave on the lower part; (4) straight above and convex below; (5) concave above and straight below; (6) concave above and convex below; (7) convex above and straight below; (8) convex above and concave below.
>
> (Leonardo's *Trattato*, quoted by Gombrich, 1976)

And this was just for noses seen in profile! A further 11 types were listed for front views.

Many centuries later, the photographer Jacques Penry invented the 'Photofit' system, which comprises sets of hundreds of variants of face features. A trained operator helps the witness to select appropriate features and to refine the emerging representation. However, although performance can be improved with trained and sensitive operators, overall evaluation of the likenesses produced by kits of this kind has shown them to be very poor. For example, in one study by Ellis, Davies and Shepherd (1978), participants rated the likenesses between the constructions produced by volunteer 'witnesses' and the people they were attempting to construct. The constructions were made by the witnesses themselves drawing the faces, or using Photofit, and they were made either with the target face *in view* or from memory. When the target face was in view – i.e. the task of the witness was simply to copy the face – then witnesses' own drawings were rated as much better likenesses than were those produced by Photofit. When reconstruction was from memory, the rated likeness obtained with both techniques dropped, and there was a slight but not significant advantage for Photofit.

Why is performance with Photofit so poor? One problem is that this kind of kit assumes that a face representation can be deconstructed into its component parts, whereas we saw earlier that representations for face recognition may be more holistic than this. Moreover, we also saw that spatial relationships between different features can be important too, but Photofit has only limited opportunities for the manipulation of such factors. Finally, there are a small number of what Ellis (1986) termed 'cardinal' features which are regularly and reliably used by people to describe and categorise faces. These are face shape, hair and age – all global dimensions which are difficult to manipulate directly with a Photofit kit.

The rapid development of powerful graphics computers at relatively low cost made it possible to develop more interactive systems which appeared to remedy some of these deficiencies. E-fit was developed jointly by researchers at the University of Aberdeen, the Home Office and the private sector. While still based around a basic kit of photographic parts of faces, there is much more opportunity for global manipulations, blending and elaboration than with Photofit, and the resulting images are much more realistic (see Figure 6.21).

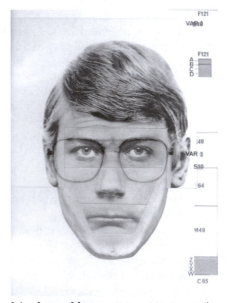

Figure 6.21 E-fit and Photofit constructions of the face of former Prime Minister John Major. Prepared by John Shepherd at the University of Aberdeen for Bruce and Young (1998).

Recently there have been large-scale evaluations of the efficacy of different types of face reconstruction system. Frowd et al. (2005a, b) examined how well one set of participants selected to be unfamiliar with particular target faces could produce composites of these that could be named by other participants who were familiar with the people depicted. This is analogous to the situation where an eyewitness unfamiliar with a criminal makes a composite used on a television programme such as Crimewatch UK in an attempt to trigger recognition by someone who knows the perpetrator. Frowd et al. (2005a) compared identification rates of composite images produced by various different systems approximately 2 hours after exposure to target photographs, to drawings produced by a police sketch artist. The composite systems compared were E-fit and PRO-fit (both similar systems based upon a Photofit-like feature selection process), the original Photofit system, and a new system called EvoFIT that works on recognition rather than recall which was under development at that time (we will describe this system later in this chapter). Table 6.2 shows the proportions of composites that were named by participants familiar with the target faces. As can be seen, identification rates were low in all tested systems. A follow-up study (Frowd et al., 2005b) had composites created about two days after initial viewing of the target – a delay more typical of real police investigations. Under these circumstances naming rates were even lower, as shown in Table 6.2. Indeed naming rates were so low that other measures of performance had to be used to compare systems. Table 6.2 also shows performance on a task where participants were asked to sort composites against a set of target identities.

Contemporary composite systems like E-fit, etc. can produce decent copies – the main problem is not with the art work. Something about the process of building an image using such systems is clearly problematic.

One important factor may be that different regions of the face are of importance for people relatively familiar or unfamiliar with the face. As we described earlier, matching and memory of unfamiliar faces is dominated by the external features – particularly hairstyle, while recognising familiar faces makes more use of the internal features. By definition, an eyewitness trying to build an image of a face from memory is trying to recall an unfamiliar face (if the person was familiar, the eyewitness could just name or otherwise describe the identity of the person committing the crime). Therefore they will have a better ability to remember

Table 6.2 Relative percentage rates of naming and sorting composites using different systems at different delays from target exposure (from Frowd et al., 2005a, 2005b).

Condition	Sketch	E-fit	PRO-fit	EvoFIT	Photofit
2 hr delay					
Naming	9.2	19.0	17.0	1.5	6.2
Sorting	81	74	72	50	49
48 hr delay					
Naming	8.1	0.0	1.3	3.6	n.a.
Sorting	54	43	41	39	n.a.

external than internal features. But the aim of a face composite is to trigger recognition by someone who knows the person depicted – for example a viewer of a programme such as Crimewatch who might phone in, or a police officer who recognises a person with previous convictions. But these people will rely more on internal features – the part of the face that the witness is less likely to be able to recollect accurately. Consistent with this, Frowd, Bruce, McIntyre and Hancock (2007a) demonstrated that the external features of constructed face composites were almost as effective as the whole face composite when the task was to match the composites against possible target faces. In contrast, the internal features of composites alone yielded much poorer matching performance. This advantage of external over internal composite features was somewhat reduced, but not eliminated, when the 'witnesses' constructing the composites were familiar with the faces they were trying to recall, suggesting that the effect reflects limitations of the composite system rather than solely unfamiliarity with the faces to be remembered. These observations have led to evaluation of systems in which an initially selected hairstyle is blurred while the rest of the features are selected, with some suggestions that this can help composite production (e.g. see Frowd et al., 2011).

How can we improve the likeness gained from composite systems?

Despite the rather poor performance of composites seen in studies by Frowd and his colleagues, there are also some indications from recent work of ways to improve the recognisability of composites. We will here describe three: combining information from different independent composites, manipulating composites through caricaturing, and developing a new system of composite construction that relies less on recall of individual features and more on recognising whole face images.

Combining composites

Bruce, Ness, Hancock, Newman and Rarity (2002) reasoned that while individual witnesses might produce composites which were poor likenesses due to errors in the depiction of particular aspects of appearance, there was no reason to think that different witnesses would make the same errors in their composites. Therefore, where there was more than one witness who had seen a particular criminal act, there might be merit in combining their individually generated composites. Two experiments reported by Bruce et al. (2002) tested the hypothesis that an 'average' composite created by morphing together two or more independent witness attempts would be better than individual witness composites, on average.

In Bruce et al.'s (2002) first experiment a rather artificial task was used. Participants ('witnesses') were asked to create a composite either by copying or by remembering one familiar target and one unfamiliar target face. Four different participants created composites of each of four familiar and four unfamiliar targets in both the 'copy' and 'memory' conditions. Another set of participants then rated how good the likenesses were between composites and the target images. They could see individual composites, '2-morphs' made of pairs of composites (i.e. combinations of two participant witness attempts), or '4-morphs' made of all four composites in a particular condition. The 4-morphs yielded significantly higher likeness ratings than the 2-morphs which were in turn better than the individual composite ratings. The ratings given to individual composites were then used to select a 'best' and 'worst' composite from the sets of four obtained for each target in each condition. Interestingly the ratings that had been given to the four-morphs were rather higher than those given to the best of the individual faces. In a final phase of the experiment, composites were shown against line-ups of six alternative faces. The alternatives were all familiar faces for the familiar targets and all unfamiliar faces for the unfamiliar targets. The task now was to decide which of the faces in the array a composite was supposed to depict. A new set of participants attempted this task and the target selection rates were compared for the 'best' and 'worst' individual composites, the 4-morph, and a condition where all four composites were shown alongside the array. The results showed, on average, significantly higher matching rates for the 4-morph, though matching performance in the unfamiliar-memory condition were low and not significantly different across the different conditions tested.

These results were encouraging enough to prompt a second experiment with greater ecological validity. In Bruce et al.'s (2002) second experiment participant witnesses were shown videos of faces that they were then required to construct from memory. Again, four different participants constructed composites of each of four different, unfamiliar female targets whose faces were shown in video. In the next phase a new set of participants rated the likenesses of the resulting composites against photographs of the targets. Again 4-morphs were rated as better likenesses than any of the individual composites. New volunteers attempted to match the composites to an array containing suitably matched distractors, and here the 4-morph condition produced the best matching when the target was present but at no increase in false positives when she was absent.

These findings and subsequent replications have had an influence on policy, since the rules of working with witnesses now allow the use of independent composites in combination.

Effects of caricaturing

The positive effects of morphing together different witness composites can also be thought of in terms of changes in distinctiveness. Because of the averaging process, a morphed witness composite will tend to be more average in appearance than any of the contributing individual composites, even though the perpetrator's face may have been more distinctive. This led Frowd, Bruce, Ross, McIntyre and Hancock (2007b) to hypothesise that an even better likeness might be created if a morphed composite was then given a modest amount of positive caricature. In general, this prediction was upheld. Positive caricaturing enhanced perceived likeness and did not reduce identification rates for morphed witness composites. For individual composites, however, anticaricaturing – making the composite more average/less distinctive in appearance – was beneficial.

In exploring the effects of caricaturing and anticaricaturing, however, Frowd et al. (2007b) found that there were substantial individual differences. For some faces, and some composites, relatively large amounts of caricaturing or anticaricaturing were beneficial. For others, very small amounts provided benefits. Individual participants also showed considerable variation in what they perceived as the best likeness as well. This led Frowd et al. to investigate the effect of presenting a full range of variation from anticaricature to positive caricature – so that individual participants could be exposed to each target in the optimum format, without knowing in advance what that should be. Experiments showed that showing a full range of caricature levels yields identification rates considerably higher than those found when the original composite, or a single caricature level, is shown.

EvoFIT as an alternative approach?

Over the past decade a different approach to composite production has been developed which harnesses witnesses' powers of recognising whole faces rather than recalling individual features. One example of this new approach is EvoFIT, developed by Frowd and Hancock (see Frowd, Bruce & Hancock, 2008 for a description). In the EvoFIT system a witness is shown a screen of face images and asked to select a small number of images that best resemble the target face. Following such choices new screens are shown in which the faces generated as choices are intended increasingly to come to resemble the witness memory for the target face. The faces which are shown and from which selection is made are not real faces but synthetic faces generated using the PCA methods described earlier in this chapter. The choices made by the witness are used in a genetic algorithm to 'breed' new choices that are likely to more closely resemble the witness memory, and this step can repeat through several iterations until the witness feels they have created the best likeness. The PCA approach also allows the faces selected to be adjusted holistically at the last stages of the process – faces can be made to look older or younger, more or less attractive, 'meaner' or more intelligent.

In early evaluations of EvoFIT its performance was similar to current recall based systems (see Table 6.2). However it has since been fine-tuned to incorporate a number of extra features and in recent studies performs well. For example, Frowd et al. (2010) report data in which resulting composites from EvoFIT were named 24.5% of the time, which compares very well with the rates shown for other systems in Table 6.2.

Witness identification of faces: Photospreads, line-ups and video parades

As well as reconstruction, the other main way in which witnesses may have their memory for faces probed is via a recognition test of some sort. This may involve looking at photographs in an album of 'mug-shots', looking at a live 'line-up' of potential offenders staged at the police station or, increasingly, at a video line-up. All these techniques have limitations.

The main problem with searching through mug-shot files is that they may be very large, and psychological experiments have shown that the chances of correctly recognising a target face fall off dramatically at later positions within a long list. In effect, the process of looking at a list of potential suspects' faces interferes with your memory for the perpetrator. One way round this problem is to pre-select a relatively small number of faces for the witness to inspect. An early Home-Office funded project at the University of Aberdeen (e.g. Shepherd, 1986) developed a system where an initial witness description could be coded by computer, and used to select from the mug-shot file a smaller number of photographs for inspection by the witness. Evaluation of such a system showed that it could produce more accurate performance from witnesses than was possible using the full mug-shot album.

Line-ups pose a range of other problems. One problem is that the volunteers who form the rest of the line may not be well-matched against the suspect on some key dimension. For example, if the witness remembers that the villain was 'very tall', and the suspect is the tallest in the line-up, then the witness may be inclined to pick out this person on this basis alone. One recommendation is that photographs of line-ups should be given to people with no connection to the original incident, along with the original witness description. A fair line-up is one where a 'dummy' witness armed with the description is unable to guess who the suspect might be with better than chance success. This procedure can also help ensure that there were not other subtle cues to the likely suspect (e.g. if he were unshaven having spent a night in custody and others in the line-up were clean-shaven this could act as a clue to the likely suspect). Wells, Small, Penrod, Malpass, Fulero and Brimacombe (1998) elaborate on these and other recommended means of ensuring that a line-up procedure is fair.

Factors like these are especially important because eyewitnesses are often highly motivated to pick someone from a line-up. They presume that the police do not go to the trouble of arranging such a thing unless they have a suspect, they are usually concerned that the suspect should not 'get away with it', and hence it is extremely important that the line-ups be constructed and administered wisely, emphasising to the witness that the suspect may not be present, and preferably conducted by an officer who does not know which person is the suspect and thus cannot give any clues – deliberately or otherwise – to the witness (see Wells et al., 1998). Leach, Cutler and Van Wallendael (2009) review further factors affecting eyewitness identification in line-ups, highlighting areas which remain controversial or where further research is still needed.

A significant change in the past decade has been the increasing use of video rather than live line-up parades, at least in the UK (see Davies & Griffiths, 2008). These have the advantage that line-up foils can be drawn from a stored data-base of many thousands of video clips, to match the suspect on key characteristics. The video parade also requires sequential inspection and thus reduces the possibility that a suspect will be identified by elimination following comparisons between simultaneously presented line-up members. It may be for these reasons that evaluations have found that video parades have been found to be fairer to the suspect (e.g. Valentine & Heaton, 1999). The video parade uses clips of people showing head and shoulders only, thus eliminating any possible use of dimensions such as height and weight – the witness must identify the face, and not the person.

Whether live or video parades are used, it is important that the same witnesses are not asked to examine photographs *and* a line-up, since there may be unintended transference of familiarity gleaned from the photographs. People are much better at knowing that a face is familiar than at knowing why it is familiar. Several notorious cases of mistaken identity have involved witnesses who identified from line-ups faces that they had already been shown in photographs.

Davies and Griffiths (2008) review some of these past cases, and describe how eyewitness testimony has been used in the English courts over the century since the first public enquiry into the case of misidentification of Adolph Beck in 1895, and again in 1904, for a series of swindles. Several victims of these frauds identified Beck each time he was convicted for crimes he did not commit. The public enquiry in 1925 concluded that identification evidence based on personal impressions was an unsafe basis for conviction. This early conclusion was reiterated by Devlin (1976) and yet mistaken identification continues to form the basis for wrongful conviction. As we see in the next section, this problem is not eradicated by the use of CCTV technology.

Beyond witnessing: CCTV on trial

Recent years have seen a huge rise in the number of crimes where video evidence of the identity of the suspect has been gathered on a security video camera at the time of the criminal act. It may seem that this reduces the need to worry about human factors in face identification, but in reality such images simply raise a new set of problems. Images captured by security cameras are often of extremely poor quality, and thus considerable interpretation can be involved in determining to whom a captured face belongs. Cameras may be set to scan a large public area, and so the images of any individual may be of very poor resolution, or the camera may be at the wrong angle from which to perceive the face. Because video images are costly to store, only a sparse sample of the frames may be captured, and these may miss the most recognisable view of a person's face. For these reasons, video evidence has not provided a simple solution to identification problems. Instead, in a number of court cases in recent years, the identity of people caught on video has been hotly debated by expert witnesses for prosecution and defence, each using different methods to attempt to prove that the suspect is, or is not, the person shown on the tape.

Research studies have demonstrated that there are substantial problems with the use of CCTV images where these may be used to attempt to verify the identity of an unknown suspect. Some of the problems are more fundamental than issues to do with image quality. In Chapter 2 we demonstrated (Figure 2.1a) how difficult it can be to decide whether or not an unfamiliar person shown even in a high quality image matches one of an array of comparison faces. Bruce et al. (1999) showed that when participants were asked to decide whether or not the person shown in a high quality video image was present in a 10-person array of faces, they were accurate on average only 70% of the time, and this was when viewpoint and expression matched between target and distractor items. Performance on this task dropped to 64% if expression was changed and 61% if viewpoint was slightly changed, averaged across target present and absent arrays. When the task was changed so that targets were *always* present and participants were told this, performance averaged only 79% correct – one in five of their choices were false. When only the internal face features of the target face were shown, with the target present on every trial, performance averaged only 49% correct. In line with the importance of external face features in processing unfamiliar faces, performance with external features alone in this task was 73% correct.

This experiment shows that even verifying the identities of unfamiliar faces across slight changes in image format can be highly error prone. It is a result that echoes that obtained in the striking experiment on photo identification cards by Kemp and his colleagues we described in Chapter 2 (see Table 2.1). Again consistent with Kemp et al. (1997), further research has shown that the results obtained by Bruce and colleagues (1999) generalise to more realistic situations. Henderson and her colleagues (Henderson et al., 2001) conducted research using footage from a filmed staged robbery in which both high and low quality video images of the robbers were taken from cameras at the event. A series of experiments examined how accurately participants could match camera images of one or other 'robber' against arrays showing the robber with distractor faces, and revealed large numbers of mistaken matches even when the high quality camera images were used. Davis and Valentine (2009) examined how well participants could match moving video footage of choreographed actions made by a 'perpetrator' against a live 'defendant'. The 'defendant' was either the same person shown on video or a distractor of similar overall appearance. Error rates across all three experiments reported in their paper were high, and very comparable to those reported in the photo-based studies reported by Bruce et al. (1999) and Henderson et al. (2001). Table 6.3 shows the results obtained in Davis and Valentine's final experiment, in which they compared the accuracy of video matching against a live target with matching against a photograph. Averaging across target present and absent trials there was little difference in accuracy for photographic compared with live target presentation.

The experiments reviewed above demonstrate very clearly that it is quite common to be misled by resemblance. Two different images of the same person can look quite different, and two images of different people can look very similar.

In 2005, in the aftermath of terrorist attacks on London transport, police officers shot and killed Jean Charles de Menezes whom they mistook for a suspect, Hussain Osman, and whose movements appeared erratic and suspicious. The physical resemblance between these two men was slight. They even came from different ethnic backgrounds. The results of experimental

Table 6.3 Percentage errors in Davis and Valentine (2009, Experiment 3) as a function of video condition and presentation mode. In Live mode, a live actor (the 'defendant') was shown alongside high quality video footage. In Photograph mode, a monochrome photograph was shown alongside the video footage. Where the identities matched the video footage, the footage may have been taken a few minutes earlier ('immediate') or a week previously ('time lapse').

Presentation mode	Culprit present immediate	Culprit present time lapse	Culprit absent
Live	16	26	41
Photo	17	41	27
Mean	17	33	34

research and tragic cases such as that of de Menezes highlight that any apparent resemblance between images of unfamiliar faces should be used to signify just that – resemblance. This is also the message that has come from the much longer history of research into identification of faces in line-ups and photospreads.

Does this mean that CCTV images are of no use in the hunt for criminals? Not at all! First, CCTV images do reveal a great deal of extremely useful information about what happened in a criminal event and also about the appearance of the wanted person. A CCTV image showing an apparently middle-aged white male robbing a bank can be used to eliminate from suspicion those of different ethnic background and of significantly younger or older age. Furthermore, even low quality CCTV footage can be useful in identifying the perpetrator by someone who knows them well. As we have seen several times, familiarity is key.

Burton, Wilson, Cowan and Bruce (1999) showed that participants were very accurate at identifying low quality CCTV footage when they were students in the same department as the lecturers who appeared in the videos, provided that the video images showed the face. Accuracy was considerably reduced when the films concealed the faces – even when clothing and gait was available. This suggests that using CCTV images in public appeals for information may be highly effective when someone recognises a personally familiar perpetrator, and indeed some high profile crimes have been aided in this way. David Copeland, the London 'nail bomber', was recognised by a work colleague from CCTV footage displayed during the desperate hunt for the perpetrator in April 1999, but unfortunately not apprehended until after his third and most devastating bomb exploded in the Admiral Duncan pub, killing three people and injuring 79.

Although the studies of photo-matching from video images reviewed above revealed that participants matching unfamiliar faces make a large number of mistaken judgements, on average, there are large variations in performance between people. In the next section we turn to consider what these individual differences tell us about the mechanisms involved in face matching.

Individual differences in face recognition and photo-matching

Individual differences in face recognition and related abilities are potentially very important. With better knowledge of these, we might be able better to assess the credibility of a witness, or to ensure that immigration officials are good at matching a real face with a passport photograph.

Megreya and Burton (2006) investigated what correlated with participants' abilities to match faces in tasks like those reported by Bruce et al. (1999). In a replication of the basic array-matching task, where targets could be present or absent from depicted arrays, overall performance from 30 undergraduate participants was 82% correct (a little higher than that observed with the same task by Bruce et al.) with a standard deviation of 12%, and scores ranged widely from 50% through to 96% – near perfect matching. Performance on this task correlated positively and significantly with a number of other perceptual and visual memory tasks, including tasks of matching objects across slight variations, speeded matching of line drawings, and finding all instances of the letter A as quickly as possible in a set of words, as well as tests of visual short-term memory and recognition memory for face images.

One recurrent factor in the tasks which predicted face matching was their requirement for participants to pay attention to local details (e.g. find letter A, ignoring the words containing them) rather than holistic impressions. This suggests that what may determine good performance in the array matching task is attention to local features of faces. This fits with what many of us seem to do in an unfamiliar face matching task – we check the hairstyles, the eyes, the noses, and anything that might offer a workable cue. In subsequent experiments this impression was confirmed when Megreya and Burton found high correlations between performance on the upright array matching task and performance on a range of tasks using *inverted* faces – whether using unfamiliar faces, familiar faces, or recently familiarised faces. So, to match faces well across slight variations produced by different camera and lighting characteristics requires a particular analytical/local processing style that is also beneficial for processing faces when these are inverted. People who are better than average at matching arrays of unfamiliar faces like those shown in Figure 2.1a are also better than average at recognising famous faces upside down.

At a more general level, within the normal (i.e. non-brain-injured) adult population we can identify people who are remarkably good – 'super-recognisers' (Russell et al., 2009) – as well as people who are remarkably poor – 'congenital prosopagnosics' (Behrmann & Avidan, 2005) – at a range of face processing tasks. Research has tended to focus on those who experience problems – as in congenital prosopagnosia – but the exceptional facility of super-recognisers may have as much to teach us. Recent evidence shows that there may be significant heritability of face processing skills (Wilmer et al., 2010; Zhu et al., 2010), so future work on individual differences and their neural underpinnings may have much to contribute to understanding how we recognise faces.

In this chapter we have reviewed what we understand about the processes underlying face recognition. We began, though, by noting that the main reason we become so good at face recognition is that, as members of a highly social species, we need to be able to recognise different people so that we can interact with them as individuals, bringing to mind pertinent facts about them that can guide these interactions. Recognising the visual pattern of a face – the topic we have been discussing here – is only one component of the more complete task of identifying a person. In the next chapter we move on to the broader set of processes involved in person recognition.

Summary

Face recognition is often considered the acme of perceptual classification skills, because we can individuate so many faces despite their often having high similarity to each other and we recognise familiar faces across substantial variations in pose, expression, and so on. We reviewed some of the main ideas and evidence about how we recognise faces including effects of distinctiveness and caricature, inversion, prototype effects, other-race and other-age effects, and the roles of different types of configural information and other potential cues to identity. The multidimensional face-space framework provides a unifying account of many of these findings, but it does not specify what the dimensions might be. We showed the value of PCA and related approaches that offer the possibility of identifying dimensions of variability based on image statistics, and how these approaches can fit with evidence of image-dependence in behavioural and functional neuro-imaging studies. Finally, we discussed how many of the insights from research on face recognition can be used in legal and forensic contexts.

Further reading

Burton, A. M., Jenkins, R., Hancock, P. J. B., & White, D. (2005) Robust representations of face recognition: The power of averages. *Cognitive Psychology, 51,* 256–284.
An impressive step forward in understanding how familiarity effects could arise, based on an appealing hypothesis.

Davies, G., & Griffiths, L. (2008). Eyewitness identification and the English Courts: A century of trial and error. *Psychiatry, Psychology and Law, 15,* 435–449
A fascinating review of the long and rather sorry history of cases of mistaken identity, including those we mention in this book, and the official enquiries whose recommendations about problems of identification evidence have not always been heeded.

Frowd, C., Bruce, V., & Hancock, P. J. B. (2008). Changing the face of criminal identification. *Psychologist, 21,* 668–672.
A longer overview of some of the developments of composite systems that we describe in this chapter.

Johnston, R. A., & Edmonds, A. J. (2009). Familiar and unfamiliar face recognition: a review. *Memory, 17,* 577–596.
Like the title says.

Maurer, D., Le Grand, R., & Mondloch, C. J. (2002). The many faces of configural processing. *Trends in Cognitive Sciences, 6*, 255–260.
One of the first papers to try really hard to unpick the different senses in which 'configural' has been used in the research literature, and the implications of its different meanings.

O'Toole, A. J., Roark, D. A., & Abdi, H. (2002). Recognizing moving faces: A psychological and neural synthesis. *Trends in Cognitive Sciences, 6*, 261–266.
Looks at how we use facial motion in recognition. Links to how motion signals we discuss in Chapter 4 (expression, lipreading) might contribute, and how the various pieces fit with Haxby et al.'s (2000) neurological model.

Beyond the face: Person perception

So far in this book we have discussed many of the kinds of information we can get from people's faces, including how we use the face's physical structure to infer characteristics such as age and sex, how we recognise emotions from facial expressions, how we use cues such as gaze to make inferences about whether someone is interested in what we are saying, and how we recognise the faces of familiar people.

In these and many other such examples, facial cues support interpersonal interaction, allowing us to make inferences about other people and to bring to mind pertinent facts we may need to recall about them. In this chapter, we will set what we can do with faces more firmly into this context of person perception by looking at how we access previously stored information about people we recognise and how face perception relates to other important sources of information such as voices. To do this, we will place particular emphasis on theoretical models that bring together and seek to explain key observations made here and elsewhere in this book.

Accessing semantic information and names

In Chapter 6, we reviewed what is known about how we recognise the faces of people we know. For faces that can be recognised, a crucial task is to bring to mind previously stored information – the things you know about these people. If you can't do this, normal social interactions with familiar people become impossible.

The information we need to access to fully identity a person includes known occupational, biographical or other personal information, such as 'Scottish former Labour Prime Minister and Chancellor with two sons' – which we put under the heading of 'semantic' information, and also may include the person's name 'Gordon Brown' – though as we will see later, names are peculiarly difficult to remember.

In 1986 we (Bruce & Young, 1986) drew an important distinction between 'visually-derived' and 'identity-specific' semantic information. *Visually-derived* semantic information refers to things you can see or infer without needing to recognise whose face it is – things like race, age, sex, as we discussed in Chapter 3. In contrast, *identity-specific* semantic information can only be accessed from recognising the face you are looking at – it refers to things you know about the person such as their occupation, where they live, or whether they like bananas, but which generally are not revealed by specific visual characteristics of their face. It is the derivation of identity-specific semantic information that most clearly links face recognition to the wider domain of person recognition, and this is what we address first.

Compared with other visual objects and shapes, faces form a special class of visual stimuli because we must nearly always individuate them – this creates different environmental demands from recognising many other visual objects. Everyday objects often need to be assigned only to relatively broad categories that maximise the visual and functional similarity between exemplars – if you are knocking a nail into a wall it is important to know that a particular object is *a* hammer, but most hammers will do the job, so knowing *which* hammer it might be is not always necessary. Face recognition presents a quite different type of problem. Recognising a face as a face does not get us very far. Instead, we need to know which individual's face we are looking at, and the smallest of differences may be crucial in determining this. This distinction is readily seen in cases of acquired prosopagnosia, where patients typically do not experience problems in classifying faces as faces, even though they cannot recognise (i.e. individuate) them (Damasio, Damasio, & Van Hoesen, 1982; Hécaen, 1981).

The relation between form and function is also different for faces and many objects. The shapes of manufactured objects are generally closely related to the functions they must perform, so that one could expect to tell fairly easily whether a novel object was likely to be a tool or a piece of furniture. This is much less true for faces. Although there are some pointers (pop stars are usually young people with exuberant hairstyles, etc.) there is a fundamentally arbitrary mapping to *identity-specific* semantic information – you can't really know whether the face of an unfamiliar young person with an exuberant hairstyle is that of a would-be pop star, actor, student or hairdresser.

Here, we will examine what studies have taught us about how we access this identity-specific semantic information. As well as considering everyday and laboratory recognition of familiar faces, we will examine some of the implications of person identification impairments caused by brain injury, and the importance of the interaction between data from investigations of normal and disordered recognition in advancing our understanding.

Recognising familiar faces and accessing identity-specific semantic information is often seen as a multi-stage hierarchical process involving sequential access to different kinds of information (Bruce & Young, 1986; H. Ellis, 1986; Hay & Young, 1982). Particularly strong support has accrued to the suggestion that the sequence involves three broad stages – first, recognising a face as familiar; second, accessing stored semantic information; and finally retrieving the person's name. Figure 7.1 shows a simple box and arrow model of these three stages. A

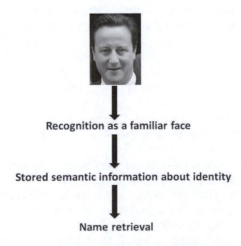

Recognition as a familiar face

Stored semantic information about identity

Name retrieval

Figure 7.1 Sequential model of familiar face identification. Courtesy of Press Association Images.

sequence of this kind formed the main identification route in the more elaborate Bruce and Young (1986) model of face recognition we introduced in Chapter 2, and that we describe in more detail later in this chapter.

One of the earliest studies that supported this sequence was conducted by Young, Hay and Ellis (1985), who collected a corpus of everyday errors by carrying out a 'diary' study in which 22 people took notes on mistakes they made in recognising people across an 8-week period. To standardise these records, they were made on forms which provided a checklist of things to note. After discounting the records made during the first week (to allow participants to learn how to use the record sheets properly), there were 922 records of difficulties and errors. Most of these records could readily be grouped into different types, some of which can clearly be considered to reflect breakdown at different levels of recognition. Here are examples of such errors from Young, Hay and Ellis' (1985) study, with brief descriptions of their salient characteristics:

1. *'I was going through the doors to B floor of the library when a friend said, "Hello". I at first ignored him, thinking that he must have been talking to the person behind me.'*

    These are failures to recognise a familiar person, who is mistakenly thought to be unfamiliar (114 records). This type of error is readily understandable when the person was of low familiarity, seen under poor conditions, or when the error was quickly corrected, but there were also a proportion of records for which such factors did not seem to apply (42% involved familiar people, 82% occurred in conditions that were not described as poor, and 58% lasted more than 10 seconds).

2. *'I was in the bank, waiting to be served. I saw a person and I knew there was something familiar immediately. After a few seconds I realized she was from a shop on campus or a secretary of one of the departments. I eventually remembered by a process of elimination.'*

    Such errors involve recognising a person as familiar, but being unable to bring to mind any other details, such as her or his occupation or name (233 records). This problem was often felt to be due to meeting someone who was not very well-known in an unexpected context. In the cases where the person's identity was successfully discovered (135 records) only 13% involved highly familiar people, and only 16% happened in contexts where that person would be expected.

3. *'I saw a poster advertising a film. I knew what films the actress was in and knew she does a lot of Beckett, but it was another minute before I could remember her name.'*

    These involve recognising the person as familiar and remembering appropriate semantic information about them, whilst failing to remember certain other details, such as her or his name (190 records). Of the cases where this problem was successfully resolved (135 records) the overwhelming majority (99%) involved inability to remember the person's name. This could happen even to highly familiar people (33% of these records), and usually lasted for some time (71% lasted over 10 seconds).

The orderliness of these types of everyday error supports the suggestion of sequential access to different types of information, in the sequence face familiarity then semantics then name retrieval, as shown in Figure 7.1. In these terms, the first example given above reflects a failure at the first stage in the model shown in Figure 7.1, the second example involves a failure at the second stage, and the third example a failure at the third stage.

However, diary studies taken alone have a number of limitations (Reason & Lucas, 1984). The most important of these are that diarists' reports might show biases, perhaps because they only report the errors they find particularly striking or easy to interpret themselves, or because they deliberately or unintentionally distort the errors in ways that make them seem more clear-cut than was actually the case.

Additional confirmation of the findings of diary studies of everyday errors has therefore been obtained from studies of errors made under laboratory conditions (Hanley & Cowell, 1988; Hay, Young, & Ellis, 1991). These studies can eliminate reporting biases, because errors can be systematically examined as they are made, yet still find the types of error predicted by the sequential access view.

Hay et al. (1991) showed 190 photos of famous and unfamiliar faces to 12 participants who were asked whether or not each face was a familiar person, what the person's occupation was, and what the person's name was. All of the errors made fell into patterns which would be expected from the hierarchical sequential access model, and examples were found for all of the types of error predicted by such a model. More importantly, there were no examples of any of the types of error which would be incompatible with a sequential access model. For example, the sequential access model does not permit errors in which a participant can name a particular face without being able to give the person's occupation. So we should never observe successful completion of the third stage in the sequence (naming) in the absence of successful completion of the second stage (accessing identity-specific semantic information). Reassuringly, this never happened (such errors were not found in Young et al.'s diary study, either).

The same point is made very effectively through a cueing technique adopted by Hanley and Cowell (1988), and Table 7.1 shows some of the data from their study. Participants who found a face they should have recognised to be unfamiliar, familiar only, or who knew who the person was but couldn't remember the name, were cued by giving them semantic information about the person (e.g. 'Brilliant cavalier Spanish golfer whose raw ability and adventurous play carried him to the top of the sport') or a card containing the initials of four famous people (one being the person in question), with blank spaces for the remaining letters (S - - - B - - - - - - - - - -, etc.). As is clear from Table 7.1, the semantic cue was most effective at promoting correct naming when participants found the face familiar only, whereas cueing with the initials was more effective when the occupation was already known. This is exactly as would be expected from a sequential access model, since people who find the face familiar only would be 'blocked' at the stage where semantic information would normally be retrieved (and hence assisted by a semantic cue more than an initials cue), whereas people who can already access the occupation but are still searching for the name should derive more benefit from an initials cue than a semantic cue (they have the semantic information already).

Table 7.1 Percentages of names successfully retrieved after cueing by semantic information or initials in Hanley and Cowell's (1988) study.

	Initial knowledge state		
	Face unfamiliar	*Face familiar only*	*Face familiar, and occupation known*
Semantic cue	41	52	35
Initials cue	12	22	47

'Blocked' access to information that should be remembered is a familiar everyday occurrence in the form of the irritating tip-of-the-tongue (TOT) state, when we seem to know everything relevant except the word we are looking for. Inability to bring to mind people's names is a particularly common cause of TOTs (Brown, 1991). Like other TOTs, these often involve partial information states in which quite a lot is known about the intended target name. Cohen and Faulkner (1986) described a person searching for the name 'Kepler' who managed to generate the candidates Keller, Klemperer, Kellet and Kendler. Although all of these were rejected, the participant knew that the target was foreign-sounding, and that Keller was the closest to it.

Another feature of many TOTs is that recall of the correct name seems to be blocked by an incorrect name that is persistently (and irritatingly) brought to mind. However, whether these subjectively blocking items play a causal role is debated. Reason and Lucas (1984) found that blocking items usually share structural, contextual or semantic features with the target, but tend to be items that have been more recently and more frequently encountered than the target itself. They suggested that blocked TOT states thus show the susceptibility to habit intrusions previously noted in other types of everyday error by Reason and Mycielska (1982). In contrast, Kornell and Metcalfe (2006) found that a delay which should help participants to forget the blocking item did not enhance the resolution of TOTs that included blockers any more than it enhanced TOTs without a blocking item, and that reminding participants of previous blockers did not affect TOT resolution either. On both grounds, they suggest blockers are a consequence, not a cause, of name retrieval difficulties.

An interesting extension of the cueing technique to investigate the sequential model of person identification was made by Brennen, Baguley, Bright and Bruce (1990) using TOT states. They induced TOT states by asking participants to name famous people from snippets of semantic information (e.g. 'The nervous man with the knife, in the shower scene in Hitchcock's Psycho'). When participants felt sure that they knew the name, but could not recall it (the TOT) they were cued either by giving the target person's initials, by showing the person's face, or by repeating the question (to control for the possibility that more time, or a second attempt, is all that is required). According to the model used in Figure 7.1, participants in a TOT state are blocked at the third stage, and should be helped only by cues about the missing name.

Results are shown in Table 7.2. The important point is that, consistent with

Table 7.2 Percentages of tip-of-the-tongue states resolved by different types of cue in Brennen et al.'s (1990) study.

Initials cue	*Face cue*	*Repeat question*
47	15	11

the simple stage model, cueing from seeing the person's face had no effect, since no more TOTs were resolved by this than by simply repeating the question. This is consistent with the model because according to such a model the face can only access the same pool of semantic information as the original question, but the blockage that creates the TOT state lies after that stage. Repeating the question is a comparison control condition that allows for the fact that simply allowing more time to resolve the TOT may in itself create some improvement.

Cases of neuropsychological impairment can also demonstrate that errors can correspond to breakdowns arising at different stages or levels of recognition (Young, 1992a). In such cases, a brain-injured patient will make characteristic errors to many seen faces. In prosopagnosia, for example, known faces seem unfamiliar (Meadows, 1974), which corresponds to error arising from failure to access the first stage in the sequence. De Haan, Young and Newcombe (1991a) reported a case in which known faces were familiar only, corresponding to a block before the retrieval of semantic information or names. In anomia, name retrieval to known faces may become problematic even though semantic information can be properly accessed (Flude, Ellis, & Kay, 1989).

To investigate this systematically with neuropsychological patients with different kinds of problem, Young and his colleagues developed tasks in which photographs of faces are presented one at a time, and participants are asked to rate familiarity, provide information about the person's identity (such as occupation), and give the person's name. The tasks included faces of 20 highly familiar famous people, 20 less familiar people, and 20 unknown people. Table 7.3 presents data from the highly familiar faces in these tasks for these three cases with contrasting patterns of impairment.

PH, who had occipito-temporal lesions caused by a closed head injury (de Haan, Young, & Newcombe, 1987a) shows the 'prosopagnosic' pattern of impaired recognition of faces. For ME, a patient with an unusual vasculitic disorder (de Haan et al., 1991a), the sense of familiarity of faces was well-preserved, but access to semantic information and name retrieval were severely compromised. For EST, who had surgery to remove a left temporal lobe tumour, only name retrieval seemed to be affected (Flude et al., 1989).

These findings are again consistent with a hierarchy of impairments corresponding to the idea that access to familiarity, occupation, and name retrieval involve sequential stages, as in Figure 7.1. There are breakdowns at each level, but those at the earlier levels affect later stages: without a sense of the face's familiarity, the occupation and name cannot be retrieved (PH); if the face is familiar but the occupation cannot be retrieved, then it can't be named either (ME); and name retrieval impairments can exist even when familiarity and occupation are available (EST). The different neuropsychological impairments

Table 7.3 Recognition of highly familiar faces by PH (de Haan, Young, & Newcombe, 1987a), ME (de Haan, Young, & Newcombe, 1991a), and EST (Flude, Ellis, & Kay, 1989). [Asterisked scores are more than 3.10 standard deviations below the control mean, p <. 001.]

	Familiarity (1–7 rating scale)	Occupation (max = 20)	Name (max = 20)
PH:	1.2*	0*	0*
ME:	5.7	7*	7*
EST:	5.2	17	3*
Control participants (N = 28):			
Mean	5.98	18.86	16.25
SD	0.51	1.15	2.81

thus parallel some of the patterns of error which arise as transitory phenomena for normal people in everyday life (Young, Hay, & Ellis, 1985).

Although none of the brain-injured patients documented in Table 7.3 could *retrieve* names of familiar people from their faces, this does not mean that they would necessarily have problems *recognising* names when shown them in print. Indeed prosopagnosic patients who have problems identifying people from their faces generally demonstrate that they do have intact knowledge of personal identities by responding relatively normally when asked about a person whose face they cannot recognise ('who is Gordon Brown?'). This reflects an important distinction between name inputs ('who is Gordon Brown?') and name outputs (finding the name 'Gordon Brown' in response to a prompt such as a face, a voice or simply a description of the person) that we will elaborate later in this chapter.

So, what happened when these three patients were tested for recognition of names rather than faces? Results showing how well they can recognise names as familiar and know to whom they belong are shown in Table 7.4.

Table 7.4 Recognition of highly familiar names by PH (de Haan, Young, & Newcombe, 1987a), ME (de Haan, Young, & Newcombe, 1991a), and EST (Flude, Ellis, & Kay, 1989). [Asterisked scores are more than 3.10 standard deviations below the control mean, p <. 001.]

	Familiarity (1–7 rating scale)	Occupation (max = 20)
PH:	6.0	19
ME:	6.2	8*
EST:	6.9	19
Control participants (N = 28):		
Mean	6.27	19.66
SD	0.63	0.84

Here we see that PH, who was unable to recognise faces at all, is completely normal at recognising names and retrieving semantic information about occupations. EST, whose problems were confined to retrieving names from faces, is quite normal at recognising names – again emphasising the difference between name input and name output. However, ME showed an interesting pattern with names appearing familiar but with an inability to retrieve information about why they are familiar – mirroring the deficit shown with faces for this patient. So in the name recognition task, ME showed the same pattern of impairment as for faces, whereas PH did not. Hence there is a difference between impairments which primarily affect the recognition of *faces*, and those which seem to involve *person* recognition regardless of the input domain. In the terms outlined in Figure 7.1, PH has an intact route to retrieving semantic information (stage 2) from name inputs, while ME is impaired at stage 2 and beyond irrespective of the input mode. Later in this chapter we will describe how both PH and ME provided further data which were critical for the development of theoretical accounts of person recognition.

Also important are patterns of impairment which do not occur. As for everyday and laboratory errors, a brain-injured person for whom name retrieval is normal from seen faces but access to occupations is impaired would clearly violate the proposed hierarchy shown in Figure 7.1, and therefore be of considerable theoretical importance. Such a deficit has been widely sought because of its critical significance, yet it is rarely reported. The only remotely persuasive cases in the literature have been DT, a French lady studied by Brennen, David, Fluchaire and Pellat (1996), and SB, an Italian lady studied by Papagno and Muggia (1999).

Brennen et al.'s (1996) case DT was tested repeatedly with a set of 20 faces of people who were famous in France, and on four occasions she could name Serge Gainsbourg, four times Catherine Deneuve, and once Christine Ockrent without giving appropriate semantic information. However, DT made many other errors (all consistent with the linear model) as well, and she was suffering a dementing illness at the time of testing (scoring 12/30 on the Mini-Mental State Test, probably because of Alzheimer's disease). In contrast, such errors have not been noted in systematic studies of groups of patients with Alzheimer's disease (Greene & Hodges, 1996; Hodges & Greene, 1998). Therefore, we are faced with the difficulty of interpreting an unusual and infrequent error pattern which is itself untypical of Alzheimer's disease and was not the dominant form of error made by DT. These data therefore need to be considered with caution. It can be tricky to establish that people with advanced dementing illnesses are approaching tasks according to the instructions given to them. As well as deficits which impact directly on face recognition, they often have problems affecting comprehension, attention, and short-term memory which can lead to their forgetting what they are asked to do, or simply doing something else.

Case SB suffered a left frontal haemorrhage that left her with a dysexecutive syndrome. Papagno and Muggia (1999) comment that she was easily distracted during testing sessions, and that only tests which required an immediate response could be used. She was able to name several famous faces, some of them consistently, and sometimes offering incorrect information with the name – 'Gorbachev, he has a factory in Pisa' – but more often giving incorrect information following further questioning where it would be difficult to rule out the possible impact of her other cognitive deficits. Like DT, SB also made other errors consistent with the linear sequential model.

Studies of everyday, laboratory and neuropsychological errors have therefore produced a number of converging findings which mostly fit the sequential access model of recognition shown in Figure 7.1 – later, we will return to why there have been occasional exceptions. Reaction time experiments have also given strong support to the sequential model. For example, faces can be classified as familiar more quickly than they can be classified by occupation, and categorisations based on occupations or other semantic properties can usually be achieved more quickly than categorisations which require access to the person's name. Such findings hold even when task demands and response requirements are carefully equated (Young, Ellis, & Flude, 1988; Young, McWeeny, Ellis, & Hay, 1986; Young, McWeeny, Hay, & Ellis, 1986). For example, all three kinds of decision can be made as binary key presses (press one key for familiar, another for unfamiliar; one key for politician, another for non-politician; one key for someone called John, another for any other name). When this is done, responses based on name outputs are slower than those based on occupations which are in turn slower than those based on familiarity.

The slower access to information about name outputs can arise even when the 'semantic' information needed seems intuitively to be more demanding. One experiment illustrating this was conducted by Johnston and Bruce in 1990. The experiment used only eight faces, repeated throughout the experiment. Four of the faces were of people called John and four called James. Half the faces were of British and half of American celebrities, and half were of dead people and half were of people still alive (e.g. two examples were John Lennon – a dead British celebrity, and John Wayne – a dead American one). The participants were shown pairs of faces and asked to verify as quickly as possible whether the two faces matched or mismatched on a dimension specified separately for each block of trials. In one block of trials the faces were to be matched by name, on another block they were to be matched on nationality, and on a further block they were to be matched in terms of whether both faces were dead or both alive. Johnston and Bruce (1990) found that all the tasks involving matching for names were conducted more slowly than any of those assessing nationality or dead–alive, even though intuitively it seems that it should be harder to retrieve information about whether a face belongs to a person who is now dead than whether they are called John.

These results can again be explained within the three-stage model of person identification. On this model, any task involving name retrieval must take longer than any task involving retrieval of information about identity, simply because name retrieval involves an additional, and time-consuming, stage.

Why are names so hard to retrieve?

Although the sequential access account proposes that information is accessed from seen faces in the order familiarity then semantics then name, this does not account for *why* name retrieval should come last in this sequence. The account redescribes, rather than explains, the phenomenon.

First we need to analyse the nature of the problem a bit more. Although our recall of names will often let us down, there is no evidence of anything like a comparable problem for name *recognition* – when we read or hear the name 'Elvis Presley', we don't usually have any trouble remembering who he was. For such reasons, Bruce and Young (1986) therefore drew a distinction between name input codes, which allow us to recognise a seen or heard name, and the name output codes involved in saying (or writing) that name. Problems arise when we have to generate a name output code in response to a face, voice or some other cue which contains no information about what the name might be.

Of course, face naming can be considered a recall task, and recall is often poorer than recognition. However, remembering an arbitrary fact, such as that Elvis Presley was American rather than British, is also a recall task, yet it does not usually cause the same type of problem (as illustrated by Johnston & Bruce, 1990). A satisfactory explanation must be sought elsewhere.

One useful approach has been to study how names and occupations are learnt in the laboratory. Cohen and Faulkner (1986) constructed brief biographical descriptions of fictitious people. Each biography contained a person's name, the name of a place associated with that person, the person's occupation and the person's hobby; for example, 'a well-known amateur photographer, Ann Collins, lives near Bristol where she works as a health visitor'. As Table 7.5 shows, recall of the people's names from these biographies was poorer than recall of the other types of information. Notice, too, that the place names were recalled relatively well – it is not simply the fact that names are proper nouns which somehow accounts for our problems in remembering them.

A similar study was carried out by McWeeny, Young, Hay and A. Ellis (1987), who taught participants a fictitious surname and occupation to each of 16 unfamiliar faces. The surnames were found to be much harder to learn than the occupations, and this was true even for items which can be used as names or occupations (Baker, Cook, etc.). It is more difficult to recall that a person's surname is Farmer than to recall that she or he is a farmer. Hence the explanation of differences between the ease of recall of names and occupations does not lie in properties of the items themselves, such as imageability, frequency, and so on.

Cohen and Faulkner (1986) suggested that occupations, hobbies and place names like Glasgow or Bristol may be semantically richer than people's names, which remain essentially arbitrary labels. There are some points in favour of this view. Cohen (1990) found that participants could remember people's possessions (e.g. that Mr. Hobbs has a dog) as well as they could remember their occupations (Mr. Hobbs is a pilot), but that recall of nonsense possessions (Mr. Hobbs has a

Table 7.5 Percentages of each type of target correctly recalled by 26 year olds in Cohen and Faulkner's (1986) study.

First names	Surnames	Places	Occupations	Hobbies
31	30	62	69	68

blick) was as poor as recall of names. Furthermore, when Cohen (1990) paired potentially meaningful names (e.g. Mr. Baker) with meaningless occupations (Mr. Baker is a ryman), it was the occupations which were worse recalled. Hence, we can make use of the imageability and meaningfulness of names, but only if this does not conflict with other semantic information about the person.

A related view was suggested by Young, A. Ellis and Flude (1988), who proposed that names are stored separately from other semantic information because nowadays they are arbitrary labels which are only occasionally required – when we see a face, we want to know who that person is, but it would be unnecessary and inconvenient if the name were constantly brought to mind. Earlier in social history, however, a name like Miller could be a significant indicator of the role or genealogy of a particular person. Moreover, names in other cultures or religious contexts may be meaningful and/or redundant – e.g. the common surnames Singh (male) or Kaur (female) in Sikh communities.

On these views, many names have nowadays acquired properties (such as semantic arbitrariness) that make them hard to recall, and this may in itself explain some of the problems of name retrieval without needing to invoke the idea that name retrieval lies at the end of a sequence of processing stages (Semenza, 2009). Consistent with this, very young children whose knowledge of people may be rather limited ('a boy in my class at school; another boy in my class at school') can sometimes find names easier to retrieve than other kinds of information (Calderwood & Burton, 2006; Scanlan & Johnston, 1997). And where an individual person is a very significant other, such as a husband or wife, retrieving their name can also be easier than their occupation (Brédart, Brennen, Delchambre, McNeill, & Burton, 2005). Later we will consider how computer-based models of person identification allow these rather subtle variations in the relative priority of semantics over names to arise, giving such models an advantage over the proposal that names are accessed at the last stage in a rigid sequence.

The Bruce and Young (1986) model

The (then) known empirical observations about the stages of retrieval of personal identities from face inputs formed the core of the face identification route in the theoretical framework for face recognition published by us in 1986. Figure 7.2 shows the full model we published then (also shown in Figure 2.15).

According to this model, when a face is viewed, a number of different kinds of analysis are conducted in parallel. These include the derivation of information about emotional states (via analysis of facial expressions), and information about visual speech (from lip, tongue and jaw movements), as well as personal identity (identity-specific and name codes). The route labelled 'directed visual processing' allows focused attention to be paid to particular physical properties of faces such as hair colour, sex or age – as might happen when you actively search for white-haired ladies of a particular age when meeting your grandmother at the railway station. Importantly, though, personal identity can only be accessed for a familiar face via activation of the appropriate 'Face Recognition Unit' (the FRU, using the

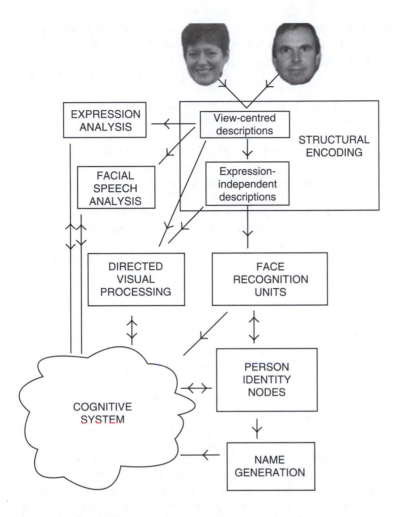

Figure 7.2 Functional model of face perception proposed by Bruce and Young (1986). First published in Bruce,V., & Young, A. Understanding face recognition. *British Journal of Psychology*, 1986, Volume 77, Issue 3, pp. 305–327, Figure 1, p. 312, John Wiley & Sons.

idea that the appearance of each known face is stored as a distinct FRU) when a suitable structural description of a viewed face matches the stored description for a known face.

Bruce and Young (1986) made it clear that the later stages of the face identification route were shared with other routes to person identity, such as hearing a voice or seeing a printed name:

A face recognition unit will respond when any view of the appropriate person's face is seen but will not respond at all to his or her voice or name.

The person identity node, in contrast, can be accessed via the face, the voice, the (written) name or even a particular piece of clothing (only access via the face is shown).

(Bruce & Young, 1986, p. 312)

Thus the model captures one input route (via the face) to a domain-independent semantic system where all the things known about a person can be accessed. On this model, then, patient PH (see Table 7.3 and Table 7.4) has problems accessing Person Identity Nodes (PINs) from face inputs, but his good performance in recognising familiar names and retrieving semantic information from names shows that access to PINs via another entry route (from a name input) is relatively normal. You can see from Figure 7.2 that this pattern might reflect problems either with structural encoding or with the FRUs themselves, and this illustrates how even a basic functional model can point you in the direction of what possibilities need to be tested.

Young, Humphreys, Riddoch, Hellawell and de Haan (1994) reasoned that one way to probe whether PH's FRUs were affected would be to test his face imagery. Theories of mental imagery suggest that imaging an item can be considered to require access to the same mental representation as would be needed to recognise it (Farah, 1989), and consistent with this fMRI data show that mental imagery for faces activates the FFA (O'Craven & Kanwisher, 2000). To test imagery for familiar faces, Young, Humphreys et al. (1994) asked PH questions about the appearance of (unseen) familiar faces (for example, 'Did Elvis Presley have fair hair or dark hair?') – these are the kinds of questions for which neurologically normal individuals report forming a mental image of the face to arrive at the answer. PH's ability to image the appearance of faces was severely impaired – he could not remember what the people he could not recognise looked like. In contrast, case HJA, who had extensive visual recognition problems for faces and many everyday objects in a context of impaired perception, showed normal face imagery. These results formed a double dissociation in which PH's vision was better than HJA's, whereas HJA's face imagery was better than PH's (Young, Humphreys et al., 1994). The interpretation that HJA's problems primarily affect structural encoding and PH's problems centre on the FRUs fits the data well. Later, we will discuss findings of 'covert recognition' for PH, and show how these can be simulated through problems at the FRU level, lending weight to this interpretation.

Clever studies by Craigie and Hanley (1993, 1997) also fit the idea that face imagery involves accessing FRUs. Craigie and Hanley (1993) looked in more detail at how we retrieve information about a person's facial appearance from being cued by their name. They showed that a form of sequential access still holds, in which identity-specific semantic information about the person's occupation has to be accessed before their appearance – that is, to form a mental image you have to go via the PIN to the FRU. In a follow-up study, Craigie and Hanley (1997) taught participants a name and an occupation for a series of faces, then asked them to match the items together. They found that choosing the correct name when shown a face was only possible if the correct occupation was selected, but that choosing the correct face when shown a name was equally dependent on first finding the correct occupation. These patterns fit the idea that sequential access happens in the recognition system whatever the entry point and target destination.

Although the examples given above show the value of an explicit functional model such as Bruce and Young (1986), several things were unclear or unknown at the time that we published this paper. What kind of representation formed the 'structural description' for a known face held in the FRU? Did PINs themselves hold all the things known about a person or were these just way-stations in to the cognitive system? How did initially separable routes for identities, expressions, etc. come together again so that subsequent actions were appropriate (e.g. at the play park you might rush to console your own child seen crying, but first look around for the parent of a crying child you knew less well)? It was also difficult to explain convincingly why different types of 'priming' (see later) had the properties they did, and particularly difficult (at the time) to explain how some prosopagnosic patients could show covert recognition of faces that they did not recognise overtly.

These deficiencies in the model led to the development of a related, but subtly different, computer-implemented system – Burton, Bruce and Johnston's (1990) 'IAC' model (for Interactive Activation with Competition). Before we outline IAC we first need to discuss in some detail the ways in which priming can affect face recognition, and how the IAC model and developments of it have simulated such effects.

Repetition and semantic priming

Priming effects have provided important insights into the organisation of mechanisms involved in the recognition of familiar people. In particular, comparisons of repetition and semantic priming have been instructive.

Repetition priming involves the facilitation of recognition of a previously seen item. Such priming is demonstrated widely in a range of recognition domains – including written and spoken words and pictured objects (Kolers, 1976; Morton, 1979; Warren & Morton, 1982). Here we are specifically interested in the patterns of repetition priming obtained in person recognition. Early studies demonstrating priming of face recognition were reported by Bruce and Valentine (1985) and A. Ellis, Young, Flude and Hay (1987). These showed significant facilitation of familiar faces seen earlier in the experiment (see Chapter 2 for an overview of the repetition priming technique). For example, recognition of Prince Charles' face is faster if his face has appeared previously in the experiment than if it has not come up before. These repetition priming effects are domain-specific – recognition of Prince Charles' face is *not* facilitated by previously having recognised the name 'Prince Charles'. The effects also show substantial image-dependence. Reduced, though often still significant, priming is found if the image recognised in the test phase of the experiment differs from the picture studied earlier.

Consider, for example, results reported by Bruce and Valentine (1985). Their participants saw faces or names of familiar people in a pretraining part of the experiment, and were then asked to make familiarity decisions (familiar

Table 7.6 Mean reaction times in milliseconds for correct familiarity decisions to familiar faces (Bruce & Valentine, 1985).

Same view as pretraining	Different view from pretraining	Name seen in pretraining	Unprimed
893	952	1000	1032

versus unfamiliar person) to faces in a second part of the experiment. Mean reaction times for correct familiarity decisions are shown in Table 7.6.

In this experiment, the 'Unprimed' condition acts as a baseline that tells us how long it takes to recognise a face that was not in the pretrained set. Notice that there was a facilitation of reaction time to the face if it had been previously seen (Same View and Different View versus Unprimed), so having seen the face in the pretraining helps you to recognise it in the test part of the experiment. In contrast, there was no significant effect of previously seeing a name on recognising the person's face (Name Seen versus Unprimed). This is important, because it shows that simply remembering who you encountered in the pretraining isn't enough to produce a benefit. For face recognition to benefit, you have to have seen the person's face, not their name – this is what we mean by saying that repetition effects are domain-specific. There was, though, additional benefit from seeing the Same View rather than a Different View of the face in Bruce and Valentine's (1985) experiment, which they attributed to an effect of visual memory of the specific photograph used. However, a subsequent study by A. Ellis et al. (1987) found that the amount of repetition priming fell as the similarity between the previously studied and test face photographs decreased.

The effects of repetition seem to be located in the face recognition system itself, since decisions about the face's expression or sex, which can be made without needing to recognise the person, do not show repetition priming (A. Ellis, Young, & Flude, 1990), and neither do decisions about what sound a face was articulating (Campbell & de Haan, 1998). Table 7.7 shows data from an experiment reported by Ellis and colleagues in which participants saw photographs of faces during a pretraining session and then were later asked to make decisions about the familiarity, expression or sex of these faces in a second phase of the experiment (A. Ellis et al., 1990). Although exactly the same photographs were used in the pretraining and test phases, only reaction times for familiarity

Table 7.7 Reaction times in milliseconds for familiarity, expression or sex decisions to familiar faces which were seen (Primed) or not seen (Unprimed) in a pretraining phase of the experiment (Ellis, Young, & Flude, 1990).

	Primed faces	Unprimed faces
Familiarity decision:	709	862
Expression decision:	552	566
Sex decision:	636	638

decisions showed any benefit. So, seeing a face earlier even in exactly the same picture does not facilitate a later judgement made about its expression, or whether it is male or female. A minor exception to this general pattern is that sex decisions can be facilitated by repetition under circumstances where the judgement is made particularly difficult (Goshen-Gottstein & Ganel, 2000).

Other experiments reported by A. Ellis et al. (1990) showed that the benefit of recognising familiarity of having seen a face before was equivalent regardless of whether the face was initially judged on sex, expression or familiarity, and Campbell and de Haan (1998) found a comparable phenomenon for lipreading, in which judging mouthed speech or judging identity in the pretraining phase of the experiment improved later recognition of identity. Again, this pattern points to the locus of the benefit of repetition priming being in the system that recognises the face's identity. When we look at a face, recognising it is involuntary – it is something we do even when we are focused mainly on some other aspect such as expression.

Repetition priming effects can be remarkably robust. Bruce and colleagues placed faces on participant recruitment posters in university halls of residence, inviting people who could recognise the faces shown to come into the laboratory to take part in face recognition experiments (Bruce, Carson, Burton, & Kelly, 1998). Unknown to the participants some of the items that had been on the recruitment posters reappeared in a face familiarity decision task in the same or different pictures, and familiarity decisions to these items were made significantly faster than to items that were novel in the experimental lists. Again priming effects were greater to faces shown in identical pictures compared with ones shown in changed pictures. These effects showed not only that priming effects can cross a change in context (from the recruitment poster to the laboratory), but also that they can last for several hours or days, between seeing the poster and participating in the advertised experiment.

More dramatic long-term priming effects of person identification were reported by Maylor (1998) who showed that young adults were more likely to correctly name faces that they had named in the laboratory 22 months earlier than novel items they had not previously seen in the laboratory. Because of the naming task used, this long-term effect may have arisen from priming of any of the stages in the identification route, including name retrieval. With pictures of objects, a priming effect after a staggering 17 years was reported by Mitchell (2006) who showed that naming of fragmented pictures benefited from earlier sight of the intact pictures in a laboratory visit 17 years earlier that several of the participants could not actually remember!

Repetition effects, then, are long lasting and domain specific, and the benefit of repetition seems to arise from the process of recognition itself. This pattern might be accounted for in various ways in the Bruce and Young (1986) model. Such an 'explanation', though, would be entirely post hoc – the benefits of repetition are not built in to the model.

Also problematic for models like Bruce and Young (1986) is the effect of the similarity between previously studied and test photographs (A. Ellis et al., 1987), which does not sit easily with the idea of an FRU that holds only the abstract essence of a face's appearance. A better conception of how an FRU might operate seems to come from Burton, Jenkins, Hancock and White's (2005) approach of averaging over instances of encountered faces (see Chapter 6), because this could still retain some information about the instances seen or allow recent encounters to have a greater influence on the average than old encounters.

A quite different pattern of priming is found with what is variously termed 'associative' or 'semantic' priming (we will later consider which is the more appropriate term, but in the research literature many authors use them more or less interchangeably). Semantic priming tasks investigate the effect of having previously recognised a closely associated stimulus – for example, the effect of having recently recognised one member of a comedy duo (e.g. Eric Morecambe) on the recognition of his or her partner (e.g. Ernie Wise). [In our examples of priming here we will use the classic British comedy duo Morecambe and Wise to illustrate even though they may not be very familiar to some of our readers. Comedy duos, like celebrity marriages, often become dated quickly and/or are very culture-specific. We did not feel that any more contemporary example we might use here would necessarily stand the test of time and place better than Morecambe and Wise.]

Table 7.8 shows data from a study in which Bruce and Valentine (1986) examined reaction times in a face familiarity decision task. Each of the familiar target faces could be preceded by a Related face prime (e.g. Eric Morecambe's face preceding the target face of Ernie Wise), a Neutral prime (an unfamiliar face), or an Unrelated face prime (e.g. Prince Charles' face preceding the target face of Ernie Wise). Different conditions of the experiment varied the amount of time between the onset of the prime and the target faces – their stimulus onset asynchronies (SOAs) – from 250 milliseconds, through 500 milliseconds, to 1000 milliseconds before each target. This was to see if any priming was confined to longer SOAs – a pattern which could be due to conscious anticipation of the face most likely to appear next. As can be seen, recognition was facilitated by related primes at all SOAs. Moreover, there was no evident 'cost' for the unrelated primes, which might have been expected if these created expectations of faces that might appear next (e.g. Princess Diana might have been consciously expected to follow Prince Charles' face at the time this experiment was conducted). The presence of strong priming at short SOAs and the absence of inhibition in unrelated trials suggest that the mechanism for these priming effects is highly automatic rather than based on participant strategies (Posner & Snyder, 1975).

Table 7.8 Reaction times (in milliseconds) for familiarity decisions to face targets preceded by Related, Neutral, or Unrelated face primes presented 250 milliseconds, 500 milliseconds, or 1000 milliseconds before each target (Bruce & Valentine, 1986).

	Related	*Neutral*	*Unrelated*
Stimulus onset asynchrony:			
250 milliseconds	782	848	855
500 milliseconds	705	804	816
1000 milliseconds	662	828	805

Semantic priming produces clear benefits on recognition that differ from repetition priming effects in two important ways. First, unlike repetition priming effects, the facilitation produced by semantic priming is very short-lived. Bruce (1986) varied the number of items that intervened between 'prime' and 'target' items in a continuous series of faces in which some items were repeated and others preceded by associates. Repetition priming effects of repeated items showed no sign of reduction as the number of intervening items varied from none (immediate repeat) to 11. Semantic priming effects were found only when prime and target followed each other immediately. Either semantic/associative priming lasts only a matter of seconds, or it is obliterated by an intervening, unassociated item. Second, unlike repetition priming, semantic priming crosses stimulus domains (for example, from recognition of Eric Morecambe's face to recognition of Ernie Wise's name) (Bruce & Valentine, 1986; Young, Flude, Hellawell, & Ellis, 1994; Young, Hellawell, & de Haan, 1988).

These differences between repetition priming and semantic priming effects imply that the sources of facilitation must arise at different loci in the recognition system. Consistent with this idea, ERP studies (see Chapter 2 for essentials of this technique) show that repetition priming affects a relatively early and topographically distinct component of the brain's electrophysiological response to a face, now known as the N250r (Schweinberger, Pfütze, & Sommer, 1995). Semantic/associative effects are in contrast more apparent in a later component of the ERP waveform, the N400.

However, precise specification of the causes of differences between repetition and semantic priming effects is difficult with a model such as that of Bruce and Young (1986). What is needed is a more tightly constrained model that can generate predictions about patterns of reaction times. For this reason Burton, Bruce and Johnston (1990) developed their IAC model, which was intended as a computer simulation of key features of the functional architecture of face and name recognition that would be broadly consistent with Bruce and Young (1986). Because it is implemented as a computer simulation, though, Burton et al.'s (1990) account is able to model in detail the effects of repetition and semantic priming and the differences between them.

Modelling repetition and semantic priming

The Burton et al. (1990) model is particularly important because priming and other effects reported in the literature arise quite naturally from the basic architecture with few additional assumptions.

The basic structure of Burton et al.'s (1990) model is shown in schematic form in Figure 7.3. The model is couched in Interactive Activation with Competition (IAC) terms – as a shorthand, we refer to it as the IAC model. It consists of active units connected to each other by modifiable links which can be excitatory (increasing the unit's activation) or inhibitory (decreasing the unit's activation). As in other interactive activation models building on the seminal work of McClelland and Rumelhart (1981), 'pools' of functional units are

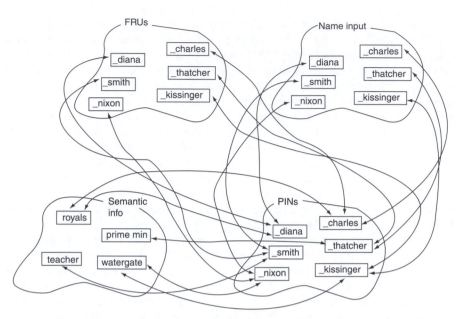

Figure 7.3 Central architecture of Burton, Bruce and Johnston's (1990) IAC model. The examples are from a bygone era, but we opted not to update them. *Un peu d'histoire* – Charles and Diana were members of the British royal family, Thatcher was Prime Minister, Nixon and Kissinger were US politicians, Mrs Smith was someone's school teacher. See text for explanation of FRUs, SIUs, etc. First published in Burton, A. M., Bruce, V., & Johnston, R. A. Understanding face recognition with an interactive activation model. *British Journal of Psychology, 81*, pp. 361–380. Copyright 1990 Wiley-Blackwell.

interconnected by bi-directional excitatory links, and within each pool the rival units compete by inhibiting each other. This inhibition becomes greater as units in a pool gain in activation, but in the absence of any input each unit's level of activation is set to decay slowly at a standard rate. There are pools of units corresponding to individual faces (face recognition units, or FRUs), seen names (name input units, or NIUs), and items of semantic information (SIUs such as politician, teacher, etc.). These are connected to each other via person identity nodes (PINs). PINs are modality-free 'gateways' to the semantic system. Inputs to PINS may come from FRUs, NIUs and (though not shown in Figure 7.3) voice recognition units too, and the PIN for a particular person will activate whichever SIUs are appropriate for that particular identity.

The Burton et al. (1990) model can be considered to be an implementation of part of Bruce and Young's (1986) model, though it also involves certain differences. The most important of these concern the PINs. Bruce and Young (1986) were unclear whether the PINs held identity-specific semantic information or enabled access to this information. Burton et al. (1990) are clear that PINs provide an interface to semantic information (the SIUs), rather than holding semantic information themselves. This in turn allows the PINs to play a key role in the identification sequence, because Burton et al. suggest that it is at the PINs where an input can be classified as familiar, rather than the FRUs or NIUs as Bruce and Young (1986) had envisaged. Thus, according to Burton et al., a face is seen as familiar when there is sufficient activity at the PIN corresponding to that person's face. This means that where a face, voice and other information are all provided, personal familiarity will be assessed from the combined activity arising from all these sources (rather than independently for face, voice, etc.).

This simple IAC model provides a neat simulation of key properties of semantic priming and repetition priming, using the assumption that familiarity is recognised when activation at the PIN crosses an arbitrary threshold.

We will look first at semantic priming. Consider what happens at the PINs for Eric Morecambe and Ernie Wise when activation is increased at the Eric Morecambe FRU (the equivalent of seeing Eric's face). Obviously, the Eric Morecambe PIN crosses the threshold of recognition quite quickly, but Burton et al. (1990) showed that activation at the Ernie Wise PIN also increases (but remains below threshold). This happens because activation is passed back to the PINs from the SIUs shared by Eric and Ernie. However, this activation does not bring the Ernie PIN to threshold, because it is simultaneously being inhibited by the more active Eric PIN.

After the input ceases, activation at both PINs decays a little, but does not return to resting level. This means that a subsequent presentation of Ernie *or* Eric will be recognised more quickly than if the activation in these PINs was at resting level. Moreover, it will not matter whether this subsequent presentation comes from Eric or Ernie's face or name, because either input route will be able to capitalise on the residual increased activation level at the relevant PIN. Note that the potential short-term 'self' priming of Eric's face or name from an immediately preceding exposure to Eric in either format is quite different from the more usually studied long-lasting but domain-specific repetition priming effect (Calder & Young, 1996).

In Burton et al.'s (1990) IAC simulation, then, the mechanism for semantic priming lies in interaction of the PINs and SIUs, and the explanation of why semantic priming will cross input domains is because the PINs can receive input from FRUs or NIUs. The short duration of semantic priming is accounted for by the fact that subsequent presentation of any face (or name) other than Eric or Ernie will drive the Eric and Ernie PINs back to resting level, because of the within-pool inhibitory links.

The mechanism for repetition priming in Burton et al.'s (1990) IAC model is different. A principle of Hebbian learning (Hebb, 1949), very commonly used in connectionist models like this, is that whenever two units are simultaneously active the connection strength between them is increased. So, after recognising Eric Morecambe's face, the connection between the Eric FRU and the Eric PIN will be strengthened, making activation of the PIN rise more quickly the next time Eric's face is encountered. Because of this strengthened connection, repetition of the face then leads to faster recognition. This explains why repetition priming effects are domain-specific, however, because it is the links between input units (FRUs or NIUs) and PINs which are strengthened, so if the face has been seen the FRU-PIN link is strengthened but this buys no advantage when it comes to recognising the name later on, and vice versa. Moreover, this mechanism can also explain why repetition priming effects are so long-lasting. The time over which a strengthened link decays can be set to be short or long, as the modeller chooses, but if link strengthening is to be any realistic analogue of learning then slow decays are more plausible than rapid ones.

This simple architecture was successful in explaining the reported difficulties in person identification by neuropsychological patients PH and ME (Table 7.3 and Table 7.4). If PH's problems lie somewhere in the FRUs or their connections to PINs, this would explain why he cannot retrieve any information overtly from faces, since these will fail to produce above-threshold activation at the PINs. Recognition and retrieval of information via name inputs can be quite normal, however. What of patient ME, who finds faces and written names familiar only but knows nothing more about the people giving rise to this familiarity? According to the IAC model, ME's problems must lie beyond the PINs which give rise to normal familiarity signals – either the SIUs are damaged or the connections from PINs to SIUs. This interpretation of ME's difficulties gave rise to the counter-intuitive prediction that ME should be able to pair up names and faces that belong together, even when she seemed to be aware of nothing other than that the face and name were each familiar. De Haan et al. (1991a) confirmed that this was the case.

Although Burton et al. (1990) were thus able to show that this IAC implementation can simulate several reported results on face recognition, at first sight there is no mechanism to account for problems in accessing name output codes (since a separate store for these is not built in to the model). However, Burton and Bruce (1992) noticed that the IAC model shown in Figure 7.3 can already account for problems in name retrieval, if it is assumed that names are stored along with other types of semantic information. A name like 'Bill Clinton' would then be linked to a single PIN (for Bill Clinton), whereas most items of semantic information would be linked to several PINs (e.g. 'politician' to PINs for Bill Clinton, Barack Obama, Tony Blair, Gordon Brown, etc.). It is a property of this type of architecture that the less interconnectivity an item has, the less easy it is to boost its activation. The SIU corresponding to 'Bill Clinton' (i.e. the output name) is inhibited by all the other SIUs within that pool and gains activation from only one PIN. In contrast, the SIU corresponding to 'politician' gets activation from PINs from all the other politicians. So this simple property can do a reasonably good job of simulating the relative difficulty of name compared with semantic information retrieval (Burton & Bruce, 1992), and ERP and behavioural reaction time studies have generated some findings that seem to fit the IAC model more easily than a fully sequential model (Rahman, Sommer, & Schweinberger, 2002). Moreover, placing the names in the same pool as SIUs may help in accounting for the paradoxical effects we noted previously in which the normal relative difficulty of accessing names and semantic information changes across development (Calderwood & Burton, 2006; Scanlan & Johnston, 1997), or in which brain-injured patients have named faces for which they did not seem to be able to offer correct semantics (Brennen et al., 1996; Papagno and Muggia, 1999).

Elegant though this seems, however, subsequent evidence has shown that the placement of name outputs within a single undifferentiated store of SIUs may not be quite right. Consider Brédart et al.'s (2005) finding that names of people with very high familiarity can in some cases be retrieved faster than other semantic information. On the standard IAC account, names of people about whom you knew a great deal should actually be even harder to retrieve than names of people about whom you knew rather little, because they will be more vulnerable to within-pool inhibitory effects. This counter-intuitive prediction is known to be false (Brédart et al., 1995, 2005). In line with most people's intuitions, it is actually *easier* to name people about whom more semantic information is known compared with equally familiar people about whom less is known.

Brédart et al. (1995) thus suggested that the system holding SIUs and name outputs is differentiated into distinct pools holding different kinds of information, as shown in Figure 7.4. On this model there might be one pool of SIUs about nationality, another for SIUs about occupation, and so forth, with names held within a pool on their own. Inhibition would occur separately within each of these pools but semantic information units of different kinds would not inhibit each other. This model is an alternative implementation of the idea that names lie at the same level as other kinds of semantic information rather than being retrieved 'last' as in Bruce and Young's (1986) model. The debate is not settled, because Bruce and Young (1986) never suggested that *all* semantic information must be retrieved before a name – only some items of semantic information were considered essential. But the introduction of implemented accounts has allowed the questions to become more precise, and offered potentially important insights. It was the development of computer models of the stages of face recognition that allowed the insight that the relative difficulty of name retrieval could arise from properties of interactive activation and the interconnectivity of different kinds of information, rather than from an immutable sequence of stages. This approach also makes it possible to understand why some names, such as those of our partners, can be retrieved more easily than semantic information, even though most names cannot. On an IAC view, the connections to our partner's name will be considerably stronger than, say, to our partner's nationality.

The attentive reader may have noticed that the computer models we have described so far in this chapter do not take real faces as their input, since the problems of representing face patterns are side-stepped by starting the simulations with activation of the FRU – the stage at which face structures have already been analysed. This is a convenient way of exploring the 'central architecture' of putative systems for person recognition, but it clearly leaves a lot missing as a complete account of face recognition.

To begin to remedy this deficit Burton, Bruce and Hancock (1999) extended the IAC model by building a perceptual 'front end' which stored representational descriptions of real face patterns and was tested with novel visual exemplars of faces known to the system. The representational descriptions used were based around the Principal Components Analysis (PCA) based representations we discussed in Chapter 6. The model encoded representations of 50 male faces in neutral expressions and was able to recognise expressive variants of these men. Associations between some of the men were created by giving some pairs of items shared SIUs. Using this extended IAC model with a psychologically plausible pattern processing front end, Burton et al. showed that the model was

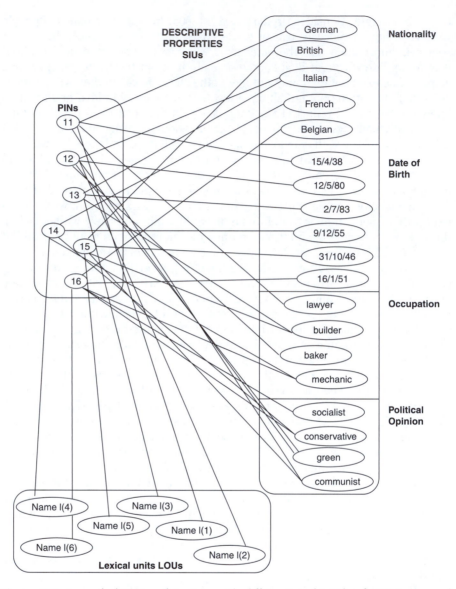

Figure 7.4 Amended IAC architecture with differentiated pools of SIUs proposed by Brédart et al. (1995). Reproduced from Brédart, Valentine, Calder and Gassi (1995).

sensitive to the relative visual distinctiveness of items and showed appropriate patterns of repetition and semantic priming using real faces.

So the core IAC model is capable of incremental extension in ways that can allow it to encode and recognise real face patterns, simulating effects of face recognition alongside more general properties of person recognition.

Where is semantic information about familiar people stored in the brain?

We have seen that a key aspect of Burton et al.'s IAC model is that a common pool of semantic information can be accessed via different, domain-specific input routes (face or name inputs, via FRUs or NIUs). Neuropsychological studies of the effects of brain injury fit this proposal well, since they show that access deficits can be domain-specific (for faces or names only) whereas impairments of the semantic information pertaining to familiar people affect all domains.

First we describe domain-specific access deficits. Newcombe and her colleagues studied groups of ex-servicemen who had recovered from unilateral shrapnel injuries affecting posterior parts of the left cerebral hemisphere or the right cerebral hemisphere using tasks which required them to decide as quickly as possible whether faces or names were those of familiar or unfamiliar people (Newcombe, de Haan, Ross, & Young, 1989). A comparison group of neurologically normal participants was also tested. The ex-servicemen with left posterior hemisphere lesions were slow to recognise familiar names but normal at recognising familiar faces, whereas the ex-servicemen with right posterior lesions were slow to recognise familiar faces but normal at recognising familiar names. These dissociable patterns of impairment did not reflect more basic visual problems. Newcombe, de Haan et al. (1989) measured the spatial contrast sensitivity function for all their participants and found that, whilst the contrast sensitivity functions of both the left and right posterior brain-injured groups were impaired overall relative to controls, there were no differences between the pattern or degree of impairment shown by the left and right groups. Moreover, at the individual case level, striking dissociations were evident between preserved or defective vision and preserved or defective face or name familiarity decision.

Further evidence for domain-specific access deficits comes from Neuner and Schweinberger (2000), who used a similar approach to Newcombe, de Haan et al. (1989) of testing familiarity decisions to demonstrate dissociable recognition deficits affecting voices as well as faces and names.

Second, we turn to loss of semantic information about people. The first case studies were reported by A. Ellis, Young and Critchley (1989) and Hanley, Young and Pearson (1989). Both patients had brain injuries affecting the temporal lobes, and especially the right anterior temporal lobe. They had severe problems in recognising famous people from their faces, names or voices. The pattern of deficit was therefore rather like case ME from Tables 7.3 and 7.4 (de Haan et al., 1991a), except that, as well as being unable to provide semantic information, these patients were not able to decide whether or not faces, names and voices were familiar. In this respect, ME seems like a more selective case in which the PINs of Burton et al.'s model can still be accessed even though semantic information has been lost, whereas in the more typical cases damage affects both PINs and SIUs.

Later studies have strongly supported the right anterior temporal lobe as a critical region for information about the identities of familiar people, and it forms part of Haxby, Hoffman and Gobbini's (2000) extended system. In contrast, the left anterior temporal lobe seems to be highly important for semantic knowledge about everyday objects, leading to striking reports of double dissociations between preserved knowledge of people and severely impaired knowledge of objects following left anterior temporal lobe damage, or severely impaired knowledge of people and relatively preserved knowledge of objects following right anterior temporal damage (Kay & Hanley, 2002; Thompson et al., 2004; Lyons, Kay, Hanley, & Haslam, 2006).

Particularly interesting (but also very distressing) variants of these disorders involve a form of neurodegenerative disease that affects the anterior temporal lobes and can itself have asymmetric effects. They often begin as seeming like a prosopagnosia, since recognition of faces is particularly obviously affected in the early stages, but become more obviously linked to person recognition from any source of information as the disease progresses (Busigny, Robaye, Dricot, & Rossion, 2009; Evans, Heggs, Antoun, & Hodges, 1995; Gainotti, 2010; Gainotti, Barbier, & Marra, 2003). Despite severely impaired person recognition and extensive right anterior temporal atrophy, Busigny et al. (2009) were able to use standard fMRI localiser techniques to find the right OFA and right FFA in their patient, who showed remarkably well-preserved ability to perceive faces in behavioural tests.

Although the right anterior temporal lobe seems to be particularly important to representing semantic properties of familiar people, it is usually left anterior temporal lobe damage that creates specific problems of name retrieval, whether for names of everyday objects or the names of familiar individuals (Gainotti, 2007; Semenza, 2009). This neurological asymmetry between retrieving names and other semantic information about familiar individuals does not sit easily alongside the IAC model's allocation of these items to a common store – but neither does it decisively rule out the possibility. Together with other evidence reviewed above, it shows that there are still questions to be answered before we can satisfactorily answer the deceptively simple question of why names are so hard to retrieve.

Covert recognition in prosopagnosia

A considerable strength of the Burton et al. (1990) IAC model is that it can provide an account of the otherwise puzzling phenomenon of covert recognition found in some cases of prosopagnosia. This is remarkable because the IAC model was not developed with this in mind.

To understand the simulation, we need to look at some of the phenomena that demonstrate covert recognition. Prosopagnosic patients usually fail all tests of overt recognition of familiar faces (Hécaen, 1981). They cannot name the face, give the person's occupation or other biographical details, or even state whether or not a face is that of a familiar person (all faces seem unfamiliar). Surprisingly, though, there is substantial evidence of covert recognition from physiological and behavioural measures (Bruyer, 1991).

In a very elegant study, Bauer (1984) measured skin conductance whilst a prosopagnosic patient, LF, viewed a familiar face and listened to a list of five names. When the name belonged to the face LF was looking at, there was a greater skin conductance change than when someone else's name was read out. Yet if LF was asked to choose which name in the list was correct for the face, his performance was at chance level. The same effect was found to personally known faces (LF's family) and famous faces he would only have encountered in the mass media.

This was a very surprising finding. In effect, Bauer had applied a classic lie-detection technique known as the 'guilty knowledge' test to show that LF had more knowledge of familiar faces than he was able to articulate in response to explicit questioning – but of course no-one concluded that LF was lying! Instead, it seemed that the SCR was able to tap into responses to faces of which LF was himself 'unaware', and another SCR study by Tranel and Damasio (1985) confirmed this by demonstrating stronger SCRs to 'unrecognised' familiar faces than to unfamiliar faces in other prosopagnosic individuals.

A crucial question concerning these findings was therefore whether such effects were restricted to physiological responses such as the SCR, or could be demonstrated in other ways. The existence of a report by Bruyer and his colleagues which used learning techniques (Bruyer et al., 1983) suggested that purely behavioural indices of covert recognition in prosopagnosia might be developed from tests which examined face recognition indirectly, by measuring its influence on some other task. Bruyer et al. (1983) showed that even though their patient, Mr. W, failed nearly all tests of overt recognition, it was easier for him to learn to give the correct names to pictures of five famous faces (i.e. to learn to associate the name 'John Kennedy' with Kennedy's face) than it was for him to learn incorrect names (e.g. to label Kennedy's face 'Richard Nixon').

A number of such indices of covert recognition in prosopagnosia have since been developed – often based on already well-established behavioural paradigms used with neurologically normal participants. For example, semantic priming has been found from 'unrecognised' faces onto the recognition of name targets (Young, Hellawell, & de Haan, 1988). In Young, Hellawell and de Haan's (1988) study, prosopagnosic patient PH was asked to decide whether printed names were those of familiar or unfamiliar people. Paradoxically, PH's reaction time for recognising a familiar *name* was facilitated if it was preceded by a related face, even though PH could not overtly recognise the related face primes. So PH, just like non-prosopagnosic adults, was faster to recognise that Ernie Wise's name was familiar when it had been preceded by the face of Eric Morecambe than if preceded by the face of Prince Charles, even though the face primes did not seem familiar to him.

A comparable phenomenon was evident for PH with a face–name interference paradigm. Again, this made use of the fact that PH could recognise familiar names. He was asked to classify names as being those of politicians or television personalities as quickly as possible, and to ignore any irrelevant faces presented alongside the names. Figure 7.5 shows examples of stimuli from a critical condition of the experiment, in which the pairings of faces and names come from opposite categories – the name 'Frank Bough' (a well-known TV presenter at the time) is placed alongside the face of the politician Neil Kinnock, and vice versa. For neurologically normal participants, the presence of a task-irrelevant distracter face from the wrong semantic category slows classification of the name – as if information about the face's semantic category cannot be ignored (Young, Ellis, Flude, McWeeny, & Hay, 1986). Remarkably, the same was true for PH (de Haan et al., 1987a, 1987b). Note that the faces in Figure 7.5 are carefully matched for sex, age and overall appearance – any interference has to come from accessing identity-specific semantic information, not general visual properties of the images.

Young and Burton (1999) summarised findings from a number of studies of covert recognition and related effects in cases of prosopagnosia. A wide variety of such phenomena has now been reported, with covert recognition being demonstrated in studies using a range of indirect methods to assess recognition

Figure 7.5 Face–name interference paradigm used to demonstrate covert recognition in prosopagnosia. See text for explanation. First published in *Face recognition without awarenesss*, Edward H. F. de Haan, Andy Young, Freda Newcombe, *Cognitive Neuropsychology*, 1987, reprinted by permission of the publisher (Taylor & Francis Group, http://www.informaworld.com).

including differential eye movement patterns (Rizzo, Hurtig, & Damasio, 1987), preference judgements (Greve & Bauer, 1990), face matching (de Haan et al., 1987a; Sergent & Poncet, 1990), and savings in relearning of familiar compared with unfamiliar identities (Bruyer et al., 1983; de Haan et al., 1987a). Importantly, such effects are evident even when overt recognition of individual faces is completely absent – with face naming, ability to give the occupation or other identifying information, and assessment of face familiarity all at chance level.

The existence of covert recognition in prosopagnosia is therefore no longer disputed – the focus has shifted onto how it is best interpreted. Initial efforts centred on the notion of some form of neurological disconnection between face recognition and awareness of recognition (de Haan, Bauer, & Greve, 1992; de Haan et al., 1987a), and this had the advantage that Schacter, McAndrews and Moscovitch (1988) showed how the same approach could be applied to a number of different neuropsychological deficits. But problems became increasingly apparent. There was no detailed account of what 'signals to awareness' might be, and attempts to describe some of the phenomena in box and arrow terms (Young & de Haan, 1988) became worryingly complex.

A definite step forward was therefore achieved with the discovery that a simple and plausible form of damage to the Burton et al. (1990) IAC model could simulate some of these behaviours. Findings of covert recognition in prosopagnosia show responses based on the unique identities of familiar faces, even though overt recognition of these faces is not achieved. The simulation involves simply halving the connection strengths between FRUs and PINs in the Burton et al. (1990) model as a proxy for 'damage' to these connections (Burton, Young, Bruce, Johnston, & Ellis, 1991; Young & Burton, 1999). The damaged network is then no longer able to classify face inputs as familiar, because the PINs cannot rise above threshold levels from the degraded face inputs. But simulations show that the damaged network continues to display semantic priming from 'unrecognised' faces because the PIN-SIU links can still pass excitation to each other even at these sub-threshold levels. The problem of understanding how covert responses can be preserved when there is no overt discrimination may thus be less intractable than it at first appeared.

The implications of this type of simulation need to be carefully considered. It does not prove that this is why covert recognition is found in prosopagnosia. What it does is to show that this is a plausible candidate mechanism, subject to the limitation that other candidates may also be discovered in due course. But because we now have a candidate mechanism for covert recognition, and because it derives from such a simple modification to the Burton et al. (1990) account of normal recognition, it helps to demystify the phenomenon. Moreover, it offers the challenge to future accounts that to better it they will need to be able to account for the wide range of phenomena already encompassed and add something more. To date, other models have failed this critical test (Young & Burton, 1999).

An obvious implication of Burton et al.'s (1991) approach is that covert recognition will not be an 'all or none' phenomenon – effects will be graded according to the functional locus and severity of damage. Newcombe, Young and de Haan (1989) had already shown that covert recognition was not found when the locus of impairment was clearly primarily perceptual, albeit 'higher-order' perception. This fitted with a more general distinction between perceptual (apperceptive) and mnestic (associative) forms of prosopagnosia emphasised by De Renzi, Faglioni, Grossi and Nichelli (1991). However, an important analysis of a series of 10 acquired cases shows that, whilst the apperceptive versus associative distinction has some value as an idealised description, these patterns actually vary in severity and shade into each other (Barton, 2008). In another case series study, covert recognition and residual overt familiarity were found to be related (Barton et al. 2001), again consistent with Burton et al. (1991). This was only for acquired cases, however. The patterns of covert effects in congenital prosopagnosia have to date been less clear (Avidan & Behrmann, 2008; Barton, Cherkasova, & O'Connor, 2001; Striemer, Gingerich, Striemer, & Dixon, 2009) – possibly reflecting different developmental trajectories in these circumstances. Acquired cases, in contrast, reflect damage to systems that are likely organised to a considerable extent in functionally equivalent ways.

A related feature of Burton et al.'s (1991) simulation of covert recognition is that it implies that the failure of recognition seen in cases of prosopagnosia need not be absolute. This fits with Sergent and Poncet's (1990) observation that their patient, PV, could achieve *overt* recognition of some faces if several members of the same semantic category were presented together. This finding of overt recognition provoked by simultaneously presenting multiple exemplars of a semantic category has since been replicated with patients PH (de Haan, Young, & Newcombe, 1991b), PC (Sergent & Signoret, 1992) and ET (Diamond, Valentine, Mayes, & Sandel, 1994). The phenomenon is very striking – the patients themselves tend to be highly surprised at being able to recognise faces overtly. The provoked recognition only happens for some semantic categories, and it reflects genuine recognition rather than laborious deduction. It isn't due to thinking things like 'if they're film stars, I guess the blonde one could be Marilyn Monroe', because when patients can't identify the category themselves they continue to fail to recognise the faces even when the occupational category is pointed out.

Sergent and Poncet (1990) suggested that their demonstration shows that 'neither the facial representations nor the semantic information were critically disturbed in PV, and her prosopagnosia may thus reflect faulty connections between faces and their memories'. They thought that the simultaneous presentation of several members of the same category may have temporarily raised the activation level above the appropriate threshold. This bears an obvious resemblance to the Burton et al. (1991) account of prosopagnosia with covert recognition. Moreover, Morrison, Bruce and Burton (2001) have shown that the IAC model could simulate provoked overt recognition with some additional assumptions.

Morrison et al. (2001) first demonstrated that an IAC simulation with damaged FRU-PIN links did not reach above recognition threshold activity at the PIN even if successive input patterns were linked to the same SIU (i.e. came from the same category). This confirms that the 'lesioned' model does not allow overt familiarity to faces even when they are semantically related. They then suggested that the act of informing the participant that all the faces came from the same category could lead to focusing attention on the SIU activation which would now be known to be relevant to their task, but might have been inhibited when it was irrelevant to the task of judging familiarity alone. Lessening any inhibition at SIU level could allow SIUs to reach threshold, which would then strengthen their links with the PINs that activate them, allowing additional support for PIN activation when the task again became one of judging familiarity. Morrison et al. showed that a simulation of this 'release from inhibition' at SIU level would indeed let previously unrecognised face input patterns trigger above threshold level activation at PINs.

This potential explanation of provoked overt recognition allows us to return to the question we raised earlier in this chapter when we mentioned that the priming arising from interactions between the PINs and SIUs is variously termed 'semantic' as well as 'associative' priming. While closely associated pairs of faces such as Morecambe and Wise yield the strongest 'semantic' priming effects (Young, Flude, Hellawell, & Ellis, 1994), weak effects can be seen when items simply share a semantic category (Carson & Burton, 2001). This is to be expected on IAC where there will be both direct links between faces that share close associations and other, albeit weaker, activations flowing by virtue of category membership. The phenomenon of provoked overt recognition in prosopagnosia shows that shared category membership of several exemplars can have significant effects in a damaged network, and this is consistent with the observations from non brain-injured participants that semantic relatedness between items can also yield facilitatory effects.

Context, appraisal and recognition

Thus far we have talked about how different sources of information about personal identity may interact with each other to facilitate or inhibit identification. The examples we have used, however, all arise within a core 'cognitive' system for person identification that Bruce and Young placed largely in isolation from wider contexts. We now turn to consider how circumstantial context and particularly the appraisal of emotional and other responses may affect person identification.

An important factor in everyday face memory which was evident in Young, Hay and Ellis' (1985) diary study is the important role played by context in our recognition of faces. We may fail to recognise even highly familiar faces encountered unexpectedly, or incorrectly dismiss them as 'lookalikes' in what seems to be an inappropriate context. The Australian psychologist Don Thomson contrived to engineer the following encounter (Thomson, 1986):

> The parents of one of my students had flown from Australia to London. Soon after, and unbeknown to the parents, their daughter and a companion also travelled to London. The daughter and I arranged that she stand at a bus stop near her parents' lodgings; the companion was to stand some distance away and observe. The daughter and the companion later reported that when the parents emerged from their lodgings and saw their daughter they stopped abruptly. The father then approached the daughter and said

hello to her. She turned to face him, and as instructed, looked straight through him. His greeting choked in his throat and he lamely concluded, 'I am terribly sorry, I thought you were someone else'.

Thomson (1986, p.121)

How can parents fail to recognise their daughter? Why did they not rush to the police and say she had been abducted and drugged by some cult? In a sense, they did correctly recognise her, and were trying to say 'hello'. The key lies in that the daughter, when confronted, behaved with a cold indifference entirely inconsistent with the feelings engendered by mutual recognition between family members. Is this a one-off? Perhaps not – we next describe how failure to gain appropriate emotional signals from people can lead to a strange delusion that the people themselves have been replaced by impostors.

The Capgras delusion offers an extraordinary example of how we can discount what would seem to be correct recognition of a familiar face – thinking instead that someone is simply not who they appear to be. Typically, patients claim that one or more of their close relatives have been replaced by near-identical duplicates in the form of impostors, robots, clones or even Martians. Joseph Capgras was a French psychiatrist who gave one of the first descriptions of this bizarre phenomenon. It used to be considered very rare (Enoch & Trethowan, 1991), but it has probably been under-diagnosed and there are now hundreds of descriptions of cases in the psychiatric literature, including many reports that this delusion can follow brain injury.

At first, it is hard to take such a delusion seriously – the claim that relatives are impostors seems so blatantly preposterous. But it is no joke, and is now recognised to carry a significant risk of violence against the alleged impostors (de Pauw & Szulecka, 1988). Violence can be extreme, including decapitating the impostor to find the wires, but this is fortunately exceptional.

Cases of Capgras delusion have been found in many cultures throughout the world, and they show a noticeable consistency of certain features. Capgras delusion patients can be otherwise rational and lucid – able to appreciate that they are making an extraordinary claim. If you ask 'what would you think if I told you my family had been replaced by impostors?', you will often get answers to the effect that it would be unbelievable, absurd, an indication that you had gone mad (Alexander, Stuss, & Benson, 1979; Young, 2000). Yet the same patients will claim that, none the less, this is exactly what has happened to their own relatives. If you ask for evidence that it is an impostor, the patients often tell you that they can *see* the difference, yet they find it hard to express this difference in words (Young, Reid, Wright, & Hellawell, 1993). Further probing will sometimes reveal more pervasive feelings that many things seem strange, unfamiliar, almost unreal (Christodoulou, 1977, 1986).

Many clinicians have seen this as a psychodynamic problem. All of us find things we like and things we dislike in our loved ones, but acknowledging the existence of the things we dislike about them can make us feel uneasy. A much discussed possibility has therefore been that the Capgras delusion is a pathological way of resolving chronic ambivalence – by splitting the relative into a good original and a bad double, the double can be hated without guilt (Enoch & Trethowan, 1991).

Like many psychodynamic hypotheses, this is ingenious but not grounded in evidence. Behaviour to the alleged impostor is more variable than would be expected on the psychodynamic account, and sometimes quite friendly (Christodoulou, 1977)! More importantly, many recent reports show that the Capgras delusion is associated with certain types of abnormal brain activity or can follow brain injury. Figure 7.6 shows the distribution of blood flow in the brain of a person with Capgras delusion (Lebert et al., 1994). Abnormalities were noted in parts of posterior cortex considered likely to be involved in our emotional reactions to visual stimuli, and faces in particular.

Bauer's (1984) study of prosopagnosia may provide a clue to what is happening. A number of researchers have suspected that there might be some kind of link between prosopagnosia and the Capgras delusion, because both types of problem affect the recognition of familiar people. This speculation has been fuelled by findings that people who experience the Capgras delusion often perform quite poorly on face perception tasks (Young, Reid et al., 1993), and that they may show neurological abnormalities in brain regions similar to those involved in prosopagnosia (S. Lewis, 1987).

Even so, the relation between these conditions must be relatively subtle – the face recognition impairments noted to accompany Capgras delusion are

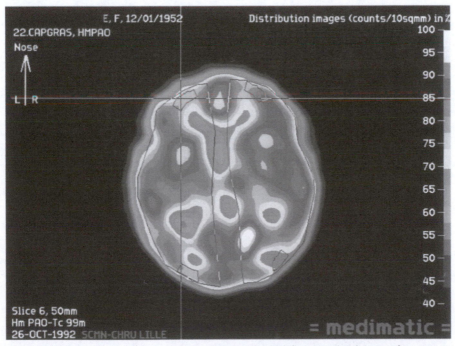

Figure 7.6 See colour plate. Image showing blood flow in the brain of a person with Capgras delusion, showing abnormal blood flow in parts of posterior cortex. First published in Lebert, F., Pasquier, F., Steinling, M., Cabaret, M., Caparros-Lefebvre, D., & Petit, H. (1994). SPECT data in a case of secondary Capgras delusion. *Psychopathology, 27*, pp. 211–214. Courtesy S. Karger AG, Basel.

nothing like as severe as those found in prosopagnosia whilst, conversely, people with prosopagnosia do not usually make delusional claims about their relatives.

Recall that Bauer tested the skin conductance response (SCR) of a person with prosopagnosia (case LF) when he was shown a familiar face and a series of names was read out to him. The SCR is usually measured by recording electrical conductivity from the finger or the palm of the hand. When we have an emotional response to something, the secretions from sweat glands caused by activity of the autonomic nervous system alter skin conductance – even very small degrees of emotional arousal can be measured in this way.

Bauer's finding was that LF showed a greater SCR change when the correct name for a face was read out than when an incorrect name was given. Yet LF could not recognise the face if asked to do so, and he could not even make an accurate verbal guess as to which was the correct name. The SCR was therefore picking up some form of non-conscious, covert recognition of the face's identity. Bauer considered that this was some form of non-conscious orienting response – he argued that emotional orienting responses and conscious recognition of identity are mediated by different neurological pathways, and that it is mainly the pathway to overt recognition which is compromised in prosopagnosia. This idea is shown in schematic form in Figure 7.7, using a face which still produces a strong emotional orienting response in many people.

From Bauer's account of his findings in prosopagnosia, H. Ellis and Young (1990) reasoned that the opposite pattern of relatively preserved conscious recognition but loss of emotional orienting responses might form the basis of the Capgras

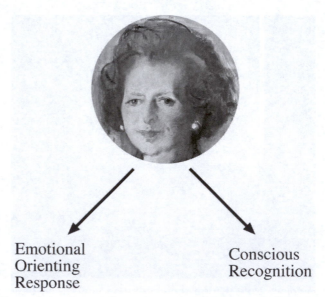

Emotional Orienting Response

Conscious Recognition

Figure 7.7 See colour plate. Schematic rendering of Bauer's (1984) proposal that emotional orienting responses and conscious recognition of identity are mediated by different neurological pathways. In Bauer's (1984) model, it is mainly the pathway to conscious recognition which is compromised in prosopagnosia.

delusion. The consequence will be that faces can be recognised, but seem somehow odd because they do not provoke the usual reactions. Lack of an orienting response might give social interactions a strange, awkward and emotionless tone – like interacting with a stranger. The impostor claim would then be a rationalisation of this highly disquieting sense of strangeness, and the delusion is primarily centred on close relatives because it is these for which the discrepancy between continuing overt recognition and absent orienting reactions will be most noticeable.

When we look at faces of people we know, then, we recognise who they are and parts of our brains set up preparatory reactions for the type of interaction that is likely to follow – an emotional orienting response. In H. Ellis and Young's (1990) account, recognising who it is and preparing for what you are likely to do (emotional orienting responses) involve separable neurological pathways, and the Capgras delusion can happen when the pathway responsible for the orienting response is affected. This theory predicts that people with Capgras delusion will not show any SCR to familiar faces. It is an important prediction because it follows directly from H. Ellis and Young's (1990) account but is not predicted by other theories.

So far, the prediction has proved valid. Hirstein and Ramachandran (1997) tested a single Capgras delusion patient (case DS) and found no SCR to personally familiar faces, and H. Ellis, Young, Quayle and de Pauw (1997) tested five patients and found no SCR to famous faces. The upper panel of Figure 7.8 shows mean SCR amplitudes to familiar (famous) and unfamiliar faces for non-deluded normal controls, five people with Capgras delusion, and for psychiatric controls taking similar medication (H. Ellis, Young et al., 1997). Only the people with Capgras delusion show no differential response to familiar compared to unfamiliar faces. However, the people with Capgras delusion also show a lack of responsiveness to all faces, so the lower panel of Figure 7.8 gives range-corrected scores which take account of this, showing that the pattern of loss of SCR to familiar faces in Capgras delusion is still found when measured in this way. In contrast, the SCRs of people with Capgras delusion to an auditory tone were normal in magnitude and rate of habituation (H. Ellis, Young et al., 1997).

Note that these studies demonstrate abnormal SCRs to faces for which the patients tested have not expressed any particular delusional beliefs, as well as for those about whom they may be deluded. Lack of responsiveness is found to *all* familiar faces in Capgras delusion, not just to the faces of people who have been subjected to the impostor allegation. This is exactly as H. Ellis and Young's (1990) hypothesis predicts.

The Capgras delusion can also be used to explore the relation between SCR and behavioural indices of recognition. Prosopagnosic patients who show covert recognition typically produce equivalent findings demonstrating covert recognition whether behavioural or physiological (SCR) indices are used (de Haan et al., 1992), suggesting that these different indices tap the same underlying phenomenon. In Capgras delusion, however, SCRs show reduced responsiveness to faces but behavioural findings of priming, interference, and so on are unaffected (H. Ellis, Lewis, Moselhy, & Young, 2000). In a way, this isn't completely surprising – the patients can recognise many familiar faces, even if they say some are not who they appear to be – but it highlights the value of detailed studies in clarifying what does need to be explained. In this instance, how the SCR is generated.

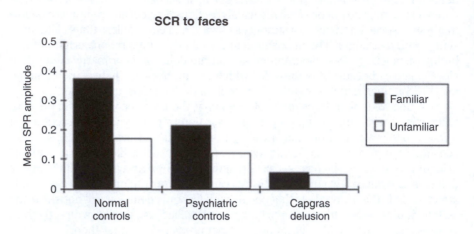

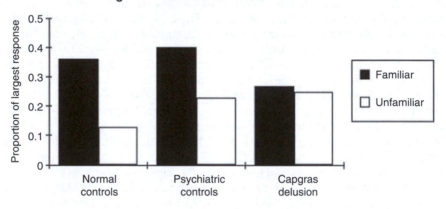

Figure 7.8 Skin Conductance Response (SCR) to familiar and unfamiliar faces in cases of Capgras delusion, psychiatric controls and non-deluded controls. The upper panel shows mean SCR amplitude in micro-Siemens, and the lower panel gives range-corrected SCRs as a proportion of each person's largest response. First published in Ellis et al. *Proceedings of the Royal Society B: Biological Sciences, 264* (1384), p. 1085. Copyright (1997) The Royal Society.

Bauer (1984) thought that SCRs to faces originate from an autonomic nervous system response that is triggered by a dorsal visual-limbic pathway through the superior temporal sulcus and the inferior parietal lobule. He suggested that this pathway 'subserves processes of selective attention and tonic emotional arousal, and is implicated in the process whereby "relevance" is attached to an attended object' (Bauer, 1984, p. 466). Thus it has multiple functions encompassing automatic emotional responses to stimuli which have personal relevance – these have been widely implicated as putative specialised functions of the right cerebral hemisphere (Bear, 1983; Van Lancker, 1991).

In discussing Bauer's model, however, it is important to keep separate his general conception that autonomic and conscious recognition involve dissociable pathways and his specific proposals concerning the underlying neurology. The neurology of Bauer's (1984) proposals has been questioned by other experts (Breen, Caine, & Coltheart, 2000; Hirstein & Ramachandran, 1997; Tranel, Damasio, & Damasio, 1995) who have none the less accepted the more general proposition that autonomic and overt indices of recognition tap different neural systems. Gobbini and Haxby (2007) have updated and extended Haxby et al.'s (2000) neurological model to better reflect the range of responses to familiar faces – including emotional responses.

Evidence can therefore be found to suggest the utility of H. Ellis and Young's (1990) general approach, though there are conflicting views about the details of how, neurologically, SCRs are lost in Capgras cases. However, H. Ellis and Young's (1990) original proposal lacked something more important. Even if you accept the premiss that the Capgras delusion represents a person's attempt at explaining powerfully abnormal perceptual experiences, nothing was said about why such a bizarre (impostor) explanation should be offered. Why doesn't a person in the grip of such an experience just say something to the effect that 'things seem very strange, but I'm not sure what's causing it'?

In fact, many people do say such things – they just get less attention from psychiatrists, neurologists and psychologists. The Capgras delusion represents the tip of a large iceberg of plausible and less plausible personal explanations of anomalous experiences. What characterises people with Capgras delusion is that they have additional problems which serve to create conditions under which extravagant explanations can be formed and sustained. For example, the suspicious mood that so often accompanies this delusion creates a bias which focuses the person's attention onto seeking external causes for their problems (Kaney & Bentall, 1989), and allows conclusions to be reached on the basis of insufficient evidence (Dudley, John, Young, & Over, 1997; Garety, Hemsley, & Wessely, 1991).

From this perspective, the Capgras delusion is due to an unfortunate interaction of problems that include both anomalous perceptual experiences and reasoning biases or impairments. This two-factor (or even multi-factor) approach can help explain other strange delusions that can co-occur with the Capgras delusion, and Langdon and Coltheart have developed it into an overarching two-factor theory of delusions in general (Langdon & Coltheart, 2000).

Other work has shown that people become (not unnaturally) preoccupied with their delusions and find it difficult to take their attention away from anything which seems relevant to the delusional belief (Leafhead, Young, & Szulecka, 1996). This heightened attention to delusion-related material may serve to make the world seem to throw up evidence consistent with the delusion, serving further to increase the bias to find relevant information. When you put it to a family member that they are someone other than they seem to be, they will typically react by treating you differently from usual, confirming that they are indeed an impostor and creating a vicious circle in which a delusion becomes almost a self-fulfilling prophecy.

Relations between voice and face recognition

We noted earlier that, like faces, voices can form a cue to recognising identity and that neuropsychological studies imply that faces and voices access a common pool of semantic information about people we know. For this reason, models of person recognition treat face recognition and voice recognition as more or less independent pathways to the same semantic information. Consistent with this, a defining characteristic of prosopagnosia is that the deficit affects recognition of identity from the face but not from other cues such as the voice. Conversely, cases of phonagnosia have been described, in which voice (but not face) recognition is impaired following acquired brain injury (Neuner & Schweinberger, 2000) or developmentally (Garrido, Eisner et al., 2009).

This hypothesis of parallel inputs for faces and voices is illuminated by further observations from cases of Capgras delusion, for which we noted that H. Ellis and Young (1990) postulated a lack of normal emotional responses linked to the face recognition input pathway. Hirstein and Ramachandran's (1997) patient, DS, thought his parents were impostors when he saw them, yet claimed it was his real parent when speaking on the telephone – as if the lack of emotional response was restricted to the visual modality, consistent with Ellis and Young's position. This observation suggests, though, that there might be a parallel form of Capgras delusion reflecting abnormal emotional responses to auditory recognition. This seemed likely because it was already known that blind people sometimes experience the Capgras delusion (Reid, Young, & Hellawell, 1993; Rojo, Caballero, Iruela, & Baca, 1991), but much stronger confirmation was found by Lewis, Sherwood, Moselhy and H. Ellis (2001). Their case, HL, was a sighted person who showed a voice-based Capgras delusion in the context of normal SCR to faces and abnormal SCR to voices.

Repetition priming effects also point to a system for voice recognition that has a similar 'functional architecture' to that used to recognise faces. Ellis and his colleagues found that exposure to voices in a pretraining phase of the experiment primed later voice recognition whereas exposure to faces did not prime later voice recognition (H. Ellis, Jones, & Mosdell, 1997). When the interval between the face and voice stimuli was reduced to the point where there were no intervening items, however, Ellis et al. (1997) did find evidence of cross-domain priming. This parallels results reported for faces and names (Calder & Young, 1996), and the pattern is explicable (even predictable) from activation at the PIN level in Burton et al.'s (1990) IAC model – as we noted previously, the PIN for a person who has just been recognised will be susceptible to cross-domain 'self' priming until its activation is suppressed by recognising someone else.

The similarity between overall architectures for face and voice recognition is further emphasised by a study by Schweinberger, Herholz and Sommer (1997), who used Hanley and Cowell's cueing technique (discussed earlier in this chapter) to demonstrate that, just like face naming, voice naming is contingent on accessing identity-specific semantic information. This is exactly as would be expected from models of the type we have discussed in this chapter, in which faces and voices converge on the same identity-specific semantics.

Recently, adaptation paradigms have been extended to the study of voice perception, with a demonstration of a contrastive after-effect in which prior adaptation to a male voice caused an androgynous voice to sound more female, and vice versa (Schweinberger et al., 2008). In the same study, Schweinberger et al. (2008) showed that adapting to seeing a (silent) talking face did not affect voice perception, showing again a separation between functional input pathways.

However, not all aspects of voice recognition are exactly comparable to face recognition. Some of the differences seem to reflect greater overall difficulty of some aspects of voice perception, perhaps resulting from the fact that we often rely on faces more heavily – we often see the face of someone who isn't talking, whereas (in the era before widespread mobile phone use, at least) hearing a voice without seeing a face is less common. Burton and Bonner (2004) played clips of the voices of characters from *The Archers*, a popular British radio soap opera (inexplicably to one of us, the other is a fan), to people who were or were not Archers fans. For the Archers fans, for whom the voices were highly familiar, decisions about the actor's sex based on their voice were quicker than for non-fans, to whom the voices were unfamiliar. As Burton and Bonner (2004) noted, a benefit of familiarity in determining sex is not a pattern usually found in studies of face recognition (see Chapter 3 and Chapter 6).

Particularly intriguing is the phenomenon that voice recognition seems to fail more often than face recognition at the subjectively irritating point where the stimulus (face or voice) can be recognised as familiar but not identified more precisely. Hanley and colleagues have studied this carefully, confirming that 'familiar only' experiences are indeed more common to voices than faces, and that this happens even when face recognition is made as difficult as voice recognition by blurring the faces (Hanley, Smith, & Hadfield, 1998; Hanley & Turner, 2000). Hanley and Turner (2000) showed how this pattern can be simulated with the IAC model if activation levels are generally lower in the voice than the face input system (through weakened VRU-PIN connections).

The IAC suggestion of pooled familiarity decisions at PIN level from separate face and voice inputs does not, however, easily account for more recent results reported by Hanley and Damjanovic (2009). They showed that when faces and voices were matched for overall familiarity and ease of recognition (achieved by blurring the faces), names and occupations were more readily retrieved from faces than from voices. This should not happen, according to IAC, since these pieces of information arise from a stage later than the PINs, where information from faces and voices has been pooled. However, Schweinberger and Burton (2003), in an approach which resonates with that discussed above to explain the Capgras delusion, suggest that there may be an additional modality-specific route to familiarity linked to the derivation of emotional responses to familiar people.

Faces and voices in person perception

Although studies of the relationship between voice and face recognition have delivered findings that can mainly be encompassed within the recognition framework we have put forward (as reviewed above), there are broader questions about how faces and voices are used in person perception that require more careful thought, since they don't assimilate quite so tidily into a rigidly 'parallel input' type of model.

For example, we saw in Chapter 4 how closely information from face and voice can be integrated in speech perception – making it in important respects an audiovisual phenomenon. The implications of audiovisual integration may be more wide-ranging than simply in facilitating speech perception, though. We are able to match characteristics of faces and voices of unfamiliar people (Kamachi, Hill, Lander, & Vatikiotis-Bateson, 2003; Lander, Hill, Kamachi, & Vatikiotis-Bateson, 2007), and even to use audiovisual information to create some form of multimodal perceptual representation of a speaker's identity (Robertson & Schweinberger, 2010; Schweinberger, Robertson, & Kaufmann, 2007). As we have also seen in Chapter 4, interactions between vocal and facial signals are evident in studies of emotion perception (Aubergé & Cathiard, 2003; de Gelder & Vroomen, 2000; Hagan et al., 2009), and even in cases of prosopagnosia (von Kriegstein et al., 2008; von Kriegstein, Kleinschmidt, & Giraud, 2006).

An interpretation of such findings has been offered by Belin and his colleagues, as shown in Figure 7.9 (Belin, Fecteau, & Bédard, 2004). What Belin

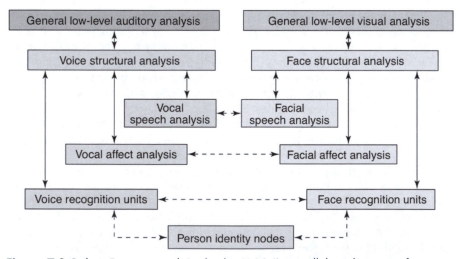

Figure 7.9 Belin, Fecteau and Bédard's (2004) parallel architecture for voice perception (left side of figure) to that suggested by Bruce and Young (1986) for face perception (right side of figure), with a common set of supramodal person identity nodes. Reprinted from *Trends in Cognitive Sciences*, 8, 3, Pascal Belin, Shirley Fecteau, Catherine Bédard, Thinking the voice: neural correlates of voice perception, pp. 129–135. Copyright 2004, with permission from Elsevier.

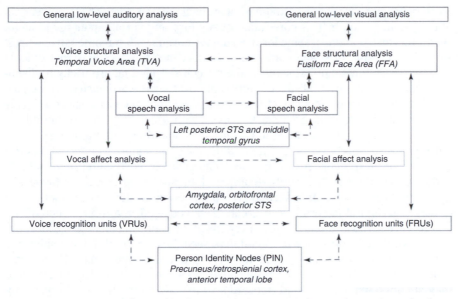

Figure 7.10 Campanella and Belin's (2007) suggested neural correlates for functional components shown in Figure 7.9. Reprinted from *Trends in Cognitive Sciences*, *11*, 12, Salvatore Campanella, Pascal Belin, Integrating face and voice in person perception, pp. 535–543. Copyright 2007, with permission from Elsevier.

et al. (2004) have done, in effect, is to suggest a parallel architecture for voice perception (left side of Figure 7.9) to that suggested by Bruce and Young (1986) for face perception (right side of Figure 7.9), with a common set of supramodal person identity nodes. Something we think is especially cunning is that Belin et al.'s (2004) schema puts vocal and facial speech analysis right next to each other, vocal and facial affect analysis close but slightly further apart, and voice and face recognition units more distant (see Figure 7.9). To our way of thinking, this neatly captures the evidence of relatively tighter coupling between face and voice for speech than for expression, and for expression than for identity. Sadly, an extension of the model, which offered suggested neural correlates for most of the putative functional components (Campanella & Belin, 2007), rather lost this spatial aspect of the schema (see Figure 7.10), suggesting that it may have been coincidental. Coincidentally or not, though, we think it reflects an important point that we will next elaborate.

What's it all about, Alfie?

The important point that is reflected in Figure 7.9 and partly missing from Figure 7.10 has to do with the extent to which demands of our social and physical environments shape the functional and neurological organisation of our brains. We have alluded to this before. We learn language mainly in face-to-face encounters in which there is a strong correlation between what we hear and the articulatory movements of the person's mouth. This correlation of auditory and visual inputs might alone favour the development of some form of audiovisual analysis, but other strong pressures in the same direction come from the fact that the speech signal unfolds quickly across time and that some of the speech sounds that are tricky to distinguish auditorily are more distinct in terms of how they are articulated on the face (see Chapter 4). Tightly coupling the analysis of auditory and visual speech signals can therefore enhance the accuracy and speed with which they are interpreted.

In contrast, when we need to recognise people they can often be seen but not heard – we might see someone at a distance, or simply wonder who is the quiet person in the corner of the room? The reduced correlation of visual and auditory recognition of identity (compared to speech perception) favours a greater degree of separation between them that is reinforced by the fact that the impact of temporal factors is also greatly reduced – once you have recognised that it is Fred who is sitting in the corner, his identity doesn't change – you would waste your time if you kept watching him to see if he became Bill. A considerable degree of modality-specificity of identity recognition mechanisms is therefore a solution that fits these influences. Because faces are so often recognised when they are not making any sound (most of us don't talk all the time), whereas only a limited number of acquaintances have to be recognised from their voice alone (e.g. on the telephone), we become much better at recognising faces than voices.

Recognising moods and emotions falls somewhere in between. A person who is afraid may scream as well as showing a facial (and bodily) expression of fear – but not always. There is a clear temporal element – a person's feelings can change from moment to moment, and there is a premium on detecting this – but the temporal constraints are not as precise as those for speech perception, where the critical differences between sounds often involve short time windows.

It will be interesting to see whether future studies bear out our opinion that the degree of dependence on multimodal integration is determined by factors such as the temporal characteristics of signals and the need for rapid responses, as outlined above and in Chapter 4, or whether multimodality is simply used for the analysis of any signals that have some degree of temporal contiguity.

One of the brain's main purposes is to make behaviour fit for the world a person inhabits, so it seems to us entirely reasonable that it should adapt itself to the contingencies that operate in that world. Some of the findings of the extent to which it can do this, though, are truly remarkable. For instance, Gick and Derrick (2009) showed that an inaudible slight puff of air on the skin affected whether a sound was perceived as aspirated or not (e.g. 'p' rather than 'b', 't' rather than 'd') – this audiotactile variant of the McGurk effect (McGurk & MacDonald, 1976) seems to be due to our brains having picked up that aspirated sounds are accompanied by a little puff of air from the speaker's mouth.

Apart from this unlikely digression on audiotactile effects, we have mainly discussed interactions between auditory and visual sources of information, but there are interactions between different domains of information within a specific sensory modality too. The Burton et al. (1990) IAC model, of course, explained interactions between seen faces and printed names, but it forms a rather specialised example that mainly relates to everyday life through activities such as reading a newspaper or a web page. Gaze is a better case in point. There is no auditory signal that is strongly correlated with a shift in gaze, but what do correlate to some extent are the eye movements and head movements that occur when we shift our focus of attention and, as we saw in Chapter 5, the brain combines information about eye and head position to evaluate gaze direction.

Another form of within-domain interaction is between the perception of faces and bodies. Body-selective regions of cortex have been found, often in proximity to face-selective regions (Peelen & Downing, 2007), and similarities and differences between neural and psychological face and body perception are beginning to be identified (Minnebusch & Daum, 2009; Urgesi, Calvo-Merino, Haggard, & Aglioti, 2007; Yovel, Pelc, & Lubetzky, 2010), as well as intriguing interactions (Morris, Pelphrey, & McCarthy, 2006).

This somewhat speculative foray into the territory of why our brains become organised in the way they are brings us to questions of development and change that we have reserved for the final chapter.

Summary

This chapter sets what we can do with faces into the broader context of other cues that support interpersonal interaction. A key requirement is that, having recognised someone (often from their face), we bring to mind pertinent information about that individual. The chapter discusses how this is done and, critically, how attempts have been made to create models that can simulate key aspects of this process. It then shows how the most successful of these models, the IAC account developed by Burton and his colleagues, offers a good fit to well-established patterns of priming and other effects and can be extended to encompass previously puzzling effects demonstrating covert recognition in prosopagnosia. The role of emotional responses in recognition is evaluated, leading to a more wide-ranging discussion of how different sources of information (especially faces and voices) are combined in interpersonal perception, set in an overarching perspective on why this may happen the way it does.

Further reading

Belin, P., Fecteau, S., & Bédard, C. (2004). Thinking the voice: Neural correlates of voice perception. *Trends in Cognitive Sciences*, *8*, 129–135.
Considers the relation between voice and face perception, offering an overall schema based on a reworking of Bruce and Young's (1986) account of face perception.

Burton, A. M., Bruce, V., & Hancock, P. J. B. (1999). From pixels to people: A model of familiar face recognition. *Cognitive Science*, *23*, 1–31.
One of the most highly-developed versions of Burton's IAC simulation of key properties of person recognition.

Ellis, H. D., & Lewis, M. B. (2001). Capgras delusion: A window on face recognition. *Trends in Cognitive Sciences*, *5*, 149–156.
Reviews what we can learn from studies of the Capgras delusion.

Gainotti, G. (2007). Different patterns of famous people recognition disorders in patients with right and left anterior temporal lesions: A systematic review. *Neuropsychologia*, *45*, 1591–1607.
Reviews deficits affecting semantic knowledge of familiar people following brain injury affecting the left and right anterior temporal lobes.

Young, A. W., & Burton, A. M. (1999). Simulating face recognition: Implications for modelling cognition. *Cognitive Neuropsychology*, *16*, 1–48.
The most complete account of covert recognition in prosopagnosia to date.

Nature and nurture

Given the multiplicity of perceptual skills we have for perceiving faces, and the many brain regions involved in face perception, a natural question concerns how this organisation comes about. Once again, the controversial figure of Sir Francis Galton looms large, this time from his study of eminent Victorian 'English men of science', to which he gave the subtitle 'their nature and nurture' (Galton, 1874). Galton was a half-cousin of Charles Darwin and is now controversial because of his interest in eugenics – a term he himself coined – which became inextricably intertwined with some of the most dreadful political events of the twentieth century.

Somewhere along the way, too, Galton's neat turn of phrase became twisted into 'Is it nature *or* nurture?' – a way of framing the topic that creates a false antithesis. All human abilities reflect some combination of genetic and environmental factors, and trying somehow to allocate these to separate baskets is often pointless because of the complexity of gene–environment interactions. As Galton's subtitle implied, what is needed is to elucidate the contributions of nature *and* nurture. Galton himself was quite clear about this, stating that nature and nurture is 'a convenient jingle of words' and that 'it is needless to insist that neither is self-sufficient' (Galton, 1874, p. 12).

Here, we will begin by asking to what extent the human infant comes into the world prepared to see faces, and how skills of face perception and recognition develop over the first few months of life and later during childhood. Observations of typical and atypical development interact with issues raised elsewhere in the book and lead us, later in this chapter, to look more closely at the question of whether faces have a 'special' status for the human brain.

Perception of faces by newborn babies

First, let us review what we know about how infants see faces. Because newborn babies have a limited repertoire of behaviour, psychologists have to devise ingenious methods to test what babies can see. This often involves measuring how long a baby looks at one pattern rather than another – given a choice of two – or how far a baby will 'track' with its own head and eye movements one kind of pattern moved in front of it compared with another. Habituation measures are also used with young infants, as we described in Chapter 2.

Fantz conducted a series of pioneering experiments in the 1960s in which he examined how long newborn infants spent gazing at objects or patterns. These were presented singly or in pairs in a looking chamber which enabled an experimenter to watch the baby's eyes and record how long infants spent looking at any specified item (Fantz, 1961). Fantz found that infants aged from 1 to 15 weeks looked more at patterns such as stripes or a bull's-eye, rather than at plain shapes. He exploited this preference for patterned over plain shapes to conduct one of the first investigations of the development of visual acuity in infants.

In humans, the visual system is fairly immature at birth. This places limits on what the baby can see, especially in terms of its ability to resolve fine detail and gradations of shading. In Fantz's experiments, a striped pattern was paired with one of uniform grey, and the width of the stripes was decreased until babies showed no preference for the patterned stimulus, indicating that stripes of this width (or 'spatial frequency', see Chapter 2) were invisible to them. This method revealed that infants showed a steady increase in the spatial frequency (roughly equivalent to the number of stripes per unit of width) they could see across the first few weeks of life. This means that for the first few weeks they will be unable to see fine detail and the world will look blurred to them, compared to an adult's. These observations have been replicated and extended since Fantz's initial investigations (Atkinson, 1995). Figure 8.1 gives an impression of what a face might look like to a 1-month-old and a 3-month-old infant, demonstrating both the initial immaturity of the baby's vision and its rapid development.

In another study Fantz demonstrated that infants ranging in age from 4 days through to 6 months showed a modest preference for a face-like pattern over a scrambled face pattern showing the same features rearranged, with the strongest preference seen in infants aged 2 to 3 months. Unfortunately, however, Fantz's scrambled face pattern was asymmetrical, and it might have been the symmetry of the face that led to the slight preference for that pattern. A further experiment presented individual patterns to babies aged 2 to 3 months, and demonstrated that they spent twice as long looking at a face than at a bull's-eye or textured pattern. This strong preference for face patterns at around 10 weeks of age was reduced in infants older than 3 months. Taken together, Fantz's

Figure 8.1 What a face may look like to a baby aged 1 month (left) and aged 3 months (right), based on our knowledge of the infant's visual abilities. Courtesy of Alex Wade.

experiments were suggestive of a preference for structure, and perhaps even a face-like structure, from early infancy, but most of the babies tested in his studies were several weeks old and so no strong conclusions could be drawn about neonatal preferences.

Against that back-drop, it was striking when a group of researchers reported clear preferences in newborns for faces when these were compared with a set of comparison patterns which were better controlled for face-like properties. Goren, Sarty and Wu (1975) used a different method to that used by Fantz. Rather than showing newborn babies static patterns and examining how much attention each item attracted, Goren et al. (1975) presented a single pattern at a time, but moved it in an arc in front of the infant's face, measuring how far the baby followed the pattern with head and/or eye movements. In this way they were able to see which of a series of moving patterns best held the baby's attention, rather than demanding the more complex discriminatory choice often required by Fantz's technique. Goren et al. (1975) compared infants' tracking of different face-shaped 'paddles' (see Figure 8.2, which illustrates the kind of patterns used) – including one showing a schematic face pattern, two showing a 'scrambled' but symmetric rearrangement of face features (only one of these is shown in Figure 8.2), and one with no features at all. The infants, who were tested just minutes after birth, showed a clear preference for the face-like over the scrambled face or blank paddles, as measured by the extent of their head and eye movements to follow each type of stimulus.

This important finding suggested provocatively that infants enter the world with some 'knowledge' of faces – or of what is face-like. Notice that the face patterns are purely schematic, not realistic. The response to face-likeness may

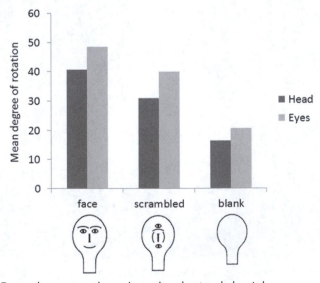

Figure 8.2 Face shapes used, and results obtained, by Johnson et al. (1991) in their first experiment.

therefore share characteristics with innate releasing mechanisms found in ethological studies of other species, where the releaser can actually be fairly simple
as it only needs to include those features that will make it distinct in the animal's
environment. Despite the potential significance of Goren et al.'s study, it remained
relatively unnoticed by developmental psychologists and those interested in face
perception until Hadyn Ellis, characteristically, noted its significance and brought
the finding to a wider community.

Ellis joined forces with Johnson and other colleagues (Johnson, Dziurawiec,
Ellis, & Morton, 1991) to replicate and extend this research. In their first experiment they compared three of the patterns used by Goren et al. (1975) – a face, a
scrambled face and a plain outline (see Figure 8.2). They obtained measurable
behaviour from 24 newborns of mean age 37 minutes. Each was tested lying
down in the experimenter's lap, who held one of the paddles above the infant and
moved it slowly in an arc to the right or left. The experimenter was not aware of
the particular pattern shown on each paddle as she moved it in front of the infant.
The entire procedure and the infant's responses were recorded on video and the
eye and head movements later measured by additional experimenters who were
also unaware of the particular conditions of the experiment or, indeed, of the
experiment's purpose. Figure 8.2 shows the results of this experiment, which
clearly replicate the initial report by Goren et al. Neonates followed the faces
further than the scrambled faces which in turn were 'preferred' to the blank
pattern, and these effects were shown for both eye and head movements.

In their second experiment Johnson et al. (1991) tested a different set of
infants with a mean age of 43 minutes, and looked at their tracking of four
different patterns shown in Figure 8.3. These included the face pattern, a pattern

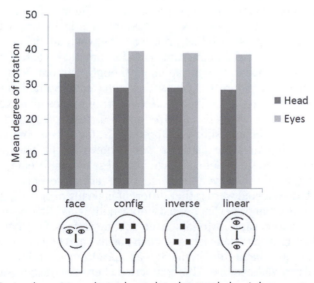

Figure 8.3 Face shapes used, and results obtained, by Johnson et al. (1991) in
their second experiment.

of dots arranged rather like two eyes and a mouth (labelled 'config'), the same dots inverted (labelled 'inverse'), and a linear but symmetrical arrangement of face features. Using the same methods as before, they obtained the results shown in Figure 8.3. Statistical analyses showed that the infants tracked the face significantly more with their eyes than the inverse and linear comparison patterns, but that eye-tracking of the face was not (quite) significantly different from the 'config' stimulus. This suggests that 'config' may be intermediate in its ability to elicit following to the face and inverse patterns, though we should point out that the findings are not completely conclusive. In this study, head movements showed no significant differences between any of the patterns. It is important to note this trend towards stronger responses to faces than other 'face-like' patterns when we come to try to understand what is responsible for the infant preferences revealed by such techniques.

Research with newborn infants presents considerable difficulties, and although not every attempt to replicate Goren et al.'s findings has succeeded, there is now a body of supportive research. Some studies have returned to using a preference method, more like that used by Fantz, to assess what newborns 'like' best in face-like patterns. In one such study Mondloch and colleagues (Mondloch et al., 1999) used a paired preference method where newborn infants were shown pairs of faces or other patterns and an observer who was blind to the actual patterns presented on each trial used the full range of their behaviours to decide which of the patterns, if either, was preferred. For example they might use the observation that the baby consistently looked first *or* looked longest at the pattern on the left or right to deduce that this was the preferred one. Using this technique of blind scoring to a flexible criterion, Mondloch et al. (1999) found that 9 out of 12 newborns of mean age 53 minutes preferred to look at a highly schematic face outline with a face-like arrangement of squares – two horizontal squares at the top, a single one below (cf. 'config' in Figure 8.3) – rather than one with the same internal shapes inverted (cf. 'inverse' in Figure 8.3). However, infants at this same age showed no preference between an elaborate schematic face pattern shown normal and the same pattern contrast-reversed, as in a photographic negative. In apparent contradiction, though, Farroni, Johnson, Menon, Zulian, Faraguna and Csibra (2005) used a preference method and found that contrast polarity did have a significant effect on preferences observed in slightly older infants (aged between 13 and 168 hours at test) measured in terms of looking time. These infants showed a preference for a face compared with an inverted face *only* when the patterns were shown in positive polarity. This apparent difference in the results reported by these two different groups should be treated cautiously, however, because there are differences between the studies. The babies tested were rather different in terms of age, slightly different methods were used and, perhaps most importantly, the choices offered to the babies were not the same. Mondloch et al.'s newborns failed to distinguish between two upright schematic faces – one in positive and one in negative polarity. Farroni et al.'s older babies distinguished an upright from an inverted face, but only when polarity was positive. This comparison between the studies shows how careful we must be to consider the details of the specific investigation when drawing conclusions about perceptual and cognitive competence.

For now, we may conclude that infants within a few minutes or hours of birth are attracted more to face-like patterns than to a range of patterns that are less like faces. What has been hotly debated is the reason for this attraction. Is it that the newborn arrives in the world prepared to respond to *faces*, and this preparedness for faces produces some degree of responsiveness to things that are a bit like faces? We already mentioned the possible parallel with innate releasing mechanisms found in other species for behaviours with high survival value. Although the implications of being innately responsive to faces are probably negligible for the *short-term* survival of a human infant – because its parents will be intelligent and resourceful enough to look after it for a while – an innate interest in faces will quickly engage an infant with its social world and strengthen parent–infant bonds by making its carers feel that the baby likes them. These are important *long-term* considerations for a species with a relatively lengthy period of infant dependence ('neoteny'). So, there is a case for something like an innate releasing mechanism that makes human babies interested in faces. The sceptic's alternative is that faces just *happen* to be preferentially attractive because of more general characteristics of the newborn's visual system.

The 'Linear Systems Model' (LSM; Banks & Salapatek, 1981) proposes that it is the fit between physical properties of visual stimuli and the infant's visual sensitivity that determines what infants look at. So if at a particular stage of development the infant cannot see any difference between stripes of different widths, then of course it cannot prefer one over another. It is the visibility of things that matters. As soon as its visual system is able to perceive stripes of a particular width then the infant – who prefers patterned to plain input – will turn to the stripes it can see. Now whether stripes are visible depends both on their spacing *and* on their contrast. A baby might be shown very faint stripes that it could not see but ones of the same width with more contrast might fall in the range that it could see. We chose the example of stripes deliberately, because LSM is derived from an approach to visual perception in which complex patterns can be described in terms of underlying spatial frequency components of particular amplitudes (cf. brightness) and phase (cf. arrangement) (see Chapter 2). According to this theory, if infants prefer faces it can be explained in terms of the visibility of their underlying spatial frequency components. And when two choices are both visible, the infant will prefer the 'brighter' thing, the one with more contrast.

Consistent with this, in a third condition of Mondloch et al.'s (1999) study, newborn babies preferred a pattern which had the amplitude of a face over one that had the phase of a face, even though it is the latter that looks more face-like to adults (see Figure 8.4). In a series of experiments, Kleiner (1987) also found that phase information appeared to be ignored by 2-day-old infants, whose preferences seemed to be dominated by the amplitudes of the patterns they saw.

Clearly, then, it is important to keep in mind characteristics of infant vision when interpreting infant preference studies. Nevertheless, Morton, Johnson and Maurer (1990) pointed out an important comparison in Kleiner's data which showed that infants prefer a pattern displaying both the phase and the amplitude of face (i.e. a face!) to one showing the amplitude of a face superimposed onto a lattice pattern with a different phase structure. So, neonates do like something that is most like a face, *provided* that the amplitude of the underlying components makes

Figure 8.4 Patterns used by Kleiner (1987) as reproduced by Morton et al. (1990). Pattern C has the phase information from the face (A) and the amplitude from the lattice (B). Pattern D has the phase of the lattice and amplitude of the face. Pattern D was preferred to C by infants in Kleiner's studies, though it looks less face-like to adults. Reprinted from *Infant Behavior and Development*, *13*, 1, Author(s), John Morton, Mark H. Johnson, Daphne Maurer, pp. 99–103. Copyright (1990), with permission from Elsevier.

this visible. Thus the work which has been influenced by the LSM reminds us that babies cannot see all the structure in the world that an adult can, but the balance of evidence still suggests that when patterns are equally visible, in terms of the amplitudes of their components, faces have the edge in terms of preference.

Other groups have taken a different tack by arguing that what guides infant preferences is the presence of patterned structure towards the *top* of the shape, so that babies will prefer upper structure to lower structure, even if the patterns are not very face-like. Simion, Macchi Cassia, Turati and Valenza (2003) summarise a number of studies that have used a preference technique in which the proportion of time infants look at each of two patterns is recorded. Infants prefer patterns in which there are more elements in the top than in the bottom part of the pattern (see Figure 8.5a), though none of the patterns shown are face-like in other respects. They sometimes even prefer a non-face like pattern with three dots high in the oval than a more face-like one with the dots arranged like 'config' (Figure 8.5b). Other studies reviewed by Simion et al. show that preferences for face-like patterns require the presence of a head 'outline' as well as feature-like blobs, and that there needs to be some congruency between these features and the outline for preferences to emerge (i.e. a feature arrangement like 'config' is ineffective if placed in a face outline which is upside-down). Simion et al. (2003) therefore conclude that apparent preferences for faces at birth may result from inbuilt preferences for patterns which are 'top-heavy' in terms of their elements, and congruent with their outlines. We should note, though, that most of the things that a newborn baby will see that have these characteristics are, of course, human faces.

Although a preference for a stronger top-half pattern may explain why two dots above one dot ('config' in Figure 8.3) is liked more than the 'inverse' pattern of one dot above two, the important point to note is that 'face' is liked best of all in the infant preference studies. So, whatever the infant is born able to do, it happens to direct its attention to faces more than other kinds of patterns. And while this may just be an accident of coincident independent pattern preferences, it seems more parsimonious to propose that infants come into the world prepared to see something a bit like faces because this itself confers some kind of benefit.

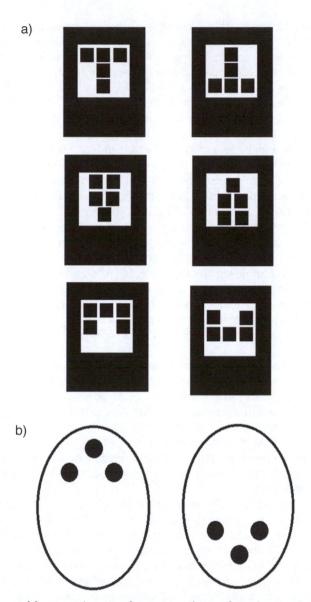

Figure 8.5a and b In each pair of patterns, the preferred one, to the left, has its features higher up in the outline. Adapted from Simion et al. (2003).

Morton and Johnson (1991) developed an ambitious theory of neonatal competence in face perception in which they likened the immature human visual system at birth to the system guiding imprinting responses in birds such as chickens and ducklings. Birds like chickens have an innate releasing mechanism that leads them to follow virtually any moving object they see after hatching. In natural circumstances, of course, this would usually be their mother

(Bateson, 1966). However, this instinctive following response is stronger to patterns which are more similar in colour to adult hens (Kovach, 1971) and the chicks learn to be more discriminating about the characteristics of adult hens in the days after hatching. By analogy, Morton and Johnson (1991) suggest that infant face preferences are based on a 'CONSPEC' mechanism that directs attention to faces of conspecifics and provides information for a 'CONLERN' mechanism that can learn about faces but does not influence looking behaviour until around 2 months of age.

Imprinting in chicks is known to be dependent on a specific forebrain region (Horn, 1986). Johnson (2005) develops the argument that the human newborn's CONSPEC mechanism involves mid-brain structures (superior colliculus, pulvinar and amygdala) which guide it towards patterns that are face-like at a general level – rather like 'config'. In adults these mid-brain structures have been thought to provide a fast-operating face perception pathway based on low spatial frequency information (Vuilleumier, Armony, Driver, & Dolan, 2003) – the kind of information that the neonate can see. Johnson (2005) suggests that it is this subcortical route in newborns that detects faces and orients them towards faces, and also that this pathway can activate those cortical areas that are specialised for face processing in adults. Indeed he suggests that it may be the particular nature of the pattern of projections from mid-brain to cortical areas that determines which cortical regions are recruited in the fully developed face processing network.

Simion, Valenza, Umilta and Dalla Barba (1998) looked at orienting to faces by newborn babies with one eye concealed, with the intention that faces shown in different parts of the visual field would project to different areas of the newborn brain. We know that in other species information from the nasal field (nearest the nose) feeds the cortical visual pathways, whereas that from the temporal field feeds cortical and subcortical structures. Simion et al. (1998) found that the face preferences in their newborn infants were found only when faces were presented in the temporal fields of the non-occluded eye, consistent with responses driven by subcortical pathways.

Findings such as those of Simion et al. lend weight to the idea of subcortical involvement in neonatal face preferences, but the CONSPEC and CONLERN theory none the less rests heavily on an analogy with what is known to happen in non-human species. Comparability across species is a plausible possibility, and the general proposition that the newborn human infant's visual abilities are dependent on subcortical centres has been around for many years (Bronson, 1974). However, it is remarkably difficult to demonstrate lack of cortical involvement in infant vision directly, and the claim needs to be weighed against a long history in psychology of underestimating infant capabilities. Indirect evidence has been considered to come from adult fMRI studies showing that activation of structures like the amygdala is weighted towards low spatial frequency information from faces (Vuilleumier et al., 2003) – findings like these are taken to be consistent with the existence of a non-cortical 'fast-track' visual pathway to the amygdala. However, we saw in Chapter 4 that amygdala responses to faces are not restricted to low spatial frequencies – for example, its responses to fear can be triggered purely by information from the high spatial frequency eye region.

To complicate matters further, the existence of an entirely subcortical visual pathway to the amygdala in humans has itself been disputed (Pessoa & Ungerleider, 2004; Pessoa & Adolphs, 2010).

For these reasons, we think it best to separate different claims made in the CONSPEC and CONLERN theory. The first claim is that there is some form of innate response to faces (CONSPEC) that guides the neonate's attention and provides information that will support learning about faces. This seems, on balance, well supported by data. A second claim is that CONSPEC is subcortically mediated. This we see as plausible, but contentious. The third claim is that the cortical CONLERN system does not operate in the first month of life. This seems difficult to establish and inconsistent with studies we will be discussing later that show learning of faces by young infants.

If we accept, then, that there is something about faces that guides the initial attention of the newborn visual system, we still need to understand more about the nature of this initial representation. What are the characteristics of CONSPEC? While the research we have discussed so far would suggest the innate face template is rather crude – something that can respond to the kinds of cartoon-like faces used in the original Goren et al. studies and may also be activated by even simpler patterns like 'config' – other work suggests something more elaborate.

Slater and his colleagues have shown in three sets of studies that babies less than 3 days of age prefer the more attractive of two faces shown to them, and that this preference appears to be driven by the arrangement of internal face features, since it is still found when external features are concealed (Slater et al., 1998; Slater, Bremner, Johnson, Sherwood, Hayes, & Brown, 2000a; Slater, Quinn, Hayes, & Brown, 2000b). Moreover, this preference disappears when the faces are inverted, so it cannot be due to some overall property such as attractive faces having nicer coloration than unattractive ones. We know from work with older infants and adults that attractive faces are more 'average' than unattractive ones (see Chapter 3), and so the attractiveness preference at birth might reflect an inborn representation that reflects what faces look like 'on average'. Johnson (2005) suggests that the kind of rudimentary representation of faces that he thinks drives subcortical orienting and hence preferences for faces might well be activated most strongly by the low spatial frequency components of more 'proto-typical' (and hence more attractive) faces.

An alternative possibility is that the attractiveness preference within a few days of birth arises from rapid experience of faces in the immediate postnatal environment. Certainly babies appear able to learn quickly about faces they meet early on – as we will see later – and assuming most babies encounter a number of faces during their first few days some kind of facial averaging could create a bias that favours attractive faces.

Whether it is cortically or subcortically mediated, inborn attentiveness to faces probably serves several functions, not the least of which is to make the baby seem interested in its caregivers, thereby encouraging them to nurture it. But we need to look harder at two assumptions that are easily made, but may mislead. These are the assumptions that learning is entirely postnatal, and that visual inputs will exclusively drive attentiveness to faces.

Intriguingly, Quinn and Slater (2003) suggested that infants might learn about their own faces proprioceptively in the womb, and this knowledge could contribute to their preferences for faces after birth. This proposal would have sounded radical had it not been for demonstrations of the importance of auditory learning *in utero*. Hepper (1988), for example, found that babies of mothers who listened to the theme music of particular soap operas while pregnant showed a preference for these same tunes postnatally! Of course, any sounds heard in the womb will be distorted. Even so, De Casper and Fifer (1980) showed that newborn babies aged 2–4 days old will suck harder on a non-nutritive teat if this leads them to hear their mother's rather than a stranger's voice, suggesting that they already know (or have quickly learned) their mother's voices. The 'non-nutritive sucking' paradigm used by DeCasper and Fifer (1980) built on earlier work on voice recognition in early infancy by Mills and Melhuish (1974), who also noted that from birth babies will turn towards the source of a sound, and that infants are more interested in their mother's face when she is talking. Mills and Melhuish (1974) suggested that this orientation to voices will help infants to learn about faces.

This is another illustration of a point we emphasised in Chapter 4, that focusing too much on faces can sometimes lead you away from something important. In this case, by asking only about the *visual* cues that make newborns attentive to faces, you might fail to pick up that because they know their mother's voice, they can use it to orient to her face. It is a good example, too, of something that will promote multimodal learning of the type we discussed in Chapter 4 – orienting to its mother's voice will help the infant to learn things about her face.

Of course, though, if babies are able to pair a familiar voice with a significant visual pattern towards which they have an inbuilt generic ('config') orientation this should further help kick-start the learning of Mum's face. An intriguing study by Sai (2005) is consistent with the suggestion that inborn knowledge of Mum's voice can help the baby learn her face. Sai reports that preference for Mum's face over the face of another woman of similar overall face type a few hours after birth was stronger in infants who heard their mother speaking after delivery than it was in infants whose mothers were somehow persuaded not to speak at all (but otherwise to interact appropriately) in the first few hours after their babies were born! The same study showed that babies looked more often at their mothers if they heard them talking than if they were silent. This is another study that would be well worth replicating.

Other studies of neonates show evidence of precocious abilities to copy facial movements and respond to facial expressions. Before discussing these, though, we will look more closely at what happens when the infant has the opportunity for postnatal learning.

The development of face perception after birth

However elaborate face preferences may be at birth, babies develop rapidly over the first months of life and these early preferences change. Johnson et al. (1991) examined preferences in infants aged 1, 3 and 5 months old using a tracking procedure. The youngest group of 1 month olds were tested in the same way we described earlier, but the older babies had to be tested rather differently. Instead of measuring how far the infant would follow a moving face-shaped paddle, as they had done with their neonates, they instead moved the baby in front of the pattern. Each of these older infants was seated on their mothers' lap on a rotating chair. The baby initially looked at the test pattern and then the chair was rotated away from the pattern. The angle at which the baby broke fixation was taken as a measure of following, since the baby had to maintain fixation by moving its eyes and/or head to compensate for the rotation of the chair.

Johnson et al. (1991) compared following of four patterns – a schematic face, 'config' (cf. Figure 8.3), and two non-face patterns which showed the same face features in symmetrical but unface-like arrangements labelled 'linear' and 'scrambled'. They found that, like newborns, the 1 month olds tracked the face pattern significantly more than all other non-face patterns, including config. For the 3 and 5 month olds there were no significant preferences, however. Mondloch et al. (1999) had also tested 6- and 12-week-old infants on the paired preference paradigm they had used for newborns. In contrast to what they observed in neonates, at 6 weeks and 12 weeks they observed no preference for 'config' over 'inverse', but strong preference for a pattern with the phase of a face over one with just the amplitude. Mondloch et al.'s (1999) contrast reversal results also showed change over the first 3 months. Six week olds showed no preference between positive and negative polarity schematic faces, while 12 week olds strongly preferred the positive contrast versions. Thus, whatever is responsible for the tracking of faces shortly after birth, its influence has dwindled 3 months later, and over that time the infant's preferences for static faces have shifted too.

One way to think about this apparent change in the early preference for face-like patterns is that it may proceed along a trajectory that involves the baby's requiring that stimuli are increasingly realistic faces before they will engage its interest. As it learns about real faces, it loses interest in purely schematic repre- sentations. According to Morton and Johnson (1991), the preferences guided by CONSPEC at birth become suppressed by cortical mechanisms that mature in the first few months. It is these cortical mechanisms (CONLERN) that are responsible for learning individual faces, and which will guide preferences by age 3 months. However, the evidence suggests that babies can learn individual faces more quickly than this – suggesting either that there may be some learning oper- ating within the subcortical structures or that the cortical learning pathway becomes functional very quickly.

Bushnell and his colleagues (Bushnell, Sai, & Mullin, 1989) demonstrated that learning the faces of significant others gets off to a very prompt start. They tested 2-day-old infants in a maternity ward. The real mother of each infant stood beside another woman, behind a screen sprayed with air freshener to mask any cues from the mother's smell. Two day olds looked significantly longer at their mother's face than a stranger's face, gazing on average around 60% of the time to their own mum. Bushnell (2003) replicated this with babies aged 3 days of age, but also looked at the correlation between the degree of preference shown for the mother and the amount of time in hours the baby had spent looking at her. The latter was established by sampling infant and mother behaviour for four

2-hour periods every day and extrapolating the total time the infant was looking at its mother from these recorded observations. There was a highly significant positive correlation between the time infants had spent looking at their mother and the strength of preference shown for her, underlining the view that this mother preference derives from rapid learning of her face.

Other studies have shown that the young infant's representation of its mother's face is initially based mainly on large, external features of the face, since their preference for their own mother is reduced or removed completely if external features are concealed or standardised (Bushnell, 2003). Their face recognition skills are not *confined* to their mothers, however. For example, Pascalis and De Schonen (1994) found that babies aged 3 to 4 days old could learn to recognise something about a stranger's face using a habituation paradigm (see Chapter 2 and later in this chapter for more on the habituation technique).

Whatever the mechanism, babies are clearly strongly influenced by their close proximity to their mothers in their early days and weeks. This manifests itself in an overall preference for a face which resembles 'Mum'. Three-to-four month olds familiarised with male faces prefer females (the novel category) when given a choice of what to look at. But infants of the same age familiarised with female faces do not prefer males later, suggesting that the familiarisation has not been sufficient to overcome an underlying preference for female over male faces. Indeed spontaneous preference for female faces is observed when babies of this same age are given a choice between female and male items, even if the hair is not shown, but not when the faces are inverted, suggesting that it is not an effect of cosmetics, etc. (Quinn, Yahr, Kuhn, Slater, & Pascalis 2002). However, it does seem to be something that has been learnt. Five out of six of a small sample of infants reared by male primary caregivers showed the opposite preference, for male rather than female faces, suggesting that the more usual female face preference is indeed due to generalisation from experience with a female mother during the first few months of life.

Earlier in this chapter we described how newborn babies look more at attractive than unattractive human faces. Interestingly, 3- to 4-month-old infants also prefer looking at pictures of domestic or wild cats (tigers) that are rated as more attractive by adults when paired with exemplars rated as less attractive (Quinn, Kelly, Lee, Pascalis, & Slater, 2008). This may suggest that the attractiveness preference shown by newborns derives from more general mechanisms that go beyond human face perception. However, it is also possible that the preference is based upon the same mechanisms that drive preference for female human faces. 'Attractive' cats appear to have visual features that might lead them to be rated more feminine in appearance – larger eyes, less elongated noses and so forth.

Over the first year of life, the human infant becomes skilled at face recognition, demonstrating abilities to recognise different categories of face (e.g. male versus female), different individual faces and so forth. Such skills are usually demonstrated using a habituation paradigm (see Chapter 2). An infant is shown an initially unfamiliar face for prolonged viewing, and it gradually gets less interested in it, and looks at it less. It is then shown a second face. If this second face looks different to the infant, it will recover its interest and start to look at it again, whereas if it looks the same its responding will remain low. Using a habituation paradigm, Fagan and Singer (1979) tested 5–6 month olds and revealed that their habituation responses seemed strongly determined by the gender or age category of a face, rather than by superficial aspects of visual appearance. For example, the babies showed release from habituation when the new face was a different sex even if the male and female exemplars looked much more similar in appearance than two different exemplars of the same sex.

Particularly interesting studies of the early development of face recognition have been conducted using such habituation techniques by Pascalis, Nelson and their colleagues. Nelson (2001) argued that face recognition skills in infancy may gradually become attuned to the kinds of faces the infant experiences regularly, in the same way that the perception and articulation of speech sounds gradually narrows to those within the native language. Pascalis, de Haan and Nelson (2002) demonstrated strikingly that while 6-month-old and 9-month-old infants could both recognise previously unfamiliar human faces, 6 month olds (but *not* 9 month olds) could also show recognition memory for the faces of macaque monkeys. This suggests that the younger infants have the capacity to recognise a wider range of faces than the older ones, including ones beyond our native species. It is reminiscent of the finding that younger infants can distinguish speech sounds beyond the range of phonemic distinctions in the infant's native language (Werker & Tees, 2005) that are inaudible to older infants and adults.

A common way to interpret such findings is to argue that becoming better at recognising the members of a common category of stimuli (be they faces or speech sounds) involves 'tuning in' to critical differences that matter in classifying them and learning to ignore irrelevant variation. This implies that if what would normally be irrelevant variations are emphasised, ability to process them should not decline. Consistent with this, Pascalis et al. (2005) showed that ability to discriminate non-human faces could be maintained by focused exposure to them. Parents of 6-month-old babies were encouraged to maintain contact with macaque faces by regularly showing their infants books of monkey faces and interacting with these. These infants retained the capacity to discriminate individual macaque faces at the age of 9 months (Pascalis et al., 2005). Likewise, Sugita (2008) was able to manipulate exposure to different kinds of faces much more dramatically in macaque monkeys, who were deprived of any faces visually from birth for many months and then faces of either monkeys or humans were introduced. These monkeys developed discrimination abilities and preferences for the kind of faces that they were exposed to.

In Chapter 6 we described the cross-race effect in adult face recognition, and offered an explanation like that above, in terms of differential exposure and consequent 'expertise'. It seems that this differential ability to recognise own-race faces also develops during the first few months of life. Kelly et al. (2005) showed that 3 month olds prefer faces of their own to those of other races, but that this preference was not present at birth. Even more dramatically, Kelly, Quinn, Slater, Lee, Ge and Pascalis (2007) showed how the capacity to discriminate between faces of different races actually *narrows* during the first year of life. They used a habituation paradigm where the infant was shown a face until it had substantially reduced the amount of time spent looking at it. The baby was then shown a pair of faces – one matching the identity of the habituated face, the other a novel face identity. Both faces in the test pair were shown in a viewpoint different from that shown in the habituation phase (e.g. habituation to a full face image was followed by a test phase showing two ¾ profile faces, or vice versa). If in this study the infant preferred to look at the novel identity from the two test faces, then it must be able to recognise that the other one matches that shown in the habituation phase, despite the change in viewpoint.

Using this method, Kelly et al. (2007) found that 3-month-old infants could discriminate own-race (Caucasian) faces *and* faces from three other racial groups. Babies at this age looked significantly more often (about 60% on average) at the novel item in the test pairs across all the race conditions tested. By 6 months of age, there was reduced ability to recognise African or Middle Eastern faces, where there was no significant preference for the novel items at test. The infants retained some discrimination of Chinese as well as Caucasian faces at this age, however. By the age of 9 months, though, the babies could only distinguish between faces from their own race. Babies at this age preferred the novel of two Caucasian faces about 60% of the time, but their choices between two Chinese, African or Middle Eastern faces were all around about 50%.

These experiments show how babies acquire face-specific expertise in their first year of life. They quickly learn to recognise the faces of their own parents, and more slowly become attuned to the kinds of faces they are regularly exposed to – human faces of their own racial group/s.

The neural mechanisms of face perception by developing infants can be studied too. Studies with fMRI are at an early stage, but it is generally not possible to use PET scanning with young infants unless this is clinically relevant. One exception of this kind was a study by Tzourio-Mazoyer, De Schonen, Crivello, Reutter, Aujard and Mazoyer (2002) who examined PET responses to faces compared with coloured patterns in a very small sample of 2 month olds in intensive care. Although the study is limited by sample size and the control materials its results were interesting, because it indicated activation by faces of areas in the infant brain which are analogous to the 'core' pathways in Haxby, Hoffman and Gobbini's (2000) neurological model of adult face perception.

Most other studies of infants have tested rather older babies using non-invasive ERP measurements (see Chapter 2), since it is possible to fit an electrode cap or 'geodesic hair net' to young infants to record their responses to different kinds of faces (see Figure 8.6). Grossman and Johnson (2007) review a number of studies which have recorded ERPs as infants view faces. Most have tested infants in the age range 3 to 12 months. De Haan, Pascalis and Johnson (2002) compared ERP responses to faces in 6 month olds and adults and found two apparently face-specific components labelled N290 and P400 in the infants that resembled in some ways the N170 seen in adults. However, the adult N170 is sensitive both to orientation and species of faces – it is smaller in amplitude and faster in latency for upright human faces than for inverted faces or the faces of monkeys. In contrast, in 6 month olds, the N290 was unaffected by inversion, but affected by face species, while the P400 was sensitive to species but unaffected by inversion.

Halit, de Haan and Johnson extended this approach to examine ERPs in younger (3 months) and older (12 months) infants. At 12 months the specificity of both components resembled the adult N170, making it unclear which of these reflected the developmental precursor of adult neural responses. At 3 months,

Figure 8.6 A baby wearing a geodesic hair net. Photo courtesy of Mark Johnson and © Michael Crabtree.

neither component showed the same kinds of specificity. This should perhaps not surprise us, since 3-month-old infants are at an age where they show consider-able plasticity in their face categorisations (cf. other race and other species studies reviewed above) and in these respects see faces rather differently from adults anyway.

Perception of expressive and social signals from faces in infancy

So far, we have examined how infants respond to facial characteristics that are, in Haxby et al.'s (2000) terms, relatively invariant. There are further remarkable demonstrations of infant competence in face perception when we turn to their responses to what Haxby et al. call changeable aspects of faces – facial expres-sions, gaze, and facial speech (see also Chapters 4 and 5).

Meltzoff and Moore (1977) reported that infants aged between 12 and 21 days of age can imitate adult facial movements including tongue protrusion, mouth opening and lip protrusion (see Figure 8.7). Later studies by the same authors (Meltzoff & Moore 1983, 1989) showed similar behaviour in newborn infants just a few hours old. An important aspect of this finding is that it seems to demonstrate that the baby must have some kind of 'map' to indicate which of its

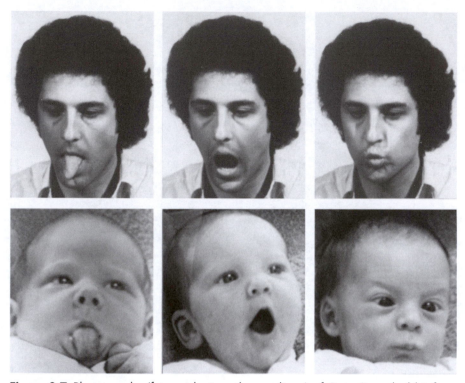

Figure 8.7 Photographs (from videotaped recordings) of 2- to 3-week-old infants imitating tongue protrusion, mouth opening and lip protrusion. From Meltzoff and Moore (1977).

own facial muscles corresponds to those of another human being, even though it has never experimented with a mirror. Such an inborn mapping could provide an important contribution to learning to make the movements necessary for speech. According to Meltzoff and Moore, infant imitation demonstrates an innate linkage between the perception and production of actions, a supramodal representation accessible by both visual and motor systems.

Since Meltzoff and Moore's original publication, a possible neural mechanism for such a capacity has been discovered in the 'mirror neuron' systems which have been much studied in the past 15 years. Mirror neurons in monkey premotor cortex respond when the monkey performs a hand action in a goal-directed way, and also when it sees such an action (Rizzolatti, Fadiga, Gallese & Fogassi, 1996). Meltzoff and Decety (2003) suggest that human infant imitation might be subserved by a human mirror neuron system, though acknowledging that there is as yet no direct evidence about whether such systems are innate in monkeys or in people.

However, such neonatal imitative ability, and its possible neural basis, remains controversial. Imitative ability in newborns runs counter to the Piagetian claim that the capacity to imitate reflects cognitive development during the first year in life and will first be seen at about 12 months of age. Certainly there is rather little evidence that older babies aged 2–12 months are capable of imitating facial movements such as tongue protrusion, and where vocal imitation is observed it is the adults imitating the infants, rather than vice versa (see Jones, 2009)! It is of course possible that an inborn imitative capacity could disappear after about 2 months – just as the inborn tendency to track face patterns declines. However, Jones (2009) maintains that the evidence for neonatal imitation per se is weaker than Meltzoff and colleagues maintain. Jones (2009) argues that tongue protrusion is a sign of arousal in the newborn infant, and that many of the apparent demonstrations of infant capacity to match an adult's facial gesture with their own can be re-interpreted as a reflection of the infant's natural response to stimuli it finds arousing. A distinction, though, needs to be drawn between imitation based upon an infant's intention and responses that may arise from more primitive neural underpinnings. It may be intentional imitation that emerges later in the baby's life.

Beyond imitation, how do young babies perceive facial expressions? Field, Woodson, Greenberg and Cohen (1982) reported that newborn infants could discriminate three different facial expressions – happiness, sadness and surprise – by showing that following habituation to one expression, infants looked longer at a live model when she changed to a different expression. This study also reported, consistent with Meltzoff and Moore's (1977) findings, that these newborn babies tended to show movements that imitated the expressions they were shown. Whether the newborn babies are interpreting perceived *emotions* at this stage remains unclear, however, since they might just be noticing and responding to changes in overall face shape between the different expressions shown. Moreover, as noted by Smith and Muir (2003) this dishabituation could have arisen because the change of expression involved a new movement by the model, attracting the neonate's attention to the changing configuration.

In Chapter 4 we described how the neural underpinnings of emotion perception involve brain structures that respond to emotions across modalities. The foundations of this crossmodal integration appear to be established early in infancy. Grossman, Striano and Friederici (2006) demonstrated that ERPs measured in infants aged just 7 months were sensitive to whether a face and a voice which followed it shortly afterwards displayed the same or different emotions.

Newborn babies are also sensitive to whether eye gaze is directed to them or not. Batki, Baron-Cohen, Wheelwright, Connellan and Ahluwalia (2000) showed 105 neonates one of two photographs in turn – an adult female face with eyes open or eyes closed. The babies looked longer at the face with open eyes (47 s on average) than the one with closed eyes (40 s on average). Farroni, Csibra, Simion and Johnson (2002) presented infants aged 1 to 5 days old a pair of photographs in which one woman gazed directly ahead and the other had her eyes averted. These newborn babies looked substantially longer at the face with direct gaze (107 s compared with 64 s) and also looked more often towards the face with direct gaze. Farroni et al. (2002) went on to record ERPs of 4 month olds to faces with direct or averted gaze and found that an N240 component (cf. the N290 discussed earlier), which was likened to the N170 in adults, showed differential sensitivity to direct versus averted gaze. Johnson et al. (2005) were able to analyse these ERPs further and suggested that the fusiform gyrus (FFA), rather than the superior temporal sulcus (STS), was largely responsible for this sensitivity to direct gaze in infants. While Grossman and Johnson (2007) contrast this finding with the STS involvement in gaze found in adults, we saw in Chapter 5 that some studies (George et al., 2001) have also found that FFA in adults can be differentially activated by faces with direct gaze. We need to differentiate between indirect effects that gaze may have on the activation of regions involved in face recognition and the perception of gaze direction itself as an indicator of social attention.

Reid, Striano, Kaufman and Johnson (2004) showed that ERPs to objects viewed by 4 month olds were sensitive to whether or not these objects had previously been cued by eye gaze, and Senju, Johnson and Csibra (2006) showed that 9 month olds showed differential ERP responses to faces depending on whether the gaze was directed towards or away from a location previously occupied by an interesting object. These studies are beginning to reveal the neural underpinnings of the development of gaze cueing and shared attention mechanisms.

However, as reviewed by Doherty (2006), even 3 year olds are far from perfect at answering explicit questions about whether a face is looking at them or not, and so the sensitivity of neural systems to gaze direction in infants may not map directly onto more explicit competence at gaze 'understanding'. For example, even though infants will often follow an adult's direction of gaze (Scaife & Bruner, 1975), Corkum and Moore (1995) showed that it was only at the age of 18 months that infants were able to use the direction in which adults turned their eyes to *predict* where an object of interest would appear, indicating that until this age they are unable to act upon the informative significance of a gaze shift. Again, we must distinguish between what we might call infant 'pre-cognitive' competence, as assessed by preference and habituation studies, and the later emerging cognitive and emotional skills of person perception. This potential mismatch between remarkable infant competence in the first year of life and the slower development of explicit childhood skill is the theme to which we turn next.

Development during childhood

So far, we have described the development of face perception skills over the first year of a child's life. What happens beyond these first months? In order to track development over the years, the methods used will typically change. A baby's abilities are inferred from how long it looks at one pattern or another, but this is a laborious, painstaking procedure. A child's ability is more often measured by its answers to questions, posed in words. This means that care has to be taken not to confuse the child's abilities at face perception and memory with their more general cognitive development. A child may fail to respond correctly to a face processing test because it cannot yet perceive the relevant face dimensions, or because it doesn't understand in the same way, or has even forgotten, the questions asked by an experimenter. To give a simple example, even though it is relatively straightforward to demonstrate that babies prefer to look at attractive faces, or prototypical faces, it would be problematic to ask young children

questions about facial 'attractiveness' or 'distinctiveness' for reasons of vocabulary alone.

A useful approach is to try to arrive at a way of testing different aspects of
face perception based around a common set of procedures. Bruce et al. (2000)
constructed simple tests using pictures of children's faces, to probe abilities to
match unfamiliar faces on identity, and to match or to recognise different expressions, gaze direction and facial speech across an age range of 4 through to 10
years. Questions were posed as simply as possible to make the tasks comprehen-
sible to the youngest age group. There was a general age-related progression
across all the tasks tested. Figure 8.8 shows some of the results of that study and
illustrates how substantial are the improvements even on simple tasks during
these early years. Matching tests which most 4 year olds failed were performed
perfectly by 10 years of age. But does this really demonstrate that children's
proficiency with faces improves so much over this timescale? To what extent is it
just that the tasks themselves require more general cognitive abilities of attention, comprehension and memory and that these themselves explain most or all
of the improved face perception performance in childhood? This is a tricky question to answer, and to show why we will look fairly closely at a series of studies
that has been highly influential but also proved difficult to interpret correctly.

As we discussed in Chapter 6, a widely shared opinion is that adult face
recognition skills seem particularly to depend on processing configural information. The idea originated in studies by Carey and Diamond, who developed the
influential theory that skilled face recognition is particularly based upon the
processing of second-order configural information (Carey & Diamond, 1977;
Carey, Diamond, & Woods, 1980; Diamond & Carey, 1977). The first-order
configuration of a face is the arrangement of eyes above nose above mouth –
violations of this destroy the 'facelikeness' of the pattern. The second-order

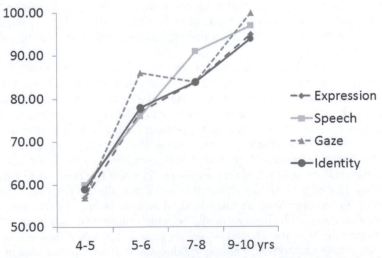

Figure 8.8 Average % correct matching of faces on four different tasks by children
in four age groups tested by Bruce et al. (2000).

configuration is the more subtle arrangement of face features within this basic face pattern. Adults are remarkably sensitive to variations in second-order config-uration – as we discussed in Chapter 6. Inverting faces seems to impair the processing of such configural information by adults, and this impairment may in part explain the disproportionate effect of face inversion on recognition of faces by normal adults. Using such observations, Diamond and Carey (1986) elab-orated a more general position that what characterises our ability to recognise faces is that through looking at them so much we have become face 'experts', and that the key to this expertise lies in sensitivity to second-order configural information.

We will have more to say about the expertise hypothesis later. For now, all that needs to be noted is that it would be reasonable to expect that becoming a face expert could take a considerable amount of time. From this theoretical standpoint, it was very interesting when initial results suggested that it might be second-order configural processing that particularly differentiated older from younger children's face recognition performance. Two different paradigms were adduced to support this claim – paraphernalia effects and inversion effects. We will consider these in turn.

Carey and Diamond (1977) found that 6-year-old children's recognition decisions in an unfamiliar face matching task seemed disproportionately influ-enced by changes in facial expression or in paraphernalia such as hats – they would pick faces as being those of the same person simply because they wore the same hat, or think they were different if they had different expressions. Such findings led Carey and Diamond (1977) to suggest that children aged around 6 years of age process faces largely on the basis of piecemeal information (i.e. isolated features, including paraphernalia), and that the configural processing that underlies mature face processing expertise develops more slowly. This hypothesised childhood 'encoding switch' from reliance on piecemeal to config-ural information forms a powerful theoretical claim because it suggests that developmental change may be qualitative (a shift from relying on featural to configural information) rather than merely quantitative (just getting better at doing the same things).

A problem with this claim was apparent in Diamond and Carey's (1977) study, since they found that young children were not fooled by irrelevant para-phernalia when asked to match faces of their classmates. So it seemed possible that young children might already be using some form of configural encoding of familiar faces – rendering the idea of a pure encoding switch less convincing. Moreover, when Flin (1985a) created unfamiliar face matching tasks with distracting paraphernalia, but manipulated the similarity of the faces, she found that young children only relied on paraphernalia when the faces were similar to each other. But later work has shown this is not actually so different from what adults do. As we discussed in Chapter 2, Hancock, Bruce and Burton (2001) point out that even adults have difficulty with unfamiliar face matching, and they resort to piecemeal, feature-based strategies as well. The key difference between adults and young children may simply be that adults have a better idea of which features to home in on, and in particular they know that a hat could well be there to fool you in a psychology experiment!

Now we turn to the findings for inversion effects. Using a recognition memory task with photographs of unfamiliar faces, Carey and Diamond (1977) and Carey et al. (1980) found that 6-year-old children, while poorer at upright face recognition than adults, were relatively unaffected by inversion of the faces. Between ages 6 and 10 years, their performance at recognising inverted faces did not change a great deal, whereas there was a strong improvement in ability to remember upright faces. This pattern was interpreted as indicating not much change in ability to use the feature-based recognition needed with inverted faces, and improvement in the configural encoding of upright faces. However, Crookes and McKone (2009) have recently argued that floor effects with younger children could explain the apparent absence or reduction of inversion effects in these earlier studies. When the task is sufficiently difficult that children are performing poorly with upright faces, it is not possible to demonstrate the same reduction in performance following inversion (or other manipulations) as can be seen in older children or adults. Crookes and McKone (2009) present a comprehensive review of studies of face recognition in childhood and demonstrate that when young children are compared with adults in tasks that avoid floor and ceiling effects, there is no evidence for qualitative differences in face processing between young children and adults, and little evidence for quantitative differences either, other than those to be expected to arise from general cognitive factors (see also Itier & Taylor, 2004). Thus a tentative conclusion is that children are actually already fairly 'expert' face perceivers, but general perceptual and cognitive abilities are needed to reveal this expertise in certain kinds of experiment.

That said, other studies have also suggested that young children are insensitive to changes in the second-order configuration of face features as defined by the spacing between different internal features – but again, there are complications of interpretation. Mondloch and Thomson (2008) for example showed 4 year olds photos of the faces of familiar classmates which were either unaltered or had their internal feature spacings altered. The children were asked to identify the 'real' version in an engaging game where they had to help a bus driver let the right person onto the bus. Children of this age appeared not to be able to discriminate between such spacing variants and performed near chance. Control conditions showed that they were able to play the game when the identities were varied in their hairstyles. Four year olds performed above chance, but still very poorly, when the test involved simply matching a target face with its 'twin' in a pair in which the foil had altered spacing. One interpretation of such findings might be that 4 year olds do not process second-order configural information in the way that older children and adults do. A different interpretation, however, could be that they find it difficult to make judgements based on subtle variations between whole faces and, given these difficulties, they tend to opt for something simpler, such as the hairstyle. A study by Nishimura, Maurer and Gao (2009) gives some support to this interpretation. They showed that 8-year-old children and adults perceived faces similarly, in terms of the overall dimensions of similarity which were extracted using multidimensional scaling of sets of 'odd-man-out' judgements. However, children tended to use a single dimension of similarity while adults were able to use multiple dimensions for individual judgements.

To complicate matters further, we saw in Chapter 6 that evidence for the importance of second-order configural information in face recognition is now seen to be less compelling than was once thought. Fortunately, what remains more persuasive is evidence of the importance of holistic configural processing, and for this the developmental evidence is also more clear.

Two widely-used paradigms for investigating holistic perception – both introduced earlier in the book – are Young, Hellawell and Hay's (1987) face composite effect (see Chapters 2 and 6) in which the alignment of two halves of different faces impedes identity decisions based on one half of the aligned composite, and Tanaka and Farah's (1993) comparison of differences between face parts seen in isolation or in a whole-face context (see Chapter 6). Both methods have been used in studies of children, and no age differences in the tendency to use holistic information have been found with the composite (Carey, 1992; de Heering, Houthuys, & Rossion, 2007; Mondloch, Pathman, Maurer, Le Grand, & de Schonen, 2007) or part-whole paradigms (Pellicano & Rhodes, 2003; Tanaka, Kay, Grinnell, Stansfield, & Szechter, 1998). The youngest participants in these studies were 4 years old, which is probably at the limit of the suitability for these methods. A comparable study using the composite technique with facial expressions – as discussed for adult studies in Chapter 4 (Calder, Young, Keane, & Dean, 2000) – found that whilst children aged 5 years and upwards improved in their ability to recognise facial expressions they always showed a composite effect (Durand, Gallay, Seigneuric, Robichon, & Baudouin, 2007).

On balance, then, there is little evidence of a fundamental change in the mechanism for perceiving and encoding faces across the 4–10 years age range. Holistic configural processing is clearly demonstrable across this age range, and evidence of a switch to greater reliance on second-order configural information is open to simpler interpretations.

A number of researchers have suggested that configural processing may be integral to the right cerebral hemisphere's superiority in various face perception tasks (Bourne, Vladeneau, & Hole, 2009). Any such specialisation does not seem to be absolute. We saw in Chapter 6 that although the right FFA shows sensitivity to feature spacing, so does the left FFA (Rhodes, Michie, Hughes, & Byatt, 2009) – at least to some extent. But the hypothesis of right hemisphere involvement in configural processing makes it interesting to know whether there might be any change in right cerebral hemisphere superiority for face perception across the age range we are discussing. However, studies using the divided visual field and chimaeric face techniques (see Chapter 2 for descriptions of these methods) as behavioural indices of right hemisphere superiority consistently report no evidence of developmental change (Aljuhanay, Milne, Burt, & Pascalis, 2010; Young, 1986; Young & Bion, 1980; Young & Ellis, 1976).

To probe the more general organisation of the face perception system in 5- to 11-year-old children, Spangler et al. (2010) used tasks that involved sorting pictures of faces on one dimension – facial identity, facial speech, facial expression or gaze direction – whilst ignoring changes in the others. They found patterns of cross-talk that were comparable to those we have described elsewhere for Garner interference in adults – in particular, identity could not be ignored when sorting facial speech or emotional expression. These findings again show no fundamental organisational changes across this age range.

Not everything is at present neatly pigeon-holed, though. In contrast to this overall picture of relatively stable organisation of childhood face skills, functional neuroimaging studies have shown that there certainly *do* seem to be changes in relevant neural structures. For example, there are changes in early components of the ERP to faces (such as the P1 and N170) across the 4 to 15 years age range (Taylor, Batty, & Itier, 2004).

Some of the most provocative findings have come from fMRI. Aylward et al. (2005) investigated activation in the fusiform gyrus (FFA) as children aged 8 through to 12 years old, and adults, looked at faces and houses. They found greater activation of the fusiform gyrus by faces in older children and adults than in the younger children. Scherf, Behrmann, Humphreys and Luna (2007) studying 5 to 8 year olds and Golarai et al. (2007) with 7 to 11 year olds drew similar conclusions. In children there is less activation of the FFA by faces than in adults. Partly as a consequence of this, the right FFA forms a larger identifiable region in adults, and these increases in the volume of tissue strongly activated by faces correlate with improved recognition memory for faces.

Cohen Kadosh and Johnson (2007) and Grill-Spector, Golaria and Gabrieli (2008) review these and other functional imaging studies. While noting the difficulties of interpreting fMRI data from children, they agree that the balance of evidence suggests that face selective regions in the ventral stream (the pathway that according to Haxby et al. results in recognition and interpretation of invariant characteristics) appear to develop slowly over several years. This is in marked contrast to an area such as the lateral occipital complex, implicated in other kinds of object recognition, which from fMRI looks much the same functionally in 6 year olds and adults. However, the slow development of the FFA could arise for a number of reasons as children meet and recognise increasing numbers of faces throughout their childhood. Thus functional changes in the FFA could result from dealing with increased numbers of faces rather than necessarily reflecting any fundamental change in the processing mechanism, and this interpretation would bring the fMRI studies into line with the behavioural findings. It will be interesting to see how this new field of fMRI with children moves forward.

Face perception and recognition across the lifespan

Of course, development does not stop at 10 or 11 years old! Here, we will look separately at development in adolescence, changes during the adult years, and at age-related cognitive decline.

First, adolescence. We left this out of our previous discussion of childhood age changes because something different seems to happen in adolescence. While face recognition as tested by explicit memory and matching tests improves steadily until the age of 10 years old, various studies have revealed an apparent dip in performance at around 12 or 13 years (Carey et al., 1980; Flin, 1980, 1985a, 1985b). The exact age of the dip in performance varies from study to study, and sometimes it takes the form of a levelling off in a previous upwardly improving trend rather than an actual decline, but it is consistently found (Chung & Thomson, 1995; Lawrence et al., 2008). The performance dip is most evident in recognition memory tasks – familiar face recognition does not seem to be affected. It is found for inverted as well as upright faces, it also extends to recognition of unfamiliar voices (Mann, Diamond, & Carey, 1979), and there is some evidence of a dip for other non-verbal stimuli such as houses and flags (Flin, 1985b).

Importantly, not all tasks show this phenomenon – so it isn't simply that adolescents don't try hard enough. We noted that familiar face recognition isn't affected, and Figure 8.9 shows performance across the range 8 to 16 years on the Embedded Figures Test (EFT, a test in which you try to find a figure which is hidden by being embedded in a more complex drawing) compared to a recognition memory test for unfamiliar faces (Diamond, Carey, & Back, 1983). Performance improves steadily on the EFT, and it improves for faces too, but with a clear dip along the way in the face data.

How could normal development make you temporarily worse at something? One possibility would be that it reflects a change in what are called 'metacognitive' abilities – the understanding we have of what mental skills we possess and

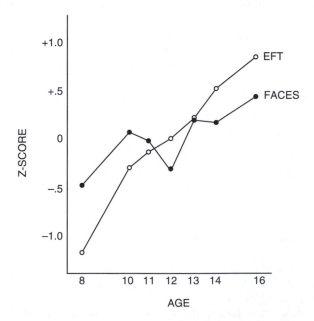

Figure 8.9 Data obtained by Diamond et al. (1983). Task performance is expressed in Z-scores and age is shown in years. Reprinted from *Cognition*, 13, 2, Rhea Diamond, Susan Carey, Karen J. Back, *Genetic influences on the development of spatial skills during early adolescence*, pp. 167–185. Copyright 1983, with permission from Elsevier.

how to make best use of them. Important studies in the 1960s had shown that a substantial component of young children's poor performance on short-term memory tasks results from the fact that they don't think (or don't bother) to rehearse the items during the memory interval – so if they are instructed to rehearse their performance improves substantially (Flavell, Beach, & Chinsky, 1966; Keeney, Cannizzo, & Flavell, 1967). Maybe the adolescent performance dip for face recognition might have a similar strategic origin?

Carey et al. (1980) investigated this possibility by using a 'depth of processing' manipulation. In the study phase of their recognition memory experiment, they asked one group of children to judge the sex of the faces (i.e. as male or female) and a second group to judge their 'likeability'. In this way, Carey et al. (1980) exerted a degree of control over the face encoding strategy. Moreover, the likeability instruction leads to deeper processing than the relatively superficial sex judgement, so it should lead to enhanced memory. As expected, the likeability judgement group showed better recognition memory for the studied faces than the sex judgement group. However, the adolescent performance dip was equally apparent regardless of the encoding strategy. This doesn't entirely rule out the possibility that some other strategic or metacognitive factor is involved, but it makes it quite a bit less likely.

Instead, Carey et al. (1980) suggested that maturational changes associated with puberty affect the right hemisphere. In support of this, Diamond, Carey and Back (1983) found that girls in the midst of puberty showed a greater decline in their face memory performance than those of the same age who were either pre- or post-pubescent. Such performance changes could arise for a number of reasons. The prolonged functional development of FFA (as revealed by fMRI) continues into adolescence (Golarai, Liberman, Yoon, & Grill-Spector, 2010). Blakemore (2008) reviews structural changes that also occur in the adolescent brain in areas relevant to face processing and social cognition, and speculates about possible neurological bases for the temporary decline in face recognition at this stage of development. That said, the phenomenon may have multiple contributory causes. Although hormonal changes may somehow be acting directly on the brain, part of the performance dip in face and voice recognition memory may be a secondary effect of accompanying cognitive changes. For instance, we saw in Chapter 3 how hormones can affect attractiveness judgements, and these perceptions of attractiveness are themselves subject to change during adolescence (Saxton, DeBruine, Jones, Little, & Roberts, 2009). Variations in perceived attractiveness may be both consequences of hormone-related influences on the brain and among the factors contributing to temporary performance disruption.

Though the adolescent findings are intriguing, we think that some of the most interesting changes occur in adulthood. This is a time that most theories treat as a period of relative stasis, yet this is far from correct – especially for face perception. Everyone has to learn lots of new faces as they progress through adulthood and encounter new people in new contexts. Young adults will meet other students in the classroom, later they will meet other parents at the school gate, and so on. New generations of young people play for our favourite football or cricket teams. Celebrities on television, actors, politicians, pop stars come and go all the time.

Faces (and names) can be remembered across long intervals. Bahrick, Bahrick and Wittlinger (1975) examined recognition of the names and faces of people taken from USA high school yearbooks. In this way, they were able to test the recognition abilities of participants across intervals ranging from 3 months to 48 years since graduation. From their data, it is clear that the ability to recognise faces and names of former classmates remains good for many years. For faces, there was virtually unimpaired performance across a 34-year interval, whereas performance for names began to fall after 15 years. Even after 48 years, more than 70% of the faces tested were recognised. Although the faces and names used in Bahrick et al.'s (1975) study would mostly have been very thoroughly learnt at high school, and there would have been some opportunity for rehearsal when participants got out their high school yearbooks (though Bahrick et al. did try to make allowances for this), one cannot but be impressed by the levels of performance achieved across such long retention intervals.

But as adults we don't just learn new faces – we have somehow to modify the representations of faces we already learnt. As we grow older, the faces of the people we have known for years change. Facial identity is classed as 'invariant' in Haxby et al.'s (2000) model, but only in the sense that it changes imperceptibly slowly. Across an entire lifetime, the changes are substantial.

Bruck, Cavanagh and Ceci (1991) (see Figure 8.10) asked people to attempt to match high school graduation photographs with pictures of the same people taken 25 years later, when they were in their early forties. Participants were shown the yearbook pictures of each person and had to choose which of ten pictures of the forty-something adults they thought matched each picture. Volunteers unfamiliar with any of the people photographed performed with an accuracy of 33% overall, which was higher than the rate of 10% which might be expected by guessing alone, but far from perfect. Participants who had been class-mates at high school were significantly more accurate (49% correct matching) but still also far from perfect at this task, and performing well below the recognition rates for photos taken during the high school years reported by Bahrick et al. (1975).

In Bruck et al.'s (1991) study, classmates were equally accurate whether the pictures to be matched showed the same or a different viewpoint, while those unfamiliar with any of the faces were better at the matches where the depicted viewpoints coincided. The above-chance performance by the strangers is presumably based in part on the perception of features which are invariant across this range of ages (e.g. the length and shape of the nose and eyes changes little over early adulthood), which are easier to compare when viewpoints match. In contrast, the performance of the familiar judges may be based more on a viewpoint-independent knowledge built up over multiple exposures to the faces at high school. In addition, Bruck et al. suggest that familiar judges may remember, for example, characteristic expressions or poses which might provide additional sources of age-invariant information on which to make these matches. Bruck et al. excluded from their sample a small number of responses to faces that volunteers reported having seen over the past 17 years, and so we can assume that the effects of familiarity which were observed did genuinely result from memories of the high-school faces which had been retained over this interval. This familiarity

Figure 8.10 Example of the test used by Bruck et al. (1991). With kind permission from Springer Science+Business Media: *Memory & Cognition*, Fortysomething: Recognizing faces at one's 25th reunion, *19* ,3, 1991, pp. 221–228, Maggie Bruck, Appendix, p. 228.

with the youthful faces allowed matching to be better than if these people were strangers, but the relatively poor performance of both groups illustrates how substantial are the changes in appearance over a 25-year interval – changes that we somehow adapt to very readily in the people with whom we retain close contact. It is only when we look back at photographs of our close friends and family taken many years earlier that we notice how much they have changed as the decades pass.

So face recognition abilities must be flexible enough to accommodate change to individuals as well as change to the population of items we know. We know, though, that we are not completely flexible in this respect, because we are better at recognising faces from a more familiar 'culture' – our own race, our own age group (see Chapter 6). But these abilities to recognise 'out-group' faces can themselves be enhanced by experience, as we saw in Chapter 6. For example, compared to adults who are not teachers, preschool teachers show enhanced holistic perception of young children's faces as indexed by the composite effect (de Heering & Rossion, 2008; Kuefner, Macchi Cassia, Vescovo, & Picozzi, 2010). Cultural experience affects some quite basic aspects of face processing too. Megreya and Bindemann (2009) showed that Egyptian adults are better at matching unfamiliar faces on the basis of their internal features, in contrast to British adults who are better with external features of unfamiliar faces. This difference is attributed to expertise with internal features in a society where women's hairstyles are concealed. They showed also that Egyptian children, whose hair is not concealed, show the typical advantage for external features of unfamiliar faces, suggesting that it is experience during adulthood that has biased processing towards internal features.

This flexibility and malleability of face recognition may be one of the environmental imperatives responsible for the protracted development of the core system for face recognition. But what exactly happens when we learn a new face, or modify an existing representation? These are really important issues about which we know far too little. They relate directly to questions about face familiarity we discussed in Chapter 6, but have wider implications.

Sadly, there is also age-related cognitive decline. When you reach the authors' age, you will have begun to realise that many things are not as easy as they used to be, and this extends to mental activities (like writing intelligible books) as well as the physical stuff. Mostly, there is not much reason to suppose that these kinds of problems are face-specific (Maylor, 1997), but memory for contextual associations does appear to decline (e.g. see Naveh-Benjamin, Shing, Kilb, Werkle-Bergner, Lindenberger, & Li, 2009) – and may help explain why so many elderly people report that they have particular problems remembering names and specific facts.

That said, some of this cognitive decline may be relatively circumscribed. For example, ability to recognise some facial expressions seems to fall off more quickly than others (Calder et al., 2003), and this may relate to changes in some of the key brain regions linked to specific emotions (see Chapter 4). However, it is difficult to be confident about what is normal and what is pathological change – an indeterminate proportion of what appear to be neurologically normal participants over the age of 55 will actually be experiencing the early consequences of neurodegenerative conditions that will only become obviously symptomatic later, and this unknown proportion will likely increase as older participants are tested. Importantly, too, standard cross-sectional designs that test performance at different ages can mistake cohort effects for age-related change. Early experiences can affect facial expression recognition (Pollak & Kistler, 2002), so who knows exactly how much factors like the prevalent 'stiff upper lip' attitudes of 50 or more years ago might have affected everyday displays of facial expressions and ability to recognise them?

Now, what on earth were we talking about?

Atypical development

So far in this chapter, we have reviewed the acquisition and maintenance of 'normal' face processing skills across the lifespan. But there is much to be learnt from atypical development as well.

In Chapter 5, we described how children with Autistic Spectrum Disorder (ASD) and Williams syndrome (WS) may process gaze differently from those who are typically developing. Children with autism seem to avoid looking at faces – and so do some of their parents (Pellicano, 2008). In contrast WS children are fixated, literally, upon them. Intriguingly, WS seems to be associated with an enlarged FFA (Golarai, Hong et al., 2010), but how do these groups perform on behavioural tasks of face perception and recognition?

Riby, Doherty-Sneddon and Bruce (2008) asked a group of WS and a group of participants with autism, along with mental-age and chronological age-matched controls, to undergo the set of face processing tasks developed for use with children by Bruce et al. (2000). They found that there were few differences between the developmentally-disordered groups and mental-age matched controls. The WS group was no better than controls on processing facial expressions of emotion or visual speech, but did do well on eye gaze tests, as we might by now expect. The group with autism was poor on eye gaze tests but generally not worse than appropriate controls on other tasks.

The different attentiveness of these two groups to faces and to the eyes in particular does, however, seem to be reflected in the ways in which they process different parts of the face when these are probed in other tasks. Riby, Doherty-Sneddon and Bruce (2009) described the performance of 15 WS and 20 participants with autism, alongside mental and chronological age-matched controls for each group – on matching faces using upper and lower face areas; on detecting changes to eyes or mouths within faces; and on deciding which face 'looks odd' following inversion of eyes, mouth or both as in the 'Thatcher illusion' (see Chapter 4). The results showed that in all tasks WS performed at a similar, or slightly better, level than mental-age controls, and, like typically developing children, they were generally better at matching faces or spotting differences based on the upper half of the face or the eyes. In contrast, participants with autism did poorly, relative to all control groups, at matching or noticing differences around the upper half or eyes of faces. They were comparable with their controls when tasks involved processing of the lower regions/mouths.

Conditions such as autism or Williams syndrome are ones where pervasive developmental disorders impinge strikingly, but not exclusively, on social perception. We turn next to consider developmental deficits that may be more (but not entirely) face-specific.

In earlier chapters we have described the neuropsychological condition of prosopagnosia – inability to recognise familiar faces. This may arise as a result of brain injury or disease, and in a congenital form in people who have been found to have problems with faces throughout their lives, quite possibly from birth. As we have seen, individuals with congenital prosopagnosia can seem remarkably normal at some aspects of perceiving faces, including the perception of gaze (Duchaine, Jenkins, Germine, & Calder, 2009), expression (Humphreys, Avidan, & Behrmann, 2007), attractiveness (Carbon, Grüter, Grüter, Weber, & Lueschow, 2010) and trustworthiness (Todorov & Duchaine, 2008).

We also noted, though, that interpreting the implications of congenital cases can be complicated because they reflect a combination of lifelong atypical development and potential compensatory strategies (Bishop, 1997). Moreover, simply listing what can *sometimes* be normal in congenital prosopagnosia – as we just did – is also a bit misleading because the profiles of strengths and weaknesses in face perception actually vary from individual to individual (Le Grand et al., 2006). Importantly, even for individuals with congenital prosopagnosia who are members of the same family – where there is a strong possibility of some form of genetic link – the symptoms remain heterogeneous (Schmalzl, Palermo, & Coltheart, 2008). This heterogeneity of the 'cognitive phenotype' is typical of various neurodevelopmental disorders that are likely due to interactions between numerous different genes and environmental factors (Bishop, 2009).

Several neuroimaging studies have investigated the FFA in congenital prosopagnosia, both structurally and functionally. These have shown activation (in terms of blood flow) of the FFA when people with congenital prosopagnosia look at faces, and an N170 electrophysiological response, despite their poor recognition (Behrmann & Avidan, 2005). So individuals with congenital prosopagnosia do not simply lack an FFA. Whether their FFA works efficiently or even in the normal manner is more difficult to establish, but it seems that structurally their fusiform gyrus (the region that includes FFA) is relatively small (Behrmann, Avidan, Gao, & Black, 2007; Garrido, Furl et al., 2009) and shows abnormal connectivity with other brain regions involved in face perception (Avidan & Behrmann, 2009; Thomas et al., 2009).

Valuable insights also come from cases of prosopagnosia caused by early acquired brain damage, when patterns of impairment can be remarkably like those found following brain injury sustained in adulthood (Young, 1992; Young & Ellis, 1989). The case described by Young and Ellis (1989) followed brain infections and associated complications during her first few years of life, after which she did not regain ability to recognise faces yet was able to learn to read. This observation that one complex visual skill (reading) can be acquired whilst another skill (face recognition) cannot be relearnt is relevant to issues we will approach directly later, concerning what processes might be face-specific.

A very interesting developmental perspective arises from examination of the development of face processing in individuals who were born with cataracts which deprived them of normal visual input in their early months or years. At a later age, the cataracts can often be surgically corrected, so through studying the consequences of early visual deprivation we can gain insight into the importance of early learning for face perception.

Mondloch, Le Grand and Maurer (2003) summarise a series of studies of people tested as adults who had visual deprivation from bilateral cataracts that were corrected on average about 4 months after birth. As adults these participants performed just as well as controls at detecting faces in high contrast Mooney face images (see Figure 8.18) and at noticing differences between faces based on changes to specific features or internal contours. They were significantly impaired, however, at noticing differences due to changes in the internal spacing or second-order configuration of features. Le Grand, Mondloch, Maurer and Brent (2004) further examined configural processing in a group of 12 people who had been treated for bilateral cataracts between 3 and 6 months of age, and who were aged between 9 and 23 years of age when tested. They modified the face composite task (cf. Young, Hellawell, & Hay, 1987) to produce a variant where participants had to decide if the top halves of two sequentially presented faces were the same or different. The faces were composites created by pairing the top half of one face with the bottom of a different one, such that the two halves were aligned or misaligned. Consistent with other studies of the face composite effect, a group of young adults, and a control group matched with the visually deprived participants, performed quite well at the task when the half faces were misaligned, but were inaccurate and slow at the task when the composite half faces were aligned. The participants who had suffered early visual deprivation, however, showed no effect of the alignment manipulation on accuracy on the task at all. They performed somewhat worse than controls when the face halves were misaligned and considerably better when the half faces were aligned. This pattern of performance is consistent with an impairment in the processing of holistic configural information which interferes with comparisons of part-faces in composites but can help these comparisons when there is no impediment from the rest of the face context.

We have noted at various points that the right cerebral hemisphere seems to be particularly involved in various aspects of face perception, and studies of early visual deprivation offer a unique insight into this. To understand why, we need to consider the early development of the visual pathways. The adult visual pathways were described in Chapter 2 (Figure 2.16), but changes during early postnatal development create a system that has some functional differences. In particular, there is evidence that sensitivity to stimuli is better in the nasal part of each retina (the part of the retina nearest the nose) during the early months. Since this is the part of the retina of each eye that projects via the optic nerve to the opposite cerebral hemisphere (see Figure 2.16), a cataract of the left eye in early infancy will have a differentially severe impact on the visual input received by the right cerebral hemisphere, whereas a cataract of the right eye will affect the visual input to the left hemisphere (Le Grand, Mondloch, Maurer, & Brent, 2003). In addition, the corpus callosum (the fibre tract that connects the cerebral hemispheres) is slow to myelinate, reducing the likelihood of effective interhemispheric integration.

Le Grand et al. (2003) were able to compare a group of people who had cataracts affecting their left eye during the first few months of life with another group who had right eye cataracts and a normally sighted control group. All were tested at least 8 years after the cataracts were removed – giving plenty of time for the brain to achieve any recovery from the effects of the deprivation, and they were tested with binocular presentation, allowing them to use the unaffected eye. As explained, a left eye cataract in infancy will differentially deprive the right hemisphere of patterned visual input and a right eye cataract will deprive the left hemisphere. Le Grand et al. (2003) were looking for any long-term consequences of this early deprivation. They found that it was only those who had had left eye cataracts whose configural face perception skills were affected, suggesting that it is specifically the right hemisphere of the brain that requires a particular kind of input for configural face processing to develop normally.

It is intriguing that the absence of visual input in the first few weeks of life can have such an effect on configural processing of faces. Early visual deprivation has other long-term effects on overall visual acuity, but Geldart et al. (2002) found that later visual acuity was not correlated with the degree of impairment in face perception. It will be interesting to see how the FFA and other areas are activated in such participants and to make comparisons with the studies of congenital prosopagnosia we discussed earlier.

Are faces the 'special ones'?

We can now return to what has proved to be one of the most contentious issues in face research – whether faces have a special status? This is a question we introduced in Chapter 1, where we outlined the idea that evolved structures in the brain are involved in face perception, but we could only touch on its ramifications at that point. Now, equipped with a much wider knowledge base, we are ready to try to disentangle some of the issues.

In one respect, the answer is obvious. It just depends what you mean by 'special' (H. Ellis & Young, 1989; Hay & Young, 1982). Faces are undeniably special in many ways that we hope this book has well illustrated. There are no other visual objects of similar importance in terms of their functions, the range of messages sent, and the complexity of non-rigid movements they exhibit. Only our bodies might come anywhere close, but – putting the pretensions of pop psychology 'body language' aside – they don't talk as well.

However, the heat in the special controversy comes from somewhere else. It arises because the claim that faces are special is often interpreted (and often intended) to mean they are understood by a specific brain region or regions – the idea that there is a specific face 'module' in the brain (Kanwisher & Yovel, 2006). To do justice to this requires that we return to some of the issues we introduced in Chapter 1, where we considered the neural systems used to perceive faces, setting them alongside other matters considered in the book, including issues of innateness and development we have tackled in this chapter.

The idea of modular organisation of brain function can be traced back to the phrenologists, and possibly beyond. It became important in modern psychology initially from evidence of dissociable neuropsychological deficits (Marshall & Newcombe, 1973; Shallice, 1988; Warrington & Shallice, 1969), but Marr (1976) gave it added force by pointing out that modularity is a good design feature for any complex system for which it is desirable to be able to modify a component without affecting the rest of the system's operational properties. This is certainly true for the brain – when you move to a new job and have to learn lots of new faces, you don't want this to disrupt your ability to recognise facial expressions. Modularity is one way to achieve this.

In an extended discussion of the concept of modularity, Fodor (1983) argued that it has a number of properties. Those we think important to discuss here are that, for Fodor, modularity is demonstrated when there is evidence for *innateness, localisation* and *specificity* of a particular function. First let us consider the question of whether our face processing abilities are *innate*.

In this chapter we have described extensive evidence that newborn babies are born with some kind of representation of the human face – at least sufficient to guide their orienting movements towards faces. This is evidence of some form of innateness, but we saw that the relationship between this relatively primitive and possibly subcortical *orienting* system and the *interpretation* of face messages by the human adult cortex is less clear, and that the system that orients attention to seen faces interacts with responses to voices that may have been learnt pre-natally. In sum, we have the impression of a neatly crafted system with both innate and prenatally learnt orienting components that will optimise the infant's chance to learn about faces, but this infant evidence doesn't tell us whether the system that does the learning is innately organised to learn about *faces* or just to learn about anything visual. The remarkable evidence of perceptual narrowing later in infancy (Pascalis et al., 2002; Pascalis et al., 2005; Kelly et al., 2007), so that as the baby becomes more skilled at perceiving faces of the kinds it has encountered it starts to lose ability to discriminate out-group faces, fits either possibility.

However, we have also seen that some people seem to be born with an inability to learn to recognise faces normally, in the form of congenital prosopagnosia. This is clear evidence for some innate system that will enable most of us to learn to recognise faces proficiently. This face learning system seems to require certain input at a critical point early in infancy. As we have seen, if newborn infants are deprived of visual input due to congenital cataract, later corrected, they fail to develop a capacity to recognise faces well (Le Grand, Mondloch, Maurer & Brent, 2003; Maurer, Lewis, & Mondloch, 2005), suggestive of there being a critical period in which the innate face learning system needs the kind of visual patterns it is designed to discriminate.

What about localisation and specificity? Although logically distinct, these properties are more difficult to keep separate in practice – the evidence often speaks to both properties at the same time, creating confusion by encouraging people almost to treat them as the same thing. We will begin by concentrating on specificity, before returning to localisation.

Does the brain use face-specific mechanisms?

There is no doubt that some parts of the human brain seem to be particularly implicated in face processing, as we introduced in Chapter 1 and elaborated in several places since. Haxby et al.'s (2000) core system comprises brain regions including the OFA, FFA and posterior STS. But, and this is much trickier, are these areas of the brain *face-specific*? It is that question that we now discuss in some detail.

Clearly, the regions in Haxby et al.'s core system exhibit a degree of differential response to faces that makes it appropriate to call them 'face-selective'. To say they are 'face-specific', though, can be taken to imply that only faces are of interest to them, and many researchers stop short of this. Haxby et al.'s (2000) framework, for example, specifies a division of processing into distinct regions deriving information about recognition, what (or who) something is (via the lateral fusiform gyrus or FFA), as opposed to information more directly relevant to interacting with that person (the posterior STS). However, Haxby et al. (2000) are careful not to prejudge the issue of whether these areas are face-specific or not and they do not themselves label them as exclusively 'face' areas.

Others are less circumspect – they see the stakes as very high, and the winner takes it all. Since the identification of the FFA by Kanwisher et al. (1997), there has been a debate about why this part of the brain is so responsive to faces. In this debate, opinions have tended to polarise into two camps. One camp maintains that the FFA is a region that is involved specifically in perceiving faces; the other camp maintains that it is involved in other tasks that require discrimination between individual items with high perceptual similarity. Typically, members of the first camp see evolution as the driving force that created the FFA, whereas members of the second camp see it in terms of acquired expertise based on configural processing.

In our opinion, this second part of the argument – evolution versus expertise – is again predicated on the false 'nature or nurture' antithesis. We can't see why an evolutionary mechanism for faces would necessarily be face-specific, and we can't see why acquired expertise and a degree of perceptual flexibility are thought to be incompatible with an evolved substrate. So we will concentrate on the first part of the argument, about whether the FFA is a face-specific region. The patterns of deficit that result from brain injury to posterior visual regions (including FFA) are relevant here. We will look at these before returning to the evidence from functional brain imaging.

Let's start with a broad perspective. Damage to parts of the ventral visual pathway can create problems in visual recognition. Traditionally, clinicians have grouped and labelled these visual recognition deficits into impairments affecting reading (alexia), object recognition (visual object agnosia), and face recognition (prosopagnosia). There is no doubt that these are clinically salient problems, but what is their relationship to each other? Remarkably, no-one looked at this systematically before Farah (1991).

Farah (1991) was interested in the question of whether different neural systems might be needed to recognise words, faces and everyday objects. To this end, she reviewed the literature on neuropsychological impairments of face, word and object recognition, examining the different patterns of deficit which had been reported by simply noting from each case report what was said to be impaired or spared. Leaving aside cases where there were problems in recognising anything at all, with three types of visual stimulus, there are six possible

Table 8.1 Summary of cases by Farah (1991). The question marks signify when Farah was not fully convinced by these case reports.

Impaired	Spared	Number of cases
Faces	Objects, words	27
Faces, objects	Words	15
Words	Faces, objects	lots
Objects, words	Faces	16
Objects	Faces, words	1?
Faces, words	Objects	1?

combinations of impaired and spared abilities for patients who have dissociable deficits. These six combinations are listed in Table 8.1, together with the number of published cases for each pattern that Farah found in the literature. Table 8.1 makes clear that whereas four of the six possible patterns seemed to crop up fairly frequently, there were at the time no fully convincing cases in which object recognition was compromised without impairment of either face recognition or word recognition.

As Farah (1991) pointed out, these patterns of co-occurrence suggest that, rather than there being three separate recognition systems for objects, words and faces, the brain may make use of two underlying systems – one which is particularly appropriate for words but is also needed for some objects, and one which is particularly appropriate for faces but is also needed for some objects. From this, she developed the proposal shown in Figure 8.11. Her idea was that a whole-based encoding mechanism is needed to represent stimuli (such as faces) which are not readily identifiable from their constituent parts (most eyes, noses, mouths are hard to recognise as isolated fragments) and hence are usually

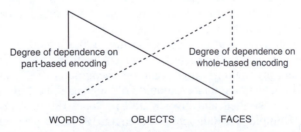

Figure 8.11 Farah's hypothesis that the brain uses two structural encoding systems. Part-based encoding is particularly appropriate for words but is also needed for some objects. Whole-based encoding is particularly appropriate for faces but is needed for some objects too. First published as Figure 2.9 on p. 368 in *Human cognitive neuropsychology: A textbook with readings*, Ellis, A. W. and Young, A. W. Psychology Press 1996, reprinted by permission of the publisher (Taylor & Francis Group, http://www.informaworld.com).

treated holistically, whilst a part-based encoding system represents stimuli which are readily decomposable into simpler nameable parts used to identify them (e.g. words into letters). A mild impairment of the whole-based encoding system could then lead to impaired face recognition only, since faces are the stimuli which place the greatest demands on this form of recognition, but more severe impairments would begin to compromise recognition of at least some objects. Similarly, mild impairment of the part-based encoding system would initially affect word recognition only, and then increasingly severe impairments would start to involve objects. The hypothesis also maps neatly onto phenomena of cerebral asymmetry if the part-based system is organised mainly in the left cerebral hemisphere and the whole-based system mainly in the right hemisphere.

For neuropsychological aficionados, a limitation of Table 8.1 is that the binary classification of abilities into 'spared' or 'impaired' categories can hide a lot of what is happening (Shallice, 1988; Young, Newcombe, de Haan, Small, & Hay, 1993). In particular, abilities that seem at first to be spared can turn out to be less intact when more carefully investigated. In this respect, a study by Moscovitch, Winocur and Behrmann (1997) is of exceptional value. They studied case CK, a person with impaired reading and object recognition but preserved face recognition following a closed head injury – the pattern corresponding to the fourth row of Table 8.1. Moscovitch et al. (1997) were able to show that CK performed as well as neurologically normal controls on face perception tasks as long as the face was upright and retained the correct pattern of spacing of internal features. If the face was inverted or fragmented in any way, however, CK performed poorly. Moscovitch et al. (1991) reasoned that CK has lost a part-based mechanism needed for the recognition of words and objects, but only required for face recognition if the face is presented in an unusual manner (such as being inverted or fragmented). In a particularly telling experiment, Moscovitch et al. (1997) showed that CK could outperform controls when searching for faces in a picture where they were hidden among overlapping rocks and trees. This happened, of course, because CK could not properly recognise the obscuring rocks and trees (due to impairment of the part-based recognition mechanism). The demonstration of a performance enhancement (however unlikely to be of real-life value) resulting from a brain injury gives a strong indication that the underlying theory is on the right lines (Kapur, 1996).

Although attractive and ingenious, Farah's (1991) hypothesis of two representational systems clearly predicts that certain patterns of deficit should not occur – the main prediction is that impaired recognition of objects with intact recognition of both words and faces should not happen. Since 1991, though, such cases have been described and investigated in detail (Rumiati & Humphreys, 1997; Rumiati, Humphreys, Riddoch, & Bateman, 1994), but they clearly remain rare.

A second prediction from Farah's (1991) account is that the recognition problems of people with acquired prosopagnosias will never be restricted only to faces, unless the deficit is very mild. This certainly fits the majority of cases, where people who lose the ability to recognise faces following brain injury are usually found to experience other object recognition difficulties as well (Barton, 2008), especially when the objects come from visually homogeneous categories (flowers, cars, birds, and so on). None the less, there are a small number of quite remarkable dissociations in the literature which are more consistent with the face-specificity hypothesis (De Renzi, 1986). For example, one man studied by McNeil and Warrington (1993) lost his ability to recognise faces following a stroke but then, post-injury, became a sheep farmer and learnt to recognise his individual sheep – correctly identifying several of them from photographs of their faces! This would not be expected if the damaged area was needed to subserve visual expertise of this sort. A similar report has been made with another case, RM (Sergent & Signoret, 1992b). When asked to recognise famous faces, RM could only identify Mikhail Gorbachev (from his birthmark) out of 300 faces shown. However, RM was very interested in cars, and was still able to give the manufacturer's name, model, and approximate year of manufacture to 172/210 pictures of cars. In this task, RM outperformed six normal controls, whose best score was 128/210.

Although they are exceptionally rare, such cases imply that the possibility of face-specific deficits must be taken seriously. But many factors need to be taken into account to arrive at a more precise interpretation, including the locations of the brain lesions themselves (often difficult to determine and encroaching on more than one region of interest) and the pre- and post-morbid interests of the individuals (RM outperformed controls at recognising cars, but 172/210 correct could still be below his pre-morbid ability). For these reasons, a lot of attention has shifted to functional neuroimaging studies, where a greater degree of experimental control can be achieved. It is time to look at these more closely.

A definite bone of contention has been whether expertise with other kinds of objects is sufficient to engage the FFA. Gauthier, Tarr and their colleagues set out to explore the expertise hypothesis more systematically by inventing a new category of artificial creatures called 'greebles' that had a variety of different features that could be varied to specify different individuals, and categories of individuals (analogous to families or types such as gender) – see Figure 8.12. They trained observers to discriminate between greebles until, after several hours of training, these heroic participants could make judgements about individual greebles with a high degree of accuracy – they had become greeble 'experts'. Some thought-provoking studies have been done (e.g. Gauthier & Tarr, 1997), though their implications remain uncertain.

For example, which parts of the brain become active when greeble experts see greebles? Does greeble expertise recruit the FFA? The answer is – yes, well, sometimes, . . . erm 'up to a point, Lord Copper'. Behrmann, Marotta, Gauthier, Tarr and McKeeff (2005) attempted to teach SM, a visual agnosic patient with accompanying prosopagnosia, to recognise greebles. He did make some progress in learning to recognise greebles, though he lagged behind control participants. Intriguingly his new skills at greeble recognition came at a cost to face recognition, which actually got a bit worse. And the greebles activated regions of the FFA that previously had been activated by faces, suggesting that the greebles had 'poached' that part of the brain. In stark contrast, though, Duchaine, Dingle, Butterworth and Nakayama (2004) described a case of a developmental prosopagnosic man who was able to learn greebles just as well as control participants with normal face recognition abilities.

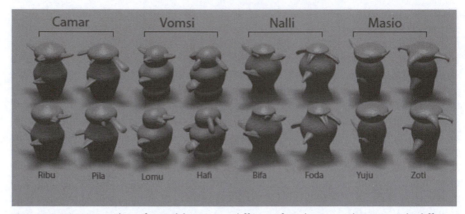

Figure 8.12 Examples of greebles. Four different families are shown, with different 'genders' shown for each family. For example, Ribu and Pila are different gender members of the Camar family. The top row shows symmetrical greeble sets used in earlier studies, and the bottom row shows asymmetrical variants developed for later work. Images provided courtesy of Michael J. Tarr.

Gauthier and her colleagues have published other findings suggesting that the FFA is activated by greebles in trained greeble-experts (Gauthier, Tarr, Anderson, Skudlarski, & Gore, 1999) and also by cars and birds for car and bird experts (Gauthier, Skudlarski, Gore, & Anderson, 2000). In related work, Rhodes, Byatt, Miche and Puce (2004) found that pictures of moths showed some activation of the FFA for participants who were lepidopterists. But other studies have failed to find FFA activated by such 'objects of expertise' (Yue, Tjan, & Biederman, 2006), or noted that FFA activation to faces correlates with behavioural measures of face recognition whereas FFA activation for other objects does not correlate so well with ability to recognise them (Grill-Spector, Knouf, & Kanwisher, 2004).

The controversy has been reviewed by McKone, Kanwisher and Duchaine (2007), who find the balance of research findings in favour of the specificity rather than expertise hypothesis. Perhaps we should not be so surprised that the greeble studies have produced some ambiguous results. The earliest versions of greebles are a little face-like (e.g. in terms of their axes of symmetry and the numbers of feature-like protruberances they have) and even later versions with reduced symmetry remain a little body-like (some of them have quite distinct head-like regions), leaving it possible that greeble-learning might itself build on other expertise for biological forms.

To further evaluate claims of face-specificity, it helps to consider brain areas that don't care so much about faces – importantly, faces are not the only visual stimuli for which there is regional selectivity of neural responses from the occipito-temporal cortex. Epstein and Kanwisher (1998) identified a Parahippocampal Place Area (PPA) that responds more to pictures of environments than faces and other stimuli, located along the ventral visual stream in the parahippocampal gyrus and the adjacent collateral sulcus. The PPA responds strongly to indoor or outdoor scenes, but shows little interest in the objects that make up such scenes (such as items of furniture) if they are not arranged into a coherent scene. Interestingly, as its name implies, the PPA is close to the hippocampus, a brain structure widely thought to play a role in spatial navigation (Maguire, Frackowiak, & Frith, 1997), consistent with the idea that the disposition of category-selective brain regions has an underlying logic.

It helps, too, to be convinced that all this apparent regional response selectivity is really going on in our everyday lives. The typical fMRI localiser scan uses a series of static images from the same category, followed by a blank interval, then a series of images from another category, another interval, and so on. To what extent does this careful but unnatural procedure artificially enhance the apparent selectivity of the regions identified?

Remarkably, the answer seems to be 'not a lot'. A delightful study by Hasson et al. (2004) shows this very clearly. Hasson et al. (2004) used standard localiser scans to identify the face-selective region in the fusiform gyrus (FFA) and the place-selective region along the collateral sulcus (PPA) for each of their participants, but for the rest of the experiment participants simply lay in the fMRI scanner watching the first half hour of Sergio Leone's film *The Good, the Bad, and the Ugly*. What Hasson et al. (2004) did was then to look at activation in the FFA and PPA, as defined by the functional localiser, to find which parts of the film caused the most activation in each area. Figure 8.13 shows stills from parts of the film where FFA activation was highest, and Figure 8.14 shows stills where PPA activation was highest. The brilliance of this approach lies in the fact that a film will intrinsically present a very wide range of images to the visual system, and identifying the frames that create the maximal response for a set of voxels carries no presuppositions about what those voxels might be doing. In this context, it is

Figure 8.13 See colour plate. Frames producing the highest activation in the face-responsive region of the fusiform gyrus (ROI shown red on underside of inflated brain). From figure 3, p. 1637 in Hasson, U., Nir, Y., Levy, I., Fuhrmann, G., & Malach, R. (2004). Intersubject synchronization of cortical activity during natural vision. *Science*, 303, pp. 1634–1640. Reprinted with permission from AAAS.

Figure 8.14 See colour plate. Frames producing the highest activation in the place-responsive region of the collateral sulcus (ROI shown green on underside of inflated brain). From figure 3, p. 1637 in Hasson, U., Nir, Y., Levy, I., Fuhrmann, G., & Malach, R. (2004). Intersubject synchronization of cortical activity during natural vision. *Science, 303*, pp. 1634–1640. Reprinted with permission from AAAS.

very striking that all 16 of the most activating parts of the film for FFA showed faces, and 12 of the 16 most activating parts of the film for PPA showed overall views of indoor or outdoor scenes.

As well as the FFA and PPA, other category-selective regions have been found in the same general region. Figure 8.15 shows regions responding maximally to faces, houses, bodies and 'other objects' on the underside of an inflated brain, with a flattened cortical representation below that relates these to well-established early visual areas that have retinotopic maps (Op de Beeck, Haushofer, & Kanwisher, 2008).

What could possibly underlie such an intricate arrangement? An interpretation that has been strongly favoured by Kanwisher and her colleagues is that evolution has shaped a degree of category-specificity in the organisation of parts of our brains (Kanwisher, 2000; Kanwisher and Yovel, 2006), but this is not the only possibility. For faces, we have already discussed the suggestion that expertise is a critical determinant (Tarr & Gauthier, 2000), but noted some of the limitations and complications of this idea.

A more general approach suggests that a strong driver of apparent category-selectivity could be retinal 'eccentricity bias' (Hasson, Levy, Behrmann, Hendler, & Malach, 2002). The suggestion here is that stimuli such as faces often require the kind of detailed analysis for which central (foveal) vision is most appropriate (see Chapter 2 for a brief discussion of properties of foveal and non-foveal vision), whereas environmental scenes (be they indoors or outdoors) require large-scale integration of features across the visual field. You can see this easily in Figure 8.13, where the faces form distinct regions within each movie frame that you can inspect regardless of the background, whereas the environmental scenes in Figure 8.14 occupy each entire frame. Since the category-selective regions are close to retinotopic visual areas (see Figure 8.15), these relative biases

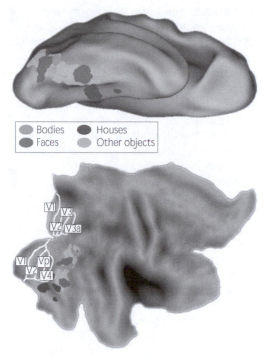

Figure 8.15 See colour plate. Regions responding to bodies, faces, houses and other objects. Reprinted by permission from Macmillan Publishers Ltd: *Nature Reviews Neuroscience*, Interpreting fMRI data: Maps, modules and dimensions, Hans P. Op de Beeck, Johannes Haushofer and Nancy G. Kanwisher, 9, 2, pp. 123–135, copyright 2008.

to depend on information from central or more peripheral regions of the visual field for interpretation of the image might underlie some of the differences in response.

More on localisation

The face-specificity versus generic expertise debate is by no means over, but a powerful study by Haxby's group shows that neither the extreme 'specificity' nor extreme 'expertise' position does full justice to the complexity of the issues – even for the single region of the FFA. Haxby et al. (2001) conducted painstaking fMRI research that showed that the broader region of ventral occipito-temporal cortex yields distinctive patterns of neural activation for various classes of object other than faces. Haxby et al. (2001) showed their participants pictures of faces, cats, houses, shoes, scissors, chairs and bottles, plus scrambled control images. They demonstrated that there were different areas that were maximally responsive to *each* of these categories. This is in itself important in making you think beyond evolutionary adaptation as the only potential contributor to category-selective responses – chairs and bottles, for instance, are comparatively recent cultural inventions.

Haxby et al. (2001) then pushed this further by showing that these apparently category-selective regions showed distinctive *patterns* of activation across each of the different kinds of object – they didn't only respond to the type of object for which their activation was maximal. For example, the region that was activated most strongly by cats was a little activated by human faces but barely at all active to houses. So from the neural response in this cat-selective part of the cortex we can actually infer something about which category of stimulus a person is looking at (a big response is cats, intermediate is faces, less still is houses) – not simply whether they are looking at cats or not.

This is a key theoretical point. Identifying regions such as FFA based on maximal neural responses can create the impression that the identified region is a processing 'module' responsible for perceiving faces. What Haxby et al. (2001) showed, though, is that you can still tell whether a person is looking at a face from brain activations recorded entirely *outside* the face-selective regions, *if* you analyse the pattern of activations rather than concentrating exclusively on the maxima. It was a timely reminder that we were simply assuming that maximal responses are what count, whereas the brain could be doing something different. Haxby et al. (2001) also pointed out that the brain regions that are seemingly cat-selective, bottle-selective, shoe-selective, and so on show a consistent topography across different individuals – they are not located at random. They suggested the brain might use some form of population coding of responses across regions of cortex arranged in terms of the visual, structural and even semantic properties of things in the world. From this standpoint, critical information is highly distributed across cortical regions, and this contrasts markedly with the more focal representations implied by naming regions FFA, PPA, and so on.

Which of these views is correct? It is not going to be easy to tell definitively, because we are relying on inferences from correlations with regional neural activity (worse, it is actually consequent haemodynamic changes, not neural events themselves – see Chapter 2). What Haxby et al.'s work shows very elegantly is that more information is available in the pattern of correlated neural activity than analyses based on category-selective regional activity routinely use. What it doesn't show is that *the brain* itself uses this information!

Some findings fit very well with the idea that the category-selective regions are indeed critical. Andrews et al. (2002) cleverly made use of the Rubin figure, which can be seen as two face profiles or a vase according to which part of the image is foreground or background (Figure 8.16). Participants viewed this image in an fMRI scanner, reporting when they saw the faces and when they saw the vase. In order to achieve sufficiently slow switches in face or vase responses needed for fMRI analysis, the participant's percept was manipulated by adding subtle contrast gradients at the boundary between the black and white regions of the figure. Seeing the Rubin figure as faces was correlated with increased activation in the FFA (as identified by a functional localiser), but not in the STS. Provocatively, this study links the FFA not just to perception of faces, but to *conscious* perception of faces. After all, the Rubin figure is physically the same whether it is seen as faces or vase – what changes is the percept.

Figure 8.16 Rubin's face–vase figure.

The important point that responses from regions like FFA are not purely stimulus-driven shows up in other studies, too. O'Craven, Downing and Kanwisher (1999) created stimuli that showed faces superimposed on houses (see Figure 8.17), with one of the images moving slowly across the other. They asked their participants to attend to the face, the house, or whichever was moving, and found that attention to faces enhanced the neural response from the FFA and attention to houses enhanced responses from the PPA. And when they recorded neural responses to faces and bodies Morris, Pelphrey and McCarthy (2006) found interactions between regions that might otherwise be considered face- or body-selective.

A further study by Andrews and Schluppeck (2004) used pictures of faces, objects and Mooney faces as stimuli (Figure 8.18). Mooney faces are high-contrast images that look like collections of black and white blobs until the face is seen. A localiser scan comparing responses to the faces and objects was used to identify face-selective and object-selective regions of cortex, which were then used as ROIs in which event-related responses to specific Mooney face images were compared between those participants who saw them as faces or as blobs. Seeing the Mooney face as a face increased activation in the FFA, but had no effect on STS or the object-selective regions of ventral occipito-temporal cortex. As for Andrews et al. (2002), this both links FFA to conscious perception of a face and shows a less graded response from other cortical regions than might be expected based on Haxby et al.'s (2001) hypothesis of a widely distributed functional representation.

Horner and Andrews (2009) took a slightly different tack by investigating the linearity of the responses of FFA and PPA to face-likeness or place-likeness. This gets directly at Haxby et al.'s (2001) claim that sub-maximal activations could be functionally significant. They identified FFA and PPA for each participant with a localiser scan, and then presented faces or houses that were systematically degraded by reducing the phase coherence of each image (see Figure 8.19). The focus of interest is in whether there will be a linearly increasing

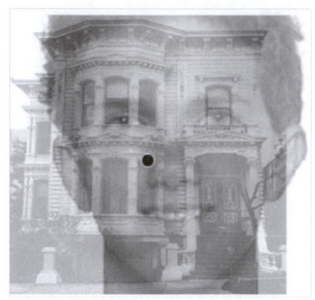

Figure 8.17 A single frame from superimposed materials used by O'Craven et al. (1999). Reprinted by permission from Macmillan Publishers Ltd: *Nature*, fMRI evidence for objects as the units of attentional selection, Kathleen M. O'Craven, Paul E. Downing and Nancy Kanwisher, *401, 6753*, pp. 584–587, copyright 1999.

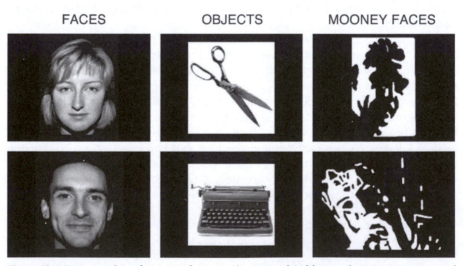

Figure 8.18 Examples of images from Andrews and Schluppeck (2004). Reprinted from *NeuroImage*, *21*, 1, Timothy J. Andrews, Denis Schluppeck, Neural responses to Mooney images reveal a modular representation of faces in human visual cortex, pp. 91–98. Copyright 2004, with permission from Elsevier.

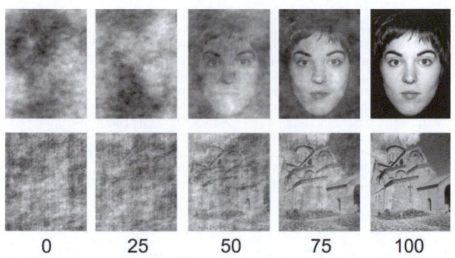

0   25   50   75   100

Figure 8.19 Examples of face and place images at different levels of % phase coherence. First published in Horner and Andrews (2009), Figure 1, p. 2630. Linearity of the fMRI response in category-selective regions of human visual cortex. *Human Brain Mapping*, 30, pp. 2628–2640. Copyright John Wiley and Sons.

activation response to the degree of face-likeness or place-likeness of each image in FFA and in PPA. Horner and Andrews did find linear responses, but only in the area that was selective for that stimulus. In other words, FFA showed a linear-response to face-likeness but not to place-likeness, whereas PPA showed a linear-response to place-likeness but not to face-likeness. So the category-selective response does seem to be graded, but only for its category of interest.

Although Haxby et al.'s (2001) claim that representations in the occipito-temporal cortex are functionally distributed is an important one, then, it is not fully supported by subsequent findings, and recent theories are beginning to incorporate parts of the distributed *and* more modular claims (Op de Beeck et al., 2008). We are optimistic that this could be a step in the right direction.

Summary

We have seen how, through what appears to be a combination of innate perceptual mechanisms and prenatal learning, the infant comes into the world ready to perceive faces and start learning about them. Infancy is a period of remarkable perceptual development, with changes that lead to an increasing specialisation for own-group faces and some consequent loss of ability for faces that do not belong in this category. During the childhood years, face processing abilities seem steadily to improve, but with little evidence of any fundamental change in mechanism. In fact, specific face recognition abilities have to be modified throughout adulthood, because of the need constantly to learn new faces and to adapt to age-related changes in the faces we already know.

Studies of atypical development due to congenital disorders or early visual deprivation offer persuasive evidence of the extent to which the development of face perception and recognition skills are influenced by neurodevelopmental factors, and this raises the question of whether faces are 'special'. We evaluated this in terms of some of Fodor's criteria for modularity, revisiting developmental evidence and introducing relevant evidence from neuropsychology and functional brain imaging. On balance, face perception does seem to fulfil Fodor's criteria of innateness, localisation and specificity, though in each case these need some qualification. Some aspects of face perception appear to be innate, but all appear modifiable through experience. There appear to be some areas of the brain particularly involved in face recognition but these also form part of a distributed network that helps us to recognise other kinds of objects too.

Further reading

Behrmann, M., & Avidan, G. (2005). Congenital prosopagnosia: Face-blind from birth. *Trends in Cognitive Sciences*, *9*, 180–187.
A concise review of some of the first cases of congenital prosopagnosia.

Grill-Spector, K., Golarai, G., & Gabrieli, J. (2008). Developmental neuroimaging of the human ventral visual cortex. *Trends in Cognitive Sciences*, *12*, 152–162.
Describes some of the studies which show the protracted development of these critical areas.

Johnson, M. H. (2005). Subcortical face processing. *Nature Reviews Neuroscience*, *6*, 766–774.
Describes the subcortical routes important in Johnson and Morton's theory of neonatal perception of faces.

McKone, E., Kanwisher, N., & Duchaine, B. C. (2007). Can generic expertise explain special processing for faces? *Trends in Cognitive Sciences*, *11*, 8–15.
A critical review of the 'expertise' hypothesis.

Pascalis, O., & Kelly, D. J. (2009). The origins of face processing in humans: Phylogeny and ontogeny. *Perspectives on Psychological Science*, *4*, 200–209.
An excellent review of some of the research on infant perception of faces we have touched on here.

Aftermath

And so, dear reader, we reach the end of our journey. We hope you found out a few things along the way. Sadly, the destination turns out to be just an arbitrary stopping point, with only the sketchiest pointer to the way ahead. By the time you read this, others will already have moved on, and some of the paths we travelled may already have been closed or diverted. That is the nature of progress in what remains a relatively new scientific area.

Where will they have gone? We don't know, but we hope we have made it clear that despite what we think has been substantial progress, some of the big questions remain unanswered. If the area has engaged your interest, there is plenty for you to do!

References

Abbas, Z.-A., & Duchaine, B. (2008). The role of holistic processing in judgments of facial attractiveness. *Perception, 37*, 1187–1196.

Adams, R. B., & Kleck, R. E. (2003). Perceived gaze direction and the processing of facial displays of emotion. *Psychological Science, 14*, 644–647.

Adolphs, R., Baron-Cohen, S., & Tranel, D. (2002). Impaired recognition of social emotions following amygdala damage. *Journal of Cognitive Neuroscience, 14*, 1264–1274.

Adolphs, R., Damasio, H., Tranel, D., Cooper, G., & Damasio, A. R. (2000). A role for somato-sensory cortices in the visual recognition of emotion as revealed by three-dimensional lesion mapping. *Journal of Neuroscience, 20*, 2683–2690.

Adolphs, R., Gosselin, F., Buchanan, T. W., Tranel, D., Schyns, P., & Damasio, A. R. (2005). A mechanism for impaired fear recognition after amygdala damage. *Nature, 433*, 68–72.

Adolphs, R., & Tranel, D. (1999). Intact recognition of emotional prosody following amygdala damage. *Neuropsychologia, 37*, 1285–1292.

Adolphs, R., Tranel, D., & Damasio, A. R. (1998). The human amygdala in social judgment. *Nature, 393*, 470–474.

Adolphs, R., Tranel, D., & Damasio, A. R. (2003). Dissociable neural systems for recognizing emotions. *Brain and Cognition, 52*, 61–69.

Adolphs, R., Tranel, D., Damasio, H., & Damasio, A. (1994). Impaired recognition of emotion in facial expressions following bilateral damage to the human amygdala. *Nature, 372*, 669–672.

Adolphs, R., Tranel, D., Hamann, S., Young, A. W., Calder, A. J., Phelps, E., et al. (1999). Recognition of facial emotion in nine individuals with bilateral amygdala damage. *Neuropsychologia, 37*, 1111–1117.

Akiyama, T., Kato, M., Muramatsu, T. Saito, F., Umeda, S., & Kashima, H. (2006). Gaze but not arrows: A dissociative impairment after right superior temporal gyrus damage. *Neuropsychologia, 44*, 1804–1810.

Akiyami, T., Kato, M., Muramatsu, T., Saito, F., Nakachi, R., & Kashima, H. (2006). A deficit in discriminating gaze detection in a case with right temporal gyrus lesion. *Neuropsychologia, 44*, 161–170

Alexander, M. P., Stuss, D. T., & Benson, D. F. (1979). Capgras syndrome: A reduplicative phenomenon. *Neurology, 29*, 334–339.

Aljuhanay, A., Milne, E., Burt, D. M., & Pascalis, O. (2010). Asymmetry in face processing during childhood measured with chimeric faces. *Laterality, 15*, 439–450.

Allison, T., Puce, A., & McCarthy, G. (2000). Social perception from visual cues: Role of the STS region. *Trends in Cognitive Sciences, 4*, 267–278.

Allport, G. W. (1954). *The nature of prejudice.* Cambridge, MA: Addison-Wesley.

Alsius, A., Navarra, J., Campbell, R., & Soto-Faraco, S. (2005). Audiovisual integration of speech falters under high attention demands. *Current Biology, 15*, 839–843.

Ambadar, Z., Schooler, J. W., & Cohn, J. F. (2005). Deciphering the enigmatic face: The importance of facial dynamics in interpreting subtle facial expressions. *Psychological Science, 16*, 404–410.

Ames, C. S., & Jarrold, C. (2007). The problem with using eye-gaze to infer desire: A deficit of cue inference in children with Autism Spectrum Disorder? *Journal of Autism and Developmental Disorders, 37*, 1761–1775.

Anastasi, J. S., & Rhodes, M. G. (2005). An own-age bias in face recognition for children and older adults. *Psychonomic Bulletin & Review, 12*, 1043–1047.

Ando, S. (2002). Luminance-induced shift in the apparent direction of gaze. *Perception, 31*, 657–674.

Andrews, T. J., Davies-Thompson, J., Kingstone, A., & Young, A. W. (2010). Internal and external features of the face are represented holistically in face-selective regions of visual cortex. *Journal of Neuroscience, 30*, 3544–3552.

Andrews, T. J., & Ewbank, M. P. (2004). Distinct representations for facial identity and changeable aspects of faces in the human temporal lobe. *NeuroImage, 23*, 905–913.

Andrews, T. J., & Schluppeck, D. (2004). Neural responses to Mooney images reveal a modular representation of faces in human visual cortex. *NeuroImage, 21*, 91–98.

Andrews, T. J., Schluppeck, D., Homfray, D., Matthews, P., & Blakemore, C. (2002). Activity in the fusiform gyrus predicts conscious perception of Rubin's vase-face illusion. *NeuroImage, 17*, 890–901.

Anstis, S. M., Mayhew, J. W., & Morley, T. (1969). The perception of where another face or television 'portrait' is looking. *American Journal of Psychology, 82*, 474–489.

Apperly, I. A. (2010). *Mindreaders: The cognitive basis of 'Theory of Mind'.* Hove: Psychology Press.

Apperly, I. A., Samson, D., Chiavarino, C., & Humphreys, G. W. (2004). Frontal and temporo-parietal lobe contributions to theory of mind: Neuropsychological evidence from a false-belief task with reduced language and executive demands. *Journal of Cognitive Neuroscience, 16*, 1773–1784.

Apperly, I. A., Samson, D., & Humphreys, G. W. (2005). Domain-specificity and theory of mind: Evaluating neuropsychological evidence. *Trends in Cognitive Sciences, 9*, 572–577.

Asghar, A. U. R., Chiu, Y.-C., Hallam, G., Liu, S., Mole, H., Wright, H., & Young, A. W. (2008). An amygdala response to fearful faces with covered eyes. *Neuropsychologia, 46*, 2364–2370.

Atkinson, J. (1995). Through the eyes of an infant. In R. Gregory, J. Harris, P. Heard, & D. Rose (Eds.), *The artful eye.* Oxford: Oxford University Press.

Aubergé, V., & Cathiard, M. (2003). Can we hear the prosody of smile? *Speech Communication, 40*, 87–97.

Avidan, G., & Behrmann, M. (2008). Implicit familiarity processing in congenital prosopagnosia. *Journal of Neuropsychology, 2*, 141–164.

Avidan, G., & Behrmann, M. (2009). Functional MRI reveals compromised neural integrity of the face processing network in congenital prosopagnosia. *Current Biology, 19,* 1146–1150.

Aviezer, H., Hassin, R. R., Ryan, J., Grady, C., Susskind, J., Anderson, A., et al. (2008). Angry, disgusted, or afraid? Studies on the malleability of emotion perception. *Psychological Science, 19,* 724–732.

Aylward, E. H., Park, J. E., Field, K. M., Parsons, A. C., Richards, T. L., Cramer, S. C., et al. (2005). Brain activation during face perception: Evidence of a developmental change. *Journal of Cognitive Neuroscience, 17,* 308–319.

Bahrick, H. P., Bahrick, P. O., & Wittlinger, R. P. (1975). Fifty years of memory for names and faces: A cross-sectional approach. *Journal of Experimental Psychology: General, 104,* 54–75.

Banks, M. S., & Salapatek, P. (1981). Infant pattern vision – a new approach based on the contrast sensitivity function. *Journal of Experimental Child Psychology, 31,* 1–45.

Baraitser, M., & Winter, R. M. (1983). *A colour atlas of clinical genetics.* London: Wolfe Medical.

Baron, R. J. (1981). Mechanisms of human facial recognition. *International Journal of Man-Machine Studies, 15,* 137–178.

Baron-Cohen, S. (1995). *Mindblindness: An essay on autism and Theory of Mind.* Cambridge, MA: MIT Press.

Baron-Cohen, S. (2005). The Empathizing system. A revision of the 1994 model of the Mindreading system. In B. Ellis & D. Bjorkland (Eds.), *Origins of the social mind.* New York: Guilford Publications.

Baron-Cohen, S. (2009). Autism: The empathizing-systemising (E-S) theory. *Annals of the New York Academy of Sciences, 1156,* 68–80.

Baron-Cohen, S., & Cross, P. (1992). Reading the eyes: Evidence for the role of perception in the development of a theory of mind. *Mind & Language, 7,* 172–186.

Baron-Cohen, S., Leslie, A. M., & Frith, U. (1985). Does the autistic child have a 'theory of mind'? *Cognition, 21,* 37–46.

Baron-Cohen, S., Campbell, R., Karmiloff-Smith, A., Grant, J., & Walker, J. (1995). Are children with autism blind to the mentalistic significance of the eyes? *British Journal of Developmental Psychology, 13,* 379–398.

Barrett, L. F., & Kensinger, E. A. (2010). Context is routinely encoded during emotion perception. *Psychological Science, 21,* 595–599.

Bartlett, J. C., Hurry, S., & Thorley, W. (1984). Typicality and familiarity of faces. *Memory & Cognition, 12,* 219–228.

Bartlett, J. C., & Searcy, J. (1993). Inversion and configuration of faces. *Cognitive Psychology, 25,* 281–316.

Barton, J. J. S. (2008). Structure and function in acquired prosopagnosia: Lessons from a series of 10 patients with brain damage. *Journal of Neuropsychology, 2,* 197–225.

Barton, J. J. S., Cherkasova, M., & O'Connor, M. (2001). Covert recognition in acquired and developmental prosopagnosia. *Neurology, 57,* 1161–1168.

Bassili, J. M. (1978). Facial motion in the perception of faces and of emotional expression. *Journal of Experimental Psychology: Human Perception & Performance, 4,* 373–379.

Bateson, M., Nettle, D., & Roberts, G. (2006). Cues of being watched enhance cooperation in a real-world setting. *Biology Letters, 2,* 412–414.

Bateson, P. P. G. (1966). The characteristics and context of imprinting. *Biological Review, 41,* 177–220.

Bateson, P. (1978). Sexual imprinting and optimal outbreeding. *Nature, 273,* 659–660.

Batki, A., Baron-Cohen, S., Wheelwright, S., Connellan, J., & Ahluwalia, J. (2000). Is there an innate gaze module? Evidence from human neonates. *Infant Behavior & Development, 23,* 223–229.

Baudouin, J.-Y., & Humphreys, G. W. (2006). Configural information in gender categorisation. *Perception, 35*, 531–540.

Bauer, R. M. (1984). Autonomic recognition of names and faces in prosopagnosia: A neuropsychological application of the guilty knowledge test. *Neuropsychologia, 22*, 457–469.

Bayliss, A. P., de Pellegrino, G., & Tipper, S. P. (2005). Sex differences in eye gaze and symbolic cuing of attention. *Quarterly Journal of Experimental Psychology, 58A*, 631–650.

Bayliss, A. P., Griffiths, D., & Tipper, S. P. (2009). Predictive gaze cues affect face evaluations: The effect of facial emotion. *European Journal of Cognitive Psychology, 21*, 1072–1084.

Bayliss, A. P., Paul, M. A., Cannon, P. R., & Tipper, S. P. (2006). Gaze cuing and affective judgments of objects: I like what you look at. *Psychonomic Bulletin & Review, 13*, 1061–1066.

Bear, D. M. (1983). Hemispheric specialization and the neurology of emotion. *Archives of Neurology, 40*, 195–202.

Beauchamp, M. S., Nath, A. R., & Pasalar, S. (2010). fMRI-guided transcranial magnetic stimulation reveals that the superior temporal sulcus is a cortical locus of the McGurk effect. *Journal of Neuroscience, 30*, 2414–2417.

Bedny, M., Pascual-Leone, A., & Saxe, R. R. (2009). Growing up blind does not change the neural basis of Theory of Mind. *Proceedings of the National Academy of Sciences, USA, 106*, 11312–11317.

Behrmann, M., & Avidan, G. (2005). Congenital prosopagnosia: Face-blind from birth. *Trends in Cognitive Sciences, 9*, 180–187.

Behrmann, M., Avidan, G., Gao, F., & Black, S. (2007). Structural imaging reveals anatomical alterations in inferotemporal cortex in prosopagnosia. *Cerebral Cortex, 17*, 2354–2363.

Behrmann, M., Marotta, J., Gauthier, I., Tarr, M. J., & McKeeff, T. J. (2005). Behavioral change and its neural correlates in visual agnosia after expertise training. *Journal of Cognitive Neuroscience, 17*, 554–568.

Belin, P., Fecteau, S., & Bédard, C. (2004). Thinking the voice: Neural correlates of voice perception. *Trends in Cognitive Sciences, 8*, 129–135.

Bell, C. (1844). *The anatomy and philosophy of expression, as connected with the fine arts* (3rd ed.). London: George Bell.

Benson, P. J., & Perrett, D. I. (1991a). Computer averaging and manipulation of faces. In P. Wombwell (Ed.), *Photovideo: Photography in the age of the computer* (pp. 32–51). London: Rivers Oram.

Benson, P. J., & Perrett, D. I. (1991b). Perception and recognition of photographic quality facial caricatures: Implications for the recognition of natural images. *European Journal of Cognitive Psychology, 3*, 105–135.

Bentin, S., Allison, T., Puce, A., Perez, E., & McCarthy, G. (1996). Electrophysiological studies of face perception in humans. *Journal of Cognitive Neuroscience, 8*, 551–565.

Benton, A. L. (1980). The neuropsychology of facial recognition. *American Psychologist, 35*, 176–186.

Benton, A. L., Hamsher, K. S., Varney, N., & Spreen, O. (1983). *Contributions to neuropsychological assessment: A clinical manual*. Oxford: Oxford University Press.

Berry, D. S., & McArthur, L. Z. (1985). Some components and consequences of a baby-face. *Journal of Personality and Social Psychology, 48*, 312–323.

Berry, D. S., & Zebrowitz-McArthur, L. (1988). What's in a face? The impact of facial maturity and defendent intent on the attribution of legal responsibility. *Personality and Social Psychology Bulletin, 14*, 23–33.

Bestelmeyer, P. E. G., Jones, B. C., DeBruine, L. M., Little, A. C., Perrett, D. I., Schneider, A., et al. (2008). Sex-contingent face aftereffects depend on perceptual category rather than structural encoding. *Cognition, 107*, 353–365.

Bickart, K. C., Wright, C. I., Dautoff, R. J., Dickerson, D. D., & Barrett, L. F. (2011). Amygdala volume and social network size in humans. *Nature Neuroscience, 14,* 163–164.

Biederman, I., & Kolocsai, P. (1997). Neurocomputational bases of object and face recognition. *Philosophical Transactions of the Royal Society, London, B: Biological Sciences, 352,* 1203–1219.

Bimler, D., & Kirkland, J. (2001). Categorical perception of facial expressions of emotion: Evidence from multidimensional scaling. *Cognition and Emotion, 15,* 633–658.

Bindemann, M., & Burton, A. M. (2009). The role of color in human face detection. *Cognitive Science, 33,* 1144–1156.

Bindemann, M., Burton, A. M., & Jenkins, R. (2005). Capacity limits for face processing. *Cognition, 98,* 177–197.

Bindemann, M., Burton, A. M., & Langton, S. R. H. (2008). How do eye gaze and facial expression interact? *Visual Cognition, 16,* 708–733.

Bindemann, M., Burton, A. M., Leuthold, H., & Schweinberger, S. R. (2008). Brain potential correlates of face recognition: Geometric distortions and the N250r brain response to stimulus repetitions. *Psychophysiology, 45,* 535–544.

Birmingham, E., Bischof, W. F., & Kingstone, A. (2009). Get real! Resolving the debate about equivalent social stimuli. *Visual Cognition, 17,* 904–924.

Bishop, D. V. M. (1997). Cognitive neuropsychology and developmental disorders: Uncomfortable bedfellows. *Quarterly Journal of Experimental Psychology, 50A,* 899–923.

Bishop, D. V. M. (2009). Genes, cognition, and communication: Insights from neurodevelopmental disorders. *The Year in Cognitive Neuroscience 2009: Annals of the New York Academy of Sciences, 1156,* 1–18.

Blair, I.V., Judd, C.M., Sadler, M.S., & Jenkins, C. (2002). The role of afrocentric features in person perception: judging by features and categories. *Journal of Personality and Social Psychology, 83,* 5–12.

Blakemore, C. B., & Campbell, F. W. (1969). On the existence of neurones in the human visual system selectively sensitive to the size and orientation of retinal images. *Journal of Physiology, 203,* 237–260.

Blakemore, S. J. (2008). The social brain in adolescence. *Nature Reviews Neuroscience, 9,* 267–277.

Blanz, V., & Vetter, T. (1999). A morphable model for the synthesis of 3D faces. *Proceedings of the 26th Annual Conference on Computer Graphics and Interactive Techniques,* 187–194.

Bodamer, J. (1947). Die Prosopagnosie. *Archiv Fur Psychaitrie und Nervenkrankheiten, 179,* 6–53.

Bodamer, M. D., & Gardner, R. A. (2002). How cross-fostered chimpanzees (Pan troglodytes) initiate and maintain conversations. *Journal of Comparative Psychology, 116,* 12–26.

Bogart, K. R., & Matsumoto, D. (2009). Facial mimicry is not necessary to recognize emotion: Facial expression recognition by people with Moebius syndrome. *Social Neuroscience, 5,* 241–251.

Bonner, L., Burton, A. M., & Bruce, V. (2003). Getting to know you: How we learn new faces. *Visual Cognition, 10,* 527–536.

Bornstein, B. (1963). Prosopagnosia. In L. Halpern (Ed.), *Problems in dynamic neurology* (pp. 283–318). Jerusalem: Hadassah Medical Organization.

Bornstein, R. F. (1989). Exposure and affect: Overview and meta-analysis of research, 1968–1987. *Psychological Bulletin, 106,* 265–289.

Borod, J. C., Cicero, B. A., Obler, L. K., Welkowitz, J., Erhan, H. M., Santschi, C., et al. (1998). Right hemisphere emotional perception: Evidence across multiple channels. *Neuropsychology, 12,* 446–458.

Borod, J. C., Santschi Haywood, C., & Koff, E. (1997). Neuropsychological aspects of facial asymmetry during emotional expression: A review of the normal adult literature. *Neuropsychology Review, 7*, 41–60.

Bourne, V. J. (2006). The divided visual field paradigm: Methodological considerations. *Laterality, 11*, 373–393.

Bourne, V. J. (2008a). Chimeric faces, visual field bias, and reaction time bias: Have we been missing a trick? *Laterality, 13*, 92–103.

Bourne, V. J. (2008b). Examining the relationship between degree of handedness and degree of cerebral lateralization for processing facial emotion. *Neuropsychology, 22*, 350–356.

Bourne, V. J., Vladeneau, M., & Hole, G. J. (2009). Lateralised repetition priming for featurally and configurally manipulated familiar faces: Evidence for differentially lateralised processing mechanisms. *Laterality, 14*, 287–299.

Bowers, J. S. (2009). On the biological plausibility of Grandmother Cells: Implications for neural network theories in psychology and neuroscience. *Psychological Review, 116*, 220–251.

Brédart, S., Brennen, T., Delchambre, M., McNeill, A., & Burton, A. M. (2005). Naming very familiar people: When retrieving names is faster than retrieving semantic biographical information. *British Journal of Psychology, 96*, 205–214.

Brédart, S., Valentine, T., Calder, A., & Gassi, L. (1995). An interactive activation model of face naming. *Quarterly Journal of Experimental Psychology, 48A*, 466–486.

Breen, N., Caine, D., & Coltheart, M. (2000). Models of face recognition and delusional misidentification: A critical review. *Cognitive Neuropsychology, 17*, 55–71.

Brennan, S. E. (1985). The caricature generator. *Leonardo, 18*, 170–178.

Brennen, T., Baguley, T., Bright, J., & Bruce, V. (1990). Resolving semantically induced tip-of-the-tongue states for proper nouns. *Memory & Cognition, 18*, 339–347.

Brennen, T., David, D., Fluchaire, I., & Pellat, J. (1996). Naming faces and objects without comprehension – a case study. *Cognitive Neuropsychology, 13*, 93–110.

Bressan, P., & Dal Martello, M. F. (2002). Talis pater, talis filius: Perceived resemblance and the belief in genetic relatedness. *Psychological Science, 13*, 213–218.

Bressan, P., & Zucchi, G. (2009). Human kin recognition is self- rather than family-referential. *Biology Letters, 5*, 336–338.

Brigham, J. C. (1986). The influence of race on face recognition. In H. D. Ellis, M. A. Jeeves, F. Newcombe, & A. Young (Eds.), *Aspects of face processing* (pp. 170–177). Dordrecht: Martinus Nijhoff.

Broks, P., Young, A. W., Maratos, E. J., Coffey, P. J., Calder, A. J., Isaac, C. L., et al. (1998). Face processing impairments after encephalitis: Amygdala damage and recognition of fear. *Neuropsychologia, 36*, 59–70.

Bronson, G. (1974). The postnatal growth of visual capacity. *Child Development, 45*, 873–890.

Brooks, K. R., & Kemp, R. I. (2007). Sensitivity to feature displacement in familiar and unfamiliar faces: Beyond the internal/external feature distinction. *Perception, 36*, 1646–1659.

Brosch, T., Pourtois, G., & Sander, S. (2010). The perception and categorisation of emotional stimuli: A review. *Cognition and Emotion, 24*, 377–400.

Brothers, L. (1990). The social brain: A project for integrating primate behavior and neurophysiology in a new domain. *Concepts in Neuroscience, 1*, 27–51.

Brown, A. S. (1991). A review of the tip-of-the-tongue experience. *Psychological Bulletin, 109*, 204–223.

Brown, G., Anderson, A. H., Yule, G., & Shillcock, R. (1984). *Teaching talk*. Cambridge: Cambridge University Press.

Brown, R., Hobson, R. P., Lee, A., & Stevenson, A. (1997). Are there autistic-like features in congenitally blind children? *Journal of Child Psychology and Psychiatry, 38*, 693–703.

Bruce, C., Desimone, R., & Gross, C. G. (1981). Visual properties of neurons in a polysensory area in the superior temporal sulcus of the macaque. *Journal of Neurophysiology, 46*, 369–384.

Bruce, V. (1982). Changing faces: Visual and non-visual coding processes in face recognition. *British Journal of Psychology, 73*, 105–116.

Bruce, V. (1986). Recognising familiar faces. In H. D. Ellis, M. A. Jeeves, F. Newcombe, & A. Young (Eds.), *Aspects of face processing*. Dordrecht: Martinus Nijhoff.

Bruce, V., Burton, M., Doyle, T., & Dench, N. (1989). Further experiments on the perception of growth in three dimensions. *Perception & Psychophysics, 46*, 528–536.

Bruce, V., Burton, A. M., Hanna, E., Healey, P., Mason, O., Coombes, A., et al. (1993). Sex discrimination: How do we tell the difference between male and female faces? *Perception, 22*, 131–152.

Bruce, V., Campbell, R. N., Doherty-Sneddon, G., Import, A., Langton, S., McAuley, S., & Wright, R. (2000). Testing face processing skills in children. *British Journal of Developmental Psychology, 18*, 319–333.

Bruce, V., Carson, D., Burton, A. M., & Kelly, S. (1998). Prime time advertisements: Repetition priming from faces seen on subject recruitment posters. *Memory & Cognition, 26*, 502–515.

Bruce, V., Doyle, T., Dench, N., & Burton, M. (1991). Remembering facial configurations. *Cognition, 38*, 109–144.

Bruce, V., Ellis, H. D., Gibling, F., & Young, A. W. (1987). Parallel processing of the sex and familiarity of faces. *Canadian Journal of Psychology, 41*, 510–520.

Bruce, V., Green, P. R., & Georgeson, M. A. (2003). *Visual perception: Physiology, psychology and ecology* (4th ed.). Hove: Psychology Press.

Bruce, V., Healey, P., Burton, A. M., Doyle, T., Coombes, A., & Linney, A. (1991). Recognising facial surfaces. *Perception, 20*, 755–769.

Bruce, V., Henderson, Z., Greenwood, K., Hancock, P. J. B., Burton, A. M., & Miller, P. (1999). Verification of face identities from images captured on video. *Journal of Experimental Psychology: Applied, 5*, 339–360.

Bruce, V., & Langton, S. (1994). The use of pigmentation and shading information in recognising the sex and identities of faces. *Perception, 23*, 803–822.

Bruce, V., Ness, H., Hancock, P. J. B., Newman, C., & Rarity, J. (2002). Four heads are better than one: Combining face composites yields improvements in face likeness. *Journal of Applied Psychology, 87*, 894–902.

Bruce, V., & Valentine, T. (1985). Identity priming in the recognition of familiar faces. *British Journal of Psychology, 76*, 363–383.

Bruce, V., & Valentine, T. (1986). Semantic priming of familiar faces. *Quarterly Journal of Experimental Psychology, 38A*, 125–150.

Bruce, V., & Valentine, T. (1988). When a nod's as good as a wink. The role of dynamic information in facial recognition. In M. M. Gruneberg, P. E. Morris, & R. N. Sykes (Eds.), *Practical aspects of memory: Current research and issues. Volume 1: Memory in everyday life* (pp. 169–174). Chichester: Wiley.

Bruce, V., Valentine, T., & Baddeley, A. D. (1987). The basis of the ¾ view advantage in face recognition. *Applied Cognitive Psychology, 1*, 109–120.

Bruce, V., & Young, A. (1986). Understanding face recognition. *British Journal of Psychology, 77*, 305–327.

Bruce, V., & Young, A. (1998). *In the eye of the beholder: The science of face perception.* Oxford: Oxford University Press.

Bruck, M., Cavanagh, P., & Ceci, S. (1991). Fortysomething: Recognizing faces at one's 25th reunion. *Memory & Cognition, 19*, 221–228.

Bruyer, R. (1991). Covert face recognition in prosopagnosia: A review. *Brain and Cognition, 15*, 223–235.

Bruyer, R., Laterre, C., Seron, X., Feyereisen, P., Strypstein, E., Pierrard, E., et al. (1983). A case of prosopagnosia with some preserved covert remembrance of familiar faces. *Brain and Cognition, 2*, 257–284.

Bull, R., & Hawkes, C. (1982). Judging politicians by their faces. *Political Studies, 30*, 95–101.

Bull, R., Jenkins, M., & Stevens, J. (1983). Evaluations of politicians' faces. *Political Psychology, 4*, 713–716.

Bull, R., & Rumsey, N. (1988). *The social psychology of facial appearance.* New York: Springer-Verlag.

Bülthoff, I., & Newell, F. N. (2004). Categorical perception of sex occurs in familiar but not unfamiliar faces. *Visual Cognition, 11*, 823–855.

Burt, D. M., & Perrett, D. I. (1995). Perception of age in adult Caucasian male faces: Computer graphic manipulation of shape and colour information. *Proceedings of the Royal Society, London, B: Biological Sciences, 259*, 137–143.

Burt, D. M., & Perrett, D. I. (1997). Perceptual asymmetries in judgements of facial attractiveness, age, gender, speech and expression. *Neuropsychologia, 35*, 685–693.

Burton, A. M., Bindemann, M., Langton, S. R. H., Schweinberger, S. R., & Jenkins, R. (2009). Gaze perception requires focused attention: Evidence from an interference task. *Journal of Experimental Psychology: Human Perception & Performance, 35*, 108–118.

Burton, A. M., & Bonner, L. (2004). Familiarity influences judgments of sex: The case of voice recognition. *Perception, 33*, 747–752.

Burton, A. M., & Bruce, V. (1992). I recognise your face but I can't remember your name: A simple explanation? *British Journal of Psychology, 83*, 45–60.

Burton, A. M., Bruce, V., & Dench, N. (1993). What's the difference between men and women? Evidence from facial measurement. *Perception, 22*, 153–176.

Burton, A. M., Bruce, V., & Hancock, P. J. B. (1999). From pixels to people: A model of familiar face recognition. *Cognitive Science, 23*, 1–31.

Burton, A. M., Bruce, V., & Johnston, R. A. (1990). Understanding face recognition with an interactive activation model. *British Journal of Psychology, 81*, 361–380.

Burton, A. M., Jenkins, R., Hancock, P. J. B., & White, D. (2005). Robust representations for face recognition: The power of averages. *Cognitive Psychology, 51*, 256–284.

Burton, A. M., & Vokey, J. R. (1998). The face-space typicality paradox: Understanding the face-space metaphor. *Quarterly Journal of Experimental Psychology, 51A*, 475–483.

Burton, A. M., Wilson, S., Cowan, M., & Bruce, V. (1999). Face recognition in poor-quality video: Evidence from security surveillance. *Psychological Science, 10*, 243–248.

Burton, A. M., Young, A. W., Bruce, V., Johnston, R., & Ellis, A. W. (1991). Understanding covert recognition. *Cognition, 39*, 129–166.

Bushnell, I. W. R., Sai, F., & Mullin, J. T. (1989). Neonatal recognition of the mother's face. *British Journal of Developmental Psychology, 7*, 3–15.

Bushnell, I. W. R. (2003). Newborn face recognition. In O. Pascalis & A. Slater (Eds.), *The development of face processing in infancy and early childhood* (pp. 41–54). New York: Nova Science Publishers, Inc.

Busigny, T., Robaye, L., Dricot, L., & Rossion, B. (2009). Right anterior temporal lobe atrophy and person-based semantic deficit: A detailed case study. *Neurocase, 15*, 485–508.

Busigny, T., & Rossion, B. (2010). Acquired prosopagnosia abolishes the face inversion effect. *Cortex, 46*, 965–981.

Butler, S., Gilchrist, I. D., Burt, D. M., Perrett, D. I., Jones, E., & Harvey, M. (2005). Are the perceptual biases found in chimeric face processing reflected in eye-movement patterns? *Neuropsychologia*, *43*, 52–59.

Cabeza, R., Bruce, V., Kato, T., & Oda, M. (1999). The prototype effect in face recognition: Extension and limits. *Memory & Cognition*, *27*, 139–151.

Caldara, R., Schyns, P., Mayer, E., Smith, M. L., Gosselin, F., & Rossion, B. (2005). Does prosopagnosia take the eyes out of face representations? Evidence for a defect in representing diagnostic facial information following brain damage. *Journal of Cognitive Neuroscience*, *17*, 1–15.

Calder, A. J., Beaver, J. D., Winston, J. S., Dolan, R. J., Jenkins, R., Eger, E., et al. (2007). Separate coding of different gaze directions in the superior temporal sulcus and inferior parietal lobule. *Current Biology*, *17*, 20–25.

Calder, A. J., Burton, A. M., Miller, P., Young, A. W., & Akamatsu, S. (2001). A principal component analysis of facial expressions. *Vision Research*, *41*, 1179–1208.

Calder, A. J., Jenkins, R., Cassel, A., & Clifford, C. W. G. (2008). Visual representation of eye gaze is coded by a nonopponent multichannel system. *Journal of Experimental Psychology: General*, *137*, 244–261.

Calder, A. J., Keane, J., Cole, J., Campbell, R., & Young, A. W. (2000). Facial expression recognition by people with Möbius syndrome. *Cognitive Neuropsychology*, *17*, 73–87.

Calder, A. J., Keane, J., Manes, F., Antoun, N., & Young, A. W. (2000). Impaired recognition and experience of disgust following brain injury. *Nature Neuroscience*, *3*, 1077–1078.

Calder, A. J., Keane, J., Manly, T., Sprengelmeyer, R., Scott, S., Nimmo-Smith, I., & Young, A. W. (2003). Facial expression recognition across the adult life span. *Neuropsychologia*, *41*, 195–202.

Calder, A. J., Keane, J., Young, A. W., Lawrence, A. D., Mason, S., & Barker, R. A. (2010). The relation between anger and different forms of disgust: Implications for emotion recognition impairments in Huntington's disease. *Neuropsychologia*, *49*, 2719-2729.

Calder, A. J., Lawrence, A. D., Keane, J., Scott, S. K., Owen, A. M., Christoffels, I., & Young, A. W. (2002). Reading the mind from eye gaze. *Neuropsychologia*, *40*, 1129–1138.

Calder, A. J., Lawrence, A. D., & Young, A. W. (2001). Neuropsychology of fear and loathing. *Nature Reviews Neuroscience*, *2*, 352–363.

Calder, A. J., Rowland, D., Young, A. W., Nimmo-Smith, I., Keane, J., & Perrett, D. I. (2000). Caricaturing facial expressions. *Cognition*, *76*, 105–146.

Calder, A. J., & Young, A. W. (1996). Self priming: A short-term benefit of repetition. *Quarterly Journal of Experimental Psychology*, *49A*, 845–861.

Calder, A. J., & Young, A. W. (2005). Understanding the recognition of facial identity and facial expression. *Nature Reviews Neuroscience*, *6*, 645–651.

Calder, A. J., Young, A. W., Keane, J., & Dean, M. (2000). Configurational information in facial expression perception. *Journal of Experimental Psychology: Human Perception & Performance*, *26*, 527–551.

Calder, A. J., Young, A. W., Perrett, D. I., Etcoff, N. L., & Rowland, D. (1996). Categorical perception of morphed facial expressions. *Visual Cognition*, *3*, 81–117.

Calder, A. J., Young, A. W., Rowland, D., & Perrett, D. I. (1997). Computer-enhanced emotion in facial expressions. *Proceedings of the Royal Society, London, B: Biological Sciences*, *264*, 919–925.

Calder, A. J., Young, A. W., Rowland, D., Perrett, D. I., Hodges, J. R., & Etcoff, N. L. (1996). Facial emotion recognition after bilateral amygdala damage: Differentially severe impairment of fear. *Cognitive Neuropsychology*, *13*, 699–745.

Calderwood, L., & Burton, A. M. (2006). Children and adults recall the names of highly familiar faces faster than semantic information. *British Journal of Psychology*, *97*, 441–454.

Calvert, G. A. (2001). Crossmodal processing in the human brain: Insights from functional neuroimaging studies. *Cerebral Cortex, 11,* 1110–1123.

Calvert, G. A., Bullmore, E. T., Brammer, M. J., Campbell, R., Williams, S. C. R., McGuire, P. K., et al. (1997). Activation of auditory cortex during silent lipreading. *Science, 276,* 593–596.

Calvert, G. A., Campbell, R., & Brammer, M. J. (2000). Evidence from functional magnetic resonance imaging of crossmodal binding in the human heteromodal cortex. *Current Biology, 10,* 649–657.

Calvert, G. A., Hansen, P. C., Iversen, S. D., & Brammer, M. J. (2001). Detection of audio-visual integration sites in humans by application of electrophysiological criteria to the BOLD effect. *NeuroImage, 14,* 427–438.

Campanella, S., & Belin, P. (2007). Integrating face and voice in person perception. *Trends in Cognitive Sciences, 11,* 535–543.

Campanella, S., Chrysochoos, A., & Bruyer, R. (2001). Categorical perception of facial gender information: Behavioural evidence and the face-space metaphor. *Visual Cognition, 8,* 237–262.

Campbell, F. W., & Robson, J. G. (1968). Application of Fourier analysis to the visibility of gratings. *Journal of Physiology, 197,* 551–566.

Campbell, J., & Burke, D. (2009). Evidence that identity-dependent and identity-independent neural populations are recruited in the perception of five basic emotional expressions. *Vision Research, 49,* 1532–1540.

Campbell, R., de Gelder, B., & de Haan, E. (1996). The lateralization of lip-reading: A second look. *Neuropsychologia, 34,* 1235–1240.

Campbell, R., & de Haan, E. H. F. (1998). Repetition priming for face speech images: Speech-reading primes face identification. *British Journal of Psychology, 89,* 309–323.

Campbell, R., Heywood, C. A., Cowey, A., Regard, M., & Landis, T. (1990). Sensitivity to eye gaze in prosopagnosic patients and monkeys with superior temporal sulcus ablation. *Neuropsychologia, 28,* 1123–1142.

Campbell, R., Landis, T., & Regard, M. (1986). Face recognition and lipreading: A neurological dissociation. *Brain, 109,* 509–521.

Carbon, C.-C., Grüter, T., Grüter, M., Weber, J. E., & Lueschow, A. (2010). Dissociation of facial attractiveness and distinctiveness processing in congenital prosopagnosia. *Visual Cognition, 18,* 641–654.

Carey, S. (1992). Becoming a face expert. *Philosophical Transactions of the Royal Society, London, B: Biological Sciences, 335,* 95–103.

Carey, S., & Diamond, R. (1977). From piecemeal to configurational representation of faces. *Science, 195,* 312–314.

Carey, S., Diamond, R., & Woods, B. (1980). The development of face recognition – a maturational component? *Developmental Psychology, 16,* 257–269.

Carmon, A., & Nachshon, I. (1973). Ear asymmetry in perception of emotional non-verbal stimuli. *Acta Psychologica, 37,* 351–357.

Carpenter, R. H. S. (1988). *Movements of the eyes.* (2nd ed.). London: Pion.

Carson, D. R., & Burton, A. M. (2001). Semantic priming of person recognition: Categorial priming may be a weak form of the associative priming effect. *Quarterly Journal of Experimental Psychology, 54A,* 1155–1179.

Chambers, P. (2007). *Body 115: The mystery of the last victim of the King's Cross fire.* Chichester: Wiley.

Chapman, H. A., Kim, D. A., Susskind, J. M., & Anderson, A. K. (2009). In bad taste: Evidence for the oral origins of moral disgust. *Science, 323,* 1222–1226.

Chawarska, K., Kiln, A., & Volkmar, F. (2003). Automatic attention cuing through eye movement in 2-year old children with autism. *Child Development, 74,* 1108–1122.

Chiroro, P., & Valentine, T. (1995). An investigation of the contact hypothesis of the own-race bias in face recognition. *Quarterly Journal of Experimental Psychology, 48A*, 879–894.

Christodoulou, G. N. (1977). The syndrome of Capgras. *British Journal of Psychiatry, 130*, 556–564.

Christodoulou, G. N. (1986). Role of depersonalization-derealization phenomena in the delusional misidentification syndromes. *Bibliotheca Psychiatrica, 164*, 99–104.

Chung, M.-S., & Thomson, D. M. (1995). Development of face recognition. *British Journal of Psychology, 86*, 55–87.

Cline, M. G. (1967). The perception of where a person is looking. *American Journal of Psychology, 80*, 41–50.

Clutterbuck, R., & Johnston, R. A. (2005). Demonstrating how unfamiliar faces become familiar using a face matching task. *European Journal of Cognitive Psychology, 17*, 97–116.

Cohen, G. (1990). Why is it difficult to put names to faces? *British Journal of Psychology, 81*, 287–297.

Cohen, G., & Faulkner, D. (1986). Memory for proper names: Age differences in retrieval. *British Journal of Developmental Psychology, 4*, 187–197.

Cohen Kadosh, K., & Johnson, M. H. (2007). Developing a cortex specialized for face perception. *Trends in Cognitive Sciences, 11*, 367–369.

Coleman, M. N., & Ross, C. F. (2004). Primate auditory diversity and its influence on hearing performance. *The Anatomical Record Part A, 281A*, 1123–1137.

Coetzee, V., Perrett, D. I., & Stephen, I. D. (2009). Facial adiposity: A cue to health? *Perception, 38*, 1700–1711.

Coltheart, M. (2006). What has functional neuroimaging told us about the mind (so far)? *Cortex, 42*, 323–331.

Cook, S. W. (1939). The judgment of intelligence from photographs. *Journal of Abnormal and Social Psychology, 34*, 384–389.

Coombes, A. M., Moss, J. P., Linney, A. D., Richards, R., & James, D. R. (1991). A mathematical method for the comparison of 3-dimensional changes in the facial surface. *European Journal of Orthodontics, 13*, 95–110.

Corkum, V., & Moore, C. (1995). Development of joint visual attention in infants. In C. Moore & P. J. Dunham (Eds.), *Joint attention: Its origins and role in development* (pp. 61–83). Hillsdale, NJ: Lawrence Erlbaum.

Craigie, M., & Hanley, J. R. (1993). Access to visual information from a name is contingent on access to identity-specific semantic information. *Memory, 1*, 367–391.

Crookes, K., & McKone, E. (2009). Early maturity of face recognition: No childhood development of holistic processing, novel face encoding, or face-space. *Cognition, 111*, 219–247.

Cunningham, W. A., Johnson, M. K., Raye, C. L., Gatenby, J. C., Gore, J. C., & Banaji, M. R. (2004). Separable neural components in the processing of black and white faces. *Psychological Science, 15*, 806–813.

Curtis, V., Aunger, R., & Rabie, T. (2004). Evidence that disgust evolved to protect from risk of disease. *Proceedings of the Royal Society, London, B: Biological Sciences, 271*, S131–S133.

Dailey, M. N., Cottrell, G. W., Padgett, C., & Adolphs, R. (2002). EMPATH: A neural network that categorizes facial expressions. *Journal of Cognitive Neuroscience, 14*, 1158–1173.

Dalton, K. M., Naewicz, B. M., Johnstone, T., Scaefer, H. S., Gernsbacher, M. A., Goldsmith, H. H., et al. (2005). Gaze fixation and the neural circuitry of face processing in autism. *Nature Neuroscience, 8*, 519–526.

Damasio, A. R., Damasio, H., & Van Hoesen, G. W. (1982). Prosopagnosia: Anatomic basis and behavioral mechanisms. *Neurology, 32*, 331–341.

Darwin, C. (1859). *The origin of species*. London: John Murray.

Darwin, C. (1872/1904). *The expression of the emotions in man and animals*. London: John Murray.

Davies, G. M. (1996). Mistaken identification: Where law meets psychology head on. *The Howard Journal*, *35*, 232–241.

Davies, G., & Griffiths, L. (2008). Eyewitness identification and the English Courts: A century of trial and error. *Psychiatry, Psychology and Law*, *15*, 435–449.

Davies, G., & Noon, E. (1991). *An evaluation of the live link for child witnesses*. London: UK Home Office Report.

Davies-Thompson, J., Gouws, A., & Andrews, T. J. (2009). An image-dependent representation of familiar and unfamiliar faces in the human ventral stream. *Neuropsychologia*, *47*, 1627–1635.

Davis, J. P., & Valentine, T. (2009). CCTV on trial: Matching video images with the defendant in the dock. *Applied Cognitive Psychology*, *23*, 482–505.

Dawkins, R. (1976). *The selfish gene*. Oxford: Oxford University Press.

de Gelder, B., & Bertelson, P. (2003). Multisensory integration, perception and ecological validity. *Trends in Cognitive Sciences*, *7*, 460–467.

de Gelder, B., Bocker, K. B. E., Tuomainen, J., Hensen, M., & Vroomen, J. (1999). The combined perception of emotion from voice and face: Early interaction revealed by human electric brain responses. *Neuroscience Letters*, *260*, 133–136.

de Gelder, B., & Vroomen, J. (2000). The perception of emotions by ear and eye. *Cognition and Emotion*, *14*, 289–311.

de Haan, E. H. F. (1999). A familial factor in the development of face recognition deficits. *Journal of Clinical and Experimental Neuropsychology*, *21*, 312–315.

de Haan, E. H. F., Bauer, R. M., & Greve, K. W. (1992). Behavioural and physiological evidence for covert face recognition in a prosopagnosic patient. *Cortex*, *28*, 77–95.

de Haan, E. H. F., Young, A., & Newcombe, F. (1987a). Face recognition without awareness. *Cognitive Neuropsychology*, *4*, 385–415.

de Haan, E. H. F., Young, A., & Newcombe, F. (1987b). Faces interfere with name classification in a prosopagnosic patient. *Cortex*, *23*, 309–316.

de Haan, E. H. F., Young, A. W., & Newcombe, F. (1991a). A dissociation between the sense of familiarity and access to semantic information concerning familiar people. *European Journal of Cognitive Psychology*, *3*, 51–67.

de Haan, E. H. F., Young, A. W., & Newcombe, F. (1991b). Covert and overt recognition in prosopagnosia. *Brain*, *114*, 2575–2591.

de Haan, M., Pascalis, O., & Johnson, M. H. (2002). Specialization of neural mechanisms underlying face recognition in human infants. *Journal of Cognitive Neuroscience*, *14*, 199–209.

de Heering, A., Houthuys, S., & Rossion, B. (2007). Holistic face processing is mature at 4 years of age: Evidence from the composite face effect. *Journal of Experimental Child Psychology*, *96*, 57–70.

de Heering, A., & Rossion, B. (2008). Prolonged visual experience in adulthood modulates holistic face perception. *PLos ONE*, *3*, e2317.

de Pauw, K. W., & Szulecka, T. K. (1988). Dangerous delusions: Violence and the misidentification syndromes. *British Journal of Psychiatry*, *152*, 91–97.

De Renzi, E. (1986). Current issues in prosopagnosia. In H. D. Ellis, M. A. Jeeves, F. Newcombe, & A. Young (Eds.), *Aspects of face processing* (pp. 243–252). Dordrecht: Martinus Nijhoff.

De Renzi, E., Faglioni, P., Grossi, D., & Nichelli, P. (1991). Apperceptive and associative forms of prosopagnosia. *Cortex*, *27*, 213–221.

De Renzi, E., Perani, D., Carlesimo, G. A., Silveri, M. C., & Fazio, F. (1994). Prosopagnosia can be associated with damage confined to the right hemisphere – an MRI and PET study and a review of the literature. *Neuropsychologia, 32,* 893–902.

DeBruine, L. M. (2002). Facial resemblance enhances trust. *Proceedings of the Royal Society, London, B: Biological Sciences, 269,* 1307–1312.

DeBruine, L. M. (2004). Facial resemblance increases the attractiveness of same-sex faces more than other-sex faces. *Proceedings of the Royal Society, London, B: Biological Sciences, 271,* 2085–2090.

DeBruine, L. M., Jones, B. C., Unger, L., Little, A. C., & Feinberg, D. R. (2007). Dissociating averageness and attractiveness: Attractive faces are not always average. *Journal of Experimental Psychology: Human Perception & Performance, 33,* 1420–1430.

Decasper, A. J., & Fifer, W. P. (1980). Of human bonding – newborns prefer their mothers' voices. *Science, 208,* 1174–1176.

Devlin, Lord (1976). *Report to the Secretary of State for the Home Department of the Departmental Committee on Evidence of Identification in Criminal Cases.* London: HMSO.

Diamond, B. J., Valentine, T., Mayes, A. R., & Sandel, M. E. (1994). Evidence of covert recognition in a prosopagnosic patient. *Cortex, 30,* 377–393.

Diamond, R., & Carey, S. (1977). Developmental changes in the representation of faces. *Journal of Experimental Child Psychology, 23,* 1–22.

Diamond, R., & Carey, S. (1986). Why faces are and are not special: An effect of expertise. *Journal of Experimental Psychology: General, 115,* 107–117.

Diamond, R., Carey, S., & Back, K. J. (1983). Genetic influences on the development of spatial skills during early adolescence. *Cognition, 13,* 167–185.

Dion, K. (1992). Physical attractiveness and evaluation of children's transgressions. *Journal of Personality and Social Psychology, 24,* 207–213.

Dion, K., Berscheid, E., & Walster, E. (1972). What is beautiful is good. *Journal of Personality and Social Psychology, 24,* 285–290.

Doherty, M. J. (2006). The development of mentalistic gaze understanding. *Infant and Child Development, 15,* 179–186.

Doherty-Sneddon, G., & McAuley, S. (2000). Influence of video-mediation on adult-child interviews: Implications for the use of the live link with child witnesses. *Applied Cognitive Psychology, 14,* 379–392.

Doherty-Sneddon, G., O'Malley, C., Garrod, S., Anderson, A., Langton, S., & Bruce, V. (1997). Face-to-face and video-mediated communication: A comparison of dialogue structure and task performance. *Journal of Experimental Psychology: Applied, 3,* 1–21.

Doherty-Sneddon, G., Bruce, V., Bonner, L., Longbotham, S., & Doyle, C. (2002). Development of gaze aversion as disengagement from visual information. *Developmental Psychology, 38,* 438–445.

Doherty-Sneddon, G., & Phelps, F. G. (2005). Gaze aversion: A response to cognitive or social difficulty? *Memory & Cognition, 33,* 727–733.

Doherty-Sneddon, G., Phelps, F., & Clark, J. (2007). Development of gaze aversion: Qualitative changes over the early school years. *British Journal of Developmental Psychology, 25,* 513–526.

Dotsch, R., Wigboldus, D. H. J., Langner, O., & van Knippenberg, A. (2008). Ethnic out-group faces are biased in the prejudiced mind. *Psychological Science, 19,* 978–980.

Driver, J., Davis, G., Ricciardelli, P., Kidd, P., Maxwell, E., & Baron-Cohen, S. (1999). Shared attention and the social brain: Gaze perception triggers automatic visuospatial orienting in adults. *Visual Cognition, 6,* 509–540.

Dubernard, J. M., Lengele, B., Morelon, E., Testelin, S., Badet, L., Moure, C., et al. (2007). Outcomes 18 months after the first human partial face transplantation. *New England Journal of Medicine, 357,* 2451–2460.

Duchaine, B., Dingle, K., Butterworth, E., & Nakayama, K. (2004). Normal greeble learning in a severe case of developmental prosopagnosia. *Neuron, 43*, 469–473.

Duchaine, B., Germine, L., & Nakayama, K. (2007). Family resemblance: Ten family members with prosopagnosia and within-class object agnosia. *Cognitive Neuropsychology, 24*, 419–430.

Duchaine, B., Jenkins, R., Germine, L., & Calder, A. J. (2009). Normal gaze discrimination and adaptation in seven prosopagnosics. *Neuropsychologia, 47*, 2029–2036.

Duchenne (de Boulogne), G.-B. (1862). *Mécanisme de la physionomie humaine ou analyse électro-physiologique de l'expression des passions applicable a la pratique des arts plastiques.* Paris: Renouard.

Dudley, R. E. J., John, C. H., Young, A. W., & Over, D. E. (1997). Normal and abnormal reasoning in people with delusions. *British Journal of Clinical Psychology, 36*, 243–258.

Dunbar, R. (1996). *Grooming, gossip and the evolution of language.* London: Faber and Faber.

Durand, K., Gallay, M., Seigneuric, A., Robichon, F., & Baudouin, J.-Y. (2007). The development of facial emotion recognition: The role of configural information. *Journal of Experimental Child Psychology, 97*, 14–27.

Easton, R. D., & Basala, M. (1982). Perceptual dominance during lipreading. *Perception & Psychophysics, 32*, 562–570.

Eberhardt, J. L. (2005). Imaging race. *American Psychologist, 60*, 181–190.

Eibl-Eibesfeldt, I. (1989). *Human ethology.* New York: de Gruyter.

Eimas, P. D., & Corbit, J. D. (1973). Selective adaptation of linguistic feature detectors. *Cognitive Psychology, 4*, 99–109.

Einav, S., & Hood, B. M. (2008). Tell-tale eyes: Children's attribution of gaze aversion as a lying cue. *Developmental Psychology, 44*, 1655–1667.

Ekman, P. (1972). Universals and cultural differences in facial expressions of emotion. In J. K. Cole (Ed.), *Nebraska symposium on motivation, 1971* (pp. 207–283). Lincoln, NE: University of Nebraska Press.

Ekman, P. (1979). About brows: emotional and conversational signals. In M. Von Cranach, K. Foppa, W. Lepenies, & D. Ploog (Eds.), *Human ethology.* Cambridge: Cambridge University Press.

Ekman, P. (1992). An argument for basic emotions. *Cognition and Emotion, 6*, 169–200.

Ekman, P. (1996). Why don't we catch liars? *Social Research, 63*, 801–817.

Ekman, P., & Friesen, W. V. (1976). *Pictures of facial affect.* Palo Alto, CA: Consulting Psychologists Press.

Ekman, P., & Friesen, W. V. (1978). *Facial Action Coding System: A technique for the measurement of facial movement.* Palo Alto, CA: Consulting Psychologists Press.

Ellamil, M., Susskind, J. M., & Anderson, A. K. (2008). Examinations of identity invariance in facial expression adaptation. *Cognitive, Affective, and Behavioral Neuroscience, 8*, 273–281.

Ellis, A. W., & Young, A. W. (1996). *Human cognitive neuropsychology: A textbook with readings.* Hove: Psychology Press.

Ellis, A. W., Young, A. W., & Critchley, E. M. R. (1989). Loss of memory for people following temporal lobe damage. *Brain, 112*, 1469–1483.

Ellis, A. W., Young, A. W., & Flude, B. M. (1990). Repetition priming and face processing: Priming occurs within the system that responds to the identity of a face. *Quarterly Journal of Experimental Psychology, 42A*, 495–512.

Ellis, A. W., Young, A. W., Flude, B. M., & Hay, D. C. (1987). Repetition priming of face recognition. *Quarterly Journal of Experimental Psychology, 39A*, 193–210.

Ellis, H. D. (1975). Recognizing faces. *British Journal of Psychology, 66*, 409–426.

Ellis, H. D. (1986). Processes underlying face recognition. In R. Bruyer (Ed.), *The neuropsychology of face perception and facial expression* (pp. 1–27). Hillsdale, NJ: Lawrence Erlbaum.

Ellis, H. D. (1986). Face recall: A psychological perspective. *Human Learning, 5,* 189–196.

Ellis, H. D., Davies, G. M., & Shepherd, J. W. (1978). A critical examination of the Photofit system for recalling faces. *Ergonomics, 21,* 297–307.

Ellis, H. D., & Florence, M. (1990). Bodamer's (1947) paper on prosopagnosia. *Cognitive Neuropsychology, 7,* 81–105.

Ellis, H. D., Jones, D. M., & Mosdell, N. (1997). Intra- and inter-modal repetition priming of familiar faces and voices. *British Journal of Psychology, 88,* 143–156.

Ellis, H. D., & Lewis, M. B. (2001). Capgras delusion: A window on face recognition. *Trends in Cognitive Sciences, 5,* 149–156.

Ellis, H. D., Lewis, M. B., Moselhy, H. F., & Young, A. W. (2000). Automatic without autonomic responses to familiar faces: Differential components of covert face recognition in a case of Capgras delusion. *Cognitive Neuropsychiatry, 5,* 255–269.

Ellis, H. D., Shepherd, J. W., & Davies, G. M. (1979). Identification of familiar and unfamiliar faces from internal and external features; Some implications for theories of face recognition. *Perception, 8,* 431–439.

Ellis, H. D., & Young, A. W. (1989). Are faces special? In A. W. Young & H. D. Ellis (Eds.), *Handbook of research on face processing* (pp. 1–26). Amsterdam: North Holland.

Ellis, H. D., & Young, A. W. (1990). Accounting for delusional misidentifications. *British Journal of Psychiatry, 157,* 239–248.

Ellis, H. D., Young, A. W., Quayle, A. H., & de Pauw, K. W. (1997). Reduced autonomic responses to faces in Capgras delusion. *Proceedings of the Royal Society, London, B: Biological Sciences, 264,* 1085–1092.

Emery, N. J., & Clayton, N. S. (2009). Comparative social cognition. *Annual Review of Psychology, 60,* 87–113.

Engell, A. D., & Haxby, J. V. (2007). Facial expression and gaze-direction in human superior temporal sulcus. *Neuropsychologia, 45,* 3234–3241.

Engell, A. D., Haxby, J. V., & Todorov, A. (2007). Implicit trustworthiness decisions: Automatic coding of face properties in the human amygdala. *Journal of Cognitive Neuroscience, 19,* 1508–1519.

Enlow, D. H. (1982). *Handbook of facial growth* (2nd ed.). Philadelphia: W. B. Saunders.

Enoch, M. D., & Trethowan, W. H. (1991). *Uncommon psychiatric syndromes* (3rd ed.). Oxford: Butterworth-Heinemann.

Epstein, R., & Kanwisher, N. (1998). A cortical representation of the local visual environment. *Nature, 392,* 598–601.

Etcoff, N. L. (1984). Selective attention to facial identity and facial emotion. *Neuropsychologia, 22,* 281–295.

Etcoff, N. L., & Magee, J. J. (1992). Categorical perception of facial expressions. *Cognition, 44,* 227–240.

Evans, J. J., Heggs, A. J., Antoun, N., & Hodges, J. R. (1995). Progressive prosopagnosia associated with selective right temporal lobe atrophy: A new syndrome? *Brain, 118,* 1–13.

Ewbank, M. P., & Andrews, T. J. (2008). Differential sensitivity for viewpoint between familiar and unfamiliar faces in human visual cortex. *NeuroImage, 40,* 1857–1870.

Ewbank, M. P., Schluppeck, D., & Andrews, T. J. (2005). fMR-adaptation reveals a distributed representation of inanimate objects and places in human visual cortex. *NeuroImage, 28,* 268–279.

Ewbank, M. P., Smith, W. A. P., Hancock, E. R., & Andrews, T. J. (2008). The M170 reflects a viewpoint-dependent representation for both familiar and unfamiliar faces. *Cerebral Cortex, 18,* 364–370.

Fagan, J. F., & Singer, L. T. (1979). Role of simple feature differences in infants' recognition of faces. *Infant Behavior & Development, 2*, 39–45.

Fantz, R. L. (1961). The origin of form perception. *Scientific American, 204*, 66–72.

Farah, M. J. (1989). The neural basis of mental imagery. *Trends in Neurosciences, 12*, 395–399.

Farah, M. J. (1991). Patterns of co-occurrence among the associative agnosias: Implications for visual object representation. *Cognitive Neuropsychology, 8*, 1–19.

Farah, M. J., Wilson, K. D., Drain, H. M., & Tanaka, J. R. (1995). The inverted face inversion effect in prosopagnosia: Evidence for face-specific, mandatory perceptual mechanisms. *Vision Research, 35*, 2089–2093.

Farkas, L. G., Katic, M. J., & Forrest, C. R. (2005). International anthropometric study of facial morphology in various ethnic groups/races. *Journal of Craniofacial Surgery, 16*, 615–646.

Farroni, T., Csibra, G., Simion, G., & Johnson, M. H. (2002). Eye contact detection in humans from birth. *Proceedings of the National Academy of Sciences, USA, 99*, 9602–9605.

Farroni, T., Johnson, M. H., Menon, E., Zulian, L., Faraguna, D., & Csibra, G. (2005). Newborns' preference for face-relevant stimuli: Effects of contrast polarity. *Proceedings of the National Academy of Sciences, USA, 102*, 17245–17250.

Feinstein, J. S., Adolphs, R., Damasio, A. R., & Tranel, D. (2011). The human amygdala and the induction and experience of fear. *Current Biology, 21*, 34–38.

Feldman, N. H., Griffiths, T. L., & Morgan, J. L. (2009). The influence of categories on perception: Explaining the perceptual magnet effect as optimal statistical inference. *Psychological Review, 116*, 752–782.

Felleman, D. J., & Van Essen, D. C. (1991). Distributed hierarchical processing in the primate cerebral cortex. *Cerebral Cortex, 1*, 1–47.

Field, T. M., Woodson, R., Greenberg, R., & Cohen, D. (1982). Discrimination and imitation of facial expressions by neonates. *Science, 218*, 179–181.

Fink, B., & Penton-Voak, I. (2002). Evolutionary psychology of facial attractiveness. *Current Directions in Psychological Science, 11*, 154–158.

Fiske, S. T., Cuddy, A. J. C., & Glick, P. (2007). Universal dimensions of social cognition: Warmth and competence. *Trends in Cognitive Sciences, 11*, 77–83.

Flavell, J. H., Beach, D. R., & Chinsky, J. M. (1966). Spontaneous verbal rehearsal in a memory task as a function of age. *Child Development, 37*, 283–299.

Fletcher, D. J. C., & Michener, C. D. (Eds.), (1987). *Kin recognition in animals*. Chichester: Wiley.

Flin, R. H. (1980). Age effects in children's memory for unfamiliar faces. *Developmental Psychology, 16*, 373–374.

Flin, R. H. (1985a). Development of face recognition: an encoding switch? *British Journal of Psychology, 76*, 123–134.

Flin, R. H. (1985b). Development of visual memory: An early adolescent regression. *Journal of Early Adolescence, 5*, 259–266.

Flin, R. H., Kearney, B., & Murray, K. (1996). Children's evidence: Scottish research and law. *Criminal Justice and Behaviour, 23*, 358–376.

Flude, B. M., Ellis, A. W., & Kay, J. (1989). Face processing and name retrieval in an anomic aphasic: Names are stored separately from semantic information about familiar people. *Brain and Cognition, 11*, 60–72.

Fodor, J. (1983). *The modularity of mind*. Cambridge, MA: MIT Press.

Fox, C. J., & Barton, J. J. S. (2007). What is adapted in face adaptation? The neural representations of expression in the human visual system. *Brain Research, 1127*, 80–89.

Franklin, R. G., & Adams, R. B. (2009). A dual-process account of female facial attractiveness preferences: Sexual and nonsexual routes. *Journal of Experimental Social Psychology, 45*, 1156–1159.

Freeman, J. B., Rule, N. O., Adams, R. B., & Ambady, N. (2010). The neural basis of categorical face perception: Graded representations of face gender in fusiform and orbitofrontal cortices. *Cerebral Cortex*, *20*, 1314–1322.

Fridlund, A. J. (1994). *Human facial expression: An evolutionary view*. San Diego, London: Academic Press.

Friesen, C. K., & Kingstone, A. (1998). The eyes have it!: Reflexive orienting is triggered by nonpredictive gaze. *Psychonomic Bulletin & Review*, *5*, 490–495.

Fright, W. R., & Linney, A. D. (1993). Registration of 3-D head surfaces using multiple landmarks. *IEEE Transactions on Medical Imaging*, *12*, 515–520.

Frisby, J. (1979). *Seeing: Illusion, brain and mind*. Oxford: Oxford University Press.

Frischen, A., Bayliss, A. P., & Tipper, S. P. (2007). Gaze cueing and attention: Visual attention, social cognition and individual differences. *Psychological Bulletin*, *133*, 694–724.

Frith, C. D. (2007). The social brain? *Philosophical Transactions of the Royal Society, London, B: Biological Sciences*, *362*, 671–678.

Fromkin, V. A., & Rodman, R. (1974). *An introduction to language*. New York: Holt, Rinehart & Winston Inc.

Frowd, C., Bruce, V., & Hancock, P. J. B. (2008). Changing the face of criminal identification. *Psychologist*, *21*, 668–672.

Frowd, C., Bruce, V., McIntyre, A., & Hancock, P. (2007a). The relative importance of external and internal features of facial composites. *British Journal of Psychology*, *98*, 61–77.

Frowd, C., Bruce, V., Ross, D., McIntyre, A., & Hancock, P. J. B. (2007b). An application of caricature: How to improve the recognition of facial composites. *Visual Cognition*, *15*, 954–984.

Frowd, C. D., Carson, D., Ness, H., Richardson, J., Morrison, L., McLanaghan, S., et al. (2005a). A forensically valid comparison of facial composite systems. *Psychology Crime & Law*, *11*, 33–52.

Frowd, C. D., Carson, D., Ness, H., McQuiston-Surrett, D., Richardson, J., Baldwin, H., et al. (2005b). Contemporary composite techniques: The impact of a forensically-relevant target delay. *Legal and Criminological Psychology*, *10*, 63–81.

Frowd, C. D., Pitchford, M., Bruce, V., Jackson, S., Hepton, G., Greenall, M., McIntyre, A. H., & Hancock, P. J. B. (2011). The psychology of face construction: Giving evolution a helping hand. *Applied Cognitive Psychology*, *25*, 195–203.

Furl, N., van Rijsbergen, N. J., Treves, A., Friston, K. J., & Dolan, R. J. (2007). Experience-dependent coding of facial expression in superior temporal sulcus. *Proceedings of the National Academy of Sciences, USA*, *104*, 13485–13489.

Gácsi, M., Miklósi, A., Varga, O., Topal, J., & Csanyi, V. (2004). Are readers of our face readers of our minds? Dogs (Canis familiaris) show situation-dependent recognition of human's attention. *Animal Cognition*, *7*, 144–153.

Gainotti, G. (2010). Not all patients labeled as 'prosopagnosia' have a real prosopagnosia. *Journal of Clinical and Experimental Neuropsychology*, *32*, 763–766.

Gainotti, G., Barbier, A., & Marra, C. (2003). Slowly progressive defect in recognition of familiar people in a patient with right anterior temporal lobe atrophy. *Brain*, *126*, 792–803.

Gallese, V., Keysers, C., & Rizzolatti, G. (2004). A unifying view of the basis of social cognition. *Trends in Cognitive Sciences*, *8*, 396–403.

Galton, F. (1874). *English men of science: Their nature and nurture*. London: Macmillan.

Galton, F. (1879). Composite portraits, made by combining those of many different persons into a single resultant figure. *Journal of the Anthropological Institute*, *8*, 132–144.

Galton, F. (1883). *Inquiries into human faculty and its development*. London: Macmillan.

Ganel, T., Goshen-Gottstein, Y., & Goodale, M. (2005). Interactions between the processing of gaze direction and facial expression. *Vision Research*, *45*, 1191–1200.

Garety, P. A., Hemsley, D. R., & Wessely, S. (1991). Reasoning in deluded schizophrenic and paranoid patients: Biases in performance on a probabilistic inference task. *Journal of Nervous and Mental Disease, 179*, 194–201.

Gardner, M. (1967). *The ambidextrous universe.* London: Penguin.

Garner, W. R. (1974). *The processing of information and structure.* Potomac, Maryland: Lawrence Erlbaum.

Garrido, L., Eisner, F., McGettigan, C., Stewart, L., Sauter, D., Hanley, J. R., et al. (2009). Developmental phonagnosia: A selective deficit of vocal identity recognition. *Neuropsychologia, 47*, 123–131.

Garrido, L., Furl, N., Draganski, B., Weiskopf, N., Stevens, J., Tan, G. C.-Y., et al. (2009). Voxel-based morphometry reveals reduced grey matter volume in the temporal cortex of developmental prosopagnosics. *Brain, 132*, 3443–3455.

Gauthier, I., Skudlarski, P., Gore, J. C., & Anderson, A. W. (2000). Expertise for cars and birds recruits brain areas involved in face recognition. *Nature Neuroscience, 3*, 191–197.

Gauthier, I., & Tarr, M. J. (1997). Becoming a greeble expert: Exploring the mechanisms of face recognition. *Vision Research, 37*, 1673–1682.

Gauthier, I., Tarr, M. J., Anderson, A. W., Skudlarski, P., & Gore, J. C. (1999). Activation of the middle fusiform 'face area' increases with expertise in recognizing novel objects. *Nature Neuroscience, 2*, 568–573.

Geldart, S., Mondloch, C. J., Maurer, D., de Schonen, S., & Brent, H. P. (2002). The effect of early visual deprivation on the development of face processing. *Developmental Science, 5*, 490–501.

George, N., Driver, J., & Dolan, R. J. (2001). Seen gaze-direction modulates fusiform activity and its coupling with other brain areas during face processing. *NeuroImage, 13*, 1102–1112.

George, P. A., & Hole, G. J. (2000). The role of spatial and surface cues in the age-processing of unfamiliar faces. *Visual Cognition, 7*, 485–509.

Gick, B., & Derrick, D. (2009). Aero-tactile integration in speech perception. *Nature, 462*, 502–504.

Gilad, S., Meng, M., & Sinha, P. (2009). Role of ordinal contrast relationships in face encoding. *Proceedings of the National Academy of Sciences, USA, 106*, 5353–5358.

Gilbert, C., & Bakan, P. (1973). Visual asymmetry in perception of faces. *Neuropsychologia, 11*, 355–362.

Glenberg, A. M., Schroeder, J. L., & Robertson, D. A. (1998). Averting the gaze disengages the environment and facilitates remembering. *Memory & Cognition, 26*, 651–658.

Gobbini, M. I., & Haxby, J. V. (2007). Neural systems for recognition of familiar faces. *Neuropsychologia, 45*, 32–41.

Golarai, G., Ghahremani, D. G., Whitfield-Gabrieli, S., Reiss, A., Eberhardt, J. L., Gabrieli, J. D. E., et al. (2007). Differential development of high-level visual cortex correlates with category-specific recognition memory. *Nature Neuroscience, 10*, 512–522.

Golarai, G., Hong, S., Haas, B. W., Galaburda, A. M., Mills, D. L., Bellugi, U., et al. (2010). The fusiform face area is enlarged in Williams syndrome. *Journal of Neuroscience, 30*, 6700–6712.

Golarai, G., Liberman, A., Yoon, J. M. D., & Grill-Spector, K. (2010). Differential development of the ventral visual cortex extends through adolescence. *Frontiers in Human Neuroscience, 3*, 1–19.

Goldman, A. I., & Sekhar Sripada, C. (2005). Simulationist models of face-based emotion recognition. *Cognition, 94*, 193–213.

Goldman, M., & Hagen, M. (1978). The forms of caricature: Physiognomy and political bias. *Studies in the Anthropology of Visual Communication, 5*, 30–36.

Goldstein, A. G. (1983). Behavioral scientists' fascination with faces. *Journal of Nonverbal Behavior, 7*, 223–255.

Gombrich, E. H. (1976). *The heritage of Apelles: studies in the art of the renaissance.* Phaidon Press Ltd: Oxford.

Goren, C. C., Sarty, M., & Wu, P. Y. K. (1975). Visual following and pattern-discrimination of face-like stimuli by newborn infants. *Pediatrics, 56*, 544–549.

Goshen-Gottstein, Y., & Ganel, T. (2000). Repetition priming for familiar and unfamiliar faces in a sex-judgment task: Evidence for a common route for the processing of sex and identity. *Journal of Experimental Psychology: Learning, Memory & Cognition, 26*, 1198–1214.

Gosselin, N., Peretz, I., Johnsen, E., & Adolphs, R. (2007). Amygdala damage impairs emotion recognition from music. *Neuropsychologia, 45*, 236–244.

Graham, R., Devinsky, O., & LaBar, K. S. (2007). Quantifying deficits in the perception of fear and anger in morphed facial expressions after bilateral amygdala damage. *Neuropsychologia, 45*, 42–54.

Graham, R., & LaBar, K. S. (2007). Garner interference reveals dependencies between emotional expression and gaze in face perception. *Emotion, 7*, 296–313.

Gray, J. M., Young, A. W., Barker, W. A., Curtis, A., & Gibson, D. (1997). Impaired recognition of disgust in Huntington's disease gene carriers. *Brain, 120*, 2029–2038.

Green, K. P., Kuhl, P. K., Meltzoff, A. N., & Stevens, E. B. (1991). Integrating speech information across talkers, gender, and sensory modality: Female faces and male voices in the McGurk effect. *Perception & Psychophysics, 50*, 524–536.

Greene, J. D. W., & Hodges, J. R. (1996). Identification of famous faces and famous names in early Alzheimer's disease. Relationship to anterograde episodic and general semantic memory. *Brain, 119*, 111–128.

Gregory, R. L. (1973). The confounded eye. In R. L. Gregory & E. H. Gombrich (Eds.), *Illusion in nature and art.* London: Duckworth.

Greve, K. W., & Bauer, R. M. (1990). Implicit learning of new faces in prosopagnosia: An application of the mere-exposure paradigm. *Neuropsychologia, 28*, 1035–1041.

Grill-Spector, K., Golarai, G., & Gabrieli, J. (2008). Developmental neuroimaging of the human ventral visual cortex. *Trends in Cognitive Sciences, 12*, 152–162.

Grill-Spector, K., Knouf, N., & Kanwisher, N. (2004). The fusiform face area subserves face perception, not generic within-category identification. *Nature Neuroscience, 7*, 555–562.

Grinter, E. J., Maybery, M. T., & Badcock, D. R. (2010). Vision in developmental disorders: Is there a dorsal stream deficit? *Brain Research Bulletin, 82*, 147–160.

Gross, C. G., Rocha-Miranda, C. E., & Bender, D. B.(1972). Visual properties of neurons in infertoemporal cortex of the macaque. *Journal of Neurophysiology, 35*, 96–111.

Grossman, T., & Johnson, M. H. (2007). The development of the social brain in human infancy. *European Journal of Neuroscience, 25*, 909–919.

Grossman, T., Striano, T., & Friederici, A., D. (2006). Crossmodal integration of emotional information from face and voice in the infant brain. *Developmental Science, 9*, 309–315.

Güntürkün, O. (1991). The Venus of Milo and the dawn of facial asymmetry research. *Brain and Cognition, 16*, 147–150.

Hadjikhani, N., & de Gelder, B. (2003). Seeing fearful body expressions activates the fusiform cortex and amygdala. *Current Biology, 13*, 2201–2205.

Hadjikhani, N., Hoge, R., Snyder, J., & de Gelder, B. (2008). Pointing with the eyes: The role of gaze in communicating danger. *Brain and Cognition, 68*, 1–8.

Hagan, C. C., Woods, W., Johnson, S., Calder, A. J., Green, G. G. R., & Young, A. W. (2009). MEG demonstrates a supra-additive response to facial and vocal emotion in the right superior temporal sulcus. *Proceedings of the National Academy of Sciences, USA, 106*, 20010–20015.

Haidt, J., McCauley, C., & Rozin, P. (1994). Individual differences in sensitivity to disgust: A scale sampling seven domains of disgust elicitors. *Personality & Individual Differences, 16*, 701–713.

Halberstadt, J., & Rhodes, G. (2000). The attractiveness of nonface averages: Implications for an evolutionary explanation of the attractiveness of average faces. *Psychological Science, 11*, 285–289.

Halit, H., de Haan, M., & Johnson, M. H. (2003). Cortical specialisation for face processing: Face-sensitive event-related potential components in 3-and 12-month-old infants. *Neuroimage, 19*, 1180–1193.

Hall, D. A., Fussell, C., & Summerfield, A. Q. (2005). Reading fluent speech from talking faces: Typical brain networks and individual differences. *Journal of Cognitive Neuroscience, 17*, 939–953.

Hallett, M. (2000). Transcranial magnetic stimulation and the human brain. *Nature, 406*, 147–150.

Hancock, P. J. B., Bruce, V., & Burton, A. M. (1997). Testing principal component representations for faces. In J. A. Bullinaria, D. W. Glasspool, & G. Houghton (Eds.), *4th Neural Computation and Psychology Workshop, London, 9–11 April 1997 – Connectionist Representations* (pp. 84–97).

Hancock, P. J. B., Bruce, V., & Burton, A. M. (2001). Recognition of unfamiliar faces. *Trends in Cognitive Sciences, 4*, 330–337.

Hancock, P. J. B., Burton, A. M., & Bruce, V. (1996). Face processing: Human perception and principal components analysis. *Memory & Cognition, 24*, 26–40.

Hanley, J. R., & Cowell, E. S. (1988). The effects of different types of retrieval cues on the recall of names of famous faces. *Memory & Cognition, 16*, 545–555.

Hanley, J. R., & Damjanovic, L. (2009). It is more difficult to retrieve a familiar person's name and occupation from their voice than from their blurred face. *Memory, 17*, 830–839.

Hanley, J. R., Smith, S. T., & Hadfield, J. (1998). I recognise you but I can't place you: An investigation of *familiar-only* experiences during tests of voice and face recognition. *Quarterly Journal of Experimental Psychology, 51A*, 179–195.

Hanley, J. R., & Turner, J. M. (2000). Why are familiar-only experiences more frequent for voices than for faces? *Quarterly Journal of Experimental Psychology, 53A*, 1105–1116.

Hanley, J. R., Young, A. W., & Pearson, N. (1989). Defective recognition of familiar people. *Cognitive Neuropsychology, 6*, 179–210.

Harmon, L. D., & Julesz, B. (1973). Masking in visual recognition: Effects of two-dimensional filtered noise. *Science, 180*, 1194–1197.

Harrison, V., & Hole, G. J. (2009). Evidence for a contact-based explanation of the own-age bias in face recognition. *Psychonomic Bulletin & Review, 16*, 264–269.

Hartline, H. K., Wagner, H. G., & Ratliff, F. (1956). Inhibition in the eye of Limulus. *Journal of General Physiology, 39*, 651–673.

Hasson, U., Levy, I., Behrmann, M., Hendler, T., & Malach, R. (2002). Eccentricity bias as an organizing principle for high-order object areas. *Neuron, 34*, 479–490.

Hasson, U., Nir, Y., Levy, I., Fuhrmann, G., & Malach, R. (2004). Intersubject synchronization of cortical activity during natural vision. *Science, 303*, 1634–1640.

Haxby, J. V., Gobbini, M. I., Furey, M. L., Ishai, A., Schouten, J. L., & Pietrini, P. (2001). Distributed and overlapping representations of faces and objects in ventral temporal cortex. *Science, 293*, 2425–2430.

Haxby, J. V., Hoffman, E. A., & Gobbini, M. I. (2000). The distributed human neural system for face perception. *Trends in Cognitive Sciences, 4*, 223–233.

Haxby, J. V., Ungerleider, L. G., Clark, V. P., Schouten, J. L., Hoffman, E. A., & Martin, A. (1999). The effect of face inversion on activity in neural systems for face and object perception. *Neuron, 22*, 189–199.

Hay, D. C., & Young, A. W. (1982). The human face. In A. W. Ellis (Ed.), *Normality and pathology in cognitive functions* (pp. 173–202). London: Academic Press.

Hay, D. C., Young, A. W., & Ellis, A. W. (1991). Routes through the face recognition system. *Quarterly Journal of Experimental Psychology, 43A*, 761–791.

Hayes, C. J., Stevenson, R. J., & Coltheart, M. (2007). Disgust and Huntington's disease. *Neuropsychologia, 45*, 1135–1151.

Hebb, D. O. (1949). *The organisation of behaviour.* New York: John Wiley.

Hécaen, H. (1981). The neuropsychology of face recognition. In G. Davies, H. Ellis, & J. Shepherd (Eds.), *Perceiving and remembering faces* (pp. 39–54). London: Academic Press.

Hefter, R. L., Manoach, D. S., & Barton, J. J. S. (2005). Perception of facial expression and facial identity in subjects with social developmental disorders. *Neurology, 65*, 1620–1625.

Hein, G., & Knight, R. T. (2008). Superior temporal sulcus - it's my area: or is it yours? *Journal of Cognitive Neuroscience, 20*, 2125–2136.

Henderson, Z., Bruce, V. and Burton, A. M. (2001). Matching the faces of robbers captured on video. *Applied Cognitive Psychology, 15*, 445–464.

Hennenlotter, A., Schroeder, U., Erhard, P., Haslinger, B., Stahl, R., Weindl, A., et al. (2004). Neural correlates associated with impaired disgust processing in pre-symptomatic Huntington's disease. *Brain, 127*, 1446–1453.

Henson, R. N. A. (2005). What can functional neuroimaging tell the experimental psychologist? *Quarterly Journal of Experimental Psychology, 58A*, 193–233.

Hepper, P. G. (1988). Fetal 'soap' addiction. *Lancet, June 11, 1(8598)*, 1347–1348.

Hershler, O., & Hochstein, S. (2005). At first sight: A high-level pop out effect for faces. *Vision Research, 45*, 1707–1724.

Herzmann, G., Schweinberger, S. R., Sommer, W., & Jentzsch, I. (2004). What's special about personally familiar faces? A multimodal approach. *Psychophysiology, 41*, 688–701.

Heywood, C. A., & Cowey, A. (1992). The role of the 'face-cell' area in the discrimination and recognition of faces by monkeys. *Philosophical Transactions of the Royal Society, London, B: Biological Sciences, 335*, 31–38.

Hietanen, J., Leppänen, J. M., Illi, M., & Surakka, V. (2004). Evidence for the integration of audiovisual information at the perceptual level of processing. *European Journal of Cognitive Psychology, 16*, 769–790.

Hill, H., & Bruce, V. (1996). Effects of lighting on matching facial surfaces. *Journal of Experimental Psychology: Human Perception & Performance, 22*, 986–1004.

Hill, H., Bruce, V., & Akamatsu, S. (1995). Perceiving the sex and race of faces: The role of shape and colour. *Proceedings of the Royal Society, London, B: Biological Sciences, 261*, 367–373.

Hill, H. C. H., Troje, N. F., & Johnston, A. (2005). Range- and domain-specific exaggeration of facial speech. *Journal of Vision, 5*, 793–807.

Hilton, J. L., & von Hippel, W. (1996). Stereotypes. *Annual Review of Psychology, 47*, 237–271.

Hintzman, D. L. (1986). Schema abstraction in a multiple-trace memory model. *Psychological Review, 93*, 411–428.

Hirstein, W., & Ramachandran, V. S. (1997). Capgras syndrome: A novel probe for understanding the neural representation of the identity and familiarity of persons. *Proceedings of the Royal Society, London, B: Biological Sciences, 264*, 437–444.

Hodges, J. R., & Greene, J. D. W. (1998). Knowing about people and naming them: Can Alzheimer's disease patients do one without the other? *Quarterly Journal of Experimental Psychology, 51A*, 121–134.

Hoffman, E. A., & Haxby, J. V. (2000). Distinct representations of eye gaze and identity in the distributed human neural system for face perception. *Nature Neuroscience, 3,* 80–84.

Hoffman, K. L., Gothard, K. M., Schmid, M. C., & Logothetis, N. K. (2007). Facial-expression and gaze-selective responses in the monkey amygdala. *Current Biology, 17,* 766–772.

Hole, G. J., & Bourne, V. J. (2010). *Face processing: Psychological, neuropsychological, and applied perspectives.* Oxford: Oxford University Press.

Hole, G. J., George, P. A., Eaves, K., & Rasek, A. (2002). Effects of geometric distortions on face-recognition performance. *Perception, 31,* 1221–1240.

Holle, H., Obleser, J., Rueschemeyer, S. A., & Gunter, T. C. (2010). Integration of iconic gestures and speech in left superior temporal areas boosts speech comprehension under adverse listening conditions. *NeuroImage, 49,* 875–884.

Hönekopp, J. (2006). Once more: Is beauty in the eye of the beholder? Relative contributions of private and shared taste to judgments of facial attractiveness. *Journal of Experimental Psychology: Human Perception & Performance, 32,* 199–209.

Horn, G. (1986). *Memory, imprinting and the brain: An inquiry into mechanisms.* Oxford: Oxford University Press.

Horner, A. J., & Andrews, T. J. (2009). Linearity of the fMRI response in category-selective regions of human visual cortex. *Human Brain Mapping, 30,* 2628–2640.

Hsu, S.-M., & Young, A. W. (2004). Adaptation effects in facial expression recognition. *Visual Cognition, 11,* 871–899.

Hugenberg, K., & Bodenhausen, G. V. (2003). Facing prejudice: Implicit prejudice and the perception of facial threat. *Psychological Science, 14,* 640–643.

Hugenberg, K., & Corneille, O. (2009). Holistic processing is tuned for in-group faces. *Cognitive Science, 33,* 1173–1181.

Hume, D. (1757). *Four dissertations.* London: Millar.

Humphreys, K., Avidan, G., & Behrmann, M. (2007). A detailed investigation of facial expression processing in congenital prosopagnosia as compared to acquired prosopagnosia. *Experimental Brain Research, 176,* 356–373.

Immelman, K. (1975). Ecological significance of imprinting and early learning. *Annual Review of Ecology and Systematics, 6,* 15–37.

Ishai, A. (2007). Sex, beauty and the orbitofrontal cortex. *International Journal of Psychophysiology, 63,* 181–185.

Itier, R. J., & Taylor, M. J. (2004). Face inversion and contrast-reversal effects across development: In contrast to the expertise theory. *Developmental Science, 7,* 246–260.

Jaquet, E., Rhodes, G., & Hayward, W. G. (2007). Opposite aftereffects for Chinese and Caucasian faces are selective for social category information and not just physical face differences. *Quarterly Journal of Experimental Psychology, 60,* 1457–1467.

Jaquet, E., & Rhodes, G. (2008). Face aftereffects indicate dissociable, but not distinct, coding of male and female faces. *Journal of Experimental Psychology: Human Perception & Performance, 34,* 101–112.

Jeffery, L., Rhodes, G., & Busey, T. (2006). View-specific coding of face shape. *Psychological Science, 17,* 501–505.

Jenkins, J., & Langton, S. R. H. (2003). Configural processing in the perception of eye-gaze direction. *Perception, 32,* 1181–1188.

Jenkins, R., Beaver, J. D., & Calder, A. J. (2006). I thought you were looking at me: Direction-specific aftereffects in gaze perception. *Psychological Science, 17,* 506–513.

Jenkins, R., & Burton, A. M. (2008). 100% accuracy in automatic face recognition. *Science, 319,* 435.

Johannson, G. (1975). Visual motion perception. *Scientific American, 232,* June, 76–89.

Johnson, D. R., & Moore, W. J. (1989). *Anatomy for dental students* (2nd ed.). Oxford: Oxford University Press.

Johnson, M. H. (2005). Subcortical face processing. *Nature Reviews Neuroscience, 6,* 766–774.

Johnson, M. H., Dziurawiec, S., Ellis, H., & Morton, J. (1991). Newborns' preferential tracking of face-like stimuli and its subsequent decline. *Cognition, 40,* 1–19.

Johnson, M. H., Griffin, R., Csibra, G., Halit, H., Farroni, T., De Haan, M., et al. (2005). The emergence of the social brain network: Evidence from typical and atypical development. *Development and Psychopathology, 17,* 599–619.

Johnston, R. A., & Bruce, V. (1990). Lost properties? Retrieval differences between name codes and semantic codes for familiar people. *Psychological Research, 52,* 62–67.

Johnston, R. A., & Edmonds, A. J. (2009). Familiar and unfamiliar face recognition: A review. *Memory, 17,* 577–596.

Jones, B. C., DeBruine, L. M., Perrett, D. I., Little, A. C., Feinberg, D. R., & Law Smith, M. J. (2008). Effects of menstrual cycle on face preferences. *Archives of Sexual Behavior, 37,* 78–84.

Jones, D. (1995). Sexual selection, physical attractiveness, and facial neoteny. *Current Anthropology, 36,* 723–748.

Jones, S. S. (2009). The development of imitation in infancy. *Philosophical Transactions of the Royal Society, London, B: Biological Sciences, 364,* 2325–2335.

Jones, W., Bellugi, U., Lai, Z., Chiles, M., Reilley, J., Lincoln, A., et al. (2000). Hypersociability in Williams Syndrome. *Journal of Cognitive Neuroscience, 12,* 30–46.

Jonides, J. (1981). Voluntary versus automatic control over the mind's eye's movement. In T. Field & N. Fox (Eds.), *Attention and Performance Vol. IX* (pp. 187–203). Hillsdale, NJ: Lawrence Erlbaum.

Kalick, S., Zebrowitz, L. A., Langlois, J. H., & Johnson, R, M. (1998). Does human facial attractiveness honestly advertise health? Longitudinal data on an evolutionary question. *Psychological Science, 9,* 8–13.

Kamachi, M., Bruce, V., Mukaida, S., Gyoba, J., Yoshikawa, S., & Akamatsu, S. (2001). Dynamic properties influence the perception of facial expressions. *Perception, 30,* 875–887.

Kamachi, M., Hill, H., Lander, K., & Vatikiotis-Bateson, E. (2003). 'Putting the face to the voice': Matching identity across modality. *Current Biology, 13,* 1709–1714.

Kaney, S., & Bentall, R. P. (1989). Persecutory delusions and attributional style. *British Journal of Medical Psychology, 62,* 191–198.

Kanwisher, N. (2000). Domain specificity in face perception. *Nature Neuroscience, 3,* 759–763.

Kanwisher, N., McDermott, J., & Chun, M. M. (1997). The fusiform face area: A module in human extrastriate cortex specialized for face perception. *Journal of Neuroscience, 17,* 4302–4311.

Kanwisher, N., & Yovel, G. (2006). The fusiform face area: A cortical region specialized for the perception of faces. *Philosophical Transactions of the Royal Society, London, B: Biological Sciences, 361,* 2109–2128.

Kapur, N. (1996). Paradoxical functional facilitation in brain-behaviour research: A critical review. *Brain, 119,* 1775–1790.

Kardong, K. V. (2006). *Vertebrates: Comparative anatomy, function, evolution.* Boston, MA: McGraw-Hill.

Kau, C. H., Richmond, S., Incrapera, A., English, J., & Xia, J. J. (2007). Three-dimensional surface acquisition systems for the study of facial morphology and their application to maxillofacial surgery. *The International Journal of Medical Robotics and Computer Assisted Surgery, 3,* 97–110.

Kaufmann, J. M., & Schweinberger, S. R. (2004). Expression influences the recognition of familiar faces. *Perception, 33*, 399–408.

Kaufmann, J. M., & Schweinberger, S. R. (2005). Speaker variations influence speechreading speed for dynamic faces. *Perception, 34*, 595–610.

Kay, J., & Hanley, J. R. (2002). Preservation of memory for people in semantic memory disorder: Further category-specific semantic dissociation. *Cognitive Neuropsychology, 19*, 113–133.

Keane, J., Calder, A. J., Hodges, J. R., & Young, A. W. (2002). Face and emotion processing in frontal variant frontotemporal dementia. *Neuropsychologia, 40*, 655–665.

Keeney, T. J., Cannizzo, S. R., & Flavell, J. H. (1967). Spontaneous and induced verbal rehearsal in a recall task. *Child Development, 38*, 953–966.

Kelly, D. J., Quinn, P. C., Slater, A. M., Lee, K., Ge, L. Z., & Pascalis, O. (2007). The other-race effect develops during infancy – Evidence of perceptual narrowing. *Psychological Science, 18*, 1084–1089.

Kelly, D. J., Quinn, P. C., Slater, A. M., Lee, K., Gibson, A., Smith, M., et al. (2005). Three-month-olds, but not newborns, prefer own-race faces. *Developmental Science, 8*, F31-F36.

Kemp, R., Pike, G., White, P., & Musselman, A. (1996). Perception and recognition of normal and negative faces – the role of shape from shading and pigmentation cues. *Perception, 25*, 37–52.

Kemp, R., Towell, N., & Pike, G. (1997). When seeing should not be believing: Photographs, credit cards and fraud. *Applied Cognitive Psychology, 11*, 211–222.

Keysers, C., & Perrett, D. I. (2004). Demystifying social cognition: A Hebbian perspective. *Trends in Cognitive Sciences, 8*, 501–507.

Kingstone, A. (2009). Taking a real look at social attention. *Current Opinion in Neurobiology, 19*, 52–56.

Kinsbourne, M. (1972). Eye and head turning indicates cerebral lateralization. *Science, 176*, 539.

Kipps, C. M., Duggins, A. J., McCusker, E. A., & Calder, A. J. (2007). Disgust and happiness recognition correlate with anteroventral insula and amygdala volume respectively in preclinical Huntington's disease. *Journal of Cognitive Neuroscience, 19*, 1206–1217.

Kleiner, K. A. (1987). Amplitude and phase spectra as indexes of infants pattern preferences. *Infant Behavior & Development, 10*, 49–59.

Kleinke, C. L. (1986). Gaze and eye contact: A research review. *Psychological Review, 100*, 78–100.

Klinge, C., Röder, B., & Büchel, C. (2010). Increased amygdala activation to emotional auditory stimuli in the blind. *Brain, 133*, 1729–1736.

Knight, B., & Johnston, A. (1997). The role of movement in face recognition. *Visual Cognition, 4*, 265–273.

Kobayashi, H., & Kohshima, S. (1997). Unique morphology of the human eye. *Nature, 387*, 767–768.

Kolb, B., Milner, B., & Taylor, L. (1983). Perception of faces by patients with localized cortical excisions. *Canadian Journal of Psychology, 37*, 8–18.

Kolers, P. A. (1976). Pattern analyzing memory. *Science, 191*, 1280–1281.

Kornell, N., & Metcalfe, J. (2006). 'Blockers' do not block recall during tip-of-the-tongue states. *Metacognition and Learning, 1*, 248–261.

Kotsoni, E., de Haan, M., & Johnson, M. H. (2001). Categorical perception of facial expressions by 7-month-old infants. *Perception, 30*, 1115–1125.

Kovach, J. K. (1971). Interaction of innate and acquired: Colour preferences and early exposure learning in chicks. *Journal of Comparative and Physiological Psychology, 75*, 386–98.

Kramer, R. S. S., & Ward, R. (2010). Internal facial features are signals of personality and health. *Quarterly Journal of Experimental Psychology, 63,* 2273–2287.

Kreifelts, B., Ethofer, T., Grodd, W., Erb, M., & Wildgruber, D. (2007). Audiovisual integration of emotional signals in voice and face: an event-related fMRI study. *NeuroImage, 37,* 1445–1456.

Kriegeskorte, N., Formisano, E., Sorger, B., & Goebel, R. (2007). Individual faces elicit distinct response patterns in human anterior temporal cortex. *Proceedings of the National Academy of Sciences, USA, 104,* 20600–20605.

Kuefner, D., Macchi Cassia, V., Vescovo, E., & Picozzi, M. (2010). Natural experience acquired in adulthood enhances holistic processing of other-age faces. *Visual Cognition, 18,* 11–25.

Kuhl, P. K., & Meltzoff, A. N. (1982). The bimodal perception of speech in infancy. *Science, 218,* 1138–1141.

Kushnerenko, E., Teinonen, T., Volein, A., & Csibra, G. (2008). Electrophysiological evidence of illusory audiovisual speech percept in human infants. *Proceedings of the National Academy of Sciences, USA, 105,* 11442–11445.

Lades, M., Vorbruggen, J. C., Buhmann, J., Lage, J., von der Malsburg, C., Wurtz, R. P., & Konen, W. (1993). Distortion invariant object recognition in the dynamic link architecture. *IEEE Transactions on Computers, 42,* 300–311.

Lander, K., & Bruce, V. (2000). Recognizing famous faces: Exploring the benefits of facial motion. *Ecological Psychology, 12,* 259–272.

Lander, K., Christie, F., & Bruce, V. (1999). The role of movement in the recognition of famous faces. *Memory & Cognition, 27,* 974–985.

Lander, K., & Chuang, L. (2005). Why are moving faces easier to recognize? *Visual Cognition, 12,* 429–442.

Lander, K., & Davies, R. (2007). Exploring the role of characteristic motion when learning new faces. *Quarterly Journal of Experimental Psychology, 60,* 519–526.

Lander, K., & Davies, R. (2008). Does face familiarity influence speechreadability? *Quarterly Journal of Experimental Psychology, 61,* 961–967.

Lander, K., Hill, H., Kamachi, M., & Vatikiotis-Bateson, E. (2007). It's not what you say but the way you say it: Matching faces and voices. *Journal of Experimental Psychology: Human Perception & Performance, 33,* 905–914.

Langdon, R., & Coltheart, M. (2000). The cognitive neuropsychology of delusions. *Mind & Language, 15,* 183–216.

Langlois, J. H., & Roggman, L. A. (1990). Attractive faces are only average. *Psychological Science, 1,* 115–121.

Langlois, J. H., Roggman, L. A., Casey, R. J., Ritter, J. M., Rieser-Danner, J. A., & Jenkins, V. Y. (1987). Infant preferences for attractive faces: Rudiments of a stereotype? *Developmental Psychology, 23,* 363–369.

Langton, S. R. H., & Bruce, V. (1999). Reflexive visual orienting in response to the social attention of others. *Visual Cognition, 6,* 541–568.

Langton, S. R. H. (2000). The mutual influence of gaze and head orientation in the analysis of social attention direction. *Quarterly Journal of Experimental Psychology, 53A,* 825–845.

Langton, S. R. H., Honeyman, H., & Tessler, E. (2004). The influence of head contour and nose angle on the perception of eye-gaze direction. *Perception & Psychophysics, 66,* 752–771.

Langton, S. R. H., Law, A. S., Burton, A. M., & Schweinberger, S. R. (2008). Attention capture by faces. *Cognition, 107,* 330–342.

Langton, S. R. H., Watt, R. J., & Bruce, V. (2000). Do the eyes have it? Cues to the direction of social attention. *Trends in Cognitive Sciences, 4,* 50–58.

Laurienti, P. J., Perrault, T. J., Stanford, T. R., Wallace, M. T., & Stein, B. E. (2005). On the use of superadditivity as a metric for characterizing multisensory integration in functional neuroimaging studies. *Experimental Brain Research, 166*, 289–297.

Lavater, J. C. (1793). *Essays on physiognomy; for the promotion of the knowledge and the love of mankind.* London: Robinson.

Lavenu, I., Pasquier, F., Lebert, F., Petit, H., & Van der Linden, M. (1999). Perception of emotion in frontotemporal dementia and Alzheimer disease. *Alzheimer Disease and Associated Disorders, 13*, 96–101.

Lawrence, K., Bernstein, D., Pearson, R., Mandy, W., Campbell, R., & Skuse, D. (2008). Changing abilities in recognition of unfamiliar face photographs through childhood and adolescence: Performance on a test of non-verbal immediate memory (Warrington RMF) from 6 to 16 years. *Journal of Neuropsychology, 2*, 27–45.

Le Grand, R., Mondloch, C. J., Maurer, D., & Brent, H. P. (2003). Expert face processing requires visual input to the right hemisphere during infancy. *Nature Neuroscience, 6*, 1108–1112.

Le Grand, R., Mondloch, C. J., Maurer, D., & Brent, H. P. (2004). Impairment in holistic face processing following early visual deprivation. *Psychological Science, 15*, 762–768.

Le Grand, R., Cooper, P. A., Mondloch, C. J., Lewis, T. L., Sagiv, N., de Gelder, B., et al. (2006). What aspects of face processing are impaired in developmental prosopagnosia? *Brain and Cognition, 61*, 139–158.

Leach, A., Cutler, B. L., & Van Wallendael, L. (2009). Lineups and eyewitness identification. *Annual Review of Law and Social Sciences, 5*, 157–178.

Leafhead, K. M., Young, A. W., & Szulecka, T. K. (1996). Delusions demand attention. *Cognitive Neuropsychiatry, 1*, 5–16.

Lebert, F., Pasquier, F., Steinling, M., Cabaret, M., Caparros-Lefebvre, D., & Petit, H. (1994). SPECT data in a case of secondary Capgras delusion. *Psychopathology, 27*, 211–214.

Leder, H., & Bruce, V. (2000). When inverted faces are recognized: The role of configural information in face recognition. *Quarterly Journal of Experimental Psychology, 53A*, 513–536.

LeDoux, J. E. (1995). Emotion: Clues from the brain. *Annual Review of Psychology, 46*, 209–235.

Lee, L. C., Andrews, T. J., Johnson, S. J., Woods, W., Gouws, A., Green, G. G. R., Young, A. W. (2010). Neural responses to rigidly moving faces displaying shifts in social attention investigated with fMRI and MEG. *Neuropsychologia, 48*, 477–490.

Leekam, S. R., Baron-Cohen, S., Perrett, D., Milders, M., & Brown, S. (1997). Eye-direction detection: A dissociation between geometric and joint attention skills in autism. *British Journal of Developmental Psychology, 15*, 77–95.

Lenneberg, E. H. (1967). *Biological foundations of language.* New York: John Wiley and Son.

Leonard, C. M., Voeller, K. K. S., & Kuldau, J. M. (1991). When's a smile a smile? Or how to detect a message by digitizing the signal. *Psychological Science, 2*, 166–172.

Leopold, D. A., O'Toole, A. J., Vetter, T., & Blanz, V. (2001). Prototype-referenced shape encoding revealed by high-level after effects. *Nature Neuroscience, 4*, 89–94.

Leopold, D. A., & Rhodes, G. (2010). A comparative view of face perception. *Journal of Comparative Psychology, 124*, 233–251.

Leppänen, J. M., & Nelson, C. A. (2009). Tuning the developing brain to social signals of emotions. *Nature Reviews Neuroscience, 10*, 37–47.

Levin, D. T., & Angelone, B. L. (2002). Categorical perception of race. *Perception, 31*, 567–578.

Levin, D. T., & Banaji, M. R. (2006). Distortions in the perceived lightness of faces: The role of race categories. *Journal of Experimental Psychology: General, 135*, 501–512.

Levy, J., Heller, W., Banich, M. T., & Burton, L. A. (1983). Asymmetry of perception in free viewing of chimeric faces. *Brain and Cognition, 2*, 404–419.

Lewicki, P. (1986). Processing information about covariations that cannot be articulated. *Journal of Experimental Psychology: Learning, Memory & Cognition, 12*, 135–146.

Lewin, R. (1993). *Human evolution: An illustrated introduction* (3rd ed.). Oxford: Blackwell.

Lewis, M. B., & Edmonds, A. J. (2005). Searching for faces in scrambled scenes. *Visual Cognition, 12*, 1309–1336.

Lewis, M. B., Sherwood, S., Moselhy, H., & Ellis, H. D. (2001). Autonomic responses to familiar faces without autonomic responses to familiar voices: Evidence for voice-specific Capgras delusion. *Cognitive Neuropsychiatry, 6*, 217–228.

Lewis, S. W. (1987). Brain imaging in a case of Capgras' syndrome. *British Journal of Psychiatry, 150*, 117–121.

Ley, R. G., & Bryden, M. P. (1979). Hemispheric differences in processing emotions and faces. *Brain and Language, 7*, 127–138.

Ley, R. G., & Bryden, M. P. (1982). A dissociation of right and left hemispheric effects for recognizing emotional tone and verbal content. *Brain and Cognition, 1*, 3–9.

Lieberman, D., Tooby, J., & Cosmides, L. (2007). The architecture of human kin detection. *Nature, 445*, 727–731.

Lieberman, D. E. (2011). *The evolution of the human head*. Cambridge, MA: The Belknap Press of Harvard University Press.

Light, L. L., Kayra-Stuart, F., & Hollander, S. (1979). Recognition memory for typical and unusual faces. *Journal of Experimental Psychology: Human Learning & Memory, 5*, 212–228.

Linney, A. D., Grindrod, S. R., Arridge, S. R., & Moss, J. P. (1989). 3-dimensional visualization of computerized-tomography and laser scan data for the simulation of maxillo-facial surgery. *Medical Informatics, 14*, 109–121.

Lippmann, W. (1922). *Public opinion*. New York: Harcourt Brace Jovanovich.

Little, A. C., DeBruine, L. M., & Jones, B. C. (2005). Sex-contingent face after-effects suggest distinct neural populations code male and female faces. *Proceedings of the Royal Society, London, B: Biological Sciences, 272*, 2283–2287.

Little, A. C., DeBruine, L. M., Jones, B. C., & Watt, C. (2008). Category contingent aftereffects for faces of different races, ages and species. *Cognition, 106*, 1537–1547.

Little, A. C., & Hancock, P. J. B. (2002). The role of masculinity and distinctiveness in judgments of human male facial attractiveness. *British Journal of Psychology, 93*, 451–464.

Little, A. C., & Perrett, D. I. (2007). Using composite images to assess accuracy in personality attribution to faces. *British Journal of Psychology, 98*, 111–126.

Liu, C. H., Collin, C. A., Rainville, S. J. M., & Chaudhuri, A. (2000). The effects of spatial frequency overlap on face recognition. *Journal of Experimental Psychology: Human Perception & Performance, 26*, 956–979.

Liu, C. H., & Chaudhuri, A. (2002). Reassessing the ¾ view effect in face recognition. *Cognition, 83*, 31–48.

Liu, J., Harris, A., & Kanwisher, N. (2009). Perception of face parts and face configurations: An fMRI study. *Journal of Cognitive Neuroscience, 22*, 203–211.

Loffler, G., Yourganov, G., Wilkinson, F., & Wilson, H. R. (2005). fMRI evidence for the neural representation of faces. *Nature Neuroscience, 8*, 1387–1390.

Lombroso, C. (1911). *Crime: its causes and remedies. Translated by H.P. Horton*. London: Heinemann.

Longmore, C. A., Liu, C. H., & Young, A. W. (2008). Learning faces from photographs. *Journal of Experimental Psychology: Human Perception & Performance, 34*, 77–100.

Lyons, F., Kay, J., Hanley, J. R., & Haslam, C. (2006). Selective preservation of memory for people in the context of semantic memory disorder. *Neuropsychologia, 44*, 2887–2898.

Macaluso, E., George, N., Dolan, R., Spence, C., & Driver, J. (2004). Spatial and temporal factors during processing of audiovisual speech: A PET study. *NeuroImage, 21*, 725–732.

MacDonald, J., Andersen, S., & Bachmann, T. (2000). Hearing by eye: How much spatial degredation can be tolerated? *Perception, 29*, 1155–1168.

MacKain, K., Studdert-Kennedy, M., Spieker, S., & Stern, D. (1983). Infant intermodal speech perception is a left-hemisphere function. *Science, 219*, 1347–1349.

MacLin, O. H., & Malpass, R. S. (2003). The ambiguous-race face illusion. *Perception, 32*, 249–252.

Macrae, C. N., Alnwick, K. A., Milne, A. B., & Schloerscheidt, A. M. (2002). Person perception across the menstrual cycle: Hormonal influences on social-cognitive functioning. *Psychological Science, 13*, 532–536.

Macrae, C. N., & Bodenhausen, G. V. (2000). Social cognition: Thinking categorically about others. *Annual Review of Psychology, 51*, 93–120.

Macrae, C. N., Hood, B. M., Milne, A. B., Rowe, A. C., & Mason, M. F. (2002). Are you looking at me? Eye gaze and person perception. *Psychological Science, 13*, 460–464.

Maguire, E. A., Frackowiak, R. S. J., & Frith, C. D. (1997). Recalling routes around London: Activation of the right hippocampus in taxi drivers. *Journal of Neuroscience, 17*, 7103–7110.

Malpass, R. S., & Kravitz, J. (1969). Recognition for faces of own and other race. *Journal of Personality and Social Psychology, 13*, 330–334.

Mangini, M. C., & Biederman, I. (2004). Making the ineffable explicit: Estimating the information needed for face classifications. *Cognitive Science, 28*, 209–226.

Mann, V., Diamond, R., & Carey, S. (1979). Development of voice recognition: Parallels with face recognition. *Journal of Experimental Child Psychology, 27*, 153–165.

Mark, L. S. & Todd, J. T. (1983). The perception in growth in 3 dimensions. *Perception & Psychophysics, 33*, 193–196.

Marr, D. (1976). Early processing of visual information. *Philosophical Transactions of the Royal Society, London, B: Biological Sciences, 75*, 483–519.

Marr, D. (1982). *Vision.* San Francisco: Freeman.

Marshall, J. C., & Newcombe, F. (1973). Patterns of paralexia: A psycholinguistic approach. *Journal of Psycholinguistic Research, 2*, 175–199.

Martens, U., Leuthold, H., & Schweinberger, S. R. (2010). Parallel processing in face perception. *Journal of Experimental Psychology: Human Perception & Performance, 36*, 103–121.

Martinez, A. M. (2003). Matching expression variant faces. *Vision Research, 43*, 1047–1060.

Mason, M. F., Tatkow, E. P., & Macrae, C. N. (2005). The look of love: Gaze shifts and person perception. *Psychological Science, 15*, 236–239.

Materna, S., Dicke, P. W., & Thier, P. (2009). The posterior superior temporal sulcus is involved in social communication not specific for the eyes. *Neuropsychologia, 46*, 2759–2765.

Maurer, D., Le Grand, R., & Mondloch, C. J. (2002). The many faces of configural processing. *Trends in Cognitive Sciences, 6*, 255–260.

Maurer, D., Lewis, T. L., & Mondloch, C. J. (2005). Missing sights: Consequences for visual cognitive development. *Trends in Cognitive Sciences, 9*, 144–151.

Maylor, E. A. (1985). Facilitatory and inhibitory components of orienting in visual space. In M.I. Posner & O.S.M. Marin (Eds.), *Attention and Performance XI* (pp. 189–203). Hillsdale, NJ: Lawrence Erlbaum.

Maylor, E. A. (1997). Proper name retrieval in old age: Converging evidence against disproportionate impairment. *Aging Neuropsychology and Cognition*, *4*, 211–226.

Maylor, E. A. (1998). Retrieving names in old age: Short- and (very) long-term effects of repetition. *Memory & Cognition*, *26*, 309–319.

McArthur, L. Z., & Apatow, K. (1983/4). Impressions of baby-faced adults. *Social Cognition*, *2*, 315–342.

McCabe, V. (1984). Abstract perceptual information for age level: A risk factor for maltreatment? *Child Development*, *55*, 267–276.

McCabe, V. (1988). Facial proportions, perceived age, and caregiving. In T. R. Alley (Ed.), *Social and applied aspects of perceiving faces* (pp. 89–99). Hillsdale, NJ: Lawrence Erlbaum.

McClelland, J. L., & Rumelhart, D. E. (1981). An interactive activation model of the effect of context in perception. Part 1: An account of basic findings. *Psychological Review*, *88*, 375–406.

McGurk, H., & MacDonald, J. (1976). Hearing lips and seeing voices. *Nature*, *264*, 746–748.

McKeefry, D., Gouws, A., Burton, M. P., & Morland, A. B. (2009). The noninvasive dissection of the human visual cortex: Using fMRI and TMS to study the organization of the visual brain. *Neuroscientist*, *15*, 489–506.

McKelvie, S. J. (1995). Emotional expression in upside-down faces: Evidence for configurational and componential processing. *British Journal of Social Psychology*, *34*, 325–334.

McKone, E., Kanwisher, N., & Duchaine, B. C. (2007). Can generic expertise explain special processing for faces? *Trends in Cognitive Sciences*, *11*, 8–15.

McKone, E., & Yovel, G. (2009). Why does picture-plane inversion sometimes dissociate perception of features and spacing in faces, and sometimes not? Toward a new theory of holistic processing. *Psychonomic Bulletin & Review*, *16*, 778–797.

McNeil, J. E., & Warrington, E. K. (1993). Prosopagnosia – a face-specific disorder. *Quarterly Journal of Experimental Psychology*, *46A*, 1–10.

McNeill, D. (1985). So you think gestures are nonverbal? *Psychological Review*, *92*, 350–371.

McWeeny, K. H., Young, A. W., Hay, D. C., & Ellis, A. W. (1987). Putting names to faces. *British Journal of Psychology*, *78*, 143–149.

Meadows, J. C. (1974). The anatomical basis of prosopagnosia. *Journal of Neurology, Neurosurgery, and Psychiatry*, *37*, 489–501.

Megreya, A. M., & Bindemann, M. (2009). Revisiting the processing of internal and external features of faces: The headscarf effect. *Perception*, *38*, 1831–1848.

Megreya, A. M., & Burton, A. M. (2006). Unfamiliar faces are not faces: Evidence from a matching task. *Memory & Cognition*, *34*, 865–876.

Meissner, C. A., & Brigham, J. C. (2001). Thirty years of investigating the own-race bias in memory for faces – A meta-analytic review. *Psychology, Public Policy and Law*, *7*, 3–35.

Meltzoff, A. N., & Decety, J. (2003). What imitation tells us about social cognition: A rapprochement between developmental psychology and cognitive neuroscience. *Philosophical Transactions of the Royal Society, London, B: Biological Sciences*, *358*, 491–500.

Meltzoff, A. N., & Moore, M. K. (1977). Imitation of facial and manual gestures by human neonates. *Science*, *198*, 75–78.

Meltzoff, A. N., & Moore, M. K. (1983). Newborn infants imitate adult facial gestures. *Child Development*, *54*, 702–709.

Meltzoff, A. N., & Moore, M. K. (1989). Imitation in newborn infants – exploring the range of gestures imitated and the underlying mechanisms. *Developmental Psychology, 25*, 954–962.

Míklosi, A., Kubinyi, E., Topal, J., Gácsi, M., Viranyi, Z., & Csanyi, V. (2003). A simple reason for a big difference: Wolves do not look back at humans, but dogs do. *Current Biology, 13*, 763–766.

Miller, G. A., & Niceley, P. (1955). An analysis of perceptual confusions among some English consonants. *Journal of the Acoustical Society of America, 27*, 338–352.

Miller, G. F., & Todd, P. M. (1998). Mate choice turns cognitive. *Trends in Cognitive Sciences, 2*, 190–198.

Mills, M., & Melhuish, E. (1974). Recognition of mother's voice in early infancy. *Nature, 252*, 123–124.

Milner, A. D., & Goodale, M. A. (1995). *The visual brain in action*. Oxford Psychology Series, 27. Oxford: Oxford University Press.

Minnebusch, D. A., & Daum, I. (2009). Neuropsychological mechanisms of visual face and body perception. *Neuroscience and Biobehavioral Reviews, 33*, 1133–1144.

Mitchell, D. B. (2006). Nonconscious priming after 17 years – Invulnerable implicit memory? *Psychological Science, 17*, 925–929

Mitchell, I. J., Heims, H., Neville, E. A., & Rickards, H. (2005). Huntington's disease patients show impaired perception of disgust in the gustatory and olfactory modalities. *Journal of Neuropsychiatry and Clinical Neuroscience, 17*, 119–121.

Mondloch, C., Le Grand, R., & Maurer, D. (2003). Early visual experience is necessary for the development of some – but not all – aspects of face processing. In O. Pascalis & A. Slater (Eds.), *The development of face processing in infancy and early childhood: Current perspectives* (pp. 99–117). New York: Nova Science Publishers.

Mondloch, C. J., Lewis, T. L., Budreau, D. R., Maurer, D., Dannemiller, J. L., Stephens, B. R., et al. (1999). Face perception during early infancy. *Psychological Science, 10*, 419–422.

Mondloch, C. J., Pathman, T., Maurer, D., Le Grand, R., & de Schonen, S. (2007). The composite effect in six-year-old children: Evidence of adult-like holistic face processing. *Visual Cognition, 15*, 564–577.

Mondloch, C. J., & Thomson, K. (2008). Limitations in 4-year-old children's sensitivity to the spacing among facial features. *Child Development, 79*, 1513–1523.

Montepare, J. M., & McArthur, L. Z. (1986). The impact of age-related variations in facial characteristics on children's age perceptions. *Journal of Experimental Child Psychology, 42*, 303–314.

Morris, J. P., Pelphrey, K. A., & McCarthy, G. (2006). Occipitotemporal activation evoked by the perception of human bodies is modulated by the presence or absence of the face. *Neuropsychologia, 44*, 1919–1927.

Morris, J. S., Frith, C. D., Perrett, D. I., Rowland, D., Young, A. W., Calder, A. J., et al. (1996). A differential neural response in the human amygdala to fearful and happy facial expressions. *Nature, 383*, 812–815.

Morris, P., Bradley, A., Doyal, L., Earley, M., Hagen, P., Milling, M., et al. (2007). Face transplantation: A review of the technical, immunological, psychological and clinical issues with recommendations for good practice. *Transplantation, 83*, 109–128.

Morrison, D. J., Bruce, V., & Burton, A. M. (2001). Understanding provoked overt recognition in prosopagnosia. *Visual Cognition, 8*, 47–65.

Morton, J. (1969). Interaction of information in word recognition. *Psychological Review, 76*, 165–178.

Morton, J. (1979). Facilitation in word recognition: Experiments causing change in the logogen model. In P. A. Kolers, M. Wrolstad, & H. Bouma (Eds.), *Processing of visible language, 1* (pp. 259–268). New York: Plenum.

Morton, J., & Johnson, M. H. (1991). CONSPEC and CONLERN – A 2-process theory of infant face recognition. *Psychological Review, 98,* 164–181.

Morton, J., Johnson, M. H., & Maurer, D. (1990). On the reasons for newborns' responses to faces. *Infant Behavior & Development, 13,* 99–103.

Moscovitch, M., Winocur, G., & Behrmann, M. (1997). What is special about face recognition? Nineteen experiments on a person with visual object agnosia and dyslexia but normal face recognition. *Journal of Cognitive Neuroscience, 9,* 555–604.

Muller, H. J., & Findlay, J. M. (1988). The effect of visual attention on peripheral discrimination thresholds in single and multiple element displays. *Acta Psychologica, 69,* 129–155.

Munhall, K. G., Kroos, C., Jozan, G., & Vatikiotis-Bateson, E. (2004). Spatial frequency requirements for audiovisual speech perception. *Perception & Psychophysics, 66,* 574–583.

Nabi, R. L. (2002). The theoretical versus the lay meaning of disgust: Implications for emotion research. *Cognition and Emotion, 16,* 695–703.

Nation, K, & Penny, S. (2008). Sensitivity to eye gaze in autism: Is it normal? Is it automatic? Is it social? *Development and Psychopathology, 20,* 79–97.

Naveh-Benjamin, M., Shing, Y. L., Kilb, A., Werkle-Bergner, M., Lindenberger, U., & Li, S. C. (2009). Adult age differences in memory for name-face associations: The effects of intentional and incidental learning. *Memory, 17,* 220–232.

Neale, M. C., Neale, B. J., & Sullivan, P. F. (2002). Nonpaternity in linkage studies of extremely discordant sib pairs. *American Journal of Human Genetics, 70,* 526–529.

Neuner, F., & Schweinberger, S. R. (2000). Neuropsychological impairments in the recognition of faces, voices, and personal names. *Brain and Cognition, 44,* 342–366.

Nelson, C. A. (2001). The development and neural bases of face recognition. *Infant and Child Development, 10,* 3–18.

Newcombe, F. (1979). The processing of visual information in prosopagnosia and acquired dyslexia: Functional versus physiological interpretation. In D. J. Oborne, M. M. Gruneberg, & J. R. Eiser (Eds.), *Research in psychology and medicine, Vol. 1* (pp. 315–322). London: Academic Press.

Newcombe, F., de Haan, E. H. F., Ross, J., & Young, A. W. (1989). Face processing, laterality, and contrast sensitivity. *Neuropsychologia, 27,* 523–538.

Newcombe, F., Young, A. W., & de Haan, E. H. F. (1989). Prosopagnosia and object agnosia without covert recognition. *Neuropsychologia, 27,* 179–191.

Ng, M., Ciaramitaro, V. M., Anstis, S., Boynton, G. M., & Fine, I. (2006). Selectivity for the configural cues that identify the gender, ethnicity, and identity of faces in human cortex. *Proceedings of the National Academy of Sciences, USA, 103,* 19552–19557.

Nishimura, M., Maurer, D., & Gao, X. Q. (2009). Exploring children's face-space: A multi-dimensional scaling analysis of the mental representation of facial identity. *Journal of Experimental Child Psychology, 103,* 355–375.

Nosofsky, R. M. (1991). Tests of an exemplar model for relating perceptual classification and recognition memory. *Journal of Experimental Psychology: Human Perception & Performance, 17,* 3–27.

Nothdurft, H.-C. (1993). Faces and facial expressions do not pop out. *Perception, 22,* 1287–1298.

Nummenmaa, L., & Calder, A. J. (2009). Neural mechanisms of social attention. *Trends in Cognitive Sciences, 13,* 135–143.

O'Craven, K. M., Downing, P. E., & Kanwisher, N. (1999). fMRI evidence for objects as the units of attentional selection. *Nature, 410,* 584–587.

O'Craven, K. M., & Kanwisher, N. (2000). Mental imagery of faces and places activates corresponding stimulus-specific brain regions. *Journal of Cognitive Neuroscience, 42,* 1013–1023.

O'Doherty, J., Winston, J., Critchley, H., Perrett, D., Burt, D. M., & Dolan, R. J. (2003). Beauty in a smile: The role of medial orbitofrontal cortex in facial attractiveness. *Neuropsychologia, 41*, 147–155.

O'Donnell, C., & Bruce, V. (2001). Familiarisation with faces selectively enhances sensitivity to changes made to the eyes. *Perception, 30*, 755–764.

O'Toole, A. J. Abdi, H., Deffenbacher, K. A., & Valentin, D. (1993). Low dimensional representation of faces in higher dimensions of face space. *Journal of the Optical Society of America A, 10*, 405–411.

O'Toole, A. J., Deffenbacher, K. A., Valentin, D., & Abdi, H. (1994). Structural aspects of face recognition and the other race effect. *Memory & Cognition, 22*, 208–224.

O'Toole, A. J., Peterson, J., & Deffenbacher, K. A. (1996). An other-race effect for categorising faces by sex. *Perception, 25*, 669–676.

O'Toole, A. J., Price, T., Vetter, T., Bartlett, J. C., & Blanz, V. (1999). 3D shape and 2D surface textures of human faces: The role of 'averages' in attractiveness and age. *Image and Vision Computing, 18*, 9–19.

O'Toole, A. J., Roark, D. A., & Abdi, H. (2002). Recognizing moving faces: A psychological and neural synthesis. *Trends in Cognitive Sciences, 6*, 261–266.

O'Toole, A. J., Vetter, T., Volz, H., & Salter, E. M. (1997). Three-dimensional caricatures of human heads: Distinctiveness and the perception of facial age. *Perception, 26*, 719–732.

Oaten, M., Stevenson, R. J., & Case, T. I. (2009). Disgust as a disease-avoidance mechanism. *Psychological Bulletin, 135*, 303–321.

Olson, I. R., & Marshuetz, C. (2005). Facial attractiveness is appraised in a glance. *Emotion, 5*, 498–502.

Oosterhof, N. N., & Todorov, A. (2008). The functional basis of face evaluation. *Proceedings of the National Academy of Sciences, USA, 105*, 11087–11092.

Op de Beeck, H. P., Haushofer, J., & Kanwisher, N. G. (2008). Interpreting fMRI data: Maps, modules and dimensions. *Nature Reviews Neuroscience, 9*, 123–135.

Osborne, C. D., & Stevenage, S. V. (2008). Internal feature saliency as a marker of familiarity and configural processing. *Visual Cognition, 16*, 23–43.

Page, M. (2000). Connectionist modelling in psychology: A localist manifesto. *Behavioral and Brain Sciences, 23*, 443–512.

Papagno, C., & Muggia, S. (1999). Naming people ignoring semantics in a patient with left frontal damage. *Cortex, 35*, 537–548.

Paré, M., Richler, R. C., ten Hove, M., & Munhall, K. G. (2003). Gaze behavior in audio-visual speech perception: The influence of ocular fixations on the McGurk effect. *Perception & Psychophysics, 65*, 553–567.

Parr, L. A., Waller, B. M., & Vick, S. J. (2007). New developments in understanding emotional signals in chimpanzees. *Current Directions in Psychological Science, 16*, 117–122.

Parry, F. M., Young, A. W., Saul, J. S. M., & Moss, A. (1991). Dissociable face processing impairments after brain injury. *Journal of Clinical and Experimental Neuropsychology, 13*, 545–558.

Pascalis, O., de Haan, M., & Nelson, C. A. (2002). Is face processing species-specific during the first year of life? *Science, 296*, 1321–1323.

Pascalis, O., & DeSchonen, S. (1994). Recognition memory in 3-day-old to 4-day-old human neonates *Neuroreport, 5*, 1721–1724.

Pascalis, O., Scott, L. S., Kelly, D. J., Shannon, R. W., Nicholson, E., Coleman, M., et al. (2005). Plasticity of face processing in infancy. *Proceedings of the National Academy of Sciences, USA, 102*, 5297–5300.

Patterson, M. L., & Werker, J. F. (2003). Two-month-old infants match phonetic information in lips and voice. *Developmental Science, 6*, 191–196.

Peelen, M. V., & Downing, P. E. (2007). The neural basis of visual body perception. *Nature Reviews Neuroscience, 8,* 636–648.

Pellicano, E. (2008). Face-processing clues to inheritance. *Current Biology, 18,* R748–R750.

Pellicano, E., & Rhodes, G. (2003). Holistic processing of faces in preschool children and adults. *Psychological Science, 14,* 618–622.

Pelphrey, K.A., Morris, J.P., & McCarthy, G. (2004). Grasping the intentions of others: The perceived intentionality of an action influences activity in the superior temporal sulcus during social perception. *Journal of Cognitive Neuroscience, 16,* 1706–1716.

Pelphrey, K. A., Morris, J. P., & McCarthy, G. (2005). Neural basis of eye gaze processing deficits in autism. *Brain, 128,* 1038–1048.

Pelphrey, K. A., Morris, J. P., Michelich, C. R., Allison, T., & McCarthy, G. (2005). Functional anatomy of biological motion perception in posterior temporal cortex: An fMRI study of eye, mouth and hand movements. *Cerebral Cortex, 15,* 1866–1876.

Pelphrey, K. A., Singerman, J. D., Allison, T., & McCarthy, G. (2003). Brain activation evoked by perception of gaze shifts: The influence of context. *Neuropsychologia, 41,* 156–170.

Pelphrey, K. A., Viola, R. J., & McCarthy, G. (2004). When strangers pass: Processing of mutual and averted social gaze in the superior temporal sulcus. *Psychological Science, 15,* 598–603.

Penton-Voak, I. S., Perrett, D. I., Castles, D. L., Kobayashi, T., Burt, D. M., Murray, L. K., et al. (1999). Menstrual cycle alters face preference. *Nature, 399,* 741–742.

Perkins, D. (1975). A definition of caricature, and caricature and recognition. *Studies in the Anthropology of Visual Communication, 2,* 1–24.

Perrett, D. I. (2010). *In your face: The new science of human attraction.* London: Palgrave Macmillan.

Perrett, D. I., Burt, D. M., Penton-Voak, I. S., Lee, K. J., Rowland, D. A., & Edwards, R. (1999). Symmetry and human facial attractiveness. *Evolution and Human Behavior, 20,* 295–307.

Perrett, D. I., Hietenan, J. K., Oram, M. W., & Benson, P. J. (1992). Organization and functions of cells responsive to faces in the temporal cortex. *Philosophical Transactions of the Royal Society, London, B: Biological Sciences, 335,* 23–30.

Perrett, D. I., Lee, K. J., Penton-Voak, I., Rowland, D., Yoshikawa, S., Burt, D. M., et al. (1998). Effects of sexual dimorphism on facial attractiveness. *Nature, 394,* 884–887.

Perrett, D. I., May, K. A., & Yoshikawa, S. (1994). Facial shape and judgements of female attractiveness. *Nature, 368,* 239–242.

Perrett, D. I., Penton-Voak, I., Little, A. C., Tiddeman, B. P., Burt, D. M., Schmidt, N., et al. (2002). Facial attractiveness judgements reflect learning of parental age characteristics. *Proceedings of the Royal Society, London, B: Biological Sciences, 269,* 873–880.

Perrett, D. I., Rolls, E. T., & Caan, W. (1982). Visual neurones responsive to faces in the monkey temporal cortex. *Experimental Brain Research, 47,* 329–342.

Perrett, D. I., Smith, P. A. J., Potter, D. D., Mistlin, A. J., Milner, A. D., & Jeeves, M. A. (1985). Visual cells in the temporal cortex sensitive to face view and gaze direction. *Proceedings of the Royal Society, London, B: Biological Sciences, 223,* 293–317.

Pessoa, L., & Adolphs, R. (2010). Emotion processing and the amygdala: from a 'low road' to 'many roads' of evaluating biological significance. *Nature Reviews Neuroscience, 11,* 773–782.

Pessoa, L., & Ungerleider, L. G. (2004). Neuroimaging studies of attention and the processing of emotion-laden stimuli. *Progress in Brain Research, 144,* 171–182.

Peterson, C. C., Peterson, J. L., & Webb, J. (2000). Factors influencing the development of a theory of mind in blind children. *British Journal of Developmental Psychology, 18,* 431–447.

Phelps, E. A. (2006). Emotion and cognition: Insights from studies of the human amygdala. *Annual Review of Psychology, 57,* 27–53.

Phelps, E. A., O'Connor, K. J., Cunningham, W. A., & Funayama, S. (2000). Performance on indirect measures of race evaluation predicts amygdala activation. *Journal of Cognitive Neuroscience, 12,* 729–738.

Phillips, M. L., Young, A. W., Senior, C., Brammer, M., Andrew, C., Calder, A. J., et al. (1997). A specific neural substrate for perceiving facial expressions of disgust. *Nature, 389,* 495–498.

Pistoia, F., Conson, M., Trojano, L., Grossi, D., Ponari, M., Colonnese, C., et al. (2010). Impaired conscious recognition of negative facial expressions in patients with locked-in syndrome. *Journal of Neuroscience, 30,* 7838–7844.

Pitcher, D., Garrido, L., Walsh, V., & Duchaine, B. C. (2008). Transcranial magnetic stimulation disrupts the perception and embodiment of facial expressions. *Journal of Neuroscience, 28,* 8929–8933.

Pittenger, J. B., & Shaw, R. E. (1975). Ageing faces as viscal-elastic events: Implications for a theory of nonrigid shape perception. *Journal of Experimental Psychology: Human Perception & Performance, 1,* 374–382.

Pittenger, J. B., Shaw, R. E., & Mark, L. S. (1979). Perceptual information for the age level of faces as a higher order invariant of growth. *Journal of Experimental Psychology: Human Perception & Performance, 5,* 478–493.

Polhemus, T. (1988). *Body styles.* Luton: Lennard.

Pollak, S. D. & Kistler, D. J. (2002). Early experience is associated with the development of categorical representations for facial expressions of emotion. *Proceedings of the National Academy of Sciences, USA, 99,* 9072–9076.

Pollick, F. E., Hill, H., Calder, A., & Paterson, H. (2003). Recognising facial expression from spatially and temporally modified movements. *Perception, 32,* 813–826.

Posner, M. I. (1980). Orienting of attention. *Quarterly Journal of Experimental. Psychology, 32,* 3–25.

Posner, M. I., & Cohen, Y. A. (1984). Components of visual orienting. In H. Bouma & D. G. Bouwhuis (Eds.), *Attention and Performance XVII: Control of visual processing.* (pp. 531–556). Hillsdale, NJ: Lawrence Erlbaum.

Posner, M. I., & Snyder, C. R. R. (1975). Facilitation and inhibition in the processing of signals. In P. M. A. Rabbitt & S. Dornic (Eds.), *Attention and performance, V* (pp. 669–682). London: Academic Press.

Putzar, L., Goerendt, I., Heed, T., Richard, G., Büchel, C., & Röder, B. (2010). The neural basis of lip-reading capabilities is altered by early visual deprivation. *Neuropsychologia, 48,* 2158–2166.

Quinn, K. A., & Macrae, C. N. (2005). Categorizing others: The dynamics of person construal. *Journal of Personality and Social Psychology, 88,* 467–479.

Quinn, P. C., Kelly, D. J., Lee, K., Pascalis, O., & Slater, A. M. (2008). Preference for attractive faces in human infants extends beyond conspecifics. *Developmental Science, 11,* 76–83.

Quinn, P. C., Yahr, J., Kuhn, A., Slater, A. M., & Pascalis, O. (2002). Representation of the gender of human faces by infants: A preference for female. *Perception, 31,* 1109–1121.

Quinn, P. C., & Slater, A. (2003). Face perception at birth and beyond. In O. Pascalis & A. Slater (Eds.), *The development of face processing in infancy and early childhood* (pp. 3–11). New York: Nova Science Publishers, Inc.

Rahman, R. A., Sommer, W., & Schweinberger, S. R. (2002). Brain-potential evidence for the time course of access to biographical facts and names of familiar persons. *Journal of Experimental Psychology: Learning, Memory & Cognition, 28,* 366–373.

Ramachandran, V. S. (1995). 2-D or not 2-D: That is the question. In R. Gregory, J. Harris, P. Heard & D. Rose (Eds.), *The artful eye* (pp. 249–267). Oxford: Oxford University Press.

Ramachandran, V. S. (1997). Why do gentlemen prefer blondes? *Medical Hypotheses, January,* 19–20.

Ramon, M., Busigny, T., & Rossion, B. (2010). Impaired holistic processing of unfamiliar individual faces in acquired prosopagnosia. *Neuropsychologia, 48,* 933–944.

Reason, J., & Lucas, D. (1984). Using cognitive diaries to investigate naturally occurring memory blocks. In J. E. Harris & P. E. Morris (Eds.), *Everyday memory, actions and absentmindedness* (pp. 53–70). London: Academic Press.

Reason, J., & Mycielska, K. (1982). *Absent-minded? The psychology of mental lapses and everyday errors.* New Jersey: Prentice Hall.

Reddy, L., Wilken, P., & Koch, C. (2004). Face-gender discrimination is possible in the near-absence of attention. *Journal of Vision, 4,* 106–117.

Reed, C. L., Stone, V. E., Bozova, S., & Tanaka, J. (2003). The body-inversion effect. *Psychological Science, 14,* 302–308.

Reid, I., Young, A. W., & Hellawell, D. J. (1993). Voice recognition impairment in a blind Capgras patient. *Behavioural Neurology, 6,* 225–228.

Reid, V. M., Striano, T., Kaufman, J., & Johnson, M. H. (2004). Eye gaze cueing facilitates neural processing of objects in 4-month-old infants. *Neuroreport, 15,* 2553–2555.

Rhodes, G. (1996). *Superportraits: Caricatures and recognition.* Hove: Psychology Press.

Rhodes, G. (2006). The evolutionary psychology of facial beauty. *Annual Review of Psychology, 57,* 199–226.

Rhodes, G., Brake, S., & Atkinson, A. P. (1993). What's lost in inverted faces. *Cognition, 47,* 25–57.

Rhodes, G., Brennan, S., & Carey, S. (1987). Identification and ratings of caricatures: Implications for mental representations of faces. *Cognitive Psychology, 190,* 473–497.

Rhodes, G., Byatt, G., Michie, P. T., & Puce, A. (2004). Is the fusiform face area specialized for faces, individuation, or expert individuation? *Journal of Cognitive Neuroscience, 16,* 189–203.

Rhodes, G., Chan, J., & Zebrowitz, L. A. (2003). Does sexual dimorphism in human faces signal health? *Proceedings of the Royal Society, London, B: Biological Sciences, 270,* S93–S95.

Rhodes, G., & Jeffery, L. (2006). Adaptive norm-based coding of facial identity. *Vision Research, 46,* 2977–2987.

Rhodes, G., Jeffery, L., Watson, T. L., Clifford, C. W. G., & Nakayama, K. (2003). Fitting the mind to the world: Face adaptation and attractiveness aftereffects. *Psychological Science, 14,* 558–566.

Rhodes, G., Michie, P.T., Hughes, M. E., & Byatt, D. (2009). The fusiform face area and occipital face area show sensitivity to spatial relations in faces. *European Journal of Neuroscience, 30,* 721–733.

Rhodes, G., & Tremewan, T. (1994). Understanding face recognition: Caricature effects, inversion and the homogeneity problem. *Visual Cognition, 1,* 275–311.

Rhodes, G., & Tremewan, T. (1996). Averageness, exaggeration, and facial attractiveness. *Psychological Science, 7,* 105–110.

Rhodes, G., Zebrowitz, L. A., Clark, A., Kalick, S. M., Hightower, A., & McKay, R. (2001). Do facial averageness and symmetry signal health? *Evolution and Human Behavior, 22,* 31–46.

Rhodes, M. G. (2009). Age estimation of faces: A review. *Applied Cognitive Psychology, 23,* 1–12.

Riby, D. M., Doherty-Sneddon, G., & Bruce, V. (2008). Exploring face perception in disorders of development: Evidence from Williams syndrome and autism. *Journal of Neuropsychology, 2,* 47–64.

Riby, D. M., Doherty-Sneddon, G., & Bruce, V. (2009). The eyes or the mouth? Feature salience and unfamiliar face processing in Williams syndrome and autism. *Quarterly Journal of Experimental Psychology, 62,* 189–203.

Riby, D. M., & Hancock, P. J. B. (2008). Viewing it differently: Social scene perception in Williams syndrome and autism. *Neuropsychologia, 46,* 2855–2860.

Riby, D. M., Jones, N., Brown, P. H., Robinson, L. J., Langton, S. R. H., Bruce, V., & Riby, L. (2011). Attention to faces in Williams syndrome. *Journal of Autism and Developmental Disorders, 41,* 1228–1239.

Ricciardelli, P., Baylis, G., & Driver, J. (2000). The positive and negative of human expertise in gaze perception. *Cognition, 77,* B1–B14.

Rinn, W. E. (1984). The neuropsychology of facial expression: A review of the neurological and psychological mechanisms for producing facial expressions. *Psychological Bulletin, 95,* 52–77.

Rizzo, M., Hurtig, R., & Damasio, A. R. (1987). The role of scanpaths in facial recognition and learning. *Annals of Neurology, 22,* 41–45.

Ristic, J., & Kingstone, A. (2005). Taking control of reflexive social attention. *Cognition, 94,* B55–B65.

Rizzolatti, G., Umilta, C., & Berlucchi, G. (1971). Opposite superiorities of the right and left cerebral hemispheres in discriminative reaction time to physiognomical and alphabetical material. *Brain, 94,* 431–442.

Rizzolatti, G., Fadiga, L., Gallese, V., & Fogassi, L. (1996). Premotor cortex and the recognition of motor actions. *Cognitive Brain Research, 3,* 131–141.

Roberts, M., & Summerfield, Q. (1981). Audiovisual presentation demonstrates that selective adaptation in speech perception is purely auditory. *Perception & Psychophysics, 30,* 309–314.

Robertson, D. M. C., & Schweinberger, S. R. (2010). The role of audiovisual asynchrony in person recognition. *Quarterly Journal of Experimental Psychology, 63,* 23–30.

Rojo, V. I., Caballero, L., Iruela, L. M., & Baca, E. (1991). Capgras' syndrome in a blind patient. *American Journal of Psychiatry, 148,* 1272.

Rosenblum, L. D. (2008). Speech perception as a multimodal phenomenon. *Current Directions in Psychological Science, 17,* 405–409.

Rosenblum, L. D., Yakel, D. A., & Greene, K. P. (2000). Face and mouth inversion effects on visual and audiovisual speech perception. *Journal of Experimental Psychology: Human Perception & Performance, 26,* 806–819.

Rotshtein, P., Henson, R. N. A., Treves, A., Driver, J., & Dolan, R. J. (2005). Morphing Marilyn into Maggie dissociates physical and identity face representations in the brain. *Nature Neuroscience, 8,* 107–113.

Rozin, P., Haidt, J., & McCauley, C. R. (1993). Disgust. In M. Lewis & J. M. Haviland (Eds.), *Handbook of emotions* (pp. 575–594). New York: Guilford.

Rozin, P., Lowery, L., & Ebert, R. (1994). Varieties of disgust faces and the structure of disgust. *Journal of Personality and Social Psychology, 66,* 870–881.

Ruiz-Soler, M., & Beltran, F. S. (2006). Face perception: An integrative review of the role of spatial frequencies. *Psychological Research-Psychologische Forschung, 70,* 273–292.

Rule, N. O., & Ambady, N. (2010). Democrats and Republicans can be differentiated from their faces. *PloS ONE, 5*, e8733, 8731–8737.

Rumiati, R. I., & Humphreys, G. W. (1997). Visual object agnosia without alexia or prosopagnosia: Arguments for separate knowledge stores. *Visual Cognition, 4*, 207–217.

Rumiati, R. I., Humphreys, G. W., Riddoch, M. J., & Bateman, A. (1994). Visual object agnosia without prosopagnosia or alexia: Evidence for hierarchical theories of visual recognition. *Visual Cognition, 1*, 181–225.

Rumsey, N., & Bull, R. (1986). The effects of facial disfigurement on social interaction. *Human Learning, 5*, 203–208.

Rumsey, N., Bull, R., & Gahagan, D. (1982). The effect of facial disfigurement on the proxemic behaviour of the general public. *Journal of Applied Social Psychology, 12*, 137–150.

Russell, J. A. (1980). A circumplex model of affect. *Journal of Personality and Social Psychology, 39*, 1161–1178.

Russell, J. A., & Fehr, B. (1987). Relativity in the perception of emotion in facial expressions. *Journal of Experimental Psychology: General, 116*, 223–237.

Russell, R. (2003). Sex, beauty and the relative luminance of facial features. *Perception, 32*, 1093–1107.

Russell, R. (2009). A sex difference in facial contrast and its exaggeration by cosmetics. *Perception, 38*, 1211–1219.

Russell, R., Duchaine, B., & Nakayama, K. (2009). Super-recognisers. People with extraordinary face recognition ability. *Psychonomic Bulletin & Review, 16*, 252–257.

Rutherford, M. D., Chattha, H. M., & Krysko, K. M. (2008). The use of aftereffects in the study of relationships among emotion categories. *Journal of Experimental Psychology: Human Perception & Performance, 34*, 27–40.

Sai, F. Z. (2005). The role of the mother's voice in developing mother's face preference: Evidence for intermodal perception at birth. *Infant and Child Development, 14*, 29–50.

Said, C. P., Moore, C. D., Engell, A. D., Todorov, A., & Haxby, J. V. (2010). Distributed representations of dynamic facial expressions in the superior temporal sulcus. *Journal of Vision, 10*, 1–12.

Salter, F. (1996). Carrier females and sender males: An evolutionary hypothesis linking female attractiveness, family resemblance, and paternity confidence. *Ethology and Sociobiology, 17*, 211–220.

Samochowiec, J., Wänke, M., & Fiedler, K. (2010). Political ideology at face value. *Social Psychological and Personality Science, 1*, 206–213.

Santos, I. M., & Young, A. W. (2005). Exploring the perception of social characteristics in faces using the isolation effect. *Visual Cognition, 12*, 213–247.

Santos, I. M., & Young, A. W. (2008). Effects of inversion and negation on social inferences from faces. *Perception, 37*, 1061–1078.

Sato, W., Kochiyama, T., Uono, S., & Yoshikawa, S. (2008). Time course of superior temporal sulcus activity in response to eye gaze: A combined fMRI and MEG study. *Social Cognitive and Affective Neuroscience, 3*, 224–232.

Sato, W., Kubota, Y., Okada, T., Murai, T., Yoshikawa, S., & Sengoku, A. (2002). Seeing happy emotion in fearful and angry faces: Qualitative analysis of facial expression recognition in a bilateral amygdala-damaged patient. *Cortex, 38*, 727–742.

Saxe, R., & Kanwisher, N. (2003). People thinking about thinking people: The role of the temporo-parietal junction in 'theory of mind'. *NeuroImage, 19*, 1835–1842.

Saxton, T. K., DeBruine, L. M., Jones, B. C., Little, A. C., & Roberts, S. C. (2009). Face and voice attractiveness judgments change during adolescence. *Evolution and Human Behavior, 30*, 398–408.

Sayette, M. A., Cohn, J. F., Wertz, J. M., Perrott, M. A., & Parrott, D. J. (2001). A psychometric evaluation of the Facial Action Coding System for assessing spontaneous expression. *Journal of Nonverbal Behavior, 25,* 167–185.

Scaife, M., & Bruner, J. S., (1975). The capacity for joint visual attention in the infant. *Nature, 253,* 265–266.

Scanlan, L. C., & Johnston, R. A. (1997). I recognize your face, but I can't remember your name: A grown-up explanation? *Quarterly Journal of Experimental Psychology, 50A,* 183–198.

Schacter, D. L., McAndrews, M. P., & Moscovitch, M. (1988). Access to consciousness: Dissociations between implicit and explicit knowledge in neuropsychological syndromes. In L. Weiskrantz (Ed.), *Thought without language* (pp. 242–278). Oxford: Oxford University Press.

Scherf, K. S., Behrmann, M., Humphreys, K., & Luna, B. (2007). Visual category-selectivity for faces, places and objects emerges along different developmental trajectories. *Developmental Science, 10,* F15–F30.

Schlosberg, H. (1952). The description of facial expressions in terms of two dimensions. *Journal of Experimental Psychology, 44,* 229–237.

Schlosberg, H. (1954). Three dimensions of emotion. *Psychological Review, 61,* 81–88.

Schmalzl, L., Palermo, R., & Coltheart, M. (2008). Cognitive heterogeneity in genetically-based prosopagnosia: A family study. *Journal of Neuropsychology, 2,* 99–117.

Schwab, C., & Huber, L. (2006). Obey or not obey? Dogs (Canis familiaris) behave differently in response to attentional states of their owners. *Journal of Comparative Psychology, 120,* 169–175.

Schweinberger, S., & Burton, A. M. (2003). Covert face recognition and the neural system for face processing. *Cortex, 39,* 9–30.

Schweinberger, S. R., Burton, A. M., & Kelly, S. W. (1999). Asymmetric dependencies in perceiving identity and emotion: Experiments with morphed faces. *Perception & Psychophysics, 61,* 1102–1115.

Schweinberger, S. R., Casper, C., Hauthal, N., Kaufmann, J. M., Kawahara, H., Kloth, N., et al. (2008). Auditory adaptation in voice perception. *Current Biology, 18,* 684–688.

Schweinberger, S. R., Herholz, A., & Sommer, W. (1997). Recognizing famous voices: Influence of stimulus duration and different types of retrieval cues. *Journal of Speech, Language, and Hearing Research, 40,* 453–463.

Schweinberger, S. R., Huddy, V., & Burton, A. M. (2004). N250r: A face-selective brain response to stimulus repetitions. *NeuroReport, 15,* 1501–1505.

Schweinberger, S. R., Pfütze, E.-M., & Sommer, W. (1995). Repetition priming and associative priming of face recognition: Evidence from event-related potentials. *Journal of Experimental Psychology: Learning, Memory & Cognition, 21,* 722–736.

Schweinberger, S. R., Pickering, E. C., Jentzsch, I., Burton, A. M., & Kaufmann, J. M. (2002). Event-related brain potential evidence for a response of inferior temporal cortex to familiar face repetitions. *Cognitive Brain Research, 14,* 398–409.

Schweinberger, S. R., Robertson, D., & Kaufmann, J. M. (2007). Hearing facial identities. *Quarterly Journal of Experimental Psychology, 60,* 1446–1456.

Schweinberger, S. R., & Soukup, G. R. (1998). Asymmetric relationships among perceptions of facial identity, emotion, and facial speech. *Journal of Experimental Psychology: Human Perception & Performance, 24,* 1748–1765.

Schyns, P. G., & Oliva, A. (1997). Flexible, diagnostically-driven, rather than fixed, perceptually determined scale selection in scene and face recognition. *Perception, 26,* 1027–1038.

Scott, L. S., & Monesson, A. (2009). The origin of biases in face perception. *Psychological Science, 20,* 676–680.

Scott, S. K., Young, A. W., Calder, A. J., Hellawell, D. J., Aggleton, J. P., & Johnson, M. (1997). Impaired auditory recognition of fear and anger following bilateral amygdala lesions. *Nature*, *385*, 254–257.

Searcy, J. H., & Bartlett, J. C. (1996). Inversion and processing of component and spatial-relational information in faces. *Journal of Experimental Psychology: Human Perception & Performance*, *22*, 904–915.

Semenza, C. (2009). The neuropsychology of proper names. *Mind & Language*, *24*, 347–369.

Senju, A., Hasegawa, T., & Tojo, Y. (2005). Does perceived direct gaze boost detection in adults and children with and without autism? The stare-in-the-crowd effect revisited. *Visual Cognition*, *12*, 1474–1496.

Senju, A., & Johnson, M. H. (2009a). Atypical eye contact in autism: Models, mechanisms and development. *Neuroscience and Biobehavioral Reviews*, *33*, 1204–1214.

Senju, A., & Johnson, M. H. (2009b). The eye contact effect: Mechanisms and development. *Trends in Cognitive Sciences*, *13*, 127–134.

Senju, A., Johnson, M. H., & Csibra, G. (2006). The development and neural basis of referential gaze perception. *Social Neuroscience*, *1*, 220–234.

Senju, A., Kikuchi, Y., Hasegawa, T., Tojo, Y., & Osanai, H. (2008). Is anyone looking at me? Direct gaze detection in children with and without autism. *Brain and Cognition*, *67*, 127–139.

Senju. A., Tojo, Y. Yaguchi, K., & Hasegawa, T. (2005). Deviant gaze processing in children with autism: An ERP study. *Neuropsychologia*, *43*, 1297–1306.

Senju. A., Yaguchi, K., Tojo, Y., & Hasegawa, T. (2003). Eye contact does not facilitate detection in children with autism. *Cognition*, *89*, B43-B51.

Sergent, J., & Poncet, M. (1990). From covert to overt recognition of faces in a prosopagnosic patient. *Brain*, *113*, 989–1004.

Sergent, J., & Signoret, J.-L. (1992a). Implicit access to knowledge derived from unrecognized faces in prosopagnosia. *Cerebral Cortex*, *2*, 389–400.

Sergent, J., & Signoret, J.-L. (1992b). Varieties of functional deficits in prosopagnosia. *Cerebral Cortex*, *2*, 375–388.

Sergerie, K., Chochol, C., & Armony, J. L. (2008). The role of the amygdala in emotional processing: A quantitative meta-analysis of functional neuroimaging studies. *Neuroscience and Biobehavioral Reviews*, *32*, 811–830.

Seyama, J., & Nagayama, R. S. (2002). Perceived eye size is larger in happy than in surprised faces. *Perception*, *31* (9), 1153–1155.

Shah, R., & Lewis, M. (2003). Locating the neutral expression in the facial-emotion space. *Visual Cognition*, *10*, 549–566.

Shallice, T. (1988). *From neuropsychology to mental structure*. Cambridge: Cambridge University Press.

Shaw, R. E., McIntyre, M., & Mace, W. (1974). The role of symmetry in event perception. In R. B. MacCleod & H. L. Pick (Eds.), *Perception: Essays in honor of J. J. Gibson*. Ithaca, NY: Cornell University Press.

Shepherd, J. (1986). An interactive computer system for retrieving faces. In H. D. Ellis, M. A. Jeeves, F. Newcombe, & A. Young (Eds.), *Aspects of face processing*. Dordrecht: Martinus Nijhoff.

Simion, F., Macchi Cassia, V., Turati, C., & Valenza, E. (2003). Non-specific perceptual biases at the origins of face processing. In O. Pascalis & A. Slater (Eds.), *The development of face processing in infancy and early childhood* (pp. 13–26). New York: Nova Science Publishers, Inc.

Simion, F., Valenza, E., Cassia, V. M., Turati, C., & Umilta, C. (2002). Newborns' preference for up-down asymmetrical configurations. *Developmental Science*, *5*, 427–434.

Simion, F., Valenza, E., Umilta, C., & Dalla Barba, B. (1998). Preferential orienting to faces in newborns: A temporal-nasal asymmetry. *Journal of Experimental Psychology: Human Perception & Performance, 24,* 1399–1405.

Singer, T., Kiebel, S. J., Winston, J. S., Dolan, R. J., & Frith, C. D. (2004). Brain responses to the acquired moral status of faces. *Neuron, 41,* 653–662.

Sinha, P. (2000). Last but not least: Here's looking at you, kid. *Perception, 29,* 1005–1008.

Sinha, P., Balas, B., Ostrovsky, Y., & Russell, R. (2006). Face recognition by humans: Nineteen results all computer vision researchers should know about. *Proceedings of the IEEE, 94,* 1948–1962.

Skinner, A. L., & Benton, C. P. (2010). Anti-expression aftereffects reveal prototype-referenced coding of facial expressions. *Psychological Science, 21,* 1248–1253.

Slater, A., Von der Schulenburg, C., Brown, E., Badenoch, M., Butterworth, G., Parsons, S., et al. (1998). Newborn infants prefer attractive faces. *Infant Behavior & Development, 21,* 345–354.

Slater, A., Bremner, G., Johnson, S. P., Sherwood, P., Hayes, R., & Brown, E. (2000a). Newborn infants' preference for attractive faces: The role of internal and external facial features. *Infancy, 1,* 265–274.

Slater, A., Quinn, P. C., Hayes, R. A., & Brown, E. (2000b). The role of facial orientation in newborn infants' preference for attractive faces. *Developmental Science, 3,* 181–185.

Smith, L., & Muir, D. (2003). Infant perception of dynamic faces: Emotion, inversion and eye direction effects. In O. Pascalis & A. Slater (Eds.), *The development of face processing in infancy and early childhood* (pp. 119–130). New York: Nova Science Publishers, Inc.

Smith, S. M., & Vela, E. (1992). Environmental context-dependent eyewitness recognition. *Applied Cognitive Psychology, 6,* 125–139.

Smith, S. M., & Vela, E. (2001). Environmental context-dependent memory: A review and meta-analysis. *Psychonomic Bulletin & Review, 8,* 203–220.

Smith, W. A. P., & Hancock, E. R. (2008). Facial shape-from-shading and recognition using principal geodesic analysis and robust statistics. *International Journal of Computer Vision, 76,* 71–91.

Solso, R. L., & McCarthy, J. E. (1981). Prototype formation of faces – a case of pseudo-memory. *British Journal of Psychology, 72,* 499–503.

Soto-Faraco, S., & Alsius, A. (2009). Deconstructing the McGurk-MacDonald illusion. *Journal of Experimental Psychology: Human Perception & Performance, 35,* 580–587.

Spangler, S. M., Schwarzer, G., Korell, M., & Maier-Karius, J. (2010). The relationships between processing facial identity, emotional expression, facial speech, and gaze direction during development. *Journal of Experimental Child Psychology, 105,* 1–19.

Sprengelmeyer, R., Perrett, D. I., Fagan, E. C., Cornwell, R. E., Lobmaier, J., Sprengelmeyer, A., et al. (2009). The cutest little baby face: A hormonal link to sensitivity to cuteness in infant faces. *Psychological Science, 20,* 149–154.

Sprengelmeyer, R., Young, A. W., Calder, A. J., Karnat, A., Lange, H. W., Hömberg, V., et al. (1996). Loss of disgust: Perception of faces and emotions in Huntington's disease. *Brain, 119,* 1647–1665.

Sprengelmeyer, R., Young, A. W., Schroeder, U., Grossenbacher, P. G., Federlein, J., Büttner, T., et al. (1999). Knowing no fear. *Proceedings of the Royal Society, London, B: Biological Sciences, 266,* 2451–2456.

Stone, V. E., Baron-Cohen, S., Calder, A., Keane, J., & Young, A. (2003). Acquired theory of mind impairments in individuals with bilateral amygdala lesions. *Neuropsychologia, 41,* 209–220.

Straube, T., Dietrich, C., Mothes-Lasch, M., Mentzel, H.-J., & Miltner, W. H. R. (2010). The volatility of the amygdala response to masked fearful eyes. *Human Brain Mapping, 31,* 1601–1608.

Striemer, C., Gingerich, T., Striemer, D., & Dixon, M. (2009). Covert face priming reveals a 'true face effect' in a case of congenital prosopagnosia. *Neurocase*, *15*, 509–514.

Sugita, Y. (2008). Face perception in monkeys reared with no exposure to faces. *Proceedings of the National Academy of Sciences, USA*, *105*, 394–398.

Sumby, W. H., & Pollack, I. (1954). Visual contribution to speech intelligibility in noise. *Journal of the Acoustical Society of America*, *26*, 212–215.

Summerfield, Q., MacLeod, A., McGrath, M., & Brooke, M. (1989). Lips, teeth, and the benefits of lipreading. In A. W. Young & H. D. Ellis (Eds.), *Handbook of research on face processing* (pp. 223–233). Amsterdam: North Holland.

Summerfield, Q., & McGrath, M. (1984). Detection and resolution of audio-visual incompatibility in the perception of vowels. *Quarterly Journal of Experimental Psychology*, *36A*, 51–74.

Susskind, J. M., Littlewort, G., Bartlett, M. S., Movellan, J., & Anderson, A. K. (2007). Human and computer recognition of facial expressions of emotion. *Neuropsychologia*, *45*, 152–162.

Tachakra, S., & Rajini, R. (2002). Social presence in telemedicine. *Journal of Telemedicine and Telecare*, *8*, 226–230

Tager-Flusberg, H., Plesa Skwerer, D., & Joseph, R. M. (2006). Model syndromes for investigating social cognitive and affective neuroscience: A comparison of autism and Williams syndrome. *Social, Cognitive and Affective Neuroscience*, *1*, 175–182.

Tanaka, J. W., & Farah, M. J. (1993). Parts and wholes in face recognition. *Quarterly Journal of Experimental Psychology*, *46A*, 225–245.

Tanaka, J. W., & Gordon, I. (2011). Features, configuration and holistic face processing. In A. Calder, G. Rhodes, J. V. Haxby, & M. H. Johnson (Eds.), *The handbook of face perception*. Oxford: Oxford University Press.

Tanaka, J. W., Kay, J. B., Grinnell, E., Stansfield, B., & Szechter, L. (1998). Face recognition in young children: When the whole is greater than the sum of its parts. *Visual Cognition*, *5*, 479–496.

Tarr, M. J., & Gauthier, I. (2000). FFA: A flexible fusiform area for subordinate-level visual processing automatized by expertise. *Nature Neuroscience*, *3*, 764–769.

Taylor, M. J., Batty, M., & Itier, R. J. (2004). The faces of development: a review of early face processing over childhood. *Journal of Cognitive Neuroscience*, *16*, 1426–1442.

Thomas, C., Avidan, G., Humphreys, K., Jung, K.-J., Gao, F., & Behrmann, M. (2009). Reduced structural connectivity in ventral visual cortex in congenital prosopagnosia. *Nature Neuroscience*, *12*, 29–31.

Thompson, D'A. W. (1917). *On growth and form* (1961 edition by J. T. Bonner). Cambridge: Cambridge University Press.

Thompson, P. (1980). Margaret Thatcher – a new illusion. *Perception*, *9*, 483–484.

Thompson, P., Anstis, S., Rhodes, G., Jeffery, L., & Valentine, T. (2009). Thompson's 1980 paper. *Perception*, *38*, 921–932.

Thompson, S. A., Graham, K. S., Williams, G., Patterson, K., Kapur, N., & Hodges, J. R. (2004). Dissociating person-specific from general semantic knowledge: Roles of the left and right temporal lobes. *Neuropsychologia*, *42*, 359–370.

Thomson, D. M. (1986). Face recognition: More than a feeling of familiarity? In H. D. Ellis, M. A. Jeeves, F. Newcombe, & A. Young (Eds.), *Aspects of face processing* (pp. 118–122). Dordrecht: Martinus Nijhoff.

Thornhill, R., & Gangestad, S. W. (1993). Human facial beauty: Averageness, symmetry, and parasite resistance. *Human Nature*, *4*, 237–269.

Tiddeman, B., Burt, D. M., & Perrett, D. (2001). Prototyping and transforming facial textures for face perception research. *IEEE Computer Graphics and Applications*, *21*, 42–50.

Tipper, C. M., Handy, T. C., Giesbrecht, B., & Kingstone, A. (2008). Brain responses to biological relevance. *Journal of Cognitive Neuroscience, 20,* 879–891.

Tipples, J. (2005). Orienting to eye gaze and face processing. *Journal of Experimental Psychology: Human Perception & Performance, 31,* 843–856.

Tipples, J., Atkinson, A. P., & Young, A. W. (2002). The eyebrow frown: A salient social signal. *Emotion, 2,* 288–296.

Todorov, A., & Duchaine, B. (2008). Reading trustworthiness in faces without recognizing faces. *Cognitive Neuropsychology,* 25, 395–410.

Todorov, A., & Engell, A. D. (2008). The role of the amygdala in implicit evaluation of emotionally neutral faces. *Social, Cognitive and Affective Neuroscience, 3,* 303–312.

Todorov, A., Loehr, V., & Oosterhof, N. N. (2010). The obligatory nature of holistic processing of faces in social judgments. *Perception, 39,* 514–532.

Todorov, A., Mandisodza, A. N., Goren, A., & Hall, C. C. (2005). Inferences of competence from faces predict election outcomes. *Science, 308,* 1623–1626.

Todorov, A., Said, C. P., Engell, A. D., & Oosterhof, N. N. (2008). Understanding evaluation of faces on social dimensions. *Trends in Cognitive Sciences, 12,* 455–460.

Tranel, D., & Damasio, A. R. (1985). Knowledge without awareness: An autonomic index of facial recognition by prosopagnosics. *Science, 228,* 1453–1454.

Treisman, A. M., & Gelade, G. (1980). Feature-integration theory of attention. *Cognitive Psychology, 12,* 97–136.

Tröster, H., & Brambring, M. (1992). Early social-emotional development in blind infants. *Child: Care, Health and Development, 18,* 207–227.

Tsao, D. Y., Moeller, S., & Freiwald, W. A. (2008). Comparing face patch systems in macaques and humans. *Proceedings of the National Academy of Sciences, USA, 105,* 19514–19519.

Tuomainen, J., Andersen, T. S., Tiippana, K., & Sams, M. (2005). Audio-visual speech perception is special. *Cognition, 96,* B13–B22.

Turati, C., Simion, F., Milani, I., & Umilta, C. (2002). Newborns' preference for faces: What is crucial? *Developmental Psychology, 38,* 875–882.

Tybur, J. M., Lieberman, D., & Griskevicius, V. (2009). Microbes, mating, and morality: Individual differences in three functional domains of disgust. *Journal of Personality and Social Psychology, 97,* 103–122.

Tytler, G. (1982). *Physiognomy in the European novel: Faces and fortunes.* Princeton: Princeton University Press.

Tzourio-Mazoyer, N., De Schonen, S., Crivello, F., Reutter, B., Aujard, Y., & Mazoyer, B. (2002). Neural correlates of woman face processing by 2-month-old infants. *NeuroImage, 15,* 454–461.

Ungerleider, L. G., & Mishkin, M. (1982). Two cortical visual systems. In D. J. Ingle, M. A. Goodale, & R. J. W. Mansfield (Eds.), *Analysis of visual behavior* (pp. 549–586). Cambridge, MA: MIT Press.

Urgesi, C., Calvo-Merino, B., Haggard, P., & Aglioti, S. M. (2007). Transcranial magnetic stimulation reveals two cortical pathways for visual body processing. *Journal of Neuroscience, 27,* 8023–8030.

Valentine, T. (1991). A unified account of the effects of distinctiveness, inversion, and race in face recognition. *Quarterly Journal of Experimental Psychology, 43A,* 161–204.

Valentine, T., & Bruce, V. (1985). What's up? The Margaret Thatcher illusion revisited. *Perception, 14,* 515–516.

Valentine, T., & Bruce, V. (1986). The effects of distinctiveness in recognising and classifying faces. *Perception, 15,* 525–536.

Valentine, T., & Heaton, P. (1999). An evaluation of the fairness of police line-ups and video identifications. *Applied Cognitive Psychology, 13,* S59–S72.

Van Lancker, D. (1991). Personal relevance and the human right hemisphere. *Brain and Cognition, 17*, 64–92.

van Wassenhove, V., Grant, K. W., & Poeppel, D. (2007). Temporal window of integration in auditory-visual speech perception. *Neuropsychologia, 45*, 598–607.

Vanezis, P., Blowes, R. W., Linney, A. D., Tan, A. C., Richards, R., & Neave, R. (1989). Application of 3-D computer-graphics for facial reconstruction and comparison with sculpting techniques. *Forensic Science International, 42*, 69–84.

Van Rullen, R. (2006). On second glance: Still no high-level pop-out effect for faces. *Vision Research, 46*, 3017–3027.

Viviani, P., Binda, P., & Borsato, T. (2007). Categorical perception of newly learned faces. *Visual Cognition, 15*, 420–467.

Vokey, J. R., & Read, J. D. (1992). Familiarity, memorability, and the effect of typicality on the recognition of faces. *Memory & Cognition, 20*, 291–302.

von Kriegstein, K., Dogan, Ö., Grüter, M., Giraud, A.-L., Keil, C. A., Grüter, T., et al. (2008). Simulation of talking faces in the human brain improves auditory speech recognition. *Proceedings of the National Academy of Sciences, USA, 105*, 6747–6752.

von Kriegstein, K., Kleinschmidt, A., & Giraud, A.-L. (2006). Voice recognition and cross-modal responses to familiar speakers' voices in prosopagnosia. *Cerebral Cortex, 16*, 1314–1322.

Vrij, A. (2004). Why professionals fail to catch liars and how they can improve. *Legal and Criminological Psychology, 9*, 159–181.

Vuilleumier, P., Armony, J. L., Clarke, K., Husain, M., Driver, J., & Dolan, R. J. (2002). Neural response to emotional faces with and without awareness: Event-related fMRI in a parietal patient with visual extinction and spatial neglect. *Neuropsychologia, 40*, 2156–2166.

Vuilleumier, P., Armony, J. L., Driver, J., & Dolan, R. J. (2003). Distinct spatial frequency sensitivities for processing faces and emotional expressions. *Nature Neuroscience, 6*, 624–631.

Vytal, K., & Hamann, S. (2010). Neuroimaging support for discrete neural correlates of basic emotions: A voxel-based meta-analysis. *Journal of Cognitive Neuroscience, 22*, 2864–2885.

Wade, N. J. (1983). *Brewster and Wheatstone on vision*. London: Academic Press.

Wade, N. J. (1998). *A natural history of vision*. Cambridge, MA: MIT: Press (Bradford Books).

Walker, R., Findlay, J. M., Young, A. W., & Lincoln, N. B. (1996). Saccadic eye movements in object-based neglect. *Cognitive Neuropsychology, 13*, 569–615.

Walker, S., Bruce, V., & O'Malley, C. (1995). Facial identity and facial speech processing: Familiar faces and voices in the McGurk effect. *Perception & Psychophysics, 57*, 1124–1133.

Waller, B. M., Cray, J. J., & Burrows, A. M. (2008). Selection for universal facial emotion. *Emotion, 8*, 435–439.

Waller, B. M., Vick, S.-J., Parr, L. A., Bard, K. A., Smith Pasqualini, M. C., Gothard, K. M., et al. (2006). Intramuscular electrical stimulation of facial muscles in humans and chimpanzees: Duchenne revisited and extended. *Emotion, 6*, 367–382.

Warren, C., & Morton, J. (1982). The effects of priming on picture recognition. *British Journal of Psychology, 73*, 117–129.

Warrington, E. K., & Shallice, T. (1969). The selective impairment of auditory verbal short-term memory. *Brain, 92*, 885–896.

Waters, K., & Terzopoulos, D. (1992). The computer synthesis of expressive faces. *Philosophical Transactions of the Royal Society, London, B: Biological Sciences, 335*, 87–93.

Webster, M. A., Kaping, D., Mizokami, Y., & Duhamel, P. (2004). Adaptation to natural facial categories. *Nature, 428,* 557–561.

Webster, M. A., & MacLin, O. H. (1999). Figural aftereffects in the perception of faces. *Psychonomic Bulletin & Review, 6,* 647–653.

Weikum, W. M., Vouloumanos, A., Navarra, J., Soto-Faraco, S., Sebastian-Galles, N., & Werker, J. F. (2007). Visual language discrimination in infancy. *Science, 316,* 1159.

Wells, G. L., Small, M., Penrod, S., Malpass, R. S., Fulero, S. M., & Brimacombe, C. A. E. (1998). Eyewitness identification procedures: Recommendations for lineups and photospreads. *Law and Human Behaviour, 22,* 603–647.

Werker, J. F., & Tees, R. C. (2005). Speech perception as a window for understanding plasticity and commitment in language systems of the brain. *Developmental Psychobiology, 46,* 233–251.

Weston, S. (1992). *Going back: Return to the Falklands.* London: Penguin Books.

Whalen, P. J., Kagan, J., Cook, R. G., Davis, F. C., Kim, H., Polis, S., et al. (2004). Human amygdala responsivity to masked fearful eye whites. *Science, 306,* 2061.

White, M. (2000). Parts and wholes in expression recognition. *Cognition and Emotion, 14,* 39–60.

Wiese, H., Schweinberger, S. R., & Hansen, K. (2008). The age of the beholder: ERP evidence of an own-age bias in face memory. *Neuropsychologia, 46,* 2973–2985.

Wiese, H., Schweinberger, S. R., & Neumann, M. F. (2008). Perceiving age and gender in unfamiliar faces: Brain potential evidence for implicit and explicit person categorization. *Psychophysiology, 45,* 957–969.

Willis, J., & Todorov, A. (2006). First impressions: Making up your mind after a 100-ms exposure to a face. *Psychological Science, 17,* 592–598.

Wilmer, J. B., Germine, L., Chabris, C. F., Chatterjee, G., Williams, M., Loken, E., et al. (2010). Human face recognition ability is specific and highly heritable. *Proceedings of the National Academy of Sciences, USA, 107,* 5238–5241.

Windmann, S. (2004). Effects of sentence context and expectation on the McGurk illusion. *Journal of Memory & Language, 50,* 212–230.

Winston, J. S., Henson, R. N. A., Fine-Goulden, M. R., & Dolan, R. J. (2004). fMRI-adaptation reveals dissociable neural representations of identity and expression in face perception. *Journal of Neurophysiology, 92,* 1830–1839.

Winston, J. S., O'Doherty, J., Kilner, J. M., Perrett, D. I., & Dolan, R. J. (2007). Brain systems for assessing facial attractiveness. *Neuropsychologia, 45,* 195–206.

Winston, J. S., Strange, B. A., O'Doherty, J., & Dolan, R. J. (2002). Automatic and intentional brain responses during evaluation of trustworthiness of faces. *Nature Neuroscience, 5,* 277–283.

Woodworth, R. S., & Schlosberg, H. (1954). *Experimental psychology: Revised edition.* New York: Henry Holt.

Wollaston, W. H. (1824). On the apparent direction of eyes in a portrait. *Philosophical Transactions of the Royal Society, London,* 247–256.

Wright, T. M., Pelphrey, K. A., Allison, T., McKeown, M. J., & McCarthy, G. (2003). Polysensory interactions along lateral temporal regions evoked by audiovisual speech. *Cerebral Cortex, 13,* 1034–1043.

Wyk, B. C. V., Hudac, C. M., Carter, E. J., Sobel, D. M., & Pelphrey, K. A. (2009). Action understanding in the superior temporal sulcus region. *Psychological Science, 20,* 771–777.

Xu, X., Yue, X., Lescroart, M. D., Biederman, I., & Kim, J. G. (2009). Adaptation in the fusiform face area (FFA): Image or person? *Vision Research, 49,* 2800–2807.

Yakel, D. A., Rosenblum, L. D., & Fortier, M. A. (2000). Effects of talker variability on speechreading. *Perception & Psychophysics, 62,* 1405–1412.

Yin, R. K. (1969). Looking at upside-down faces. *Journal of Experimental Psychology, 81,* 141–145.

Young, A. W. (1982). Methodological and theoretical bases of visual hemifield studies. In J. G. Beaumont (Ed.), *Divided visual field studies of cerebral organisation* (pp. 11–27). London: Academic Press.

Young, A. W. (1986). Subject characteristics in lateral differences for face processing by normals: age. In R. Bruyer (Ed.), *The neuropsychology of face perception and facial expression* (pp. 167–200). Hillsdale, New Jersey: Lawrence Erlbaum.

Young, A. W. (1992a). Face recognition impairments. *Philosophical Transactions of the Royal Society, London, B: Biological Sciences, 335,* 47–54.

Young, A. W. (1992b). Visual perception. In I. Rapin & S. Segalowitz (Eds.), *Handbook of neuropsychology, volume 7: Child neuropsychology* (pp. 1–14). Amsterdam: Elsevier.

Young, A. W. (2000). Wondrous strange: The neuropsychology of abnormal beliefs. *Mind & Language, 15,* 47–73.

Young, A. W. (2011). Disorders of face perception. In A. J. Calder, G. Rhodes, M. Johnson, & J. Haxby (Eds.), *The handbook of face perception* (pp. 77–91). Oxford: Oxford University Press.

Young, A. W., Aggleton, J. P., Hellawell, D. J., Johnson, M., Broks, P., & Hanley, J. R. (1995). Face processing impairments after amygdalotomy. *Brain, 118,* 15–24.

Young, A. W., & Bion, P. J. (1980). Absence of any developmental trend in right hemisphere superiority for face recognition. *Cortex, 16,* 213–221.

Young, A. W., & Burton, A. M. (1999). Simulating face recognition: Implications for modelling cognition. *Cognitive Neuropsychology, 16,* 1–48.

Young, A. W., & de Haan, E. H. F. (1988). Boundaries of covert recognition in prosopagnosia. *Cognitive Neuropsychology, 5,* 317–336.

Young, A. W., & Ellis, A. W. (1985). Different methods of lexical access for words presented in the left and right visual hemifields. *Brain and Language, 24,* 326–358.

Young, A. W., & Ellis, H. D. (1976). An experimental investigation of developmental differences in ability to recognise faces presented to the left and right cerebral hemispheres. *Neuropsychologia, 14,* 495–498.

Young, A. W., & Ellis, H. D. (1989). Childhood prosopagnosia. *Brain and Cognition, 9,* 16–47.

Young, A. W., Ellis, A. W., & Flude, B. M. (1988). Accessing stored information about familiar people. *Psychological Research, 50,* 111–115.

Young, A. W., Ellis, A. W., Flude, B. M., McWeeny, K. H., & Hay, D. C. (1986). Face-name interference. *Journal of Experimental Psychology: Human Perception & Performance, 12,* 466–475.

Young, A. W., Flude, B. M., Ellis, A. W., & Hay, D. C. (1987). Interference with face naming. *Acta Psychologica, 64,* 93–100.

Young, A. W., Flude, B. M., Hellawell, D. J., & Ellis, A. W. (1994). The nature of semantic priming effects in the recognition of familiar people. *British Journal of Psychology, 85,* 393–411.

Young, A. W., Hay, D. C., & Ellis, A. W. (1985). The faces that launched a thousand slips: Everyday difficulties and errors in recognizing people. *British Journal of Psychology, 76,* 495–523.

Young, A. W., Hay, D. C., McWeeny, K. H., Flude, B. M., & Ellis, A. W. (1985). Matching familiar and unfamiliar faces on internal and external features. *Perception, 14,* 737–746.

Young, A. W., Hellawell, D., & de Haan, E. H. F. (1988). Cross-domain semantic priming in normal subjects and a prosopagnosic patient. *Quarterly Journal of Experimental Psychology, 40A,* 561–580.

Young, A. W., Hellawell, D., & Hay, D. C. (1987). Configurational information in face perception. *Perception, 16,* 747–759.

Young, A. W., Humphreys, G. W., Riddoch, M. J., Hellawell, D. J., & de Haan, E. H. F. (1994). Recognition impairments and face imagery. *Neuropsychologia, 32,* 693–702.

Young, A. W., McWeeny, K. H., Ellis, A. W., & Hay, D. C. (1986). Naming and categorizing faces and written names. *Quarterly Journal of Experimental Psychology, 38A,* 297–318.

Young, A. W., McWeeny, K. H., Hay, D. C., & Ellis, A. W. (1986). Access to identity-specific semantic codes from familiar faces. *Quarterly Journal of Experimental Psychology, 38A,* 271–295.

Young, A. W., Newcombe, F., de Haan, E. H. F., Small, M., & Hay, D. C. (1993). Face perception after brain injury: Selective impairments affecting identity and expression. *Brain, 116,* 941–959.

Young, A. W., Perrett, D. I., Calder, A. J., Sprengelmeyer, R., & Ekman, P. (2002). *Facial expressions of emotion: Stimuli and tests (FEEST).* Bury St. Edmunds: Thames Valley Test Company.

Young, A. W., Reid, I., Wright, S., & Hellawell, D. J. (1993). Face-processing impairments and the Capgras delusion. *British Journal of Psychiatry, 162,* 695–698.

Young, A. W., Rowland, D., Calder, A. J., Etcoff, N. L., Seth, A., & Perrett, D. I. (1997). Facial expression megamix: Tests of dimensional and category accounts of emotion recognition. *Cognition, 63,* 271–313.

Young, S. G., & Hugenberg, K. (2010). Mere social categorization modulates identification of facial expressions of emotion. *Journal of Personality and Social Psychology, 99,* 964–977.

Yovel, G., & Kanwisher, N. (2005). The neural basis of the behavioral face inversion effect. *Current Biology, 15,* 2256–2262.

Yovel, G., Pelc, T., & Lubetzky, I. (2010). It's all in your head: Why is the body inversion effect abolished for headless bodies? *Journal of Experimental Psychology: Human Perception & Performance, 36,* 759–767.

Yovel, G., Tambini, A., & Brandman, T. (2008). The asymmetry of the fusiform face area is a stable individual characteristic that underlies the left-visual-field superiority for faces. *Neuropsychologia, 46,* 3061–3068.

Yue, X., Tjan, B. S & Biederman, I. (2006). What makes faces special? *Vision Research, 46,* 3802–3811.

Zajonc, R. B. (1980). Feeling and thinking: Preferences need no inferences. *American Psychologist, 35,* 151–175.

Zaretsky, M., Mendelsohn, A., Mintz, M., & Hendler, T. (2010). In the eye of the beholder: Internally driven uncertainty of danger recruits the amygdala and dorsomedial prefrontal cortex. *Journal of Cognitive Neuroscience, 22,* 2263–2275.

Zebrowitz, L. A., & Rhodes, G. (2004). Sensitivity to 'bad genes' and the anomalous face overgeneralization effect: Cue validity, cue utilization, and accuracy in judging intelligence and health. *Journal of Nonverbal Behavior, 28,* 167–185.

Zhu, Q., Song, Y., Hu, S., Li, X., Tian, M., Zhen, Z., et al. (2010). Heritability of the specific cognitive ability of face perception. *Current Biology, 20,* 137–142.

Author index

Subject index